Also by Rashmi Singla

ETHNIC MINORITY YOUTH IN DENMARK: About Their Psychosocial Situation (*co-author Juilo G. Arenas*)

YOUTH RELATIONSHIPS, ETHNICITY & PSYCHOSOCIAL INTERVENTION

THE ONE AND ONLY—HOW ETHNIC MINORITY YOUTH IN DENMARK FORM INTIMATE RELATIONS: Conflict and Intervention

NOW AND THEN—LIFE TRAJECTORIES, FAMILY RELATIONSHIP AND DIASPORIC IDENTITIES: A Follow-up Study of Young Adults

Intermarriage and Mixed Parenting, Promoting Mental Health and Wellbeing

Crossover Love

Rashmi Singla
Roskilde University, Denmark

First published 2015 by
PALGRAVE MACMILLAN

Palgrave Macmillan in the UK is an imprint of Macmillan Publishers Limited,
registered in England, company number 785998, of Houndmills, Basingstoke,
Hampshire RG21 6XS.

Palgrave Macmillan in the US is a division of St Martin's Press LLC,
175 Fifth Avenue, New York, NY 10010.

Palgrave Macmillan is the global academic imprint of the above companies
and has companies and representatives throughout the world.

Palgrave® and Macmillan® are registered trademarks in the United States,
the United Kingdom, Europe and other countries.

ISBN 978–1–137–39077–6

This book is printed on paper suitable for recycling and made from fully
managed and sustained forest sources. Logging, pulping and manufacturing
processes are expected to conform to the environmental regulations of the
country of origin.

A catalogue record for this book is available from the British Library.

Library of Congress Cataloging-in-Publication Data
Singla, Rashmi.
    Intermarriage and mixed parenting, promoting mental health and
    wellbeing : cross over love / Rashmi Singla.
        pages cm
    Summary: "The world is currently witnessing a significant growth in
    marriages across ethnic borders, but relatively little is known of how
    discourses of 'normal' families, ethnicity, race, migration, globalisation
    affect couples and children involved in these mixed marriages. This book
    illuminates the reality of mixed marriage though intimate stories drawn
    from the lives of visibly different couples. The testimonies describe rich
    possibilities and bitter disappointments, offering lessons for services
    promoting mental health and wellbeing, and for improving psychosocial
    intervention. The book will be of interest to academics in anthropology,
    sociology, psychology and social work, as well as practitioners including
    psychologists, counsellors, school advisors, and health workers"
    — Provided by publisher.
    ISBN 978–1–137–39077–6 (hardback)
    1. Intermarriage—Psychological aspects.   2. Families—Psychological
    aspects.   3. Parenting—Psychological aspects.   I. Title.
    HQ1031.S557 2015
    306.85—dc23   2014023274

I dedicate this book to Suraj Kumari Jain, Narendra Lal Jain and Grethe Holten, my mother, father and a close friend respectively, who are no longer with us, although their inspiration and blessings remain

Contents

Tables and Figures

Tables

Figures

Foreword

Around the globe, one of the most striking demographic trends is the increase in 'mixed' populations. In many countries, mixed relationships and people of mixed parentage are increasingly visible. This visibility is illustrated by the categorising of 'Generation E.A.' (Ethnically Ambiguous) by the *New York Times* in 2003 and the steady flow of publications on 'mixed-race studies', 'biraciality' and mixed relationships. Yet terminology is not universal. It is produced in particular countries with specific histories that make certain ways of referring to and understanding mixedness feasible and acceptable. Publications on mixed relationships and people of mixed parentage are, however, unevenly distributed across countries. For understandable reasons, given its history of settlement, enslavement and migration as well as its size, the USA has a greater volume of published work on mixedness than most other countries.

In that context, this book is highly innovative in illuminating mixed white Danish and South Asian relationships in Denmark. As the author, Rashmi Singla, explains, this has been almost entirely neglected in Danish literature. The focus on Denmark is, therefore, one of the major contributions made by this book in chapters that engage with international literature and present findings from the exploratory study that informs the text. That contribution is deepened by the historicising of racialisation and mixed relationships within the Danish context. Singla draws on Ifekwunigwe's (2004) four global pillars of racial mixing (political economic power; slavery; structural status and gender hierarchies) and points out that slavery is an unacknowledged part of Danish history.

An examination of recurrent themes in the literature of the last 20 years serves to illuminate the contrary currents that characterise this area. For example, recognition and inclusion are cross-cut by themes of exclusion; celebration of mixity coexists with suspicion and vilification of people of mixed parentage, who are at one and the same time subjected to racist practices and viewed as emblematic of convivial multicultures. In a shifting demographic context, the experiences associated with mixedness and the identities ascribed to, and taken up by, those of mixed parentage have been an important focus of much literature.

Singla has clearly spent time in careful reading of a broad range of literature in this field and critically engages, for example, with what she refers to as the 'three ages of mixed-race studies' (pathology, celebration and critique). As a result, her writing is theoretically informed and methodologically eclectic, drawing on sociocultural psychology, intersectionality and the phenomenology of sexual desire and notions of the everyday. It is this theoretical grounding that gives the text its cutting edge. Singla explores the dynamics of partnering and parenting 'across borders', particularly 'intermarriages' in couples who are visibly ethnically different, where one is a member of the South Asian diaspora. To that end, Singla interviews ten adults from six couples. Since she is a longstanding clinical psychologist, Singla draws on her psychosocial clinical work with two couples to inform her aim, encapsulated in her subtitle, of promoting mental health and wellbeing.

Singla shows that the couples have come together along various, differentiated trajectories and highlights the importance of family acceptance, of balancing multiple identities and of having fun. She demonstrates, however, that the couples presented here share much in common with other parents in terms of parenting responsibilities, desires and differentials of power and privilege. The great advantage of focusing on a small sample is that the couples come to life in the pages of the book and Singla therefore succeeds in her aim of adding nuance to this field of study and of promoting mental health and wellbeing for mixed couples and families.

As mixed parentage continues to burgeon in many countries, it is likely that the Danish trend will be for the mixed population to grow. This pioneering text is likely to stimulate other publications documenting and analysing experiences and examining the historically situated and socially constituted nature of mixedness. It is, therefore, likely to help to increasing recognition of people in mixed relationships and of mixed parentage within and beyond Denmark.

Ann Phoenix
Institute of Education
University of London
July 2014

Acknowledgements

The book you are reading is the product of the contributions of a number of persons.

I would like to acknowledge and express my sincere thanks to the participants in the empirical study and the practice case studies who volunteered to take part in the research. They opened their minds and hearts to share their experiences of being intermarried, thus making the book possible.

Thanks are due to Frida Dunger (Roskilde University) for being part of the research team during the first phase and conducting the data collection with enthusiasm and sensitivity, and to Dagny Holm (Roskilde University) for contributing to the data analyses with openness and adding unique dimensions. I am grateful to Ruta Maksimaviciute for patiently helping with the references and the quantitative part of the book, tasks which I could not have completed alone.

Gratitude is also due to the Department of Psychology & Educational Studies, Roskilde University, especially to the Head of Department Anders Siig Andersen, Professor Lars Dencik, Professor Jan Kampmann and Associate Professor Thomas Gitz-Johansen, for providing ongoing support for the book project and for their trust in my research plans. I also thank Associate Professor Neerja Sharma, Lady Irwin College, Delhi University, India, for inspiring me to research over the last four decades. I further wish to express my gratitude to Dr Suman Fernando for mentoring me for the past two decades.

Special thanks go to my colleagues: Associate Professor Azhar Hussain, for helping me with the statistics, and Associate Professor Bodil Pedersen, for critical comments. The comments and suggestions of sociologist Sayaka Osanami Törngren and of psychologist Enlisa Khanna led to important changes and are much appreciated. I also express my gratitude to the research group 'Gender, Body and Everyday Life' at Roskilde University and the members of Society for Intercultural Psychology, Denmark for thought-provoking discussions.

I thank Lucy Williams, Sociologist and Senior Researcher, for longstanding professional inspiration, and Associate Professors Stephen Carney and Bjarne Sode Funch for their interest and encouragement. Special thanks go to the three anonymous referees, Nicola Jones and Elizabeth Forrest at Palgrave Macmillan.

I thank my children – Kunal, Ketan and Devika as well as my daughter-in-law Ruheen – for supporting me and freeing me from some family duties to allow me to concentrate on the writing in Denmark. My siblings in India – Kamini, Rita and Mukul, and especially my eldest sister Chitra – have long been my distant pillars of strength – sincere thanks to all of them. Finally, special gratitude goes to Jawahar, my life partner for more than three decades, for making our everyday life smooth, having faith in my visions, supporting and encouraging me to achieve them.

The book's shortcomings are my own; reading and meaning-making is now your responsibility.

A rainy May day in Denmark, 2014

1
Intimate Relationships across Ethnic (and Other) Borders

This book is about the kind of intimate relations across ethnic borders that are gaining attention academically and politically as well as in service provision at international levels. It explores the dynamics of such relations, especially intermarriages between *visibly ethnically different couples*, characterised by differences in phenotypes such as physical and facial characteristics, skin colour and hair type. This book includes primarily an empirical study (Singla & Holm, 2012), in which one partner is Danish and the other originates from South Asia (India or Pakistan), at times also implying marriage between citizens and non-citizens.

Both study and book were motivated by my search for studies of 'mixedness' – partnering and parenting across different ethnic backgrounds which, in a Danish context, was almost futile and indicated a very limited availability of research. The exploratory study covered in the book attempts to answer questions related to intermarriage dynamics and to the negotiation of 'mixedness' by couples. Inspired by international studies of these phenomena, the objective is to explore new concepts and understandings of 'mixedness' and 'intermarriage', which have been relatively ignored in studies of diversity, migration, minority/majority relations as well as in family science in Denmark. A further motivation for this book was the lack of attention given to intermarried couples and the absence of their own voices in public and academic discourses. Thus the main research question I tackle is how ethnically intermarried couples negotiate their everyday lives and the parenting of their children.

Intermarried couples are often seen as *problems* mainly because their own voices are not heard. As A. Barbara stated in *Marriages Across Frontiers*, 'Cross-cultural marriages have the advantage of giving advance warning of what every couple must eventually face – that they are

1

different from each other' (Barbara, 1989, in Breger & Hill, 1998, p. 186). Partners in all marriages are different from each other, while couples marrying across ethnic borders may be different on some dimensions and similar on others. My goal is to create a nuanced picture of how it is to be an intermarried couple and what kind of dynamics, harmony and struggles they experience. This is an attempt to go beyond 'problematisation' to a more balanced and context-sensitive consideration of the dynamics in the nexus between intimate relations and ethnic boundary crossing. Drawing from studies in other parts of the world, especially from Asia, this book challenges the Eurocentrism of the emerging field which intersects Family Studies, Global Studies, Counselling, Psychotherapy and Migration Studies, generating new insights. My aspiration to increase awareness of these intimate relationships across borders has resulted in this book, which covers a relatively new area of study and uniquely expands the remit of research into the applied fields of *teaching* and *practice*.

Ethnic 'mixedness' is a subject related to the experiences of couples who have formed intimate partnerships across ethnic borders. It focuses on their experiences as parents and weaves in concern for their mental health and wellbeing. I perceive ethnicity as an axis of differentiation and identification, with social, historical and personally felt aspects; aptly termed as 'ethnicity in the head' and 'ethnicity in the heart' by Banks (1996 in Verkuyten, 2005). This concept is developed further in Chapter 2.

The terms 'intermarriage' and 'mixed marriage' are used in this book since they are recognised in most of the literature from the UK and Europe and it is accepted that no one term is used by couples who are married across these borders; the issue of terminology is discussed further in the next chapter.

One of the basic premises of this book, inspired by the science of intimate relationship (Fletcher et al., 2013), is that individuals are alone and incomplete but that isolation can be banished or at least ameliorated when humans pair off and experience the intimacy that can only be gained in close, emotionally connected relationships. Giles (2006) invokes the concept of sexual desire as a response to our gendered human conditions. Such intimacy can be experienced as highly romantic, sexual relationships. One understanding is that for most people the goal of forming a permanent or long-term, sexual liaison with another person is a pivotal goal in life in which a massive outlay of energy is invested. The conditions for the search for an intimate partner have changed due to the current process of globalisation, especially the popularisation of the Internet since the 1990s, and this changing pattern is another premise of this book. Globalisation processes – involving increased movements across borders – have broadened the range of potential partners for many people, leading to close intimate relationships among persons who may be geographically distant and may never have met each other without these increased movements.

Mixed marriage could mean marriage between a person originating from South Asia and a native Dane. This book studies marriages in which either spouse has migrated to get married or the spouse's parents have migrated to Denmark, and thus the spouse is perceived as part of the South Asian diaspora in Denmark – referred to here as the 'diasporic spouse' or reunified spouses. Diasporic belonging also implies a prioritising of ethnic identity and that the spouse is from an ethnic minority, while the Danish spouse is from the ethnic majority. The couples in the empirical study are, therefore, from the Global North (Denmark) and Global South (South Asia – India and Pakistan) and are studied in the Danish context. The themes emerging from this research, however, are applicable in many other contexts outside Denmark, albeit with local variations. This is not just another book on marriages because it presents intimate stories from real life, foregrounding the rarely heard voices of migrants as outsiders and thus making an important and unusual contribution.

Internationally there is an increasing political, public and intellectual interest in mixing and mixedness, people from a 'mixed' or 'inter' racial and ethnic background and people partnering and parenting across different racial and ethnic backgrounds (Edwards et al., 2012). This interest mirrors debates related to difficulties in terms of personal relationships and psychological processes associated with negative assumptions, such as 'identity confusion' on one hand and the positive assumption that mixed race people have a stronger genetic profile and are more beautiful, healthy and intelligent on the other. However, both these subnormal and supra-normal conceptualisations stem from the same premise that people from mixed backgrounds are somewhat different from mono-racial people (ibid.).

1.1 Intermarriages in a global perspective

Globalisation is a phenomenon with both geographical and ideological dimensions, being worldwide as well as universal, It involves with many life domains, including social relationships, life course, labour market affiliations, religious belongings and so on. Issues of love, intimate partnership and marriage cross many of these conceptual levels of globalisation. As this book attempts to take a broad view of mixed intimate partnerships, it aims to highlight the challenges and delights of cross-border marriages and intimate relationships that extend over countries and continents.

The phenomena of love and marriage across ethnic and geographical borders are powerful analytical tools as they provide a glimpse into the complex interconnections between cultural, economic, interpersonal and emotional realms of experience (Padilla et al., 2007). These phenomena have implications for people of mixed heritage who could benefit from more optimal social conditions, recognition, support, more sympathetic immigration and legal provisions and better health and social services if these global forces were better understood. These phenomena have hardly been scientifically explored in the Scandinavian/Danish context and this book is an attempt to do so. By focusing on the personal level, it attempts to explore how these people in intermarriages between South Asians and Danes enact, resist or transform social discourses of love and marriage within the specific historical and cultural context of contemporary Danish society.

International migration is a central aspect of globalisation and it facilitates modern, fluid, identities relating to transnational family life. Such family relationships across national borders are characterised by strong and sustainable ties between the person and a network of relatives based in other countries – including the country of origin – and they present new opportunities for family formation and lifestyles. An increasing number of people have ties to networks across geographic locations which may result in, or be the result of marrying across national or ethnic and/or racial borders. Intermarriage can be viewed as a by-product of the movement and migration of people as well as a driver of migration and, for whatever reasons, in the last few decades an increasing number of couples with markedly different ethnic origins and cultural backgrounds have chosen to live together. The global development in transnational family patterns and migration (intermarriage, transnational adoption, etc.) is thus changing and challenging traditional family forms, ideologies and values, as well as the ways of defining 'family', 'kinship' and 'marriage'. The boundaries of what is recognised as 'family' have become less clear according to sociologist Beck-Gernsheim (2002, pp. 104 ff.) who points to the tension between globalisation and individualisation in relation to the lifestyles and dynamics of new types of family and relationship patterns. She refers to them as the *post-familial family* (ibid., p. 10) where intermarriage is viewed as a result of free individual choice in a globalised world. The post-familial family is thus characterised and problematised by ethnic and racial differences internally and externally in relation to the majority population and dominant discourses in any given country of residence. Such trends towards 'intermarriage' and transnational identity are not just private decisions, they are seen as a challenge to politicians and social researchers in many European countries including Denmark where intermarriage has become a politically explosive issue (ibid., p. 105). It is not my intention to problematise mixing, however, as it offers both challenges and delights, enriching potential at societal, interpersonal and personal levels, but rather to illuminate both the problematic and celebratory aspects. This echoes Palriwala & Uberoi (2008), authors within the field of marriage migration and gender, who write that '...without discounting the abuses...social scientific attention to the intersection of marriage and migration needs to go beyond "victimisation" to a more balanced and context-sensitive consideration of changing dynamics in the nexus of marriage and migration' (ibid., p. 24).

At the same time, attention is directed to the increasing role of electronic media in the formation of intimate relationships between partners of different nationalities, races, ethnicities, sexualities and classes on the global scene. The Internet allows individuals to virtually connect and to transcend ethnic and national borders (Whitty & Carr, 2006). However, Agathangelou & Killian (2009) argue that this nullification of borders does not evade sexualising and racialising processes but reinscribes people within the racial and sexual matrices of violence and recolonisation. 'In crossing of borders to seek sexual intimacies, people do not just pass any borders and do not choose just any people' (ibid., p. 112).

There has been little scientific research regarding intermarriage and the psychosocial aspects are underexplored, even in the international context. Sookoor, Moodley & Pinto (2011) point out that in the American and Canadian contexts the paucity of mixedness research has led to the reinforcement of mythologies about ethnicity, race, sexuality, gender and identity. Mixed race and interethnic partnerships are seen as exotic, erotic or pathological. Even in Canada, a country with a declared policy of multiculturalism and relatively high degree of mixing across ethnic groups, there is very little research on the lived experiences of individuals in interethnic relationships. In the USA, Sherif, Trask & Koivunen (2007) reflect on how interethnic coupling affects marital processes, the retention of cultural traditions, assimilation and rearing of children.

Studying mixedness in close relationships such as marriage and relationships between parents and children of mixed parentage is significant. It provides a vehicle for examining ideologies surrounding race and ethnicity, ethnic relationships, and the role of social sciences in the construction and deconstruction of categories such as race and ethnicity. Moreover it is important for comprehending the self-understandings and strengths of society as argued by Root (1992). The multi racial/ethnic person's understanding of her or himself can enhance society's understanding of intra- and inter-group relations, identity and resilience. According to Wu (2011), in Canada, studying interethnic couple relationships is important not only because they reflect other aspects of diversity in families today, but also because of their potential impact in terms of social inclusion and self-identification within particular visible minority groups, particularly for subsequent generations.

The study of intermarriages provides insights into the lifestyle practices of the modern family, into integration processes and into alternative perspectives on minority and majority processes. Last but not least it provides insights into the intergenerational transmission of ethnic and cultural practices among children of mixed parentage.

Before proceeding further, I elaborate the conceptualisation of intermarriage and the salient terminology being used in the book.

1.2 Towards a conceptualisation of intermarriage

Intimate partnerships across ethnic, national and racial borders are embedded in broad social and historical structures and are also situated in specific geographic and social contexts. This makes the right terminology for the phenomena difficult for an international readership as there is no one term agreed upon by scholars or the lay readers. In a global comparative study of mixedness and multiracialism through census classification in 87 countries, Morning (2012) notes that terminology used in census questionnaires in the Americas, Asia, Europe and Africa varied according to how these regions' histories of colonialism, slavery, migration and political boundary shift. *Race* as a census item is used virtually exclusively by New World former slave societies (such as the USA and Brazil) but hardly features on European or Asian censuses. The term *race* is often conflated with ethnicity in academic, political, media and everyday understandings, although *race* hinges on beliefs about essential biological characteristics. Multiracialism is thus perceived by Morning (2012) as distinct from multi-ethnic, multicultural or multinational.

In the present study, the dynamic concepts of 'interracial mixing' and 'mixed race' highlight the contested nature of 'race' as a 'scientific' idea which attaches hierarchical meanings to physical differences as discussed by Ifekwunigwe (2004). Additionally, these hierarchies create, explain, justify and maintain social inequalities and injustices and underlie differential access to privilege, prestige and power, being differentially informed by structural factors such as gender, generation, social class, locality, colour and sexuality.

These issues, among others, will be taken up further in Chapter 2 of this book through a discussion of the historical variability of racial boundaries (Dencik, 2009; Song, 2009). For now it is important to note that there are different terms in use to denote intimate relations across ethnic borders and that all these terms are to some extent social constructions and axes of differentiations at different levels in different temporal and spatial contexts.

In Denmark, the prevalent term is ethnic intermarriage or intercultural marriage (in Danish – *etniske blandede ægteskaber, tværkulturel ægteskab*, Poulsen, 2012; Liversage, 2012). In Germany the term is bi-national or mixed nationality marriage (Fleischer, 2012; Beck & Beck-Gernsheim, 2014). In the Americas the term is interracial or multiracial (Karis & Killian, 2009; Rastogi & Thomas, 2009; Kenney & Kelley, 2011). In South Asia, especially in India, the common term is international marriage or *Euro Asian/Anglo-Indian* which, on another level, has a congruence with terms such as *interstate* or *inter-community* marriage to denote marriage between a North Indian and a South Indian (Bhagat, 2009) and when the partners belong to different dominant social groups. Some of these marriages may involve different faiths or religious belongings and may be considered as interfaith/religious marriage. Marriages between Jews and non-Jews have been investigated in Scandinavia – in Sweden, Finland and Norway, where a rising rate of religious intermarriages is indicated (Dencik, 2009).

In agreement with Song (2009), it is noted that in some cases racial, ethnic and religious intermarriage may coincide and it may be difficult to distinguish between them. There may be overlapping between the diverse categories of belonging as a White Christian (Protestant) Dane can marry a person from India who is Christian (Catholic) or a person who is Hindu; in the first case there is crossing of ethnic boundaries, while in the second both ethnic and religious boundaries are crossed.

Song's conclusion, that the increasing rate of intermarriages between black and white Britons as well as Indians and whites suggests that being 'mixed' may be becoming increasingly unremarkable, can be debated but can hardly be transplanted to the Danish context.

By 1991, Cottrell had already reviewed existing studies in the field of cross-national marriages and added to the conceptualisation of intermarriage by presenting three general types: Colonial or War brides (the result of one nation's military or colonial presence), the second type is educated Western and non-Western couples (which involves highly educated individuals who lived abroad as students or professionals), while the last type is Western (Western couples who share similar cultures). According to this typology, the present study is primarily concerned with the second type.

In their recent book, Beck & Beck-Gernsheim (2014) use an umbrella term – 'world-family' perceived as loving relationships and other forms of relationship between people living in, or coming from, different countries. Although there may be many forms, the commonality is that these people are the focal points at which different aspects of the globalised world literally become embodied. In my view, this term is too vague and broad as it includes many different groups. It is relevant to consider for the present book that there are various types of mixed marriages, some of which may involve movement across geographical borders and may be considered as transnational marriage involving cross-border marriage migration. In a seminal book about global marriage, Williams (2010) understands cross-border marriage migration as migration that results, at least in part, from a contractual relationship between individuals with different national or residency statuses such as citizen or non-citizen. For the migrant cross-border spouses this entails a loss of formal citizenship status and restrictions in their rights in their country of settlement. For the current purpose, it is pertinent to note that marriage migration may take place within the same ethnic communities linked across international borders by practical, emotional and symbolic ties *or* between ethnic groups, where the partners may have little knowledge of the lives or expectations of their new spouses (ibid., p. 120). The latter forms the primary subject of this book and alludes to increasing use of the Internet (Whitty & Carr, 2006), social networking, work, education, travelling and so on. In addition there can be marriage through brokering agencies, the so-called commercially arranged marriage migration or *commodified marriage* (see Lu, 2005; Yang & Schoonheim, 2006, cited in Williams, 2010). In this context, the term *transnational marriage*

(Beck-Gernsheim, 2007), marriage within established communities and ethnic communities across nation states such as the Indian diaspora and *incipient transnationalism* (Williams, 2010; Constable, 2013), when the spouses' communities are *not yet linked* but in which the migrant spouse may develop transnational sensibilities and logics in the future, are relevant.

The term for the spouse moving from another country to Denmark, the country of settlement in the present study, is the *diasporic spouse*, as the person is assumed to be a part of South Asian (Indian/Pakistani) diaspora irrespective of whether they have migrated themselves or whether their parents migrated. More specifically the term *reunified spouse* is used for a marriage migrant. Williams (2010) uses the term migrant cross-border spouse, which is perceived as not being sufficiently precise for the current purpose as 'the border' may be interpreted at many levels.

Lastly, while dwelling on terminologies, we can say that all marriages, by definition, are mixed to some extent as marriage is a union of two persons and/or families belonging to different (nuclear) families, irrespective of the ethnic group, community, nationality and involvement of the family – marriage implies mutual adaptation (Singla, 2006). However belonging to *visibly* different groups with different phenotypes adds another dimension to these marriages and is one of the focus points of this book.

The term ethnic intermarriage or mixed marriage is the most appropriate in the Danish context and for this book, due to the significance attached to phenotypes in everyday life. This is further emphasised by Danish studies of exclusion processes among transnational adoptees, especially from countries like South Korea and India, who have different phenotypes than the majority population (Myong, 2009; Holm, 2010; Breuning, 2012). Aspinall & Song (2013) also emphasise the continuing significance of phenotypes observable physical differences in social relationship formation and everyday life activities in the UK.

Despite the terms intermarriage and mixed marriage being criticised as being culturally essentialist and implying that the people can be effectively separated by a perceived attachment to one group (Williams, 2010) and apparently overlooking simultaneous multiple belonging (see discussion of the concept of intersectionality in Chapter 2), these terms are meaningful in Scandinavian migration studies, family studies, counselling and psychosocial services and hopefully in the wider public understanding, where these issues are largely overlooked. Lastly, these terms are gaining increasing acceptance in the academic world as reflected by some recent publications in Europe (Ifekwunigwe, 2004; Osanami Törngren, 2011; Edwards et al., 2012; Aspinall & Song, 2013, King-O'Riain et al., 2014).

I admit, though, that the use of these terms epitomises the basic dilemma of how to challenge stigmatising simplistic discourses without promoting them. This book also overlooks some complexities in the field, especially the intimate relations between adults who are themselves children of mixed parentage. As one of my students commented, 'You are studying intimate relationships between Danes and Indians/Pakistanis. What about my friend whose father is Indian and mother is Danish? Now she is married to a native Dane. Will you consider this as an intermarriage?' Similarly, I met a young woman whose mother was Danish and her father originated from Pakistan. She sought psychosocial counselling about her conflicting intimate relationship with a young Pakistani man. The counselling ended well according to her and she ended that relationship and is now in a successful one with a Danish man. Is it an intermarriage?

My answer to the student is that these relationships are intermarriages, but not the ones being explored in the present book, which is just one of the first steps in exploring these issues in the Danish context. As a researcher, one can choose not to focus on some complexities as a point of departure and hope that others will take up the challenge and explore further.

1.3   Strengthening mixed partnering and parenting: applied aspects

In contemporary Western society, around 40% of marriages end in divorce (Kalmijn, 2010). There is an assumed increased risk for disruption in ethnic intermarriages as compared with ethnic homogamous marriages, though this is challenged in recent research by Irastorza & DeVoretz (2009). This issue is taken up further in Chapter 8. Kenney & Kenney (2012) highlight myths and stereotypes that pervade Western society which suggest that the individuals who couple interracially are dysfunctional, are attempting to make a statement or have ulterior motives for marriage. Motives speculated upon include quests for the exotic, sexual curiosity and promiscuity, economic and social status or achievement, domination, potential citizenship, rebellion against society or family, low self-esteem or racial self-hatred. Ibid further claim that persons of colour are more willing to accept children of interracial unions than are white people and that the difficulties faced by interracial individuals and families are based on race and ethnicity thinking and overlook contextual aspects.

The present book attempts to move beyond these myths and stereotypes by giving voice to couples themselves and by covering issues related to strengthening the couples' relationships through health promotion, prevention of psychosocial problems and counselling in case of conflicts.

In line with Hahlweg et al. (2010) I argue that the quality of family life is fundamental to the wellbeing of the wider community as the stability of the family has a pervasive influence on the psychological, physical, social, economic and cultural wellbeing of almost all its members including the parents as well as the younger generation. In a context where society overlooks mixed couples and children, it is all the more important to consider strengthening mixed partnering and parenting, which has the potential to improve the quality of life and health status of the family, including future generations.

In Europe it is only in the past couple of decades that these issues have received increased academic attention and they have been researched as specific 'mixed identities' (Alibhai-Brown, 2001; Tizard & Phoenix, 1994; Beck-Gernsheim, 2002; Ifekwunigwe, 2004; Suki Ali, 2003; Cabarello et al., 2008; Song, 2009; Osanami Törngren, 2011; Aspinall & Song, 2013). The term 'visibly ethnically different households' (Phoenix, 2011) enables us to see the commonalities in two different kinds of 'non-normative' contexts involving negotiations of mixedness in everyday life: transnational adopted children as well as intermarried couples and their children. The main focus here is on the latter category but the former is touched upon to some extent.

I am aware that children with the same parents can also have different shades of skin colour and be affected by 'colourising' (Cunningham, 1997 in Phoenix, 2011), yet there is limited knowledge about the dynamics of mixed parenting. Inspiration can be found in works based on applied aspects such as multiracial couple therapy and family counselling (Rastogi & Thomas, 2009). Studies from the American setting on raising multiracial children (Wehrly, Kenney & Kenney, 1999; Root, 2001; Nakazawa, 2003) are useful, but have a rather different theoretical framework than the one used in this study.

There are two different tendencies in the European context regarding the strengthening of mixed parenting. One tendency is to perceive the mixed couples as ordinary (Cabarello et al., 2008) and the other is to focus on their conflictual situation (Hahlweg et al., 2010). According to Cabarello et al.'s (2008) in-depth study, the parents see their families as ordinary and are not constantly preoccupied with culture clashes. Indeed, ideas about dichotomous culture clashes are difficult to sustain in the face of the fact that parents in mixed relationships may be mixed themselves. Parents are, however, in the process of negotiating a sense of belonging for their children and dealing with society's reactions to differences. Hahlweg et al. (2010) point out that diversity in partner assumptions can be positive in a relationship where partners are able to draw on the wisdom and strengths of their backgrounds even while these differences can be a source of conflict. They further argue that interventions bring about changes in couples from diverse cultures. They recommend interventions both for *promoting* positive resources and wellbeing and *preventing* serious problems while the couple is still happy or at least in the early stages of distress; the goal of the preventive effort being to increase positive exchanges and solve relationship issues. Furthermore, *universal preventive programmes* are mentioned, as they target an entire population, for example all couples planning marriages, rather than focusing on high-risk groups which include intermarried couples. For couples already experiencing conflict and distress, counselling and therapy is recommended. Few couples, however, actually use counselling or treatment services when they experience a deteriorating relationship. Even when they ask for help, the data on the long-term outcomes indicates that in many cases, counselling is undertaken too late to repair the damage of many years of destructive conflict.

This book deals primarily with persons who constitute 'ordinary' mixed couples, supplemented by two case studies of persons who contacted psychosocial services and issues of counselling and therapy are considered further in the final chapter. I have combined the experiences of ordinary couples with two clinical cases. This combination of 'good' practices among the participants in the study and the clinical cases form the basis for health promotion, prevention and counselling suggestions for mixed partnering and parenting.

1.4   The book's structure

The book's nine chapters aim to provide an introduction to the phenomenon of intermarriage in relation to mental health and wellbeing, focusing on an empirical study leading to a deeper understanding aimed at informing scholars and researchers as well as mental health practitioners.

Chapter 2 sets the scene for the phenomena of intermarriage historically and currently, and it delineates the broader field of mixedness studies through the three ages and conceptualisations of ethnicity and *race* in the Danish context. This chapter highlights the eclectic theoretical framework combining sociocultural psychology with intersectionality that underpins this study. Methodological aspects, ethical issues and the analytic themes make up Chapter 3.

Chapters 4, 5, 6 and 7 examine salient analytical themes with the point of departure being the 'getting together' including the issues of identity and gender dynamics discussed in Chapter 4. While managing the everyday as their life course changes, the couples' system dynamics evolve with the relationship over the time and this forms the basis for Chapter 5. Parenting issues and the dominant strategies used by the couples in socialising their children are analysed in Chapter 6. The local context as well as the broader context in which the couples live, with emphasis on transnational relationships, is examined in the Chapter 7.

Chapter 8 brings together the different themes mentioned above and focuses on the overall analytic concept mental health and wellbeing of the participants within the three predominant post hoc categories of conflictual, ambivalent and supportive relations. Two supplementary cases from psychosocial counselling which consider good practice are included in Chapter 9, with the aim of contributing to a better understanding of the implications of intermarriage for health promotion, problem prevention, counselling and psychotherapy.

Dilemmas involved in the process of empirical research and future perspectives for teaching, research and practice in this field are explored in Section 9.5, Concluding Thoughts, at the end of Chapter 9.

We now turn to an examination of the phenomenon of intermarriage within the Danish context with a point of departure being a historical perspective, challenging the myth of Danish homogeneity (Jenkins, 2011) and moving beyond the assertions about identity confusion and a pathologically focused research agenda. In addition, current discourses about intermarriages along with the perspectives on strengthening mixed partnering and parenting are presented.

2
Setting the Danish Scene and Mixedness Concept

> There is a journey we all must make into our past in order to come to terms with our future.
>
> (Larsen, 2008, p.17)

This chapter sets out to highlight the phenomenon of intermarriage in Denmark from a historical context, as well as by analysing current demographic patterns and statistics.

A conceptual understanding of mixedness comprises the second part of the chapter, which includes discussion of identity and mixedness, *'othering'* processes and the relationship between 'us' and the *other*, followed by the theoretical framework comprising primarily the cultural historical approach, intersectionality and the phenomenological perspective to sexual desires.

In order to explore the Danish context regarding intermarriages, especially marriages across ethnic and colour borders, it is relevant to consider the historical background to intimate meetings between Danes and *others* in line with the cultural historical theoretical approach. The epigraph lucidly illustrates significance of including the past to comprehend the phenomenon in the present and future.

2.1 Historical background

In order to grasp the complex and dynamic expectations of couples in intimate partnerships, an appropriate point of departure is Alibhai-Brown's conclusions from an empirical study of mixedness in the UK.

One overwhelming conclusion I reached while researching this book [2001] was that however mixed race couples and mixed race children choose to live their lives, they cannot shake off historical baggage or isolate themselves from the assumptions and bigotries of the outside world. These attitudes infiltrate their lives.

(Alibhai-Brown, 2001, p.14)

This quotation shows clearly how a deep understanding of mixed marriages entails taking into account the major aspects of the 'historical baggage' in Denmark, especially as there is a dominant discourse about ethnic homogeneity in Denmark (Jenkins, 2011). This section considers historical aspects and attitudes related to intimate relationship formation across ethnic borders in the Danish context, a rather overlooked theme in the Danish history of domination and resistance. This discussion forms a broad background to the exclusion/inclusion dynamics highlighted by the participants in the empirical study at interpersonal and structural levels. I draw on the four global pillars of 'racial' mixing (in figure 2.1) as described by Ifekwunigwe (2004) to provide a framework, which enables us to position the Danish situation and relate it to social outcomes in specific geographical contexts of similar historical processes. Put simply, we consider if 'mixed-race' communities have been socially engineered in the Danish context. Were the grand ideologies of *scientific racism* mere rationalisations for European and especially Danish greed in the form of exploiting indigenous riches (such as slaves, land and sugar)? Crucially we consider how the past informs the contemporary mixedness debates (Figure 2.1).

In the Danish context, as for the rest of Europe, the period of colonisation and slavery, which began around 1500, sets a point of departure for the formation of images of the 'other' as persons belonging to another 'race'. Although mainstream Danish history from the seventeenth century hardly mentions African slaves, Frank Larsen (2008), emphasises that about 100,000 black Africans were used as slaves by Danes, including in Denmark, from the seventeenth century until the official end of slavery in 1848. This historical amnesia, a 'forgetting' of the slaves and their descendants, is indicative of the 'homogenisation' processes overseeing social diversity in Denmark. The relationship to the *other* (in this case Danes who can trace their family history back to slaves) was complex and problematic.

The history of these *Others* indicates that some have created an equal place in Danish society and from recognition of this taboo, an almost ignored part of the Danish history, we can learn about the examples of potential of human capacity. There are positive as well as negative aspects in these narratives; however the official 'silence' about these unions reflects the response of the state to such intimate partnership formation

They have overcome extreme violence, poverty, discrimination and systematic racism. They have broken the chains of the heaviest social inheritance and adapted to the modern society as equal and worthy.

(ibid., p.288, own translation)

This quotation tells us something about the failure of official discourses to reflect the reality of society and how the contribution of slaves to Danish prosperity and industrialisation has not been recognised.

Another similar taboo and forgotten part of Danish history is related to the phenomenon of the human exhibition display of exotic human beings in the zoological garden and Tivoli (a historical amusement park in a garden setting) in Copenhagen from the 1870s to 1910, these people were regarded as wild, uncivilised and very different from the Danish public (Andreassen & Henningsen, 2011). These consisted of so called 'exotic' persons from distant countries and were sometimes displayed for periods (some months) in reconstructions of their 'natural habitats', where they carried on their everyday life activities and the spectators could gaze at them.

These exhibitions reflected the fears, restrictions and practices related to racial mixing, and demonstrated how marrying across racial borders,

Political Economic Power-Producing	*Slavery*
1. European expansion, settler colonisation and imperialism led to displacement, marginalisation and subordination	2. The importation of 'non-European' slaves and indentured labourers to meet local labour needs contributed to the economic development of Europe and North America and the underdevelopment and depopulation of other parts
Structural/Status-defining	*Gender hierarchies*
3. Race/colour hierarchies–'White' European supremacy and 'indigenous' or 'non-white' inferiority assumed and backed-up by nineteenth-century 'scientific racism'	4. Majority/European men positioned at the top, majority/European women positioned below them, followed by minority/non-European men. Minority/non-European women are positioned at the very bottom and subject to sexual exploitation

Figure 2.1   Four global pillars of 'racial' mixing
Source: Abridged version of figure from Ifekwunigwe, 2004, p.7.

especially for Danish women, could be interpreted as a sign of emotional cosmopolitanism and protest against the dominant patriarchal system. The descriptions of different groups from 'exotic' parts of the world – China, India, Ghana – contained narratives as well as criticism of Danish women's romantic and sexual interest in the exhibited men. In that period, mixing across 'race' borders was a central and integrated part of race discussion and related to race hierarchy and social Darwinism. Racial mixing was perceived as a threat to the existing power and race hierarchies (Andreassen & Henningsen, 2011, p.188).

The European 'race' and its culture considered itself superior to others. As in the European colonies, racial mixing was forbidden in Denmark, but an attraction and fetishism of the *other* was recognised. Danish women's intimate relationships with these men were regarded as a lack of loyalty to the Danish (patriarchal) perceptions of Danish women belonging to Danish men. Marriages between Asian men and Danish women resulted in the women losing their Danish citizenship as it followed that a wife and any children would take the husband's nationality. Cultural researcher Nava (in Andreassen & Henningsen) interprets white women's intimate relationships with non-white men as an expression of 'an inner, experienced, *home oriented*, localised and gender wise cosmopolitanism'. She argues that such relations should be interpreted as an expression of openness in relation to the alien and the different – a form of emotional cosmopolitanism. It can also be interpreted as a rebellion against the national patriarchal gender oppression or as representing the choice of sexual freedom. It is important to note, based on Andreassen & Henningsen (2011), that despite scientific criticism of racial mixing, in everyday life, people did mix socially and romantically across nations in the past and are still mixing. These narratives document the presence of mixed marriages and the negative social reactions to them.

Thus it can be concluded that legal sanctions against miscegenation in Denmark, such as women losing Danish citizenship, have strengthened ethnic homogamous patterns and have, to an extent, stigmatised mixed marriages. These patterns draw comparisons to more comprehensive anti-miscegenation laws and pathologisation of 'mixed-race' children in eighteenth- and nineteenth-century Europe and America (Ifekwunigwe, 2004).

It is important to acknowledge this era of Danish history, since failing to recognise that racism and colonisation was a central part of the Danish past risks repeating the actions and ways of thinking at that time. There is a risk that continuing to privilege whiteness comes at the cost of the non-white and thus the inclusion of this history will hopefully influence the present and the future.

Other waves of migration in Danish history include the movement of Dutch people (approximately 150 families) to the Amager/Dragoer area in the sixteenth century in accordance with the royal invitation to come to Denmark to cultivate vegetables. These families didn't intermarry in the first few generations but did so later. In the seventeenth century, approximately 60 so-called 'Potato German' families settled in Jutland. In addition there were approximately 3,000 Polish migrants who settled in the Lolland area in the nineteenth century (Østergaard, 1983 in Krag, 2007). These migrants gradually intermarried, but were not considered 'racially' different from the majority population. Still, these historical facts indicate that the main discourse of Danish homogeneity can be questioned.

Beck-Gernsheim (2002), focuses on the topicality and controversial nature of the basic issues involved in determining 'mixed families' by considering *two classifications* from a spectrum of possibilities: society may classify people within a clear-cut category (for example in the USA), or society may devise new categories that signal the in-between status of such groups and persons (for example in Nazi Germany, where mixed-race couples and their children were persecuted).

Theoretically these classifications can be understood as social constructions producing their own paradoxes and contradictions. In the course of the nineteenth and twentieth centuries, Jews in Germany had gained civil rights and citizenship, and some Jews perceived themselves to be linked more closely with their non-Jewish surroundings through intermarriages leading to fixed families (ibid.). A twofold strategy was adopted by the Nazi regime to reverse the process of assimilation of Jews to make dissimilar those who had become so similar. On the one hand Jews were represented as the *other* by constructing a distorted image of them as spongers and parasites, while a special legal status for Jews excluded them and robbed them of their civil rights. To deal with the issues of 'mixedness' between Jews and non-Jews, intermarriages were forbidden and marriages were categorised as 'simple mixed marriages' and 'privileged mixed marriages', while children who were already born were categorised as 'grade one half-breeds' and 'grade two half-breeds' based on the religion of their grandparents. Three or four Jewish grandparents made one a 'Jew', regardless of one's own religion; two Jewish grandparents resulted in a *Mischling* ('half breed') First Grade; a single Jewish grandparent defined the *Mischling* Second Class; while an individual without any Jewish grandparent was to be considered 'German-blooded'. This fourfold classification was to replace the old dichotomous scheme of 'Aryan' vs. 'non-Aryan'.

The echoes of these terms of yesteryear extend into the present and the terms for couples and families crossing the 'race' borders are still unclear. In Germany the term 'mixed families' was used to refer to marriages between 'Aryans & Non-Aryans' (Kleiber & Gomusay, 1990 in Beck-Gernsheim, 2002), which is why in people's minds today mixedness is bound with Nazi policy and legislation. Similarly the term 'multiracial', used in the USA, has historical burdens of its own, derived from the slave period in the USA and sinister biological connotations from the Nazi period. Thus in Germany, the terms binational or multinational (or bicultural or multicultural) marriages are prevalent and as Beck-Gernsheim (2002) eloquently pinpoints, these expressions run into difficulties when applied retrospectively to earlier periods of history. This is further discussed in Chapter 9 under mixed race identities. I have discussed the German case in some detail as it illustrates the influence of political ideology on the phenomenon of intermarriage and also has relevance for the Danish context.

'Mixedness' had (and has) a negative connotation in Germany and to some extent in Scandinavia, not least when viewed in a historical postwar perspective. The persecution of women who had relationships with German soldiers during the Nazi occupation in Denmark (1939–1945), the so-called Field Mattresses, German girls (in Danish *feltmadrasser, tyskertøser*), suffered from social exclusion, public punishment and humiliation. It is estimated that during the occupation around 50,000 women were involved with German soldiers and at least 5,500 children (maybe more) were born as a result of these relationships. The social judgement on these women was hard and they were seen as traitors and prostitutes (Drolshagen, 1999). A similar fate was shared by women in other European countries after the Second World War and children of such unions grew up surrounded by silence, secrecy, isolation and shame. The children of soldiers of an occupying force and local women are typically objects of exclusion, and thus these 'mixed' children were not accepted by society – a further example is the case of Japanese-American offspring of soldiers in Japan (Murphy-Shigematsu, 2002).

In the 1960s and 1970s a sizeable number of 'labour migrants' from Turkey, the former Yugoslavia and Pakistan arrived in Denmark before the 'migration-stop' in 1972. Many of these came as single men and some cohabitated with Danish women. In the late 1970s and 1980s, however, migrant men began to bring wives and families from their countries of origin. Some interethnic marriages and cohabitation continued, some secretly, and the population of children with mixed parentage grew. Despite the reality of these relationships, and of these children, the Danish state has not acknowledged them as persons belonging to a specific category. A probable explanation might be the preference to maintain the myth of Danish homogeneity. As a result, these couples and children have been almost invisible in the media and in society, although there is a political focus on the phenomenon which has led to restrictions and the social engineering of intermarriages. Within ethnic minority families, even among young people, homogamy is prevalent, especially for those with a Muslim background, for whom it is important that the future partner should be a Muslim. Some parents, however, prefer Danish spouses for their children, rather than accepting marriages with other minority groups as there are reciprocal prejudices among different groups (Loua, 2012).

The presence of continuing racial prejudice was also indicated in 2014 through the use of the term *negro* (Danish term *neger*) for black persons by a member of parliament. This illustrates a disparaging and derogatory attitude towards persons with a different phenotype from that of the majority population. Jenkins (2011) also notes use of this term in the Danish context in his empirical study. A critical response to that member of parliament by a journalist of Kenyan origin places it as racism.

> I understand how much you cherish your freedom of expression, but your freedom does not give you liberty to belittle other people because of the colour of their skin using vilifying words. That is what *racism* is.
>
> (Khadudu, 2014, p. 1)

2.2 Intermarriage in contemporary Denmark

Intermarriage in Denmark is not just the concern of the partners involved but has become the object of public regulation through policies related to citizenship and entry, residence and rights to work in Denmark. Immigrant family patterns have become an issue of increasing public and political debate in the Nordic countries and during recent decades, concerns have been raised about citizenship and national identity, family reunification and provisions in immigration law.

Since 2002, Danish family migration legislation has tightened to reflect changing political attitudes towards immigration and transnational marriages. One result is 'the 24 years rule' (Law 365) that regulates the age of the spouses applying for entry residence and subsequent rights to work through intermarriage (irrespective of ethnic background). Publicly articulated reasons for the law were stated as to reduce and regulate immigration in Denmark and to give priority to the integration of immigrants already living in the country. Its secondary purpose was to strengthen efforts to prevent arranged and forced marriages (Rytter, 2007, p. 26).

By these restrictions and by using the law to control who can marry whom, from where, and when, the possibilities for marriage migration were limited. Law 365 came into effect in the summer of 2002 and set out specific requirements concerning the spouses' ages. Both partners – according to the requirements – must be at least 24 years old, they must have sufficient housing space and the Danish partner must be in a position to support the incoming partner financially. In addition, the partner already residing in Denmark must deposit a sum (approx. 50000 DKK/10000US$ in 2013) as a bank guarantee to ensure that financial support for the incoming partner will be forthcoming in the future. Finally, both the partners must be able to demonstrate they have a connection with Denmark. Clearly, these regulations have made family reunification especially difficult to achieve. These new requirements have reduced the number of foreign applicants approved to marry Danish citizens and the number of visas granted reduced from 6,499 in 2001 to 2,787 in 2006. As a result, many Danish citizens migrate to Sweden, where they can use their rights as EU citizens to bring their spouse from abroad, get married and live there Rytter (2007, pp. 26–27). He explains that this solution (also called the 'Swedish' model), had by 2005 been adopted by 600 Danish citizens living in Skåne, Sweden, and on that basis it can be estimated that by 2014 the total number of intermarried couples in southern Sweden must be a few thousand.

Political restrictions on intermarriage instrumentalise conceptions of how family life is formed and 'done'/practised and they make clear how marriages should *not* be 'done'/practised. Equally, marriages in which family plays a significant part in partner selection are perceived by law as inappropriate and thus provide a normative understanding of how 'family' life should be done/practised and demonstrate who is considered as a legitimate choice of partner. We can learn much about how the state views marriage from an analysis of these recent changes in the law. Marriage to non-citizens is made more difficult, so it is presumably considered as undesirable and as not a 'normal' or legitimate choice. This prohibition applies however, equally if a white Dane wishes to marry a Kenyan, a Pakistani Dane marries a Pakistani or a white Dane marries a white American.

The law tells us much about cultural discourses and values concerning 'real' families and normality: about *us* and *others*. At the same time migration legislation shows us how the state discriminates and excludes 'abnormal' family lifestyles. Chapters 7 and 8 of this book seek to discover how discourses about 'normal' families, ethnicity, race and migration affect people involved in intermarriages. How are dilemmas raised by dual (or multiple) citizenship, family legislation and immigrant laws connected? Undoubtedly, legal restrictions create practical barriers to gaining resident permits and Danish citizenship, etc., but what about the intimate and emotional aspects of intermarriage? Do attitudes towards immigration and intermarriage affect ethnic identity, sense of belonging and emotionality? Are there cultural costs and problems with intimate partnership linked to these attitudes? When social and legal processes are changing – and in this case changes are dramatic – it is of great importance to investigate the social effects of political restrictions in relation to the subjective experiences of the people involved and affected.

Intimate partnerships across borders are affected by issues related to ethnicity on both abstract and concrete everyday life levels. In the first place these issues involve just the couple, but later on the wider family may be involved. As Fernandez (2010) succinctly points out, by bringing race into the home, the couples force families and friends into an inescapable and relentless confrontation with racial issues, which primarily applies when intimate partnership formation is across colour borders and when people of different phenotypes are involved. In Denmark there has been some attention directed towards mixed marriages in popular media and literature in the past few decades. Branner (1983) had a series of interviews with mixed couples, including an Indian-Danish couple, in a national newspaper as these marriages were perceived to highlight the problems and advantages. Recently Rashid & Højbjerg (2007) have published an autobiographical novel about their Pakistani-Danish marriage, while Painuly (2014) has published a novel about life of a young Indian girl and her family living in Denmark, which among other issues, focuses on mixed marriages between Indians and Danes. However, there has not yet been any academic, systematic study of intermarriage in Denmark. This book is an attempt to fill this gap and it aims to explore both the possibilities and limitations of intimate couple formation across ethnic borders, with a special focus on South Asian and Danish mixed marriages.

2.3   Love, relationships and intimacy in the twenty-first century

When exploring intermarriage in the Danish context, a relevant point of departure is Giddens' study of changing forms of intimacy (1992, 1999) in Western societies. For Giddens, changes in intimate partnership formation are related to globalisation, urbanisation and industrialisation and there is a general trend towards the free choice of spouse. There is by no means a complete correlation, but extended family systems are usually associated with arranged marriages, especially within South Asian ethnic minorities. Due to the increasing influence of affective individualisation and romantic love as well as the above-mentioned processes, marriage by arrangement is under strain in the European context and is taking new forms, for example by using the Internet (Whitty & Carr, 2006, Willerton, 2010). In fact it can be argued that white elites are now arranging marriages through new technology by using dating websites. The parental generation of South Asian communities is also adapting to these changes to some extent by introducing young people and allowing them to interact and decide for themselves in Western countries such as the UK and Denmark. The younger generation – especially those residing and working in urban areas – often claim the right to choose their own partners. Thus the trends towards individualism and love matches are also seen amongst South Asian families. However, Giddens (1992) describes the South Asian young people as having a 'distinct' pattern with parental expectation to conform to norms of cooperation, respect and family loyalty. It seems that Giddens exaggerates the inflexibility of culture and overlooks the degree to which South Asian youngsters in European societies are exposed to an individualistic social environment at school. He notes only that South Asian young people of both genders are demanding greater consultation in the arrangement of their marriage, but he does not perceive their demand for greater freedom in the choice of a marriage partner and in ongoing intergenerational negotiations. However, the latest demographic data indicates an increase in marriages across ethnic borders in Western societies, even among South Asian groups in the UK (Song, 2012).

Romantic love as a part of marriage has become paramount in contemporary societies, invoking the concept of pure relationships where individualism and self-satisfaction is the chief objective: 'romantic love seems to be a normal part of human existence, rather than a distinctive feature of modern culture... the emphasis on personal satisfaction in marriage has raised expectations which cannot be met, and this is one factor involved in increasing rates of divorce' (Giddens, 1992, p.398).

There is an irony to all this emphasis on pure relationships and choice, as even in the Global North, the idea of *entirely love-based* relationships is a fiction as in the regimes of choice most people still tend to marry people much like themselves (Padilla et al., 2007, p. xviii), though there is a relative increase in intermarriages. In other words, people usually fall in love with people 'like' themselves, whether ethnically, culturally or through shared interests. A critical reading of the concept of the pure relationship implies that the material aspects of current Euro-American kinship systems are deliberately obscured. Furthermore, the notion that modern conjugality is only about affection and emotion contrasts sharply with the demographic data on extramarital sex and gendered effects of divorce, which show that sex is more frequent *outside* of marriage and that money is much more *within it* – as motivators for relationships than the ideology of pure relationships suggests (ibid.). We can be critical about this claim by Padilla et al. yet the material aspect of intimate relationships should not be overlooked.

Focusing on the issue of marriages in the Danish context, Jakobsen (2001) argues that partnership formation is an individual's personal project, though this freedom has its price. Seeking help in couple formation is perceived as embarrassing and it is seen as 'wrong' if intimate partnership formation has to be 'arranged' in any way.

> The meeting between the two should be just by chance, surrounded by mystic and miraculous atmosphere... The problem is that if the miracle doesn't happen by itself or doesn't take place for years, the blame is on the individual alone. One of individualism's negative sides is that the person is just left to him/herself, to own the fate.... and a miracle. It is not easy to live under the cultural condition of individualism and such expectations related to marriage.
>
> (Jakobsen, 2001, pp. 66–67)

This freedom implies that some people manage partnership formation better, easier and faster than others. In a study by Luth (2011) in Denmark, love is underlined as the primary reason for marriage. After a year or so love 'goes over', increasing the risk of divorce within three years (Statistics Denmark, 2012). At the same time Vaughn (2010), argues in a discussion of relationships, sexuality and culture that, while many Western countries view marriage as the culmination of romantic love, in many Asian and African countries less emphasis is placed on romantic love which is considered a selfish and weak reason to enter into marriage. Arranged marriages are viewed as more than simply a union between two individuals – they are seen as alliances between two families. This oversimplified dichotomy between Western and South Asian marriages is problematised in Section 2.7 and in Chapter 3. Trends in marriage patterns are changing globally with increasing urbanisation as well as globalisation and Counts, cited in Vaughn (2010, p. 120), argues that marriage has become more joyful, more *loving* and more satisfying for many couples than ever before in history, though one can question what evidence is there for his claim. However, he also claims that at the same time marriage has become more optional and brittle, which is statistically indicated by high rates of marriage and cohabitation dissolution. These two strands of change cannot be disentangled. In agreement with Padilla et al. (2007) we can conclude that the role of love in marriage provides a lens that reveals many aspects of culture, economics and interpersonal and personal values.

The complex picture of marriage within majority populations in Western Europe makes clear the extra dimensions, greater possibilities and risks for those entering into mixed marriages. According to Romain (1996, p. 5), in interfaith marriages or marriages across religious divisions which may be indicators of intermarriage from the point of view of family, the cardinal question is if it will work, as a common fear is that marriage is hard enough at best of times, so why add to your potential difficulties? Marriage, additionally, can be wonderful or horrendous depending on the couple, the effort they put into the relationship and the support they receive from others. This applies even more to mixed marriages. Successful ones can be enriching, with the partners bringing two vastly different sets of experiences and expectations which are intertwined to form a new and creative household. For unsuccessful couples, though, such marriages may be like a minefield, with differences constantly jarring and exploding at unexpected moments. Romain further points out:

> There are plenty of mixed-faith marriages somewhere in between these extremes, which jog along uneventfully most of the time but face periodic crises at seasonal observances or cycle-of-life moments.
>
> (ibid., p. 5)

In the globalised world, there is increasing in contact between persons of different ethnic and cultural backgrounds, especially among 'global nomads' – people whose parents are diplomats, academics or international business executives who do not feel that they belong to 'one culture' (Breger & Hill, 1998; Romano, 2008). Alternatively, Kang Fu (2008) points out that various forms of social control continue to limit interethnic marriages echoing the border patrolling tendencies discussed by Aspinall & Song (2013), which are discussed later in Chapter 4. This continues, despite the repeal of anti-miscegenation regulations in Nordic countries and elsewhere the law that restricted access to marriage partners solely on the basis of 'race', and allowed whites to maintain their social and economic advantages (in the USA for example).

Dutch studies (Kalmijn, 2010) found that interethnic marriages experience higher disruption rates than endogamous marriages and these studies point out that intermarriages receive less social support from family and other social network members, which may partly explain the higher divorce rates.

Kleist (2011) has studied how children are brought up in bicultural West African-German families in Germany and she concludes that there is a high potential for conflicts as the relatedness-oriented and autonomy-oriented strategies expressed by the respective spouses are very different. The relatedness-oriented strategy emphasises relations with the extended family, while the focus is mainly on the individual person in the autonomy strategy. Through the introduction of new theoretical concepts such as 'racial literacy' see chapter 6 and 'ethnic capital', Twine (2010) analyses dynamics of social control among white women who have established 'transracial' intimate partnerships and have had children with black men (primarily of African/Caribbean heritage). Adding nuances to understandings of social control, Twine discovered that some of these women are made *hyper visible* as transracial mothers of 'children of colour' or mixed children. Such relationships can promote an increased racial consciousness and an ability to negotiate racism, both from the relationship with the partner and his extended family and from female friends. The increasing number of children of black (Afro-Caribbean) fathers and white mothers provides social scientists with cases to examine how white parents interpret, negotiate and counter racial hierarchies to train their children to align themselves with racial and ethnic minorities (ibid.). These families have been relatively overlooked or they have been presented as pathological when studied. Such research focuses on the psychosocial problems that can arise from not feeling like a full member of any one racial group see also chapter 9, King-O'Riain et al. (2014) regarding mixed peoples' encounter with racism and exotisation. In the early twentieth century there was prevalence of the idea that mixed-race children were inferior to white or black children. This is clearly not true, but mixed-race children are sometimes seen as more physically attractive than their peers, though they may face challenges such as higher rates of risk.

There are hardly any in-depth Danish studies regarding phenomena associated with mixedness – including attitudes to intermarriage – but a recent doctoral thesis focusing on intermarriage across ethnic and racial boundaries in Sweden has implications for Denmark, given that it is a neighbouring country with many cultural and socio-political similarities. In this Swedish study on majority society's attitudes towards interracial marriages, dating and childbearing, Osanami Törngren (2011) indicates that the majority of Swedes could imagine getting involved in interrelationships and would not react negatively if a family member was involved in such a relationship. The study, however, emphasises the undeniable role of *visible difference* and the idea of race, which is congruent with Twine's (2010) *concept of hypervisiblity* of the mixed children and their white mothers. There is a conflict between the Swedish ideology of individual choice, which in theory allows the crossing of the boundaries between *us* and *others*, and the sense of group position (ibid., p. 239). In Osanami Törngren's analysis of attitudes, a hierarchy of preferences for a partner was explicit. The comparison of the Swedish responses to groups showed that after Scandinavian the next preferred were Central/Eastern Europeans and Latin Americans followed by South/East Asians, with African and Middle Eastern groups being least preferred as marriage partners. These categories based on 'ethnicity' are vital here, as for the UK and American readers, South Asian and East Asian are very different and South East Asians may not be included, yet in the Swedish context four of these groups – *African, Latin American, Middle Easterner* and *South/East Asian* have been also used by Allan Pred (2000, 2004 in Osanami Törngren, 2011 p. 91).

In the qualitative part of Osanami Törngren' s research, social and religious similarities were named as the basis for choice of the first two groups – Central/Eastern Europeans and Latin Americans – while the last three – South/East Asian, African and Middle Easterner – were associated with the idea of difference. Avoiding references to *visible differences* and instead directing attention to *problems* relating to cultural, social and religious differences (also identified in studies such as Bonilla-Silva2010, in Osanami Törngren, 2011) is a typical way of talking within 'colour blind' ideologies. As an ideology, *colour blindness* attempts to consider people strictly as individuals, ignoring or de-emphasising racial or ethnic membership. In other words, race or ethnicity should not matter in the way people are treated, and is an ideology held by the majority about, or towards, minority persons (Blaine, 2013). At the same time, ethnic minority persons may also hold this ideology, as discussed later in Chapter 6. However, the critics of colour blindness argue that race or ethnicity is relevant, since discrimination related to these categories persists in society, revealed (among other ways) through the negative stereotypes about ethnic minority persons.

As the present book focuses on intermarriage between South Asians and Danes, the stereotypes about South/East Asians presented in Osanami Törngren's study are relevant here. In contrast to identification of Europeans as 'like us', the idea of visible difference and religious difference was named with the groups originating from Asia and Africa. Thus there is a clear hierarchy of preference in the respondents' expressions of the desirability of relationships with someone of another origin. In other words, the majority of respondents favour someone who is not identified with visible, religious, economic and social differences. Osanami Törngren concludes that visible differences have a *master position* and evoke the perception of difference. The following perceived differences were communicated about South/East Asians:

- Traditional and patriarchal culture
- Thai women [persons originating from countries such as Vietnam, China and the Philippines were hardly mentioned]
- non-demanding, hard-working
- 'not European'. (Osanami Törngren, 2011, p. 219)

These perceived differences work against the individuals' being seen as symmetrical partners in marriage. The Swedish respondents reported feeling that South/East Asians were much less of a threat than Africans and Middle Easterners as they face less discrimination and difficulties integrating and have a less negative image than Africans and people from the Middle East. Still South/East Asians were less preferred, probably owing to their characterisation as visibly non-European. This corresponds to a study by Johnson (2007) on Russian brides that reported how some American men felt Russians made good wives as the children would look like their (white) American husbands.

Osanami Törngren argues convincingly that seeing difference and categorising a group of people is a functional process, but meanings and feelings attached to visible differences have to be problematised.

Efforts not to discuss the issue of race and the role of visible differences would not decrease prejudice and racism but would perhaps allow prejudice and racism to thrive beneath a *colour blind* ideology.

(ibid., p. 249)

In the present study, I cast light on visible differences both theoretically and empirically, and the explicit use of Phoenix's (2011) concept of *ethnically visibly mixed families* confirms this attention. In addition to the earlier mentioned pathology discourse regarding mixed children, Bastrop (2010) implies a relatively problematic psychosocial functioning for such children. Another viewpoint, the 'mixed-race faces are prettier' meme, is related directly to hybrid vigour – the biological phenomenon that predicts that cross-breeding leads to offspring that are genetically fitter than their parents. Hybrid vigour, according to Dawkins (2012), makes mixed-race people somehow biologically different and prettier than non-mixed (non-white) people by nature. Besides, there are social understandings of young black men as 'baby fathers' – the father of an infant who is not married to or in an exclusive relationship with the mother. In the Danish context, the term *perker* (Paki) is used as a derogatory term for persons with an ethnic minority background and half-Paki (in Danish *halv-perker*) for mixed-race children. These terms make a further exploration of related processes and discourses imperative.

On the whole, we can sum up the current trends regarding ethnic intermarriages in the West, and especially in Denmark, as being characterised by the salience of discourses of 'romantic love', the increasing number of such marriages and the lack of direct legal restrictions. However, social control and restrictive family reunification rules in Denmark continue to affect and limit these relationships to some extent. This exists alongside the historical negative social response, such as official silence and the collective amnesia about the children of intimate encounter with *others*, for example the slaves and the 'exotic persons' exhibited in the seventeenth to early twentieth centuries. The statistics presented in Section 2.4 indicate the relative increase of such marriages and these tendencies demonstrate the paradox that while such intimate relationships are hyper-visible, both in the country of residence and the country of origin for the diaspora partner, there is still no categorical mode of belonging in the Danish context, unlike the category of 'mixed race' in the USA and the UK.

2.4   Statistical information

Only a limited breakdown of data relevant to this population information is available and there are many aspects of intermarriage in Denmark that remain unclear. However, a demographic study by Botelho (2002) analyses some of the salient features of mixed marriage in Denmark using the definition of mixed marriage as binational marriage, that is, the legal union between partners of different nationalities (citizenships). Intermarriages, according to Botelho, show a gradual increase, from 6.8% in 1977 to 12.4% in 1999 when taken as a percentage of mixed marriages in relation to the total number of marriages contracted during the period under consideration. At the time of Botelho's study, the average percentage of mixed marriages is around 10% of all marriages, corresponding to the numbers of mixed marriages in other European countries such as France and Germany. Overall, more women than men married non-citizens until 1994, since which time more males than females have intermarried. These gender-related marriage patterns are delineated later in chapter.

In Denmark, marriages between Danes and Britons account for 6.5% of all intermarriages, followed by marriages between Danes and Norwegians (6%), Danes and Germans (5.6%) and Danes and Swedes (4.6%). Botelho (2002) argues that the high number of partners of such nationalities is not surprising given their ethnic and cultural proximity to Danish society and the well-established immigration flows since the 1970s. It is likely that immigration accounts for the intermarriages between Danes and partners of nationalities with different cultural and religious backgrounds, such as Turks and Pakistanis (among others). Already more than a decade old, Botelho's study pointed to the relatively high number of partners with nationalities, such as Thai and Philippino, who have neither cultural proximity nor immigration history in Denmark. A gender analysis shows that intermarriages with partners from Thailand, the Philippines, Poland and the former states of the Soviet Union are mainly contracted by Danish males, while intermarriages with English and Turkish partners are mainly contracted by Danish females. Based on explanations in the American literature, Piccard (1989 in Botelho, 2002) describes imagery of these women as domestic, docile and subservient, corresponding to negative racist stereotypes, perceived as positive by some men.

Constable, in 'Love at First Site' (2010), challenges as well as confirms some of these stereotypes by studying the role of Internet technology in framing romantic and marital desires. Focusing on the relevance of bodies as images and bodies as matter in the virtual world and in the real world, she suggests that bodies are very much present in cyberspace and that they most often continue to be imagined in highly conventional racial and gendered terms. However, at the same time the Internet allows for new sorts of imaginative possibilities. In Denmark also, the Internet is being used increasingly to establish contact with potential partners, both at the national and international levels, using sites such as www. dating.dk among others.

Statistical bricolage (Figure 2.2)

Figure 2.2 Intermarriages in Denmark in 2012

Irrespective of whether a future spouse is met during a stay in another country, getting in contact during a person's visit to Denmark, connecting via the Internet or meeting through transnational networks, there is a clear pattern of increase in the number of mixed marriages. The overall statistics (Statistics Danmark, 2012) show a relative increase in marriages between Danish citizens and non-citizens from 1990 to 2012 – from 4% to 6% of all the marriages taking place during the year (see Table 2.1). There is a clear gender difference with Danish men marrying non-citizens almost twice as often as women compared with Danish women marrying non-Danish men during 2012 (see Table 2.1), much lower than Botelho's estimate. A similar pattern is described in 2010 by Poulsen (2012), who found that out of 3,022 marriages between Danes and foreigners, 859 Danish women were married to foreign men, while

Table 2.1 Ethnic Danish origin persons married to persons of other ethnic origins, 2012

Men	2,499
Women	1,186
Total	**3,685**

2,163 men were married to foreign women, a trend mentioned earlier. The Danish women were mostly married to German, British and other Scandinavian citizens, while Danish men were married to some women from Western counties such as Poland and Germany, though mostly married to women from non-Western countries (1,421 marriages), mostly to women from Thailand and the Philippines. Regarding the intimate relation formations, are the focus of this study, marriages between ethnic Danes and South Asians (Indian/Pakistani) show a small increase (Figure 2.3).

The following figures and tables show similar patterns to those in Sweden and Norway, thus adding a broader Scandinavian understanding to marriages between the natives and South Asians. Figure 2.4 depicts the number of marriages between Swedes and Indians/Pakistanis, while Table 2.2 shows that in both Sweden and Norway there are children with native and Indian or Pakistani parents. It is noticeable that there is a larger number of marriages between natives and Indians in Sweden when compared with Norway. Table 2.3 indicates the number of children in Denmark with Danish and sub-continent parents from India and Pakistan. The number of Danish-Pakistani couples is higher

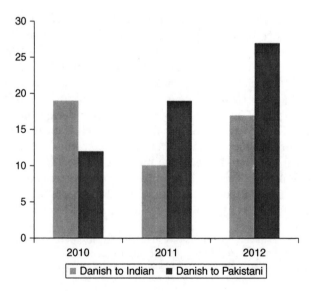

Figure 2.3 The number of mixed marriages by foreigners' country of origin, 2010–2012 (ethnic Danish with ethnic Indian/Pakistani)
Source: Statistics Denmark 2012.

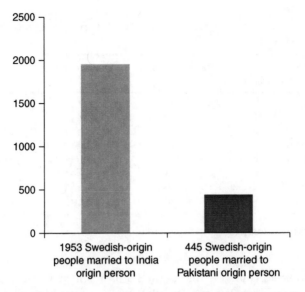

Figure 2.4   The number of mixed marriages by foreigner's country of origin, 2012 (ethnic Swedish with ethnic Indian/Pakistani)
Source: Statistics Sweden, 2012.

Table 2.2 Number of children with ethnic Norwegian/Swedish and Indian/Pakistani parents, 2012

Norwegian-born with one Norwegian and one Indian parent	851
Norwegian-born with one Norwegian and one Pakistani parent	3,638
Swedish-born with one Swedish and one Indian parent	6,435
Swedish-born with one Swedish and one Pakistani parent	1,180

Source: Sweden, Norway Statistics 2012.

than Danish-Indian couples, and this is similar to the figures in Norway related to the level of migrant populations in these countries. Regarding persons originating from Pakistan and India, immigrants and descendants living in Scandinavia in 2013, total numbers is 50,000, out of which in Denmark the number is 7775 from India and 22415 from Pakistan.

Other relevant data relates to Jewish/non-Jewish marriages in Scandinavia based on Dencik's (2009) work covering Sweden and Norway: 31% and 43% Jews are married with non-Jew, total figures, without differentiating between males and female. It is interesting to be note that 57% of respondents were married, while 8% were cohabiting.

Table 2.3   Number of children of mixed parentage in Denmark (children under 18 years, one parent is ethnic Dane, while the other is of Asian origin, 1 January 2009)

Mother/Father's country of origin	Danish Mother	Danish Father	Total
India	244	152	396
China	77	515	592
Pakistan	516	144	660
Philippines	175	2,117	2,292
Thailand	161	3,044	3,205
Japan	71	283	354
Rest of Asia	5,326	1,941	7,267
Total	**6,570**	**8,196**	**1,4766**

Source: Special extracts, Statistics Danmark, 2010.

It is interesting to note that in the Danish context, the major *us* and *others* categorising is between Danish (Christians) and Muslims. The sensational focus of the mass media is on the rejection of mixed marriages between 'Danes' and 'Muslims', illustrated by a survey conducted by CIR (Centre for Studies in Islamism and Radicalisation Processes, 2010) which found that 42% of Danish parents would not accept a Muslim son-in-law or daughter-in-law. 52% stated they would, yet negative media depictions can be interpreted both as a negative attitude towards mixed marriages in general and as the media's tendency to exaggerate the relative lack of acceptance of marriages across borders – in this case religious ones. Otherwise the Danish scene is characterised by a tendency to ignore these intimate mixings statistically but to be very aware of them in a political context. This is thought-provoking as in Denmark data is collected on almost every life domain.

In recognition of the increasing numbers of intermarriages, both in the Danish and global contexts, challenging the assumption that these marriages are inherently problematic and of relatively high risk is important, as is seeking to enhance relationships and strengthen couples.

2.5   Mixedness

When we focus on mixedness, there is a negation of race, as the products of mixed couples are neither one thing or the other but both and

they represent a melting away of 'racial signifiers', be these cultural,
physical or political.

(Olumide, 2002, p. 3)

Having introduced a conceptualisation of intermarriage leading to
mixedness in the Chapter 1, we can now examine the temporal background against which the field of 'mixedness studies' is developing,
followed by conceptualisation of identity and intermarriage. Lastly, the
theoretical framework of the empirical study is presented.

2.5.1   The three 'ages' of 'mixed-race studies'

Drawing upon Ifekwunigwe's international analysis in the area of
mixedness/mixed-race studies (2004), we can delineate three different
phases in understanding mixedness in close relationships, as couples
and among the children of mixed parentage in European and American
contexts.

1. The age of pathology – represented by 'discourses of hybrid degener-
   acy' and 'maladjusted social types'
2. The age of celebration – which challenged the damaging perspectives
   of 'mixedness' and which understood identity as fluid and complex
3. The age of critique – when multiracialism began to replace 'mixed-
   race' and present mixedness as shifting, contingent and as multilayered identity markers.

These phases cannot be transplanted directly into the Danish context
as they are primarily based on wider Euro-American contexts where
the practices of slavery and colonisation were more predominant, in
terms of time and scale, than in Scandinavia. Nevertheless, the relative
lack of academic and social attention to the issue of mixedness in the
Danish context makes these phases a source of inspiration for grasping
the dynamics of mixed partnering and parenting.

1. 'The age of pathology'. The nineteenth century was characterised
by a dominant discourse on mixedness as a transgression of so-called
pure 'racial boundaries' that would lead inevitably to degeneration.
Images of the dark-skinned people as barbaric and sexually rampant
were common (Alibhai-Brown, 2001) yet since the seventeenth century in India, the East India Company had encouraged the growth of
a 'Eurasian'/Anglo-Indian population. White men who married Indian
women and had children with them were given financial gifts for commercial reasons related to trust-building among the native population

and the high cost of travelling back to England for those who had families there.

Later, in the eighteenth and nineteenth centuries, the 'Eurasians' faced prejudice as the divide between the so-called civilised Europeans and the Asians deepened. Travelling across the continent and from India to England became easier and *disapproval* of mixed relationships was a consequence. The change in attitudes to the Anglo-Indian population provides lucid historical evidence of the impact of structural aspects on societal understanding of mixedness. Similar impact is seen in the UK, where the first Asian migrants married white women but later have married 'back home'.

Despite different geographical contexts, in 'the age of pathology' mixed 'race' people of all backgrounds and histories have tended to have similar characteristics attributed to them. In the 'race'-conscious society of the eighteenth and nineteenth centuries, the dominant ideology treated mixed-race individuals as somehow less than whole people (Mengele, 2001 in Ifekwunigwe, 2002). There was official opposition of 'race mixture' and it was argued by medical professionals that it led to contamination of Europeans – biologically and culturally – and that people of mixed origins were physically inferior and psychologically unstable, as earlier mentioned (Jonsson, 2009). See also chapter 9.

The racist notion of hypo-descent (placing the offspring in the 'low' status group) and a drop of 'black blood' led to further pathologisation of the mixed-race persons. Although oppression has many forms, a commonality in oppressive processes is the hierarchical interpretation of difference, and negative stereotypes mark this phase of dealing with mixedness.

2. 'The age of celebration'. In the 1990s, a number of authors (notably Root, 1992; Spickard, 1992), many of them identifying themselves as persons of mixed parentage, questioned linear or one-dimensional models of identity and argued in favour of multidimensional models that allowed for the possibility of simultaneous membership and multiple, fluid identities with different groups. In the American context, Spickard points out that before the last third of the twentieth century, multiracial individuals did not generally have the opportunity to choose identities for themselves and emphasised that, 'A mixed person should not be regarded as Black or White, but as Black *and* White, with access to both parts of his or her identity' (Spickard, 1992, p. 151).

In a similar way, the historian Frederickson (1981) argues that attitudes to mixing across ethnic and racial borders are inextricably linked to the ideas of *white supremacy*, that is, to the attitudes, ideologies and associated policies connected with white European domination over the 'dark' population. This theory and practice assumes that white Europeans (mainly of Anglo-Saxon and Northern European origin) are superior to non-Anglo Saxon peoples, especially people originating from Africa and Asia. This is considered by many as a taboo theme and receives insufficient exposure in academic writing.

Despite the legacy of white supremacy, there has been an increase in the number of mixed persons and census classifications which respond to 'racial subjectivities' in the USA and Canada in the form of multiple reporting on ethnic/race origin. Dual heritage options in the British census have led to more nuanced and positive understandings of being mixed. These narratives break with the characterisation of the ethnically mixed person as a tragic figure and multidimensional theories examine these phenomena. Parker & Song (2001) further confirm that people of mixed descent reveal the arbitrary and contested logic of categorisation underpinning racial divisions as their self-narratives reveal complex identities, beyond these simplistic divisions.

In Denmark, there are still no specific categories in the official statistics where mixed persons can place themselves. Morning (2012) suggests five approaches to the counting of mixed people and the Danish approach can be classified as non-recognition. We can hardly place the Danish attitude to mixedness in the second phase and the 'age of critique' is preferable to some extent.

3. *'The age of critique'*. In this 'age' there is still more focus on processual aspects as *multiracialism* replaces 'mixed race' as the dominant paradigm in the postmodern landscape. Ifekwunigwe (2002) points out that scholars continue to grapple with unresolved tensions between identification and categorisation as well as structure and agency.

Beck-Gernsheim (2002) argues that the increase in 'mixed families' is still viewed differently according to the observer's perspective. There are still many who view intermarried couples with suspicion and mistrust, probably as the result of xenophobic prejudices. For others, such couples represent open-mindedness and boldness, probably confirming cosmopolitanism and emphasis in the community of humanity. Such persons dare to look across the frontiers, to see through arbitrary and random categories and to resist the power of habit. However, this is also an overly simplistic way to view the life situation of persons in mixed families. There remains a need for broad, complex understandings which consider the intersections of different categories and subjectivities.

There are potentials in relationships across the ethnic borders and there is a dialectical relationship between the processes of identity, minoritising, majoritising and mixedness. We have to be aware of the underlying dominant ideologies which have been succinctly conceptualised as three major ideological perspectives on diversity by Blaine (2013) – the melting pot, multiculturalism and colour blindness.

As Olumide (2002) argues, those who use 'race' or ethnicity as an ideology to mobilise resistance as well as those who claim racial superiority, can have no interest in an independent and free-thinking mixed-race group. However, people who regard mixed race as symbolic of a desirable and generalisable social condition must also be mindful that real lives are supported or limited by changing social responses, as illustrated earlier by example of Euro-Asians in seventeenth century in India, Jewish – German marriages in pre- second world Germany. She emphasises:

> They may well become the 'psychological misfits' or 'half-caste' problem of tomorrow, should the whims of political and economic expediency shift. This has happened throughout the history of mixed race people.
>
> (ibid., p. 179)

In order to examine the world of the ethnic intermarried couples and children of mixed parentage in Denmark, the conceptualisations and perspectives delineated in Ifekwunigwe' s three ages are useful. The last two ages reflect the dominant paradigm but they are intertwined and the traces of yesterday extend into the present. The official silence and the collective amnesia regarding encounters with *others*, as in Denmark's history of slavery, remain an overlooked topic.

2.5.2   Identity, intermarriage and 'mixedness'

Intimate partnerships between members of minority and majority communities, which may include mixed marriages, challenges the stereotypical views about the division of society into *us* and *others*. They are also seen as a test of integration between the 'newcomers' and native populations, reflecting unresolved tensions between identifications and categorisations (Alba & Nee, 2003).

In order to comprehend identity and subjectivity of the person we turn to Valsiner & Rosa (2007), who perceive our human world as a culturally constituted world of human relationships in constantly reconstructed environments. Thus human beings are fully *social* – in the sense of their dependence upon the social contexts they create for themselves. Yet, they are simultaneously uniquely personal – subjective and affective. This dialectic between the social and personal forms a thread of continuity which is taken up in Section 2.7. For now, an intimate personal-level identity involves a gendered idea of personhood *self* in contrast to the *other*.

An ethnic intermarriage involves the willingness to accept the *otherness* of the partner (Breger & Hill, 1998). In addition, on the level of personal social interaction, the gendered self must fit into the existing family structure and the prevailing moral discourses within a broader matrix of political and economic relationships. The following analysis of mixed marriages and identity reminds us of the earlier mentioned border-patrolling and is discussed again in Chapter 4.

Mixed marriages are often treated with suspicion precisely because they call into question the boundaries between *self* and *other* (Breger & Hill, 1998, p. 9). When people partner across ethnic, national and/or racial borders, they are also making practical decisions about how to live in transnational families and they are constructing identities as couples. In other words, they are forming their own kind of 'togetherness' (which will include different elements to non-mixed couples) and they are building 'a new intercultural reality' (Beck-Gernsheim, 2002, p. 133). This reality is what is considered 'mixedness' in this book. What can this mixed identity contain? In contrast to what is this being negotiated? As pointed out above, intermarriage brings to light new forms of identity formation and opportunities for multiple, categorical intersections.

People in mixed families – and children in particular – have a large number of social categories into which they negotiate identity and belonging. The dynamics of identity raise problems in terms of attempts to measure and categorise individuals along simple dimensions. Not only does this indicate the complexity of multiple identity process and show how identities are constantly variable, renegotiated and changing, but it also brings to the surface the need to rethink conventional categories of ethnicity (Danish, Indian, white, black, Hindu, Christian, etc.) to allow for the concept of 'mixedness'. Song & Aspinall (2012) invoke the term 'master status' (coined by Everett Hughes in 1945) with special reference to race/ethnicity, as a category which – in most social situations – will dominate all others. Their recent social surveys show that race has lost its position to family and religion (in the South Asian and black groups) and (amongst young mixed-race people) categories of age/life-stage and study/work (though this can be perceived as too much of a generalisation and has limitations for broader application). At the same time, Song & Aspinall, 2012 suggest that identity attributes work through each other via intersectionality. In the UK, race appears to be less important than a 'Muslim' identity and the increasing importance of 'mixed race', and the fragmentation of identity now means that race is increasingly interwoven into other attributes, such as religion. This study aims to explore these aspects in Danish context.

Identities shift alongside historical and situational circumstances and, employing a main concept in feminist social psychology, the concept intersectionality emphasises the relationship between multiple identities and multiple racisms.

As Bhavnani & Phoenix, write 'The forms of racism are varied and, indeed, racism itself is a set of processes whose paradigms are shifting away from mainly bio-logistic considerations to include cultural and national ones' (1994, p. 5). When identities are shifting, so too are the boundaries of racism, so it is important to investigate the processes of oppression and structured inequalities, along with the processes of identity in intermarriages and mixed families. The 'nature' of racism is shifting to reflect other forms of oppression and unequal social process, which themselves are connected to social categories that are more difficult to recognise, such as colour blindness and racialisation. It is important to pay attention to fixed identity processes as well as to more fluid ones. For example, changing multiple identities and the gap between the fluid academic understandings and the continuing essentialist rigid perception of mixedness in the quantitative studies and the general public is important.

2.6   Categorisation, ethnicity and race

Intermarriages challenge images of family and normality, or as Beck-Gernsheim (2002) puts it, intermarried couples constitute 'a problem of social order' as they do not fit into normal parameters. According to her the people who challenge national or cultural classifications are a disruptive factor in social mechanisms as they cannot be represented within the usual clear-cut categories; they are often seen as 'misfits'. Their existence (for the State as for the ordinary citizens) is shifting and ambivalent, not to say dubious or suspect (Beck-Gernsheim, 2002). Processes related to intermarriages have largely been studied within the context of the USA and the UK and I am aware of the fact that there is a difference in the understandings of race between these two countries. However, the concepts of 'race' prevalent elsewhere are rarely used in the Nordic countries. The concept of ethnicity is prevalent in Scandinavia, where cultural aspects are predominant and phenotypes are barely explicitly named, though are present in the background.

It is useful to use Spickard's (1992) conceptualisation that both 'race' and ethnic group are in essence the same type of generalisation as they are both defined on the basis of social criteria. Race and ethnicity both assume descent from a common set of ancestors and a shared culture, from clothing to child rearing. At the same time, race and ethnicity can be seen as a positive tool, a source of belonging, mutual help, creating a sense of personhood that helps locate individuals psychologically and perhaps, politically. These categories create exclusion from certain groups as well as inclusion in others. From the point of view of the dominant group, Spickard emphasises:

> ... these distinctions are a necessary tool of dominance. They serve to separate the subordinate people as *other*. Putting simple, neat racial labels on dominated peoples – and creating negative myths about the moral qualities of those peoples – makes it easier for the dominators to ignore the individual humanity of their victims.
>
> (ibid., p. 150)

In Scandinavia, in this case Denmark, we can conclude that concepts of ethnicity and race are used, commonly indicating an overlap between ethnicity, race and the processes of exclusion. Overt acts of racism have declined, although discrimination continues in other forms: *colourism*, a recently acknowledged insidious 'ism' (Meszaros, 2013;Hall, 2012) and focus on the observable character of physical differences is invoked to comprehend the interconnected processes of exclusion, upholding white hegemony. Besides, concepts of ethnicity and race coexist and there is an overlap between ethnicity, race and the processes of unequal distribution of rights and privilege. They are both therefore, tools of dominance.

Another interpretation of race and ethnicity from Norway follows linking racism to a shift from a biological to an ethnic categorisation of the *others*.

> Both Nazi Germany's devastating legacy and the end of colonialism and direct control of countries in the developing world has led the term 'race' into dishonour within the social sciences. There are currently few who worry about the introduction of 'inferior

racial elements' in the immigration debate, but there are, however, many who are concerned about integration of 'foreign culture' and 'culturally distant' immigrants.

Instead of a biological categorisation of people in 'racial' groups, we have today culturally categorised people into 'ethnic groups'. A result of this paradigm shift is that 'cultural collisions', rather than the unfortunate consequences of race mixing, are the subject of both popular and scientific attention in the immigration debate.

(Loona 1995, author's own translation from Norwegian)

We could add that social changes such as the end of slavery, critique of pathologisation, anti-orientalism related to criticism and part-rejection of the concept of 'race', have led to the use of the concept of ethnicity in countries such as Denmark and Norway. This focus places biological aspects in the background and brings the cultural ones to the fore. Downplaying biological and phenotypical differences could be one of the reasons for the problem of categorisation, meaning that 'mixed' persons are nearly invisible in the Danish statistics, psychological services and underprioritised in the academic literature, too.

The categories used are what can be described as clear-cut categories or single ethnic categories, such as Indian, Pakistani, Danish, Muslim and Christian. Thus possibilities for a public acceptance of double ethnic belonging such as Danish-Indian are rather limited. One illustration is that parents with different citizenships have to choose which citizenship they want for their newborn child. Denmark is one of a handful of EU member states that does not allow dual citizenship. Danes can be born dual citizens, but they cannot go on to obtain a second citizenship later in life without forfeiting their Danish citizenship. Thus both Danes living in other countries and foreigners living in Denmark remain frozen out of public services and political engagement in the countries where they have chosen to reside if they are unwilling to sever ties with their country of heritage. Though the issue has been taken up in the Danish Parliament during 2013 on the initiative of the Danish Institution for Human Rights (DIHR), Danes Worldwide and the dual citizenship campaign group (Neergaard, 2013), and it was finally approved in June 2014 to be implemented in summer 2015 (Hamilton, 2014).

When it comes to racial categories in a European context (except in the UK) they become even more blurred, confirming the central use of race categories mentioned earlier in relation to New World former slave societies (Morning, 2012). We do not talk about race, or operate with racial categories, which makes it very difficult to discuss and investigate unequal social structures and oppressive, exclusion processes as discrimination, radicalisation and racism.

Transnational adoption researcher Line Myong defines 'race' as the blindness of ethnicity (Myong, 2009, p. 25). Her explanation has its roots in the shameful and terrible history of Europe before, during and after the Second World War, which relates the concept 'race' to Nazi ideology. She argues that race is an aspect within minority research in Europe but now it is placed under a broader term – ethnicity – because notions of 'race' are so deeply subordinated by dominant colour blindness which also apply to the Danish context to a large extent. She notes that on the one hand, Danishness is a white category, which requires white body signs, that is how one gets included and recognised as a Dane. On the other hand, there are also a lot of other things that make up Danishness. This is where it becomes paradoxical. In Denmark we have a story that we are colourblind, we are not racists, in Denmark means race nothing. But it does.

Bringing in the results from the aforementioned study by Osanami Törngren (2011) in Sweden, talking in a colour blind manner is divided in four broad ways: origin does not matter, the idea of culture, gender equality and individual choices. These colour blind explanations contain two contradictory ideas; one that focuses on difference and one that disregards differences. These understandings of colour blindness also apply in the Danish context to large extent.

Therefore, race is connected with biology, and the belief that people can be divided into distinct biological groups according to skin colour, each with its distinct physical and psychological characteristics (Tizard & Phoenix, 2002,p. 2): a notion almost every social scientist distances themself from.

Within feminist psychology and contemporary Danish feminist contexts there have been discussions concerning and ignoring the importance of 'race' and racialisation (Hasse, Henningsen & Søndergaard, 2002). Research on minorities in a Scandinavian context has mainly considered members of minority communities as objects of investigation using methods which further marginalise them rather than focus on relationships between the majority and minority. Therefore it is necessary to look at how the minority as well as the majority are constituted by using inclusive methods. The complexity of identity formations intrinsic to intermarriage then challenges such views and methods, and can be a productive way to extend migration and minority research. Intermarriages can be perceived as a constellation between minority and majority, and thus considered as a prism through which inclusion and exclusion processes, discrimination, integration and so on, can be studied. In studying these phenomena we should include the analysis of power and privilege as noted by mixed-race researcher Ali (2012). Forms of alignment and refusal, whether named as racial, ethnic or cultural, require an analysis of power, privilege and a critical engagement with the politics of recognition (ibid., 2012, p. 179).

At the same time I acknowledge that there is hierarchical placing of different ethnic groups in the Danish/Scandinavian context, where some ethnicities are linked to disfavoured racialised categories. This is explored later in this chapter.

2.7 Theoretical framework

In this book I have used an integrative framework for understanding mixedness and analysing the experiences of the research participants. This is based on my conviction that an appropriate way to deal with the wide range of approaches to intermarriages and mental wellbeing is through a theory-knitting approach that focuses on different levels of explanation.

The integrative theoretical framework of this study is based on a socio-cultural psychological approach, which is the result of various historical dialogues within psychology, sociology and anthropology (Valsiner & Rosa, 2007). An important part of this is intersectionality. As mentioned earlier in the discussion on identity, human beings are social as well as uniquely personal – subjective, affective and individually goal-oriented. The human psyche is capable of setting its own goals for action and even of creating images of the world and of itself to create a better understanding and to inform the future. Psychology as a discipline is concerned with *what* and *who psyche is*. This may be one of the reasons for the tensions and dialectics within theoretical psychology, but it helps to explain how 'what psyche is' is related to 'who psyche can be' in a particular social/cultural/historical context (ibid, pp. 30–32).

Within this approach the relevant directions for the present exploration of mixed marriages in Denmark are both the historical cultural embeddedness of the phenomena as well as its social and subjective meaning constructions. In Chapter 2 I have followed this approach to show the importance of historical and cultural understanding of Danish society in relation to the phenomena presented here.

Furthermore, another method taking a similar approach – the Trajectory Equifinality Model (TEM) (Sato et al., 2007) – has been included. Through this model it is possible to contact individuals who have arrived at the equifinality point, considered as the present state, through vastly different life course trajectories. The study participants are at the equifinality point of mixed marriages. Their choices are influenced and restricted by social, cultural and ethical conditions, which are analysed in the subsequent chapters. The TEM is also perceived as an aspect of the life course perspective. This is itself an interdisciplinary perspective focusing on both agency and structure at the same time and thus affective as social, geographical dimensions are included (Levy, et al., 2005). Among the salient aspects of the agent's life course are the multiple categories of belonging presented below as intersectionality.

2.7.1 Intersectionality, social constructionism and sexual desire

Intersections and junctions of ethnicity, class, gender and other important forms of social stratifications (Crenshaw, 2011), bear upon family, work relationships and the life course.

Reviewing intersectionality, Crenshaw (2011) considers it as an analytical, heuristic or hermeneutic tool designed to amplify and highlight specific problems. Crenshaw does not regard it as a 'grand' theory but rather as a theory of discrimination. It is now widely accepted that the intersectional approach, as a social constructionist approach, is important in understanding social relationships. According to Phoenix (2006), it provides an ontological framework which establishes that social existence is never singular, and that everybody belongs simultaneously to multiple categories that mutually constitute each other. These categories are historically and geographically located, comprising power relations that shift over time. However, it is further argued by Phoenix that it is important to recognise that these categories operate at different levels and have different logics. The three categories mentioned by Crenshaw (1994) – ethnicity, gender and class or socio-economic position – can be considered as the 'Big Three' that are most frequently invoked in social analyses. It is important, however, to move beyond these three categories to include categories such as age, nationality and locality (Moodley, 2011; Phoenix, 2011). Intersectionality encompasses issues of differences in power as well as diversity and promises an almost universal applicability, useful for understanding any social practice, any individual or group experience, any structural arrangement or any cultural configuration. I use this analytical tool here to focus on both the individual and the social levels, to contribute to the linking of the personal with wider social processes.

I reflect on the critical conceptualisations of social constructionism and sexual desire by Giles (2006), which analyse the social construction-ist appeal to free us from biological constraints and to place us within the human world of culture. The problem here, however, is that in the same stroke as we are set free from biology we become swept up into a prison of cultural controls. Invoking the phenomenological theory, sexual desire is perceived as an existential need with its origin in our gendered human condition – an awareness of the emptiness of one's own gender, as something that is empty and thus in need of filling. Giles highlights:

> ... sexual desire is neither created by our biology nor by cultural pre-scriptions. It is rather our own response to our human condition. We are still, of course, constrained to respond, but that is part of what it means to be human.
>
> (ibid., p. 237)

Sexual desire is thus received as a response to the human condition and is determined by neither biology nor culture, though constrained by both. This active understanding of human beings and sexual desire has relevance for grasping the drivers of intimate relation formation across cultural borders because the sexual desire forms an integral part of romantic love and consequent partner selection. In discussing the structure of being in love, Giles (2004) notes that what has been written about love in various epochs and cultures suggests that the experience of love is one that is common to humankind, an observation that in turn suggests that something is amiss with the social constructionist account. Giles is critical of romantic love being considered as just a Western phenomena and emphasises its universal nature, though with local variations, a point which is taken up again in chapter 3 under a discussion of so-called 'love' and 'arranged' marriages. He underlines a connection between romantic love and sexual desire, perceiving them as existential needs:

> ... since sexual desire seeks continuous fulfilment, and since such fulfilment is usually available within the structure of a romantic relationship, it is understandable that sexual desire often leads us on to the desire of love. The fulfilment of romantic love, as has

been shown, involves more than the fulfilment of sexual desire, but without the seeds of sexual fulfilment it is doubtful that the desire of love could ever grow.

(ibid., p. 188)

Thus love is more than sexual desire yet some students of modern social science are of the opinion that one emotion underlying marriage is sexual gratification, termed as 'erotic tendency'. Patny (2013/1940), however, debates this point of view in the Indian context and makes a point that has a broader relevance:

... social pundits consider sexual feelings and erotic tendency not only important but essential for the institution of marriage, but they also opine that the overall state of marriage should not be physiological only.

(Patny, 2013/2040, p. 7)

Sexual attraction alone cannot ensure a stable and lifelong relationship. Patny's conclusion is that the institution of marriage is not complete without the social, cultural and religious aspects prevalent in society. Valsiner, 2014 also argues that sexuality is a minor part belonging to general function of alimentation, as human affective processes are built upon sensual experiences of the total body.

Summing up the phenomenon of ethnic intermarriages in Denmark highlights the numerical increase as well as the official, paradoxical approach. Although historically such intimate partnership formation between the majority *us* and the *others* – they have been seen as almost taboo, resulting in a collective amnesia. The current situation is also further paradoxical as these marriages, with their implied mixedness, are not statistically registered, unlike in the multi-ethnic societies like the UK and the USA. There are no official categories recognising mixedness, yet there are increasing restrictive policies regarding reunification with spouses from countries outside Europe, which includes large numbers of visibly different spouses. These policies mirror the paradoxes of colour blind ideology with two contradictory ideas – mixedness including intermarriages as almost invisible in official statistics but placed centrally in terms of restrictive immigration policies.

A conceptualisation of identity as a sense of personhood, and of intermarriage as acceptance of *otherhood*, forms a bridge for presenting an integrative theoretical framework for the primary empirical study comprising a major part of this book. The sociocultural psychological approach forms the broad background for the historical and social presentation of intermarriage phenomena, combined with a life course perspective which includes both agency and structure. Thus the framework formed for analysing the narratives includes subjective, affective aspects, as well as the broader social geographical aspects such as exclusion processes and transnationalism to be considered in Chapter 7.

The next chapter is intended as a context chapter for the empirical study and introduces the participants, sampling techniques and analysis.

3
Intermarried Couples and Their Experiences

This chapter introduces the primary empirical study and is intended to provide context and some information about research methodology. The point of departure relates to sampling technique and a consideration of the ethical challenges faced. The data collection process is also described. I discuss here the issue of sample size, the number of research participants and subsequent generalisation because it is an important one in qualitative research and there is often discussion about *researcher-based* and a *reader-based analytical generalisation*. Finally I outline the study participants and provide their major demographic features as well as short biographical notes.

3.1 Methodological challenges and limitations

As stated in Chapter 1, throughout this book I have attempted to use the following basic rules for discussing and presenting my research:

- Writing in a form that will communicate with practitioners as well as academics.
- Including enough research data and direct quotations from participants to allow readers to make their own interpretation of the material.
- Explaining the data collection and analysis procedures clearly.
- Describing the context of the study, including not only the 'pre-understandings' of the researcher but also the social and institutional environment in which the research took place.

This section focuses on the methodological aspects. As data was collected in two separate phases, the data for the empirical study consists of two parts. In the first part the sample consisted of couples where one spouse was of South Asian (Indian or Pakistani) origin and the other a native Dane. Data was collected specifically to explore aspects of intermarriages in Denmark during the spring of 2010, and was carried out by the young Swedish researcher Frida Dunger who was affiliated to the research project. The couples belonging to the aforementioned categories were recruited through various social networks, discussed further below. As the principal researcher, I developed the interview guide and devised a data collection strategy. Strategic sampling was used covering a broad range of participants by contacting key people in relevant social networks. This was done in collaboration with Frida Dunger, who is married to a Dane and is fluent in Danish, Swedish and English. Though she didn't speak all participants' mother tongue, yet there was linguistic flexibility and no interpreter was required (Dunger, 2010).

After analysing the original data and while preparing this book, in Spring 2014 I supplemented the original data with two case examples from an NGO providing psychosocial services. These involved couples where one partner was Danish and the other originated from Pakistan or India (Singla, 2003, 2014).

In line with Mahtani's reflections upon the challenges of mixed-marriage methodologies (2012), the research team agreed that the interviewer's own situation (being in a mixed marriage Swedish-Danish) contributed to establishing a rapport with the participants. However, we agree with Mahtani that light-skin privilege also informs important bases for identification, which the interviewer didn't share with the diasporic spouses, only with the Danish ones. There are, additionally, other social cleavages which structure life worlds, such as social class, political activism, age and personality type and drawing from Mullings (1999), attention was paid to the situated knowledge of both parties in the interview leading to trust and co-operation. The team aimed for a balance of proximity and distance between the researcher and the participant (Chaudhary, 2008), created by awareness and the active invoking of commonalities and differences. In line with Kleinman & Copp (1993), we regarded the participants as our 'teachers' and there were ongoing discussions between the junior researcher who interviewed the participants and me regarding feelings related to the encounter during the data collection, analysis and dissemination of results. Another researcher, Dagny Holm, was also affiliated to the project during the analysis phase (Singla & Holm, 2012) and contributed especially to the gender aspects of the themes. Again following Kleinmann & Copp (1993), we attempted to be aware and attentive to our feelings as researchers and discussing them with colleagues and other professionals rather than ignoring troubling feelings or becoming distant.

For our purposes, participants are the teachers and we their students... We believe that there is such a thing as the right amount of empathy and we expect our good feelings to grow incrementally over time... we experience emotions simultaneously. Hence we do not just feel good or bad, comfortable or uncomfortable – Distancing will not solve the problem. We will probably have the nagging feeling that we are not doing things right. This is good because confronting our negative feelings and our fear of incompetence can help us begin analysis.

(ibid., pp. 29, 33–34)

We managed to keep an ongoing focus on the emotions of shock, disbelief and anger aroused by both narratives of the participants regarding exclusion, colourism by family or society and reading the almost taboo and relatively overlooked literature about Denmark's historical complicity in slavery and exhibiting persons from countries such as China, India and Ghana in the late nineteenth and early twentieth centuries. Furthermore, inspired by Kleinmann & Copp (1993), we got in touch with scholars in other parts of the world who were interested in similar phenomena and grappling with related themes. We attempted to focus on our analytic assumptions and contacted our colleagues, believing that communicating with others about our problems would make us less vulnerable to charges of incompetence or weakness. The following appeal by Kleinmann & Copp (1993) has been influential for us and is shared with other readers in a similar research situation.

Let us acknowledge our *interdependence*. We can give up the individualist model and instead create interdisciplinary networks and informal groups that encourage us to give and receive intellectual and emotional support. In our experience, having cooperative contexts in which to think, talk and write make us work better and feel better.

(ibid., p. 57, author's italics)

The participants were recruited through key people in the mixed couples's networks who functioned as *gatekeepers* (Sanghera & Thapar-Bjokert, 2007), they were contacted using phone and e-mails. Interviews were conducted primarily in Danish and English. The research was conducted in line with ethical standards defined by the Nordic/Danish Psychological Association. The participants consented to be interviewed for academic purposes, were assured of confidentiality through the use of pseudonyms and by the alteration of some identifying details.

In relation to the later, supplementary data, the couples who ear lier had psychosocial intervention in the NGO (described in detail in Chapter 9) were contacted by telephone and email and their permission was sought and granted to use their case notes for academic purposes. In-depth interviews (Kvale & Brinkmann, 2009) were conducted with 10 adults, due to pragmatic reasons in Copenhagen and its suburbs where the couples resided. Though one interview was conducted through Skype due to the couples' recent shifting to Hong Kong. The participants in this study were between 21 and 61 years old and had been married from between a few months to 27 years at the time of the interview.

The research is based primarily on persons who constitute 'ordinary' mixed couples, supplemented by two case illustrations of persons who had contacted psychosocial services (see Chapter 9). The interviews have some limitations, such as restricted focus on religious/spiritual affiliations in the research questions – for example the researcher who conducted the interviews didn't probe deeper into the meaning of these phenomena for couple's getting together, managing everyday life, etc. Additionally it would have been relevant to have explored the spouses' placing of religiosity and spirituality in terms of the parenting of their children. I have not been able to highlight these aspects.

In this qualitative research, we recognise that the position of the researcher, as that of any other human being, is a combination of background, professional training, values, political standing, personality, etc. This recognition brings into the open the need to be highly conscious of this position based on postmodern concepts of experience, interpretation and construction. The research team deliberated about the probable researcher effect and this is discussed below.

Firstly we recognise that holding a clearly subjective position is more the rule than the exception and we argue that it can be seen as a useful tool for the researcher. With regard to transparency and research clarity, I describe my position as a psychologist, researcher and academic originating from India and residing in Denmark since 1980. I am not ethnically intermarried, yet have friendships and collegial networks across racial, ethnic, national, gender, faith and discipline borders. Since 1981 – more than three decades – I have worked with the issues of family relationships, inclusion, exclusion and psychosocial intervention in Denmark, at times in collaboration with colleagues in India due to my academic affiliations. I have researched and practiced primarily with ethnic minorities in Denmark focusing on the changing social and political context, especially since 2001. I have observed an increasing polarity between the ethnic majority and the ethnic minority in Denmark into *us* and *others*. This has motivated me to explore new areas. I began to investigate an area in which ethnic majority and ethnic minority were meeting as (equal) human beings, thus leading me to the phenomenon of partnering and parenting across ethnic borders.

I do not claim to be able to generalise from the results based on in-depth interviews with just ten persons plus the two cases studies, yet drawing from Kvale & Brinkmann (2009), a claim to *analytic generalisability* is made. This generalisation pertains to a broader applicability beyond the specific cases. *Analytical generalisation* rests upon rich contextual descriptions and includes the researcher's argumentation for the transferability of the interview findings to other subjects and situations.

Kvale & Brinkmann (2009) further emphasise:

> ... the validity of the generalisation hinges on an analysis of the similarities and differences between the original and the present case, on the extent to which the attributes compared are relevant ... which presupposes 'thick description'.
>
> (ibid., p. 263)

To further illustrate this point, in the present study the ways of managing everyday life among the ten participants capture some salient aspects of relationships in which the partners belong to different categories – race, ethnicity, religion, region, nation, caste and so on. Thus the processes and the theoretical conceptualisations analysed from the participants' narratives can be applied more broadly, taking into account the similarities and differences mentioned above.

I concur with Kvale & Brinkmann (2009) that there is both a *researcher-based* and a *reader-based analytical generalisation* and in addition to rich specific descriptions, I have attempted to offer arguments for my findings. In terms of reader-based analytic generalisation, it is hoped that the reader will judge whether the findings may be applied to a new situation on the basis of contextual description of the study. This happened when I presented this research project to a conference in Bangalore, India (Singla, 2012). A number of audience members commented that some of these results were similar to *Inter-community*/inter state North Indian–South Indian intermarriage and referred to a popular book dealing with marriage between one partner originating from Punjab (North India) and the other from Tamil Nadu (South India) (Bhagat, 2009). The audience members were able to draw on the analytical generalisation and see the similarities (differential norms, practices, values, language) and differences (same religion, phenotypes, socioeconomic placing) between the couples described in this research study and the book (ibid., 2009).

3.2 Presentation of the research participants

Figure 3.1 is included to give the reader a brief overview of the research participants (Figure 3.1).

All participants belong to middle- or upper middle-class, well-educated families and the following biographies attempt to capture salient aspects of their psychosocial position, thus contributing to the subsequent analysis.

Sabita and Robert

Sabita, the youngest participant at 21 years old, introduced herself as 'Danish of Indian origin' and had been married for just two months at the time of interview. She is the only child of highly educated and well-placed parents from India, who migrated to Denmark 25 years ago. She is emotionally close to her grandparents and her extended family in India, with whom she usually spends summer holidays. She was born and raised in an upper class suburb of Copenhagen, attended a private international school and studied in a prestige university in the USA.

Robert is 'Danish and of Danish origin'. He lived in a similar neighbourhood to Sabita and attended the same university as her. He has close emotional ties to his grandmother and he has a highly paid job in Hong Kong. Sabita is learning Chinese.

Having met each other as Danes in the USA, their ethnic differences were unremarkable during the first phase of their contact.

Katja and Rajiv

Katja, 32, who introduced herself as 'Danish, with Danish parents', has been married for three years. She originates from Fynen and her parents are divorced and remarried, having mid-level jobs. She has a number of siblings from the same parents and some *bonus* ones from her parents' subsequent relationships. She has lived in a middle-class Copenhagen neighbourhood for the past three years. She has a master's degree and works full-time in a dynamic organisation.

Rajiv introduced himself thus: 'I am from India ... Indian'. He grew up in a city in India, his father has a high status, well-paid job and mother is non-employed. He has one older sister and 'a million cousins', implying a large extended family. He has a master's degree and has worked in

Name Gender	Age	Country of birth	Country of origin	Citizenship	Residence, period	Married since	Children: gender, age
Sabita F	21	Denmark	India	Danish	Hong Kong, two months	Two Months	Pregnant
Robert M	25	Denmark	Denmark	Danish	Hong Kong, two months	Two months	
Raaka F	42 (arrived as adult)	India	India	Indian	Denmark, Three years	Eight years	Daughter, 7
Klaus M	44	Denmark	Denmark	Danish	Denmark	Eight years	Daughter, 7
Katja F	32	Denmark	Denmark	Danish	Denmark	Three years	Daughter, 1
Rajiv M	35 (arrived as adult)	India	India	Indian	Denmark, Three years	Three years	Daughter, 1
Cecilia F	37	Denmark	Denmark	Danish	Denmark	Four years	Daughters, 9 months and 2
Sam M	36	Denmark	India	Danish	Denmark	Four years	Daughters, 9 months and 2
Marlik F	52 (arrived as adult)	Russia	Pakistan	Danish	Denmark, 27 years	27 years	Son, 15 and daughter, 25

Figure 3.1 Research participants and case examples

Name Gender	Age	Country of birth	Country of origin	Citizenship	Residence, period	Married since	Children: gender, age
Lars M	61	Denmark	Denmark	Danish	Denmark	27 years	Son, 15 and daughter, 25
Nihla F	28 (arrived as pre-teen)	Pakistan	Pakistan	Danish	Denmark, 19 years	Seven years (getting divorced)	Sons, 3 months and 3
Mads M	33	Denmark	Denmark	Danish	Denmark	Seven years (getting divorced)	Sons, 3 months and 3
Saida* F	40 (arrived as pre-teen)	Pakistan	Pakistan	Danish	Denmark, 29 years	One year	Sons, 11 and 14 (from earlier marriage)
Brian* M	45	Denmark	Denmark	Danish	Denmark	One year	Son, 20 (from earlier marriage)
Mira* F	27 (arrived as adult)	India	India	Indian	Denmark, Four years	Three years (divorced)	No children
Mark* M	28	Denmark	Denmark	Indian	Denmark	Three years (divorced)	No children

*Case examples

Figure 3.1 (Continued)

creative industries such as advertising. He was previously married to an Indian for a short period, though they divorced. Currently he is self-employed part-time in the health sector. The couple have an infant daughter. Their ethnic and job identities were prominent as they met each other in a city in India.

Cecilia and Sam

Cecilia introduced herself as 'Danish', from South Zealand and the youngest of three siblings. Her working-class parents encouraged her to mid-level education. After maternity leave, she got a part-time secretarial job.

Sam is introduced by Cecilia as a 'Danish citizen' and an 'Indian guy'. He was born and raised in Denmark by mid-level educated working Indian parents who moved to Denmark four decades ago. He lost his father some years ago. He has a younger sibling and a large extended family in India and other countries. Sam has a degree in business and is employed in a very well-paid job in the private sector. They met at their common workplace in Denmark so their ethnic belongings and work identity were moderately important.

Nihla and Mads

Nihla is 29 years old introduced herself as 'Pakistani' with 'Danish citizenship' and she immigrated to Denmark when she was nine years old with her divorcee mother and three younger siblings from a big city in Pakistan. She is mid-level educated and worked as a social educator before she went on maternity leave. Mads is 'Danish', grew up in Copenhagen as an only child and has a close relationship with his ill grandfather. He has mid-level education and is working in a private firm. They have a four-month-old son and an older son who is three. They are going through divorce proceedings and they presented their ethnic belonging as simultaneously foregrounded and underplayed.

Raaka and Klaus

Raaka, 42, introduced her nationality as 'Indian'. She has five older siblings and grew up in a city in India. She has a master's-level education. She worked in a Danish multinational firm in India and since moving to Denmark, she is partly self-employed as a consultant.

Klaus, 44, identified his nationality as 'Danish'. He is from a small town in South Jutland and has one younger sister. He is an engineer and is employed by a Danish multinational firm which relocated him to

India for a period. He is currently posted in Denmark. The couple have been married for ten years and have a seven-year-old daughter.

As both Raaka and Klaus are affiliated to the same religious sect, so their ethnic origins are less important to them than their shared spiritual identity.

Marlik and Lars

Marlik, 52, is the oldest female participant in the study and she introduced herself as 'originally Pakistani' and a 'diplomat child' born in Moscow. She was raised in a number of countries and has two sisters. She is a journalist and currently works freelance. Lars, 61, the oldest male participant, is a Dane from West Jutland. Both his parents are deceased and he has two sisters with whom he has very limited contact. He works in the police force and has converted to Islam of which he says 'my faith is between Allah and me'. They have been married for 27 years and have a 25-year-old daughter and a 15-year-old son.

The couple live in an upper middle-class neighbourhood and their common faith is foregrounded, while their ethnic belonging is downplayed.

Case Example 1: Saida and Brian

Saida, 40, and Brian, 45, had been together for four years when they sought psychosocial intervention from the NGO Transcultural Therapeutic Team (TTT). The first visit was on Brian's initiative to work with their 'uncertain couple relationship'. Saida grew up partly in Denmark with her Pakistani Muslim parents and four siblings (who also live in Denmark). Her parents live partly in her parents' ancestral village in Pakistan for a few months every year. She is mid-level educated as a social educator (in Danish, *socialpædagog*). At the time of her initial contact with Brian, she had been separated from her coethnic husband Nadar, who was a distant relative and who was living in Pakistan when the marriage was arranged by the both their families. Nadar and Saida have two teenage sons who live with Saida. Brian was born into a Christian family and both his parents were dead at the time of his first contact with TTT. He was divorced from his first Danish wife (who was an alcoholic) two decades ago, and he has one adult and one teenage child with whom he has limited contact. He was doing well economically in his own media services business.

Case Example 2: Mark and Mira

Mark, 28, contacted TTT requesting psychological intervention for his wife Mira, 26. They had been married for three years but there were problems related to her adaptation to life in Denmark and in their couple relationship. Mira is a transnational marriage migrant, an Indian citizen born and brought up in an affluent, upper middle-class Hindu family in an Indian city. She has two older sisters who immigrated to the USA for further education and who settled there. Mark was born in Denmark and raised in a small Danish town in a working-class family. He regards himself as born Christian but otherwise an atheist. He has one older brother living in the same town as his parents. Mark's parents encouraged higher education and he studied at master's level. During his internship in India he met Mira in an academic environment. More details and analyses are presented in Chapter 9.

3.3 Analytical focus and the main themes

As previously discussed, the project's researches cover subjective identity, intimate relationships, mental health and wellbeing. The themes for the study are contingent on both the empirical material as well as academic work from the intermarriage and family research field.

The analytical investigation focuses on meaning-making processes and the negotiation of identity in everyday interactions and social practices expressed in the narratives of the project's participants. The aim is to illustrate some dynamics within intermarriage related to mental wellbeing perceived as identity formation and relationships. The overall objective is to encourage a sensitive approach to research which avoids further marginalising of people by focussing only on the marginalised minority, but includes the relationship between minority and majority.

The analysis focuses on the meaning-making process of everyday interactions of people living in intermarriage, by including both *what* they tell and *how* they express themselves.

The *what* refers to the content of the narrative and the participants' choice of social categories through which to negotiate their identity and sense of belonging. The reading strategy is to capture the relation between *us* and *others* and analyse what is constructed as obvious and normal and how subject positions are legitimated and explained as (un)natural in the given context/narrative. The intersectional approach presents tools to investigate how the meanings of social categories can change over time in various narratives involving the broader social/political setting in the same interview.

The *how* refers to an analytical focus on the (self-) presentation and subjective positioning in the meaning-making process, including the construction of non-problematic and problematic subject positions. This meaning-making process from the raw data (comprising the participants' narratives and the extensive notes and telephone interviews as well as reflections from the two clinical cases) requires combining one's academic and analytical skills with psychological and practitioner skills. This mixing of skills and foci is a strength of the book as most of the studies in the field are, on one hand, empirical studies of 'ordinary' persons or couples – for example Poulsen (2012) – with limited focus on promotion, prevention and intervention of mental health and wellbeing. On the other hand, the other seminal studies in the field centre around couples with problems dealing with psychotherapy (Rastogi & Thomas 2009) and couple enhancement (Hahlweg, et al. 2010) among others. This analyses attempts to combine both the everyday life experiences and the psychosocial practioners' experiences, which is pointed as a unique aspect of the book.

The following major themes emerged from a combination of the theoretical concepts and a close reading of the interview material that comprises the subsequent chapters. Relevant international studies are used to discuss the findings and make them broader and more internationally relevant.

1. Getting together – "falling in love"
2. Managing everyday life
3. 'Mixed' parenting ideals and practices
4. Local Lives in a Transnational Context
5. Living 'private life in the public gaze': Mental health & wellbeing

This chapter has aimed to highlight that the participants in the empirical study have been interviewed with sensitivity and with awareness of differences and similarities between themselves and the researchers. The narratives of strategically chosen participants – one spouse a native Dane and the other originating from South Asia (India/Pakistan) – have been analysed within a theoretical framework including an intersectionality perspective, resulting in an array of themes that form the subsequent chapters of the book. Chapter 4 begins the analysis by focusing on how the partners originally came into contact with each other, and the participants reflect on memories of their weddings and family dynamics.

4
Getting Together – 'Falling in Love'

This chapter begins with a delineation of theories of general intimate partner selection within social psychology. It attempts to answer the question of how people from different ethnic backgrounds come together. The answers to this question within this sample show a commonality of coming together for the participants through the process of falling in love combined with pragmatic aspects, despite highly varied contextual factors.

These narratives about meeting and 'falling in love' reflect dominant discourses of love and marriage much as they exist in a Western society like Denmark. Furthermore, the chapter covers the couples' personal motivations, memories of the wedding ceremony and dynamics based on analysis of their subjective narratives related to the formation of marriages across ethnic borders.

4.1 What brings intimate partners together?

The complex issue of what brings people together in intimate relationships has been examined intensively by Fletcher et al. (2013), who studied ideal mates for long-term relationships in New Zealand. Groups of men and women wrote down characteristics that described their own ideal partners and asked another group of students to rate how much importance they placed on each ideal in the context of a romantic relationship. Using factor analysis, the items revealed tripartite categories of mate preference structure:

a) warmth/trustworthiness
b) attractiveness/vitality
c) status/resources

Citing a wealth of cross-cultural research, the authors found that the first two categories are judged in much the same way across and within cultures, while status and resources were not judged in the same way. They also found characteristic gender differences in what men and women want in an intimate partner and these differences are also strikingly similar around the world. To illustrate this point, men tend to value physical appeal more than women, but are less interested in status and resources. Furthermore, in the mate selection process, women are typically more cautious than men in indicating romantic interest, while they pay a lot of attention to their own attractiveness. Men, on the other hand, are more interested in flaunting their status, wealth and ambitiousness (ibid., p. 153). According to Fletcher et al. (2013), these universal mate selection processes point to an evolutionary psychological explanation, yet they also indicate that these strategies are flexible and alter according to an array of factors such as the goals, cultural constraints, environmental conditions and the availability of partners. One can question the universality of these processes as much regarding intimate partner selection is also based on the contextual social control and gender norms.

A preference for homogamy is another theory related to the formation of intimate relationships. This theory maintains that similarities in background and shared characteristics such as race, ethnicity, religion and other demographic features play a major part in this process and lead to good partner formation (Surra et al., 2006). A number of studies (Glenn, 1984; Olumide, 2002) have criticised this theory for not taking into account heterogamous intimate partnership formation and not including features such as personality. Killian (2013) points out that many interracial couples are similar in regard to education and social class. The analysis in the next section sheds light on what happens in heterogamous or ethnically exogamous relationships, such as the couples who participated in this study.

We now consider two sides of love – passionate and companionate love – which have informed a good deal of scientific work (Fletcher et al., 2013). On the basis of Berscheid & Walster (now Hatsfield) (1974) in ibid., *passionate love* is a state of intense longing for union with another, a feeling that is aroused particularly in the early stages of the romantic relationship. 'Falling in love', an expression used by a number of participants in the present study, is described as when 'there is a heightened sense of excitement associated with experiencing new and novel activities with a partner ... there is also typically an air of uncertainty in new relationships along with some daydreaming about the future and a dawning realisation that long-held dreams and goals may be fulfilled' (ibid., p. 170). In contrast, companionate love combines feelings of intimacy (closeness and connection), commitment (decision to remain in the relationship over both the short and long term) and deep attachment towards others, romantic or otherwise, who occupy an important part of our lives. Romantic relationships typically contain a mixture of both passionate and companionate love.

In terms of the participants in the present study, the convoluted process of starting a relationship includes a discussion of their motivations, focusing on the early stages emphasising passionate love and their descriptions of events based on their memories. For some of the participants, the marriage is brand new and the wedding ceremony is a recent memory, while for others it is at a distance.

Time notwithstanding, the memories of how the couples got together and the awareness of what keeps them together is a significant part of their narratives about love and marriage.

4.2 Getting together using the Trajectory Equifinality Model (TEM)

In order to grasp the complex and intriguing process of coming together, the Trajectory Equifinality Model (TEM), mentioned in Section 2.7, is applied. This model brings to fore similarity in the courses of different trajectories of the ten participants. Their coming together across ethnic borders is a point of similarity – forming the Equifinality Point (EFP) – which is reached via many different pathways.

The participants in this study met each other in different ways and in different locations, including UK, USA, Denmark, India and Pakistan. Some of them met in the workplace, some through their studies and some in social settings. Common to all the participants is the construction of marriage though discourses of *colour blind* love, which is raised above cultural differences, ethnicity and race. The following analysis has the construction of 'love' as an overall idealisation and identification and as the object of investigation it is useful in understanding the relationships discussed here. 'Love marriage' is usually understood as an alternative to 'arranged marriage' and is associated with individualism and the decline of family authority. It is not regarded merely as a Western institution but has spread throughout the entire world via the media of film and entertainment in the West; love marriage is above all, an ideology, saying little about the practices that accompany it (Borneman, 1996, p. 32).

However, I would like to challenge this dichotomy of 'love and arranged' vis à vis West and East, as there have been traditions of love marriage alongside arranged marriage in the East just as in the West. One example is the self-selection 'Swayambar' by Sita and Drupadi in the Indian epics *Ramayana* and *Mahabharata*, respectively. Ganesh (1999) argues that in countries like India, girls and women are not passive recipients of gendered socialisation but are active agents who attempt to shape their immediate realities, albeit within the overarching cultural values of the desirability of marriage as well as its inescapability, the auspiciousness of the married state and the emptiness of remaining unmarried. Traditions of love marriage have been carried out alongside arranged marriage forever, although there may be higher numbers of marriages in which family plays a significant part in partner selection in South Asian countries. According to a recent survey on Indian marriages, 69% of marriages were arranged, while partners themselves made the choice (so called love marriage) in 31% of marriages. It should be noted at the same time that the new generation is open to love marriage too as youngsters want to make their own choices (Times of India, 2014).

These narratives related to falling in love, meetings, wedding ceremonies and everyday marriage practices reveal some of the challenges and enrichments inherent in the institution of intermarriage. They also show the negotiations, compromises and conflicts the couples have experienced in terms of cultural differences, immigration laws, cultural/religious norms, gender roles andfamilial and societal expectations. Because some of the participants are Danish citizens, immigration law and regulations have not affected their everyday lives together, but for others they play a part in the stories about living in intermarriage in Denmark. The participants' narratives show that even though the construction of love draws upon discourses involving the two people within the marriage, they are not the only ones involved in the scene on which their married life is played out. The parental generation and the extended family are also present in these processes. The categories described below have been constructed to help comprehend significant features drawn from the narratives. It is important to note that these categories can overlap and that these beginnings have an enduring effect into later life.

Analytical categories:

1. 'Met at work': foregrounding ethnic differences.
2. 'Danes in the US'/'Cosmopolitans in Mumbai': foregrounding the 'national'/Cosmopolitan identity.
3. Joint identity and 'destiny': foregrounding the 'chance' factor.

The next part of this chapter focuses on each of these categories in turn and relates them to the empirical evidence.

4.2.1 'Met in the office': foregrounding work identity

With an increase in women's participation in the labour market at different levels, including in multinational corporations, the workplace is gaining significance as an arena where potential intimate partners meet. In multi-ethnic workplaces, there can be encounters between persons with different ethnic backgrounds intersecting with different career trajectories. This may occur despite oppressive structures of racism, sexism and classism and these encounters can lead to attractions. An example of this is Klaus, an IT project manager, who has worked with Indian companies often during his career. Around the year 2000, he was offered the opportunity to work in India for an extended period of time. While he was working there he met Raaka, an Indian colleague, and this is how he reflects upon moving to India and to the formation of their intimate relationship.

> *I was old when I met Raaka ... and I think that I had been living a life, where ... I was very much concerned with my career. ... It was the work that moved me there ... that was the sole purpose of that trip. It was not that I was thinking that I would get married in India or anything. But just before I moved to India I started to get more involved, with the thought process of thinking of having a wife or a girlfriend, you know, something steadier came up real to me ... that was a changing time of life that year before. I also think that the fact that I took the decision to move to India alone, like that, hmm, when I think about it today. It was a big decision for me, but at that point of time. It was a natural decision for me. It is difficult for me to explain.*

The sole purpose of leaving Denmark for India, he explains, was an individualistic business decision and, he continues *the family came as a second thought.* In some ways the two motivations are not separable. The change of lifestyle, working position and location also changed his attitude towards family formation. His thoughts of the possibilities of building a family increased parallel to his plans to relocate to India the year before. He constructs a priority in the narration of his motivation for changing lifestyle: work before family, where family becomes a secondary agenda. Yet, he tells how his attitude towards marriage is a part of his concerns and, along with moving and changing his lifestyle, the idea or dream of family and marriage has grown. It is difficult for him to explain and he does not cite 'marriage' or family plans as the sole purpose of the relocation decision. Possibly, this prioritising *love–work* would result in a troublesome or unwanted subject position: 'man seeking wife', and be connected to 'failure' in reaching his family dreams in Denmark.

Furthermore, a discourse about masculinity and stereotypical gender roles within the *marriage industry* – the commodified marriage market – is somehow implicitly rejected. By refusing to foreground a narrative of finding a wife in India, he evades the problematic and stigmatised stereotype position as a 'customer in the commodified transnational marriage market' (see Chapter 1). For further analysis of masculinity and the marriage industry, the work of Schaeffer-Grabiel (2006) is helpful. She focuses on how Western men feel replaceable and alienated by women in Western societies, and sees the search for love in non-Western countries as a way of going *back* to the older gender roles and values, for which India is known, while not in the same sense as Thailand and Philippines. Baggoe-Nielsen & Gitz-Johansen (2006), as well as Spanger (2013), highlight these aspects in the Danish context, and this is discussed further in Chapter 8.

Klaus's narrative about his getting together with Raaka is constructed as unproblematic and, as he puts it, a 'natural' involvement.

> *We met at work.... When I got an opportunity to work in India, I lived there and came there with... we met in the office, she was marketing manager and I was project manager for the team that was delivering software services to Denmark. So that is where we met: in the office.*

Raaka also confirms that they met in a workplace with an international atmosphere where their work identity was the common denominator.

Interviewer: *What were you doing there?*

Raaka: *I was doing, trying to sell... I was in marketing, software in that company, but I was working with Denmark actually. International marketing and Denmark was one of the places I had to work with. But we met in India.*

Interviewer: *You had a lot of contact with international people or international environment?*

Raaka: *Yes, for sure, I had some amount of contact.*

Raaka, however, describes the development of their relationship at a personally and temporally critical point, where Klaus's personality attributes and especially his egalitarianism gender-wise, made him a suitable match for her.

And when I met Klaus it seemed more equal from my point of view. But there were also many other factors. I was at a point of time where I didn't want to marry. And I met someone who really attracted me in that way, mentally and way of thinking and that matter. And I was also at a break point with my family and I had a lot of physical issues I was facing, it was completely, I just wanted to get out of my family: escape. And I needed to be in a relationship at that time.

However, their decision raised some difficulties with her extended family and the community. These difficulties are explained as being due to the cultural expectations expressed by her family towards an intercultural marriage with a Danish man, who didn't belong to her significant social categories such as caste (an ancient Indian social stratification category based on ascribed position and profession) and religion – Hindu.

In India it would be almost impossible to imagine that you can have your daughter or son marrying with someone from outside your religion, country and caste. . . . when you marry, you marry within your own caste . . . . So, I imagined a lot that it would be a problem, but it turned out that it wasn't a problem . . . my mother had problems . . . but my siblings didn't have. I spoke with my sister . . . they [her sister and her sister's husband] were quite happy with the idea that I would like to marry a Dane.

She further describes the negotiations related to acceptance of her marriage within the extended family, especially involving one of her elder sisters and her husband, who has been a 'mother substitute' for Raaka. At the time of the interview, that sister was with Raaka in Denmark as she had recently lost her husband. Raaka wanted to support her during this crisis period.

I spoke with my sister, who is practically my mother actually, the one who is staying with us, and whose husband passed away recently. They have been my parents practically speaking. They have, she is 20 years older and

> *she has mothered me all the time....My mom was totally against the idea...Because she thought my dad would not like it.*

She describes her mother's concerns as fear of judgement and exclusion from the Indian family and by society at large. Partner selection in India is a complex process involving religions, region, socio-economic placing and caste. Thus the salient part played by the community was clarified. The major obstacle to marriage with a foreigner was not about Raaka moving away from India but about potential sanctions from important social networks for the family as well as Raaka. Some family members, especially her father, felt embarrassed in relation to their community and extended family and thus preferred a simple, inexpensive wedding ceremony. Her narrative reminds us of a mild version of 'border patrolling', as downsizing the ceremony becomes a way of controlling movement across the caste/community boundaries. This is both as a preventive measure – warning those who might cross boundaries about the sanctions they would suffer – and a penalty – punishing those who do (Smith & Jones, 2011 in Aspinall & Song, 2013).

Raaka clarifies the complex situation:

> *...we cannot come together with the family or friends and that would be a lot of question marks if you married a foreigner. But, my dad was very cool about it. He said, 'okay, she wants to marry him, it is fine'. So, my mother was like 'oh'. Then it was like 'okay, we have to have a big marriage and we have to do this'...and that he was against, he wanted to have it discreet. No, 'now she is marrying a foreigner let's have a simple marriage'...he didn't want to use his money. But before he has been saving money.*

Raaka explained that there was acceptance from the extended family, including both paternal and maternal uncles, aunts and their children (cousins), but her father insisted on a discreet simple wedding and didn't want to invest his savings in an elaborate wedding ceremony.

> *In India, the family is the extended family, the cousins the uncles – they never had any problem, they accepted it. They have known him all the time and they love to invite us all over, and we have very good relationship with my part of the family in the extended family, all the cousins.*

This narrative on the one hand illustrates how what was thought to be a potentially problematic situation (the father's disapproval) wasn't a problem but, on the other hand, it also illustrates the boundary marker of acceptance/resistance to the mixed marriage within the family, in terms of the father's hesitance to pay for a large/traditional celebration of the wedding ceremony. Thus there is partial acceptance of the marriage with a foreigner. Her father's attitude towards the wedding ceremony would have been different had she chosen to marry a man of the same religion and caste as the family. The compromise is to hold a discreet marriage at low cost. The marriage was, at the time of the interview, ten years back, but Raaka still chooses to bring the episode to the forefront. This may be to illustrate the roots of her now broken relationship with a part of her family (including her father due to internal conflict between two of her siblings). The positioning of herself outside the family norms is told as both a sacrifice and deliberate break with her family as well as a personal independent choice reflecting the complexity of her motives. Her narrative illustrates that the beginning of the marital relationship and the related conflicts have partly affected the later family dynamic, leading to conflicts between the parent and child generations.

Her marriage with Klaus is construed as 'less valued' – not quite disapproved of but connected with embarrassment – illustrated by the 'cheap' wedding with relatively few guests. This may have been due to a transgression of the community endogamous norms, despite the apparent acceptance by the extended family. Cultural expectations towards intermarriage and the opinions of significant others play a role in the construction of the marriage as (un)problematic. The timing of marriage was also influenced by the family's insistence on avoiding cohabitation in the Indian context. We can conclude that they married sooner than they might have done elsewhere, given that the scope for dating was rather limited due to the community and extended family's negative attitude towards cohabitation.

Later in the interview, Raaka mentions their belonging to an international religious sect 'we have done a lot of spirituality . . . that is what connected us'. Their work, combined with their affiliation to an international religious sect, was among the reasons for their getting together. However, Raaka emphasises that she is a Hindu [the religion she was raised with] as well as a member of the sect. She explains.

. . . I think that all my wins have come because of the sect. Today I'm a happy person, and I have made my marriage work.

Klaus, on the other hand, doesn't directly mention their affiliation to the sect but points to his positive evaluation of Hinduism and spirituality in India. He is very positive about his wife's personality traits, especially in relation to her spirituality.

> *I don't have an issue with it, because the same for me. For me it is just, I actually find it that it is good. I think that Hinduism is a way of life and has a lot of good directions for people and I think that it is a good way of, you live with it. I live with it in India. This is one of the things that interested me in the first place about India. I have always been interested in understanding religion and where we are coming from and stuff like that. And, in India there are so many answers and you find so many interesting people because there is spiritualism there, and that spiritualism is another thing that I would say is that I appreciate about her. Of course that she is a wonderful woman and a fantastic person, but that fact that she has the spiritual part, the fact that she is very . . . That she has a very close part to the spiritual and that she lives, she thinks like a spiritual being and that is something that interests me.*

This section of his story directs attention to his being attracted by opposites and shows him grounding their relationship in the ecosystem of the religious, spiritual affiliation, which takes the focus away from the racial/ethnic differences in relation to getting together. That said, the issue of ethnicity and cultural difference gains salience regarding parenting and that is taken up further in Chapter 7. Klaus's family did not feature at all in narratives of the couple's getting together and this can be understood as showing how a Danish male participant may focus less on the natal family and reflect the individualism of Danish society.

Klaus and Raaka's narratives illustrate lucidly some of the inherent problematic processes of intermarriage both as social exclusion from part of the family of origin and inclusion as a couple and as part of the workplace. The problematic relationship with a part of Raaka's Indian family has consequences for their marriage and some years later they decide to move to Demark. Considering the macro perspective, their relationship can be perceived as an example of *global hypergamy* – marriage into the wealthy Global North from the poor Global South (Constable, 2004). However, Raaka and Klaus's narratives add nuance to simplistic understandings of the phenomenon, indicating that the circumstances of their coming together have significant meaning. The beginning of their relationship was not motivated by wealth differentials but by commonalities in their workplace, partnership formation motives and spiritual chemistry.

The narrative of Cecilia, a native Dane, and Sam, of Indian heritage, born and raised in Denmark, has similarities with Klaus and Raaka's as they also met in the workplace – this time in Denmark. Here she normalises this practice by emphasising its frequency:

> ... *we met at work, where a lot of people meet. At that time, we were both working quite a lot and we began making jokes you know that, 'well we have to be together because we don't see any other people' and then one thing led to another and we started dating and we have been together ever since.*

Contrary to Klaus, Cecilia didn't have much international experience before she married Sam, and Raaka had almost no international travelling before she left India. However, Cecilia describes her home atmosphere as being open, especially due to father's personality.

> *No, not really [contact from other, countries, nationalities]. But, I think that our home has always been open to people, no matter who they were or what background they come from. So I think that, my father was a very social person. So I think that gave me a sense of you know, being welcoming people, you know and seeing 'who are you' before you judge.*

Continuing in the same vein, Cecilia invokes the different traditions of intimate relationship formation in Sam's culture of Indian heritage, although he was born and raised in Denmark. Rather than pointing to Sam's different ethnic background, cultural differences are centralised along with the emphasis on the romantic aspect of the relationship. Cecilia discussed introducing a potential marriage partner as being an important point of difference based on some stereotypical views that bringing a person home in the 'Indian culture' means the matter is serious, implying that it is not so in 'Danish culture'. Cecilia's contention is not supported by Root's (2001) delineation on the issue of introduction of the girlfriend/boyfriend to the family in the Western (American/European) context. She notes that for most people, bringing someone home to meet the family signals a serious intention and sons as well as daughters want their families to like their new partner:

> *Yes, we fell in love, and then we took it one step at a time. I think it was more difficult for Sam than for me, because they have other traditions and in my home, if I had a boyfriend I could bring him home, even if it was,*

you know I had known him for a week. But in Sam's culture you would expect not to bring a person home until you were quite sure that this was the right person for you. So I guess there is a big difference, so I didn't meet his family for quite a long time, which for me was a little bit difficult to understand, like 'why?' But, that, I know now (laughs).

At the same time, there was an initial negative reaction to their getting together from her mother, especially before she met him, reflecting the negative stereotypes about ethnic minority men, emphasising fathers who might kidnap their children.

...I was raised in a very old-fashioned Danish way, I would say. My entire family was Danish, hmm...with old-fashioned traditions you know. Really, really Danish. And I remember when I met Sam for the first time, and the first time my mom was shocked actually, when she found out that he was not Danish: 'are you sure that this is what you want and do you know about his culture, do you know about his background?' And she was scared out of her mind, I mean she was thinking that 'oh if you have children with him, he will take them away from you, and you will never see them again'. You know she was scared.

Cecilia's narrative brings out the commonality in situation with Raaka and Klaus as employees in the same workplace along with awareness and conflicts due to the cultural practices and related stereotypes about the *other* in the initial phase. This 'getting together' phase reminds us of Merton's (1941) classical social exchange theory regarding exogamy with a partner of a lower socio-economic status (SES) possessing features such as 'white/majority status' that can compensate for the higher socio-economic partner status as 'ethnic minority'. However, the nuances of Cecilia's narrative highlight that in getting together the material, pragmatic logics do not preclude love and sexual desire. Moreover, the other participants' narratives, for example those with a similar socio-economic status like Sabita and Robert, contradict this theory.

To conclude, the narratives of these two couples – Raaka and Klaus and Cecilia and Sam – reveal the different trajectories of reaching the equifinal point of getting together across the ethnic borders, with disparate degrees of family support and resistance as well as different emphasis on commonality of workplace, ethnic and cultural differences and spiritual/religious belonging. There may initially be different perceptions of a 'suitable partner' – belonging exclusively to the same ethnic/community/caste group – in marriage among the parental generation for Raaka and Cecilia. However, their narratives showed that there can be acceptance of the son-in-law belonging to the *other* group through negotiations involving interaction with siblings for Raaka and familiarity through contact for Cecilia.

4.2.2 'Danes in the US'/'Cosmopolitans in Mumbai': foregrounding the 'national'/Cosmopolitan identity

Weddings are significant in many, if not most cultures, and are bound by traditions, expectations and ideals. Expectations related to mixed weddings are no exception. However, the positioning and choices the couples make are told as an interplay with *significant others* as well as with society. The participants in this study understand their marriages in the light of other people's reactions towards intermarriage, cultural discourses of love, inherent differences related to their experiences and other concerns. The outcomes described below shows a positive personal story of mixedness, flexibility and happiness.

Sabita was born and raised by her Indian parents in Denmark in an international elite environment along with strong connections to her country of origin – India. She moved to the USA from Denmark at the age of 17 to do her bachelor degree at a prestigious university. During her stay there she met her Danish husband, Robert. They met at a social event for Danish students, where they were in fancy dress:

> ...we actually met in...university. He is Danish and of Danish origin and he came to the university on Fullbright scholarship to do a master's program in finance. And, hmm...it was about 2 years ago we met sort of at a 'Dansker aften' [Danish evening].

The commonality of shared Danish nationality in a foreign context, that of an elite international educational background, combined with growing up in the upper/upper middle-class geographical area, has brought them closer and indicates the intersection between nationality, socio-economic belonging and territoriality. Sabita describes their attraction due to the aforementioned factors along with other qualities such as warmth, trustworthiness, attractiveness, vitality, status and resources (Fletcher et al., 2013). She positions herself and Robert highly in the socio-economic status and ambitious category, despite her being an ethic minority and his being an ethic majority, thus refuting Merton's social exchange theory of intermarriages referred to earlier. The compatibility is expressed vividly through the metaphor of feeling 'like home'.

> *It went really quickly from that, because we had a lot in common. We had both grown up in Denmark, but had sort of similar mindset that we kind of wanted to go out and you know try to get some of the best, get a very good education and try to get into a very good institute. And sort of have that, I really like that sort of intellectual, strife of ambition. It pushed us both out and it is sort of compatible. So it felt immediately 'like home' when we talked to each other.*

Like Raaka, Sabita narrates how her Indian family hold ambiguous opinions and cultural expectations towards intermarriage in the context of their being part of the upper caste of Brahmin, part of a Hindu diaspora closely interconnected to the family in country of origin.

> *Some of my cousins have not yet married, but I would be surprised if some of them did have an inter-racial marriage. Most of them...are a lot more religious and conservative, so even though they have been very happy for Robert...I don't think...that they would choose someone who is not Indian.*

She also emphasises the prevalence of another form of marriage among her extended family members living in India as the family belongs to Tamil Brahmin caste with high regional status and traditions of homogamy as described by Kalpam (2006). She is emotionally close to them, even though they are more conservative than she is.

She shows an awareness of her diasporic position, and describes her father's negative reaction when she told her parents about Robert and the marriage plans.

> *...we are very close [parents]. That is, I think a part of the 'Indianness', that is something that I definitely have from my parents. So, I mean there was never any question about me moving out when I was 16–17 or anything like that.*

Interviewer: *So it was accepted that you found your boyfriend yourself?*

Sabita: *No, I think, I think it was very ambiguous. I think that my parents kind of knew that it was a distinct possibility...I told my parents right away and I think then my dad just thought it was a bad dream. He was very typically fatherly about it, where my mother was more like wanted to know. I think in many other families this is something that happens when you are 16 or something, but (laughs) it happened some years later. And they didn't really know what it was.*

For Sabita, sharing the process with her parents was important, though not without reflection. She further explains that Robert wanted her to tell her parents right away but she was apprehensive about telling them until she was sure herself, and this was related to the way she has been raised. Subsequently, there was acceptance from the family and a common understanding of the *seriousness* of the matter implying sacredness to some extent.

It is not that I'm scared to tell them, but it is like they protected me for so long and I don't want to do anything stupid. It is something that is very sacred, it is not casual. In one way I'm glad that I'm raised that way.... So at the time when Robert wanted to propose, my parents were much more prepared and he was already family then and it was sort of expected. He, I mean they [parents] treated him like a son, because if you are serious about this, then you are family.... My parents wanted to know if he was very serious also if they were going to let me date him and see each other. You can wait to get married, but we need some sort of... to know that he was serious about it.

In spite of initial parental doubts, ambiguity and intergenerational negotiations, there was a high degree of parental involvement in Sabita and Robert's wedding. Both families contributed resources in arranging the wedding ceremony once the seriousness of the relationships was confirmed. The extended family from different countries such as India, the USA and Canada participated in the wedding, which was a mixture of Brahmin and Danish rituals. The memories of her wedding ceremony are positive though reflecting oversimplified binary: European version as civilised.

...At the wedding we had an Indian ceremony in the morning and all my uncles and relatives flew over... they were very enthusiastic about it. In the evening we had more of a European, civilised wedding with cocktails at a reception and all of that. So it was very mixed.

Sabita countered cultural scepticism and expectations by creating an individualistic and independent subject position and narrated her story in an untroubled way outside the family norm, by carrying out the wedding in her own (mixed) way.

Sabita and Robert had been married a couple of months before the interview. They had some cultural concerns about marriage in relation to norms and expectations as a young couple awaiting their first child immediately after their marriage. Here ethnicity, age, education, socio-economic position and location intersected as they had to get married in a hurry owing to their romantic, sexually active dating partner status being unacceptable to her family.

> *I think that all the talk about us being married quite young and we are going to have children quite young, is a bit more of a cultural shock for him than it is for me, but also for me, because I did not think that it was all going to happen so soon. One of the reasons is that it is pretty normal in my family to get married so young, but not so for me, because the schools that I went to or the careers that I had thought for myself, hadn't that picture of a child so early. So it is still sort of a surprise or a shock for me.*

In the context of education and career plans, the primary concern for Sabita can be interpreted as her life course trajectory and the relatively early pregnancy. Her anxiety about impending parenthood seems to marginalise concerns about the ethnic differences between herself and her spouse. Invoking her diasporic interconnections, she clarifies that early marriage and parenting is in contradiction to her subjective *Western values*, which assume an elite education and a career for 5–6 years. Traditional middle-class Indian values, which involve women getting married in their early twenties, seem to be less salient for Sabita, as they may be different in a transnational elite Indian family. In my opinion, Sabita paints an unnuanced, reductionist picture of upper/upper middle-class educated Indian women in the metropolis where the age of marriage is increasing due to women's education and career paths (Davar, 2005; Khalakdina, 2011). I would like to problematise Sabita's assumption of difference between Indian and Danish culture when persons concerned are 'international' elite with high levels of education.

> *I have always thought that, well your career kind of ends when you have kids. Once you have kids you can't really do, your relationships are kind of put on a hold and that are things like which I have to overcome, because I didn't think that I would be dealing with them so soon, I thought more that I would be working 5–6 years and then have children so in that sense I had much more a sort of the more Western expectations.*

Additionally Sabita formulates her uncertainty about the intriguing process of how to be sure about finding the right person – the metaphorical *one and only* – through the following comment:

> ... *there are some questions that I feel that I will never be able to answer, you know how you were saying that what sort of things that connect you and things that will make you work as a couple. It is very much the same question as many of my friends from the university were asking when I told them that he had proposed and that we were going to get married, 'oh how do you know that he is the one', that sort of question is hard to answer*

Within this framework of paradoxically 'feeling at home' and feeling uncertain at the same time, Sabita negotiates identity for her marriage in differences and similarities. For example, in the narrative about her meeting with her newly wedded husband at a get together for Danish students at an elite University in the USA:

> ... *we had a lot in common. We actually went to school and kindergarten just next to the same station. So it felt immediately 'like home' when we talked to each other.*

The shared ethnic national category 'Dane' and the shared elite student position formed the foundation of their future relationship. The similarities of being raised in Denmark is narrated as a shared reference point, along with the desire to get a good education, a career and explore the world. Here the national category – *Danish* steps into the foreground in the story about their commonalities.

Later in the interview her response to a question about their connectedness is based on fundamental emotional understanding and expresses awareness of differences in food consumption practices like her being vegetarian and his eating meat. This issue is taken up again in Chapter 5.

> *I'm not even sure if it is things like education or career or the thing that we like to move around. I think that those things are easier to find between people that have had about the same upbringing as you and grown up the same place or someone who has a similar cultural background ... I think a lot of things that connect me and Robert are much more fundamental, are a lot more emotional. We have a lot of differences in other things, like what we like to eat; I like to eat vegetarian and he does not.*

She positions their marriage as different from other couples with the same upbringing, cultural background and local belongings. By this differentiation she raises a basic question about the understanding of these belongings as contextual. In the USA, these belongings and intersections were perceived as similar, brought them together and led to the feeling of being 'home' with each other. Back in Denmark, their ethnic and cultural differences now separate them, both within the relationship, and with regard to other kinds of marriages. The 'home', first constructed as a commonality, no longer has that special connectedness. Their similarities, such as intellectual drive, ambition and the desire 'to move around', are easier to find in marriages within the same ethnic group, she says. It becomes 'special' or 'normal' in her narrative that they have found those similarities *across* ethnic borders. The similar locality and nationality change meaning in this context and, combined with the ethnic category of Indian, require her to negotiate their joint couple identity.

The (Indian) ethnic belonging she identifies herself with separates her from her husband in comparison with what she calls 'couples with similar cultural backgrounds'. She positions herself and her marriage outside the norm by constructing a discourse of similarities in upbringing in the similar neighbourhood, despite differences in heritage and cultural background, which do not fit together. These differences, or not being normal, she narrates as a positive position for them by continuing:

> ... but I think that we have much more than that, something beyond that.

Their position in the academic elite is not enough to characterise their relationship, which underlines her position outside or beyond a 'normal' marriage. But the identification to a non-ethnic category as an academic elite, still opens the possibility for maintaining a normal married identity raised above culture and cultural differences. Her negotiations include challenging expectations and her personal positioning in relation to dominating norms of marriage and the age becoming a parent for the first time. This age, on average, is 29 in Denmark (Statistics Denmark, 2013), while Sabita will become a mother at the age of 22. Additionally, in reaching the equifinal point of forming a mixed intimate relationship, her trajectory indicates independence, albeit a choice that has been highly influenced by interplay with *significant others* (Mead, 1934) and the social reactions towards intermarriage.

According to Schaeffer-Grabiel, futuristic ideals of flexibility and mobility are a way to idealise intermarriage (2006, p. 4) and they open up the possibility of cosmopolitan citizenship of the world. This is a general discourse that the project participants, including Sabita and Robert, draw upon. Cosmopolitan identity is also emphasised by Katja, who met Rajiv in a setting which was foreign for her. They met in Mumbai in India while she was doing an internship as part of her master's studies. She was introduced to Rajiv through a common friend and an intimate relationship developed soon after.

And then we started hanging out as friends and eh yeah a couple of months later 'love' (laughing).

Rajiv answered in the interview that the reason he came to Denmark was Katja, whom he met through a musician friend in Mumbai. The narrative below documents their reciprocal attraction based on common interests.

And finally we ended up meeting and we really liked each other. It was so nice. And then she was travelling around, and then she came back to Mumbai. We were already together in the first trip and we spend the last 12 days together and then she left and we were always in touch and then when I came back from Africa, that was when she said, like ok. That was when I really felt that there would be a future with her and that I felt something for her. But she had felt so all the time, but she didn't really want to talk about it about it because she felt that I was still married like. Married yeah [in the process of a consensual divorce from his Indian wife, after two years of marriage].

When asked about the reaction of those close to them about their mixed relationship, Katja described the mostly positive reactions of the people around her. The exception being the mother of one of her close friends, who reacted negatively by displaying shock at seeing Rajiv's picture and focusing on his hierarchically negative phenotype as 'black'.

Eh just one of my closest colleagues, her mother, I only met her once, but she is Dansk Folkeparti [member of the Danish national far right party] ... she knew that I had an Indian husband and it was totally fine, but then my colleague showed her picture of us at some point and she was like 'oh my God he is black' and then she told me and I was like 'okay that's really weird' (laughing) what does she expect, he is from India so yes he is black, so that's the only thing that I really noticed.

Furthermore, she described her grandmother's negative stereotype of India as 'a terrible country, bringing up a baby there is totally insane', though she rejects it as just 'grandmother talk' and points to positive acceptance of Rajiv:

It has nothing to do with him, she loves him, but she is happy that we chose Denmark and not India.

On the other hand, Rajiv emphasises his positive experiences with Katja's large family, complete with step-parents and a large number of step- and biological siblings, as well as her friends.

... her parents live there, and that was the only thing, I think that I have blended nicely, it was so kind, they were so kind all her friends and they welcomed me, and that was really cool.

In summing up, the equifinality point of being an intermarried couple for Katja and Rajiv was reached through a pathway of being romantically bonded in the context of India, where their mutual attraction and Rajiv's privileges and power as a successful professional in India were pivotal. The ethnic differences and family reactions were in the background. However, for the two Danish-Pakistani couples – Lars and Marlik and Mads and Nihla – the setting for their getting together was Denmark and in the next section we turn to their trajectories of becoming intermarried couples.

4.2.3 Joint identity and 'destiny': foregrounding the 'chance' factor

Marlik, who had been married for 27 years at the time of the interview, credits her marriage to Lars to the hands of fate by saying several times that it was *destiny* that brought them together. When questioned about meeting her husband, she clarifies:

My husband! I met him when I was studying in London and I came on a study trip to Copenhagen, it was just the destiny I met him (laughs). We liked each other and later on we fell in love and then we got married and then he came and visited me in England and ... that's how.

Furthermore, she points to her young age when she fell in love and got married, saying that she had hardly pondered the matter. Still, she was not inclined to marry an economically well-placed person from her country of origin, due to her negative feeling about displaying wealth.

> *I never thought about I should marry a Pakistani or if it should be easier for me in that way, I was 22 and studying when I met my husband so I didn't really think about it, in Pakistan if you have money it's just a show-off... and I didn't want that.*

Lars, her husband, also confirms the narrative about getting married when he was a student who was yet to reflect on married life.

> *We were students and we met each other through some common friends. I was a glad bachelor and had not given marriage much thought.*

When questioned about his life course being different if he had married a Dane, Lars mentions that he had not thought about it. He emphasised that he had converted to Islam, and perceived his faith as a relation between himself and *Allah* and didn't even think of other marital possibilities.

Marlik's narrative about getting together highlights the intersection between international belonging, ethnic identity and socio-economic status, as well as belonging to a diplomat family. She negotiates her ethnic and national belonging along these lines:

> *I don't consider myself as a migrant... I have lived in so many countries as a diplomat child and I have the identity that I am what I am.... I felt when I came here I'm not a guest worker. I came here because I fell in love with a man, he fell in love with me... in that way my relationship has been very natural, and it could have been anywhere.*

Schaeffer-Grabiel, 2006 emphasises how marrying across ethnic, national and racial borders opens the possibility for new positions in the global space to be raised (or imagined to be raised) above gender and racial hierarchies. She underlines the *regenerative* aspects of intermarriage in the twenty-first century, in contrast to the *pathological* focus of earlier times which were discussed in Chapter 2. In the present study, Raaka and Klaus, and to some extent Katja and Rajiv, concur with this position, which is further taken up in Chapter 6 in relation to parenting.

> Unlike nineteenth-century constructions of racial mixing as degenerative, in this instance foreign genes are constructed as regenerative. This shift in racial construction connects with individualistic ideals of multiculturalism in the global marketplace. Once again, diversity and race are advertised as products that promise to bring one closer to nature, towards one's 'true self' and to contribute to the making of 'natural' gender and racial hierarchies.
>
> (Schaeffer-Grabiel, 2006, p. 341)

Nihla's intermarriage with Mads was also by chance. On meeting Mads, she said:

> Nihla: *We met each other at a bar (laughs).*
> Interviewer: *In?*
> Nihla: *In Denmark....He initially, when we met each other, before we got married, and we were very serious about getting married and all that...I may seem like a Danish girl, I may talk and act like any other Danish girl but there is still a difference; there is still a significant difference in the way that I see my future.*

Her statement highlights how deeply entrenched these differences are. Unlike the other participants, Nihla brings up the issue of Pakistani identity at several points in the interviews, including the theme of getting together and their current process of divorce. The narratives are both multilayered and self-contradictory as she concludes the interview by negating her own and Mads's ethnic belonging, as well as differences, thereby foregrounding the similarities of having been raised in Danish society. These contradictions and paradoxes are highly relevant for comprehending the affective dimensions of this intermarried couple's trajectory, since although Nihla and Mads are about to end their relationship, similar dynamics can also be are perceived – albeit to different extent – in other couples' conflicts.

> *...I don't see our relationship being like Mads being Danish and me being Pakistani, not at all. For me, he could be Egyptian and I could be the same. I mean I don't think it would matter of course....I think also because*

I have been brought up in this society that our differences, even out like that, and we don't have as many.

The basic dilemma of accepting or rejecting the ethnic position is reflected here. The narrative being raised above ethnic and racial hierarchies and being similar yet different emphasises the possibility of being several things at the same time. According to Verkuyten (2005, p. 149), in our globalising world, interconnections and mixings of all kinds take place. The narratives about identity in this study are about having multiple ethnic belongings where different ethnic categories are suppressed or highlighted in different situations. Verkuyten emphasises Gloria Anzalduas's concept of 'mestizaja consciousness' (cited in ibid.), where people of mixed ancestry cope by developing a tolerance for contradiction and ambiguity. The possibility of 'juggling cultures' somehow contradicts the 'normal' and somewhat reductionistic understanding of ethnic belonging and conflict with the cultural categorisation mentioned earlier.

Social psychologists as a whole are not very interested in the messier categories of human affairs. Social identities are predominately studied as unitary categories with relatively clear-cut boundaries They are seen as reciprocally and mutually exclusive structures, such as male/female, black/white, minority/majority. Most studies consider two distinct groups at one time and pay no attention to more 'problematic' positions and definitions that are intermediate and at the boundaries or borders (Verkuyten, 2005, p. 150). The participants in this study are not persons of mixed ancestry (though some are parents of mixed children), yet a number of them, especially the diasporic or reunified spouses, are operating in a pluralistic mode. Terms for mixing processes – such as creolisation, syncretism, dual identification and hybridisation – prevalent in cultural and globalisation theories and post-structural terms, can be applied to them.

To summarise, it is clear that the participants' constructions of identities in this study occupy complex hybrid identities and use (ethnic) categories that conflict with the notion of homogeneous and defined identities. Intermarriage can be viewed as 'border-crossing' and the spouses as inhabiting socially mixed borderland positions by both identifying with their 'origin ethnicity', and their spouse's ethnicity as well as the identity they build. Sometimes ethnicity is in 'sameness' and sometimes it is in 'difference', sometimes this results in problematic positions and sometimes not.

Normatively, 'hybridity' and related terms in academics, to some extent in public understanding. are used to critique ethnic boundaries and essentialism, and to valorise mixture and change.

The space of the hybridity is transgressive, and hybridity is celebrated as an innovative and creative power...hybridity is preferred because it emphasises 'togetherness-in-difference' rather than 'living-apart-together' (Verkuyten, 2005, p. 153).

The point to be made here is that hybrid identities are advantageous and may be unavoidable identity strategies in mixed marriages.

We can conclude the 'getting together' of mixed couples – the equifinality point of forming intimate relationships through the Trajectory Equifinality Model (TEM) – through three different pathways, where disparate categories and belongings are highlighted, leading to emphasis on the differential privileges and power. Although some of the participants are aware of the processes of exclusion and discrimination, the dominant reason for mixed marriage is *falling in love*, which implies sexual desire and attraction (Giles, 2006). At the same time these couples endeavour to follow the social norms of marriage in the society in which they are living (Patny, 2013). This is not expressed here as an act of political activism and/or social resistance, as was also the case in Killian's (2013) study of interracial couples. It is noticeable that the same conclusion about falling in love being a common motive for the mixed couples across racial borders is reached by Root (2001) in her pioneering study of interracial marriages in the USA.

Ironically, theories that attempt to explain interracial marriages rarely address the subject of love. Interracial couples married for the same reason that motivated other couples – first and foremost love – falling in love seems to dissolve differences, minimises the serious faults of the other person and infuses one's life with a sense of specialness (ibid., p. 114).

Initial meetings at work, irrespective of meeting in the diasporic spouse's country of origin or in the country of residence, emphasises the commonality and the related values implied – in other words it is just 'normal' to meet at work. For some couples belonging to an international religious sect places ethnic differences, as well as the original religious belonging, in the background. However, for other mixed couples, meeting in the workplace doesn't make the ethnic differences less important.

Another trajectory for the equifinality point of mixed relationship formation is through common *national identity* in a foreign setting, where initially the socio-economic, the educational status and common *cosmopolitan* values play a vital role.

Lastly, the pathway of getting together can be primarily perceived as a destiny factor leading to romance, where ethnic differences are presented in a contradictory manner in intersection with the life course position and/or current couple crisis. Despite the differential pathways highlighting the dialectic between differences and similarities, changing patterns of privileges and power are present in the narratives, be they in the foreground or the background. These beginnings and pathways to meeting influence the participants' life trajectories throughout their relationships. It is significant to note that there are many ways for the couples to get together and begin relationships across ethnic borders and my observations highlight just some of the types of meetings. Irrespective of the ways in which couples get together, in line with Rosenblatt (2009) and these narratives, we can conclude that the different contexts and circumstances of the couples coming together may have differing meanings and result in one couple dealing with issues quite differently from another.

5
Managing Everyday Life

This chapter deals with maintaining intermarried relationships through the life course. It follows on from the previous chapter's discussion of the 'getting together' narratives of the couples characterised by the centrality of love. Some theoretical conceptualisations of love – both in society in general and within close relationships – forms the first section of this chapter, while the second section presents an everyday life approach to studying the management of mixed couple life. The third section delineates a three-stage ontogenetic (relating to the developmental history of individual within its own lifetime) division.

I have found it relevant to consider a life course perspective to enable comprehension of the complexities of intermarried dynamics over time. The life course approach (Levy et al., 2005) studies how transitions are regulated by normative representations as well as by life experiences and their interpretations. The data is analysed by using the life course stages: *The Honeymoon Phase, Family Establishment Phase* and *Settled Phase*, with the focus on gender and cultural differences.

5.1 Love, marriage and modernity

Modern attitudes to love, marriage and family relations have been theorised in a sociological perspective, for instance by Ulrich Beck and Elisabeth Beck-Gernsheim, who describe how traditionally clear definitions of love and marriage have been replaced with new individualised ways of living and loving. They argue that one of the main features of what they refer to as the 'new era' is:

a...collision of interests between love, family and personal freedom. The nuclear family, built around gender status, is falling apart on the issues of emancipation and equal rights, which no longer conveniently come to a halt outside our private lives. The result is the quite normal chaos called love... love will become more important than ever and equally impossible.

(Beck & Beck-Gernsheim, 1995, pp. 1–2)

As mentioned earlier, Anthony Giddens proposes the concept of 'the pure relationship' – a relationship built upon romantic love relations and upon trust, which become a condition for 'ontological safety – a sense of order and continuity in regard to an individual's experiences'. Traditional relationships are subject to change due to the reflectivity of modernism, which opens up an area where the 'traffic rules' of the traditional family patterns are revised. Yet this reorganisation contains a paradox or conflict between autonomy and dependence (Giddens, 1994, p. 64) or between individualisation and traditional family structures.

Individualisation means that men and women are released from the gender roles prescribed by industrial society for life in the nuclear family. At the same time this aggravates the situation, they find themselves forced, under pain of material disadvantage, to build up a life of their own by way of the labour market, training and mobility, and if need be to pursue this life at the cost of their commitments to family, relations and friends.

(Beck and Beck-Gernsheim, 1995, p. 6)

Individualisation therefore is, on one hand, the freedom to choose and be responsible for oneself, but on the other hand to be dependent on internalised demands or social conditions, which entail social transformation with practical implications. So the very conditions which encourage individualism produce new, unfamiliar dependencies: you are obligated to standardise your own existence. This dominant tendency of individualisation is criticised additionally to create new forms of dependencies such as social media dependency, FOMO – Fear of Missing Out – essentially an addiction to information technology (Social Media Today, 2014).

Furthermore, I shed light on the nature and content of love and intimate relationships. These relationships have been central themes in many stories, plays and songs since the beginning of recorded history. An analysis by Jankowiak & Fischer (1992), based on folklore, ethnographies, etc., confirms the universality of romantic love perceived as unexpected, spontaneous spurt of passion often leading into the individual choosing to enter into a committed relationship; their work found its presence in 167 out of 174 studies, even though scientific study of these themes began only a few decades ago. Although romantic love was not specifically described by any of the sample societies' researchers, results demonstrated that romantic love is indeed a human universal. To assess the sample universe accurately Jankowiak & Fischer (1992) designed a set of criteria, which served as an indication of whether the societies studies possessed romantic love. For a society to suggest that romantic love is regularly experienced within that culture, that society must meet at least one of the following five criteria: accounts depicting personal anguish and longing; the use of love songs or folklore that highlight the motivations behind romantic involvement; elopement due to mutual affection; native accounts affirming the existence of passionate love; and the ethnographer's affirmation that romantic love is present.

With 88.5% of the sample universe showing evidence of romantic love they concluded that romantic love is a human universal though with cultural variations. As mentioned in Chapter 4, the intimate relationships typically contain a mixture of both passionate and companionate love. However, the absence of companionate love in particular can spell trouble for the long-term stability of relationships. Lastly, we examine the *maintenance* of love and intimacy as this chapter also deals with ontogenetic, developmental and historical aspects of intermarriages.

Fletcher et al. (2013) have considered the connections between passionate and companionate love and they answer the question of how to keep the fire and love alive as follows:

Maintaining *interpersonal trust* ... a key ingredient of love ... trust captures the degree to which individuals can count on current partners to meet fundamental needs and facilitate important goal ... The cardinal features of trust center on a partner's emphasising partners' dependability (i.e. being able to count on the partner for comfort and support during difficult times) and faith in the future(i.e. being confident that the partner will always be available and supportive in the future) ... the development of trust involves the personalities of the partners as well as the shared experiences.

Partners in the relationship should participate together in novel and arousing activities. Engaging in such experiences with a partner recreates experiences more typical of the early stages of relationship and breaks the monotony. Stoking the sacred fire of desire can potentially be as simple as making an effort to seek out new and exciting adventures with your partner.

(ibid., pp. 179–181)

Capitalisation refers to sharing positive news with the partner as it requires self-disclosure, open communication and the partner's enthusiastic response.

Expression of gratitude to partners can also contribute to maintenance of love and intimacy.

Though these suggestions can be criticised for being too simplistic and primarily pertaining to Western societies, they have implications for supporting mixed marriages in the modern world, and these supportive mechanisms are taken up in the last chapter of this book. Over the past four decades the dissolution of marriage by divorce has been on the rise in a number of Western countries, with the peak time for divorce being after four years of marriage. Given these conceptualisations of love and intimacy, it is imperative to study how the participants manage their relationship in everyday life and the next section offers some theoretical reflections on this.

5.2 The management of everyday life

Paradoxes in everyday life analysis show how the couples manage to balance between individualism and being part of a couple and a parent. To carry out research within an everyday life perspective is to see, hear and learn from the research participants within their social relations, while at the same time remaining aware of their attitudes towards and the handling of social circumstances.

How are the social conditions and possibilities adjusted within their current life situation, and how do they handle social limitations? How do they, with others, maintain and change society and thereby create it? (Beck-Jørgensen, 1994, p. 12, author's translation).

Within an everyday life perspective, people's actions, opinions/points of view and experiences are the central object of research. The methodological challenge is to be found in the balance between the exceptional and the unexceptional, or in the conflict between the comfortable and the uncomfortable, the known and the unknown. We need to disentangle this contrary mixture of forces to see how their entanglement figures in everyday life (Highmore, 2002).

The point is that everyday life has its fundamental 'obviousness' – activities, habits, routines, etc. – that create a certain continuity and 'normality'. Therefore, it is a methodological challenge to disentangle the 'abnormal' from the 'normal' in order to form a nuanced comprehension of the everyday life of the participants.

People construct and structure their everyday life though different strategies and adjustments, as an ongoing meaning-making process. Hence the narratives are analysed to depict the participants' construction of their everyday life by using different identity strategies, while also forefronting some aspects of married life depending on their place in the life course (relating to how long they have been married). They attach importance to different problems and advantages concerning cultural differences. The participants in this study depict different phases of life course, not least as they are aged between 21 and 61 and have been married from between a few months and 27 years. Thus, their narratives indicate different adjustments towards marriage, their life situation and everyday practices.

Overall, some common values emerge in the analysis of the empirical material, for example compatibility, integration, tolerance and flexibility, displayed in different ways and from different perspectives. They represent examples of coexistence between two people from very different backgrounds, and provide us with knowledge about their facing everyday life challenges.

5.2.1 The three phases

In the following analysis, I have divided the participants into three phases determined by their position in the life course and their marriage situation. The 'phases' are based on the empirical material presented here and, as such, should be considered as ad hoc and specific to this project. These phases are drawn from the study data and are not based on other work. They may seem a bit simplistic and not all participants have not gone through these phases as the sample is general, at the same time 'cross-sectional', covering a wide range of married life period from a few months to 27 years. As we can see, social and social temporal categories such as age, working, career status, ethnicity and race intersect in different ways in their narratives about marriage.

The honeymoon phase

In the first years of married life, cultural and other differences are perceived as an interesting and positive part of the relationship – especially as the initial attraction between the partners is associated with a positive approach to differences. In this phase, some of these differences are hardly noticed as factors that require working out or negotiation. Besides, in this phase there is often a great sense of mobility and mixing, apparent and/or real. Within discourses of passionate love, problems are rarely focused on, the couples 'experiment' with compromise and are driven by career opportunities and future plans. Attitudes towards the future and the world at large are generally positive.

Family establishment

The next stage in married life is characterised by more conflicting positions, since differences may become perceived as problematic. Passionate love declines and the risk of marriage dissolution increases. 35%–40% of marriages end in dissolution in Western countries 46% in Denmark and one of the major reasons why people divorce is extra-marital sexual activity (Fletcher et.al., 2013). However, both forgiveness of betrayal and the willingness to sacrifice boost relationship wellbeing and reduce these risks. In the construction of work–life balance gender roles, different parenting styles and new ways of life are practiced and negotiated. At the same time, a clearer joint identity takes shape. In addition, couples face the challenges of living a transnational lifestyle.

The settled phase

The last stage describes couples who have been together for a longer period of time – over a decade. They have lived in the same country for some years and have 'settled down'. These couples have relationships characterised by less mobility and with a strong construction of joint identity, shared opinions and identities based on *we*. Of course, even in the most harmonious intimate relationships, conflicts and negative attributions occur. In this stage companionate love is more strongly related to relationship satisfaction, though there is still a mix of both passionate and companionate love. Arguments and differences in everyday life are expressed as a 'natural' part of living, and are therefore not seen as threatening to the marriage. In the next sections I discuss these phases in more detail analysing the empirical data.

5.3 Couples in the honeymoon phase

As the title of this section indicates, this stage of marriage reflects how these newly wedded couples or newly established relationships are characterised by the novelty of the relationship and by new everyday life routines. During this phase decisions on where to live and future plans must be taken. A combination of excitement about a new lifestyle and opportunities, along with an openness towards social worlds, are the dominant aspects. Compromises and problems are viewed as superficial and are toned down in favour of excitement over future plans. Nevertheless, daily compromises play a role in the narratives collected and are negotiated as larger or smaller personal sacrifices.

Recently married Sabita, for example, identifies herself strongly with being a vegetarian during the interview (see Chapter 4), and tells how food is, and has been, a concern for her in relation to the compromises she has made for her relationship:

> *I have disapproved of non-vegetarians and didn't think it was the pure form of eating. Actually I wasn't so aware of that I had so strong thoughts on it, and I thought that if I was getting married to someone who ate meat I would never cook for him and he could kind of have his own section in the fridge . . . and our children are definitely not going to eat meat. . . . And now I cook meat and I eat fish . . . I didn't realise that there were things that I was so narrow-minded about.*

For her, the compromise of cooking meat and eating fish should not be understood as shallow or less important than the challenges other couples face as being a vegetarian is an integral aspect of her ethnic identity as a Tamilian Indian. The quote illustrates the changes and compromises newly established couples explore. To put it in another way, everyday compromises in the honeymoon phase can be viewed as a first level of practical adjustments, where the couples 'fall into place' and move towards a joint identity formed from two radically different personal points of view, habits, norms, etc. This practical adjustment is clear in the interview and is expressed as a radical change in her former ways of living and a change in her self-identification.

Beck-Gernsheim, 2002 stresses that intermarried couples, more than others, are repeatedly forced into crucial identity decisions. What to give up? What to keep? What is important to me and to us? This can place them under constant strain or, at worst, lead to the breakdown of the relationship. On the other hand, this offers them the chance to remain more open with each other in everyday life, and to risk new starts over and over again.

This stage in life may be one in which personal development and change is at stake – when one's own philosophy of life and self-awareness is confronted and challenged – but in a world presented as being of opportunities and with a mind open for change. Analysing within a full life course perspective, this phase of life is exciting as there is openness towards challenge and it can be considered as a positive life transition. It can be seen in Sabita's case that she is open for transformations and adaptational processes, all of which characterise the honeymoon phase.

Other aspects characterising this period of time are mobility and hybridity. All the interviewed couples relate stories of how they moved or travelled a lot in the first period of their marriage. For some this is because they met each other outside Denmark and have been following a transnational lifestyle for some years. Katja and Rajiv, for example, had been travelling frequently before they met in India and fell in love during the first phase of their contact. Klaus and Raaka moved back and forth between India and Denmark for several years at the beginning of their marriage. Sabita and Robert, as mentioned earlier, met in the USA, lived in New York and were, at the time of the interview, living in Hong Kong. Sabita and Robert's movements are driven by study and/or work opportunities and they are both focused on their respective studies and careers, prioritising investment in career and search for opportunities work-wise. Sabita makes it explicit:

I think that we have much more than that, something beyond that. But of course education is something that we relate to and that is why we put a lot of value in academic elitism and that kind of merit or scholarly merit.

Similarly, Klaus and Raaka retrospectively describe how their newly wedded situation was built upon a lot of future plans and their shared openness and flexible attitude towards the world and its opportunities:

Klaus: ... we got an opportunity to move back to India after we had shifted to India, having been 2.5 years in India. Why not? It was a good opportunity workwise, we also have our plans that we want to start our own company. And that was fine. It worked out well that way ... continuing the Indian way or do something else.

These quotes document the common characteristics of the honeymoon phase: many future plans, an open-minded and flexible attitude towards geography and future and investment in career and work.

Retrospectively Marlik, who has been married for 27 years, also explains what the world looks like when you are young and newly wedded:

> *When you are young you meet a guy, and say ok he's the one and you get married, at that time you just see him, you don't see the geographic area . . .*

To conclude, this early phase is the first step into an intermarried lifestyle characterised by greater potential for mobility and positivity towards opportunities and future plans. Romano (2008) describes a similar attitude to a successful intermarried lifestyle as a 'spirit of adventure and curiosity towards the world'. The spirit that had first led them into the relationship often remains during the marriage and sometimes helps them to deal with, confront or challenge the ambiguities that can *accompany a cross-cultural existence* (ibid., p. 184). The couples to share a joint reference point in their investment in their careers. As pointed out in the Chapter 4, the establishment of the intermarriage can cause conflict in the early stage with family, and challenge cultural expectations. This, however, is related as a personal choice or positive freedom. Furthermore, the honeymoon phase is characterised by excitement about the construction of a new identity, both practically and emotionally. Attempts to build up a new 'joint identity' brought a lot of differences in viewpoints and habits (cultural or otherwise) to the foreground, but is described as positive self-awareness and a positive process creating a new self-image/identity. Similarly, on the basis of an analysis of 20 intermarried couples' experiences in the USA, Killian (2013) posits that successful construction of a new *couple identity* and/or family identity stems from:

1) The common ground, the extent to which couples share personal beliefs, goals and values
2) The achievement of a mutual respect and positive valuing of partner differences, without which partners could become locked in intractable conflicts
3) The active inclusion and integration of portions of each partner's ethnic heritage in the new family, including traditions, rituals, and personal routines from both families of origin, and
4) The agreement on how the partners will deal with and present themselves to the outside world. (ibid., p. 121)

Although we can see common ground in the form of workplace, religious commonality and some of the earlier mentioned strategies for developing a couple and mixed family identity, the transnational relationships of these mixed couples indicates more mobility and plans for mobility in the honeymoon phase. However, the families become more rooted in one place as the marriage develops. Time passes, which also contributes to or challenges the joint couple identity.

5.4 Couples in the family establishment phase

After the first step into married life – which we have termed as the honeymoon phase – other compromises and challenges come into the foreground. Many couples married for some years become parents and choose a place to live for a longer period of time. They seem to struggle with different aspects of their daily lives. The narratives illustrate a stronger or more prominent *we* as an indication of a more established joint identity, but differences in culture and personality between the spouses seem to be a greater challenge to everyday life. Family is the keyword in these narratives and compromises within marriage in relation to practical arrangements, parenting, gender roles and attitudes towards external social conditions are foregrounded in the interviews. This stage can be described as a 'reality confrontation' period. Everyday life with its established routines and cultural differences is challenging, creating possibilities for making relationship-specific arrangements as well as risks for destructive conflicts.

> … both partners must achieve the 'construction of a new intercultural reality', build an 'intercultural life world' or a 'binational family culture'. They act within a space that has been little structured beforehand, as two different worlds meet within it. In this situation, for which there is no preparation and no defined rules, the partners have to work out arrangements of their own.
>
> (Beck-Gernsheim, 2002, p.133)

The next section will analyse, in some detail, narratives of gender and love which redefine conceptualisations.

5.4.1 Family establishment – gender roles

One can no longer define relationships between two persons of different gender just in terms of sexuality, affection, partnership, parenthood and so on, due to changing social norms – including feminism. We need to include wider social, political and economic inequalities, as well as professional and personal inequalities. Family relationships are intrinsically affected by job and income, marriage, education opportunities and mobility.

The complexity of gender and power structures brings to the light a paradox: 'the more equal the sexes seem, the more we become aware of persistent and pernicious inequalities between them' (Beck & Beck-Gernsheim, 1995, p. 13).

Cecilia and her husband Sam met each other at their workplace. They were both very committed to their respective careers and were working a lot, which she describes as a joint identity that served as a 'common ground' for their relationship. Asked to reflect on their marriage, she states:

> ...*I was quite an independent woman. I was raised independently and actually for many, many years I didn't want children, because I wanted to have a career and I wanted to live that life. But I guess it changed when I met Sam, and when I became older. And I wouldn't change it now.*

There has been a change in Cecilia's lifestyle after her marriage to Sam and their building of a family. She had been working in marketing for several years and was very committed to her work. She identifies herself (retrospectively) as an independent career woman, but at the time of the interview was working part-time as a secretary and was partly on maternity leave. She is now more focused on a family lifestyle than on having a competitive career and describes how her husband's ethnic minority background, as an Indian born and raised in Denmark, plays a part in her decision to concentrate on the family rather than her career:

> *Coming from his background, the women do all the practical stuff...it is still a little bit old-fashioned....He has never done these things and I don't think that he realises the work you put into it. But I like it, and it is a choice that I have made, to say that, now he has his chance to do his career. We have two small children and, my philosophy is like, when we said that we should have children I said: 'I don't want children, if I don't have time for them'. So...I have made that choice. He hasn't. I guess, since I have made that choice, it would be stupid of me to, when he comes home after a long day, say that: 'you have to vacuum because we have to be equal'.*

Equality and gender roles are negotiated as a personal choice, through an interplay between cultural expectations and resources for parenting. She has decided to spend more time with the children and she expresses satisfaction with her situation. Gender is perceived as a 'cultural thing' and as a personal choice, and thereby an equal position. In their negotiation of power, she positions herself as an independent, and thereby, powerful woman.

> *If you had asked me 10 years ago if I would have been a 'stay-at-home mom' more or less, I would have said: 'definitely no'. I don't know if that has anything to do with culture, I mean that has just been part of getting older and wiser, I guess.*

This interpretation indicates that she does not want to be seen as oppressed or forced into a gendered position because of her own interpretation of her husband's cultural norms. Instead, she cites discourses about gender roles and practical things as restructured by cultural gender role expectations. This is an example of a power struggle that is repeated during the interview, and which also concerns categorisation imposed upon her from people outside of her immediate family, for example by the staff at her daughter's kindergarten:

> *I think that that the roles we have now, when Sam is working and I am at home, might be perceived by them as cultural, which they are not. So I guess that might be the only thing that they think, that Sam is maybe not there enough and doing what they expect from a Danish guy to do. But that, for us, it is not a cultural thing.*

She draws upon discourses of 'normal' gender roles, and how roles 'should' be divided in relation to an (imagined) prejudging categorisation towards their family lifestyle. By saying that their/her decision-making has nothing to do with culture, she narrates herself out of an oppressed gender position and takes up an individualistic position driven by personal choice.

This illustrates contradictions between how she perceives herself and how (she believes) other people see her. Furthermore, it illustrates conflicting narratives between how she understands her husband's lack of participation in the everyday running of the household and cultural expectations of gender roles. He was not raised as a 'Danish guy' and therefore was not brought up with the same expectations regarding gender roles and related household duties. The gender roles are narrated as cultural differences, yet she rejects that her 'being at home' has anything to do with culture. Cultural expectations of gender roles in a mixed marriage are cited. She understands how others could perceive the notion of inequality and several times during the interview she defends her position as a housewife, by stating that their 'traditional' gender roles are the result of her own free will. She rationalises their choices and the pattern they have settled into indicates a family lifestyle which includes more rather traditioinal, sort of static gender roles and practical arrangements between work and the household.

In Cecilia and Sam's situation, Sam is the primary economic provider and Cecilia takes care of the family, parenting and the household. Cecilia's narrative can be viewed as a picture of individualisations' contradictions, the conflict between personal demands, family demands and societal expectations. It is possible that the gendered 'power struggle' is an example of her 'getting used to' her new lifestyle. It is a way of negotiating a new identity and thereby occupying, accepting and defending a position as an independent 'stay-at-home mother'. At the same time she does not talk about a practical power struggle *with* her husband in their everyday life, which she finds unnecessary.

The reverse tendency of transformations concerning gender roles is played out in the lives of another Danish participant, Katja, and her Indian husband Rajiv. As with Cecilia and Sam, their everyday life is structured around family and work, but Rajiv is the one working part-time, while Katja works full time and even over time. The gender roles are different too, as Katja declares: '*I am the one in-charge*'. Katja's narrative can be interpreted to invoke a power aspect to her position as an economic provider. 'Equality' is negotiated differently:

> *I don't feel that I'm more important in the family or that I have to take a bigger responsibility or anything like that, it's just we have just divided things like that now, both are equally important and he is doing a big thing on the home front right now he can take Sonia to the [institution]...and all that...so that's nice.*

Rajiv explains how they 'do gender' their own way in order to maximise personal freedom and ideals of flexibility and satisfaction. He emphasises the availability of time and how being prosperous time-wise is a major aspect of his wellbeing.

> *...we have a very unique relationship....I have never felt compelled to work; I love to teach yoga....My objective in life is not to have a lot of*

money, but to have a lot of time. I can spend time with her [their daughter Sonia] and I can play music. So, that I only want to earn the money that makes us comfortable. Katja earns a lot of money anyway, so that we are cool with.

He expresses satisfaction with his life and with how roles play out in practice, so as not to interfere with his independence. He emphasises that economy is not a big concern for him as his values are freedom and the availability of time that he unproblematically defines as a powerful position. He attempts and manages to avoid time poverty in his life situation.

The phenomenon of time poverty is highly prevalent among urban well-to-do families where both parents work full-time. It is interesting, though, that Katja underlines her position as powerful due to her accepting this status, and later stresses the equality within her relationship. Rajiv underplays the economic perspective, *it doesn't matter*, yet freedom does. Even though Katja and Rajiv's ways of handling gendered power structures are different from the traditional – or Cecilia and Sam's – Rajiv does not feel the same need to defend his position as a male as strongly as Cecilia does hers as a female.

With regard to mixed marriage and family discourses about freedom, being unique can be viewed as more socially accepted and therefore a more powerful discourse than one about traditional gender roles. Both Rajiv and Cecilia create different subject positions as a *stay-at-home dad* and *stay-at-home mom* respectively. They both construct their positions as driven not only by personal choice, but also as an expression of orientation towards the areas of responsibility which they evaluate as desirable for maintaining their masculinity and femininity respectively. For men it is typically career, though for Rajiv importance is attached to time-related richness and freedom. For women responsibility is still related to home and children, as analysed through Cecilia's narrative.

Cecilia furthermore draws on different discourses of family and work in her construction of herself as an independent woman. Somehow it seems easier for her to do so within discourses of work and career than for family investment. This may be because traditional gender roles are prescribed and therefore not considered as driven by personal choice. Rajiv and Katja on the other hand break away from the traditional roles and present their family lifestyle as unique, with the freedom to build their own patterns. Their narratives seem to result in powerful and less powerful social subject positions where, according to my interpretation, Rajiv holds a more powerful position than Cecilia for the time being, though one can question if Cecilia would agree with this interpretation.

To construct as an individualised project opens up opportunities to 'do gender' in a different way, owing to ideals of flexibility and freedom. This is an example of how gender and economic status intersect as Cecilia's husband Sam has a well-paid director's job in the private sector. The 'doing' of gender roles is experienced by them in the tension between freedom/individuality and social expectations.

This indicates a fluid construction of normality as Cecilia adapts traditional gender role as a *stay-at-home mom* and Rajiv and Katja create individualistic gender and power structures with a *stay-at-home dad* that suits their values and lifestyle. A Danish study (Mortensen, 2014) about couple relationships when women are the primary breadwinners shows both continuity and change in the gender roles related to societal expectations. In the last ten years, the number of 'breadwinning' women such as Katja has increased from 25% to 33% and for most couples it works out well – as it does for Katja and Rajiv despite their ethnic differences. They manage to organise themselves against the culture-bound stereotypes and gender images. However, there is still a gap between gender equality as an ideal and gender i.1 practical, everyday life, because most research in Scandinavia shows that it is still women who have the major responsibility regarding the household and children – alongside their participation in the labour market. These gender positions and everyday practices continuously interplay. The couples' shared images of the world are continuously being negotiated, questioned, shifted, replaced and/or reaffirmed.

The above analysis illustrates how the project participants 'do gender' in different ways in their self-narrations. They find and use different strategies and ways to carry out practices. Rajiv and Katja break from traditional gender roles and gendered activities in order to define their 'own' flexible lifestyle, and meet their joint objectives. While in this phase Cecilia indicates adjustment to a more traditional gendered positioning, her challenge is to balance individual wishes of being a good parent and the Danish cultural expectation of being a full-time, working woman.

5.4.2 Family establishment mixed marriage phase – when love is (re)defined

One of the couples interviewed, Nihla and Mads, are placed in the phase of family establishment and were, at the time of the interviews, going through a divorce after three years of marriage. It is not just their marriage situation that separates them from the other participating couples in this study; the interview situation is different as well. Here, both of them were present during the interviews and they meddle in and comment on each other's answers. This may explain why the interviewer can be heard in the quotations obviously hesitating and why she finds it difficult to ask direct questions about their impending divorce. However, this unusual interview situation brings a dynamic aspect into the analysis by presenting an ongoing and active power struggle to define marriage in the temporal background of a destructive conflict.

The following quotation illustrates both the couple's negotiation of 'truth', as well as their meaning-making process and (re)definition of marriage. Nihla states when questioned about her perception of marriage before she met Mads.

> *Marriage to me then . . . and now, is a piece of paper. I mean it's a practicality. We got married after knowing each other for a really short time, and for me it was a question of having defined marriage as a relationship. . . . If that paper makes it easier for us to live together then why not get it? And I was like: 'Okay, if you are getting married why not do it with butterflies in the stomach?' And that's what we did.*

Nihla here elaborates that the marriage was the easiest way to reconcile 'cultural' expectations from her family members. She explains how the decision was partly taken because her family forbade cohabitation before marriage reflecting the dominant ethnic group value. Such an intimate extended relationship was not acceptable at all. Continuing, she indicates that it was partly to satisfy the extended family members in Denmark and her mother, that the marriage took place: *'They are happy and pleased, I'm happy and pleased.'*

This explanation demonstrates the symbolic value of getting married. What she also indicates is that love is defined through relationships, and that *'butterflies in the stomach'* demonstrates her uncertainty as well as a symbol of being in love. Nihla and Mads's dialogue lucidly shows how there are transformations in the understandings of the institution of marriage and their commitment to it.

Mads told Nihla about his perception of her change in attitude before and after marriage:

> *you lived more the Pakistani rules, you acted more Pakistani . . . You talked about marriage before, and I saw it in a totally different way . . . I never*

heard you talk about marriage as just a paper before...I always thought that this marriage was an important thing to you.

Nihla: *Yeah it was it was an important relationship for me. But I'm just saying like bottom line it's just a piece of paper...I remember all this rumour when we had these discussions with Cathy why you wouldn't marry me, and then you would always say it's just a piece of paper, and now I say yeah it is just a piece of paper, but why fight it?*

Their changing and evolving position about the acceptance of marriage as a serious institution is illustrated by their dialogue. Earlier in their relationship Mads did not consider marriage seriously, while it was a serious matter for Nihla. This situation is highlighted again in the interview with Mads. Here he defends his intentions and position as a loving and committed man:

Mads: *I always thought of getting married at some point but it just made sense getting married because she acted like she took it very seriously.*

Nihla: *I did!*

Mads: *This means a lot and therefore I was very proud getting married and it was not just a piece of paper for me.*

The interview situation illustrates a power struggle – the power to define or redefine their marriage and intentions, negotiation of truth and power positions. By expressing an individual attitude towards marriage, Nihla distanced herself from their marriage, which Mads takes as a rejection of their past. Maybe due to the situation that they are in, Nihla's statement is understood by Mads as a rejection of their marriage and that the marriage is being emptied of its meaning, love and commitment. His interpretation of her as changed from being very Pakistani to less Pakistani also indicates how deeply entrenched ideas of differences associated with specific ethnicity are, for instance, commitment to marriage is considered Pakistani!

The dialogue becomes a negotiation of who had the right intentions, during which Mads positions himself as a seriously committed husband and Nihla as unrecognisable and changed. Somehow, he doubts her original intentions, and she has to defend herself. The joint identity, their common objective and their commitment is no longer visible, and the marriage is not defined by romance but by a symbolic 'piece of paper'. Nihla states that their divorce has nothing to do with culture; she relates it to a change of personality. Yet those two explanations can hardly be completely separated in the narration. Mads challenges this separation as he associates Nihla's personality with a cultural and ethnically rooted understanding of commitment and marriage. Earlier in the relationship, he was the one who did not want to get married (demonstrating his lack of commitment) but now it is Nihla who is not committed as she now considers the institution of marriage as 'just a piece of paper'. The *companionate love* (Fletcher et al., 2013) between them seems to be absent in this family establishment phase of their marriage.

This phase shows how personal/cultural differences are present in everyday practices such as compromises concerning gender roles in relation to career and family life. Similarly, investments made in terms of personal goals and self-determination to legitimise and defend positions play a role in constructing a unique identity. Finally, it shows how differences in personality, changes in understandings and the emergence of communication gaps become prominent when 'togetherness' no longer exists, as in the case of any failing marriage.

In managing everyday life with all its visible and invisible, acknowledged or overlooked differences, there are many ways of dealing with these differences after the first honeymoon phase of excitement and passionate love is over. The strategies employed by the couples can be delineated as decentralising differences which may include the silencing of history, exoticisation of the *other*, living with cultural contradictions and developing cultural consciousnesses (Killian, 2013). Our analysis indicates that these strategies can overlap as in case of Cecilia and Mads, whose narratives reflect both the ignoring of differences as well as the exoticising some of the spouse's cultural practices. Nihla and Mads's relationship mirrors conflicts related to both culture and personality differences, as they constitute each other in accordance.

Taking a sociocultural psychological perspective Valsiner & Rosa (2007), constructive means of resolving disappointment and anger, tolerance of individual differences, respect for each other's decisions are such as some of the characteristics that enable a family to operate smoothly in general. They also determine to a large extent how a family would accept an ethnically mixed marriage (Root, 2001). In the case of Nihla and Mads, a constructive way of resolving disappointments caused by an array of tension points seems to be absent, leading to disruption and the subsequent dissolution of the couple's relationship. Giblin (2014) notes that power struggles are common with blame, judgement, criticism and defensiveness as outcomes. Ideally, couples learn about forgiveness, accommodation and interdependence along with finding a space for separateness in this stage. This hasn't happened for Nihla and Mads as the companionate love seems to be subsequently disppear.

5.5   Couples in the settled phase

By naming the third phase the 'settled phase' I underline that couples who have been married for several years express a calmer or more 'laid-back' attitude towards marriage and everyday practices. Conflicts between career identities and family and gender roles have moved into the background. In other words, couples are more settled. Career-wise they have chosen their path, the 'we' that is a fundamental of a married identity is established. However, but differences are visible, not as compromise, but more as acceptance and are expressed with pride and love. A symbiosis, an acceptance of differences has taken place, which to some extent is peaceful.

Raaka and Klaus have been married for ten years, and at the time of the interviews had just moved back to Denmark from India. They have been shifting back and forth for some years, as mentioned earlier. Although they have married just for a decade, they are placed within this phase because of their social characteristics. First of all, this couple is more settled down and, as they have taken a decision to stay in Denmark for a longer period of time, they are not travelling as much as before. Furthermore, they express other family values, such as parenting and gender roles, more than the other participating couples. For example, Klaus explains their decision to stay in Denmark for the long term:

And that was a conscious decision ... it is Denmark for the next 20 years ... We are not moving anywhere because for her [daughter Sonia's] sake we try to keep the school and everything. And it is tough, because we have had a life where we have been moving around. And I have been travelling a lot and Raaka has been travelling a lot and we have had fairly high position jobs and, it's like compromise. Now you have to do it a little bit differently. One thing is that we have work but we have to do it in a different pace, in a little different way. Business is still there, but it is kept in a different focus ... That is important during this period. That has been like a journey for us ... when I met Raaka in India we worked 12 hours a day both of us ... it was work, work, work and suddenly you get a child and you start thinking oh, we need to relax a little bit, at least now we propose a different view.

There is a significant age difference between the couples in the second family establishment phase and those placed in the third phase of the married life course. These older couples have gained more experience both in life and in marriage. They have made some compromises and as Raaka says:

> *We know from practical experience. That you can't have it all...And I know my priorities, and now put my 100% focus on family and career second. Earlier it was career and I didn't get my family.*

The above quotation indicates experiences of the 'phase of establishment' as a separation of career and of family lifestyle. Furthermore, Raaka expresses how she has realised that the struggle of conflicting positions is no longer a concern as she has decided her priority and made a choice for this phase of life course (Levy et al., 2005). She is aware of the fact that she can't have both family and career and this acknowledgement for her is related to the intersection of gender and minority status in Denmark. Klaus has maintained more of a career focus while Raaka has given it up.

Another important feature partly characterising the settled phase is illustrated in the quotation above. The couples speak about their hopes and dreams in terms of *we*. The joint identity is more defined, outspoken and strongly expressed. They follow 'one line', as Klaus says, and this underlines their similarities and a common mindset. Two cultures but one line – following the same goals, values, beliefs and priorities – highlights how they separate problems in different levels of importance and shows a level of understanding beyond race and ethnicity. At the same time they both emphasise spirituality and religion as joint reference point and as the most important shared value see also chapter 7, section 7.2.

> Klaus: ...*we can have some heated arguments...we have very different views on...politics...about spending money. Raaka is very concerned about spending, very good attitude actually. I have a bit different. Sometimes you must spend to gain...I think that is also good...It is a good combination. But in that way we can have heated arguments...but we have a similar kind of purpose. We believe that this is the right thing for us. We believe that there are some things that we want to do...And, that purpose, keep us on the right track...We have the same sort of line, the same direction. We are not sitting and discussing to do this or that. It's*

> *both of us in a line. The things we are discussing are smaller things . . . It is not the whole purpose of our life.*

'That's the way it is' and 'it's obvious' are not phrases used by the couples in the earlier phases of married life. Problems and arguments are here seen as a 'normal' part of married life and seem to be a commonality for the couples in this phase.

What is also clear is the toned-down attitude towards arguments – they are more relaxed and 'safe' because of their joint experiences shared through living together over a long period. Problems are placed in perspective, some large-scale and some small-scale. They have been living and learning, getting to know each other's differences and similarities. They complement each other and their marriage seems to be in balance, although they have different temperaments. They have managed to create a new sense of connection as they learn more about each other's strengths, vulnerabilities and differences, finding a new balance of separateness and togetherness, independence and intimacy as described by Giblin (2014). This does not mean they do not have quarrels about cultural practices but not about significant cultural differences, as they are able to perceive their situation in the companionate love framework where they have lived through struggles. On the whole they seem to have a calm attitude towards their everyday life as they report hardly any quarrels about gender roles and they have accepted the divisions related to careers and household duties. For Raaka and Klaus things may seem smooth, yet we have to be attentive to the situation for other couples for whom this phase can be characterised by the continuity of chronic conflicts and disharmony, where the problems that need to be dealt with have been repressed or have simply become a part of everyday life.

5.5.1 Cultural differences and a joint identity

As discussed earlier, a predominant *we* is interpreted as an expression of a common identity, constructed on a mixed identity – combining ethnicity, race, religion, gender and so on. Olumide (2002) refers to the complex concept of 'mixed race' as a condition that focuses on commonality-based aspects and the sharing of common elements of lived social experiences:

> The mixed race refers then to common experiences over time and space of those who had been socially defined as mixed or mixing race. It is a loose term, not intended to suggest rigidity in any form.

Rather than being a checklist of experiences which 'ought' to have been had, it is an acknowledgement of commonality amongst some very diverse groups. This commonality has the markings of a common history and provides the basis for group identity and political vision. Mixed race is never a community based on shared phenotypic features, common language or cultural artefacts. Rather, it is a group based on shared elements of lived social experience... of infinite variet, but with identifiable common features.

(Olumide, 2002, p. 4–5)

Following Olumide's conceptualisation, intermarried life in a more established phase can be considered as a product of lived experience and a mixed group identity. In this context it is a product of compromise and connected cultural differences. Yet couples do not necessarily construct their problems as cultural:

Marlik: *Like any marriage we have had problems too, but I don't see these problems as intercultural. I see them as two individuals living together, of course you clash. Like two sisters or two brothers or two Danish people. It is not because we are having some cultural conflict.*

Distinguishing between the participants' perception of problems related to belonging to different cultures from existential problems which all couples may face can be analytically useful.

Following Marlik's statement about marriage as a construction there is hardly any significance attached to cultural differences. By identification with a narrative about 'a normal marriage' she rejects the significance of culture. Olumide (2002) argues that the possibilities of group solidarity lie in the ability to transcend race. Mixed marriage constructed within discourses of colour-blindness implies an identity strategy attempting to consider people strictly as individuals, de-emphasising racial or ethnic group membership.

Yet the 'cultural' aspects stick to the stories about intermarried life, mostly when the problems are told in past or retrospectively.

Klaus had some worries about the cultural differences at the beginning of their marriage:

I had some ideas that it could be an issue... that we had to travel back and forth all the time and... It was going to be expensive; it is not a cheap solution for life. I also thought about... getting kids [them being] in between and needing to understand both cultures. But then again, that was a short

> *movement of thought, because I think it is a huge strength that we have*
> *that background.*

It is worth noting that he also speaks himself into a 'same' background because he lived in India, knows the culture some spouses in mixed marriages and thus underlines his and Raaka's sameness.

Another way to comprehend problems within intermarriage in everyday life is presented by Raaka, in whose narrative commonality is foregrounded:

> *It's not because we don't have our challenges, it's just because we don't look*
> *at them as challenges ... it is not because we are intercultural that we have*
> *tolerance ... we are two individuals that have similar thoughts ... we agree*
> *on them, we make things work. We try not to look at the negatives.*

Instead of emphasising differences, there are investments in similarities and joint experiences, practices and values. An investment in sameness can be viewed as an identity strategy by which couples claim social inclusion or, as Ann Phoenix (2008) formulates, 'claim liveable lives' by constructing the abnormal into 'normal' narratives of lived married life.

As Raaka outlines above, the couples strongly identify themselves as (especially) tolerant people implying ethnicity's external and objective aspects, which also explains why, in this phase, couples such as Raaka and Klaus attach importance to politics, integration and to how Danes perceive ethnic minorities. Williams (2010) and Ballard (2004) present a picture of some members of South Asian diaspora in Britain being more traditional than their privileged counterparts in the country of origin. This tendency is seen to some extent in Raaka's narrative, as she shows initiative and activity as a relatively newly arrived person, in contrast to her other coethnics who have been living in Denmark for a longer period, including both the so-called first and second generation.

These narratives from the participants present a nuanced understanding of managing everyday life through a plurality of strategies which present an optimistic perception of mixed couples. The extended family and their social networks contribute to managing the challenges of everyday life. However, these narratives presented in chapter 5 focus primarily on the couple relationships due to methodological limitations and analytical focus on the broad contex tin chapter 7.

Using the management of everyday life as an analytic theme within an ontogenetic – developmental, historical – framework, highlights the dominant features of the three phases in which the participants are placed. This framework proved to be useful for comprehending the temporal dynamics. The honeymoon phase, characterised by passionate love, excitement, potential for mobility, willingness to change and reluctance to focus on differences, especially those perceived as negative. The second phase, identified as the establishment phase, is the phase when reality is confronted and where everyday life, routines and differences – including the negative ones – have to be addressed. Sharing, valuing differences and validating each spouse's ethnic, family heritage in forming a common culture can lead to a positive couple identity. Positioning gender centrally, analyses show that the dominant values are *being a good mother, avoiding time poverty* and the personal gender related choices such as being a *stay-at-home mom or dad.* Lack of togetherness, 'we-ness', companionate love, sense of commitment, constructive resolution of disappointment and anger in this phase may lead to conflicts, disruption and the possible dissolution of relationships. In the third stage there is a sense of acceptance, reconciliation, living with the differences and the *we* identity represents a balance between the personal demands and the couple demands. Chronic conflicts and disharmony can, however, characterise this phase, and this theme is covered in chapter 8 and 9. Ongoing negotiations, dialogue and communication leads to compromises among the couples in the context of sociocultural norms and expectations, addressing the tension between personal freedom and commitment to their relationship, the extended family and the broader context of their lives. Children have a central place in the developmental history of these mixed couples and families and thus, still focussing on the couples, parenting is explored in the next chapter.

6
Mixed Parenting Ideals and Practices

Starting from the admittedly scarce literature and theoretical conceptualisations regarding the processes of socialisation in the context of multi-ethnicity, the primary focus in this chapter is on the processes of parenting in visibly ethnically mixed couples and households (Phoenix, 2011), represented by the participants in the present study. The objective of this book is not to focus solely on the troublesome elements in mixed couple relationships and parenting, because mixed relationships may be culturally and socially enriching and expand the world-view of the partners involved. One illustration of these positive features is that the children of mixed heritage may have linguistic and cultural advantages compared with monocultural children. According to Tizard & Phoenix (2002, p. 1), people worry about 'mixedness' of children of mixed parentage, rather than seeing them as fortunate constellations (or as the inheritors) of two cultures.

6.1 The future generation and racial literacy

There are, however, real risks for developing potential conflicts in mixed relationships where social processes such as *racial discrimination* and exclusion are not addressed. In addition, the partners may perceive basic developmental issues such as parental control and discipline radically differently. Parents who acquire racial literacy (Twine, 2010) identify racism as a serious problem and actively prepare their children to cope with it, due to or in spite of the parents' majority group ethnic heritage.

Family is perceived as one of the structures that guides as well as limits the constructive process of internalisation, providing the critical link between an individual and a collective (Chaudhary, 2007). The family as a whole is constituted of a dynamic adjustment between different members – such as adults and children, grandparents and parents, siblings and so on – and belonging to the family implies the sharing of a value system, resources, space and time. The focus of this chapter is on parenting and on the relationship between parents and children, where the parents as the intermarried couple may have rather different value systems as a starting point. It is noticeable that interracial and interethnic partnering does reduce fertility in Chinese-white and Asian Indian-white intermarriages in the American context (Kang Fu, 2008). Still, these results indicate that intermarried couples have transcended group boundaries, which may involve different value systems.

In the Indian/South Asian context, the central binding force for the family is the belief in its centrality in the life of an individual, whereas individualising processes are central aspects in the late modern Danish context, as discussed in Chapter 2. Family relationships are presumed to be lifelong and the socialisation of young children's strong interconnectedness (not necessarily interdependence) is the norm, although these relationships and each individual's life is believed to range between independence and interdependence on an imaginary continuum (Chaudhary, 2007, pp. 531–533).

The intergenerational transmission of life worlds, values and norms, is one of the major functions of the family. In spite of parenting becoming an increasing focus of Danish academic and policy debate, there is little empirical research into ethnicity, parenting and family life, which is required to understand the context of migration, ethnicity, socio-economic circumstances, multiculturalism and racism (Skytte, 2007). Literature from the British context (Barn et al., 2010), exploring the views and experiences of 'ordinary' parents of young children growing up – among others in South Asian endogamous as well as mixed households – is drawn on and combined with Twines's (2010) longitudinal field research with mixed children of white mothers in Leicester. A review of academic literature on these issues shows that the intersections of ethnicity, social class, parental employment patterns and family type are evident and discussed under three emerging themes of *social relationships, public/private concerns* and *ethnic and racial socialisation including racial literacy*, combining Barn et al. (2010) and Twine (2010).

Social relationships, understood as contact with family and friends, varied across ethnic groupings. However, ethnic minority families reported more frequent contacts with *the wide family network* than the majority 'white' families, who reported more frequent contact with friends. At the same time non-availability of some family members, such as grandparents, was an important concern for the families.

Public/private concerns seem to be most evident among ethnic minority families and one illustration is less willingness to vocalise the problematic aspects of their children's behaviour. At the same time, most parents wished to be involved in their children's education regardless of ethnic background and socio-economic status. Asian parents especially those comprising the South Asian diaspora, placed an enormous importance *on the value of education*; something less prominent among the 'white' group. Barn et al. (2010) emphasise that good education is regarded as significant for combating racial discrimination and minimising social exclusion. Respect for teachers, discipline and self-discipline are regarded as the cornerstones of a good education.

Ethnic and racial socialisation including racial literacy is challenging for the minority parents and children as religious and ethnic identities are important in informing how they raise their children. Barn et al. (2010) show that there is a wide diversity in how parenting is performed. A focus on the fathers indicates that most want to have a close relationship with (and be a friend to) their children and that they actively distanced themselves from what they saw as *typical Asian father* behaviour, characterised as remote and authoritarian. They further underline how fathers who worked long hours are not necessarily absent from personal care-giving, but are more likely to devote themselves to *quality time* at home – to activities such as playing and reading.

The additional task of giving positive messages about differences and diversity has wide implications for the family as well as for 'significant others', such as professionals. This goes along with the usual task of creating a positive nurturing and supportive environment. To some extent, these processes are similar to the concept of *racial literacy*, relating to an analytical orientation and a set of practices that reflect shifts in perceptions of race, racism and whiteness, though there are some fundamental differences in the British context (Twine, 2010) and in the Danish context. In the British context, the concept was developed with the explicit focus on the observable character of physical differences, especially the colourist focus on skin colour. In Denmark there is no direct focus on physical differences but rather on the cultural differences (see also Chapter 2, Section 2.2).

The components of *racial literacy* are as follows:

1) The definition of racism as a contemporary problem rather than a historical legacy.
2) An understanding of the ways that the experience of racism and racialisation are mediated by class, gender inequality and heterosexuality.

3) Recognition of the cultural and symbolic value of whiteness.
4) An understanding that racial identities are learned and an outcome of social practices.
5) The possession of a racial grammar and vocabulary to discuss race, racism and antiracism.
6) The ability to interpret racial codes and racialised practices. (Twine, 2010, p. 92)

Twine (2010) concludes that racial literacy is not an automatic consequence of establishing an intimate relationship with someone who is black, as there were only a minority of white respondents in her study (approximately 25%) who developed racial literacy. However, she also argues that *racial literacy* in practice presents a dilemma for the white parents in providing their children with the resources they need to cope with the various forms of racism they may encounter in public institutions such as schools. Providing a conceptual framework for understanding how white parents respond to racial hierarchies, three discursive and material practices are noted. Firstly by the provision of conceptual tools: discussing racism with the children and sharing their own experiences can lead to the acquisition and transmission of racial logics and probably black-/ethnic minority-oriented networks. Secondly, by designing black-/ethnic minority-centred home interiors the visual and material culture of homes can be used to counteract their, impoverished visual representation in the mainstream media; parents may purchase, collect and display visual art, toys, books and music which 'idealise' the black/ethnic minority group. Thirdly, developing cultural practices, such as hairstyling and heritage cooking, the ethnic capital can be enhanced, reflecting Bourdieu's (1997) symbolic capital concept.

6.2 Negotiating parenthood

Continuing in line with the main focus of the present study, our concern is to further deepen understandings of how intermarried couples who are parents of mixed children deal with issues in parenting their children. Due to limited Danish literature such as differences, similarities, exclusion (Refsing, 1998; Poulsen, 2012), we turn to conceptualisations developed by Alibhai-Brown (2001); Suki Ali (2003); Caballero et al. (2008) and Aspinall & Song (2013) from the UK, Root (1992, 1996); Sengstock (2009); Kenney & Kenney (2012) and Killian (2013) from the USA, who have focused specifically on the mixedness phenomena. Based on these insights, we can see that the mixed parents show highly diverse ways of dealing with the issues of parenting, yet are all in the process of dealing with the difference and belonging in relation to the identity of their children. According to Miriam Stoppard (2006), 'To form a lasting relationship, you have to be strong and determined. That's true for everybody, and especially true in inter-racial relationships.' Global qualities such as strength and determination are especially important in mixed relationships including parenting. Still, there are negotiations of differences among the parents. I name these three basic approaches as:

Single (or belonging to one camp); mixed and open or cosmopolitan. It is important to point out that each approach has underlying key features:

- In the first, single approach, only one parent's background is stressed and a sense of belonging is promoted through that. Parents could emphasise values and norms associated with the particular heritage and perceive it as transcending other differences. According to Root (1996), there may be a struggle for inclusion and legitimacy in the 'traditional' ethnic communities. Belonging to one camp can be related to the power position of the group or to other inclusion/exclusion dynamics such as children of black/white couples being brought up with a largely black identity.
- In the second, mixed approach, simultaneously belonging to 'both camps', children's mixed racial and ethnic background is emphasised. According to Cabarello et al. (2008), there are two aspects to this approach. Parents can encourage their children to acknowledge and engage with the different parts of the heritage through the sense of *specific mix*. The second main aspect of a mixed approach is engagement with difference and belonging through *a general notion of mixedness*. There is a shaping of a shared identity among racially mixed people see also Olumide, 2002 in chapter 5, section 5.5.1. Exploring the social movements related to mixedness in the USA, we can note that being mixed can be perceived as a dominant aspect of identity.
- In the third approach, open or cosmopolitan, the key feature is that the children are encouraged to think beyond ethnic and racial labels, as they are not necessarily seen as rooted in their particular racial or ethnic backgrounds. To some extent there is a struggle to dismantle dominant racial ideology and group boundaries and to create *connections across communities into a community of humanity*. There are three main ways of doing it. Being a *cosmopolitan* 'citizen of the world' or belonging to the 'community of humanity' (Root, 1996) is one of the ways. This approach can also be manifested through the concept

of *an organic self,* where children are encouraged to develop and be true to their potential and abilities. According to Cabarello (2008), the concept of *choice* is indicative of the open approach. Children are encouraged to focus on their options in terms of whether or not they adopt, leave aside or continue their parents' racial, ethnic or religious backgrounds. As earlier mentioned, yet another facet of this approach is *colour/ethnicity transcendence,* where race or ethnicity is considered incidental to how children should be seen or viewed by others.

These approaches, however, should be seen as dynamic and can be present as a mixture of approaches for some parents and as contextually changing for others. There may be some overlap in these categories, yet the dominant aspects are the main reason for placing of the narratives in a particular category. Parents may negotiate divergent approaches in different contexts and temporal perspectives, combining and holding complex views drawn from the three basic approaches.

As with any other categorisation, we have to be careful in using them as tools of analysis as they are meant to promote our understanding of complex phenomena, not for placing the mixed parenting practice into rigid categories. These approaches make explicit the many ways of socialising the children and for ethnic and racial socialisation there is no universal way for parents to bring up their children. At the same time we should pay attention to the findings of an array of empirical studies that show the importance attached to mixedness may vary depending on a multitude of factors, including structural aspects of society, the wider social attitudes related to differences, the geographical and demographic placing of the family.

Mixedness may not be the only concern for the parents as there are also 'ordinary' concerns that occupy any parent, such as safety, health, parental unity over disciplinary boundaries, drug and alcohol abuse, gang violence and teenage pregnancy.

The next section of this chapter analyses the participants' narratives within these conceptualisations, keeping in mind that close relationships are not the only arena of love and affection but are also settings for experiencing more disruptive emotions such as anger (Schoebi et al., 2011). There are a variety of family and family-like ways of life across Europe and in the countries the partners originate from. While this plurality is by no means a new phenomenon, Rauschenbusch (2010) sees it as a result of growing cultural diversity – the mixing of new realities and old ideals related to the family. Although no alternative to the family way of life has emerged in contemporary society, yet there is increasing discrepancy between wish and reality. Therefore, the following analysis of mixed parenting based on the narratives of the participants attempts to cover both the wish and the reality.

The participants have a wide range of parenting experiences as the ages of their children varies from four months to 25 years (and one is pregnant with her first child). The involvement of grandparents in socialising at different levels is another theme which emerges in the analysis, closely intertwined with parental understanding and practices. I will discuss the empirical data applying each of the three approaches to parenting mixedness in turn.

- Single/one camp approach
- Mixed approach
- Open approach

6.3   The 'single' approach

Cecilia is a mother of two daughters, one two-and-half years old and the other 9 months old. She is married to Sam and monolingualism is an important part of their parenting. She emphasised her husband and mother-in-law's attitude to children's bilingualism, which she did not agree with. Danish is the primary language of communication within the family as the father was not fluent in Punjabi, his language of heritage. She discusses the linguistic issue as a contentious one since her mother-in-law and husband want the elder daughter to learn 'Indian' (Punjabi). For Cecilia just a few words and greetings is enough, and she would prefer her daughters to learn English as a second language as she considers it to be more relevant. She rejects the idea of her daughter learning 'Indian' in school, considering it exaggerated or 'overkill'. Although she has never been to India, she has the erroneous impression that everyone can speak English in India – a country with a population of 1.2 billion, yet only the educated there, estimated at 100 million or 10% of the population, are English-speakers (India Tribune, 2014).

> *I think that we have some issues with language, that is. When my mother-in-law and husband think that they should learn Indian. Hmm ... (pause) and I might think that it is not that important. Eh, because they are so young you know, and my husband doesn't speak Indian, so I find it a little bit strange maybe that she should learn Indian, you know. And all people in India more or less speak English. So I think that it would be a much better idea to teach her English than Indian. Of course we have taught her*

some small words like milk and water and greeting people and I think that
is fine. But going to school to learn Indian might be a little overkill, which
is the only thing that we have.

Furthermore, she points to her perception of 'Indian' food as another
issue of difference, though one that is not as problematic as language.
Her observation refers to the salience of food in the everyday lives of
Indians as pointed out by Chaudhary (2005) and Smith (2003). The
paternal grandmother wants the children to eat a lot of food and also
Indian-style food to some extent.

...oh maybe it is the food, I mean they eat all the time. And like my
mother-in-law is very focused upon on the girls 'oh do they eat enough, do
they get enough to eat?'

However, she is aware of the differences in the socialisation practices
of her own and her husband's family, further complicated by the presence of a mother-in-law who is perceived as simultaneously 'Danish and
Indian' having lived in Denmark for more than three decades. Cecilia's
description reflects how deeply these ideas of difference are entrenched
and the focus is on the differential socialisation in the two cultural
contexts. The maternal grandmother is conspicuous by her absence in
the narrative regarding parenting. Cecilia alludes to some disagreements
regarding children and her own strength in dealing with these issues.

Because there are differences, because I have been raised one way and Sam
has been raised another way, but of course that my mother-in-law is very
Danish, but she is also Indian. And of course sometimes, it comes to the
surface and we do not always agree, because I am a strong woman, and
I know what I want.

Moreover, Cecilia is able to appreciate her husband's positive qualities
in different family roles as a parent, son and a spouse. At the same time
she points to the commonality of strong family bonds for herself and
her husband. With humour she expresses her own and Sam's different
ideas of children's freedom in the future relating to independence and
(inter)dependence between the parents and the children, especially adolescent and adult ones. He would like them to stay at home until they
are older than Cecilia considers an appropriate age to move out.

No not for the moment, but they are so small. I guess when they get older,
(laughs) when they get a little bit older, their father would like to, you

know, keep them in the house until they are 35 (laughs). While I guess that I would be more like, 'go out and have some fun'.

Her narrative shifts from potentially contentious differences to positive similarities, which form the basis for significant relationships between the maternal as well as the paternal family. Sam's upbringing in Denmark makes it easy for her to focus on his both cultures, and his unique personality as a caring, affectionate family member.

But he is a loving father, he is a loving son and he is a loving husband. He would do anything for his family...I think that from the very beginning, Sam's family means a lot to him and my family means a lot to me...And it has been important for us that our girls get to meet their families and know that they are part of a strong family, and two strong cultures as well...bonus that you have two cultures (laughs). I think that it is fun, that it is interesting.

Cecilia emphasises the positive aspects of the bicultural situation and aspires to socialise her children through both cultures, albeit in a rather abstract manner. When further questioned about the positive or 'fun' aspects, she points to her realisation of the fundamental human similarities across different communities and the significance of positive, loving relationships in the family. These fundamental human similarities are seen as a gift, which can be interpreted as an aspect of the *open approach* to mixed parenting.

And, that I think for our girls as well, it will be a gift. It would be learning in tolerance, towards other people, towards the world, as it is becoming more and more mixed. Hmm...and that I hope that we can raise two girls who have tolerance towards other people and who have empathy towards differences. That is my hope, and that for me is a gift, definitely....But I guess, that the fun is that you find out that it is actually not that different and in any family, the base is love.

The issue of parental unity over discipline is a significant issue in parenting and the gender positions. Cecilia's narrative regarding her own strictness contrasting with Sam's lenient attitude confirms the importance of this aspect in a situation regarding an Indian spouse. It is important to understand the intersections of these practices across socio-economic positions, gender roles, work situation, kinship and family matters (Chaudhary, 2007). Cecilia related this disciplinary difference to Sam's work position as a managing director with high temporal demands, as well as his gendered masculine position as the primary breadwinner. Her comments about these cultural understandings of masculinity raise questions about culture as a meaning system and a system of actions Valsiner, 2008. She wishes to socialise the children in her own way in the future as she expects Sam to follow the Indian socialisation practice by which adult children continue to reside with the parents if there is no marital, education or work reason for moving out. These narratives underline how mixed parenting is not just about ethnic mixedness but also about the same concerns of parents with shared ethnic backgrounds.

Well, I think that I am the strict person (laughs). And I think that my husband and his mother, you know they allow the girls to do anything (laughs), and I think that is the main difference. My husband, I think, hmm – because I think that he sees them much less than I do, so when he is finally with them he just wants to spoil them, and he just does not want to say no, because he does not want problem, any problems with them. But just to have a good time with them when they are there. That bothers me sometimes (laughs), but I don't know if that is culture or not.

Her description of Sam's contact with his daughters seems congruent with earlier delineated (section 6.1) Barn et al.'s (2010) description of being an engaged father focusing on quality time with the children, trying hard not to be remote and unavailable despite limited time limitations. The main parenting responsibility falls to Cecilia, whose own values accept taking the primary parenting role. Her narrative continues by pointing to their basic similarities in approach, despite their differences in faith (Christianity and Sikhism respectively). Referring to her mother's initial worry about her marrying an Indian, Cecilia emphasises the commonalities: discovering the similarities between her spouse and herself is perceived as the fun part of being a mixed couple.

'oh if you have children with him, he will take them away from you, and you will never see them again.' You know she was scared. Then she met Sam, and it hasn't been any problem since (smiles). But I guess, that the fun is that you find out that it is actually not that different and in any family, the base is love. The base is commitment to each other. Hmm ... right and that you are not that different you know when it comes down to it. You

know if you are a Muslim, Sikh or Christian, your values are in fact the same.

Despite this positive view, she also expresses her concern about raising mixed children in a country where ethnic minorities face discrimination. When questioned about the children's future and her concerns, she says:

I think that the biggest concern is for the girls, I mean if it continues to go down this road, it could be difficult for them. Hmm ... (pause) and maybe if they find a future husband from a different country .... Respect for other human beings until you know that person. That is something that I miss in society today.

Cecilia is worried about socialising her children into an environment of exclusion for certain groups of population. The historical experiences of exclusion and stigmatisation of the *other* (Andreassen & Henningsen, 2011) directly affect these understandings to some extent. Contemplating the future, she names the potential spouses for her daughters and their possible mixed marriages in a context of limited acceptance of visibly different persons. In some ways Cecilia's situation as intimate partner of a visible minority and mother of mixed children can be characterised as 'insider-outsider'. Twine (2010) has developed the concept of racial literacy in the British context and expands on parental strategies of countering racism; some of these strategies are relevant in a Danish setting. The phenomenon of racial stereotypes and stigmatising are reminiscent of Cecilia's mother's fear of her Indian son-in-law running away with the children. At the same time it is pointed out that the nursery staff's comments on Cecilia being a 'stay-at-home mom'. These examples make it plain how Cecilia has herself become racialised by marrying a man identified as ethnically different and becoming a mother of mixed children. Her children are very young still but she has aspirations for them and worries about their spouses in the distant future.

Cecilia's approach to parenting is complex and the 'single' camp approach seen in her narratives is primarily expressed with regard to language. She is not able to accept bilingualism for her children as the father himself hasn't learnt his mother tongue. She also demonstrates other approaches to mixedness by eulogising biculturalism as a gift for children and the open approach through an emphasis on tolerance. A gender-focused analysis of parenting reveals that Cecilia, as a mother, seems to have the major responsibility for parenting with a father who is occupied by work-related demands, though he is perceived as nurturing and loving. There is both support and some interference from the paternal grandmother in raising the children. In the Danish study of Japanese-Danish intermarried couples, Refsing (1998) concludes that Japanese mothers took over most of the responsibility concerning the children, describing how in most cases the husbands readily fell into the routines that confirmed the expectations of their Japanese wives. However, the husbands held the firmly expressed opinion that the fact their wives were Japanese and not Danish made no difference at all. The issue raised here by Cecilia's example and the Japanese mothers' example is that the gender-related responsibility for primary parenting seem to be among women deeply ingrained, irrespective of ethnic belonging.

In contrast to Cecilia, whose narratives are analysed in this section, Marlik seems to share the responsibilities with her husband. Their adult children have been socialised primarily into the mother's and father's religious practices (through conversion) as well as into geographical/cultural practices. Marlik differentiates between family relationships in Pakistan and Denmark as close and distant respectively. She illustrates this view by her own frequent contact with her parents (when they were alive) and ongoing and frequent contact with a sister living in London. Lars, apparently, has very limited (twice a year) contact with his two sisters who live in Denmark. Within this dichotomisation of close and distant relationships, Marlik makes an effort to ensure her children have contact with both the maternal and paternal family. The nature of this contact is different, however, because of the very limited contact with the paternal side. The maternal extended family played an important part in the children's lives as they visited their grandparents frequently when they were alive and now they continue to visit their aunt and her children.

> Yeah the bonds are not so close, like he has only two sisters now, he doesn't have his parents anymore, so it's very important to have contact with them. It's important for my kids to know my family and to know their roots, and that's why we travel to London every year, so that my children should know where I belong, in the same way I want them to know their Daddy's roots and his family, so, but we do take initiative to call them and invite them, they are very formal.

For Marlik, both the family relationship and the shared religious belonging to Islam are important as Lars converted to Islam before they got married. She wants her children to be aware of their religious identity. Like Raaka and Klaus, Marlik engages with the different parts of the family's heritage through a sense of a *specific mix* – where the ethnic and religious identities of both the parents are important. She uses the metaphor of roots in a broad sense to include extended family relations and cultural as well as religious self-perception.

> *The roots are your family and not where you are born, I was born in Moscow and all that so. I feel roots belong to your family and not geographical to a place in Pakistan, and that is important, they should know their mother's sister and their kids and roots are also their culture and religious identity, that is also important, they should know why we are Muslims, and what is Islam, so that is also their roots.*

Marlik gave her daughter freedom to move out to her own apartment when she got a job three years ago – she wanted to move out like her friends had. However, her daughter chose to move back with the parents after three months as she didn't want to live alone. This pattern of migrants' children staying with their parents longer than the children of majority ethnic groups is shown in published statistics. According to Statistics Denmark (2010/2013), among 25-year-olds with non-Western descendents, 35% of men and 27% of women live with at least one of their parents, while similar figures for 25-year-olds with a Danish background is 11% for men and 5% for women. However, it is imperative to point out that Marlik's children would be categorised as 'Danish' by Statistics 2010/2013, as they have one parent who is originally Danish. There is no category specifying children/persons of mixed parentage, so these statistics are of rather limited value to this study. Irrespective of the objective formal categorisation, in accordance with Marlik's subjective understanding, the relatively longer co-residence of an adult daughter is related to the mother's close family values. In her judgement, she chooses to overlook the less close family relation heritage on her father Lar's side. In the extract below, she challenges her colleague's notion about children moving out in order to gain independence by countering that it can be done later in life. In other words, Marlik's narrative destabilises the hegemonic discourse connecting moving out of the parental home with autonomy. Furthermore, her narrative confirms the prominent position of mother as discussed earlier.

> *... of course my children are more attached to us, my daughter is 25 and she got a job 3 years ago, she got her own flat, we helped her in that here*

in this area because she said all her friends were moving out about when they were 20 and all. Then we said well you can also get a flat, it's right nearby, and be on your own and then you at least know it. Then she moved and after 3 months she moved back here, and said why should I stay alone? So we have given her that attachment, that she also values it a lot, so I have very close contact to my family in that way my children have those values through me, . . . my colleague says they have to be independent, I say they have their whole life to be that.

When questioned about raising children of mixed parentage, Marlik referred to the similarity of psychological factors expressed as *mentality* between her and Lars. She added that religion is another subject they agree on:

Well my husband luckily, he has the same mentality as I have so we haven't had any problems in bringing up the children, religion was a thing we talked about and they should know, my husband said yes.

At this point it is relevant to include Lars's self-perception as a religious convert who feels he doesn't have to prove his religiosity to others; for him it is something between himself and God. Daneshpour (2009) discusses Muslim intercultural marriages and notes that spirituality and religion may be a major source of conflict between Muslim and Christian partners. However, there may not be conflicts if one partner converts to the religion of the other, both keep their own faith and if they decide not to interfere with the faith of the other or if both drift away from faith or refrain from any formal religion.

There are many who when they convert, go completely off the rails. They have to prove something, but my faith is just between me and Allah I have nothing I need to prove to anyone else.

He goes on to compare marriage in Pakistan and Denmark. Though Lars's comment seems quite polarised within the love/arranged marriage binary, yet, he managed to add nuances to the oversimplified understanding of different forms of marriages among these groups, especially regarding the absence of positive emotions among Pakistani couples.

The large difference between Pakistani and Danish marriage is that Muslim marriage is arranged which means you take it easy and love is allowed to grow. In Denmark, the person is in love and gets married and then comes everyday.

Regarding the future, he answers that he plans to continue living in Denmark as his children live here; this reflects his attachment to the children and confirms that mixed parenting does not concern only mixedness but also hopes, plans and visions about the future, as is the case for most parents.

Marlik mentioned that her parents were very open and raised her well. She also emphasised that she visited her parents every other year when they were alive. In spite of the geographical distance, they were important in socialisation of the children.

I think my parents moulded us, for me a child is like wax, it's the parents who mould the ideas, my parents were very open, they gave me good education, and encouraged us in learning language and they were always giving us the guidelines, what is good for us ... when my mother was alive focus was in Pakistan we visited her every second year, and my children they loved Pakistan (laughing). They think it was nice and different, they enjoyed it. We are from the capital city Islamabad, and from there we would go and show them different places, big cities, so they got to know that country too.

The narratives of Cecilia and Lars as the Danish parent and Marlik as the diasporic parent of mixed children in different age groups (pre-schoolers in the case of Cecilia and Sam and adults in the case of Marlik and Lars) indicates a high degree of concern and awareness about the children's mixedness. By focusing on Danish as the first language and English as the second, with just a few words of Hindi/Punjabi such as Paani (water), Doodh (milk), Cecilia has been placed in the 'single' camp position. Notwithstanding that, she shows some strategies of racial literacy as well. Marlik and Lars have inculcated Islamic faith values along with the continued interdependence between parents and the adult daughter through continued co-residence. Marlik's narrative can be interpreted to invoke some racial literacy strategies such as frequent and in-depth contact with the diasporic family and the country of origin, thereby maintaining an ethnic network.

In an anthropological study of marriage migration in Denmark, Poulsen (2012) illustrates differential parenting strategies used by parents where one is Danish and the other of South Asian background. The South Asian parent Megha from Bhutan tells her children that they are

Danish but their mother is from Bhutan, because she doesn't want her children to grow up with confusion of feel being 'half of each', thus she emphasises belonging to 'one camp', being Danish very explicitly. On the other hand, her Danish husband Martin explains to the children that they are from both Denmark and Bhutan, explicitly entailing a mixed identity. This example illustrates the plurality of strategies used by parents as well as two different strategies used by two parents.

A similar strategy is illustrated by research among West African-German families in Germany (Kleist, 2011) where socialisation goals and parental ethnographies are seen as an organised set of expectations, ideas and beliefs that are influenced by cultural norms and values. By including both West African mothers and fathers, the effect of gender norms is analysed and Kleist concluded that German mothers were the most *autonomy oriented*, followed by German fathers. West African mothers as well as fathers were mainly *relatedness oriented*. Although there is a high potential for conflict since strategies are experienced very differently, these qualitative interviews deepen our knowledge of the strategies used for solving conflicts and navigating these differences.

The next section illuminates the primary placing of narratives within mixed parenting and is informed by the work of scholars of mixed race such as Olumide (2002), Ifekwunigwe (2004), Sedmark (2012) and Aspinall & Song (2013).

6.4   The 'mixed' parenting approach

The narratives of Raaka and Klaus demonstrate mixed parenting as they teach their seven-year-old daughter Clara about her mixed origins linguistically as well as culturally, combining both her parental national affiliations. Raaka is married to Klaus and moved to Denmark six months before the data was collected. They are planning to stay in Denmark until Clara finishes school. This is the second time they have moved back to Denmark. For Raaka and Klaus, their daughter Clara's educational trajectory is the main reason for moving to Denmark, yet they also emphasise and miss the spirituality of India. Regarding parenting, Raaka focuses on the *specific mix* of the Danish and the Indian cultures. She explains the positive dimensions of both backgrounds, such as the value of respect and education in the East. Denmark is perceived as a relatively relaxed society that is less competitive when compared with India. She strives to mix these relative strengths to provide the optimal socialisation of her child and she talks about how she actively mixes the best features, through some oversimplified stereotypes about both India and Denmark.

> *But we like it, we think it can be a 'fordel'* [Danish for advantage] *for her, she gets both the Western and Eastern culture. There are a lot of good things in both cultures. She has the most amazing possibilities. East has a lot of respect, East has lot of importance to education, to knowledge, which she gets, and she is a brilliant child. Denmark is less competitive, which is also good for her. I would like her to be a child to be relaxed and also learn other things in life, not just books and education. India is very spiritual. So it is very good values she has that she can get both. Not the extreme . . . we like to take the best of both.*

However, Raaka is also deeply aware of the problems and conflicts involved in her young daughter's subjective understanding of differences in everyday practices as well as the hierarchical positioning of phenotypical differences such as skin colour. This awareness of racialisation, based on biological features and expressed as Clara's wish to be a Dane, is tackled by a mixed parental approach accompanied by an attitude of patience. At the same time Raaka is also aware of the positive implication of the double belonging as providing experience in adapting to a new environment. With humour, Raaka points to the Indian way of addressing people in India where, unlike in Denmark, kinship terms mostly such as uncle, aunty, brother, sister are used, rather than just names.

> *It's, hmm . . . difficult for the child, to understand two different cultures. In India you would never address an older person by name, everyone is an aunty or aunt, but she lived here, grew up here and suddenly she turn around and says: 'grandma is Rasa'. It is a small example, but sometimes it can be difficult for the child, but it can also be fun for the child. She gets a lot of exposures, and I think that she enjoys it. She likes to believe that she is 100% Danish. First, she would like to be Danish, she wants to be white.*

Raaka also discusses Clara's wish to be perceived as a Dane and become a Dane after reference to her painting, which was noticed by the interviewer. The painting depicted the faces of family members, where the father and the daughter are pink and the mother is brown. But Clara has black hair, like her mother and the father has red hair. According to Raaka, Clara's painting her Danish father and herself in the same pink colour reflects her wish to be like him, though the black hair colour like the mother can be interpreted as a partial acceptance of the reality of being a child of mixed parentage. To some extent this is congruent with extensive research in the social sciences pointing to mixed children's wish to belong the dominant white group related to 'white privilege' (Addison & Thomas, 2009) – the social privileges of light-skinned persons in comparison to dark-skinned ones. This confirms that skin colour/pigmentation and the resulting colourism hierarchy – as part of the observable differences in the physical features in wider society – are also reflected among members of visibly ethnically different families in diverse contexts such as Sweden, USA and Philippines as discussed by Törngren Osanami, 2011; Killian, 2013; Meszaros, 2013 and also discussed under the concept of colourism. As a parent, Raaka is optimistic that with age Clara will get a realistic understanding of her dual cultural belonging and perceive it as an advantage. She considers that Clara's dual racial and ethnic background is a rooted and factual part of her identity. She attempts to make Clara aware of these differences through the process of racial literacy mentioned earlier in section 6.1.

Early from the beginning, she was like, all Danish, speak Danish and they have red hair and all Indians speak Hindi. She has an obsession with whiteness. Sometime she will start to understand the difference, it is not just she has a problem with my colour. She just thinks that she is Dane. She is more Dane than Indian. She believes that she is 100% Dane and 50% Indian.

Raaka and Klaus's parenting can be analysed mainly as a 'mixed' approach and there is some parental agreement on the significant values to be transmitted to the child. Raaka also emphasises the issue of parental unity on discipline, in which she is strict and Klaus is rather permissive. However, she also refers to her own 'double standards' regarding her lack of acceptance of his scolding their daughter, while she does so herself. It is noticeable that she essentialises this strictness and attributes her authoritarian attitude to her Indian background.

No [disagreement] not on the value sets we want to give her. We have disagreements on a day-to-day basis. He can raise his voice, which I can't accept to a child. I get totally pissed off if he does that. I can raise my voice, but he should not (laughs). It is also bad thing with me. I am very strict with her and that he doesn't like. He is more relaxed, 'don't be so strict, she is just a child', he says. But I have certain rules, and we follow rules. That comes from my Indian background.

The complexities of mixed parenting become explicit when Raaka resorts to personal-level dynamics, such as reciprocal compatibility, in order to comprehend how they deal with everyday life problems and conflicts. Furthermore, she mentions the spiritual level as an explanation for their compatibility and overall agreement regarding parenting, thus adding nuances to the intrapersonal and interpersonal levels of understanding.

> *It is not that we don't have our challenges. . . . We address them, we are positive people and that has nothing to do with being Dane or in an intercultural marriage. I don't think that it is because we are intercultural that we have tolerance. I just think that we are two individuals that have similar thoughts and it's just because maybe our spiritual karmas.*

Klaus, in contrast, directs his focus to the linguistic mixing in parenting Clara and hardly brings in the spiritual dimension. According to him, one of the reasons for their shifting to India again was to create optimal conditions for Clara to learn her mother tongue – Hindi. At the same time I am aware that mother tongue doesn't necessarily mean her mother's language, but the language that is closest to the person's heart – and we can discuss which it is in Clara's case. For Klaus and Raaka both the father's and the mother's language are important as they want to encourage bilingualism.

Clara's Hindi and English learning in a metropolitan city in India has been significant for her multilingualism. The parental consensus is about mixed parenting through providing her both Indian and Danish language and schooling. Klaus pinpoints that it was a big help for them as a couple that they lived in India, because he gained experience and was accepted into the family.

> *There was actually another purpose as well. Clara was at the time going to kindergarten here and we felt that it would be a good idea for her to go back and also get the Hindi language. So she went to a Hindi school in the metropolitan city in India, and you know, she picked up Hindi within one year and that is very good for her to know, because now she has this foundation that she can handle English, Danish and Hindi and it helps her a lot in terms of communication with family and also in a later stage. So that was important for us to give her that cultural background . . . we took a different decision when she got the age where she can start school in Denmark, because we could see that at that time, we could either continue the Indian way or do something else.*

Raaka is aware of the challenges involved in moving across borders and also of Clara's positive development in various institutions, which Raaka sees as building her mental robustness. She emphasises the positive evaluation of her daughter by her daycare institutions and schools, thus dismantling the myths about poor functioning and patronisation of mixed children.

> *We have moved but she has not had a problem. Most Danish psychiatrists would say 'oh that is bad'. But she is the most wonderful child, the happiest child. Any kindergarten or school she has been to have said 'oh we want five of Clara'. She has not been affected by the changes.*

Along with the mixed approach, Klaus discusses the significant transformation in their work–life balance related to parenthood, which reflects the 'ordinary' concerns of parents. Raaka is in a flexible self-employment situation in order to be able to spend time with Clara and to support her. Time is a valuable resource for the family as they aim for temporal prosperity.

Later Klaus expresses his aspiration about providing 'a good life' in which work and life are balanced similar to Rajiv and Cecilia in chapter 4.

> *But it was work, work, work and suddenly you get a child and you start thinking oh, we need to relax a little bit. What we have done is that I work like a normal work day, but Raaka has been kept free, so that she can take her courses and start her own business.... We can manage this way, because for us we are not into, earning money is fine to a certain level, but the time and family ... I would say that we have a lot of hope that we are going to bring up our kid in a way that she can manage herself to have a good life.*

The participants in this study show that mixed approaches to parenting children include an appreciation of the significance of grandparents, thus bringing out the *intergenerational aspects* of parenting through vertical relationships. However, the role of paternal grandfather is not mentioned at all by Klaus, who is an otherwise highly concerned father involved in planning their daughter's educational trajectory.

A study of ethnically mixed families, mainly Italian-Slovenian families from the former Yugoslavia, shows how they have been marked by profound political changes after independence in 1991. Though conducted in a different political context than Denmark, Sedmak's research

(2012) notes that most of the children accept the cultural, linguistic, religious and other differences which characterise their parents. The parents are from Italy and Slovenia, and are therefore geographically, phenotypically and culturally similar, yet the families have been affected by political upheavals. The processes of identity-related confrontations are similar to the mixed families at the centre of this study. The children's lives include a general social context, which shows how:

> Potential issues children born into ethnically mixed families have to confront – concerning self-declaration of nationality, identity construction, shame of a 'wrong' surname, or 'wrong' affiliation of their mother or father – are the result of intolerant and nationalistic attitudes in their environment, rather than intrinsic to the ethnic diversity of their parents per se.
>
> (ibid., p. 66)

In addition, Sedmak directs *attention to parenting* by emphasising that parents often want to teach their children about their ethnically mixed origins and to explain the positive aspects of their family's ethnic backgrounds. She concludes that most parents leave the decision of national affiliation to their children and do not force them into exclusive declaration. The findings have some similarities to Klaus and Raaka's parenting of Clara. To sum up, Raaka and Klaus show a high level of agreement regarding a mixed approach to parenting and a shared emphasis on a *good life* for their daughter, accompanied by ongoing negotiations about their differences in parental unity regarding discipline.

6.5   The 'cosmopolitan' parenting approach

In diverse contexts, some mixed couples and their children do not perceive themselves monoethnically, even when forced into exclusive declaration of nationality. They may resort to broad identities such as 'citizen of the world' or 'member of the human race'. Such parenting practices are illustrated by the narratives of Rajiv and Katja as well as those of Nihla and Mads.

For Rajiv and Katja, parents of Sonia, their a one-year-old daughter, both paternal and maternal grandparents play an important role in raising the child, nevertheless, her identity and sense of belonging are not rooted in any particular ethnic background. When questioned about the couple's agreements and disagreements regarding his daughter's socialisation, Rajiv's narrative about universal morality indicates that he is thinking beyond narrow ethnic and religious categories. For him basic moral values are significant.

> *Both of us are sending out the same message to her and I think that fundamentally we want to give her a solid life, with good life values. That is my priority, like you know in Denmark. I have seen it at the yoga classes, if you mention the world moral or morality, people start to move strange. It is a bad word apparently, but it is very important. It is the foundation for any spiritual ... it is that your basic moral function is strong.*

These moral values may seem rather abstract. However, he further describes values such as not telling lies or hurting others as he emphasises that no one wants to be hurt or lied to. Rajiv's narrative can be interpreted as expressing cosmopolitan and organic notions of the self which underline the universal aspect of these values.

> *It is simple ... do you like to be lied for, no. Okay so don't lie. Do you like being hurt, ok don't hurt. It is universal.*

However, along with these universal values, there is also a desire to teach the child the diasporic parent's mother tongue as it represents a connection to the specific region in the country of origin and the positive aspects of the cultural heritage, such as intellectual traditions. He is also aware of the possible limited significance of his mother tongue Bangla (language in the state West Bengal, India).

Thus he concludes this narrative by stressing that the 'tools' should be made available to child so she can choose later in life.

> *We are talking about the language now right, and she speaks Danish and I speak Bangla. We have known a lot of couples that are mixed, and they speak their respective language to the children. I give her all the tools that she needs and then she makes the choice and whatever she finds interesting in the language, or pursue her call.*

It is remarkable that other mixed couples socialising their children to bilingualisms are cited as source of inspiration. These visions about bi/multilingualism have to be understood in relation to the reality of almost no organised teaching of Asian languages for children in Denmark. This indicates that such hopes may be unrealistic or limited to informal, everyday level mother-tongue learning (Holmen, 2011).

In a critical discussion of the desire to raise bilingual children among English-German couples in Germany and Belgium, Piller (2009) indicates that parents of small children are full of hope for their children's bilingualism, whereas mixed parents of older children often exhibited a palpable sense of failure. Bilingualism is hard work and the responsibility is squarely placed on the minority parent. This hard work is usually invisible, like other emotional work in the family, and is made more difficult by the lack of support from broader society. Rajiv's plans, combined with the findings from Piller's study, reflect the gap between ideals and the real-life situation. This relates to the complex nature of parenting where the dominant idea of an open-minded approach within the family combines the diasporic parent's cultural and lingual background.

This approach can be considered as a *colour blind approach* and does not reflect how race and ethnic differences are constructed within power relations. Colour blindness as an ideology attempts to consider people strictly as individuals, ignoring or de-emphasising ethnic group membership. As Root (2001) points out, regardless of the truth of the statement that we are all members of the human race, race does make a difference to how people are treated. While Rajiv does not report direct racial or ethnic discrimination (see Chapter 7 for a more detailed discussion), he is still subject to a racialising gaze and identification by others as ethnically ambiguous, or as an Indian. At the same time he wishes to encourage bilingualism in his daughter and he to prepare her for name-calling, to defend herself against the childhood taunts of 'half-paki', 'coconut' and 'zebra'. If race is not discussed at home, the child may perceive that the parents do not understand or know how to cope with racial or ethnic taunts and they may feel unassisted in coping with such experiences through formulations such as 'race/ethnicity doesn't matter'. The effective parenting of mixed-race children thus entails some preparation and reflection involving the previously mentioned concept of racial literacy. Grandparents can contribute to the socialising process and, as Rajiv points out, his parents were joyous at his daughter's birth and they sent a substantial economic gift for the child.

> *But, they gave quite a lot of money to Sonia when she was born, not quite a bit in Danish standards, but quite a bit in Indian standards. And, that, it is very difficult to send things from India.*

The Danish partner, Katja, also emphasises the close contact between her parents and her daughter, even though they live in Funen, two hours drive away. Visiting them every other month is perceived as a high frequency of contact between the generations, as compared with the very limited intergenerational contact among the Danes described by Indian anthropologist Reddy (1991) after he lived for a year in Denmark. According to Katja, Sonia's birth has resulted in more frequent visits from her parents.

> *I see my parents quite a lot. I'm very close to my siblings, my brothers and I see my parents quite a lot, we go there almost like every second month or something.*

> *... after I gave birth, hmm ... well of course that influenced ... in the sense that they certainly come and visit much more than they used to because it is a little easier, before we could just go there. My mother is very happy to come here and babysit Sonia of course (laughing).*

She also mentions that although her divorced parents have new partners, there is close contact with them as well as with her biological siblings and *bonus* siblings (parents' new partners' biological children from the earlier relationships). She seems to be highly positive about her life which comprises a couple relationships, a child and a job, and she uses the metaphor 'vacation' for her life implying excitement, happiness and activities, rather than a passive, boring, routine everyday life (Highmore, 2002).

> *Yes I'm very happy, it's super exciting and we both really love to make a lot of plans, doing things, so that's, my mum always told me that there is an everyday life as well, but we always feel like we are on a vacation (laughing) so that's really nice.*

Katja's narrative about parenting contributes to our understanding of her positive impression about current life transitions. Her husband Rajiv's flexibility and cooperation regarding parenting is much appreciated in this life phase, which would be demanding and stressful without support from a partner or other family members see chapter 5, section 5.4.1. The division of household chores between the couple reflects the power position between the partners and can be a bone of contention between them, especially if we draw gender to the foreground and consider dominant discourses of South Asian males. This holds that men with origins in South Asia, especially those from the upper middle-class, are unwilling to share household work (Rastogi, 2009).

> *It's great because I have a husband who is very flexible, who can bring and pick up the child from the daycare, he takes part in everything and we are*

very equal and...it's not like, he is not traditional in that aspect at all, he is the one that cooks as well, so it's very, yeah, there are no stereotypes there.

Furthermore she is aware that Rajiv's special work situation (he works 15–20 hours a week) has an important bearing on his primary parenting function, while she has a demanding full-time and well-paid job. The sharing of parental duties to this extent wouldn't have been possible if the spouse had a demanding full-time job similar to Katja's. The gender roles are partly transformed and influence the parenting pattern, which is open and cosmopolitan, hardly following the 'old-fashioned' parenting style of the South Asian diaspora, where the fathers are supposed to be without the 'diaper-duty gene' (Rastogi, 2009). Rajiv is a highly engaged and emotionally attached father who spends a lot of time with his child.

so we've been able to bring up the child together and I've had a lot more freedom than some of my friends who are mothers as well, 'cause he could just take care of her when I had to do something, I'd never been so much to the hairdresser.

At the same time, Katja is aware of the potential differences they may have regarding the extent of freedom given to the child when she gets older. With a point of entry being the example of *drunken teenagers*, she expects that Rajiv will be more restrictive than her, as she has been socialised under permissive parental conditions (Mørch, 2001).

Interviewer: *Have you had any disagreements in bringing up your daughter?*

Katja: *Umm I think the only thing we disagree about is that I think with good reason but Rajiv really, not hates that's a very strong word, but he feels very strongly about when he sees young kids twelve, thirteen, fourteen on the streets in no clothes walking around late at night maybe even being drunk, and it's not a disagreement 'cause I totally agree, But maybe he feels a little stronger about how you should keep your children at home than I do because I've also grown up with a lot of freedom myself, and he is definitely more used to your parents telling you what to do and what you should study and whatever, He fought a long way to be himself in that aspect. Whereas I mean we usually grow up with being supported in what we do and that's a different perspective. But he is very aware of letting her become whatever she's supposed to be and not pushing her in any direction.*

These reflections indicate a risk for potential conflicts in mixed relationships where some of the basic developmental conditions for children, such as parental control and discipline, are perceived as different. It is remarkable that Rajiv has neither anticipated such conflicts nor mentioned his own restrictive upbringing. This situation implies that anticipated future conflicts may be based on presumptions and negative stereotypes of the spouses' upbringing under 'restrictive condition'. These presumptions play an important role in couple dynamics, power conflicts and probable psychosocial intervention.

Katja explicitly expressed that Rajiv is not restrictive and expects him to be supportive; a viewpoint also expressed by him. This similarity of parenting principles can be interpreted both as an open approach to parenting and a sign of the couple's positive mental health.

For Nihla, who moved to Denmark when she was nine years old, there was simply no awareness of categories such as race and nationality when she lived in a big city in Pakistan and attended a school there. Her meeting with the *others* in the Danish context made her conscious of her own ethnic minority background, illustrating the circumstantial approach to ethnicity (Verkuyten, 2005). Belonging to the majority group and the upper middle-class in Pakistan, her ethnic background was the 'norm', taken for granted and not questioned.

. . . you know what, I never thought about race umm or nationality or those things before I came to Denmark.

At the time of the interview, Nihla was separated from her Danish husband Mads and was in the middle of divorce proceedings, thus the focus was not only on parenting, but also on their impending break-up.

When questioned about their two small children's upbringing, she stressed the 'mixed' belonging of the children rather than her own country of origin. She emphasises her Pakistani background and her husband's Danish belonging. In this way she presents an essentialist dichotomy with this narrative:

I mean I am not confused about where I am from, I'm Pakistani and I think for them they are going to be . . . and his mom is going to be Pakistani and his dad is going to be Danish, obviously he is going to be more Danish and more influenced by this culture than mine, being raised here.

Later, however she distanced herself categorically from the ethnic categories for her children thus implying an open approach to parenting. She wishes ideally to ignore ethnicity.

I don't know like, for me I'm gonna like focus as little on culture on ethnicity as possible. 'Cause that ultimately it has nothing to do with anything you know or well it does but it really shouldn't!

At the same time, her distancing is not complete, as she is prepared to add some aspects of her 'original culture', which she evaluates as positive. As with Rajiv and Katja, she expects the children to choose for themselves the extent to which they identify with Pakistani culture.

And I mean the Pakistani culture is going to be a part of their life as big or small as they would like it to be. But I mean I hope a positive addition.

Nihla's narrative directs our attention to the apparent paradoxes and complexities involved in parenting children of mixed heritage for some couples. Daneshpour (2009) argues that it is through the children's issues that all other problems surface and must be confronted; he perceives parenting conflicts as battles over some basic differences in values or beliefs. Though Nihla wants to move away from narrow categories, some aspects of Muslim cultural practices are still included in the parenting of the children. According to Sedmak (2012), there is an expectation that children can take the decision later so long as the parents prepare them for the choices. One can question how realistic this is, as for both couples – Rajiv and Katja as well as Nihla and Mads – the children are young (between four months and three years old) and the broad context exigencies are not fully taken into account, given how unpredictable social and political circumstances can be. Both couples live in a multi-ethnic metropolitan environment, which is an important factor in shaping their parenting patterns. The views and responses of the extended family and the social network also influence these practices.

In order to sum up this analysis of the parenting patterns of mixed couples, we have to attempt to understand the dynamic forces that promote the formation of ethnically mixed couples and affect the socialisation of children of these relationships. According to Root (2001, p. 137), the birth of an ethnically mixed child, especially in visibly different families, introduces the following issues that are rarely relevant in same ethnicity families:

- It permanently records the interethnic relationship
- It creates difference – ethnic blood kin
- It can change people's perception of a parent's race
- It potentially changes the ethnic proportions and cultural norms within a family
- It provokes reflection on ethnic/racial socialisation, congruent to the earlier mentioned concept of racial literacy, especially giving the white mothers a crash course in 'racial self-defence'.

'What about the children?' is a significant and common question for parents in a mixed relationship and they address it in a variety of ways, showing concern and reflection. Our research findings explicitly indicate this, irrespective of the age of the children or the couple. However, this is not congruent with the findings in Killian (2013)'s study in the USA involving 20 mixed couples and it is perhaps surprising that most of his research participants expressed little or no concern about what their multicultural children's lives would be like. However, half of the participants in Killian's study expressed a profound hope and optimism that their children would not be perceived as 'different' or become scapegoats. Two discourses informed this optimistic world-view. Resisting a focus on skin colour and the dominant biological construction of race, several couples decentralised the topic and avoided references to differences in colour, hair texture and facial features among family members. Other couples denied such differences as superficial, relatively insignificant and unworthy of the attention or 'hype' bestowed upon them by the popular media and mainstream society (ibid., p. 111.). Thus these parents of mixed children highlight the hope that historical problems and continuing patterns will not influence their children's future opportunities.

According to Killian's analysis, these parents employ individual strategies such as 'determination and will-power', though these couples hardly participate in a collective addressing of the issue. These findings are partly similar to the parenting patterns observed in Cecilia's narrative in the present study, which displays optimism about her daughters' capacity to develop 'tolerance towards others', though she does perceive the world as becoming 'more and more mixed', thus she includes the broad context in an abstract manner. In some ways the couples adopting a cosmopolitan stance in the present study can be perceived as optimists.

Killian (2013) also describes how some parents express concern and worry about children in American society where 'personal traits are often attributed on the basis of skin pigmentation' and where blacks are placed as 'minorities' in terms of both proportion and relative limited power and privileges in society. In the present study, this 'worrying' attitude is partly reflected in the first part of Raaka's narrative describing the pink and brown colour complex, however, she is later actively optimist about her daughter's mixed-identity development.

These narratives entail various ways of developing racial literacy among mixed children. Close contact and knowledge about diasporic parents' country of origin – a strategy employed by Marlik and Lars – is one way of strengthening the children's ethnic identity and making them aware and proud of their parental culture. Rajiv and Katja's vision of their daughter's trilingualism (Danish, Bangla and English) and Raaka and Klaus's strategy of providing both a fundamental mother tongue (Hindi) and Danish education for Clara are also illustrations of how parents can support racial literacy. On the other hand, Cecilia emphasises Danish as the main language for her daughters and expressly excludes the paternal family language (Punjabi). Still, she perpetuates tolerance and openness in her daughters as a white mother of mixed children, thus inculcating racial literacy to some extent. Although racial literacy is a demanding analytical process, these participants are active in attempting to develop a conscious awareness of the ways in which ethnicity and transnationalism shape their children's lives.

By way of contrast, Poulsen (2012) expresses a 'worrying' attitude towards mixed marriages in her Danish study, when she points out that the arrival of children in intercultural marriages makes the culture meeting visible in more than one way. A new consideration is required to 'your', 'mine' and 'our' culture. It raises concrete questions such as which values are important in socialisation? Should the child be circumcised? Should the child eat pork? How do we create conditions for the child to develop an identity without feeling split? Her empirical analysis is rather pessimist and can be criticised for overemphasising the individual cultural aspects and overlooking broader societal aspects.

A study which includes a more optimistic perspective towards parenting in mixed families is that of Sengstock (2009), which examines the self-identification of mixed-background adults in the USA, focusing on their retrospective experience about achieving success in multicultural families. The results are also applicable to the discussion in Chapter 9 of this book, which deals with the practical implications of mixed relationships. Sengstock's analysis includes a variety of mixedness, both visibly different families as well as those which are phenotypically simi-lar but culturally different, yet the lessons learnt from the respondents' experience are relevant to add a comparative perspective to the pat-terns emerging from the present study. These can be used not only in mixed families, but also in other mixed groups to some extent. The main lessons learnt are that parents have a critical role in providing support and developing close family ties in spite of cultural (and sometimes even geographical) distance. They have the ability to focus on shared simi-larities, distinguishing between important and unimportant differences and the value of a supportive social setting.

The *critical role of parents in providing support* to the children is signifi-cant, as they can provide information about both sides of the children's heritage and present children with the two (or more) options. The term used for provision of options is sometimes termed 'a cafeteria approach to culture' (Sengstock, 2009, p. 159) which may sound some-what derogatory. In the present study, Raaka and Klaus are relevant examples of parents who have provided not only information but also bilingual competences to their daughter Clara. Rajiv and Katja also have similar visions regarding Sonia's future linguistic competences. How-ever, in practice providing linguistic options is a challenge and very hard work for parents. It is noticeable that bilingualism, with acquisition of the diasporic parent's language – Urdu – is not mentioned by Marlik as well as Lars. Notwithstanding this, Marlik and Lars have travelled fre-quently with their children to different countries associated with their maternal grandparents in order to develop strong ties with the diasporic family.

This example documents the second lesson learnt about developing close ties in spite of cultural and geographical distance. In the present empirical study, a number of couples attempt (successfully) to main-tain contact with their family in distant countries through the use of the Internet. One such is Rajiv who has established communication between Sonia and his parents in India through Skype, a phenomenon forming the basis for the concept of distant love by Beck & Beck-Gernsheim (2014). Similarly, close ties are maintained between Katja and her family living in another Danish city through frequent travel-ling. No such pattern of contact can be seen between Lars's children and his siblings, who live in Jutland, indicating the lack of close ties.

Ability to focus on shared similarities is another way of accentuating common cultural patterns and minimising the importance of differ-ences among successful mixed families according to Sengstock (2009).

This is illustrated well by Raaka's example in the present study as she meets and shares everyday life concerns with her Danish in-laws by attempting to communicate in Danish, despite ethnic and religious differences. With the extended families' common focus on daughter Clara, the other differences are minimised. Similarly Rajiv and Katja manage relationships with both sides of the family in spite of dramatic cultural differences and defining some differences as 'unimportant' through their cosmopolitan approach. Rajiv and Katja's narratives emphasise another pattern indicative of successful mixed families as they share an ability to distinguish between cultural dimensions which are important for them and those which are not. For Rajiv and Katja, the in-laws' different religions – Christianity and Hinduism respectively – are not critical to their membership of an extended family and it makes sense to ignore them as being open-minded and tolerant is important to them. They plan to socialise Sonia within both religions to some extent so that she feels free to adopt whichever she would find most appealing. It is relevant to note with Sengstock (2009) that this practice can lead to divergent patterns among siblings, though this issue is not within the scope of the present study.

Another noticeable result of the present empirical study is the different focus on discipline and freedom for the couples' children. Both Danish women, Cecilia and Katja, expect their diasporic husbands to be more protective and indulging than themselves, whereas Raaka regards herself as more strict, owing to her Indian background. These differences are, however, negotiated in different settings in various ways, depicting an acceptance of tensions and ambiguity in the couples' strategies of parenting.

Finally, *a supportive social setting* is particularly significant to the development of good relationships in mixed families, as mixed people whose social environment has been positive and supportive have been found to be more comfortable with their mixedness (Sengstock, 2009). Furthermore, hierarchical positioning of the ethnic group to which the partly belong is also significant. Nakazawa (2003), in her parent's guide to raising mixed children, points to an increase in their number in American society and expresses a hope for a relative breaking-down of divisive racial barriers. A restructuring of belief systems which essentialise differences between races could make society a better setting for mixed families and their children. This directs our attention to Danish society as a setting for the participants in the present empirical study. A setting in my understanding is perceived as the broad context including both the local as well transnational aspects, when one of the spouses in the intermarried couple has their origins in another country. Supportive settings need to provide sensitivity to the ethic and cultural differences and to the feelings of the person. At the same time, due to the potential negative conflicts involved in cross-border relationships, parents and professionals providing psychosocial services need to anticipate the possibility – indeed the probability – of negative encounters which may create difficulties, and be prepared to minimise their impact upon the children. There is still an ongoing *worry stance* in the study of mixedness, which assumes that mixed individuals demonstrate more psychological difficulties and behavioural problems than their monoethnic peers (see Chapter 2 for different 'ages' of mixedness). At the same time, it is relevant to note the voices of the mixed persons themselves; some studies reveal strength and resources in mixed children and youth (Bang, 2010; Aspinall & Song, 2013; Maxwell, 1998). The following conclusions by Maxwell (1998) illustrate these voices, implying the significance of parenting including both/multiple sides of mixedness, based on an empirical study of relatively economically privileged mixed young people, rather similar to the children of couples in the present study.

> Despite the problems encountered these respondents evaluate as an asset their mixed inheritances. They felt that to be a mixed-culture person is more interesting, gives more flexibility and a broader outlook and interest in other cultures. A mixed heritage can foster an ability to cross cultures, to understand and relate to others, empathise with the exploited and sufferings of the Third World and may contribute towards combating racism.
>
> (ibid., 1998, p. 227)

To sum up, we can note that the three lessons learnt pertaining to the parenting of mixed children are: the *critical role of parents in providing support* to the children as they play an important role in children's comfort with their multi-ethnic origins, including the racial literacy concept; developing the *ability to focus on the shared similarities*, by developing close ties with both sides of the family despite cultural and geographical distances, and lastly, being part of a *supportive social setting*.

The social settings – the local and the transnational – are covered in Chapter 7. Finding similarities within differences and distinguishing between important and unimportant differences have direct implications for everyday parenting practices for the intermarried couples, as well as for professionals dealing with their psychosocial intervention – a theme which is covered in the last chapter of the book.

The parenting of mixed children is thus influenced by ethnicity, gender, religious belonging and socio-economic belonging, as well as broad contextual factors in both the local as well transnational settings. We turn to local life in transnational contexts in the next chapter.

7
Local Lives in a Transnational Context

This chapter deals with the broader social context that mixed couples live within, both in the country of residence and in the diaspora spouse's country of origin. Along with a focus on everyday practices and activities within the marriage, participants express their attitudes towards broader social questions and conditions that lie outside their intimate relationship, including those concerning religion and politics. The treatment the mixed couples – especially the diasporic spouses – meet in broader society reveals the extent to which their humanity is recognised and how human the receiving society is, as expressed by Tutu in 2014: 'When we oppress others, we end up oppressing ourselves. All of our humanity is dependent upon recognising the humanity in others.' These aspects of their narratives reflect wider social attitudes – in other words the 'outside' rather than 'inside' as delineated by Cabarello, Edwards & Puthussery (2008). While 'outside' and 'inside' have been analytically separated here, it is acknowledged that in real life they are closely intertwined.

In exploring the divorce risk of international couples, Irastorza (2013) attempts to develop a comprehensive theoretical model which includes individual, cultural and environmental factors rather than just cultural factors based on the country of origin and religion of both spouses. Following Irastorza, I utilise the term 'liability of foreignness' in order to invoke some of the broad contextual factors (including the migration-related environmental factors). This term includes the difficulties the spouse has to face when entering the labour market of the country of residence and can involve factors such as lack of local language, knowledge of market rules and local labour experience, professional certification required in the new setting and discrimination.

The newly arrived spouses – especially when the intimate partnership formation has been a personal decision, and when the person is not migrating within a transnational community – face the complexity of negotiating belonging. Network formation is but one part of this multifaceted concept and in some situations the conventional denominators of nationality, religion, socio-economic background and educational level do not serve as common ground that belonging can be built upon.

Focusing on the broad local context, where the intermarried couples live their everyday life, Denmark is a Nordic country with a welfare state model that forms the basis for a healthcare system and entails many rights. The Nordic welfare state model emphasises egalitarian and extensive benefit levels, wealth redistribution and promotion of gender equality and maximisation of labour force participation. Citizens in Nordic countries benefit from free education, universal healthcare and public services that provide an elaborate social safety net. Hence, the Nordic model is widely regarded as a benchmark with regard to economic and social performance. Denmark ranks highest on the OECD's list of the top ten nations with the highest social mobility, along with rest of the Nordic countries (Overland et al., 2014).

In spite of its egalitarian aspirations, Denmark's changing political landscape is characterised by increasing polarisation between the different socio-economic and ethnic groups; one illustration is the Mohammad cartoon crisis implying exclusion processes and Islamophobia (Hussain, 2011) despite a dominant discourse of homogeneity (Jenkins, 2011). Historical exclusionary processes for *others* has already been discussed in Chapter 2 and current changes reflect the discourse of the 'death' of multiculturalism in Europe, for example following the 7 July 2005 bombings in London (Allen, 2007) and Germany's Chancellor Merkel declaring the death of multiculturalism, judging it as having 'failed utterly' (Connolly, 2010). These discourses at the Danish national level and in powerful, wealthy countries at European level form the basis for saying that Denmark is a society which tends to view multi-ethnicism and multiculturalism in a negative light.

With this backdrop, the next section presents experiences of the intermarried couples placed within the post hoc categories negative, positive and indifferent. These categories are analysed from their narratives with the point of departure in the negative experiences of inclusion in the receiving society within the framework of politics and integration.

7.1   Negative experiences in the receiving society

In this research project we found some of the participants' views reproduce prevailing political discourses of integration, ethnicity and race and some use personal experience as examples of those discourses.

It is noteworthy is that the Danish partners express a more strongly negative view of Danish integration politics and attitudes towards immigrants than their 'foreign' partner. As described earlier in this chapter, the problems experienced by the participants are anchored in *outside* circumstances as well as *inside* ones. Politics is perceived as an *outside* circumstance but in close interplay with the *inside* ones.

The positioning of the diasporic partner as the 'victim' of the Danish system is an example of the interplay between outside and inside circumstances. Lars explains how his wife Marlik, a journalist, has been discriminated against in her workplace in Denmark. To some extent this indicates that interracial intimacy is a dynamic, micro-political site where white members of interracial families can learn to develop a critical analysis of how race and racism operates in their lives, as discussed by Twine, 2010. Moreover, through interracial intimacy they may learn to distinguish between their whiteness and white supremacy as an ideology, as well as their position of structural advantage affected by the interrelated factors of socio-economic placing, gender, generation, sexuality and locality.

> *I have felt with her. For example those things she has gone through, and sometimes you get bitter. She has been treated very badly. She was working in a position for 20 years, and at the office there were some people who felt, that you weren't supposed to employ a female migrant, so they made life miserable for her.*

One possible interpretation is that Lars is constructing a victim position for Marlik and emphasises her exclusion at her workplace. Marlik's narration also focuses on her not thriving in Denmark in the beginning, though attributes it to climatic conditions.

> *I came here in the winter months, it was so cold...I felt like I was in a prison...I lived in Moscow and there it can be really cold...minus 20 degrees, but you don't feel the cold, but here it was minus 5 and it was hitting you, I used to cry sometimes. I'm leaving, I can't stay here, it was so hard.*

Lars and Marlik have been married for 27 years and somehow it seems easier for couples in the settled phase to express their feelings and problems of living in a different country. Given that the problems occured some time ago, the couple might now find them easier to describe and reflect upon them.

It is noteworthy that Lars is also positioning himself out of the (Danish) norm, emphasising his own broad horizons as well as human commonalities. He is critical towards the lack of tolerance of difference and he employs irony to describe Denmark as a wonderful place:

> *I behaved differently during my youth. I felt I could identify more with foreign cultures, and I did not like the Danish mentality against foreigners...today, Denmark is a wonderful place to be still. There are so many opinions and prejudices among Danes and that is really frightening. I really do experience a lot of that in my job. The politics is awful. Today everybody means the same and has the same prejudices.*

Lars is critical about the current exaggerated focus on cultural differences in which the cultural practices of foreigners are placed low in Danish societal hierarchy. He also makes an appeal to draw attention to the commonalities between the majority and the minority – for common humanity. In the light of the lessons learnt from the study by Sengstock (2009), Lars's appeal to look for similarities instead of talking about differences is congruent to the lesson about *focusing on the similarities* in social relationships in multi-ethnic groups mentioned by Sengstock (2009) in Chapter 6.

> *I think that my horizons as a person have grown. Both in terms of my people managing skills, my understanding of other people's problems and tolerance towards differences: when people are different. Because I think that...we try, in Denmark, to make people the same, when people are a little bit outside these scope of 80%, it is like: 'what do we do with this?' Back in line that is good in some ways. It makes things easier, but...there is no development. I think that new things and new positive things...They happen from these persons that look a little different at things, it is about seeing the common. When we talk about culture we look at the differences. Why don't we look about the things that are the same, they are absolutely the majority. I mean, one of the learnings that I had, was that I had these impressions from Asia, that I thought I knew how they are, and they are like that. But when you get to know people they are exactly like us, they have the same problems, they have the same thoughts.*

Analysing Lars's narrative we can draw the conclusion that people who express positive attitudes of understanding and tolerance towards differences in personal life may also express a similar attitude with regard to their work life to some extent. Lars, a policeman, describes how a culturally and religious mixed identity may create possibilities for different strategies and actions which influence each other. His narrative indicates the influence of locality in his self-understanding of where his wife is positioned. He places her as a sophisticated and knowledgeable person while he positions himself as a simple person who has been raised in a rural area. His interpretation is contrary to the stereotypical understandings of minority and majority.

> *It has affected me a lot spiritually and emotionally. In the beginning I was more a Muslim that she was. She was raised in a modern family, I am just a country boy, who likes fixed points in life.*

He relates how he has met with a lot of judgemental behaviour since he converted to Islam, which was difficult for some Danes to accept. He strongly identifies himself as an open-minded, tolerant man, different from other Danes whom he categorises in general as judgemental. For people like Lars, intermarriage can be considered as an identity project with religious, spiritual and political aspects.

Mads also criticises Danes as being clannish and ethnocentric, rejecting mixed intimate relations and his Danish network is 'pressing' him to select a mate who is one of *us* (Danish), after his divorce from the *other*, Nihla.

> *...my view on Danish people has changed too, for the worse I think in many points. Not...racism but the Danish people are so, clannish in some ways...Helping me to find a new girlfriend who has to be Danish.*

Similarly, in the present study the Danish female participant Katja points to her experiences of being subject to a gaze in public spaces, both in India and Denmark. Although she attempts to rationalise being 'noticed' as non-judgmental and related to peoples' interest, it can be interpreted as a relatively negative experience for the visibly different intermarried couples.

> Interviewer: *Do you experience being noticed when you walk around as a couple?*
>
> Katja: *Mm not really, no, maybe only in an interesting way, that we look different and that is interesting, but not in a negative way, not in a judgmental way, I mean people notice us of course both here and in India.*

She condemns the discriminatory practices in the Danish system regarding mixed marriages and the restrictive immigration rules and comments on the exclusion of spouses from the labour market, invoking the psychosocial aspects related to lack of recognition in society. However, she doesn't mention her own spouse Rajiv's specific situation.

> *Well eh only that we are really experiencing that some of our friends have a lot of problems in their relations, and it is not necessarily because they as people not really work together anymore. It is because as a foreign partner [it] is very hard to be in Denmark. It is based on well, they can't get a job and they can't do what they really want it do . . . it's really sad so it's just if you could do something on the practical front so that they could just relax and be happy together and focus on the things that are actually important, it's very difficult for them and it is not really about money but it's about you as a person having an identity being recognised in society.*

Supporting this view, Raaka comments that it was difficult for her to get a job in Denmark corresponding to her qualification, implying the exclusion of foreigners from the labour market. Here is Raaka's own description:

> *At that time I wanted to go back to work, after two years, but then I could not find a job in Denmark. It was very, very difficult to get a job in Denmark . . . If there is a foreigner coming in, and this is only if it is a necessity, if there is a position where they can't find a Dane. Then 'okay, cheap labour or whatever'. It is easier to have a Dane, they have the same humour, and they have the same language. 'Uh a foreigner, that must be something new about this person, and I have to learn and it is so difficult'.*

She also criticises the exclusion of ethnic minorities from the process of finding solutions to problems related to ethnic minorities in society and considers that society is closed and unwilling to adapt. She emphatically points to the barriers that newcomers meet in being accepted into Danish society, implying ethnic minority exclusion from the labour market, a subject well documented by Jensen (2011) in a lucid analysis of exclusion processes which come to light during the job interview.

At that time it was very irritating. I also had a very low self-confidence, because I also know that many Danes are much closed. This is my observation. I think that Danes are very lazy. Not because they don't like foreigners and I don't think that they are very racist, but they are very lazy. They don't like to open up and to accept newcomers. It is too much of an effort....Also frustrating is that I'm willing to change and to adapt your culture, not changing but adapt...More politically speaking, more culturally wise it was frustrating that people don't open up. It is a much closed society in that way, mentally very closed....That was frustrating. What frustrates me now is that I read a lot of news and I follow politics a lot and I point towards all the politics of foreigners that Denmark has...Completely wrong when they talk about foreigners and when they talk about integration, and when they talk about problems they have with foreigners...Because I'm a foreigner and they don't just ask me and what the solution could be.

Furthermore, she invokes a positive example of India, her country of origin, and its example of dealing with linguistic differences. She appeals for increased acceptance of diversity in Denmark.

The problem is the foreigner, I know, but who are the foreigners, what are the problems? I know that I'm on tape, but I feel you cannot give them language and degrade them. India has 25 national languages and you have one. We still move around state to state without understanding each other's language. We can still live with each other, and work with each other.

Raaka is also wary of Denmark being increasingly intolerant with regard to the religious sect they belong to and she has a vision of moving back to India.

But I can't say it openly in Denmark, which I did a few times and people were just like 'uhhh' and some people would not like to talk to me. In India you can do that...we both feel that India is more spiritual. We have more freedom to follow our spirituality there. Here you get branded if you say you follow a specific path, because people don't have understanding. It doesn't matter if you are a Catholic, a...member of a religious sect. You get branded and that is irritating.

One way to deal with such differences is to see the common positive aspects, such as the aspiration to work, to use one's skills and gain social recognition. Olumide (2002) argues on the basis of interviews with mixed-race participants that some have given very positive views of their abilities to move easily despite differences. They consider themselves as bridge-builders but at the same time point out these skills may not be acknowledged as they may challenge the status quo of hierarchical division.

Some people have occupied the moral high ground and offered skills assessments of themselves as 'bridge-builders' or peacemakers in situations of prevalent-race thinking. This is at some distance from the ways in which mixed race is most usually constructed – as an inherently problematic, confused and isolated situation.

> This is not by any means to suggest that inter-group skills are universally acknowledged as valuable... In the meantime, such skills are ignored, undervalued or attacked. They threaten to undermine the interests secured through social division.
>
> (ibid., 2002, p. 9)

In the present study Raaka, and to some extent Rajiv, assess themselves as bridge-builders, although they are spouses in a mixed-couple relationship and not mixed in the genetic sense as conceptualised by Olumide (2002).

The analyses also demonstrate that Danish partners such as Lars and Katja are highly aware of and critical about the discrimination that ethnic minorities, including immigrant spouses, face in Denmark. Similar patterns are also documented by Poulsen (2012) in her study of marriage migrants in Denmark.

> It can be daunting for migrants to experience anti-immigrant attitudes... it can lead to some intercultural couples to give up residence in Denmark because they find it discriminatory and insulting. It applies to both Western and non-Western immigrants. It surprises the new arrivals in Denmark to encounter terms such as 'second' or 'third generation' immigrant, terms which are perceived as discriminatory and racist as they are associated to migrants with a specific skin colour.
>
> (ibid., p. 120)

Poulsen's analysis points to exclusionary processes in society which she argues apply to dark-skinned persons, implying the continuing phenomenon of colourism mentioned earlier. A study by Grewal (2009), conducted in the USA among South Asian and Arab Muslim Americans, provides a nuanced insight into the ways colour, race and class play an important role in the choice of marriage partner and how interracial marriage may be connected to preferences for lighter-skinned mates. Contrasting the attitudes of parents to their children, it is suggested that questions of colour and race are experienced differently across the generations. Grewal's findings describe ideologies of colour and racial prejudices – colourism – that focus on the other observable physical differences, especially among the parental generation. Preference for light skin colour is found not only among white and black, but also among South Asians and Arabs and in the Far East – in fact everywhere to a large extent.

In the present study Lars is highly aware and critical about the discrimination which his spouse Marlik encountered in her workplace of two decades and at the same time he is also critical of the overall lack of tolerance and Danes' negative prejudices against 'foreigners'. It is probably his own position, as an open-minded police officer who has converted to Islam, which contributes to his sensitivity towards the exclusionary processes in society and he too considers himself to be a bridge-builder. In contrast to Lars's awareness, it is thought-provoking that in the US context Killian (2013) concludes that a number of white partners, especially white male partners among the interracial couples, don't 'notice' the discriminatory processes. He elaborates:

> In light of White partners' tendency to *not notice*, black partners may choose to remain silent about their daily experiences or take on the task of directing attention and making case as each event or experience occurs. Whether or not they are successful in opening dialogues with their partner about suspected racist incidents, black partners will continue to adopt a stance of vigilance, to invest considerable energy in monitoring incidents, and to tolerate ambiguity in the face of the many small, sometimes subtle acts of hostility that occur in a racist society.
>
> (ibid., p. 146)

Historical processes of racial discrimination related to slavery and the segregation of the native population in the USA may explain why white partners may not notice racism. Their 'liberalist' views about individuals possessing 'equal' opportunities for success are threatened by the black partners' discourse about unequal power and privilege. The last vestiges of *legal segregation* in the USA were ended on 12 June 1967, with the *Lovings vs. Virginia* case, but attitudes take longer to change. As late as 1987, a full 20 years after the case, only as 48% of Americans said it was acceptable for blacks and whites to date, so from this we can see that it was in the not-so-distant past that anti-miscegenation sentiments were predominant. More recently, the number of people indicating that such relationships are acceptable has jumped to 83%, according to the Pew Research Centre (2010). The centre estimated that one in seven new marriages in the USA is now interracial, while in 1961, the year President Obama's parents married, only one in 1,000 marriages were between a black person and a white person. Today, it's one in 60 (Shay, 2010).

In Denmark, the Danish male partners Lars and Klaus show a clear awareness of the liberalist discourse, and racism has not been so blatant and explicit. At the same time, Katja's experience of *gaze* – being noticed in both the country of residence, Denmark, and the spouse's country of origin – reminds us of the dynamics of the observable character of physical differences. Although some might say I am labouring this point, it is relevant to invoke a poignant description by Sengstock (2009):

> It is perhaps belabouring the obvious to note that the physical character of racial differences ensures that they are constantly observable, even to the casual onlooker. Only people with racial differences look different – all the time.
>
> (ibid., p. 65)

He further quotes the experience of one of his racially different research participants, who felt *not being subjected to gaze* during her visit to Hawaii, with its broad racial spectrum.

> I wasn't being looked at as different – that I didn't feel that I stood out to any extent walking down the street or hanging out – or whatever.
>
> (ibid., p. 65)

Although the mixed couples in the present study are subject to gaze when they are together and not when the spouses are in their native countries alone, the lucid description of being noticed is relevant for comprehending this subtle, non-verbal process. However, at the same time there could be a preference for non-white exotic spouses in

Denmark, as in the UK and in the Far East – in fact everywhere due to a variety of reasons, among others myths regarding non-demanding wives as discussed by Osanami Törngren (2011) (see Chapter 2), a preference for submissive life partners, Baagøe-Nielsen & Gitz-Johansen (2006), and the commodification of intimacy (Constable, 2004).

7.2 Positive experiences in the receiving society

The diasporic partners' positive experiences in relation to their social environment are also evident in the narratives of the participants in contrast to Raaka's critical narrative about lack of openness from Danes. Raaka is active within her ethnic minority group and she helps to integrate others into the network. It is noteworthy that Raaka has the resources and vision to provide assistance to others from her country of origin in adapting to Denmark, despite her own negative experiences mentioned in the previous section.

We are Indians and we also help Indians to integrate with the Danes and the whole society . . . Most Indians that are coming in are mostly coming for work, they have no interest in living in Denmark. They want to earn and just go back. So, we help them to integrate, because as long as they are here, it is a very different culture and a lot of them are here for a couple of years and then they go back, because they can't, they have not had help to understand: the weather is very different, food is difficult, they don't have anyone to talk to. So, what we do is that we facilitate them and to make them feel comfortable living in Denmark, so that they can carry on with their career instead of going back.

At the same time, her work in helping Indians is a bridge-building position grounded in her business experiences, she is pragmatic and has adapted to Danmark without being too nostalgic.

I don't have this network because I need an Indian network, not at all. It is more like, that I know that I can help Indians, but all Asians, they are my business area. So, it just matches with my business also. I love to help and facilitate them, to be comfortable. Because I have come across so many sad stories and I have seen people face challenges. So it is interesting that I can help through this network and that is the reason. I'm strange, I don't miss Indian food or Indian people, language. I don't miss anything (laughs).

She is both optimistic and confident about her abilities to contribute to broader society and to her own development through her qualifications and experiences.

> *I think that I can contribute. I can add to the society and to myself. I would like to build up that business ... I'm a multi tasker in daily life, but when it comes to taking a decision of career or something and then everything goes in to that to make it successful.*

It is paradoxical that Raaka views herself as 'well integrated', while her husband Klaus positions her as a victim. Raaka's earlier narratives about being active and contributing to society emphasise her agency and challenges studies such as Cottrell, 1991; Breger & Hill, 1998; Refsing, 1998. These studies regard Asian wives as victims of circumstances, supporting a simple idea of global hypergamy, focusing on the economic aspects, directing attention away from dimensions of emotions such as love and spirituality. In contrast to the myths that may be more prominent in the media than in academic works, Raaka is neither poor nor does she marry a man who is above her on the socio-economic ladder. She belongs to a middle class family and has a skilled, office job. Commenting on her agency and active responses, Klaus positions her as *an untypical Indian* and *not Indian anymore*, thus confirming his negative stereotype about passive Indian women. Raaka explains her strong motivation for learning the Danish language because of her husband's extended family's monolingualism and her wish to be included in family communication.

> *I learned the language very fast. I believe in life, I take life and learn things on a necessity and I have a necessity. My in-laws do not speak a word of English. Most of Klaus's family don't speak English at all, just a few cousins ... I did not want to be an outsider. I didn't just want to sit and look at them and get bored.*

Additionally, Raaka's following analysis of herself underlines her similarity with 'masculine', controlling Danish women and how this can be considered as a reason for her positive experiences in Danish society.

> *I think that the Danish women specifically are more men than women. They have more male qualities then female qualities (laughs) not negative about it but, I'm quite a Danish woman, my husband says. Control freak and all that, Danish women are control freaks ... Because they are independent, they have their own mind and they can express themselves and they*

would like to be equal, and that is what Danish men (laughs) don't want, equal relationship.

However, she excludes her own husband from the category of Danish men who seek asymmetrical relationships with foreign women whom they can control. She seeks an egalitarian relationship with her husband and at the same time criticises the asymmetrical power relationship between male and female among Indian couples, where males are positioned as superior 'lords'. Her narrative can be interpreted as her positive attitude to a relatively more symmetrical power relationship in marriage with a Danish spouse.

Klaus is an exception, he got someone, I don't know. Maybe he thought that he could control me (laughs)...I didn't want to get married to an Indian, because I can't be in control. Indian tradition is that the man takes the lead role, he is the Lord in the family. Maybe that was definitely not my taste.

Another position of 'well integrated' is constructed by Marlik, who perceives herself as becoming 'Danish' after the initial phase; she now feels integrated or settled down:

When I travel for four weeks I start missing my life here at home, so then I feel ok I'm becoming more Danish.

Both Raaka and Marlik have achieved an integration style of acculturation – this can be explained as the option where some degree of cultural integrity is maintained, while at the same time participating as an integral part of the larger society (Berry, 2011). They also seem to be managing their marriages well, which concurs with a study to understand the psychological and marital wellbeing of European spouses of Arabs in mixed-ethnic/faith marriages in Israel. The results show that women who adopt an integration style of acculturation in adapting to a new cultural environment, achieved a high level of marital satisfaction and marital intimacy (Abu-Rayya, 2007).

On the other hand Nihla, who has been partly raised in Denmark, hardly reflected on national and racial differences, so processes of exclusion came as an unwelcome surprise when she was an adolescent and positioned as an immigrant. Perceived as the *other* who would be (potentially) disliked by a Danish biker (stereotyped as dangerous), this was Nihla's first experience of explicit rejection by her significant others, her classmates and her study project group members. Her own social network made her aware of her position as the outsider that she herself had not appreciated.

> *I didn't think about it before, I was going to a regular Danish school and eh and we were doing this project in my class and I had to do this interview and a girl from my group said how we interview this biker, and I was like 'well eh okay, I don't know what we will ask him but sure'. Then she said 'I'm not sure we should take you along'. I said 'oh why?' and she said 'because some of them don't like immigrants'. That's the first recognising I have of thinking like, okay there is a distinction between you and me, before that I never thought of that.*

In the processes of feeling left out, alertness and ambiguity are not just about social structures in everyday life but are also increasingly about identity. Narratives in this study indicate that institutional circumstances and the macro-level situation have a deep impact on people's lives on the micro level. This impact was even stronger than I had anticipated as an engaged researcher. It is pointed out by Daneshpour (2009), regarding Muslim-Christian marriages in the USA, that there may be complications due to social but not legal restrictions (a non-Muslim male/female who wishes to marry a Muslim woman/man or may be expected to convert to Islam) and that individuals might lack useful, unbiased information for their relationship formation and maintenance.

These broader issues related to societal attitudes, viewed from my perspective, have asserted themselves as one of the most thought-provoking findings of this study. At the very centre of the study is the complex relationship between the macro and the micro, the broad context and personal life. The everyday life and decisions of the intermarried couples, especially where recent marriage migration is involved – as for Rajiv and Raaka – is highly influenced by current political circumstances at any given point in time.

There is an organisation in Denmark 'Marriage without borders' (Marriage without Borders/Ægteskab Uden Grænser, 2014), whose aims are to ensure the rights of Danish citizens to freely choose their spouse and live in Denmark regardless of the spouse's nationality. They seek to ensure proper and humane treatment during the process of seeking visas and residence permits for foreign spouses and their children and to help promote respect for Danish-foreign couples. Although none of the couples in the present study are members of this organisation, they are aware of the discrimination and the restrictive practices that caused this group to form.

Killian's (2013) research, based on the analysis of mixed couples in the USA where no direct linking of socio-political views and mate selection was evident, concludes that most couples wish to be 'ordinary and normal'. In their *non-political stance*, these couples are not so different from most couples who choose not to define themselves in political terms of a larger socio-political framework. Most of these couples have the extra dimension of being interconnected to the diasporic spouses' family in their lives, and their network in the country of origin and in several other localities. This issue is covered in the subsequent main section.

7.3   Indifferent experiences in the receiving society

Rajiv migrated to Denmark in 2006, four years before the interview. When questioned about his move, he talked about falling in love and a shared discussion he and Katja had had as to who should move so that they could be together. It was decided that he should move because of his flexible work situation. The process was cumbersome but he didn't judge it as being tough, given that it worked out well.

> ... *Would it be easier for her to move or for me to move? 'Cause, it was easier for me to move, because my life was very flexible, and I was doing music, doing yoga and I can do that everywhere. So, that then, we started applying, going through that millions of paper work, and that was all that. But it wasn't a nightmare for me, it was a smooth process. I think it worked out.*

He describes the whole migration procedure almost without any critical comment, implying an indifferent attitude to the migration procedure despite its being characterised by restrictions and control. He comments on the lack of voting rights for migrants, but he is otherwise indifferent to the negative aspects of the procedure.

Interviewer: *So, now you have a Danish citizenship?*
Rajiv: *No, you can't have that. You get in and you can have a resident permit. And basically the first two years you get a visa on your passport, that lets you stay here and work here and get all the facilities that a Dane would get except that you can't vote and you don't have any rights to a pension and stuff like that. But, then after two years they renew it.*

He explains his current status as a person holding a permanent residence card and their daughter's automatic Danish citizenship based on her mother's citizenship. This shows improvement in the legal rights of the unified spouse when compared to the historical situation in the nineteenth and early twentieth centuries, as mentioned in the Chapter 1, when Danish women and their mixed children followed the 'foreign' father's citizenship. It is interesting to note that children and wives followed the husband/father's citizenship according to the law in the Netherlands until very recently.

I have a little card, and which I should carry with me all the time. And, then after two years it can be renewed for three more years, and then I have a choice. If I want to apply for a citizenship or if I want to keep my Indian...She [daughter Sonia] has become Danish, because the laws are here apparently that the child takes the nationality of the mother straight away. We don't apply for it, and that is okay, because, yeah we probably spend more time here than in India.

On the whole, Rajiv seems hardly to be affected by the immigration process or the process of moving to Denmark, but he did express his first impressions of a large supermarket in the very first phase of arriving to Denmark. He states:

For me it wasn't even a big move, because it wasn't a cultural shock. In the beginning yeah, yes I mean, I remember the first time in Føtex [supermarket], I thought wow, this is paradise.

Rajiv can be seen as a flexible person who is not too attached to his coethnics; he neither misses them nor attempts to contact them, though he has Indian contact through his teaching activity.

...from language school I know a lot of people from Mexico and South America and all these kind of, but I knew one Thai girl, but she has completely disappeared, I don't know where she is. I have met a couple of random Indians on buses and, but I don't know any Indians, except from Nishant...but he comes for yoga.

However, Rajiv's narrative indicates that he is aware of some difficulties at the macro/structural level related to Danish language learning, getting appointments with medical specialists and so on. He does recognise, though, that the support, appreciation and acceptance from his wife

Katja at the personal/micro level is a major contributor to his subjective perception of the immigration process as unproblematic and smooth.

> *I don't give it much thought but, of course it has not been easy right. No, I mean that I know that at this point, learning a language that you don't use any other place in the world, so you question everything right, and then little things frustrate me sometimes. Doctors, for example, they are free and that is cool, but then it is so difficult to get some specialised time and something like that. And then you think, how is this any better? Everything is so smooth and nice and Katja is very thankful that I made the move and I am very thankful that I could get accepted so nicely. So it is very, very good.*

He is also appreciative of the structural functioning and the openness and 'spaciousness' of Danish society. In addition he expresses his appreciation of the relative economic equality in Denmark and criticises the corruption in India, his country of origin.

> *But I love the fact that systems work and have a basic sense of respect for each other. The space and that is good ... Nobody is hungry, nobody here has ever experienced hunger in their entire life. The homeless people are not even hungry. So that is a big, big thing. Denmark is the least corrupt country in the world. Did you know that? Number one. India is number 83.*

When questioned about the racialising *gaze*, that is, being looked at as a visibly ethnically mixed couple, Rajiv downplayed the phenomenon and considered it as a pleasant experience. This is different to some extent from his wife Katja's narrative described earlier in this chapter. His rationale is that his indeterminate physical appearance (Aspinall & Song, 2013) means he is not pigeonholed into a stigmatised Indian identity but misrecognised as a Jamaican. He further explained that a Jamaican can be perceived from two different angles: in a positive way by someone as a person who loves Bob Marley, or negatively as someone who smokes marijuana 24 hours a day. His narrative challenges the simplistic assumption that mixed couples are always exposed to a negative gaze. Rajiv's indeterminate physical appearance and dreadlocks may be the reason for being subjected to a different, non-stigmatised gaze.

> Interviewer: *What about when you walk around as a couple on the street. Do you feel that you are being watched?*

> Rajiv: *No, not really. In a nice way, sometimes, in a nice way. It is no one like 'oh weirdo'. Most of them think that I am from Jamaica or something, because of my hair* [Rajiv has dreadlocks]. *They don't think that I am from India or something like that. I'm not being stared at or anything like that.*

To sum up the participants' understanding of local life and their processes of inclusion in the local context, it is pertinent to consider the current Danish society symbolised by an illusion of 'homogeneity' as historical-cultural construction characterised by a collective amnesia and official silence regarding mixedness through past centuries (see Chapter 2). The shadows of the past combined with twenty-first-century anxieties have influenced present immigration policy, which is reflected in the negative experiences of some participants – especially the Danish partners' critique of exclusionary and discriminatory practices. To some extent, the current Danish package of regulations restricting the reunification of spouses (introduced in 2001) reflects the current political climate. This climate may be characterised by the concept of 'Fortress Europe' defended from encroachments from outside. Moreover, Beck & Beck-Gernsheim (2014) discuss the transformation of attitudes towards multiculturalism and towards viewing migrant women as victims.

> Multiculturalism, formerly extolled as achievement of modernity, has now become suspect as a naive, unworldly, utopian dream. The latest slogan is 'integration' and it has become mandatory for new immigrant...They [books about 'women as victims'] deal with women as the victims of honour killings, forced marriages, circumcision and oppression, women as objects of archaic customs, ritual practices and patriarchal violence.
>
> (ibid., p. 101)

Unfortunately, this focus on women's victimhood – such as Lars's positioning of Marlik in the workplace and Klaus's positioning of Raaka as victim of racial discrimination – minimises and to some extent neglects the women's agency, resistance and their positive strategies to cope with such external demands. However, these women are not positioned one-sidedly as victims – their husbands also point out their resources and strengths. Nevertheless there are remarkable gender-related gaps in the subjective and others' perception of the diasporic spouses.

Raaka and Marlik perceive themselves as 'well integrated' and the male diasporic partner Rajiv refutes such victim status. Their accounts show them as active human beings with resources and agency. Almost all the participants are aware of the difficulties involved in adapting to a new context, such as exclusion from the labour market, learning a new language, adapting to a different healthcare system, being subjected to negative stereotypes (especially related to religious/spiritual belonging) and dealing with the *gaze* of people to differing extents. At the same time they are aware of the 'liability of foreignness' creating hindrances to their participation, such as the recognition of their qualifications in the labour market and the positive aspects such as 'spaciousnes', smooth system functioning, relative economic equality. The intersection of gender, socio-economic placing and competences has contributed to partial labour market inclusion for them due to their qualifications, experiences, personality attributes and the spouses' support.

Raaka, at the time of the interview, hadn't managed to get a job corresponding to her master's level qualification. Despite looking for a year so, she decided to begin her own consultancy business. Marlik acquired a qualification to work as a journalist, while Rajiv didn't seek a job but became self-employed working part-time. Underpinning the analysis of these narratives is the importance of encouragement and support from the surroundings – especially from one's own spouse – to counter negative social stereotypes and exclusion at various levels. Raaka's suggestion 'to include the foreigners themselves in finding solutions' could be useful for working in this complex field. The broad context for the diasporic partners also includes their country of origin, discussed below.

7.4 Transnationalism and diasporic relations

Diaspora can be defined as a process of *dispersal*, and the dispersal of populations from an original locality which implies distance and the importance of maintaining or creating connections. It becomes a major goal to reduce or at least deal with that distance (Dufoix, 2008). Diaspora here is not perceived in the classical, narrow sense of the Jewish diaspora, which is based on one movement out, never to return again and rootlessness. In a relatively broader sense, it is defined as moving away from the country of origin and maintaining some connections despite distance.

The subjective features of the diaspora direct attention to the multiple meanings of diaspora perceived as a social form, a type of consciousness and mode of cultural production/consumption (Vertovec, 2000). As a social form, diaspora is concerned with relationships, networks and economic strategies across borders, while consciousness is based on multi-locality, both *here* and *there* interconnecting with others, sharing the 'roots' and 'routes'. Lastly, diaspora as mode of cultural production is seen as a transnational cultural phenomenon, with a flow of media images and messages as connectors.

Kalra, Kaur & Hutnyk (2005) argue that diaspora shifts attention away from viewing migration as a one-way process in favour of an understanding of the complex transnational identities. They conceptualise it as both a *positive embracing* of transnational affiliation in context of the South Asian post-colonial history and a defensive posture by communities in the face of a hostile host telling them they *do not belong*. Diaspora is about the ongoing political, socio-economic, psychological and cultural ties. It is about ambivalence and exclusion, including an understanding of diaspora as an emotional construct based on memory and loss. *Myth of return* as an archetype of diaspora is also significant.

Castles (2006) emphasises transnationalism as a relevant research perspective for studying these groups but one that is hardly used in Denmark. Transnationalism encompasses diaspora and includes day-to-day links between two or many countries (Rai & Reeves, 2009). Kivisto & Faist (2010) use the term 'transnational social spaces' to describe two or more national states that become a part of a single new social space. Transnationalism occurs when disaporic people and communities have managed to remain connected to and involved in their countries of origin. Al-Sharmani & Tiilikainen (2014) attempt to define transnational family life by highlighting strong and sustainable ties between the person and a network of family and relatives based in other countries (including and not limited to the home country). These ties consist of regular communication, sharing resources and family burdens and processes of decision-making that take into account the welfare and interest of other relatives in this transnational family network.

There are large variations in transnational relationships and engagements, given that not all immigrants are involved in transnationalism. These variations are related to gender, family structure and life course positioning. On the basis of an empirical study of Pakistani transnational connections in the UK, Charsley (2013) emphasises that young people have relatively less transnational engagement when compared to their parents, unless they get married to a spouse from the same country of origin. However, she refers to their future selves, suggesting that they may become more connected to the country of origin and other countries in later phases of life.

Given that they have not gone through many of the life course events... young people are likely to be less transnational than their parents, or indeed perhaps their future-selves. If they contract a marriage in Pakistan, this may change and new dreams, hopes and transnational involvements emerge.

(ibid., p. 59)

In order to analyse transnational processes, the 'migrated/diasporic' partners' relationships with their country of origin and relatives in other parts of the world are important for intermarried couples. In analysing their narratives I categorised them post hoc and placed the participants into three categories: *intense, moderate* and *limited*, based on the nature and frequency of the social contact and economic strategies combined with the diasporic consciousness. These indicate the dominant patterns of contact with the country of origin for the participants – some overlapping is, however, unavoidable.

It is important to grasp the complex relation between national and local practices and connect them to the broader migration context both in a vertical as well as a horizontal sense. Here, intergenerational and filial piety and sibling responsibility are important, though dependant on generational, gender and socio-economic positions. One can also question if transnationalism links back to the country of origin or links to a range of countries and places. One superficial conclusion that can be drawn from this research is that diasporic partners who have moved to Denmark as reunified spouses – such as Rajiv and Raaka – demonstrate a relatively more intense pattern of transnationalism than Sam, Sabita and Nihla, who were either born and raised wholly or partly in Denmark. The analysis below adds nuance to this assumption.

7.4.1   Intense transnational connections

Rajiv maintains frequent contact with India, his country of origin, both through travelling and Internet technologies such as Skype. He communicates not only with his extended family in India but also in other countries.

With the aunts [in the USA and UK] I am the black sheep in the family. I am very bad in keeping contact with everybody. But they are sending, but sometimes I write to them, but sometimes I call, I hate sms'ing, so I call most of the time by Skype.

He travels once or twice a year to India, but considers this to be infrequent as his expectation at the time of marriage was that he would make more frequent visits. Life events (Levy et al., 2005), such as the birth of a child, are one of the major factors for explaining this frequency, confirming the significance of such life course events in current everyday life.

> *Our original plan, what I was told when we moved to Denmark was that 'Oh darling you can go back to India whenever you feel like. You can go every three months if you want.' Of course it does not work like that. In the beginning I think that every six months we were going, but now, it is once a year. This last time I did a trip on my own because Sonia [daughter] was too small to travel.*

His narrative illustrates the diverse objectives of his trips to the country of origin, such as to give concrete financial advice to his father, to further develop competences or to relax.

> *We have to figure out the situation and someone has to take all that over, because they [parents] are getting old and want to simplify their life, you know they have a big house, which they are taking care of all the time ... so I took a one month trip and I was in [city name] for a few days and then I went up into the mountains in a beautiful township and studied yoga, and stayed there in an ashram.*

He has no financial responsibility towards his family in India. On the contrary, his parents have been contributing economically for their granddaughter by depositing some money in her name. However, it is noticeable that Rajiv has a very limited Indian network in Denmark, though he has close emotional ties with the extended family in India and in the UK and the USA where some of his relatives live, through the Internet and Skype.

> Interviewer: *Your relatives, do they all still live in India?*
> Rajiv: *Yeah, no, one of them has been living in the UK all her life. She is a doctor, a psychiatrist, but now she has retired. And another one has been in the US all her life, but now she is spending more time in India. She is quite old.*

The youngest research project participant, Sabita, is also from India. She is closely connected with her country of origin as she visits her grandparents in India every summer.

Oh, yes we are actually very close to my grandparents who live in India and quite a few of my uncles. My father's side of the family is quite big. He has 7 siblings and some of them are in India. We actually go back every summer a few weeks. When I was younger my mother and I spent 3 or 4 months there, the summer holiday and a bit more. We stayed there with my grandparents.

At the time of the Skype interview, Sabita lived in Hong Kong, and thus it is relevant to focus on her contact with Denmark as well as India. In addition, she has contact with her extended family members in the USA, which is also part of her complex transnational social space (Faist & Kivisto, 2010).

Right now I live in Hong Kong. So, I graduated from a prestigious American university this summer in June and my husband graduated last year from the same university as well and moved to Hong Kong. So now I have joined him here.

Due to her emotional closeness to her grandmother and her feeling of belonging to India, she describes her plans to visit India which is supported by her husband, Robert. She even emphasises Robert's close relationship with his grandmother.

I speak to my grandparents on both sides once a week, at least. Sometimes a little bit more and sometimes a little less. There is always a lot of dialogue...I think that now, I will be travelling more with Robert. I will try to coordinate; Robert has actually not been to India yet, so I think that when he gets a bit more vacation we will definitely be going. That will be our next trip. Besides that, we do it very frequently in the family.

Sabita and Robert's focus on filial piety towards grandparent (Trask & Koivunen, 2007) is a significant aspect of their transnationalism as well as a common value for both of them. This value related commonality seems to transcend ethnic differences and challenges the negative stereotypes regarding filial piety in Danish families. Sabita states:

On my mother's side, my grandmother and I are very close and she is always talking about how she is making...for me. Normally presents are sent to Copenhagen and then my parents bring them to Hong Kong if they are going. So definitely packages are being sent and a lot of exchange of gifts and so on. Definitely my grandmother does a lot of that. Both I and Robert have close relationships to our grandmothers; they are endearing people who have always had a spot for us.

Furthermore, Sabita emphasises Robert's and her own background in an upper-class Danish suburb and their shared upper socio-economic status in Denmark are a commonality between them see chapter 4, section 4.2.2. Robert supports her in remaining connected to her extended family in India.

These narratives illustrate how close emotional relationships can be maintained with family members in the country of origin and other countries by visiting as well as through the Internet and social media. This is also confirmed by the narratives of Pakistanis in the UK (Charsley, 2013; Williams, 2010; Kalra et al, 2005), twice- or thrice-migrated Indians in the UK (e.g. from Uganda) Bachu (1999), Indians directly from India in the UK, both the older migrants viewed as 'not quite Indians' by the newer migrants and newly arrived skilled migrants (Raghuram & Sahoo 2008). These studies also conclude that 'being' transnational is greatly facilitated by improvements in communications and by the increasing affordability of travel. (It should be noted that the newly arrived Indians, perceive the Indians living in the UK for some decades as 'not quite Indians', due to their acculturation.)

7.4.2   Moderate transnational connections

Similar to Rajiv, Raaka does not have a close Indian network in Denmark, but she is an active member of an Internet network.

Indians in Denmark, Hmm... we try to, we are Indians and we also help Indians to integrate with the Danes and the whole society. That is the purpose, it is not just to have a place where we meet to have a cup of coffee. We have that, our women's club and children's club, where children meet and... We have these Hindi classes and they learn Hindi and they can learn about their history and we have book club, where they can exchange Indian books... And that is what the club does.

She is, however, not nostalgic about India and does not lament her lack of Indian contacts in Denmark, contrary to theoretical knowledge about enhanced involvement with the everyday life practices in the country of origin for relatively new arrived migrants (Berry, 2011).

It is more like, that I know that I can help Indians... I'm strange; I don't miss Indian food or Indian people, language. I don't miss anything.

Raaka explains that she broke off contact with one of her brothers and her father in India some years back. At present she has a relationship with just one brother, two sisters and her mother. She considers herself as a person with a limited need for contact.

> ... *even during the first three years when I lived here at that time I had contact with parents also, I'm not the person who calls too much and talks to people. I write mails, even I keep in contact I don't have that craving. I keep in touch sort of. The last six months I have been calling my sister, because she lost her husband, so then it means more responsibility ... I don't like too much near contact with anyone. I like my independence.*

It is paradoxical that despite emphasising her independence, her behaviour indicates interdependence towards extended family members. Raaka is aware of her responsibilities towards them and fulfils her duties, not only when a sister was widowed but also in regard to her parents' residence. She invited her widowed sister to stay with her in Denmark for a period just after her husband's death. Regarding remittances, she explains about the financial support she has offered through purchasing a couple of apartments. Her husband Klaus is co-owner of the apartments, which indicates his supportive stance towards her family.

> *When we travel we take some souvenirs and small things, but it is definitely not as many other foreigners do ... What we did was, I had a necessity to find a place for my parents, because they lived with me, and I got married and I moved out and I knew that they need a place to live. So we bought, me and Klaus, two apartments actually and we settled our parents in one of them and in the new apartment my brother lived so that he could take care of them.*

An analysis of Raaka's narrative indicates her filial piety through her responsibility towards her parents, and at the same time she also shows a sense of responsibility towards some of her siblings. These coexist with a contentious relationship with her father and a couple of her brothers. Through this we can see that there can be transnational ties in particular domains of life, without frequent ongoing communication and high affective involvement with some extended family members.

7.4.3 Limited transnational connections

Nihla, who migrated to Denmark with her divorced mother and siblings, has rather limited contact with Pakistan, her country of origin, in relation to both visits and economic strategies. Her visits to her grandmother in Pakistan were infrequent due to the families' socio-economic situation and the cost of living in Denmark. As Nihla's mother also lives in Denmark and they have no contact with the divorced father in the country of origin, Nihla's transnational involvements are limited.

Nihla, however, points out that her mother telephones regularly and travels every year to Pakistan to spend time with her own mother, confirming transnational relationships with intergenerational variation. This is a pattern that is similar the earlier mentioned study of transnational Pakistani connections (Charsley, 2013) in this chapter, section 7.4. Crucial life junctures, such as the demise of parents or divorce from the coethic partner are shown to be factors that lead to less binding contact with the country of origin or to the diasporic community in the country of residence. Additionally, Charsley's study concludes that young people are likely to be less transnational than their parents, even if they develop these links later in life. This argument applies well to Nihla, however, it hardly applies to Sabita, thus challenging such generalisations.

> *I talk to them regularly and I go to Pakistan when there is an occasion 'cause you have to fit it in with other places you want to travel as well, with vacation, with job, with school you know many things, it's not always like my mum goes often I think every year, right? [Nihla asks Mads] 'Yeah' [Mads says] yeah for me I've having been there for the last three years because of the kids this and that, and before that it was maybe like every second year or something.*

At the same time Nihla expresses her longing for the country of origin, especially the culinary aspects.

> *Like my mom, when she goes to Pakistan she gets me she brings me food (laughs) because I get homesick for the food as well.*

Nihla is aware of the absence of contact between her grandparents and her children, though there is some contact with her divorced husband Mads's parents.

> *And with his grandfather really sick, they were still lucky they got to see each other often. Not often but that they had the opportunity you know,*

and they. Yeah Mads' grandmother had seen our kids like my grandmother hasn't.

For Marlik, married for 27 years, her current contact with Pakistan, her country of origin, is rather limited but there was relatively more contact and visits when her children were young. The purpose has been to confirm the family relationships as well as experience new places.

Oh I'm in contact with them, my father was a diplomat and the last post he had was in Iran, he passed away there, so when my parents were in Iran we were visiting them. When my mother was alive we visited her every second year, and my children love Pakistan (laughing). They think it was nice and different, they enjoyed it. We are from the capital city Islamabad, and from there we would go and show them different places, big cities, so they got to know that country too.

Marlik reminds us that she had no need to send remittances home as her family is well off. She also mentions how her family supported her economically at the beginning of her marital life. Her narrative illustrates the changing economic strategies with the life cycle (Levy et al., 2005).

It depends, if your family is poor like I know some from Thailand and Philippines, they send money because their family is poor, but I don't have to send them money in fact sometimes I asked them to send me some money (laughing). Because in the start I didn't have much money.

In contrast to Marlik, who currently has a limited relationship with her country of origin, Sam has not visited his country of origin for the last two decades, despite the presence of extended family there. He has, however, had some contact with family members in the UK and Canada.

To sum up, these narratives of transnationalism complicate an array of myths regarding the diasporic spouses and their relationship to their countries of origin, despite this very small and cross-sectional sample. These results are still thought-provoking, since most work on transnationalism is conducted with families where both partners are from 'elsewhere'. There is an intense and frequent transnational contact between two of the participants – Rajiv and Sabita – who can be considered as a marriage migrant and a child of first-generation migrants respectively. Another marriage migrant, Raaka, has less frequent contact with her family in India, her country of origin. This data suggests that it is the strength of the extended family relationships across the national border that influences contact, rather than the migration pattern itself.

Both Rajiv and Sabita use Internet-based communications technology – Facebook, Skype and so on – to strengthen the vertical as well as the horizontal relationships in the country of origin, emphasising the contact with their parents, grandparents, aunts and cousins. Rajiv has sustainable ties with his parents as he is involved in their welfare and in family decision-making processes. Raaka has close though not frequent contact with some members of her biological family. She and Klaus show how mixed couples can override frontiers and the control of nation states as well as break free from the conventions of the normal family as the dynamics of the world market tightens its grip on both external and internal reality (Beck & Beck-Gernsheim, 2014).

Raaka still fulfils traditions of filial piety by providing housing (apartments) for her parent and a sibling in the country of origin. Her husband Klaus is supportive of her economic strategy of helping her family. Simultaneously she supports her eldest sister at a time of crisis by inviting her to visit Denmark after her recent widowhood. Her narrative challenges media-driven stereotypes of marriages in which there is an asymmetry of rights and resources in the relationship between the sexes, with women having a lower position. These relationships across the borders confirm that transnationalism implies reciprocal sharing of the joys and sorrows across the borders and is seen among several other diasporic communities, for example among Turkish women in Denmark, who provide care and economic support to their families in the country of origin (Mirdal, 2006).

The nature of the contact also changes with the life course phase as seen in Marlik's narrative: she has been married for the past 27 years and her parents are both deceased. At the time of interview, her transnational contacts were rather limited as she only visits a sister in the UK sometimes. In the past, however, she had frequent contact and visited her parents regularly. Similarly, Nihla has limited contact with her country of origin, as her grandmother who lives there is very frail. Her own children are young, but her mother (who resides in Denmark) visits Pakistan every year, documenting intergenerational variation in transnational engagement and relationships.

We cannot generalise about the nature of transnational contact on the basis of structural categories such as type of migration, gender and socio-economic belonging only. The intersection of these categories with subjective aspects such as the nature of relationships especially the affective domain, the agency of the persons involved and the choices made is important. This is well illustrated by the narrative of Cecilia in describing her husband Sam, who was born and raised in Denmark and has almost no contact with his country of origin as his Indian parents (first generation of immigrants), chose not to maintain links with India. He has, however, visited extended family members in the UK and Canada. His infrequent contact with India may be inferred from his related to his Danish spouse Cecilia not having visited India but having ongoing contact with her sister-in-law in Canada. Sam's lack of Indian language (Hindi/Punjabi) and the current monolingualism of his young daughter may be related to the nature of his family's relative lack of transnational involvement and relationships with the parental country of origin.

Taken together, these narratives illustrate how practices and choices in a particular domain and life course phase influence and intersect with behaviour patterns and practices in other life domains and life phases. Consequently our understanding of a simplistic definition of transnationalism is challenged, as not all migrants can be considered to be diasporics and having ties with the parental country of origin as well as other countries. Maybe transnationalism is more about the quality of the contact especially the emotional, affective aspects and if it affects daily life, or whether relatives are involved in vital decisions. Should transnationalism be perceived as a dynamic, changing process depending on the life course, the nature of everyday life and the broader context as illustrated by the participants' own voices? The interactional affective processes emerge as the salient aspect of the couples' life situation rather than their objective categorisation as first-/second-generation. This has been lucidly documented by the variation in Sabita and Sam's transnational ties with their country of origin. Furthermore, research related to ethnically intermarried, mixed couples (Joshi & Krishna, 1998; Kelley & Kelley, 2012; Killian, 2013) has shown that interactional processes and personality variables play a significant part in marriage satisfaction and success, in interaction with broader aspects. The next chapter deals with the issues of mental health and wellbeing perceived within interactional framework, by bringing together the earlier mentioned 'outside' and 'inside' aspects.

8
Living 'Private Life in the Public Gaze': Mental Health and Wellbeing

One of the key issues being investigated in this book is the wellbeing of the intermarried couples in relation to various life domains. In the previous chapter, we found that these couples are influenced both by 'outside' and 'inside' aspects and in this chapter an attempt is made to bring these aspects together, among others, through the concept of *gaze*. By drawing on the narratives, I examine the mental wellbeing of the couples, not in a narrow clinical sense, but in terms of self-understanding and significant relationships.

8.1 Intersections of the private and the public: bringing the themes together

The broad context of this study includes the *gaze* to which persons who are phenotypically different to the 'white' majority population in Denmark are subjected. Mixedness is an ignored, neglected and to some extent stigmatised phenomenon. As already discussed, Danish attitudes are influenced by cultural and historical dimensions that have become taboo and largely forgotten. Only a few now will talk openly about the superiority of the white race, yet many researchers argue that earlier prejudices and stereotypes about 'race' have been substituted by a form of cultural racism (Andreassen & Henningsen, 2011). One of the basic assumptions of this book is that focus on the observable aspects of physical differences (Sengstock, 2009) including colourism, intertwined with cultural racism which is still influential in Danish public discourse.

How do these participants, as people who constitute a visible and ethnically different couple, respond to the *gaze*, and to the processes of exclusion, stigmatisation, potential pathologisation and sensationalisation? How do they prepare the next generation, among other ways by encouraging racial literacy? Attaching salience to race and ethnic differences is just one strategy, as noted by Aspinall & Song' (2013), in an analysis of mixed-race people's experiences of misrecognition. They appeal for a reconsideration, rather than assuming the automatic salience of certain race or ethnic identities over others. In line with the results of Killian's (2013) examination of the centrality of 'race' and significance attached to 'race' by the mixed couples, the following two dominant strategies are delineated. These dominant strategies are perceived as recurring patterns among the participants in the present study, taking into account the intersections with life course, parenting as well as broader context.

- Awareness, racial literacy
- Indifference

These two strategies discussed in the following sections to demonstrate how the research participants in this study employed them in their everyday lives.

8.2 A strategy of awareness and racial literacy

Raaka and Cecilia's narratives indicate an awareness of the discrimination processes they confront in different social domains such as the labour market, the stereotypical views of family members and personnel in the children's daycare institutions. They are critical about state policies related to immigration as discussed in the Chapter 7, section 7.1 reflecting similar views to the persons positioned to express the discourse 'race matters' in Killian's study (2013) discussed above. It is noteworthy that it is Raaka and Cecilia, Indian and Danish participants respectively, who point to racist incidents, as some people notice and name such incidents while others don't. Klaus, Raaka's Danish husband, hardly comments on racial discrimination, implying that some white partners employ a discourse professing a lack of awareness of the discrimination their ethnic minority partners face. Raaka and Cecilia's responses are those of people who have negative experiences related to their mixedness as a couple and a family, because they also find such experiences intrusive and suggestive of unwelcome attributions of difference, though they are no less real. At the same time it is important to note, with Dunn (1998), that there are a number of variables, such as specific context, personal, are psychological and socio-political awareness that influence the *salience and silencing* of particular identities.

Being in the family establishment phase, Raaka and Cecilia are both aware of the implications of mixed phenotypes for their children. Their young children are aged from nine months old to seven years and, as mothers, they have reflected upon ways to strengthen the children, albeit through different means. For Raaka, bilingualism and knowledge of the country of origin through primary education in India is the way ahead, while for Cecilia it is through teaching tolerance and openness to her daughters.

8.3   A strategy of indifference

Sabita, Robert, Katja and Rajiv seem to be indifferent to the *gaze*, which can be partly related to their life course phase as they have been married for a month and three years respectively and romantic love between them (Giles, 2004; Patny, 2013/1940) may be the dominant aspects of their life situation. They can be placed as couples whose narratives can be interpreted to express a 'race does not matter' discourse (Killian, 2013). In Killian's study, 14 of the 20 couples interviewed demonstrated constraining rules of non-engagement on the topics of racial difference, history and race relations.

Some examples of such rules are: pushing the topic of family history into margins at personal level; partner history, and family rituals, traditions not being brought to the couples' marriages at dyadic level, implying selective or elective amnesia; the white partner displaying a tendency to 'not notice' discourses about unequal power and privilege.

> Primarily ignoring, overlooking and underplaying the *gaze* and the other implications of racism in the short term 'may represent an adaptive strategy in a racist society, but over time such strategies can precipitate and/or sustain amorphous, conflicted, or fragmented racial and ethnic identities that can be detrimental to both the partners and the next generation of the family system'.
>
> (ibid., p. 149)

This quote from Killian presents rather pessimistic long-term consequences of ignoring or being indifferent to gaze. There are other more constructive dynamics of comprehending this indifference to 'race matters'. For example, Sabita's self-identification – as *Danish of Indian origin* and her upbringing in the international environments, attending school and an elite American University – directs our attention to following explanations for such indifference by Song & Aspinall (2012), in a British context:

1. Participants considered themselves to be 'British', regardless of 'colour'.
2. Race in cosmopolitan settings such as London, where degrees of conviviality and mixing are high, meant that being of any hue or mixture was regarded as unremarkable – in many situations at least.

These explanations cannot be transplanted into the Danish context, but Sabita's self-perception as having been born and raised in Denmark, combined with the cosmopolitanism she has encountered, can be considered as a partial reason for her not noticing the exclusionary processes and subscribing to a 'race does not matter' discourse. In addition, it should be pointed out that Sabita became aware of her 'Indianness' when she moved back to Denmark from the USA, where it formed one part of her constitution of racial identity interwoven with other dimensions of identification and belonging such as nationality, territoriality, country of origin, and membership of an urban metropolis with a cosmopolitan character. Her responses confirm that in such investigations participants' simultaneous positioning in various categories related to ethnicity, gender, socio-economic class and so on, is significant. The cosmopolitanism of an upper-class suburb in Copenhagen can hardly be questioned, but one can question how cosmopolitan the other regions of Denmark are. Besides, attaching relatively less importance to ethnicity as a dominant identity marker can be another reason for indifference to a racialising gaze. For Sabita, her life course phase and her study and work emerges as her dominant identity. For Katja as well, being in the honeymoon phase of marital life course overrides alternatives.

My analysis of the narratives show how ethnicity, gender and socio-economic belonging change the importance of other interactions and contexts such as Katja's Danish belonging and her position as a mother and a working woman. These positions gain salience at different points in the interview as she carries multiple identities. Despite these changes, some belongings become more salient than others, such as religious identity possibly being more dominant, and perceived as 'master identity', which is discussed below.

For Marlik – and to some extent for Raaka – their religious identities are paramount at the expense of their racial/ethnic identity. When focusing on them as couples, it is noticeable that for Marlik and Lars their Muslim religious identity is important, while for Raaka and Klaus their membership of a religious sect becomes salient. According to Aspinall & Song (2013), the centrality of religious identity among South Asian groups is shown in some British surveys, such as the Citizenship survey, in which a third of Pakistanis and a tenth of Indians chose it as their 'master' identity. Moreover, they note that second-generation British Muslims value both their religion *and* their nationality as Britons and do not regard the two as being in conflict with one another.

Marlik and Lars can be interpreted as placing their religious identity as central, while also attaching importance to their being Danish.

Despite the absence of comprehensive empirical studies about mixedness in the Danish context, it can be concluded that indifference to racial matters can hardly be reduced only to those which intersect with a number of other belongings. Similarly, it can be concluded that racial literacy – a conscious, critical awareness of the ways in which racism shapes and structures one's intimate life – does not come simply by being in a mixed relationship, but by attending to racial logics and practices (Twine, 2010). It is a demanding process, especially when it comes to transmitting it to the children. In Chapters 6 and 7, we see Raaka attempting to develop racial literacy in her daughter Clara.

The discussion above has reflected on the consequences of different strategies on the mental health and wellbeing of the persons involved, and argues that underplaying *gaze* and forms of racism in society may have negative consequences in the long term. The second section addresses this theme.

8.4   Mental health and wellbeing

In this study we adopt a broad definition of mental health, inspired by the WHO (World Health Organisation) formulation. According to this, mental health refers to a broad array of activities directly or indirectly related to the *mental wellbeing* component included in the WHO's definition of health: 'A state of complete physical, mental and social wellbeing, and not merely the absence of disease'. This definition encompasses the promotion of wellbeing, the prevention of mental disorders, and the treatment and rehabilitation of people affected by mental disorders.

Mental health then, is not just the absence of mental disorder. It is defined as a state of wellbeing in which every individual is encouraged to realise his or her own potential and can cope with the normal stresses of life, can work productively and fruitfully and is able to make a contribution to her or his community (WHO, 2014).

This definition can be criticised, however, for emphasising an action orientation and excluding the spiritual aspects of human existence.

I would like to explicitly include a spiritual aspect to the understanding of mental health and wellbeing. Accordingly, being mentally healthy in the present study refers to a state of psychological, social and spiritual wellbeing. It is interpreted through a sense of identity and through significant social relationships, which may involve contradictions and complexities for the intermarried couples and their children. It is also acknowledged here that physical and mental health are inextricably linked. Poorer mental health operationally defined as 'moderate' or 'languishing' can lead to increased physical health problems, time off work, limitations in people's daily lives and to poorer psychosocial functioning. As the focus here is on mental health and wellbeing, rather than on mental illness, it is relevant to consider that people with good mental health are typically able to:

a. Develop emotionally, creatively, intellectually and spiritually.
b. Take initiative to develop and maintain mutually satisfying personal relationships.
c. Encounter the problems, find solutions and learn from them. (Mental Health Foundation, Lee, 2006)

This description goes beyond a narrow understanding of mental health based on the absence of illness and psychiatric dysfunction are not considered here as this research is based on 'ordinary' mixed couples, supplemented by a couple of clinical case examples. I also include discussion of the concept of mental health promotion, which is seen as an umbrella term that covers a variety of strategies aimed at positively affecting mental health in general. The encouragement of individual resources and skills, and improvements in the socio-economic environment are among the strategies used.

In line with the above understanding of mental health promotion and inspired by the earlier mentioned study of mixed families by Caballero, Edwards & Puthussery (2008), I include individual as well as environmental aspects. This work argues that not only *interpersonal relationships* within families matter, but also that *the responses of others* to their mixedness are significant. Primary sources of distress may be related to macro-cultural or systemic influences consisting of social messages, family influences or (lack of) acceptance from the community as well as micro-cultural individual differences (Bhugra & De Silva, 2000). However, these can also function as sources of strength and comfort when family and the community network can provide support and solutions in times of crisis.

Some of the most significant issues in mixed intimate partnerships and parenting can be the responses of the others. In a study of the sociology of mental health, Simon (2007) documents a variety of social influences on subjectively experienced feelings as well as expressive behaviour and he argues that there is growing recognition that social life includes both rational and non-rational (i.e. emotional) forces as human beings are both cognitive as well as affective beings. These social influences lead to some socially disadvantaged persons – including those with lower socio-economic status and the unmarried – feeling more distressed than their more advantaged peers. At the same time he underlines complex gender differences in the experience of mental health problems. Simon finds that while women have higher rates of *internalising* emotional problems such as depression and anxiety, men have higher rates of *externalising* emotional problems such as substance abuse. The intersections of gender, race and class are an important part of the mutually constitutive 'matrix' of social categories that contribute to identities and power relation. Religion however, as a social category, is often overlooked. Such oversight can only result in limited analysis and leaves pathways to social inclusion and exclusion concealed. The issue of religious belonging is reflected in the present study to reflect the degree to which it was expressed by the participants themselves and four participants explicitly mentioned religiosity and/or spirituality in their narratives.

In this chapter we turn our attention to an analysis of mental health and wellbeing of the intermarried subjects based on their empirical narratives and expressed emotional situation. Following the life course perspective (Levy et al., 2005) mental health and wellbeing can be traced to a number of factors, among them expected life events termed *on-line markers* and *off-time markers*, non-normative transition or undesirable life events (McAdams, 2005). The off-time markers are unexpected and usually considered *stressful*. However, positive and/or negative values assigned to these life events and transition processes depends on the person's interpretation of qualitative environmental harmfulness and *environmental support* to the event.

While reflecting on the life course, it is relevant to point out that the shift to a more intimacy oriented family ideal occurred in the USA and Europe at a historical moment when the combination of declining fertility and gains in life expectancy meant that there were suddenly many years of married life during which couples were not raising children (Padilla et al., 2010, p. xxvii). In our analysis of the mental health of couples who have been married for a long period, the dynamics of relationships *aside* from parenting also become important.

The flip side of family life, invoking oppression, conflict and violence, also needs to be considered in any discussion of mental health and wellbeing of intermarried couples, even though researchers may be wary of asking questions about this area of family life. Issues of power, privilege and oppression may be involved in the everyday struggles which can constitute a dark side to the family. These struggles may be related to the active racial contexts and connected to the white privilege of one partner and the 'powerlessness' of the *other* partner (Lee, 2009 in Rastogi & Thomas). In this chapter, I address issues of privilege, equity and fairness in working with conflicts and their resolution among the mixed couples. Some narratives from the study by Rastogi & Thomas (2009) show complex emotions and processes such as internalisation of negative stereotypes and anger related to exclusionary processes, for example 'being immigrant is not as good as White', 'You are a reflection and extension of me, my trophy'. At the same time I agree with Romano, who argues that commitment to the relationship and ability to communicate are two salient factors for a successful marriage across racial and ethnic borders (Romano, 2008).

As most of the participants in the present study are 'ordinary' mixed couples rather than couples in psychosocial crisis, the focus is on positive mental health and wellbeing. This study attempts to understand their lived experiences and everyday life practices as well as their negotiation of everyday life challenges. Nonetheless, our analysis indicates some commonalities concerning conflict and different coping strategies. It may be perceived as being normative, yet we can identify some strategies that contribute to positive mental health and wellbeing involving flexibility in the gender roles as well as a focus on the 'fun' of being in a mixed relationship. However, we have to keep in mind that these strategies are dynamic and related to wellbeing through the life course. Our analytical focus here is on couples who are in the family establishing phase – not in the honeymoon nor the settled phase – and our analysis places them in the post hoc categories:

- Conflictual relations and unfulfilled expectations.
- Ambivalent relations and gender dynamics.
- Supportive relations and 'fun part' emphasis.

These categories illustrate different levels of mental health and wellbeing. As pointed out in Chapter 5, the honeymoon phase is characterised by enthusiasm, excitement and so on; the reclining phase by calmness and togetherness and a generally positive attitude towards married life, whereas the family establishing phase is characterised by greater diversity of attitudes to the marriage, related to practical as well as emotional challenges. I am aware of the diverse views and varied experiences of the intermarried couples (Kenney & Kenney, 2011, 2012) and of the methodological limitations. The interview setting may lead participants to answer in an *expected* way, which may not reflect their current situation fully. The couples in the family establishing phase are positioned in the above three categories and are discussed in detail in the next section.

8.4.1   Conflictual relationships and changing positions

In this analysis of the mental health and wellbeing of intermarried couples and their different post hoc categorisations, one of the primary categories is conflictual relationships, defined as the relationship characterised by disharmony, disagreements and destructive conflicts. Nihla and Mads are placed in this category as they are going through the process of divorce, but in-depth comment on their mental health is not possible because of the limitations of this data. The interview included both partners and the researcher did not feel able to ask a number of questions as it is a research interview and not therapy or a diagnostic interview.

Their dialogues do provide some insight into the dynamics of their identity strategies and the transformations in their positions.

In industrialised Western countries, approximately 40% of marriages end in divorce. Data from Hahlweg et al. (2010) indicates that children are involved in 70% of these divorces and about 50% of the divorces occur in the first seven years of marriage. 10–25% of couples live in stable but unhappy relationships for various reasons, including the financial implications of divorce and personal and cultural expectations. There may be an increased risk of disruption in interethnic marriages according to Kalmijn et al. (2010, 2012), and it is no surprise to find such conflicts and disruptions in intermarriages. Often, there is a pathogenic public, media as well as academic view of divorce in mixed marriages and focus may be placed upon the stresses as well as adverse outcomes associated with marital break-up. Though Hahlweg et al. (2010, p. 6) note that divorce can offer an escape from an unhappy, abusive, conflictual or demeaning marriage and can represent an opportunity to build a new, more harmonious relationship. At the same time these authors point to marital distress and destructive marital conflict as major generic risk factors for many types of dysfunction and psychopathology that may have long-lasting consequences for the children. It is thought-provoking that 75% of divorced men and 66% of women get remarried within three years with idea of building a new, more harmonious, fulfilling relationship, even though the divorce rate in second marriages is even higher than in first marriages. However, a simple unidirectional model of causality between marital distress and psychopathology is inadequate. We can though agree here that marital distress and individual disorders reciprocally influence one another.

The relationship between Nihla and Mads can be seen as indicative of negative mental health as well a desire to escape from a conflictual marriage within this theoretical framework. The transformations in Nihla's attitude towards marriage as 'a piece of paper' and Mads's interpretation of this as a rejection of their past implies a power struggle – the power to define or redefine their marriage and intentions, negotiation of truth and power positions, see chapter 5 section 5.4.2. The common objective of love, commitment and taking the marriage seriously is no longer seen in their intimate couple relationship. Using conceptualisations of passionate and companionate love (Fletcher et al., 2012), their situation may be understood as companionate love failing to develop to replace the passionate love. For Nihla, it is personality and individual aspects which play an important part in the relationship. When questioned about the effect of her migrant situation on the couple relationship, she answers:

> *I think it does has a big impact but it is hard to tell like I don't know I say you know going in to every relationship your personality plays a big role in your wants and your likes and dislikes. I think that maybe my personality played a role in my wants and needs and like yeah, I don't know if that has much to do with the fact that I am Pakistani.*

At the same time she emphasises the ethnic aspect in her self-understanding by pointing to the norm of filial piety – the adult children's duty towards the old, frail parents. She plans to take care of her divorced mother in her old age and had conveyed this to Mads during the period of their courtship.

> *Initially when we met each other before we got married, and we were very serious about getting married and all that, I told him okay one day my mum is going to get old. I may seem to look like a Danish girl I may talk and act like any other Danish girl but there is still a difference. There is*

> *still a significant difference in the way that I see my future eh and for me when my mum gets old she is not going to stay in a nursing home, she is going to stay with me, and there is no way in hell she's going to live alone and not doing okay.*

In light of Nihla's narratives, we hear that Mads interprets her as changed from *being very Pakistani to less Pakistani*, and this also indicates the split between them and the change in their previously well-understood positions. Now Nihla explains that the institution of marriage was a means of legitimising their living together, as cohabitation was not acceptable to her mother and the extended family.

> *... we got married after knowing each other for a really short time eh and for me it was a question of having defined marriage as a relationship that is certified okay? Eh and for me if that paper makes it easier eh for us to live together then why not get it?*

We can interpret that personal and cultural differences are intertwined in Nihla and Mads's understandings and everyday practices. When questioned about Mads's qualities, Nihla's answer further illustrates this complexity by describing his positive qualities of being composed and protective towards her:

> *...qualities about Mads, eh that's a tough one in the middle of a divorce... there is something very calm about him, always be cool, calm, collected...Mads, through these eight years has been my 'magic eight ball'...Mads, represents the society where you don't necessarily need to get married.*

Nihla's attitude towards marriage becomes explicit when she responds to a question about the increased media focus on marriages between Danes and partners from less-rich countries. Using the example of Thai women in Denmark, she underlines reciprocity and perceptions of women's motive of having a better life for themselves and their children.

> *... But in this sense the guy has a need for something, and the girl is giving it to him, and she needs something else and you know it's an exchange of goods. And that happens in any relationship, and they do it to survive, a little more than survive but create a better life for their kids.*

More focused queries about their own everyday life and the issues involved in parenting directs our attention towards conflicts and attempts at negotiation. The classic issue of 'circumcision of male children' and 'pork eating' gain salience in Nihla and Mads's negotiation of mixedness. These religious-based practices symbolise their own socialisation and have deep meaning for her.

> *About the 'snap' I think like about the circumcision, like Mads, didn't see any point of this, whereas for me it's like eating pork. You know it's not like, it's like not eating pork it's something that I'm yeah I have been brought up with this notion that that is what you should be doing. And then there is some scientific evidence thing that it is more hygienic . . . somebody had to win that battle.*

For Nihla as a Muslim, the circumcision of a male infant – a custom that is virtually non-existent among the Christian majority population in the Scandinavian countries – is significant, while Mads, as a Christian finds it irrelevant. For Jews, as for Muslims living in Scandinavia, circumcision is a powerful and irreversible identity marker, especially if the father is born (and thus, circumcised) in a mixed marriage between a Jew and a non-Jew. The general rule seems to be 'like father, like son' (Dencik, 2009, p. 84). Thus the conflicts between Nihla and Mads become understandable when contextualised through comparison with Jewish intermarriages and the issue of circumcision in Scandinavia. However, it should be noted that for Mads as a Christian, this practice is not important. As mentioned in Chapter 6, in line with Daneshpour (2009), I argue that these parenting conflicts reflect deeper philosophical value disagreements which have not been resolved between Nihla and Mads.

The destructive conflicts on these issues reflect contradictions and ambivalences when Nihla negates the ethnic belonging as a reason for the conflictual relationship, while at the same time pointing towards the essential Pakistani aspect in her. In the beginning of her relationship with Mads, one possible interpretation is that her initial focus is on unique individual aspects of her partner, his personality, in the relationship, pointing towards the colour-blind ideology (see Chapter 2).

Intersectionality could be useful in comprehending the conflicts between these young partners, where the categories of ethnic belonging intersect with gender, age and individual qualities and are transformed with the passage of time. Nihla's own essentialising of her ethnicity by considering herself 'Pakistani' in the beginning and later rejecting ethnicity as a basis for interpersonal conflicts, confirms the dynamic nature of these concepts.

> *Probably, that I don't see our relationship being like Mads, being Danish and me being Pakistani, not at all. For me, he could Egyptian and I could be the same I mean I don't think it would matter ... In the beginning I used to say that you know what we may not be able to hear it or see it, but I am Pakistani (laughs). It [is] hidden underneath all this Danish culture.*

She addresses most of their differences to diverse cultural understandings, yet the ethnic aspect of their intimate marriage problems is rejected. This is a common feature in the narratives and reflects contradictions and complexities for the intermarried couples and their children. In some ways her narrative reflects a *race does not matter* discourse. There is some kind of separation between cultural differences in general and the specifics of intimate relations in the narratives. This dichotomy and separation between cultural differences in general and the participants' own ethnic belongings, has been perceived as a 'survival strategy' or defence mechanism by Romain (1996).

On the whole, these transformations in identity strategies, combined with the conflicts related to culture-specific issues such as circumcision and eating pork, have led to receding commitment and not 'taking the marriage seriously'. The consequent disruption and dissolution of the marital relationship has resulted in divorce. At the same time, it is noticeable that there is almost no mention of the 'fun part' of the differential belonging in Nihla and Mads's narratives. As earlier mentioned, the empirical methodical limitations hardly provide a basis for casting light on the deeper power dynamics and the part played by the 'the significant others' regarding the conflictual situation.

8.4.2   Ambivalent relations and gender position

Using the concepts of systemic macro- and micro-cultural influences that ethnic intermarried couples may experience, we can focus on family members and social reactions to the marriage. An analysis of Cecilia's narrative indicates that her mental health is characterised by limited wellbeing and implicit conflicts.

Cecilia expressed awareness of different patterns of romantic love relations in her Danish family and in her spouse Sam's Indian family, in which one would expect not to bring a person home until it was certain that they were the right person.

I didn't plan it. I didn't plan to marry an Indian guy. We fell in love, and then we took it one step at a time. I think it was more difficult for Sam than for me, because they have other traditions than in my home ... so I didn't meet his family for quite a long time, which for me was a little bit difficult to understand.

At the same time, Cecilia describes her mother's initially sceptical views and fears towards her 'foreign' boyfriend. It was rather unexpected for her mother, who had lived in an 'old-fashioned' manner, without much international exposure. This attitude changed after she met Sam, but her initial reluctance to accept him reflects the overall community discourse to intimate partnership across ethnic borders which is dominated by negative stereotypes of ethnic minority fathers 'kidnapping' their children and implies the concept of border-patrolling mentioned in Aspinall & Song (2013). Discussions in Chapter 2 show how this attitude is prevalent in Denmark and a preference for homogamy reflects a belief that whiteness is normative and the standard, and that ethnic minority people should marry other ethnic minority people.

Before I met Sam I was raised very old-fashioned Danish, I would say. My entire family was Danish with old-fashioned traditions you know. Really, really Danish. And I remember when I met Sam for the first time, my mom was shocked actually, when she found out that he was not Danish: 'Are you sure that that is what you want and do you know about his culture, do you know about his background?' And she was scared out of her mind, I mean she was thinking that 'oh if you have children with him, he will take them away from you, and you will never see them again'.

However, Cecilia points out that Sam was born and raised in Denmark, which made it quite easy for them. Mentioning her sharing of experiences with a Canadian sister-in-law married to Sam's cousin in Canada, she explains the problematic aspects involved in being a daughter-in-law in an Indian family. These issues are also raised in Joshi & Krishna's (1998) article about English and North American daughters-in-law in Hindu families. Issues of deference to elderly family members, gender roles in various domains, food-related customs (such as serving males first), negotiation of privacy and intimacy, shared care and extended families' 'protective care' can be potentially problematic for them. However, these authors also emphasise the cultural and psychodynamic benefits of cross-cultural marriages, especially in relation to the reframing mechanisms (referring to Paris & Guzder, 1989), and point out that most of these marriages were successful. Cecilia voices her difficulties in being in the position of daughter-in-law with differential expectations:

> *But of course there are differences, and sometimes it is difficult to be the one, the wife of a son, an Indian son especially, I guess.*

Furthermore, Cecilia discussed the particular family dynamics related to her mother-in-law's early widowhood and her resulting responsibility for raising two sons as a single mother. She notes her understanding of the Indian 'division of labour' in a household, which is stereotypical and 'old-fashioned' according to her narrative. In addition, she refers to the mother's and mother-in-law's common experience of being a widow.

> *But Sam has a very strong mother and she means the world to him and his brother, and, she became a widow quite early as well, as my mom. But she did everything for her boys and she still does . . . .*

> *Coming from his background, the woman does do all the practical stuff. I mean it is still a little bit old-fashioned.*

Although Cecilia is able to add nuances to her stereotypical understanding of the gender-based division of household chores, these patterns are a source of considerable ambivalence and psychological conflict for her. They reflect a deep-seated idea of difference.

> *So, that I would guess that a Danish mother would have raised her son a little bit different, but I don't know, because you know sometimes when I speak to my Danish friends whom are married to Danish guys, it is sometimes the same.*

Discussing statutory parental leave for their nine-month-old daughter, Cecilia wishes that Sam would take part of the leave, yet she understands his limitations and her own wish to be with their infant daughter. According to Danish law, the father of a newborn has a right to two weeks' leave, while the rest of the period of six months can be shared between the parents. She doesn't see the point in Sam taking leave during the six months, yet she mentions it as a kind of paradox and defends their position. This is one of the reasons that she has been analytically positioned in the ambivalent category. On the one hand she wants to be a good mother, taking care of the children without temporal restrictions, but on the other hand she wants her husband to be there as an active parental figure, which creates a dilemma for her.

This ambivalence characterises Cecilia's attitudes in a number of life domains and it affects her wellbeing. She expresses these decisions as her own choice yet she still aspires to gender equality. Her gender function positioning illustrates the dilemma between the dominant social discourse of gender equality in parenting, shown by statutory paternal leave and her current situation of being the sole caretaker and 'stay-at-home mother' which she tolerates and passively accepts. Economic aspects, such as Sam's position as a managing director, also play a part in understanding this situation. She uses humour to explain the situation, yet some contradictory aspects of symbolic violence and tendencies of oppression can be interpreted in her narrative.

I mean, of course that I wish that he would take maybe one month, maybe two months, but it should not be because I want him to. Because, I would love to have the full maternity leave, because I love to spend time with the girls, you know. So, sometimes of course when you hear your friends saying: 'my husband is taking the next two months of the maternity leave'. I go, 'oh I wish it was my husband'. But on the other hand, Sam is Sam, and I knew who he was before I married him, and I would like my kids to survive (laughing).

Normatively she uses humour to avoid a problematic subject position related to gender equality position with her husband like those of her friends. In the same breath, Cecilia points out that she is accepted by her husband Sam's family and her family has accepted Sam, yet there are a few examples of togetherness and she underlines her mother-in law's ambivalence towards her. The issue of ethnic background is brought to the forefront as she mentions her mother-in-law's assumed expectation of an Indian daughter-in-law. When Cecilia questioned her about this issue, the mother-in-law focused on her son's happiness rather than ethnicity. This dialogue indicates a positive vertical relationship – a relatively harmonious relationship between the two generations. The conflicts between Cecilia and her mother-in-law are resolved as there are negotiations and dialogue based on reciprocal respect for the differential socialisations they have experienced. However, from the earlier analysis see chapter 6, section 6.1 we can recollect the conflicts and concerns related to everyday life, such as food consumption practices and language at home.

We are very blessed: we have family that has accepted me and on this side and my family has accepted him ... there are differences, because I have been raised one way and Sam has been raised another way, but of course that my mother-in-law is very Danish, but she is also Indian. And of course sometimes, it comes to the surface and we do not always agree, because I am a strong woman, and I know what I want ... I mean that I guess that she deep down dreamt about her son marrying an Indian girl. And I guess I asked her actually one time, and she said that: 'what means most to me is that Sam is happy'. And that has been in the back of my mind, so any differences we have had, has always been solved.

Cecilia is not completely satisfied with all aspects of her marriage, including her relationship with her mother-in-law.

However, the mother-in-law emphasised her son's happiness as being paramount and thus accepts Cecilia, despite her belonging to the ascribed ethnic category Danish. Cecilia's mental health and wellbeing is also influenced by negative stereotypes and the dominant political discourse about ethnic minorities in Denmark.

When asked about the feeling of 'being looked at' as an visibly ethnically mixed couple, she defends herself and Sam from this broad discourse by emphasising that the harsh negative stereotypes apply to other ethnic minority groups, not Indians. She adds nuance to his ethnic background, making it acceptable that they are together. She is aware of her husband's *otherness* but downplays it. This strategy can be interpreted as a 'rationalisation' defence mechanism to cope with a difficult and anxiety-provoking situation. Cecilia emphasises that these systemic and macro-cultural influences do not affect her everyday life, yet she reflects about them.

In general I think that, if I should be quite frank, that the Danish people should be ashamed of the politics we have in Denmark in regard to foreign people. I think that relations between especially Muslims and other cultures have been quite dramatic in the last 4–5 years, and, and I think it is a shame that one party in Denmark has that kind of power.

I think that sometimes people look at us. But, I guess that the fact that he is Indian makes it a little bit easier actually. I think it has been difficult if he was from Iraq or Iran with another background.

Cecilia expresses the 'fun aspect' of her interethnic marriage, and refers to the process of finding similarities in spite of difference. She notes the possibility of travelling to different countries around the world where various family members reside. This implies transnational ties in other countries.

> *I guess that the fun is that you find out that it is actually not that different and in any family, the base is love... We have a large family and we can travel round the world and see his family, and I find that a gift as well.*

On the whole, ambivalence and dilemmas characterise Cecilia's mental health and wellbeing as she is simultaneously influenced by her own conflicting attitudes and those of Sam's mother. Conflicting discourses about gender equality, of being a good mother and a housewife are key here, however, Cecilia is able to negotiate to some extent with her mother-in-law, though less so with her husband, and she manages the situation by taking decisions like being a stay-at-home mother and describing them as being her own choice, thus negating cultural aspects.

This analysis indicates some traces of psychological oppression and economic power strategies in Cecilia's coping with the challenges of marriage, which affect her wellbeing to some extent. With some negotiation, humour, realistic awareness of economic factors and acceptance of power imbalance, she is able to manage an everyday life and conflicts with ambivalence. She is both positive about the decisions as her own, yet defensive and uncomfortable about not having a job and about her husband's limited participation in parenting the children. Thus, on the whole, the institution of marriage is not a threat for Cecilia, despite some tendencies towards internalising psychological problems.

8.4.3 Supportive relationships and emphasis on the 'fun part'

Rajiv and Katja displayed a high level of positive mental health and wellbeing at the time of the interview. Rajiv mentions his first homogamous marriage in India, which lasted one-and-a-half years and ended in a divorce, saying, 'we were too young'. He learnt from the experience and became a different person. Now he emphasises that he does not have worries about his and Katja's relationship as a couple, indicating marital satisfaction and wellbeing, which can be understood in the biographical context of the welcome he experienced on his arrival in Denmark.

> *For me it wasn't even a big move, because it wasn't a cultural shock... I think that I have blended nicely, it [her family] was so kind,*

they were so kind all her friends and they welcomed me, and that was really cool. The first few friends I had were her friends, alright. And, then so that, I have just... It has really strengthened this.

His positive reception by the Danish in-laws, combined with current regular contact with her family and friends has supported his wellbeing. It is further strengthened by his contact with his family of origin through Skype and other means and through visits to India. As a marriage migrant he is susceptible to a number of acculturative stresses related to migration and resettlement that impact on some people (Greenman, Young & Johnson, 2009), but the positive relations, inclusion and welcome has become a source of strength. However, it is worth noting that during the first phase, Rajiv used a strategy of withdrawal, which he felt was acceptable due to the space and openness in the Danish society.

In the beginning I had this habit of actually withdrawing... I was like in the shell, but I enjoyed that. Because in Denmark you can really have a lot of space, it is quiet here and I enjoy it, I have so much space and time to do my thing, read and music and these things.

Gradually he felt included and developed a sense of belonging to Denmark. He stated that after a hectic trip to India he considered his home was Denmark and India was now a place he visited.

We hadn't really had any quiet time and it was and that was the first time I really felt that 'oh now we are going home – (ohm)'. And that really, like wow did I really say that? Yes we are going home and this is home. India is the place where I visit family and friends.

Possibly Rajiv has found a 'hiding place', a place to 'relax' in Denmark, associated with wellbeing and satisfaction with new beginnings. We can recollect Marlik's narratives, who did not find the same enjoyment in being alone in a new country, and Raaka who moved to Denmark to get away from the relational pressures in her country of origin. Their narratives indicate different motives and different life strategies to cope with the initial phase of adapting to a new country.

Considering factors related to micro-cultural individual differences mentioned earlier, Rajiv is highly appreciative of his wife's accepting attitude, calmness and her positive outlook on life, which forms the basis for living life at the same pace and sharing similar life goals.

> *Okay, one is calmness. I have never seen her angry till today. You know her anger is if she, if she gets angry, she will just become quiet and then cry for two minutes and that is the only anger I have seen. She never gets angry or shouts, or uses harsh words, so that is the biggest human quality if you don't get angry, because in yoga, you know I teach a lot about that...She finds a bright side to everything, always. That is very beautiful and she is all the time focusing on the beautiful and being positive, so these are the basic yeah, fundamental qualities that I appreciate.*

Their sense of wellbeing is further reflected by his expression of *perfection* regarding their relationship, engaging in activities together and their agreement on how to socialise their daughter Sonia. Katja expresses her concern about future potential disagreements regarding their daughter's freedom, though appreciates that he doesn't *push* her right now. Rajiv is aware of the challenges related to their differences of opinion on issues such as bilingualism and the limited chance of his daughter Sonia learning her father's mother tongue in Denmark see chapter 6, section 6.5. Still, Rajiv and Katja agree to create choice for their child and subjective experiences such as making the best of potential. Concepts such as *destiny* are present in their narrative. Katja mentions her parents' unhappy marriage and highlights the significance of interpersonal relationships for a sense of marital harmony and fulfilment.

> *I didn't maybe have the best starting point from my parents in the sense that that was not a very happy marriage...I think that we are on the same pace right now, totally. We have the same dreams and priorities. We have the same pace...yeah...it is perfect...it is very special, it is very unique, and it has become like that naturally. I think that both of us are doing what we are destined to do.*

Against the *backdrop* of these narratives, it is noticeable that Katja emphasises the absence of problems in their own couple relationship, implying fulfilment of sexual desire and romantic love, leading to a positive interpersonal relationship and marital satisfaction – in spite of structural hindrances. She appreciates her husband's flexibility regarding his gender function position, thus overcoming the systemic and macro-cultural difficulties through negotiating the micro-cultural aspects. They aim to create balance between individualism on one side and being part of a couple and society on the other.

> ... *Quite a few of our friends have a lot of problems but luckily we haven't experienced anything like that....I have a husband who is very flexible, who can bring and pick up the child from the daycare, he takes part in everything and we are very equal and...it's not like, he is not traditional in that aspect at all, he is the one that cooks as well so it's very yeah there is no stereotypes there.*

Katja emphasises the fun aspect of their marriage, describing it as being on a 'vacation', while she regards Danish-Danish marriages as being boring, predictable and routine. She adds that in contrast, their marriage offers a number of opportunities and possibilities, especially related to international experiences and to open, cosmopolitan strategies.

> ... *it's super exciting and we both really love to make a lot of plans, doing things, so that's, my mum always told me that there is an everyday life as well, but we always feel like we are on a vacation (laughing) so that's really nice...but I mean now we have all options open in the sense that we can stay here for more or less so long as we want to, as long as we follow the rules of course, and eh we can go to India and that's as much home as staying here or we can go to a third place, and I think it's probably much easier for us to go abroad than for others Danish-Danish couples in the sense that we have a lot of [experience] in going abroad and we make sure that we have long holidays every year (laughing) it's good.*

Focusing on the strength of mixed marriages is another strategy to avoid problematic positioning. Cultural differences are not presented as problems within Rajiv and Katja's narratives, but are identified as enrichment or as the 'fun' part in the marriage. Their experiences are categorised as positive aspects of being a mixed couple, as an alternative to the problematic, worrying and pathologising discourse delineated in Chapter 1 & 2.

Of course people notice them, their phenotype differences, the observable character of physical differences including skin colour and hair (primarily Rajiv's) and other's responses have been discussed in Chapter 7. In their everyday life, these are narrated as positive differences, whereas Cecilia does not like how the nursery teachers think about her and her husband and her perception that they position them in 'cultural boxes' which assume gender inequality. The fun is *because of*, not despite, cultural differences and/or because of partners' *otherness*.

To be different, as described by these couples, demands adjustment in their everyday lives. Intermarriage is perceived as an optimistic experiment that makes the relationship especially lively and interesting (Beck-Gernsheim, 2002, p. 135) and this conceptualisation of intermarriage is illustrated by how the participants talk about the 'fun part' of being married to a foreigner or a visibly ethnic minority person.

Although one can get the impression that the focus on 'fun' and 'open options' implies an overlooking of the problematic subject positions, this hardly seems to be the case for Rajiv and Katja. Their positive mental health is related to marital satisfaction and wellbeing and can be understood through both their systemic, interpersonal and personal factors. The process of 'getting together', the early welcome and the current relationship with both families, flexibility in the gender positions and focus on the 'fun' aspect of intermarriage are all important along with an awareness of structural limitations. Invoking the concept of the *liability of foreignness* delineated in the previous chapter, which refers to the difficulties spouses can face in entering the labour market of the country of residence (Irastorza & Devoretz, 2009) it can be argued that Rajiv has relatively low liability on the adaption side due to his professional competencies in the health sector as a yoga teacher. He has also felt welcome (a favourable integration environment), which has contributed to his mental wellbeing and also indicates a high likelihood of marriage survival, marital harmony and satisfaction.

This conclusion has valuable implications for sustaining wellbeing in such intimate partnerships for counselling as well as psychotherapy. Analysing good practice in the everyday lives of 'ordinary' couples can contribute to further development of psychosocial services for supporting such couples as well mixed families and this is covered in Chapter 9.

In this analysis of mental health and wellbeing of the participants in the empirical study, two overarching themes related to ethnic hierarchies and the significance of love emerges. In the last section of this chapter, I further analyse these two themes.

8.5 Overarching themes: stereotyping, racial and ethnic hierarchies

Even though love is narrated as being colour blind, and therefore raised above ethnicity or race, these categories can refer to discourses about love in a less positive way. When compared with other couples, intermarried couples are exposed to both prejudices viewed with suspicion, as well as ethnic and racial hierarchies, as well as to challenges based on notions about 'true' love.

Beck & Beck-Gernsheim (1995), taking a sociological point of view, suggest that love has become a 'new religion' in the privacy of the home or in the office of divorce lawyers and marriage counsellors. This is a relevant point within this context. The transformation process towards individualisation opens up the possibility of new identities which have huge implications for people's experience of personal stability. Following this thought, discourses of love build a regime of truth wherein certain forms of marriage can be legitimated and justified on the behalf of others. Examples of stereotyped narratives about other intermarried couples confirm this point. Bech-Jørgensen calls this the exercise of symbolic power. By drawing upon dominant discourses of love and marriage, power is acquired to organise the dominant understanding of the world (Bech-Jørgensen, 1994, p. 18).

> Lars, the eldest Danish participant states: *There is a huge difference in intermarriages between Thai and Pakistani people [Danes marrying]. The Thais do need the marriage more, and will do everything for their husbands, when they finally move to Denmark, then the husband acts in a totally different way, and then the marriage falls apart. It is different with a Muslim, because it is not that easy for a Dane to marry within that culture, you have to convert to Islam, etc. So I would without a doubt prefer arranged marriages. There are many Danish men whom travel to Thailand to 'buy a slave', and many marriages fall apart because other people judge them. If the couples meet each other in the country [where they both live] then most of them succeed.*

We see from this quote that an array of categories are mixed up in the telling of stories of intermarriage, locality, religion and gender. Baagøe Nielsen & Gitz-Johansen (2006) have analysed the differential expectations and power struggles between Danish men and their spouses from countries such as Thailand, while Spanger (2013) has written about the many meanings ascribed to love by female Thai migrants selling sex and concludes that to a certain extent, the borders between migration, sex work and marriage are fluid. According to Lars, however, for a long-lasting intermarriage, it is the same religion and country of residence that matter, and he devalues an intermarriage between a Thai woman and a Danish man. In the narrative, Lars places himself in a less troublesome position by identifying another kind of intermarriage

(Thai female to Danish male) as problematic. He sees this as partly due to the comparative ease of getting married, the element of inequality and not knowing each other before the marriage. It is illogical that he supports arranged marriages but is critical over this form of marriage. A further problematic factor is the judgemental attitude towards such marriages that Lars has expressed very directly. Analysis of Lars's narratives combined with the findings from studies such as Baagøe Nielsen & Gitz-Johansen (2006), Osanami Törngren (2011) and Spanger (2013), lead to the conclusion that there are ethnic and religious hierarchies – albeit fluid – within discourses of intermarriages in Denmark (as well as the rest of Scandinavia) challenging the dominant discourse of egalitarianism and homogeneity.

This perspective offers us a way to perceive marriage in society and makes explicit the identification with *true romantic love* that has become a social discourse, which characterises modern society, implies exclusion of some groups.

The participants in this study are 'stakeholders' in 'romantic love' as they point out their experiences of love and thus create equality in the narratives. One doesn't have to be Danish to be in a romantic love relationship and Giles (2004) has documented the universality of romantic love, even though debates in the Danish media appear to deny this. The categorisation of *us* and *others* implies that 'forced marriages' and 'arranged marriages' in the Western understanding are not based on love, thus denying 'love' to some groups. Emphasising love becomes a way to legitimise intimate couple relationships and to allow the inclusion of a cultural narrative about love marriage which avoids potential exclusion.

Such stereotypes and categories direct our attention to 'visible differences' – the observable character of physical differences and the attention visibly different couples receive from external sources. Invoking Katja's narratives, we can see her realistic attitude to hers and Rajiv's visibility and the problems faced by intermarried couples in Denmark. She mentions being subjected to *gaze* of others, both in the country of residence and Denmark and in India.

> . . . we *look different and that is interesting, but not in a negative way, not in a judgmental way, I mean people notice us of course . . . both in Denmark and in India.*

Katja also mentioned her friend commenting on Rajiv as 'black', thus focusing on his phenotype, though this term is used as an umbrella term in political sense in the UK, and to some extent also in the academic arena in Denmark.

> *...she was like 'oh my god he is Black' and then she told me and I was like 'okay that's really weird' what does she expect, he is from India so yes he is black, so that's the only thing that I really noticed.*

She also mentions her partner's situation in the labour market and the difficulty of getting a job corresponding to his competence.

> *...as a foreign partner is very hard to be in Denmark and it is based on well they can't get a job and they can't do what they really want to and they feel that they have the competences of doing something.*

8.5.1   Overarching theme: in the name of love

The romantic love discourse can legitimise a minority position. As Marlik argues, one is not a guest worker or an immigrant when one has moved to a country because of 'romantic love'.

> *I'm not a guest worker, I came here because I fell in love with a man and that is it, so in that way my relationship has been very natural, it could have been anywhere.*

Marlik is both critical and nuanced about so-called 'marriages of convenience' and commercially arranged marriages that take place between the women from the Global South and men from Denmark (Baagøe Nielsen & Gitz-Johansen, 2006). She attempts to find positive emotions in such relationships.

> *They* [the females] *come from Thailand and the Philippines... and can't speak the language, coming from small towns, very poor. The woman needs a better life, the man needs someone who can take care of the home. You can call it convenience marriage from both sides. I don't think that they have so many problems, there must be love there as well.*

This significance attached to romantic love in perceiving other couples and the commonality of 'falling in love' explicitly expressed in the couples' getting together, as discussed in Chapter 4, directs attention towards this phenomenon of love linked to sexual desire (Giles, 2008). At a sociological level, the emergence of romantic love is linked with the rise of the 'narrative of the self' type of self-identity. The discourse of romantic love is said to have developed from the late eighteenth century (Giddens, 1992). He notes that that romanticism, the eighteenth- and nineteenth-century European macro-level cultural movement, is responsible for the emergence of the novel – a relatively early form of mass media. The growing literacy and popularity of novels fed back into the mainstream lifestyle and the romantic novel proliferated the stories of ideal romantic life narratives on a micro-level, giving romantic love an important and recognised role in the marriage-type relationship. He even asserts that intimate social relationships have become 'democratised', so that the bond between the marital partners has little to do with external laws, regulations or social expectations, but is based on the internal understanding between two people – a trusting bond based on emotional communication. Where such a bond ceases to exist, modern society is generally happy for the relationship to be dissolved.

Though the present study doesn't support the above assertion that 'outside' aspects such as the legal regulations are not important, the narratives of the mixed couples show that the marital bonds between the spouses are highly significant for their mental health and wellbeing. Moreover, Giddens's assertion about 'happy societal acceptance of relationship dissolution' is rather problematic.

However, in current Danish society, dissolution of marriage is an acceptable possibility for Nihla and Mads, as their relationship is characterised by destructive conflicts and disharmony, implying that the emotional bond–companionate love (Fletcher et al., 2013) – has ceased to exist between them.

On the other hand, analysis of the data placed Rajiv and Katja in the category of supportive relationships as they are perceived to experience positive mental health characterised by an emotional bond as well as companionate love. Their focus is on the 'fun part' of being together, and on the supportive exchanges and relationships with the extended families of both spouses. Furthermore, a perception of creativity and broad possibility is a characteristic of persons placed in within the supportive relationship category. The gendered position as partly stay-at-home father is subjectively perceived of as the result of time schedule flexibility and the extended family, and the network of friends are seen as accepting, curious and welcoming. Similarly (Root, 2001) observes that blending into a family implies shared definitions of family, network, expectations of closeness, positive attitude and the openness of the extended family. Katja and Rajiv's focus on *universal morality* indicates thinking beyond ethnic categories to being a part of the community of humanity and elements common with Ali's discussion of a post-race focus (Ali, 2003). Congruently, a focus on the 'fun part' highlights positives and opportunities, such as increased choices in food, greater creativity and contact with relatives in two countries, as expressed by Katja and Rajiv. This is an example of a positive way that being in a mixed couple may contribute to positive mental health. For Lars and Marlik, the dominant discourse of love plays a salient part and *in the name of love* they position themselves as different from other couples (particularly Thai-Danish), while simultaneously emphasising the negative stereotypes which they refute in relation to themselves.

A cosmopolitan approach to being in a mixed relationship implies a transcendence of the narrow categorisation of *us* and *others* and focuses on the commonality of being a member of the human community. This approach could be recommended for couples for whom there is an exaggerated focus on the difference. Furthermore, foregrounding the 'fun part', the positive and creative aspects expressed by the participants in the study, shows the importance of this way of thinking as a resource for mixed couples.

In the last section of this chapter we can sum up by emphasising that the broad analysis of the mental health and wellbeing of the mixed couples indicates a continuum from conflictual, contentious relations to relationships characterised by harmony. The sense of fulfilment some achieve implies this continuum from poor mental health to positive mental health and wellbeing. Both the personal and the social – families and network – influence wellbeing. The *internal*, personal and family aspects, such as realising plans, mixing everyday practices and focusing on the 'fun part', are in interplay with *external* aspects such as formal and informal acceptance of the intermarriage in society, dominant gender roles, recognition and inclusion. The positive aspects on both levels contribute to the couples' wellbeing. The overarching salience of ethnic stereotypes as well as their hierarchical placing and romantic love, points to the commonalities among the mixed couples, despite variations in their mental health and wellbeing.

In the Danish context, where issues of mixedness are largely marginalised, counselling therapy services which are sensitive to mixed relationships and mixed parentage are needed. A focus on managing the practices and conditions of everyday life, not just as an abstraction but as concrete decisions and actions, are also suggested as a part of counselling. In line with the intersectionality framework in the present study, Rastogi & Tomas (2009) argue that in psychotherapy with multicultural couples multiple areas of diversity intersect with each other and should be considered at every step of couple counselling. Furthermore, they pinpoint reflection and gaining skills on how to form the all-important alliances with couples in the context of both the counsellors and therapists. These multilayered and complex realties taken up in detail in the final chapter which may be considered as the applied part of the book.

9
Implications for Strengthening Mixed Partnering and Parenting: Counselling and Psychotherapy

This final chapter is the result of many epistemological as well as ethical reflections and brings insights from my clinical practice into this research. Besides working as an academic since 2000, in the Department of Psychology and Educational Studies at Roskilde University along with affiliation to Interdisciplinary Studies in Health Promotion and Health Strategies, for the past three decades I have been working as a clinical psychologist, providing counselling and psychotherapy. My clients have included, among others, ethnically mixed couples and families, ethnic minority youths, their families and transnational adoptees. It has been a challenge to combine the research-based results from the present study focussing on 'ordinary', intermarried couples with positive mental health and wellbeing, with insights from my psychosocial practice. A survey about the psychotherapeutic activities of psychologists in Denmark (Jacobsen, Nielsen & Mathiesen, 2013) in a Danish psychological journal *Psykolog Nyt*, made me aware that just 2% of psychologists in Denmark have a Ph.D. degree along with a specialisation in psychotherapy Thus only a few psychologists possess "double competence" which combines clinical practice experiences with research experience. Besides it was pointed that about 7% have a minority background like me while 93% have majority Danish background. At the same time significance of qualitative research in enhancing counselling and psychotherapy has been highlighted emphatically by McLeod, 2012. This has convinced me that using the lived experience of intermarried clients along with empirical study results would be useful as a source of knowledge for readers from both the academic and practice fields.

The term *psychosocial intervention* is used an umbrella term which includes both counselling and psychotherapy. The former tends to be problem-based and shorter term, while the latter is more concerned with personal insights – there is, however, a lot of overlap (Singla, 2004, p. 284). Dissemination of psychosocial intervention experiences related to mixed couples in Denmark became very important when I contacted other mental health service providers. This exploration revealed that there are services offering couple therapy and educational courses for couples including PREP (Prevention and Relationship Enhancement Program), among others (Center for Familieudvikling, 2014). There is no particular focus on mixed couples, couples across ethnic and national borders, however, practitioners reported that 'we treat them like any other couple', demonstrating the dominant discourse of colour blindness within the field of psychosocial services.

While reflecting on these issues and on my practice-based experiences, I was immensely inspired by Murphy-Shigematsu (2002), a mixed Japanese-American professor, whose moving descriptions of multicultural encounters are based on his own case narratives from counselling practice. He poignantly appeals for the dissemination of a combination of theoretical and practical knowledge, in order to improve the conditions for professional counsellors, psychotherapists, psychologists and other scholars of the phenomenon, as well as for the clients. According to him, counselling is an encounter that involves the self-understanding of the counsellor as much as that of the client, as also stated by Jung in: 'The psychotherapist, however, must understand not only the patient; it is equally important that he understands himself' (Jung, 1965, p. 134). Murphy-Shigematsu explains his approach to counselling and criticises the narrow Western/American counselling practice:

> Counselling is presented as a powerful way of assisting human development through challenging and reworking old and established patterns of experiencing self, others and the world... Counsellors [in mainstream American practice] are trained to strive to make clients more independent, told never to give advice, advised to avoid self-disclosure, and warned not to accept gifts. But these kinds of guidelines are based on cultural values that are not shared by everyone. In my work with people of different cultural backgrounds I have violated all of the above rules when it seemed to be appropriate for effective therapy.
>
> (Murphy-Shigematsu, 2002, p. 103)

As discussed above, working with mixed couples involves values and practices which are not part of mainstream Western understandings in a professional context (in which ethnic minority groups are not endowed with the cultural traits that have been imposed upon them in a rigid and stereotypical way). Thus the cases presented here take into account diverse world-views and aim to avoid distancing and objectifying individuals or relying on stereotypes of other cultures.

German and other European contexts are relevant regarding the enhancement of couple relationships and prevention of couple distress (Hahlweg et al., 2010). They argue that the field of couple therapy and preventative work has made great strides over the past decades and practice innovations continue to evolve as theoreticians, researchers and clinicians employ research findings to benefit couples and families. Although these views can be critiqued as modernist, they are not irrelevant – persuasive research and practice-based knowledge should be disseminated. It is imperative to provide support to strengthen and promote mental health among couples, especially intermarried couples, who are a relatively ignored group in this field. For all these reasons I have decided to include two cases from my practice at the non-governmental organisation (NGO), which fulfilled the criterion used in the research study – that one of the spouses is of South Asian heritage and the other originates from Denmark, thus comprising a visibly ethnically different couple in the current Danish context.

Before presenting the cases, a few lines about the NGO I have been associated with are required. TTT (Transcultural Therapeutic Team) works with ethnic minority youths and their families and was established in Copenhagen in 1991 (Arenas & Singla, 1995; Singla, 2003). The TTT ethos is inspired by intercultural psychotherapeutic perspectives (Fernando, 2010) and offers broad psychosocial interventions with families of different cultural backgrounds from that of mainstream Danish culture. Culture is perceived here and by the organisation as a dynamic and complex meaning system, rather than as a simplistic or static concept. At the same time, the structural and political dimensions of inequality are considered as it is felt that these families' needs cannot be met without a consideration of the effects of wider society upon them.

Starting from concrete case examples, this chapter presents the demographic details, intervention process and a discussion of the cases. In the subsequent section, the case-based experiences are combined with relevant results from the empirical study to present lessons for good practice. The final sections move beyond the cases to include some empirical results and discuss their implications for health promotion, problem prevention and psychosocial interventions discussed in other relevant studies. The concluding section includes considerations regarding the aforementioned areas, reflections on broader social policies and suggestions for research.

9.1 Case example 1: her exit and his threshold – an act of balancing

Saida, 40, and Brian, 45, had been together for four years when they sought psychosocial intervention from TTT in the first instance. It was on Brian's initiative to work with the *uncertain couple relation*. Brian chose to contact TTT for the intervention since he felt that a psychologist familiar with Saida's culture would be able to appreciate the cultural nuances impacting on their relationship. Saida agreed with him. She grew up partly in Denmark with Muslim Pakistani parents and four siblings, while her parents live partly in Denmark and in their ancestral village in Pakistan for a few months of the year. She is educated to a middle level as a social educator (in Danish: *socialpedagog*). At the time of contact, she had been separated from her former (coethnic) husband Nadar, who was a distant relative living in Pakistan when the marriage was arranged by their families. Nadar and Saida have two teenage sons. She considered her relationship with Nadar as a 'dry relationship', and Brian told me that there had been very limited emotional or sexual contact between Saida and Nadar. After her separation from Nadar, she trained as a social educator and was working in a children's daycare centre, although she was not satisfied with the atmosphere at her workplace. She was seeking a divorce from Nadar and a major dilemma for her was whether to divorce in accordance with the law in her country of origin (Islamic Sharia law). She wanted to marry Brian in a religious ceremony in Denmark which would entail his conversion to Islam and a ritual in a local mosque. For her, a mixed marriage implied partial *exit* from her family and the Pakistani ethnic group as a mixed marriage with a Christian Danish person was forbidden by her parents, some of her siblings and the extended family.

Brian was born in Denmark, is a Christian and both his parents were deceased at the time of his contact with TTT. He had divorced from his Danish wife (who was an alcoholic) two decades earlier. He had one adult child with whom he had limited contact and his primary family ties were with Saida and her children. He had his own business in media services, which was doing well financially. Saida and Brian had met through the business, where she was initially a customer. His attitude is supportive, loving and caring towards Saida and her children which matters a great deal to her. She describes how she is worried about her family's reaction at her being in a relationship with Brian and that she is frustrated when she is away from him. For Brian, the main issue is the lack of acceptance and openness from Saida's family, which he considers to be a reflection of gender discrimination, since one of Saida's brothers has a Danish wife, who is accepted by the family. One of Saida's sisters is married to a Dane and she has been excluded by the family, although Saida had clandestine contact with her.

9.1.1 TTT's intervention

The TTT intervention lasted for almost two years and included both individual and couple sessions. After several sessions, professional help was sought for Saida's two teenage sons. Thus there were a couple of sessions with the young sons as well. The primary language spoken during counselling was Danish, but there was some mixing with Punjabi and Urdu in communicating with Saida.

9.1.1.1 *Her partial exit strategy, mutual love and family resistance*

At the start of therapy, as counsellor, I focused on drawing a map of Saida and Brian's psychosocial relations and positioning in the life course phase, which confirmed the significance of their 'mutual companionate love' and empowered them. The social aspects of historical silencing and taboos related to mixed marriage in Danish society and in the Pakistani community were discussed and were used to contextualise the issues and develop strategies to confront the exclusion processes. Saida reflected on the gender-based differential acceptance of mixed marriage within her own family and I focused on the injustice, oppression and gender-based discrimination involved in the acceptance of her brother's marriage to a Danish woman and the rejection of her sister's marriage to a Dane.

She decided to go ahead with the legal divorce in Denmark (though not in Pakistan) from her husband Nadar without informing the extended family in Pakistan or telling them about her new relationship. She told her family in Denmark she was planning to divorce Nadar and they attempted to dissuade her. She still avoided full cohabitation with Brian but travelled on vacations with him. They were both able to focus on the positive and 'fun' aspects of their relationship and be supportive and nurturing towards each other. Saida maintained contact with her family of origin, though with a reduced frequency. She respected their wishes about not involving the extended family in the country of origin regarding the separation from Nadar, thus maintaining *face*, and she deepened her contact with the sister who had also married a Dane. She continued her insistence on having a religious (Islamic) wedding ceremony with Brian.

On my suggestion, her sons had a couple of sessions with me where they clarified their acceptance of Brian as a caring figure and that they had almost no emotional ties with their biological father. Brian's parenting of the young sons played an important part in Saida's difficult decision about seeking a divorce and continuing the intimate relationship with Brian.

9.1.1.2 His threshold, partial acceptance of the cultural practices and finding a balance

Brian was aware of the dilemmas Saida faced and the contentious family relations that related to marriage migration and cultural practices, such as endogamous marriage. He realised that gender made a difference to the acceptance of ethnic difference and he accepted that religion is a bearer of identity that explained Saida's insistence on his conversion. These practices coexisted with his recognition of Saida as an intelligent, active, caring, committed and romantic partner who needed human and temporal support to work through her dilemmas and conflicts. Gradually, Brian developed strategies to support her and nurture the young sons as he was committed to being an active father figure in contrast to the boys' passive biological father. He was able to see his own cultural embeddedness as an individual with rather limited vertical relationships, owing to the deaths of his parents a decade before he sought psychosocial help for his uncertain couple relation with Saida. Brian expressed his sense of exclusion from Saida's family and attempted successfully to establish contact with her Danish brother-in-law. In the counselling session there was focus on the missing family support, rigid attitudes of the Saida's family and an acceptance of such processes as survival strategies in such interethnic marriages.

Issues related to power and privileges were engaged with in line with Addison & Thomas (2009), we discussed how persons can be privileged along some dimensions of identity and how oppressed and privileged identities can intersect within the same person. I emphasised that I was privileged as a highly educated academician but at the same time a member of the *other* visible ethnic minority in Denmark. The differential privileges and disadvantages associated with their positions were highlighted. The power asymmetry – due to Brian's majority position and Saida's minority position – was partly balanced by Saida's middle-level education and affiliation to the labour market. TTT's intervention enabled them to discuss these sensitive issues while containing the influence of Saida's family and the social stereotypes related to ethnic minorities and mixed marriages.

When the intervention ended by the couple's and my mutual agreement, Saida was legally divorced from Nadar and she was relieved about this. Saida and Brian were partly cohabiting and the sons showed an increased acceptance of Brian. Five years later I contacted the couple by telephone to seek their permission to include their case in this book. Permission was granted and a telephone interview took place with both partners.

Brian was continuing with his business and Saida was satisfactorily employed as social educator in an institution for homeless people. They had an Islamic marriage four years back, after his conversion. They were having a sexually and emotionally fulfilling life by emphasising the 'fun aspect' of their situation, especially by travelling on vacations and sharing parental functions. Saida's eldest son is staying with her and Brian. He works in an IT firm, although he is relatively socially isolated. Her second son is studying hotel management and was managing well socially and in his studies. There is still no open acceptance of this intimate relationship from Saida's family, but there is a tacit tolerance of the situation from both sides.

On the whole the couple's relationship was positive, despite some difficulties related to the extended family. Saida's father was terminally ill and she expressed hopes that he would be able to accept their mixed intimate relationship before he died. The death of a family member is significant and can be an integral aspect of mixed-family dynamics, especially against the backdrop of lack of acceptance and resistance. Root (2001) discusses how some family patriarchs hold so much power that although other family members might not agree with them deep down, they dare not stand up to them. There can also be closure when a patriarch who had opposed a mixed marriage repents on their deathbed and gives the couple his blessing. Time will reveal Saida's father's final response to her mixed relationship.

9.1.1.3   Discussion of first case example

In this case, an intersectional, gender and life course framework was shown to be constructive in identifying and resolving the multiple conflict areas.

These areas were:

- Marital status – separation/divorce and mixed marriage.
- The extended family and parental acceptance of the new relationship.
- Issues of parenting and children's acceptance and inclusion.

For each area, both partners had to consider various aspects of their gender position, their familial and cultural expectations, their own life course position, societal reactions and renegotiations of their own needs in the context of the current couple relationship. Through the psychosocial intervention Saida managed to find a new way of resolving her dilemma. She had to choose between a formal divorce from her husband Nadar or continue the relationship with him. In the former choice, there was the risk of a breakup with a part of her extended family. While in the latter choice there was a risk of breakup with Brian. She became aware of her own and her children's need for a caring, loving person in the family and she managed to confront Nadar with the need to end the relationship legally without involving the whole family. He agreed to sign the divorce papers, which paved the way for her marriage to Brian.

Brian agreed to convert to Islam as he realised this had great personal significance for her. He perceived it as pragmatic solution. Talking this through with a counsellor made Brian aware of the exclusionary processes Saida had encountered in relation to the extended family and the surrounding network – especially within the Pakistani community in Denmark – caused by her separation from her first husband. Charsley (2013) describes a decreased transnational and local community involvement for Pakistani women living in the UK as divorce and subsequent marriage to a non-Muslim may imply partial exit and estrangement from the community.

Moreover, Saida's limited inclusion and dissatisfaction at her workplace was also addressed. This all led to a focus on issues that had been avoided or minimised, both in their couple relationship and in the psychotherapeutic conversations. Both Brian and Saida were able to move beyond the negative societal stereotypes of 'rigid majority man' and the 'passive minority woman'. These discussions involved paradoxes, ambiguities and compromises from both sides, which they were learning to live with. The intersection between the couple's life course phase – in this case in mature middle age – stable affiliation to the labour market, common acceptance of need for stability as well as nurturance for children and partial empathy for the extended family in the country of residence and country of origin contributed to their couple relationship and family life, which was well suited to the psychosocial intervention.

9.2 Case example 2: moving back and forth, the power of stereotypes and making up her own mind

Mark, 28, contacted TTT requesting psychological intervention for his wife Mira, 27. They had been married for three years but she was experiencing problems related to her adaptation to her new country of residence and in their couple relationship. Mira is a marriage migrant spouse. She is an Indian citizen and was born and brought up in an affluent, upper middle-class family in an Indian city. She has two older sisters who immigrated to the USA for further education and are settled there. Mark is Danish, born and raised in a small town to a working-class family. He has one older brother living in the same town as their parents. Mark's parents encouraged him to study to master's level. During an internship in India he met Mira in an academic environment, where they realised they shared a number of similarities such as academic interest and ambition, leisure time activities, travelling and an interest in jazz. They were sexually attracted towards each other and fell in love like 'any other young couple' on the campus. He returned to Denmark but the relationship continued. After a year, they decided to get married in India and, after that, Mira moved to Denmark. After the honeymoon phase, the couple begun to experience conflicts and Mark took the initiative to contact TTT as he was looking for a professional who could speak fluent English and who had understanding of foreigners' problems in Denmark.

9.2.1 TTT's intervention

The intervention in TTT lasted for almost a year and consisted of individual sessions with Mira, a few sessions with Mark and two couple sessions. The primary language spoken was English, although there was some mixing with Hindi in communication with Mira and Danish in communication with Mark.

9.2.1.1 *Her expectations, reality confrontation ... both here and there*

Part of TTT's intervention involved some detailed mapping of Mira's life, her migration narrative and analysis of her psychosocial network. As the youngest child in a progressive, well-educated and well-to-do family in an Indian city, Mira had privileges such as an elite education and encouragement to concentrate on academic as well as social activities. She was raised in a household where all the daily chores were done by maids and servants. Moving to Denmark, she was confronted with limited economic means and a responsibility for a household without any help, since Mark worked part-time as a project researcher on a three-year temporary contract. Her expectations of a European standard of living and freedoms were shattered. She faced additional challenges in her everyday life as she was a strict vegetarian according to Hindu religious observance.

Her encounters with the in-laws in the small Danish town were characterised by opposition. Her mother-in-law was rather conservative and xenophobic and was critical of Mark's choice of partner and of their economic situation. In contrast, her father-in-law was open and supportive. Mira experienced racial discrimination as a visibly different minority woman in public spaces of the local area, although her academic environment was supportive.

The intervention focused on a comparative analysis of her life conditions in the country of origin and in Denmark within a framework of the intersection between gender, age, socio-economic position, educational level and the regional (metropolis/small town) aspects. Both material and emotional issues were taken up as the household finances and chores became *hot-button* issues for Mira, resulting in everyday life conflicts. During the sessions, potential solutions were considered, as were Mira's transnational connections with her country of origin as a couple of trips to India – financed by her parents – added to the complexity of the situation.

Particular issues related to the continued intergenerational interdependence between her parents and her were taken up in the intervention, inspired by delineation of Indian Women in psychotherapy (Guzder & Krishna, 2005). Moreover, during the course of the intervention the issues of exclusion were brought up, both in the sessions with Mira and in the couple sessions. Mira managed to get a part-time job in the academic world related to her educational qualification, but still the couple conflicts, the symbolic violence of the division of labour, superiority, inferiority and subjugation continued. She became more focused on her future in the academic world, making relevant enquiries and investing resources in various possibilities.

Gradually, through the course of intervention, Mira began to complain more strongly about the effects of being subjected to the *gaze* of people both in some areas of Denmark as well as in India, especially the intense curiosity and looks of surprise and confusion. She even mentioned facing obtrusive questions about her personal life in both contexts, while Mark hardly seemed to notice or be bothered about this *gaze* and questioning of their relationship.

The phenomenon of *othering* – the hierarchical placing of differences, especially phenotypical differences – and the negative stereotypes associated with Asian women in Denmark/Europe played an important part in the counselling. Through these dialogues, Mira began to challenge discourses of *the exotic* and *power*, as well as the privileges attached to belonging to the minority and majority in Denmark and India respectively. In psychotherapy, acknowledging her position within and outside of family life encouraged her to expand her academic pursuits, social networks, economic independence and transnational nurturing ties, which empowered her. Attempts were made to focus on Mira and Mark's similarities, such as the educational values, political beliefs and shared music interests to counter the dominant discourses associated with them as an interethnic couple emphasising boundaries or differences Karis & Killian, 2009), though this resulted in limited success.

9.2.1.2   The power of stereotypes, Global North/South hierarchies and the division of labour

The point of departure for the intervention provided by TTT was Mark's referral of Mira who he described as 'well educated, with a cosmopolitan outlook, thinking that she understood how the world functioned'. He had emphasised her 'loss of identity' and her 'focus on her limitations such as her inability to cycle' in the process of adapting to Denmark. He also emphasised her feelings of anxiety, especially after she suffered a physical attack by a drunk person one evening in the local neighbourhood. From Mark's perspective, Mira was a victim and only she needed psychotherapy to help her adapt to living in Denmark. His perception of Mira's country of origin and her family background was dominated by his placementing of India and Indian families within his rigid, colonial thinking. The stereotypes of Asian women as better mothers, as warmer, more sexual and less outspoken than Western women constructed within the global economy (Schaeffer-Grabiel, 2006) also seems to have influenced Mark's attitude to Mira in the Danish context.

After many sessions with Mira alone leading towards a more realistic and nuanced understanding of material and emotional differences and similarities with Mark, it was imperative to include Mark in the intervention. First he was invited for individual sessions, where the focus was on his part in the problems faced by them as a couple. The sessions were professionally highly challenging as they were characterised by Mark's victim blaming, alienation, perpetuation of gender inequality and preference for the status quo. I maintained that as a professional engaged in psychosocial intervention I had to overcome my hesitation to discuss race, ethnicity and other dimensions of privilege and oppression and to become comfortable hearing about my privileged identity as an academician, practitioner and researcher. I attempted to account for my privileges and make a responsible use of my situationally granted power as a psychologist with university affiliations to guide Mark and Mira into the academic possibilities and clarify their future visions.

From the beginning, however, Mark was resentful when I suggested that he needed to 'see colour' and to recognise the privileges associated with his majority ethnic background in the Danish context. In addition, he became withdrawn and defensive about his family, especially his mother, when the thematic focus was directed towards his family. The psychotherapeutic intervention encouraged *racial literacy* by attending to racial logics that organise media depictions, especially about the exotic, passive Asian women, and suggested ways in which racism could have shaped and structured their intimate life. Attempts to interpret, analyse and resist these logics and practices brought about few transformations in Mark's views towards Mira, her situation and the families in Denmark and/or in India. Focusing on Mira's transnational relationships, both on the vertical ones with her parents in India and the horizontal ones with her siblings and their spouses in the USA, brought attention to an *extension of victim blaming* directed towards Mira. It was difficult for Mark to see the situation from any perspective other than from his own and he could barely perceive the symbolic violence involved in their relationship as there was no use of physical violence from his side. It became apparent that Mark had not acquired *racial literacy* through simply being in an interethnic marriage but demanded much from him as a labour-intensive analytical process. He came to express awareness of the depth of the differences between himself and Mira and in the later sessions even began to allude to separation as a solution.

In the first sessions with Mark, there were difficulties in placing his actions along a continuum of power and control. Gradually, however, my focus on the cultural stereotypes associated with the *passive Asian woman*, and the *superior white man* began to make sense to him, especially when combined with an intersectional framework linked to post-colonial thinking (Poddar, 2013) and the life course perspective. This loosened his defensiveness and allowed him a sense of personal accountability; his social responsibility became less burdensome. Although he was supportive of Mira's academic pursuits to a degree, the everyday life conflicts about household chores and his dichotomous developed/undeveloped, Global North/South attitude towards Mira's country of origin India, in comparison with Denmark, continued.

The three sessions where both Mira and Mark were present made the distance between their perspectives explicit and prepared them for new choices aimed at minimising long-term hostility and the mutual blame game. I encouraged Mark and Mira to stop focusing on each other's shortcomings, while at the same time Mira was encouraged not to feel guilty about serious problems in her relationship and use her active agency as an appropriate response to the symbolic violence and control. After a couple sessions, it was decided to stop the TTT intervention, as Mira and Mark agreed to separate from each other for a period of a few months as Mira had the opportunity to move to another city in Denmark to continue her academic pursuits.

9.2.1.3   Follow-up

Two years later, when I contacted Mira telephonically to get her permission to include the case in this book, I was informed that Mira and Mark had had a 'peaceful separation followed by an undramatic divorce by mutual consent'. I conducted a brief telephone interview with Mira as well as Mark.

Mira was living in another Danish city and pursuing doctoral studies in her academic field in collaboration with Indian and American institutions. She was primarily pursuing her academic path which facilitated her continued residence in Denmark, despite divorce from Mark. She expressed that she was *doing well* and was academically progressing. Her family had been highly nurturing and supportive and she had developed a trusting social network with coethnic, Danish and international students. She spoke to Mark once in a while and there had been some reparation from his side and forgiveness from hers. Lastly, she added that she is dating another international scholar residing in Denmark but that her plans for getting married were on hold but that the idea of another *mixed marriage* in distant future was a possibility.

Mark informed me that he had got job as a high school lecturer in a suburb and was no longer engaged in international research projects. He had remarried in the year before to a middle-level educated young Danish woman he had known from his high school. He was getting on with life in a peaceful manner and had managed to continue some contact with Mira.

9.2.1.4   Discussion of second case example

The following multiple areas of conflict and irreparable damage to the couple relationship can be seen in this case through the use of a framework combining intersectionality, post-colonialism and transnationalism.

- Negative stereotypes, issues of power and privileges at macro and micro level.
- Division of responsibility, financial duties and household chores.
- Extended family and family-in-law issues.

In each area, the couples were made aware of their own perspectives, the distance between them, the discourses that dominated their thinking and the consequences of these. Attempts were made in intervention to negotiate their own needs in the context of the couple relationships. At macro level negative and degrading stereotypes of India as a Global South country with high level of poverty and corruption hardly corresponds to Mira's upper-class, well-educated family, and created confusion for Mark, who had over-focused on these stereotypes. Similarly, stereotypes of South and East Asian women as hardworking and non-demanding (Osanami Törngren, 2011) combined with Mira's Hindu background and vegetarianism contributed to make her 'exotic', which again influenced Mark's perceptions.

When Mira and Mark met in India, Mark was overwhelmed by the Indian setting and found the perceived differences attractive. Later, on moving to Denmark, racial prejudices emerged and, as a result of the perception of these differences, Mira was positioned as a *victim*, over-focusing on her shortcomings, her anxiety and her loss of positive aspects identity. Her agency made him uneasy, especially in situations when he was confronted with cultural and social aspects in Mira, for example that: 'She is intelligent, progressive and industrious', which could not easily be fitted into his negative stereotypes. The issues of privilege and oppression, especially in the intersection of oppressed and privileged identities in the same person, were important and challenging.

Stereotypical thinking made the division of household chores a contentious issue for them. Mark expected Mira to be a 'hardworking' housewife who would do all the household chores, even while working part-time in an academic job. Mira had been raised in a household where the chores were done by servants and I empathised with her experience of being raised as the youngest child in an upper middle-class family with privilege and power. At the same time I encouraged her to adapt to the current situation and to reframe these values. Furthermore, Mark's mother's conservative and xenophobic attitudes made the situation more difficult for Mira, especially during frequent visits to Mark's home town, while her own parents and sisters empowered her to find new ways of living. Later, her own social network of other international students contributed to her ability to cope with the situation. Mira continued to value the opportunities for academic development and independence, which were shared by her family in India and the USA.

Mark's unwillingness to share household work led to discussion about gender roles among Indian women and Danish men, but Mark's rigid attitude towards the division of work and to their financial problems didn't 'soften' and husband and wife were not able to support each other in these areas, despite encouragement to communicate their emotional and everyday life difficulties to each other. For whatever reason, they didn't manage to nurture each other's needs and expectations in relation to household chores and the extended family, though they began to understand the power dynamics better.

Along with gender and transnationalism, I took up the intersection between cultural practices and geographical locality in the intervention. I reflected on Mira's feelings of missing the extended family in everyday life, something which was partly countered by digital technology – Skype, emails and so on. Mark's lack of cooperation led to a fear of abandonment, which was exacerbated by the *gaze* she was exposed to especially in Mark's small home town. However, Mira's supportive father-in-law sustained her through a turbulent married life and the later period. Lastly, discussion of these dynamics promoted an understanding of the similarities and differences for both Mira and Mark which led to a peaceful dissolution of this intimate relationship across the borders. The intervention's results may not be optimal, but it can be concluded that a peaceful dissolution of a malfunctioning relationship between the two partners and continued contact is a positive outcome from a long-term perspective. Couple psychotherapy's objective was not just prolonging the relationship at any cost, but also to create dialogue, negotiation and compromise.

9.3   Lessons learnt – combining empirical research with clinical practice

The knowledge gained by going through just two cases from the practice can be questioned, but I refer again to the concept of analytic generalisation (see Chapter 3). I argue that there is significance in combining the lessons learnt from the empirical research with those from clinical practice. Academic literature in the area of intermarriage is mostly divided either in empirical research or clinical studies; this book attempts to move beyond this division by combining the two. The analyses of the narratives in the empirical research showed some ways of relating to the challenges of mixedness and being a mixed family. Congruently, the clinical cases demonstrated ways of dealing with psychosocial problems, despite the individual variation. The combination has resulted in the following broader points.

9.3.1 Balancing different family and world-views

In the Danish context, recent publications dealing with ethnic minority families and especially emphasising issues affecting young women (Danneskjold-Samsøe, Mørck & Wagner, 2011; Nielsen, 2011; Loua, 2012) have covered some empirical and practice-based aspects, but a focus on mixedness is conspicuous by its absence. The significance of involving the extended family in interventions was explicitly discussed in Nielsen (2011) as family conflicts cannot be resolved by breaking the bond between young people and the rest of the family. The two clinical cases illustrate lucidly that family inclusion considers aspects related to the life course and to transnational practices in accordance with the TTT's three principles of family inclusion, broad context-level inclusion and multiple identity focus (Singla, 2003, 2014). Oversimplified concepts of individualistic and collectivistic duality have to be reconsidered as this popular duality disguises the various degrees to which they apply in individual cases. Every individual experiences variability in individualism and collectivism the context of the life course (Chaudhary, 2007) as illustrated by the narratives of the present empirical study participants such as Marlik and Sabita, who I have placed in different phases of couple relationship as presented in Chapter 5.

The lessons learnt from their narratives are to support the family relationships across generational and national borders in ways that are appropriate to the relevant life phase; which includes supportive relationships between the grandparents and their grandchildren. The close emotional intergenerational bond between Sabita and Robert and their respective grandparents are a source of strength and this is also the case for Marlik's children. Similarly, continuing positive intergenerational relationships between Mira and her Danish father-in-law (as well as her own parents in the country of origin) became a source of sustenance. These good practices indicate that, in the counselling and psychotherapy of mixed couples with psychosocial problems, intergenerational relations – across and within national borders, especially for the diasporic partner – should be explored and included. This can be a challenge for professionals working with mixed couples, since including the extended family may seem inconsistent with the dominant discourse of individualisation. According to Murphy-Shigematsu (2002) however:

> Various struggles emerge in our attempts at simultaneously understanding both the client's worldview and our own, and

balancing these issues is an art of therapy…balance is a construct. In multicultural counselling that involves the identification of diverse or even conflicting culturally learned perspectives without necessarily resolving the differences.

(ibid., p. 111)

In accordance with the TTT's principle of inclusion of the broad context, it is important to create a comfortable setting, where the ethnic minority clients can bring up her or his experiences of exclusion in wider society. As in the case of Mark and Mira, the majority partner may think that the minority partner is exaggerating some episodes of exclusionary processes and can perceive them as being 'hypersensitive' or 'paranoid'; thus racial literacy issues have to be addressed with sensitivity. Killian (2013) similarly emphasises that professionals should listen carefully to the partners, privileging their own voices and understandings. He suggests what should be considered before deciding on suitable interventions:

… a therapist must recognise the ways the couples connote and *negotiate difference*, detect their *implicit rules* for presenting themselves in public and the therapy room, and learn about the *couple identity* they have formed together'.

(ibid., p. 202, emphasis added)

Furthermore, as in the case example of Saida and Brian and in line with the sociocultural psychological framework of this study, the ethnic minority partner's experiences of exclusion and racial discrimination should be placed in both historical and current social contexts. This would confirm that experiences are legitimate and the response is not exaggerated.

Another lesson learnt from the case examples and the empirical study narratives is about balancing multiple identities and the dominant identity in accordance with the TTT's principle of validating multiple identities. Research studies on intimate relationship satisfaction (Giles, 2008; Fletcher et al., 2013) have indicated that micro-level aspects such as personality variables and interactional processes are stronger predictors of marital satisfaction than macro-background factors such as a couple's age, race or socio-economic status. This further confirms the significance of subjective aspects for couple interventions and in Mira's case is illustrated by her balancing of multiple identities as an upper middle-class woman and daughter in India, a marriage migrant and daughter-in-law in Denmark, a young person, a research scholar and so on. The TTT intervention evolved to focus on her dominant identity as a scholar and as an active person with intellectual and social resources, which eventually led to the long-term solution to her conflictual situation as an intermarried migrant in Denmark. Professionals working with mixed couples should be aware that ethnicity, gender and socio-economic belongings are not entirely separable entities but intersect with each other as parts of an interdependent system. Thus Mira's experiences of sexism, racism and ageism in the internal and external domains are interconnected. The professional has the responsibility of bringing up the issues of oppression and privileges. Addison & Thomas (2009) use the term *double bind to* apply to the conflicts experienced by clients – especially visibly different ethnic minorities – when they are oppressed by those who are allegedly acting benevolently towards them. By failing to see the relevance of race and ethnicity to the client and their problems, they are displaying an 'anxiety-provoking neutrality'. Furthermore, they point out that some clients may *censor* comments on racism in the presence of the privileged white people, instead choosing to remain silent.

9.3.2 Fun and the serious aspects of life – levity and gravity

Focus on fun and positive aspects at the couple level show how perseverance and mutual support in everyday life emerge as factors strengthening relationships both for the participants in the empirical study and in the case examples. Emphasising the richness, humour and the liveliness of forming an intimate relationship across ethnic borders is crucial for Katja and Rajiv as well as Saida and Brian, described in Chapters 4 and 9, respectively.

Through these narratives I have attempted to offer examples of how cultural and psychodynamic benefits of intermarriages, especially related to reframing mechanisms, are important for maintaining the mental health and wellbeing of the couples. Classic examples of valuing each other's traditions by celebrating Christmas, as well as Diwali, can be seen as having *double fun*, instead of half or none. Similarly, recalling descriptions of Saida and Brian, I highlight how recreational activities – such as travelling together – contributes to humour and gaiety in life, which in turn strengthens them to face conflicts with the extended family and social stereotyping.

Fun and humour can be found during the psychotherapeutic process, as well as in everyday life, and this also brought out hope and optimism. Optimism and pessimism have to be balanced however, as Murphy-Shigematsu (2002) notes:

> Balancing optimism and pessimism is therefore a source of tension. Without hope, therapy is powerless. The connections of hope and health are increasingly being documented and optimism is recognised as a form of emotional intelligence that enhances wellbeing. Too much optimism may deprive some persons of the necessity of seeing themselves and their situation clearly. Practical solutions become difficult when the client indulges in excessive and false hope... we [counsellors] are both helpful and limited in our power to heal. A lack of faith in our ability is obviously self-defeating. But an unjustified sense of our own importance in healing our clients will cause us to miss opportunities to empower them.
>
> (ibid., p. 114)

With this lesson learnt about the balance between levity and gravity, optimism and realism in health promotion, problem prevention and psychosocial intervention of mixed couples, I approach the final lesson drawn from this research.

9.3.3   Relating to similarities and differences: inter- and intra-ethnic couples

The narratives of the research participants and the case examples demonstrate that human beings are simultaneously similar and different, and that they have been placed in particular categories. Categorisation, by definition, sorts objects based on assumptions of difference and similarity. This may sound simplistic but it is at the heart of questions about similarity and differences between the interethnic married couples and intra-ethnic couples. It is fruitful to compare these ethnically intermarried couples to intra-ethnically married couples. What are the similarities and differences between their experiences and how do they respond to the various life course phases identified in this study as well as to the unique aspects of their situation?

An anonymous reviewer of this book manuscript commented during the writing process that:

> Reading through the quotations – at some points I was forgetting that these are 'mixed' partnerships, and I suppose that is one of your points – that mixed partnerships are just like other partnerships.

The issue of similarity and difference is important and exists simultaneously. As discussed in Chapter 6 on parenting, mixed parents deal with issues such as safety and ambition for their children in similar ways to other parents. Killian (2013) notes that interracial couples are same as intraracial couples in at least two ways:

1. They experience the same major milestones and life-cycle transitions, and
2. When partners come together to form any couple and/or family, they are not emptied of power. Differentials of power and privilege are always there, even in Black-Black and White-White couple formations, even if such differences are naturalised, deprioritised, or depoliticised by those couples.

(ibid., p. 198)

In the present study, we can see how differential strategies of centralisation and decentralisation of partner differences affects their choice about whether or not to focus on incidents of racial exclusion. Danish Katja centralised the cultural differences between her socialisation and her ethnically Indian husband Sam – who was born and raised in Denmark see Chapters 5 and 6. She was prepared to name some incidents of racial discrimination, such as her mother's initial suspicion about 'Indian fathers', thus displaying some level of racial literacy. By contrast, Danish Cecilia and Indian Rajiv decentralised such differences and foregrounded cosmopolitanism, stressing their shared membership of a community of humanity. They hardly named any incidents of racism. In a similar way, Mira and Mark also decentralised their differences in the first phase of their contact but later these differences hit them, and Mark especially was highly influenced by the negative stereotype of the *non-demanding, hardworking Asian woman*. This apparent contradiction in Mark and Mira's relationship can be considered as an understandable one; they were like any young couple in love during the first phase of the marriage life course. After all, they met as students and were affected by sexual desires and attractions despite separation and distance.

Viewed in a different way, Mark and Mira's dynamics are highly complex as moving to Denmark made them aware of Global North/South differential discourses (Ifekwunigwe, 2004) as well as negative stereotypes about Asian women and European men. These differences, initially seen as attractive and exotic, became a source of conflict and frustration. Awareness of these dynamics and actions at different levels foregrounded gender issues and problematised the dynamic with the extended family (Rastogi, 2009). For Mark and Mira, these issues led to conflict and to the eventual dissolution of their relationship. Katja and Rajiv's claim to cosmopolitanism and harmony, like Mira and Mark's, saw them construct themselves like any other couple, as essentially ordinary. This approach seems understandable and less paradoxical in the context of *individualised romantic love* and an act of *resistance* to pathologisation and sensationalisation related to colourism.

One of the lessons learnt through research and clinical practice is that professionals and their clients have to move beyond the dichotomy of similarity and difference. I agree with Murphy-Shigematsu (2002), who argues that difference and sameness are not mutually exclusive and both clearly exist and must be understood through a client's cultural contexts. He further states that the sensitivity of the professional to a client depends on balancing the shared humanity, shared cultural commonalities and the personal uniqueness. Identity then, at these universal, group and individual levels, is fluid.

> A client may focus on individual needs at one moment, at another on an issue related to reference group identity, while at still another time on universal human experience. The counsellor flexibility strives to relate to that which is salient at that moment . . . significant to recognise that people are more alike than different and clients often consult us [professionals] about problems in living that transcend culture and have little or nothing to do with race or ethnicity.
>
> (ibid., pp. 117–118)

9.4 Implications for psychosocial intervention – counselling and psychotherapy

The case examples, combined with the empirical study, make a contribution to our understanding of wellbeing and positive mental health in the context of globalisation, where intimate relationships are formed across ethnic borders. At the same time, however, I hope that the case of an 'unsuccessful marriage' – such as Mira and Mark's and Nihla and Mads's – do not lead to the further pathologisation of mixed marriages.

I aim to add nuance to the phenomenon and to avoid one-sided negative stereotypes and problematisation. Inspired by the strength-based approach (Killian, 2013), it is imperative in my view to develop a simultaneous focus on the merits and perils, opportunities and limitations of such relationships in order to contribute to mental health promotion, problem prevention, counselling and psychotherapy for distressed couples. After all, positive interactional processes and personality features relate closely to marital happiness and success. As mentioned at the beginning of this chapter, there are almost no institutions focusing on psychosocial intervention for mixed couples in Denmark (Center for Familieudvikling, 2014). The State Administration, Ministry of Internal and Economic Affairs (http://www.statsforvaltningen.dk/) deals with, among other matters, divorces, child custody and child support and there is no particular focus or special consideration for mixed couples or ethnic minority couples (consultant state administration, 2014). Thus, in order to understand the particular needs and issues facing mixed couples in relevant areas, it is imperative to establish and further develop relevant institutions within the field of psychosocial services. The dominant discourse of colour blindness in these areas and in the field generally may serve an important function of guiding couples to navigate their intimate relationships and everyday lives, but in the long term may constrain their abilities to engage with the complexities of living in an ethnically stratified society such as a multi-ethnic Denmark.

Throughout this book I have attempted to add nuance to an ignored and neglected area of migration studies, South Asian studies and family studies, as well as the counselling and psychotherapy fields. I have done so in a variety of ways, including bringing in the voices of spouses in mixed marriages; introducing life course and exclusion processes and considering the role of diaspora as a part of the theoretical framework for comprehending mixed marriages. In addition I have considered concepts of sexual desire and love in a predominantly structural and instrumental view of intimate partnership formation and made concrete suggestions for providing a range of appropriate forms of support such as health promotion and counselling services. I am aware of crossing disciplinary boundaries by moving across the social sciences, from social, psychological, anthropological and ethnographic studies to clinical and social work disciplines and have tried to use psychosocial family counselling and therapy disciplines in a life-enhancing manner. This cross-disciplinary movement has its own promises and pitfalls, but hopefully more of the former than the latter.

The implications of this study are that researchers and practitioners need to pay simultaneous attention to internal and external aspects in an inclusive counselling practice. In everyday life, the internal is closely intertwined with the external and the divide is more of an analytical dichotomy – albeit a useful one for practical purposes – than a real one. With regard to 'outside' factors, this book reaffirms the significance of ethnicity and colourism in the wider social context and confirms that the both partners' positions on domains such as an acceptance of legal systems and societal exclusion/inclusion processes are salient, as they influence power relations and privileges. Awareness of historical/cultural discourses related to mixedness and to being *visibly different*, collective amnesia and official silence about the Danish encounters with the visible *others* (Larsen, 2008; Andreassen & Henningsen, 2011) is relevant and important for dealing with the often unspoken issues relating to the current exclusion of the couples, even while the dominant narrative of couples is that 'race does not matter'. Getting inspiration from a recent study of global mixed race, including in Denmark's neighbouring country Germany, attention is directed towards a number of theoretical and contextual issues. A person can be positioned as Danish – if one parent is Danish – in Denmark, as German in Germany, even if one of the ancestors is German (Nandi & Spickard, 2014), as a migrant in Holland, if one parent is migrant (Kalmijn, 2012), or as mixed race in the UK (Aspinall & Song, 2013). German practices illustrate the complexity further. The citizenship in Germany has been consistently based on the principles of *jus sanguinis* – principle of descent – in contrast to the principle of *jus soli*, the law of place of birth, as in France. However, in 2000, an opening was made, so that native-born children of permanent resident migrants can apply for citizenship after completion of their education in German schools. Still the overriding idea of unitary German folk defined in terms of blood ancestry, determining membership of German society, is rather uneven. This principle leads to understanding that 'one drop rule' of German citizenship would lead to social acceptance. Germans perceive Muslims and Africans as non-Germans – even if they are citizens and taxpayers. It turns out that mixed people whose non-German ancestors are white enjoy readier access to membership than do those whose non-German parentage hails from Africa, Asia or the Middle East according to Nandi & Spickard (2014).

Despite these complexities and variations, based on a global study of mixed race King-O'Riain et al. (2014) conclude that one thing mixed people around the world may have in common is their continued encounter with mixed racism and exoticisation in global marketing and popular culture. Moreover, there is the dilemma of being caught between two socially recognised categories: it is common that people are pressured to choose one, or being thought of as a suspect or 'less authentic'. This is being contested globally and the need for new categories is evident.

Similarly, the *liability of foreignness*, referring to the difficulties experienced by the reunified spouse in the labour market (Irastorza &

DeVoretz, 2009), directs our attention to the diaspora spouse's placement in the labour market and shows how a lack of recognition of educational qualifications or professional and social competences gained elsewhere is important practically and emotionally.

On a macro level, raising awareness and addressing how the complexity of identity issues in society are important in research, policy and services, this book is an effort to rectify the situation in Denmark. Perhaps a continued failure to notice these persons may seem an easy way out, but as a social scientist and a practitioner I feel a sense of responsibility. When questioned by a national radio journalist in 2011 about the attitudes of daycare personnel and teachers towards mixed children, I was unable to answer as there is almost no scientific research on these issues in Denmark (Hemming Hansen, 2011). This lack is also emphasised by Bille (2011) in an article about children of mixed parentage in Denmark. Highlighting the positive aspects of mixing is vital for challenging some dominant discourses which consider mixed marriages as a social problem. Promoting recognition of 'mixedness' for intermarried couples and their children can be positive for other issues, such as problematic life course transitions, that bring mixed couples to counsellors.

Practical support, a welcoming attitude and acceptance from social networks such as friends, neighbours and close and extended family also contribute to couples' wellbeing. There can be hindrances prior to marriage such as resistance from both sides of the family and lack of acceptance from social networks, because, despite increase in interethnic marriages, the borders between ethnic groups can still be patrolled from both sides in many instances. Although partners can and do choose to be with the person they love, there may be social consequences (Karis, 2009; Aspinall & Song, 2013) and these may be significant in the counselling process. There can be ongoing barriers in the everyday life of the couple or the diasporic partner and subtle derogatory and disparaging communication, such as the *gaze* of people, suspicion, *othering* processes, exclusion from privileges and social communities, which should be explored and addressed. Eroticisation of the diasporic partner reflects a process of sexualisation, mystification and objectification of female, ethnic minority or 'black' partners by their male spouses. Exploring and addressing racial literacy is important while providing intervention for mixed couples with children.

Practitioners in psychosocial services have to take up the responsibility of addressing the issues of discrimination, oppression and privileges, thus avoiding the 'anxiety-provoking neutrality around race and culture' and moving beyond self-censorship on racism and silence.

Practitioners have to overcome the fear of discussion of race and other dimensions of privilege, without it being uncomfortable. As these issues are complex, their attention should be drawn to the intersection of oppressed and privileged identities in the same person, and changes in these depending on the context. As McGoldrick (2005 (cited in Addison & Thomas, 2009, p. 17) wrote 'the more power and privilege we have, the harder it is to think about the meaning of the rage of the powerless'

Paying attention to the intersections between multiple belongings and everyday life practices is vital for counselling and psychotherapy. More concretely for dealing with counselling and psychotherapy of the distressed couples, Christensen (2011) describes a 'unified protocol' for couple therapy based on principles of the contextualised conceptualisation of problems, the modification of dysfunctional behaviour, the fostering of productive behaviour emphasising strengths and encouraging positive behaviours.

Snyder & Gasbarrini (2010) recommend integrative approaches to couple therapy transcending one theoretical modality, while Rastogi (2009) recommends focusing on the role of gender, power and privilege. A suitable way to deal with distressed couples is to combine these two recommendations. In line with the intersectionality framework in the present study, Rastogi & Thomas (2010) discuss psychotherapy with multicultural couples where multiple areas of diversity intersect with each other and these complexities should be considered at every step of counselling. They also recommend that counsellors gain skills in forming the all-important alliances with couples in the context of their multilayered reality.

Cosmopolitanism as an approach to being in a mixed relationship implies a transcendence of the narrow categorisation of *us* and *others* and places a focus on the commonality of being a member of the community of humanity. This approach could be productive for couples for whom there is an exaggerated focus on difference, and a limited ability to focus on the common humanity. An overarching discourse of 'colour does not matter' and 'colourism/race talk is transgressive' may be an adaptive strategy in a racist society in the short term, but over time can lead to fragmented identities which are detrimental to the couples and the next generation.

Thus inclusion of mixed practices may be useful in counselling couples who totally overlook the practices and experiences of one spouse – usually the diasporic one.

These approaches may be useful for dealing with differences which are not embedded in ethnicity but in other categories, such as religion or age. I invite counsellors and psychotherapists to work within ethical and social justice frameworks, in line with Moodley (2011), involving the multiple identities of the client. Almeida (2009) also uses the concept of the intersectionality of culture, gender and class in dealing with South Asian couples in conflict in the USA. Furthermore, foregrounding the 'fun part', the positive and creative aspects expressed by the participants in the study, implies a resource perspective with a focus on the *opportunities, strengths* and *potentials*.

In the Danish context, where issues of mixedness are largely marginalised, counselling therapy services sensitive to mixed relationships and mixed parentage are recommended. They are rarely available to couples at affordable prices and are not based on promoting health. Often the available services are directed only at situational problem-solving and hardly integrate the compromises and reconnections in the marriage. Enhancing the mixed couples' resources can be attained by focusing on concrete practices and conditions in everyday life, which is also recommended as part of counselling.

9.5 Concluding thoughts

This book has highlighted both enhancing aspects and risk factors which influence the mental health and wellbeing of intermarried couples in Denmark. The Danish situation has been contextualised by an interplay with current international literature from other countries, primarily from the USA, the UK, Japan, Germany and India. The everyday life of these mixed couples, their mental health and wellbeing is affected by the intersection of the 'big three' categories of ethnicity, gender and socio-economic status, with other categories such as life-course phase, diasporic belonging and transnational practices contributing. The concept of colourism throughout directs attention to the significance of phenotypes among the *visibly ethnically different* couples and their children in the Danish context. I feel that as a social scientist and a clinical psychologist, addressing the official amnesia and silence about the historical stigmatising of and current exclusion visible *others* in Denmark is part of academic and an ethical responsibility.

Despite the dominant discourse of Danish homogeneity there is an increase in ethnic diversity, including the number of mixed marriages. This is not due to migrant marriages – since the package of regulations restricting the entry of marriage partners in 2001 – but due to the presence of Danish citizen ethnic minorities. These restrictions are paradoxical when considered against the backdrop of democratic principles of freedom and the right to choose. The mixed couples in the present cross-sectional study indicate an awareness of these restrictions and related exclusionary processes such as the public *gaze* and *othering*. The focus on visible differences requires management through different practice in everyday life and through different phases of the life course. On the other hand, the narratives also emphasise commonality and that the dominant reason for getting together and forming their mixed marriage is *falling in love*, implying sexual desire and attraction. This commonality counters dominant discourses of commodification in mixed marriages, especially those related to marriage migration. A limitation of the present study is that it is based on strategic sampling, which doesn't allow broad generalisation. However, through analytic generalisation, I conclude that these couples endeavour to follow the social norm of marriage and romantic love in the society they are living in.

The *internal*, personal and family aspects, such as realising plans, mixing everyday practices, and focusing on the 'fun part', are in interplay with *external* aspects such as formal and informal acceptance of intermarriage in society, dominant gender roles, recognition and inclusion. Some of the practices analysed in the study, combined with reflections from the two clinical case examples, contribute to positive mental health and wellbeing, and thus form a basis for health promotion, prevention of psychosocial problems and counselling of those couples who experience problems. It is important for researchers, policymakers and health practitioners – including counsellors – to work together to improve the social situation and mental wellbeing of the people in mixed relationships and especially of their children.

Suggestions for further research follow from the basic ideas behind this book. Both national and international comparative studies of intermarriage phenomena with spouses originating from different countries using both quantitative and qualitative methods are currently lacking. Not only marriages between majority and minority, but also among specific minority groups should be included. Future studies should include family dynamics, such as relationships between parents and their children in a longitudinal perspective. In addition, the attitudes towards mixedness of 'the significant others' in the children's lives – the daycare providers and teachers – should be explored to enhance their acceptance and promote the children's mental health and wellbeing. Finally, relevant policies and services promoting their mental health, the prevention of problems and for counselling should also be explored systematically, assuming that these exist.

In line with Murphy-Shigematsu (2002), I also consider that research-ing and writing about psychosocial intervention are political acts that require taking a stand, depending on the purpose and the audience. As my purpose is to illuminate the phenomenon of mixed marriage mixedness and to challenge bias, my audience is comprised of fellow professionals, scholars, social workers and others concerned with social equity and equality.

Raising awareness and addressing related issues of multiple identity, exclusionary processes, recognition of differences equity and equality in society is important in the research field of policy and psychosocial ser-vices. This exploratory study is an initial step in Denmark. Nuanced per-spectives and promoting recognition intermarried couples and mixed children are vital for challenging negative stereotypes and discourses of mixed marriages as being inherently problematic. Hopefully the intermarried couples' own voices presented here have succeeded in adding some of these nuances and in providing a foundation for establishing and further developing relevant policies, organisations and psychosocial services.

Bibliography

Abu-Rayya, H. (2007) 'Acculturation, Christian Religiosity, and Psychological and Marital Well-being Among the European Wives of Arabs in Israel', *Mental Health, Religion & Culture* March, 10(2), 171–190

Addison, S. & Thomas, V. (2009) 'Power, Privilege, and Oppression: White Therapists Working with Minority Couples' in Rastogi, M. & Thomas, V. K. (eds.) *Multicultural Couple Therapy* (New Delhi: Sage), pp. 9–27

Agathangelou, A. & Killian, K. (2009) 'Electronic Attachments: Desire, the Other, and the Internet Marital Trade in the 21st Century' in Karis, T. & Killian, K. (eds.) *Intercultural Couples: Exploring Diversity in Intimate Relationships* (London: Routledge), pp. 111–144

Alba, R. & Nee, V. (2003) *Remaking the American Mainstream: Assimilation and Contemporary Immigration* (Cambridge, MA: Harvard University Press)

Ali, S. (2012) 'Situating Mixed Race Politics' in Edwards, R., Ali, S., Cabarello, C. & Song, M. (eds.) *International Perspectives on Racial and Ethnic Mixedness and Mixing* (London: Routledge)

Ali, S. (2003) *Mixed-Race, Post-Race, Gender: New Ethnicities and Cultural Practices* (Oxford: Berg)

Alibhai-Brown, Y. (2001) *Mixed Feelings: The Complex Lives of Mixed Race Britons* (London: Women's Press)

Alibhai-Brown, Y. (1999) *True Colours: Attitudes to Multiculturalism and the Role of Government* (London: Institute for Public Policy Research)

Allen, C. (2007) 'Down with Multiculturalism, Book-burning and Fatwas', *Culture and Religion: An Interdisciplinary Journal*, 8(2), 125–133

Almeida, R. V. (2009) 'Couples in the Desi Community: The Intersection of Culture, Gender, Sexual Orientation, Class and Domestic Violence' in Rastogi & Thomas (eds.) *Multicultural Couple Therapy* (New Delhi: Sage), pp. 277–295

Al-Sharmani, M. & Tiilikainen, M. (2014) *Transnational Migrant Families: Norms, Laws, and Lived Realities.* Available at: http://www.sfi.dk/Default.aspx?ID= 12506 (accessed 9 April 2014)

Andreassen, R. (2013) *For the Sake of Nation: Regulations of Inter-Racial Intimacies.* Paper presented in Intimate Migrations Conference, 3–5 April, Roskilde University

Andreassen, R. & Henningsen, A. F. (2011) *Menneske Udstilling: Fremvisninger af Eksotiske Mennesker i Zoologiske Have og Tivoli* (Copenhagen: Tiderne Skifter)

Arenas, J. & Singla, R. (1995) *Etnisk minoritetsungdom i Danmark – om deres psykosociale situation* (Copenhagen: Dansk Psykologisk Forlag)

Aspinall, P. & Song, M. (2013) *Mixed Race Identities* (Basingstoke: Palgrave Macmillan)

Baagøe Nielsen, N. & Gitz-Johansen, T. (2006) *Mænd i migrationsægteskaber – fortællinger om hverdag og vold i danske mænds samliv med udenlandske kvinder* (Roskilde Universitet & Ligestillingsministeriet). Available at: http://www.lige .dk

Bang, H. A. H. (2010). Negotiating Identities Among Children of Mixed Parentage (Unpublished Master Dissertation) Department of Psychology and Educational Studies Roskilde University

Barbara, A. (1989) *Marriage Across Frontiers* (Philadelphia: Multilingual Matters Ltd/Bardalio)

Barn, R., Das, C. & Sawyer, A. (2010) *Family Group Conferences and Black and Minority Ethnic Families* (London: Family Rights Group)

Beck-Gernsheim, E. (2002) *Reinventing the Family: In Search of New Lifestyles* (West Sussex: Wiley)

Beck-Gernsheim, E. (2002) 'Transnational Lives, Transnational Marriages: A Review of the Evidence from Migrant Communities', *Europe Global Networks*, 7(3), 271–288

Bech-Jessen, F. (2008) 'Kærlighedens Anatomi' [The Anatomy of Love], *Kristeligt Dagblad*, 4 July

Bech-Jørgensen, B. (1994) *Når hver dag bliver hverdag* (Copenhagen: Akademisk Forlag)

Beck, U. & Beck-Gernsheim, E. (1995) *The Normal Chaos of Love* (London: Polity Press)

Beck, U. & Beck-Gernsheim, E. (2014) *Distant Love: Personal Life in the Global Age German Fernleibe* (2011) translated by R. Livingstone (Cambridge: Polity)

Berry, J. (2011) *Integration and Multiculturalism: Ways Towards Social Solidarity.* Papers on Social Representations, 20, 2.1. Available at: http://www.psych.lse .ac.uk/psr/PSR2011/20_02.pdf (accessed 9 April 2011)

Bhagat, C. (2009) *Two States: The Story of My Marriage* (New Delhi: Rupa Publications)

Bhavnani, K. & Phoenix, A. (1994) *Shifting Identities, Shifting Racisms: A Feminism & Psychology Reader* (New Delhi: Sage)

Bhugra, D. & De Silva, P. (2000) 'Couple Therapy Across Cultures', *Journal of the British Association for Sexual and Relationship Therapy*, 15, 183–192

Bhui, K. (1999) 'Common Mental Disorders Among People with Origins in or Immigrants from India and Pakistan', *International Review of Psychiatry*, 11(2/3), 136–144

Bille, M. (2011) 'Mixede børn har fordele', *Børn & Unge*, 2. Available at: http://www.bupl.dk/iwfile/BALG-8DHBQG/$file/02_2011_Allesider.pdf (accessed 11 May 2014)

Blaine, B. (2013) *Understanding the Psychology of Diversity* (New Delhi: Sage)

Bonfanti, S. (2013) *Indian Diasporas and the Crafting of an Intimate Imagery: The Case of Second-Generation Punjabis in Italy.* Paper presented in Intimate Migrations Conference, 3–5 April, Roskilde University

Bourdieu, P. (1986) 'The forms of capital' in J. Richardson (Ed.) *Handbook of Theory and Research for the Sociology of Education* (New York, Greenwood), 241–258

Borneman, J. (1996) 'Until Death Do Us Part: Marriage/Death in Anthropological Discourse', *American Ethnologist*, 23(2), 215–235

Botelho, V. (2002) *Patterns and Trends of Mixed-Marriage in Denmark*, Danish Center for Demographic Research, SDU, Working Paper No. 25

Branner, J. (1983) 'Mand og Kvinde gør den største forskel' [Man and Woman Makes the Biggest Difference], *Politiken*, 2 June

Breger, R. & Hill, R. (eds.) (1998) *Cross-Cultural Marriage: Identity and Choice* (New York: Berg)

Breuning, H. D. (2012) *Betydninger i adoptivlivet* [Meaning in the Adopted Life], unpublished Master's thesis, Department of Educational Psychology, Danish School of Education

Caballero, C., Edwards, R. & Puthussery, S. (2008) *Parenting 'Mixed' Children: Negotiating Difference and Belonging in Mixed Race, Ethnicity and Faith Families* (York: Joseph Rowntree Foundation)

Castles, S. (2006) *Migration, Citizenship and the European Welfare State: A European Dilemma* (with Carl-Ulrik Schierup and Peo Hansen) (Oxford: Oxford University Press)

Center for Familieudvikling (2014) Center for Family Development. Available at: http://www.familieudvikling.dk/ accessed (31 October 2014)

Center for Studies in ISlam & Radicalisation Processes (2010) www.cir.au dk/en accessed 22.11.2014

Charsley, K. (ed.) (2012) *Transnational Marriage: New Perspectives from Europe and Beyond Research in Transnationalism* (London: Routledge)

Charsley, K. (2013) *Transnational Pakistani Connections: Marrying 'Back Home'* (London: Routledge)

Chaudhary, N. (2004) *Listening to Culture: Constructing Reality from Everyday Talk* (New Delhi: Sage)

Christensen, A. (2010) 'A Unified Protocol for Couple Therapy' in Hahlweg, K., Grawe-Gerber, M. & Baucom, D. H. (eds.) *Enhancing Couples: The Shape of Couple Therapy to Come* (Göttingen: Hogrefe), pp. 33–46

Chaudhary, N. (2007) 'The Family: Negotiating Cultural Values' in Valsiner J. & Rosa, A. (eds.) *The Cambridge Handbook of Sociocultural Psychology* (Cambridge: Cambridge University Press)

Christensen, A. (2010) 'A Unified Protocol for Couple Therapy' in Hahlweg, K., Grawe-Gerber, M. & Baucom, D. H. (eds.) *Enhancing Couples: The Shape of Couple Therapy to Come* (Göttingen: Hogrefe), pp. 33–46

Connolly, K. (2010) 'Angela Merkel Declares Death of German Multiculturalism', *The Guardian*, 17 October. Available at: http://www.source.ly/10zAC# .U0VLDalwDXR (accessed 9 April 2014)

Constable, N. (2010) 'Love at First Site? Visual Images and Virtual Encounters with Bodies' in Padilla, M., Hirsch, J., Munoz-Laboy, M., Sember, R. and Parker, R (eds.) *Love and Globalization* (Nashville, TN: Vanderbilt University Press), pp. 252–271

Constable, N. (2004) *Cross-Border Marriages: Gender and Mobility in Transnational Asia* (Philadelphia, PA: University of Pennsylvania Press)

Constable, N. (2013) *Temporary Intimacies, Transnationalism and Failed Cross-Border Marriages*. Paper presented in Intimate Migrations Conference, 3–5 April, Roskilde University

Consultant, State Administration (2014) *Psychologist Enlisa Khanna, Personal Communication*, 22 April

Cottrell, A. B. (1991) 'Cross-National Marriages: A Review of the Literature', *Journal of Comparative Family Studies*, 21(2), 151

Crenshaw, K. (2011) 'Demarginalizing the Intersection of Race and Sex: A Black Feminist Critique of Anti-discrimination Doctrine, Feminist Theory, and Anti-racist Politics' in Lutz, H., Virvar, M. T. H. & Supik, L. (eds.) *Framing Intersectionality: Debates on a Multi-Faceted Concept in Gender Studies* (Farnham: Ashgate), pp. 25–42

Daneshpour, M. (2009) 'Bridges Crossed, Paths Traveled: Muslim Intercultural Couples' in Karis, T. & Killian, K. (eds.) *Intercultural Couples: Exploring Diversity in Intimate Relationships* (London: Routledge), pp. 207–228

Danneskiold-Samsøe, B., Mørck, Y. & Sørensen, B. W. (2011) *Familien betyder alt Vold mod kvinder i etniske minoritetsfamilier* (Copenhagen: Frydenlund)

Davar, B. (2005) *Mental Health of Indian Women* (New Delhi: Sage)

Dawkins, M. (2012) *Clearly Invisible: Racial Passing and the Color of Cultural Identity* (Waco, TX: Baylor University Press)

De Graaf, P. M. & Kalmijn, M. (2006) 'Change and Stability in the Social Determinants of Divorce: A Comparison of Marriage Cohorts in the Netherlands', *European Sociological Review*, 22, 561–572

Dencik, L. (2005) *Mennesket i postmoderniseringen – om barndom, familie og identiteter i opbrud* [Human Beings and Postmodernization – On Childhood, Family and Changing Identities] (Værløse: Billesø & Baltzer)

Dencik, L. (2009) 'Kosher and the Christmas Tree: On Marriages Between Jews and Non-Jews in Sweden, Finland, & Norway' in Reinharz, A. & DellaPergola, S. (eds.) *Jewish Intermarriage Around the World* (London: Transaction Publishers), pp. 75–87

Dufoix, S. (2008) *Diasporas* (Berkeley, CA: University of California Press)

Dunger, F. (2010) *Making Sense of Intermarried Identities*, unpublished project report, International Development Studies, Roskilde University

Dunn, R. G. (1998) *Identity Crises: A Social Critique of Postmodernity* (St. Paul, MN: University of Minnesota Press)

Drolshagen, E. (1999) *Det skal de ikke slippe godt fra: kvinderne som forelskede sig i de tyske soldater under besættelsen* (oversat fra Tysk af Annette Pedersen) (Copenhagen: Schønberg)

Edwards, R., Ali, S., Caballero, C. & Song, M. (2012) *International Perspectives on Racial and Ethnic Mixedness and Mixing* (London: Routledge)

Faist, T. & Kivisto, P. (2010) *Beyond a Border: The Causes and Consequences of Contemporary Immigration* (New Delhi: Sage)

Fernandez, N. T. (2010) *Revolutionizing Romance: Interracial Couples in Contemporary Cuba* (New Brunswick, Quebec: Rutgers Press)

Fernando, S. (2010) *Mental Health, Race and Culture* (third edition) (Basingstoke: Palgrave Macmillan)

Fleischer, A. (2012) *Migration, Marriage and the Law: Making Families Among Cameroonian 'Bush Fallers' in Germany* (Berlin: Regiospectra)

Fletcher, G., Simpson, J., Campbell, L. & Overall, N. (2013) *The Science of Intimate Relationships* (West Sussex: Wiley-Blackwell)

Frederickson, G. (1981) *White Supremacy: A Comparative Study of American and South African History* (Oxford: Oxford University Press)

Ganesh, K. (1999) 'Patrinelael Structures and Agency of Women: Issues in Gendered Socialization' in T.S. Saraswathi (ed.) *Culture, Socialization and Human Development: Theory Research & Application* (New Delhi: Sage), pp. 235–254

Giblin, P. (2014) *Stages of Growth in Marriage*. Available at: http://www.foryourmarriage.org/stages-of-growth-in-marriage (accessed 31 October 2014)

Giddens, A. (1992) *The Transformation of Intimacy: Sexuality, Love and Eroticism in Modern Societies* (Cambridge: Polity)

Giddens, A. (1999) *Runaway World: How Globalization Is Reshaping Our Lives* (London: Profile)

Giles, J. (2008 *The Nature of Sexual Desire* (Lanham, MD: University Press of America)

Giles, J. (2006) 'Social Constructionism and Sexual Desire', *Journal for the Theory of Social Behaviour*, 36(3), 225–238

Gilroy, P. (2000) *Between Camps: Nations, Cultures & the Allures of Race* (London: Allen Lane)

Glenn, N. D. (1984) 'A Note on Estimating the Strength of Influences for Religious Endogamy', *Journal of Marriage and Family*, 46(3), 725–727

Greenman, P. S., Young, M. Y. & Johnson, S. M. (2009) 'Emotionally Focused Therapy with Intercultural Couples' in Rastogi, M. & Thomas, V. K. (eds.) *Multicultural Couple Therapy* (New York: Sage), pp. 143–165

Grewal, Z. (2009) 'Marriage in Colour: Race, Religion and Spouse Selection in Our American Mosques', *Ethnic and Racial Studies* 32(2) February, 323–345

Guzder, J., & Krishna, M. (2005). 'Mind the Gap: Diaspora Indian Women in Psychotherapy', *Journal of Psychology and Developing Societies: A Journal*, 17(2), 121–138.

Hall, S. (1991) 'Old and New Identities: Old & New Ethnicities' in King, A. (ed.) *Culture Globalisation and the World System – Contemporary Conditions for the Representation of Identity* (St. Paul, MN: University of Minnesota Press)

Hasse, C., Henningsen, I. & Søndergaard, D. M. (2002) 'Køn og Magt i Akademia' in Borchorst, A. (ed.) *Kønsmagt under forandring* (Copenhagen: Hans Reitzel), 110–129.

Hahlweg, K., Baucom, D., Grawe-Gerber, M. & Snyder, D. (2010) 'Strengthening Couples and Families: Dissemination of Interventions for Treatment and Prevention of Couple Distress' in Hahlweg, K., Grawe-Gerber, M. & Baucom, D. (eds.) *Enhancing Couples* (Göttingen: Hogrefe), pp. 3–29

Hemming Hansen, K. (2011) Hvid udenpå sort indeni (White Outside and Black Inside) Danarks Radio P1 Program Interview Among Others with Rashmi Singla First Broadcast 26 January 2011 http://www.dr.dk/arkivP1/Feature/Udsendelser/2011/06/26092027.htm (accessed 31 October 2014)

Highmore, B. (2002) *Everyday Life and Culture Theory: An Introduction* (London: Routledge)

Holm, Dagny (2010) '*Adopteret – og hvad så?*' [Adopted – So What?], Unpublished Master's Dissertation – An Integrated Thesis on Cultural Encounters and Psychology, Institut for Psykologi og Uddannelsesforskning, Roskilde University

Holmen, A. (2011) 'At tage udgangspunkt i det kendte: Om brug af modersmålet ved tilegnelsen af et nyt sprog' [Taking the Point of Departure in the Familiar: Using Mother Tongue for a New Language Acquisition], *Sprogforum*, 51, 47–55

Hussain, M. (2011) Copenhagen: Muslims in Europe – A Report on 11 EU Cities. At Home in Europe Project. Available at: www.opensocietyfoundations.org/sites/default/files/a-muslims-europe-20110214_0.pdf (accessed 31 October 2014)

Ifekwunigwe, J. O. (2004) '*Mixed Race Studies*' – A Reader (London: Routledge)

India Tribune (2014) http://www.indiatribune.com/index.php?option=com_content&id=9705:india-worlds-second-largest-english-speaking-country&Itemid=471 (accessed 30 November 2014)

Irastorza, N. & Devoretz, D. (2009) *Factors Affecting International Marriage Survival: A Theoretical Approach.* Available at: http://www.sfu.ca/~devoretz/lecturenotes/sem9.pdf (accessed 22 November 2013)

Jacobsen, C.H., Nilesen, J. & Mathiesen, B. B. (2013) Hvem er de dankse psykoterateuter: danske psykologer som psykoterapueter articleserie 1 (Who Are the Danish Psychotherapists) in Psykolog Nyt 18, pp. 16–18

Jakobsen, T. P. (2001) 'Arrangeret Ægteskab eller Kontakt annonce' in Reumert, P. (ed.) *Familiens Psykologi: Dens udvikling og dynamik* (Copenhagen: Gyldendal Uddannelse), pp. 48–67

Jankowiak, W. R. and Fischer, E.F. (1992) 'Cross-Cultural Perspective on Romantic Love', *Ethnology*, 31(2) (April), 149–155

Jenkins, R. (2011) *Being Danish: Paradoxes of Identity in Everyday Life* (Copenhagen: Museum Tusculanum Press)

Jensen, I. (2011) *Jobsamtaler med etniske minoriteter* (first edition) (Frederiksberg: Roskilde Universitetsforlag), p. 131

Johnson, E. (2007) *Dreaming of a Mail-order Husband: Russian-American Internet Romance* (Durham: Duke University Press)

Jonsson, P. (2009) *Interracial Marriage: Is Life Tougher for Biracial Kids?* Available at: http://www.csmonitor.com/USA/Society/2009/1016/p02s16-ussc.html (accessed 18 March 2014)

Joshi, M. & Krishna, M. (1998) 'English & North American Daughters-in-Law in the Hindu Joint Family' in Breger, R. & Hill, R. (eds.) *Cross-Cultural Marriage: Identity and Choice* (New York: Berg), pp. 171–191

Jung, C. J. (1965) *Dreams, Memories and Reflections* (New York: Vintage)

Kalmijn, M. (2012) 'Longitudinal Analyses of the Effects of Age, Marriage, and Parenthood on Social Contacts and Support', *Advances in Life Course Research*, 17(4), 177–190

Kalmijn, M. (2010) 'Country Differences in the Effects of Divorce on Well-being: The Role of Norms, Support, and Selectivity', *European Sociological Review*, 26(4), 475–490

Kalpagam, V. (2008) 'America *Varan*' 'Marriage Among Tamilian Brahmins: Preferences; Strategies and Outcomes' in Palriwala, R. & Uberoi, P. (eds.) *Marriage, Migration and Gender* vol. 5 (New Delhi: Sage), pp. 98–123

Kalra, V., Kaur, R. & Hutnyk, J. (2005) *Diaspora & Hybridity* (New Delhi: Sage)

Kang Fu, V. & Wolfinger, N. (2011) 'Broken Boundaries or Broken Marriages? Racial Intermarriage and Divorce in the United States', *Social Science Quarterly*, 92(4), 1096–1117

Kang Fu, V. (2008) 'Interracial–Interethnic Unions and Fertility in the United States', *Journal of Marriage and Family*, 70(3), 783–795

Karis, T. & Killian, K. (eds.) (2009) *Intercultural Couples: Exploring Diversity in Intimate Relationships* (London: Routledge)

Kenney, M. & Kenney, K. (2011) *Contemporary Multiple Heritage Couples, Individuals, and Families: A Generation with Diverse Views and Varied Experiences*, Metissage, Mestizaje, Mixed 'Race', and Beyond, Keynote in 6th Critical Multicultural Counselling and Psychotherapy Conference, OISE (Ontario Institute for Studies in Education), University of Toronto, 7 June 2011

Kenney, M. & Kenney, K. (2012) 'Contemporary Multiple Heritage Couples, Individuals, and Families: Issues, Concerns, and Counseling Implications', *Counselling Psychology Quarterly*, 25(2), 99–112

Khadudu, Z. (2014) 'Dear Esben Lund: "Neger" Is a Dirty Word', *Copenhagen Post*, 7–13 February

Khalakdina, M. (2011) *Human Development in the Indian Context: A Socio-cultural Focus* (New Delhi: Sage)

Killian, K. (2013) *Interracial Couples, Intimacy & Therapy: Crossing Racial Borders* (New York: Columbia University Press)

King-O'Riain et al. (2014) *Global Mixed Race* (New York: New York University Press)

Klienmann, S. & Copp, M. (1993) *Emotions and Fieldwork: Qualitative Research Methods* (Thousand Oaks, CA: Sage)

Kleist, A. (2011) 'Child Rearing in Bicultural Families: Socialisation Goals and Parental Ethnotheories in West African-German Families' in de Lopez, Kristine Jensen & Hansen, T. G. B. (eds.) *Development of Self in Culture: Self in Culture in Mind*, vol. 1 (Aalborg: Aalborg University Press), pp. 41–63

Krag, H. (2007) *Mangfoldighed, Magt og Minoriteter. Introduktion til Minoritetsforskningens Teorier* (Copenhagen: Forlaget Samfundslitteratur)

Kvale, S. & Brinkmann, S. (2009) *Interviews: Learning the Craft of Qualitative Research Interviewing* (New Delhi: Sage)

Larsen, A. F. (2008) *Slavernes Slægt* (Kins of the Slaves) (Copenhagen: Denmark Radio)

Lee, M. (2006) *Mental Health Foundation*. Available at: http://www.mentalhealth .org.uk/content/assets/PDF/publications/getting-on-full-report.pdf (accessed 8 February 2014)

Levy, G., Goff, S. & Widmer, J. M. (eds.) (2005) *Towards an Interdisciplinary Perspective on the Life Course* (Amsterdam: Elsevier)

Liversage, A. (2012) 'Divorce Among Turkish Immigrants in Denmark' in Charsley, K. (ed.) *Transnational Marriage: New Perspectives from Europe and Beyond* (London: Routledge)

Loona, S. (1995) Kultur og identitet i det flerkulturelle samfunn. Tema nr.: Psykologi i en verden i forandring, *Tidskrift for norsk psykologforening*, 8

Loua, I. (2012) *Når Aicha løber hjemmefra: Psykosocialt Arbejde med Etniske Minoritetspiger* [When Aicha Runs Away from Home: Psychosocial Work with Ethnic Minority Girls] (Copenhagen: Hans Reitzel)

Lutz, H., Virvar, M. T. H. & Supik, L. (eds.) *Framing Intersectionality: Debates on a Multi-Faceted Concept in Gender Studies* (Farnham: Ashgate)

Mahtani, M. (2012) 'Not the Same Difference; Notes on Mixed-Race Methodologies' in Edwards, R., Ali, S., Caballero, C. & Song, M. (eds.) *International Perspectives on Racial and Ethnic Mixedness and Mixing* (London: Routledge), pp. 156–168

Marriage Without Borders/Ægteskab Uden Grænser (2014) Available at: http:// www.aegteskabudengraenser.dk/ (accessed 9 February 2014)

Maxwell, A. (1998) 'Not All Issues Are Black or White: Some Voices from the Off-spring of Cross-Cultural Marriages' in Breger, R. & Hill, R. (eds.) *Cross-Cultural Marriage: Identity and Choice* (New York: Berg), pp. 209–228

McAdams, D. (2005) 'Studying Lives in Time' in Levy, G., Goff, S. & Widmer, J. M. (eds.) *Towards an Interdisciplinary Perspective on the Life Course* (Amsterdam: Elsevier)

Mcleod, J. (2011) *Second Edition Qualitative Research in Counselling and Psychotherapy* (London: Sage)

Mead, G. H. (1934) *Mind, Self and Society from the Standpoint of a Social Behaviorist* (New York: University of Chicago Press)

Merton, R. K. (1941) 'Intermarriage and the Social Structure: Fact and Theory', *Psychiatry*, 4(3), 361–374

Meszaros, J. (2013) *A Desire for the Exotic: Racialized Desires Within the Philippines Romance Tour Industry*. Paper presented in Intimate Migrations Conference, 3–5 April, Roskilde University

Mirdal, G. M. (2006) 'Stress and Distress in Migration: Twenty Years After', *International Migration Review*, 40, 375–389

Mixed Race Kids (2014) Available at: http://www.huffingtonpost.com/marcia-alesan-dawkins/what-the-mixed-kids-are-always-so-beautiful-meme-really-means_b_3792596.html (accessed 11 January 2014)

Moodley, R. (2011) *Outside the Sentence: Readings in Critical Multicultural Counselling and Psychotherapy* (Toronto: CDCP)

Morning, Ann (2012) 'Multiraciality and Census Classification in Global Perspective' in Edwards, R., Ali, S., Caballero, C. & Song, M. (eds.) *International Perspectives on Racial and Ethnic Mixedness and Mixing* (London: Routledge), pp. 10–22

Mortensen, S. K. (2014) 'Når Anna tjener mere end Anders' [When Anna Earns More Than Anders], i *Psykolog Nyt*, 6, 2–15

Murphy-Shigematsu, S. (2002) *Multicultural Encounters; Case Narratives from a Counseling Practice* (New York: Teachers College Press)

Myong, L. (2009) *Adopteret: Fortællinger om transnational og racialiseret tilblivelse* (Copenhagen: Danmarks Pædagogiske Universitetsskole, Aarhus University)

Mørch, S. (2001) 'Social identitet og integration hos etniske unge' [Social Identity and Integration Among Ethnic Youth], *Psyke & Logos*, 22(1), 224–243

Nakazawa, D. J. (2003) *Does Anybody Else Look Like Me?: A Parent's Guide to Raising Multiracial Children* (Cambridge: Da Capo Press/Lifelong Books)

Nandi, M. & Spickard, P. (2014) 'The Curious Career of the One-Drop Rule: Multiraciality and Membership in Germany Today' in King-O'Riain, R. C., Small, S., Mahtani, M., Song, M. & Spickard, P. (eds.) *Global Mixed Race* (New York: New York University Press), pp 188–212

Neergaard, S. (2013) 'Law Allowing Dual Citizenship Likely to Pass in Parliament', *Copenhagen Post*, 23 April

Nielsen, F. (2011) *Tværkulturel Konfliktmægling; Familiekonflikter blandt etniske minoritetsborgere* [Cross-cultural Conflict Mediation] (Copenhagen: Hans Reitzel)

Olumide, J. (2002) *Raiding the Gene Pool: The Social Construction of Mixed Race* (London: Pluto Press)

Overland, G., Guribye, E. & Lie, B. (eds.) (2014) *Nordic Work with Traumatised Refugees: Do We Really Care* (New Castle Upon Tyne: Cambridge Scholars Press)

Padilla et al (2007) (eds.) *Love and Globalization: Transformations of Intimacy in the Contemporary World* (Nashville, TN: Vanderbilt University Press)

Painuly, A. (2014) *Where Do I Belong?* (New Delhi: Rupa Publications)

Palriwala, R. & Uberoi, P. (2008) *Marriage, Migration and Gender*, vol. 5 (New Delhi: Sage)

Paris, J. & Guzder, J. (1989) 'The Poisoned Nest: Aspects of Exogamous Marriage', *Journal of American Academy of Psychoanalysis*, 17(3), 493–500

Parker, D. & Song, M. (2001) *Rethinking 'Mixed Race'* (London: Pluto Press)

Patny, L. (2013/1940) *Marriage and Our Society* (translated from Hindi by Meenakshi Nayar) (Jaipur: Jaipur Printers)

Pew Research Centre (2010) *Millennials: A portrait of Generation Next*. Available at: http://www.pewsocialtrends.org/files/2010/10/millennials-confident-connected-open-to-change.pdf (accessed 31 October 2014)

Phoenix, A. (2006) *Interrogating intersectionality: Productive ways of theorising multiple positioning*. Kvinder, Køn & Forskning, 2–3, pp. 21–30.

Phoenix, A. (2008) 'Claiming Liveable Lives: Adult Subjectification and Narratives of 'Non-Normative' Childhood Experiences', in Kofoed, J. & Staunaes, D. (eds.) *Magtballader (Adjusting Reality)* (Copenhagen: Danmarks Pædagogiske Universitetsforlag), pp. 178–193

Phoenix, A. (2011) 'Psychosocial Intersections: Contextualizing the Accounts of Adults Who Grew Up in Visibly Ethnically Different Households' in Lutz, H., Virvar, M. T. H. & Supik, L. (eds.) *Framing Intersectionality: Debates on a Multi-Faceted Concept in Gender Studies* (Farnham: Ashgate), pp. 137–152

Piller, I. (2009) 'I Always Wanted to Marry a Cowboy'. Bilingual Couples, Language and Desire' in Karis, T. & Killian, K. (eds.) *Intercultural Couples: Exploring Diversity in Intimate Relationships* (London: Routledge), pp. 53–70

Poddar, P. (2013) *Cultural Encounters Post Colonialism*. Professor Inaugural Lecture, Roskilde University, 15 October 2013

Poulsen, P. (2012) *På tværs og På Trods: Om Ægteskabsmigration i Danmark* [On the Contrary and Despite: About Marriage Migration in Denmark [(Copenhagen: Frydenlund)

Qian, Z. (2005) 'Breaking the Last Taboo: Interracial Marriage in America', *Contexts*, Fall, 33–37

Raghuram, P. & Sahoo, A. (2008) 'Thinking "Indian Diaspora" of Our Times' in Raghuram, P., Sahoo, A., Maharaj, B. and Sangha, D. (eds.) *Tracing an Indian Diaspora* (New Delhi: Sage), pp. 1–28

Rai, R. & Reeves, P. (eds.) (2009) *South Asian Diaspora: Transnational Networks & Changing Identities* (London: Routledge)

Rashid, R. & Højbjerg, J. (2007) *Bag Sløret* (Copenhagen: People's Press)

Rastogi, M. & Thomas, V. K. (eds.) (2009) *Multicultural Couple Therapy* (New Delhi: Sage)

Rastogi, M. (2009) 'Drawing Gender to the Foreground: Couple Therapy with South Asians in the United States' in Rastogi, M. & Thomas, V. K. (eds.) *Multicultural Couple Therapy* (New Delhi: Sage), pp. 257–275

Rauschenbusch, T. (2010) *New Realities, Old Ideals*, German Youth Institute (DJI) Bulletin Available at: http://www.dji.de/bulletins (accessed 15 September 2011)

Reddy, P. G. (1991) *Sådan er danskerne!: En Indisk Antropologs Perspektiv på det Danske Samfund* (Mørke: Grevas)

Reddy, P. G. (1998) *Danske Dilemmaer* (Mørke: Grevas)

Refsing, K. (1998) 'Gender Identity and Gender Role Patterns in Cross-Cultural Marriages: The Japanese-Danish Case' in Breger, R. & Hill, R. (eds.) *Cross-Cultural Marriage: Identity and Choice* (New York: Berg), pp. 193–208

Reinharz, A. & DellaPergola, S. (eds.) (2009) *Jewish Intermarriage Around the World* (New Brunswick, Quebec: Transaction Publishers)

Romano, D. (2008) *Intercultural Marriages: Promises and Pitfalls* (revised edition) (Boston, MA: Intercultural Press)

Romain, J. (1996) *Till Faith Us Do Part: Couples Who Fall in Love Across the Religious Divide* (Hammersmith: HarperCollins Publishers)

Root, M. P. P. (ed.) (1992) *Racially Mixed People of America* (Thousand Oaks, CA: Sage), pp. 3–11

Root, Maria P. P. (ed.) (1996) *The Multiracial Experience: Racial Borders as the New Frontier* (Thousand Oaks, CA: Sage)

Root, M. P. P. (2001) *Love's Revolution: Interracial Marriage* (Philadelphia, PA: Temple University Press)

Rosenblatt, P. C. (2009) 'A Systems Theory Analysis of Intercultural Couple Relationships' in Karis, A. & Killian, K. D. (eds.) *Intercultural Couples: Exploring Diversity in Intimate Relationships* (New York: Routledge), pp. 3–20

Rytter, Mikkel (2007) 'Partnervalgets grænse: Dansk-pakistanske Ægteskabsmigranter i Sverige', *Dansk Sociologi*, 3, 25–46

Rytter, Mikkel (2013) 'Family Upheaval: Generation, Mobility and Relatedness Among Pakistani Migrants in Denmark', *EASA Series*, 21

Sanghera, G. & Thapar-Bjokert, S. (2007) 'Methodological Issues: Gatekeepers and Positionality in Bradford', *Ethnic and Racial Studies*. 1 (20)

Santos, B. (2006) with Nunes, J. & Menes, M. *Opening up the Canon of Knowledge and Recognition of Differences.* Available at: http://www.boaventuradesousasantos.pt/media/Introduction%283%29.pdf (accessed 31 October 2014)

Sato, T., Yasuda, Y., Kido, A., Arakawa, A., Mizoguchi, H. & Valsiner, J. (2007) 'Sampling Reconsidered: Idiographic Science & the Analysis of Personal Life Trajectories' in Valsiner, J. & Rosa, A. (eds.) *The Cambridge Handbook of Sociocultural Psychology* (Cambridge: Cambridge University Press), pp. 82–106

Saulny, S. (2011) 'In Strangers' Glances at Family, Tensions Linger'. Available at: http://www.nytimes.com/2011/10/13/us/for-mixed-family-old-racial-tensions-remain-part-of-life.html (accessed 16 October 2011)

Schaffer-Grabiel, F. (2006) 'Planet-Love.com: Cyberbrides in the Americas and the Transnational Routes of U.S. Masculinity', *Journal of Women in Culture and Society*, 31(2), 331–356

Schoebi, D., Wang, Z., Ababkov, V. & Perrez, M. (2011) 'Affective Interdependence in Married Couples' Daily Life: Are There Cultural Differences in Partner Effects of Anger?', *Family Science*, 1(2), 83–92

Sedmak, M. (2012) 'When Ethnicity Became an Important Family Issue: The Case of Slovenian Istria' in Edwards, R., Ali, S., Caballero, C. & Song, M. (eds.) *International Perspectives on Racial and Ethnic Mixedness and Mixing* (London: Routledge), pp. 57–72

Sengstock, M.C. (2009) with Javed, A., Berkeley, S. & Marshall, B. *Voices of Diversity: Multi-culturalism in America* (New York: Springer)

Simon, R. F. (2007) *Contributions of the Sociology of Mental Health for Understanding the Social Antecedents, Social Regulation, and Social Distribution of Emotion, Mental Health, Social Mirror* (New York: Springer), pp. 239–274

Shay, C. (2010) 'Loving Day', *Time*, Friday 11 June

Singla, R. (2003) Ungdom og etnicitet, Udfordringer i modernitetens landskabet *Psykologisk Set* vol.20, nr. 51

Singla, R. (2004) *Youth Relationships, Ethnicity and Psychosocial Intervention* (New Delhi: Books Plus), pp. 4–14

Singla, R. (2006) *Den eneste ene – Hvordan Etniske Minoritetsunge i Danmark Danner Par*, Konflikt og intervention (2006). Available at: http://www.akademia.dk (eBook)

Singla, R. (2008) *Now and Then – Life Trajectories, Family Relationships and Diasporic Identities: A Follow-up Study of Young Adults* (Copenhagen: Copenhagen Studies in Bilingualism)

Singla, R. (2010) *Intermarriage, Children of Mixed Parentage and Mental Health: Life Course and Psycho Social Intervention Perspectives.* Paper presented in Symposia Cross Border Relationships: Changing Paradigms & Psychosocial Challenges IACCP, 7–10 July, Melbourne

Singla, R. (2011) 'Plugged in Youth: Technology and Transnationalism Among South Asian Diaspora in Scandinavia' in German, Myna & Banerjee, Padmini (eds.) *Migration, Technology and Transculturation: A Global Perspective* (St. Charles, MO: Lindenwood University Press), pp. 141–164

Singla, R. (2012) *Health Promotion & Counseling in Context of Mixedness: Intermarried Couples & Parenting of Children and Mental Well Being.* Keynote Presentation Second International Conference on Counseling, Psychothrapy and the third Congress of Integrating Traditional Healing into Counseling, Psychotherapy and Psychiatry, Bangalore: Christ University 4–6 January

Singla, R. & Holm, D. (2012) 'Intermarried Couples, Mental Health and Psychosocial Wellbeing: Negotiating Mixedness in the Danish Context of "Homogeneity"', *Counselling Psychology Quarterly*, 25(2), 1 June 2012, 151–165

Singla, R. (2014) 'Psychosocial Intervention with Ethnic Minority Families in Denmark' in Overland, G., Guribye, E. & Lie, B. (eds.) *Nordic Work with Traumatised Refugees: Do We Really Care* (New Castle Upon Tyne: Cambridge Scholars Press), pp. 245–260

Skytte, M. (2007) *Etniske Minoritetsfamilier og Socialt Arbejde*, 3. udg. (Copenhagen: Hans Reitzel)

Social Media Today (2014) 'Technology: Are You Suffering from Fear of Missing Out?'. Available at: http://socialmediatoday.com/contentmoney/1604246/technology-are-you-suffering-fomo (accessed 6 April 2014)

Song, M. (2009) 'Is Intermarriage a Good Indicator of Integration?', *Journal of Ethnic and Migration Studies*, 35(2), 331–348

Song, M. (2012) 'Making Sense of "Mixture": States and the Classification of "Mixed" People', *Ethnic and Racial Studies*, 35(4), 565–573

Song, M. & Aspinall, P. (2012) '"Mixed-Race" Young People's Differential Responses to Misrecognition in Britain' in Edwards, R., Ali, S., Caballero, C. & Song, M. (eds.) *International Perspectives on Racial and Ethnic Mixedness and Mixing* (London: Routledge)

Sookoor, M., Moodley, R., Pinto, G., Hall & Wu R. (2011) *Narratives and Lived Experiences of Men in Interethnic/Interracial Relationships – Preliminary Findings of a Focus Group.* Paper presented in Metissage, Mestizaje, Mixed 'Race', and Beyond, 6th Critical Multicultural Counseling & Psychotherapy Conference, OISE (Ontario Institute for Studies in Education), 7–8 June

Spanger, M. (2013) 'Doing Marriage and Love in the Borderland of Transnational Sex Work: Female Thai Migrants in Denmark'. *NORA – Nordic Journal of Feminist and Gender Research*, 21(2), 1–27

Spickard, P. (1989/1992) *Mixed Blood: Intermarriage and Ethnic Identity in Twentieth-Century America* (Madison, WI: University of Wisconsin Press)

Spickard, P. (with Joanne L. Rondilla) (2007) *Is Lighter Better? Skin-Tone Discrimination Among Asian Americans* (Lanham, MD: Rowman and Littlefield)

Snyder, D. K. & Gasbarrini, F. (2010) 'Integrative Approaches to Couple Therapy: Implications for Clinical Practice, Training and Research' in Hahlweg, K., Grawe-Gerber, M. & Baucom, D. H. (eds.) *Enhancing Couples: The Shape of Couple Therapy to Come* (Göttingen: Hogrefe), pp. 47–60

Stanners, P. (2012) 'Dual Citizenship Delayed at Least Another Year', *Copenhagen Post*, 13 October

Statistics Denmark (2010/2012/2013) *Befolkning, 10*. Available at: http://www.dst.dk (accessed 12 December 2010, 25 November 2013)

Stoppard, M. (2006) *The Mirror*, 27 January Advice Column

Surra, C., Gray, C., Boettcher, T., Cottle, N. & West, A. (2006) 'From Courtship to Universal Properties: Research on Dating and Mate Selection, 1950–2003' in Vangelisti A. & Perlman, D. (eds.) *The Cambridge Handbook of Personal Relationships* (New York: Cambridge University Press), pp. 113–130

Tharp, R. (2009/1970) 'Psychological Patterning in Marriage' in Gry A. L. (ed.) *Man, Woman and Marriage: Small Group Processes in the Family* (Piscataway, NJ, Transaction Publishers), pp. 62–95

The State Administration (2014) *State Authority Belonging to Ministry for Economic Affairs and the Interior*. Available at: http://www.statsforvaltningen.dk/ (accessed 23 April 2014)

Times of India (2014) Most Indians still prefer arranged marriages p.1 http://timesofindia.indiatimes.com/life-style/relationships/man-woman/most-indians-still-prefer-arranged-marriages/articleshow/33655556.cms (accessed 29 November 2014)

Tizard, B. & Phoenix, A. (2002) *Black, White or Mixed Race? Race and Racism in the Lives of: People of Mixed Parentage* (revised edition) (London: Routledge)

Törngren, Osanami, S. (2011) *Love Ain't Got No Color? – Attitude Toward Interracial Marriage in Sweden*, Ph.D. thesis, Malmö, Studies in International Migration and Ethnic Relations, No. 10

Trask, S. & Koivunen (2007) 'Trends in Marriage and Cohabitation' in Trask, S. & Hamon, R. (eds.) *Cultural Diversity and Families: Expanding Perspectives* (New Delhi: Sage), pp. 80–99

Tutu, D. (2014) Campaigning to Make a Difference. Liverpool: International Slavery Museum. Available at: http://www.liverpoolmuseums.org.uk/ism/collections/legacies/index.aspx (accessed 16 October 2014)

Twine, France Winddance (2010) *A White Side of Black Britain: Interracial Intimacy and Racial Literacy* (Durham, NC: Duke University Press)

Valsiner, J. & Rosa, A. (2007) *The Cambridge Handbook of Sociocultural Psychology* (Cambridge: Cambridge University Press)

Valsiner, J. (2008) *The Social and the Cultural: Where Do They Meet? Meaning in Action: Constructions, Narratives, and Representations* (Tokyo: Springer), pp. 273–287

Valsiner, J. (2014) Valsiner for Oslo 2014 Summer Schhol NAP ad. pdf.

Vaughn, L. M. (2010) *Psychology and Culture: Thinking, Feeling and Behaving in a Global* Context (East Sussex: Psychology Press)

Verkuyten, M. (2005) *The Social Psychology of Ethnic Identity* (East Sussex: Psychology Press)

Vertovec, S. (2000) *The Hindu Diaspora: Comparative Patterns* (London: Routledge)

Wehrly, B., Kenney, K. & Kenney, M. (1999) *Counselling Multiracial Families (Multicultural Aspects of Counselling And Psychotherapy)* (Thousand Oaks, CA: Sage)

Whitty, M. & Carr, A. (2006) *Cyberspace Romance: The Psychology of Online Relationships* (Basingstoke: Palgrave Macmillan)

WHO (2014) 'What Is Mental Health?' Available at: http://www.who.int/features/qa/62/en/index.html (accessed 8 February 2012)

Willerton, J. (2010) *The Psychology of Relationships* (Basingstoke: Palgrave Macmillan)

Williams, L. (2009) *Imagining Cross Border Marriage: Personal and Official Narratives of Marriage and Migration.* Paper presented in COST Meeting, 21–22 October, Oslo

Williams, L. (2010) *Global Marriage: Cross-Border Marriage Migration in Global Context* (Basingstoke: Palgrave Macmillan)

Wu, R. (2011) *A Narrative Inquiry into the Lived Experiences of Chinese-White Heterosexual Couples Within a Canadian Context.* Paper presented in Metissage, Mestizaje, Mixed 'Race', and Beyond, 6th Critical Multicultural Counselling & Psychotherapy Conference (OISE, Ontario Institute for Studies in Education), 7–8 June

Yancey, G. A. & Yancey, S. W. (eds.) (2003) *Just Don't Marry One: Interracial Dating, Marriage and Parenting* (Cleveland, OH: Judson Press)

Index

CPSIA information can be obtained at www.ICGtesting.com
Printed in the USA
LVOW09*2125030615

440991LV00003B/214/P

Fodor's 92
Bermuda

Fodor's Travel Publications, Inc.
New York and London

ISBN 0-679-02018-7

"America's Rebel Colonies and Bermuda: Getting a Bang for Their Buckwheat" is excerpted from *Bermuda Journey*, by William Zuill. Copyright © 1946 by William Edward Sears Zuill. Reprinted by permission of the Estate of William Edward Sears Zuill.

"Bermuda's Hidden Landscapes," by William G. Scheller, first appeared in the May/June 1991 issue of *Islands*. Copyright © 1991 by William G. Scheller. Reprinted by permission of the author.

"Following in the Tracks of the Bermuda Railway," by Ben Davidson, was originally published as "Off Bermuda's Beaten Track." Reprinted with permission from *Travel & Leisure*, November 1987. Copyright © 1987 by American Express Publishing Corporation. All rights reserved.

Fodor's Bermuda

Editor: Jillian Magalaner
Contributors: Suzanne E. De Galan, John DeMers, Honey Naylor, Peter Oliver
Art Director: Fabrizio LaRocca
Cartographer: David Lindroth
Illustrator: Karl Tanner
Cover Photograph: Andrew McKim/Masterfile

Design: Vignelli Associates

Special Sales

Fodor's Travel Publications are available at special discounts for bulk purchases (100 copies or more) for sales promotions or premiums. Special editions, including personalized covers, excerpts of existing guides, and corporate imprints, can be created in large quantities for special needs. For more information, write to Special Marketing, Fodor's Travel Publications, 201 East 50th St., New York, NY 10022, or call 1–800–800–3246. Inquiries from the United Kingdom should be sent to Fodor's Travel Publications, 20 Vauxhall Bridge Rd., London SW1V 2SA.

Contents

Maps

Foreword

For their help in preparing this guide, we would like to thank the Bermuda National Trust; Connie Dey; Elsbeth Gibson; Stephen Martin of Bermuda Small Properties; David Mitchell for the Bermuda Collection; Jacqueline Pash of Porter/Novelli; Judy Blatman of Princess Hotels; Vivian Guerrero of Trust House Forte; Charles Webbe and Pam Wissing of the Bermuda Department of Tourism; Lisa Weisbord and Georgetta Lordi of Hill & Knowlton; and Jim Zuill of the Bermuda Book Store.

While every care has been taken to assure the accuracy of the information in this guide, the passage of time will always bring change, and consequently, the publisher cannot accept responsibility for errors that may occur.

All prices and opening times quoted here are based on information supplied to us at press time. Hours and admission fees may change, however, and the prudent traveler will avoid inconvenience by calling ahead.

Fodor's wants to hear about your travel experiences, both pleasant and unpleasant. When a hotel or restaurant fails to live up to its billing, let us know and we will investigate the complaint and revise our entries where the facts warrant it.

Send your letters to the editors of Fodor's Travel Publications, 201 E. 50th St., New York, NY 10022.

Highlights'92 and Fodor's Choice

Highlights '92

In May 1991, **Northwest Airlines** began service from Boston to Bermuda, and negotiations for flights from Detroit to Bermuda are underway. Also in the spring, **United Airlines** began flights from Dulles/Washington to Bermuda.

The luxury **Bermudiana** which has been closed since 1988, will reopen as an executive time-share property, but at press time no date had been set for its opening. Occupying 1,500 feet of south shore beachfront (formerly the home of the Banana Beach Hotel, the Flamingo Hotel, and the Golden Hind Restaurant), the luxury **Ritz-Carlton** is set to open in 1994. The cost of the project: $180–$200 million. **St. George's Club,** an exclusive and ultramodern time-share and hotel property in the town of St. George's, is expanding its facilities in 1991: Eight new units and another restaurant are to be added.

On November 3, 1990, Princess Margaret officially opened the Clocktower Specialty Retail Center at the Royal Naval Dockyard. The luxury, split-level mall houses shops, many of them branches of Hamilton shops, as well as a pastry shop and tearoom. Dockyard, a former shipyard of the British Royal Navy, is currently under development as a tourist attraction on the island's west end.

Tavern on the Green, a popular restaurant in the Botanical Gardens, closed in 1990. The building was slated to be converted into an information and interpretative center for visitors to the gardens. Operated by the Bermuda Botanical Society, this facility will also include a souvenir shop, a tearoom serving light lunches, and office space.

In 1991, businesses in Bermuda suffered a slump as a result of the U.S. recession. In a move to accommodate cruise-ship passengers (and increase sales), shops in Somerset Village will stay open until 10 PM on Wednesday nights during the cruise season. Shops in St. George's (including east end branches of Trimingham's, A. S. Cooper's, Archie Brown's, and Smith's) will remain open until 6 PM on Wednesday nights during the 1991 season. Shoppers in St. George's will be entertained by a peripatetic trio that will roam through the shopping areas.

Fodor's Choice

No two people will agree on what makes a perfect vacation, but it's fun and helpful to know what others think. We hope you'll have a chance to experience some of Fodor's Choices yourself in Bermuda. For detailed information about each entry, refer to the appropriate chapter.

Beaches

Chaplin Bay

Horseshoe Bay

Somerset Long Bay

Warwick Long Bay

Favorite Outdoor Activities

Offshore wreck diving

Snorkeling at Church Bay

Golfing at Port Royal Golf & Country Club

Running or riding through the dunes at South Shore Park

Favorite Sights

Pink-and-white cottages dotting the island

Pipers going at full tilt on the green at Ft. Hamilton

The children's room at Verdmont

The astonishing blues and greens of the sea

Statues by Desmond Fountain

Pastel Hamilton from the deck of a ferry

The narrow alleys in St. George's

The view from Gibb's Hill Lighthouse

Lodging

Cambridge Beaches *(Very Expensive)*

Horizons & Cottages *(Very Expensive)*

The Reefs *(Very Expensive)*

The Princess *(Expensive)*

Rosedon *(Expensive)*

Waterloo House *(Expensive)*

Oxford House *(Moderate)*

Pretty Penny *(Moderate)*

Little Pomander Guest House *(Inexpensive)*

Salt Kettle House *(Inexpensive)*

Restaurants

Waterlot Inn *(Very Expensive)*

Plantation *(Expensive)*

Black Horse Tavern *(Moderate)*

Colony Pub *(Moderate)*

Once Upon a Table *(Moderate)*

Dennis's Hideaway *(Inexpensive)*

Special Moments

The ferry ride from Hamilton to Somerset

Driving around the island in a London cab

Browsing through the Bermuda Book Store

Watching the Gombey Dancers

Swimming and sunning at Horseshoe Bay

Taste Treats

A Dark and Stormy (or two or three) at Casey's Bar

Diet destroyers at Fourways Pastry shops

Burgers at the Ice Queen at 3 AM

A rum swizzle at the Swizzle Inn

Shark hash at Dennis's Hideaway

ATLANTIC OCEAN

WEST END

Ireland Island N. ■ **Royal Naval Dockyard**
(Bermuda Maritime Museum)

Cruise Ship
Dock

Ireland Island S.

Boaz
Island
Waterford
Is.

Cobbler's
Island

Clarence
Cove

Devonshire
Dock

Sea Gardens

Malbar Rd.

Spanish
Point

Spanish

PEMBROKE

DE

Watford Br.

Hamilton

Front St.

Somerset
Island

SANDYS

Somerset Rd.

Great Sound

Cruise Ship
Dock

Hawkins
Island

Hamilton
Harbour

Middle Rd.

Somerset Br.

Spicelands
Riding Centre

Harbour Rd.

PAGET

Spring
Benny's
Bay

Middle Rd.

Little Sound

WARWICK

Middle Rd.

South Rd.

Warwick Long Bay

West Whale
Bay

SOUTHAMPTON

Gibb's Hill
Lighthouse

Horseshoe
Bay

N

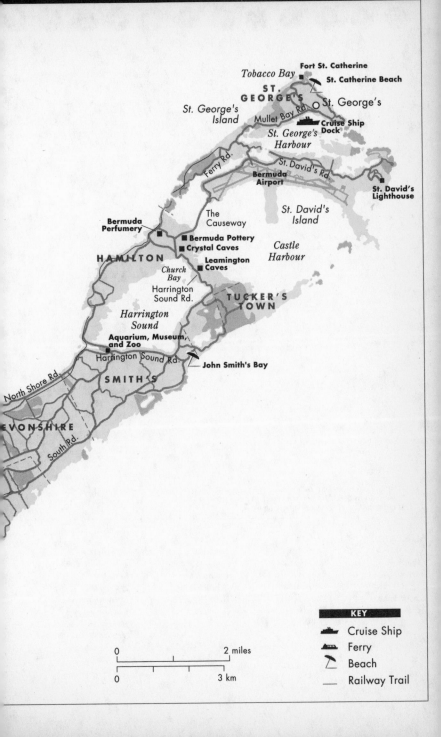

KEY

🚢 Cruise Ship

⛴ Ferry

⛱ Beach

— Railway Trail

World Time Zones

Numbers below vertical bands relate each zone to Greenwich Mean Time (0 hrs.).
Local times frequently differ from these general indications,
as indicated by light-face numbers on map.

Algiers, **29**	Berlin, **34**	Delhi, **48**	Istanbul, **40**
Anchorage, **3**	Bogotá, **19**	Denver, **8**	Jerusalem, **42**
Athens, **41**	Budapest, **37**	Djakarta, **53**	Johannesburg, **44**
Auckland, **1**	Buenos Aires, **24**	Dublin, **26**	Lima, **20**
Baghdad, **46**	Caracas, **22**	Edmonton, **7**	Lisbon, **28**
Bangkok, **50**	Chicago, **9**	Hong Kong, **56**	London (Greenwich), **27**
Beijing, **54**	Copenhagen, **33**	Honolulu, **2**	Los Angeles, **6**
	Dallas, **10**		Madrid, **38**
			Manila, **57**

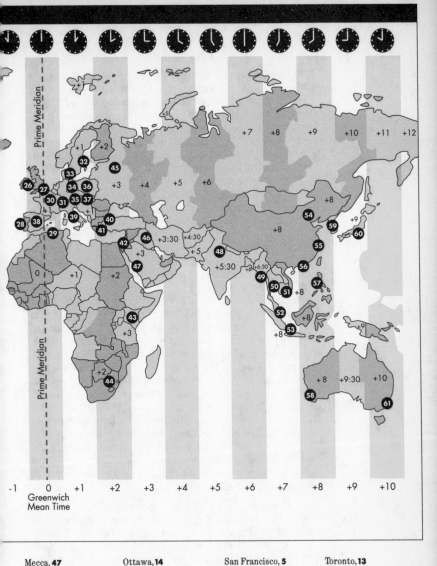

Introduction

B asking in the Atlantic 508 miles due east of Cape Hatteras, Bermuda is one of the wealthiest countries in the world—average per capita income is $20,000. Bermuda has no income tax, no sales tax, no slums, no unemployment, and no major crime problem. Don't come to Bermuda expecting a tropical paradise where laid-back locals wander around barefoot drinking piña coladas. On Bermuda's 20 square miles, you will find neither towering mountains, glorious rain forests, nor exotic volcanos. Instead, pastel cottages, quaint shops, and manicured gardens are indicative of a more staid, suburban way of life. As a British diplomat once said, "Bermuda is terribly middle-age"—and in many ways he was right. Most of the island is residential; the speed limit is 20 mph; golf and tennis are popular pastimes; the majority of visitors are over 40 years old; restaurants and shops are expensive; and casual attire in public is frowned upon. The population of 54,000 is 61% black and 39% white, but Bermudians speak the Queen's English in the Queen's own accent. White Bermudians, in particular, have strived to create a middle-class England of their own. And like almost all colonies, the Bermudian version is more insular, more conservative, and more English than the original. Pubs, fish-and-chips, and cricket are just outward manifestations of a fierce loyalty to Britain and everything it represents (or used to represent). A self-governing British colony, with a Parliament that dates to 1620, Bermudians love pomp and circumstance, British tradition, and Bermudian history. Great ceremony attends the convening of Parliament; marching bands parade through the capital in honor of the Queen's official birthday; regimental bands and bagpipers reenact centuries-old ceremonies; and tea is served each afternoon.

Bermuda wears its history like a comfortable old coat—land is too valuable to permit the island's legacy to be cordoned off for mere display. A visitor need only wander through the 17th-century buildings of St. George's, now home to shops and private residences, to realize that Bermudian history remains part of the fabric of life, with each successive generation adding its own thread of achievement and color. Indeed, the island's isolation and diminutive size have forged a continuity of place and tradition almost totally missing in the United States. Walk into Trimingham's or A. S. Cooper & Son department stores, and you are likely to be helped by a descendant of the original founders. The same names from history keep cropping up—Tucker, Carter, Trott—and a single lane in St. George's can conjure up centuries of memories and events. Even today, the brief love affair in 1804 between Irish poet Thomas Moore and the married Hester Tucker—the "Nea" of his odes—is gossiped about with a zeal usually reserved for the transgressions of a neighbor. Bermuda's attachment to its history is more than a product of its size, however. Through its past, Bermuda invokes its own sense of identity and reinforces its relationship with Britain. Otherwise, cast off in the Atlantic more than 3,445 miles from London (yet only 508 miles from the United States), Bermuda would probably have succumbed to American cultural influences long ago.

Since the very beginning, the fate of this small colony in the Atlantic has been linked to that of the United States. The crew of the *Sea Venture*, whose wreck on Bermuda during a hurricane in 1609 began the settlement of the island, was actually on its way to Jamestown in Virginia. Indeed, the passenger list of the *Sea Venture* reads like a veritable *Who's Who* of early American history. Aboard were Sir Thomas Gates, Deputy Governor of Jamestown; Christopher Newport, who had led the first expedition to Jamestown; and John Rolfe, whose second wife was Princess Pocahontas. In succeeding centuries, Bermuda has been a remarkable barometer of the evolving relationship between the United States and Britain. In 1775, Bermuda was secretly forced to give gunpowder to George Washington in return for the lifting of a trade blockade that threatened the island with starvation. In the War of 1812, Bermuda was the staging post for the British fleet's attack on Washington, DC. And with Britain facing a national crisis in 1940, the United States was given land on Bermuda to build a Naval Air Station in exchange for ships and supplies. As recently as 1990, Prime Minister Thatcher and President Bush held talks on the island.

The fact that Bermuda—just two hours by air from New York—has maintained its English character through the years is obviously part of its appeal for the more than half-million Americans (89% of all tourists) who flock here each year. More importantly, however, Bermuda means sun, sea, and sand. This bastion of Britain boasts a mild climate year-round, pink beaches, turquoise waters, coral reefs, 17th-century villages, and splendid golf courses (Bermuda has more golf courses per square mile than anywhere else in the world).

Bermuda did not always seem so attractive. After all, more than 300 wrecks lie submerged on those same reefs where divers now frolic. William Strachey, Secretary-elect for Virginia and a passenger on the *Sea Venture* in 1609, wrote that Bermuda was "a place so terrible to all that ever touched on them—such tempests, thunders and other fearful objects are seen and heard about those islands that they are called The Devills Islands, feared and avoided by all sea travellers above any place in the world." For the crew of the *Sea Venture*, however, the 181 small islands that comprise Bermuda meant salvation. Contrary to rumor, the islands proved to be unusually fertile and hospitable, supporting the crew during the construction of two new ships, in which they departed for Jamestown on May 10th, 1610.

Shakespeare drew on the accounts of the survivors in *The Tempest*, written in 1611. The wreck of the *Sea Venture* on harsh yet beneficent Bermuda—"these infortunate (yet fortunate) islands," as one survivor described them—contained all the elements of Shakespearean tragicomedy: That out of loss something greater is often born. Just as Prospero loses the duchy of Milan only to regain it and secure the kingdom of Naples for his daughter, Admiral Sir George Somers lost a ship but gained an island. Today, Bermuda's motto is "Quo Fata Ferunt" (Whither the Fates Carry Us), an expression of sublime confidence in the same providence that carried the *Sea Venture* safely to shore.

That confidence has largely been justified over the years, but concerns have recently been raised about congestion, overfishing, reef damage, and a declining quality of life. Nearly 600,000 visitors a year are the golden eggs that many Bermudians feel are now killing the goose. In the face of such an influx of tourists, the behavior of some service employees, particularly bus drivers and young store clerks, has become sullen and rude. Traffic jams leading into Hamilton, the island's capital, are no longer a rarity, despite the fact that families can only have one car and car rentals are prohibited. In 1990, the government restricted the number of cruise-ship visits to four per week, citing the large numbers of passengers who add to the congestion but contribute little to the island's coffers. Instead, the Bermuda Department of Tourism hopes to attract a wealthier clientele (Bermuda's tourists are already among the most affluent anywhere), preferably during the less-frequented winter season, when golf and tennis are the island's major attractions.

When all is said and done, however, Bermuda's problems stem from a surfeit of advantages rather than a dearth, and almost every island nation would gladly inherit them. The "still-vexed Bermoothes" is how Shakespeare described this Atlantic pearl, but the author of *The Tempest* may have changed his tune if he had had a chance to swim at Horseshoe Bay, or hit a mashie-niblick to the 15th green at Port Royal. Who knows, instead of referring to a storm-wracked island, *The Tempest* might have been Shakespeare's reaction to a missed putt on the 18th.

1 Essential Information

Before You Go

Government Tourist Offices

The **Bermuda Department of Tourism** has offices in the following locations:

In Bermuda Global House, 43 Church Street, Hamilton HM 12, Bermuda, tel. 809/292–0023, fax 809/292–7537.

In the United States 310 Madison Avenue, New York, NY 10017, tel. 800/223–6106, in NY 800/223–6107, or 212/818–9800 in New York City, fax 212/983–5289; 235 Peachtree Street NE, Suite 2008, Atlanta, GA 30303, tel. 404/524–1541, fax 404/586–9933; 44 School St., Suite 1010, Boston, MA 02108, tel. 617/742–0405, fax 617/723–7786; Randolph-Wacker Building, Suite 1070, 150 North Wacker Drive, Chicago, IL 60606, tel. 312/782–5486, fax 312/704–6996; John A. Tetley Co. Inc., 3075 Wilshire Blvd., Suite 601, Los Angeles, CA 90010–1293, tel. 800/421–0000 or 800/252–0211 in CA, fax 213/487–5467.

In Canada 1200 Bay Street, Suite 1004, Toronto, Ont. M5R 2A5, tel. 800/387–1304, fax 416/923–4840.

In the United Kingdom Bermuda Tourism, BCB Ltd., 1 Battersea Church Road, London SW11 3LY, tel. 071/734–8813, fax 071/352–6501.

Tour Groups

The majority of visitors to Bermuda opt for independent travel packages. Group tours are scarce for good reason: Because the island is just 20 square miles in size (slightly smaller than Manhattan), it's easy to get around on your own via taxi or moped. Furthermore, Bermuda is a resort destination, offering sun-and-sea vacations that require little organization. An incredible number of packages is available from tour operators, airlines, and travel agencies. Some are land only; others include round-trip airfare. Which package you choose will depend mostly on your pocketbook. Accommodations range from small guest houses to super-deluxe resorts. As usual, you get what you pay for.

When evaluating any tour, be sure to find out: (1) exactly what expenses are included, particularly side trips, meals, entertainment, taxes, and tips; (2) the ratings of all hotels on the itinerary and the facilities they offer; (3) the additional cost of single, rather than double, accommodations if you are traveling alone; and (4) the number of travelers in your group. Note whether the tour operator reserves the right to change hotels, routes, or even prices after you've booked, and check the operator's policy regarding cancellations, complaints, and trip-interruption insurance. Many tour operators request that packages be booked through a travel agent; there is no additional charge for doing so.

Listed below is a sampling of operators and packages to give you an idea of what is available. For additional resources, contact your travel agent or the Bermuda Department of Tourism.

Package Deals for Independent Travelers

In the United States　**Bermuda Travel Planners** (420 Lexington Ave., Suite 401, New York, NY 10170, tel. 212/867–2718 or 800/323–2020) offers a wide selection of four- to seven-night air/hotel packages that include a sightseeing cruise, meal plan of your choice, discount coupons, and other perks.

Globetrotters (139 Main St., Cambridge, MA 02142, tel. 617/621–9911 or 800/999–9696), **Travel Impressions** (465 Smith St., Farmingdale, NY 11735, tel. 516/845–8000 or 800/284–0044), and **Pan Am Holidays** (139 Main St., Cambridge, MA 02142, tel. 800/THE-TOUR) offer a dozen hotels and a range of departure dates from which you can choose. Packages are available for three to seven nights and include round-trip airfare.

Delta Dream Vacations (Certified Vacations, Box 1525, Ft. Lauderdale, FL 33302, tel. 800/872–7786) has four-night air/hotel packages in small and large hotels, guest houses, housekeeping cottages and apartments, and cottage colonies.

American Express Vacations (Box 5014, Atlanta GA 30302, tel. 800/241–1700, or 800/282–0800 in GA) offers three- and seven-night stays at several hotels; extra nights are available. Airfare is not included.

GoGo Tours (69 Spring St., Ramsey, NJ 07446, tel. 201/934–3500 or 800/821–3731), a veritable supermarket of hotel packages, offers a range of accommodations for a minimum three-night stay; airfare is not included. Bookings are available only through travel agents.

Other experienced operators include **Friendly Holidays** (1983 Marcus Ave., Lake Success, NY 11042, tel. 516/358–1200 or 800/221–9748) and **Martin Empire Tours** (66 Canal St., Boston, MA 02114, tel. 617/742–8887 or 800/232–8747).

In the United Kingdom　**Cadogan Travel** (Cadogan House, 9–10 Portland St., Southampton SO9 1ZP, tel. 0703/332661) offers the widest range of holidays in Bermuda, with 10 hotels and nine houses all situated by the sea. Some of the houses also have pools.

Caribtours (161 Fulham Rd., London SW3 6SN, tel. 071/581–3517) offers a variety of guest houses, cottages, and apartments, as well as all-inclusive couples-only holidays at the Harmony Club.

Kuoni Travel (Kuoni House, Dorking, Surrey RH5 4AZ, tel. 0306/740500) offers a number of holiday packages at Bermuda hotels, many with free nights or other special offers, and also features all-inclusive holidays at the adults-only Harmony Club.

Silkcut Faraway Holidays (Meon House, Petersfield, Hants. GU32 3JN, tel. 0730/65211) offers a variety of beach-based vacations, some in small hotels with no more than 15 rooms, and other more expensive packages in resorts.

Tradewinds Faraway Holidays (Station House, 81–83 Fulham High St., London SW6 3JP, tel. 071/731–8000) sells vacations in several Bermuda properties; many packages include golfing fees, entertainment, meals, tennis, and other amenities.

When to Go

Bermuda has a remarkably mild climate that seldom sees extremes of either heat or cold. During the winter (December–March), temperatures range from around 55°F at night to 70°F in the early afternoon. High, blustery winds can make the temperature feel cooler, however, as can Bermuda's high humidity. The hottest part of the year is between May and mid-October, when temperatures range from 75°F to 85°F, but 90°F is not uncommon in July and August. The summer months are somewhat drier, but rainfall is spread fairly evenly throughout the year. Bermuda depends solely on rain for its supply of fresh water, so residents usually welcome the brief storms that interrupt the pleasant weather. In August and September, hurricanes moving northward from the Caribbean sometimes batter the island.

During the summer season, the island teems with activities. Hotel barbecues and evening dances complement daytime sightseeing excursions, and the public beaches are always open. The one drawback, however, is the high cost of staying in a hotel. The pace during the off-season slows considerably. A few of the hotels and restaurants close, some of the sightseeing boats are dry-docked, and only the taxis and the St. George's minibus operate tours of the island. The majority of hotels remain open, however, slashing their rates by as much as 40%—similar rates apply during shoulder seasons (March–April and October–November). The weather at this time of year is perfect for golf and tennis, and visitors can still rent boats, tour the island, and take advantage of the myriad special events and walking tours offered (*see* Festivals and Seasonal Events, below).

Climate What follows are average daily maximum and minimum temperatures for Bermuda.

Jan.	68F	20C	May	76F	24C	Sept.	85F	29C
	58	14		65	18		72	22
Feb.	68F	20C	June	81F	27C	Oct.	79F	26C
	58	14		70	21		70	21
Mar.	68F	20C	July	85F	29C	Nov.	74F	23C
	58	14		74	23		63	17
Apr.	72F	22C	Aug.	86F	30C	Dec.	70F	21C
	59	15		74	23		61	16

Weather Trak provides information on more than 750 cities around the world—450 of them in the United States. Dialing 900/370–8725 will connect you to a computer, with which you can communicate by touch tone at a cost of 75¢ for the first minute and 50¢ a minute thereafter. The computer plays a taped message, which tells you to dial a three-digit access code for information on your destination. The code is either the area code (for cities in the United States) or the first three letters of the name of the foreign city. For a list of all access codes, send a self-addressed stamped envelope to Cities, Box 7000, Dallas, TX 75209, or call 214/869–3035 or 800/247–3282.

Festivals and Seasonal Events

Precise dates and information about any of the events listed below are available from the Bermuda Department of Tourism (*see* Government Tourist Offices, above).

January   **Jan. 1: New Year's Day** is a public holiday.

ADT International Marathon & 10K Race, in which top international runners participate, is open to all. Contact Bermuda Track & Field Association (Box DV 397, Devonshire DV BX).

January–February   **Bermuda Festival** attracts internationally known artists for a series of concerts, dances, and theatrical performances (*see* Chapter 10, The Arts and Nightlife).

February   **Golden Rendezvous Month** includes special events designed for older travelers.

Bermuda International Open Chess Tournament, open to visitors and residents, takes place at one of Bermuda's major hotels. Contact Bermuda Chess Association (Box HM 1705, Hamilton HM GX).

Annual Regional Bridge Tournament is held at a major hotel. (Bermuda Bridge Club, 7 Pomander Rd., Paget PG 05).

Lobster Pot Tournament is an annual Pro-Am Invitational played at Port Royal Golf Course.

Bermuda Valentine's Mixed Foursomes, open to all golfers, is played annually at the St. George's Golf Club and the Port Royal Golf Course. Contact Tournament Chairman (Bermuda Golf Company, Box GE 304, St. George's).

Bermuda Square Dance Convention, held at a major hotel, features internationally renowned callers. Participants are welcome. Contact Bermuda Square Dance Convention (Box 145, Avon, MA 02322, tel. 617/963–0713).

Annual Bermuda Rendezvous Bowling Tournament, open to all bowlers, is sanctioned by ABC and WIBC. Cash prizes are awarded. Contact Warwick Lanes (Box WK 128, Warwick WK BX, tel. 809/236–5290).

Bermuda Golf Festival, a two-week event held at six courses, includes tournaments for men, women, juniors, and seniors of all abilities. Contact the 1992 Bermuda Golf Festival (GD/T Sports Marketing Inc., 5520 Park Ave., Box 395, Trumbull, CT 06611–0395, tel. 800/282–7656 or 203/373–7154 in CT).

March   **Bermuda All Breed Championship Dog Shows & Obedience Trials** draws dog lovers from far and wide to the Botanical Gardens in Paget.

Annual Street Festival on Front Street in Hamilton includes marching bands, Gombey Dancers, and a variety of activities.

Bermuda Super Senior Invitational Tennis Championship is an annual tournament held at the Coral Beach & Tennis Club in Paget.

Bermuda Horse & Pony Association Spring Show features jumping, driving, and Western and flat classes at the Botanical Gardens in Paget.

Bermuda Amateur Golf Championship for Men is played at the Mid Ocean Club in Tucker's Town.

Bermuda Diadora Youth Soccer Cup attracts teams from a variety of Atlantic nations, including the United Kingdom, the United States, Canada, and several Caribbean nations.

March–April   **Palm Sunday Walk** is an annual stroll organized by the Bermuda National Trust.

Good Friday is a public holiday and traditionally a kite-flying day.

Easter Rugby Classic annually features current international athletes competing at the National Sports Club in Devonshire.

Bermuda Easter Lily Pro-Am Golf Tournament for Ladies takes place at St. George's Golf Club. Contact the Tournament Chairman (Bermuda Golf Company, Box GE 304, St. George's GE BX, tel. 809/297–8067).

Bermuda College Weeks, an annual fling for American college students on spring break, offers a program of free events. Included are beach parties, dances, free lunches, boat cruises, calypso, rock bands, limbo shows, and a steel-band concert. Admission to each event is free with a complimentary "College Week Courtesy Card," which is issued to all college students with student identification. Dates vary to coincide with U.S. college vacation periods (*see* Student and Youth Travel, below).

April   **Agricultural Exhibition,** similar to a county or state fair, takes place annually at the Botanical Gardens in Paget.

The Peppercorn Ceremony, an annual event undertaken amid great pomp and circumstance, celebrates the payment of one peppercorn in rent to the government by the Lodge of St. George No. 200 of the Grand Lodge of Scotland for their headquarters in the Old State House in St. George's.

April–May   **Open Houses and Gardens Tours,** sponsored by the Bermuda Garden Club, give visitors the chance to walk through many of Bermuda's historic homes. Most of these houses are closed to the public during the rest of the year.

International Race Week pits sailors from the United States, the United Kingdom, Canada, and other countries against Bermudians in a series of races on the Great Sound. Sunfish and sailboard races are held in Shelly Bay.

April–November   **Beat Retreat Ceremony** is performed twice monthly by the Bermuda Regiment Band, the Bermuda Isles Pipe Band with Dancers, and members of the Bermuda Pipe Band. The historic ceremony is performed alternately on Front Street in Hamilton, King's Square in St. George's, and Dockyard in the West End. No performances are given in August.

May   **Bermuda Heritage Month** features a host of cultural, commemorative, and sporting activities. The highlight is Bermuda Day, a public holiday that includes a parade at Bernard Park, a half-marathon (13 miles) for Bermuda residents only, and a Bermuda dinghy race in St. George's Harbour.

Tornado North American Championship consists of a yacht race in the Great Sound, in which visiting international yachtsmen compete with Bermudians.

Trans-At Daytona–Bermuda Yacht Race is a yacht race from Daytona Beach in Florida to Bermuda.

The Pathmark Tennis Classic, played in Bermuda since 1978, is an annual preview to the U.S. Open, bringing to the island such top-flight women players as Steffi Graf, Jennifer Capriati, and Zina Garrison. The event is held at one of the major hotels.

June   **Bermuda 1–2 Single-Handed Race,** hosted by St. George's Dinghy & Sports Club, is a yacht race from Newport, Rhode Island, to Bermuda. Thirty to 35 yachts sail single-handed Newport–Bermuda, and return double-handed Bermuda–Newport.

Queen Elizabeth II's Birthday is celebrated in mid-June with marching bands parading down Front Street in Hamilton.

Marion–Bermuda Cruising Yacht Race, from Marion, Maryland to Bermuda, is sponsored by the Blue Water Cruising Association of America, the Beverley Yacht Club in Marion, Maryland, and the Royal Hamilton Amateur Dinghy Club in Bermuda.

July **Marine Science Day** at the Bermuda Biological Station for Research (11 Biological La., Ferry Reach, St. George's., tel. 809/297–1880) gives visitors a rare opportunity to learn about marine research from the special perspective of a mid-ocean island.

August **Cup Match Cricket Festival** is a two-day match between East and West End cricket clubs. Held at the Somerset Cricket Club (Broome St., Sandys) or the St. George's Cricket Club (Wellington Slip Rd., St. George's), the match is one of the most festive occasions of the year and attracts thousands of fans who gather to picnic, chat, and dance.

September **Labour Day** is a public holiday featuring a wide range of activities, including a march from Union Square in Hamilton to Bernard Park.

October **Columbus Day Regatta Weekend,** sponsored by the Royal Bermuda Yacht Club, features keel boats competing in the Great Sound.

October–November **Omega Gold Cup International Match Race Tournament** is an exciting series of one-on-one yacht races in Hamilton Harbour.

The Convening of Parliament is preceded by the arrival of His Excellency The Governor, in plumed hat and full regalia, at the Cabinet Building on Front Street in Hamilton.

November **Nov. 5: Guy Fawkes Night,** which originated from a plot to blow up the Houses of Parliament in Great Britain, is celebrated in Bermuda with music by the Bermuda Regiment Band and the Bermuda Isles Pipe Band, the traditional burning of the Guy Fawkes effigy, food, and a half-hour fireworks display. All the festivities take place in the Keepyard of the Bermuda Maritime Museum in the Royal Naval Dockyard.

Bermuda All Breed Championship Dog Shows & Obedience Trials take place at the Botanical Gardens in Paget (*see* March, above).

World Rugby Classic pits former international rugby players against the best players from Bermuda in a match at the National Sports Club (Middle Rd., Devonshire).

Remembrance Day is a public holiday in memory of Bermuda's fallen soldiers and those of its allies. A parade, with Bermudian, British, and U.S. military units, the Bermuda Police, and veterans' organizations, begins at Front Street in Hamilton.

December **Hamilton Jaycees Santa Claus Parade** brings Father Christmas to Front Street, along with bands, floats, majorettes, and other seasonal festivities. St. Nick will also be present at the West End Junior Chamber Santa Claus Parade and the St. George's Junior Chamber Silver Bells Santa Comes to Town Parade.

Bermuda Goodwill Tournament for Men is an annual golf event, played on four courses.

Bermuda Goodwill Professional Championship (Golf) for junior

and senior divisions, is played at the Mid Ocean Club in Tucker's Town.

Dec. 24: Christmas Eve is celebrated with midnight candlelight
services in churches of all denominations.

Dec. 25: Christmas is a public holiday.

Dec. 26: Boxing Day is a public holiday when Bermudians traditionally visit their friends and family. A variety of sports activities are also held, and the Bermuda Gombey Dancers can turn
up anytime, anywhere.

What to Pack

Clothing Bermudians are more formal than most Americans when it
comes to dress. Although attire tends to be casual during the
day—Bermuda shorts are acceptable, even for businessmen—
cutoffs, short shorts, and halter tops are inappropriate. Swimsuits should not be worn outside pool areas or off the beach;
you'll need a cover-up in the public areas of your hotel. Joggers
may wear standard jogging shorts but should avoid appearing
on public streets without a shirt. Bare feet and hair curlers in
public are also frowned upon. In the evening, almost all restaurants and hotel dining rooms require that men wear a jacket
and tie and that women dress comparably. For women, tailored
slacks with a dressy blouse or sweater are fine, although most
Bermudian women wear dresses or skirts and blouses. Bermudian men often wear Bermuda shorts (and proper knee socks)
with a jacket and tie.

During the cooler months, you should bring lightweight woolens or cottons that you can wear in layers, depending on the va-
garies of the weather; a few sweaters and a lightweight jacket
are always a good idea, too. Regardless of the season, you
should pack a swimsuit, a cover-up, sunscreen, and sunglasses,
as well as an umbrella and raincoat. Comfortable walking shoes
and a tote bag for carrying maps and cameras are a must. If you
plan to play tennis, be aware that many courts require proper
whites and that tennis balls in Bermuda are extremely expensive—bring your own balls if possible.

Miscellaneous An extra pair of glasses, contact lenses, or prescription sunglasses is always a good idea; it is important to pack any prescription medicines you use regularly, as well as any allergy
medication you may need. Bermuda uses 110-volt, 60-cycle al-
ternating current, so travelers from the United States won't
need converters or adaptors for electrical appliances. Most
cruise ships that use different voltages carry adaptors for elec-
tric razors. Pack light, because porters and luggage trolleys
can be hard to find at New York airports, the main departure
point for flights to Bermuda.

Carry-on Luggage Airlines generally allow each passenger one piece of carry-on
luggage on international flights from the United States. The
bag cannot exceed 45 inches (length × width × height) and
must fit under the seat or in the overhead luggage compart-
ment.

Checked Luggage Passengers are generally permitted to check two pieces of luggage, neither of which can exceed 62 inches (length × width ×
height) or weigh more than 70 pounds. Baggage allowances
vary slightly among airlines, so check with the carrier or your
travel agent before departure.

Taking Money Abroad

The Bermudian dollar is on a par with the U.S. dollar, and the two currencies are used interchangeably. American money can be used anywhere, but change is often given in Bermudian currency. Try to avoid accumulating large amounts of this money, which is difficult to exchange for U.S. dollars in Bermuda and expensive to exchange in the United States. Loose change can be placed in marked boxes in the departure lounge at the airport—all donations go toward charity.

Most shops and some restaurants accept credit cards, but most hotels on the island insist on other forms of payment. Some take personal checks by prior arrangement (a letter from your bank is sometimes requested). U.S. traveler's checks are accepted almost everywhere. The most recognized traveler's checks are **American Express, Barclay's, Thomas Cook,** and those issued through major commercial banks such as **Citibank** and **Bank of America.** Some banks issue checks free to established customers, but most charge a 1% commission fee. Remember to take the addresses of offices where you can get refunds for lost or stolen traveler's checks. In Bermuda, the American Express representative is L. P. Gutteridge Ltd. (L. P. Gutteridge Bldg., Bermudiana Rd., Hamilton, tel. 809/295–4545). Thomas Cook is represented by Butterfield Travel Ltd. (75 Front St., Hamilton, tel. 809/292–1510).

Getting Money from Home

There are at least three ways to get money from home:

1) Have it sent through a large commercial bank that has a branch where you are staying. The only drawback is that you must have an account with the bank; if not, you'll have to go through your own bank, and the process will be slower and more expensive.

2) Have it sent through American Express. If you are a cardholder, you can cash a personal check or a counter check at an American Express office for up to $1,000; $200 will be in cash and $800 in traveler's checks. A 1% commission is charged on the traveler's checks. You can also receive money through an American Express MoneyGram, which enables you to obtain an unlimited amount of cash. It works this way: You call home and ask someone to go to an American Express office—or an American Express MoneyGram agent in a retail outlet—and fill out an American Express MoneyGram. It can be paid for with cash, or American Express, MasterCard, or Visa. The person making the payment is given a reference number and telephones you with that number. The American Express MoneyGram agent calls an 800 number and authorizes the transfer of funds to the American Express office or participating agency in the city where you are staying. In most cases, the money is available immediately on a 24-hour basis upon presentation of identification and the reference number. Fees vary with the amount of money sent. For $300, the fee is $35; for $5,000, the fee is $175. For the American Express MoneyGram location nearest your home and locations in Bermuda, call 800/543–4080. You do not have to be a cardholder to use this service.

3) Have money sent through Western Union (tel. 800/325–6000 in the United States). If you have a MasterCard or Visa, money

can be sent for any amount up to your credit limit. If not, have someone take cash or a certified cashier's check to a Western Union office. The money will be delivered to a bank where you are staying. Fees vary with the amount of money sent: For $1,000, the fee is $50; for $500, the fee is $40. There is a $5 fee for credit card charges.

Cash Machines The Bank of Bermuda's 10 branches have automatic teller machines (ATMs). Using a Visa card with your personal identification number (PIN), you can withdraw up to $500 a day in Bermudian currency for a fee. The service is available 24 hours a day. Virtually all U.S. banks belong to a network of ATMs, and some banks belong to more than one. The Plus network plans to extend its automatic teller service to Bermuda within the next two years. Call 800/THE-PLUS to locate machines in a given city. Check with your bank for information on fees and the amount of cash you can withdraw on any given day.

What It Will Cost

Bermuda imports everything from cars to cardigans, so prices are high. In fact, the most common complaint of visitors to Bermuda is the high cost of a vacation on the island. At an upscale restaurant, for example, be prepared to pay as much for a meal as you would in New York, London, or Paris. The average cost of dinner in a chic restaurant is $50–$70 per person—$100 with drinks and wine. Upscale restaurants, however, are not your only option. The island abounds with little coffee shops, where locals and thrift-minded tourists can eat hamburgers and french fries for about $4. The same meal at a restaurant costs about $12.

Hotels add a 6% government tax to the bill and, instead of tips, a 10% service charge or a per diem dollar equivalent. Other supplemental charges include a 5% "energy surcharge" at small guest houses, and a 15% service charge at most restaurants.

Sample Costs A cup of coffee costs between 80¢ and $2.50; a mixed drink $3–$5; a bottle of beer $1.75–$5; and a can of Coke about $1. A 15-minute cab ride will set you back about $15 including the tip, and a pack of Kodak 110 cartridge film, with 12 exposures, costs about $3.95.

Passports and Visas

U.S. Residents You do not need a passport or visa to enter Bermuda if you plan to stay less than six months, although you must have onward or return tickets and proof of identity (original birth certificate with raised seal, voter's registration card with photo; a driver's license is unacceptable). If you have a passport, bring it to ensure quick passage through immigration and customs. For further information, check with the **British Embassy** in Washington (3100 Massachusetts Ave. N.W., Washington, D.C. 20008, tel. 202/462–1340).

Canadian Residents Canadians do not need a passport to enter Bermuda, though a passport is helpful to ensure quick passage through customs and immigration. A birth certificate or a certificate of citizenship is required, along with a photo ID. To obtain a passport, send your completed application (available at any post office or passport office) to the **Bureau of Passports, External Affairs**

(Ottawa, Ont. K1A OG3). Include $25, two photographs, a guarantor, and proof of Canadian citizenship. Application can be made in person at the regional passport offices in Edmonton, Halifax, Montreal, Calgary, St. John's (Newfoundland), Victoria, Toronto, Vancouver, and Winnipeg. Passports are valid for five years and are nonrenewable. A visa is not required to enter Bermuda.

U.K. Residents British citizens require a valid passport or a British Visitor's Passport to enter Bermuda. Passport application forms are available from most travel agents and major post offices, or contact the **Passport Office** (Clive House, 70 Petty France, London SW1H 9HD, tel. 071/279–3434). The cost is £15 for a standard 32-page passport, £30 for a 94-page passport. British Visitor's Passports, valid for one year only and nonrenewable, cost £7.50. All applications must be countersigned by your bank manager or a solicitor, barrister, doctor, clergyman, or justice of the peace and must be accompanied by two photographs.

Customs and Duties

On Arrival In addition to personal effects, visitors entering Bermuda may bring in duty-free up to 50 cigars, 200 cigarettes, and one pound of tobacco; one quart of wine and one quart of liquor; 20 pounds of meat; and other goods to the value of $30. You should not import plants, fruits, vegetables, and animals without an import permit from the **Department of Agriculture, Fisheries and Parks** (Box HM 834, Hamilton HM CX, tel. 809/236–4201; fax 809/236–7582). Any amount of foreign or Bermudian currency may be imported. Remember, though, that merchandise and sales materials for use by conventions must be cleared with the hotel concerned before you arrive.

On Departure
U.S. Residents If you are bringing any foreign-made equipment from home, such as cameras, carry the original receipt with you or register it with U.S. Customs before you leave (Form 4457). Otherwise, you may end up paying duty on the equipment when you return. U.S. citizens go through U.S. Customs at the Bermuda airport before departing from the island. A $15 departure tax ($5 for children between 2 and 11) is also levied at the airport; a $60 port tax is included in cruise-ship fares.

You may import up to $400 worth of foreign goods duty-free, as long as you have been out of the country for at least 48 hours and you haven't made an international trip in 30 days. Each member of the family is entitled to the same exemption, regardless of age, and exemptions may be pooled. For the next $1,000 worth of goods, a flat 10% rate is assessed; above $1,400, duties vary with the merchandise. Travelers 21 or older are entitled to bring in one liter of alcohol, 100 cigars (non-Cuban), and 200 cigarettes. Only one bottle of perfume trademarked in the United States may be imported. However, no duty is charged on antiques or works of art more than 100 years old. Anything exceeding these limits will be taxed at the port of entry and may be taxed additionally in the traveler's home state. Gifts valued at under $50 may be mailed to friends or relatives at home duty-free, but you may not send more than one package per day to any one addressee; in addition, packages may not include tobacco, liquor, or perfumes costing more than $5.

Canadian Residents Canadian residents have an exemption ranging from $20 to $300, depending on the length of stay out of the country. For the $300 exemption, you must have been out of the country for one week. For any given year, you are allowed one $300 exemption. You may also import duty-free up to 50 cigars, 200 cigarettes, 2.2 pounds of tobacco, and 40 ounces of liquor, provided these items are declared in writing to customs on arrival and accompany the traveler in carry-on luggage or checked-through baggage. These restrictions apply for absences of at least seven days and a maximum of one year. If you are out of Canada for less than seven days, but for a minimum of 48 hours, there is a $100 exemption, with the same restrictions on alcohol and tobacco products. Personal gifts should be mailed as "Unsolicited gift—value under $40." Request a copy of *I Declare*, the Canadian Customs brochure, for further details. Copies are available at local customs offices.

U.K. Residents British residents may import duty-free: (1) 200 cigarettes or 100 cigarillos or 50 cigars or 250 grams of tobacco (if you live outside Europe these allowances are doubled); (2) one liter of alcohol over 22% volume or two liters of alcohol under 22% volume (fortified or sparkling wine) or two more liters of still table wine; (3) two liters of still table wine; (4) 60 milliliters of perfume and 250 milliliters of toilet water; and (5) other goods to the value of £32, but not more than 50 liters of beer or 25 cigarette lighters. For further information, contact **HM Customs and Excise** (Dorset House, Stamford St., London SE1 9PS, tel. 071/620–1313).

Traveling with Film

The cost of film on Bermuda is exorbitant, so bring all the film you need with you from home. If your camera is new, shoot and develop a few rolls before leaving home. Pack some lens tissue and an extra battery for your built-in light meter. Invest about $10 in a skylight filter: It will protect the lens and reduce haze.

On a plane trip, never pack unprocessed film in luggage you plan to check; if your bags get X-rayed, say good-bye to your pictures. Always carry undeveloped film with you through security and ask to have it inspected by hand. (It helps to keep your film in a plastic bag, ready for quick inspection.) The old airport scanning machines, still in use in some countries, use heavy doses of radiation that can make a family portrait look like an early morning fog. The newer models used in all U.S. airports are safe for anything from five to 500 scans, depending on the speed of your film. The effects are cumulative, however. You can put the same roll of film through several scans without worry, but you're asking for trouble after five scans. If your film gets fogged and you want an explanation, send it to the **National Association of Photographic Manufacturers** (550 Mamaroneck Ave., Harrison, NY 10528). The association will try to determine what went wrong. The service is free.

Staying Healthy

Sunburn and sunstroke are chronic problems for summer visitors to Bermuda. On a hot, sunny day, even people who are not normally bothered by strong sun should cover themselves with a long-sleeve shirt, a hat, and long pants or a beach wrap. These are essential for a day on a boat, but are also advisable for midday at the beach. Also carry some sunscreen for nose, ears, and other sensitive areas such as eyelids and ankles. Keep drinking liquids but, above all, limit the amount of time you spend in the sun until you become acclimatized.

No special vaccinations are required for a visit to Bermuda. If you have a health problem for which you might have to purchase prescription drugs while in Bermuda, have your doctor write a prescription using the drug's generic name—brand names can vary widely.

The **International Association for Medical Assistance to Travelers (IAMAT)** is a worldwide organization offering a list of approved English-speaking doctors whose training meets British and U.S. standards. Contact IAMAT for a list of physicians and clinics in Bermuda that belong to this network. **In the United States:** 417 Center St., Lewiston, NY 14092, tel. 716/754–4883. **In Canada:** 40 Regal Road, Guelph, Ontario N1K 1B5. **In Europe:** 57 Voirets, 1212 Grand-Lancy, Geneva, Switzerland. Membership is free.

Insurance

Travelers may seek insurance coverage in three areas: health and accident, lost luggage, and trip cancellation. Your first step should be to review your existing health and home-owner policies; some health-insurance plans cover health expenses incurred while traveling, some major medical plans cover emergency transportation, and some home-owner policies cover the theft of luggage.

Health and Accident Several companies offer coverage designed to supplement existing health insurance for travelers:

Association of British Insurers (Aldermary House, Queen St., London EC4N 1TT, U.K., tel. 071/248–4477) gives free general advice on holiday insurance.

Carefree Travel Insurance (Box 310, 120 Mineola Blvd., Mineola, NY 11501, tel. 516/294–0220 or 800/343–3149) provides coverage for emergency medical evacuation and accidental death and dismemberment. It also offers 24-hour medical phone advice.

Europ Assistance (252 High St., Croyden, Surrey CRO 1NF, U.K., tel. 081/680–1234) is a proven leader in the holiday-insurance field.

International SOS Assistance (Box 11568, Philadelphia, PA 19116, tel. 215/244–1500 or 800/523–8930), a medical assistance company, provides emergency evacuation services, worldwide medical referrals, and optional medical insurance.

Travel Assistance International (1133 15th St. NW, Suite 400, Washington, DC 20005, tel. 202/331–1609 or 800/821–2828) provides emergency evacuation services and medical referrals 24 hours a day.

Travel Guard International, underwritten by Transamerica Occidental Life Companies (1145 Clark St., Stevens Point, WI 54481, tel. 715/345–0505 or 800/782–5151), offers reimbursement for medical expenses with no deductibles or daily limits and emergency evacuation services.

Wallach and Company, Inc. (243 Church St. NW, Suite 100D, Vienna, VA 22180, tel. 703/281–9500 or 800/237–6615) offers comprehensive medical coverage, including emergency evacuation services worldwide.

WorldCare Travel Assistance Association (1150 South Olive St., Suite T–233, Los Angeles, CA 90015, tel. 213/749–0909 or 800/666–4993) provides unlimited emergency evacuation, 24-hour medical referral, and an emergency message center.

Lost Luggage On international flights, airlines are responsible for lost or damaged property at rates up to $9.07 per pound (or $20 per kilogram) for checked baggage, and up to $400 per passenger for unchecked baggage. If you're carrying valuables, either take them with you on the plane or purchase additional insurance for lost luggage. Some airlines will issue extra luggage insurance when you check in, but many do not. Insurance for lost, damaged, or stolen luggage is available through travel agents or directly through various insurance companies. Luggage-loss coverage is usually part of a comprehensive travel-insurance package that includes personal, accident, trip-cancellation, and sometimes default and bankruptcy coverage. Two companies that issue luggage insurance are **Tele-Trip** (Box 31685, 3201 Farnam St., Omaha, NE 68131, tel. 800/228–9792), a subsidiary of Mutual of Omaha, and **The Travelers Corporation** (Ticket and Travel Dept., 1 Tower Sq., Hartford, CT 06183, tel. 203/277–0111 or 800/243–3174). Tele-Trip, which operates sales booths at airports and also issues insurance through travel agents, will insure checked luggage for up to 180 days; rates vary according to the length of the trip. The Travelers Corporation will insure checked or hand luggage for $500–$2,000 valuation per person, also for a maximum of 180 days. The rates for one to five days for $500 valuation is $10; for 180 days, $85. Other companies with comprehensive policies include **Access America, Inc.,** a subsidiary of Blue Cross-Blue Shield (Box 11188, Richmond, VA 23230, tel. 800/334–7525 or 800/284–8300); **Near Services** (450 Prairie Ave., Suite 101, Calumet, IL 60409, tel. 708/868–6700 or 800/654–6700); and **Travel Guard International** and **Carefree Travel Insurance** (*see* Health and Accident, above).

Before you go, itemize the contents of each bag in case you need to file an insurance claim. Be certain to put your home or business address on each piece of luggage, including carry-on bags. If your luggage is lost or stolen and later recovered, the airline will deliver the luggage to your home free of charge.

Trip Cancellation Flight insurance is often included in the price of a ticket paid for with American Express, Visa, or other major credit card. It is also usually included in combination travel-insurance packages available from most tour operators, travel agents, and insurance agents.

Student and Youth Travel

Like everyone else, students arriving in Bermuda must have confirmation of hotel reservations, a return plane ticket, a photo ID, and proof of citizenship, such as a passport, birth certificate, or a signed voter's registration card. There are no youth hostels, YMCAs, or YWCAs on the island. During Bermuda College Weeks (*see* Festivals and Seasonal Events, above), however, special student rates are offered at hotels and guest houses, restaurants, pubs, and nightclubs.

The **International Student Identity Card (ISIC)** entitles fulltime students to reduced fares on local transportation; discounts at museums, theaters, and sports events; student charter flights;

and many other attractions. If purchased in the United States, the $14 cost of the ISIC card also includes $3,000 in emergency medical coverage, $100 a day for up to 60 days of hospital coverage, as well as a toll-free phone number to call in case of emergency. Apply to the **Council on International Educational Exchange** (CIEE, Dept. ISS–50 205 E. 42nd St., New York, NY 10017, tel. 212/661–1414). In Canada, the ISIC is available for $CN 12 from **Travel Cuts** (187 College St., Toronto, Ont. M5T 1P7, tel. 416/979–2406).

Travelers under age 26 can apply for a **Youth International Educational Exchange Card (YIEE)** issued by the **Federation of International Youth Travel Organizations** (81 Islands Brugge, DK-2300 Copenhagen S, Denmark). The services and benefits provided by the YIEE card are similar to those offered by the ISIC card. The YIEE card is available in the United States from CIEE (*see* above) and in Canada from the **Canadian Hostelling Association** (CHA, 1600 James Naismith Drive, Suite 608, Gloucester, Ont. K1B 5N4, tel. 613/748–5638).

Council Travel, a CIEE subsidiary, is the foremost U.S. student travel agency specializing in low-cost charters, and the exclusive U.S. agent for many student airfare bargains and student tours. CIEE's 80-page *Student Travel* catalogue and *Council Charter* brochures are available free from any Council Travel office in the United States (enclose $1 postage if ordering by mail). Contact the CIEE headquarters in New York (*see* above) to locate the nearest Council Travel office.

The **Educational Travel Center** (438 N. Frances St., Madison, WI 53703, tel. 608/256–5551) is another student-travel specialist worth contacting for information on student tours, bargain fares, and bookings.

Traveling with Children

Publications *Family Travel Times* is a newsletter published 10 times a year by **Travel with Your Children** (TWYCH, 80 Eighth Ave., New York, NY 10011, tel. 212/206–0688). A one-year subscription ($35) includes access to back issues and twice-weekly opportunities to call in for specific advice.

Getting There On international flights, children under age 2 not occupying a seat pay 10% of the adult fare. Various discounts apply to children from ages 2 to 12, so check with your airline when booking. If possible, reserve a seat behind one of the plane's bulkheads, where there's usually more legroom and enough space to fit a bassinet, available from the airlines. At the same time, ask about special children's meals or snacks—most airlines offer them. See TWYCH's "Airline Guide," published in the February 1990 and 1992 issues of *Family Travel Times*, for more information about children's services offered by 46 airlines.

Regulations about infant travel on airplanes are in the process of being changed. Until these changes are finalized, however, if you want to be sure your infant is secure, you must bring your own infant car seat and buy a separate ticket. Check with the airline in advance to be sure your seat meets the required standard. For the booklet **"Child/Infant Safety Seats Acceptable for Use in Aircraft,"** write to the Federal Aviation Administration

(APA-200, 800 Independence Ave., SW, Washington, DC 20591, tel. 202/267–3479).

Baby-sitting Services In Bermuda, few hotels cater to children (*see* Chapter 9, Lodging), and others actively discourage parents from bringing them. Nevertheless, baby-sitting can usually be arranged through the hotel or guest house upon advance request. The charge is $4–$8 per hour, and sitters expect paid transportation. Check with your hotel for specifics.

Home Exchange

Exchanging homes is a surprisingly low-cost way to enjoy a vacation abroad, especially a long one. The largest home-exchange service, **International Home Exchange Service** (Box 190070, San Francisco, CA 94119, tel. 415/435–3497), publishes three directories a year. Membership, which costs $45, entitles you to one listing and all three directories. Photos of your property cost an additional $10; listing a second home costs $10. **Loan-a-Home** (2 Park La. 6E, Mount Vernon, NY 10552, tel. 914/664–7640) is popular with academics on sabbatical and businesspeople on temporary assignment. There's no annual membership fee or charge for listing your home, but one directory and a supplement cost $35.

Hints for Disabled Travelers

The Bermuda Chapter of the **Society for the Advancement of Travel for the Handicapped** (SATH, 26 Court St., Brooklyn, NY 11242, tel. 718/858–5483) publishes the *Access Guide to Bermuda for the Handicapped Traveler*, available free of charge.

The **Information Center for Individuals with Disabilities** (Ft. Point Pl., 1st floor, 27–43 Wormwood St., Boston, MA 02210, tel. 617/727–5540; TDD 617/727–5236) offers useful problem-solving assistance, including lists of travel agents who specialize in tours for the disabled.

Moss Rehabilitation Hospital Travel Information Service (1200 W. Tabor Rd., Philadelphia, PA 19141–3009, tel. 215/456–9600; TDD 215/456–9602) for a small fee provides information on tourist sights, transportation, and accommodations in destinations around the world.

Mobility International USA (Box 3551, Eugene, OR 97403, tel. 503/343–1284) is an internationally affiliated organization with 500 members. For a $20 annual fee, it coordinates exchange programs for disabled people around the world and offers information on accommodations and organized study programs.

Travel Industry and Disabled Exchange (5435 Donna Ave., Tarzana, CA 91356, tel. 818/368–5648) publishes a quarterly newsletter and a directory of travel agencies and tours to Europe, Canada, Great Britain, New Zealand, and Australia, all specializing in travel for the disabled. Annual subscription fee is $15.

Hints for Older Travelers

The **American Association of Retired Persons** (AARP, 1909 K St., NW, Washington, DC 20049, tel. 202/662–4850) has two programs for independent travelers: (1) the **Purchase Privilege**

Program, which comes with membership, offers discounts on hotels, airfares, car rentals, RV rentals, and sightseeing; (2) the **AARP Motoring Plan,** provided by Amoco, furnishes emergency road service and trip-routing information for an annual fee of $33.95 per person or couple. (Both programs include the member and member's spouse, or the member and another person who shares the household.) The AARP also arranges group tours through **American Express Vacations** (Box 5014, Atlanta, GA 30302, tel. 800/241–1700 or 800/637–6200 in GA). AARP members must be 50 or older; annual dues are $5 per person or per couple.

When using an AARP or other discount identification card, ask for reduced hotel rates at the time you make your reservation, not when you check out. At participating restaurants, show your card to the maître d' before you're seated, because discounts may be limited to set menus, days, or hours. When renting a car, be sure to ask about special promotional rates that may offer greater savings than the available discount.

Elderhostel (75 Federal St., 3rd floor, Boston, MA 02110–1941, tel. 617/426–7788) is an innovative educational program for people 60 and older. Participants live in dorms on any of 1,200 campuses around the world. Mornings are devoted to lectures and seminars; afternoons to sightseeing and field trips. Fees for two- to three-week trips, including room, board, tuition, and round-trip transportation, range from $1,800 to $4,500.

Mature Outlook (6001 N. Clark St., Chicago, IL 60660, tel. 800/ 336–6330), a subsidiary of Sears Roebuck & Co., is a travel club for people over age 50. It offers hotel and motel discounts and a bimonthly newsletter. Annual membership is $9.95; there are currently 800,000 members. Instant membership is available at participating Holiday Inns.

The **National Council of Senior Citizens** (925 15th St., NW, Washington, DC 20005, tel. 202/347–8800) is a nonprofit advocacy group with about 5,000 local clubs across the country. Annual membership is $12 per person or per couple. Members receive a monthly newspaper with travel information and an ID card for reduced hotel and car-rental rates.

Saga International Holidays (120 Boylston St., Boston, MA 02116, tel. 800/343–0273), an affiliate of Elderhostel, specializes in group travel for people over age 60. A selection of variously priced tours allows you to choose the package that meets your needs.

Further Reading

The late William Zuill, a well-respected historian, wrote extensively about the island. Published in 1945 and now somewhat outdated, Zuill's 426-page *Bermuda Journey: A Leisurely Guide Book* provides a fascinating look at the island and its people, with historical notes and anecdotes. The book was scheduled to go out of print in 1990, so check with the Bermuda Book Store in Hamilton (tel. 809/295–3698) to see if it's available. (Proprietor Jim Zuill is the author's son.) William Zuill's other books include *The Wreck of the Sea Venture*, which details the 1609 wreck of Admiral Sir George Somers's flagship and the subsequent settlement of the island, and *Tom Moore's Bermu-*

da Poems, a collection of odes by the Irish poet who spent four months on Bermuda in 1804.

W. S. Zuill, the son of the noted historian, wrote *The Story of Bermuda and Her People*, a recently updated volume tracing the history of the island from the *Sea Venture* wreck to the present. *Bermuda*, by John J. Jackson, contains an abundance of facts on Bermudian business, economics, law, ecology, history, as well as tourist information. John Weatherill's *Faces of Bermuda* is a marvelous collection of photographs, and those curious about the legendary Bermuda Triangle can read about its history in *The Bermuda Triangle Mystery Solved*, by Larry David Kusche.

For a charming account of growing up in Bermuda during the 1930s and 1940s, refer to *The Back Yard*, by William Zuill's daughter Ann Zuill Williams. Two books for a younger audience are Willoughby Patton's *Sea Venture*, about the adventures of a young boy on the crew of the ill-fated ship in 1609, and E. M. Rice's *A Child's History of Bermuda*, which tells the story of the island in terms children can understand.

Arriving and Departing

From North America by Plane

Airport and Airlines The **Civil Air Terminal** (Kindley Field Rd., St. George's) is on the east end of the island, approximately 9 miles from the center of Hamilton and 17 miles from Somerset.

Airlines with direct flights to Bermuda include **American Airlines** (tel. 800/433–7300) from New York (JFK and LaGuardia), Boston, and Raleigh/Durham; **Continental** (tel. 800/525–0280) from Newark; **Delta Airlines** (tel. 800/221–1212) from Boston and Atlanta; **Pan Am** (tel. 800/221–1111) from New York's JFK airport; **USAir** (tel. 800/428–4322) from Baltimore, Philadelphia, and New York's La Guardia; and **Air Canada** (tel. 800/776–3000) from Toronto, with connections from all over Canada.

Flying Time From New York, Boston, Raleigh/Durham, and Baltimore, the flight to Bermuda takes about two hours; from Atlanta, 2½ hours; and from Toronto, 2¾ hours.

Enjoying the Flight Unless you're flying from the West Coast or Britain, jet lag won't be a problem. If you're lucky enough to be able to sleep on an aircraft, request a window seat to curl up against; those who like to move about the cabin should request aisle seats. Bulkhead seats (located in the front row of each cabin) have more legroom, but seat trays are attached rather awkwardly to the arms of the seat rather than to the back of the seat ahead. Generally, bulkhead seats are reserved for the disabled, the elderly, or parents traveling with babies.

Discount Flights The major airlines offer a range of tickets that can lower the price of any given seat by nearly 70%, depending on the day of purchase. As a rule, the further in advance you buy the ticket, the less expensive it is and the greater the penalty (up to 100%) for canceling. Check with the airlines for details. The best buy is not necessarily an APEX (advance purchase) ticket on one of the major airlines, because these tickets carry certain restrictions: They must be bought in advance (usually 21 days); they restrict your travel, usually requiring a minimum stay of seven days and a maximum of 90; and they penalize you for changes—voluntary or not—in your travel plans. But if you can work around these drawbacks (and most travelers can), they are among the best fares available.

Charter flights offer the lowest fares, although departure days are usually limited. It can be especially difficult to find a charter going to Bermuda, but if you do manage to secure a seat, be prepared for late departures. Don't sign up for a charter flight unless you've asked a travel agency about the reputation of the packager. It's particularly important to know the packager's policy on refunds in the event of a canceled flight; some agents advise travelers to purchase trip-cancellation insurance if they are booked on a charter flight. Check the Sunday travel sections of newspapers for the advertisements of charter operators.

Other discounted fares—up to 50% lower than the cost of APEX tickets—can be found through consolidators, companies that buy blocks of tickets on scheduled airlines and sell them at wholesale prices. Tickets are subject to availability, so passengers should have reasonably flexible travel schedules. Here again, you may lose all or most of your money if you change plans, but you will be on a regularly scheduled flight with less risk of cancellation than on a charter. As an added precaution, consider buying trip-cancellation insurance. Once you've made a reservation, call the airline to confirm it. Many consolidators advertise in newspaper Sunday travel sections.

Travelers willing to put up with some inconveniences in return for substantially reduced airfares may be interested in flying as air couriers. An air courier is someone who accompanies shipments (documents or packages) between designated points. There are two sources of information on courier deals: (1) A telephone directory, which lists courier companies by the cities to which they fly, is available for $5 (plus a stamped, self-addressed business envelope) from **Pacific Data Sales Publishing** (2554 Lincoln Blvd., Suite 275-F, Marina Del Rey, CA 92091); (2) *A Simple Guide to Courier Travel* can be purchased for $14.95 (includes postage and handling) from the **Carriage Group** (Box 2394, Lake Oswego, OR 97035, tel. 800/344–9375).

Another option is to join a travel club that offers special discounts to its members. Among such organizations are **Discount Travel International** (114 Forrest Ave., Narberth, PA 19072, tel. 215/668–7184), **Moment's Notice** (425 Madison Ave., New York, NY 10017, tel. 212/486–0503), **Travelers Advantage** (CUC Travel Service, 49 Music Sq. W, Nashville, TN 37203, tel. 800/548–1116), and **Worldwide Discount Travel Club** (1674 Meridian Ave., Miami Beach, FL 33139, tel. 305/534–2082). Always compare the cut-rate tickets offered by these organizations with APEX tickets on the major airlines.

Smoking   As of February 1990, smoking is banned on all routes within the 48 contiguous states; within the states of Hawaii and Alaska; to and from the U.S. Virgin Islands and Puerto Rico; and on flights of under six hours to and from Hawaii and Alaska. The rule applies to both domestic and foreign carriers. On a flight where smoking is permitted, you can request a nonsmoking seat during check-in or when you book your ticket. If the airline tells you no seats are available in the nonsmoking section, insist on one: Department of Transportation regulations require carriers to find seats for all nonsmokers on the day of the flight, provided they meet check-in time restrictions. These regulations apply to all international flights on domestic carriers, but the Department of Transportation has no jurisdiction over foreign carriers.

Between the Airport and Hotels
By Taxi

Taxis meet all flights in Bermuda and are readily available at the airport. The approximate fare (not including tip) to Hamilton is $15; to St. George's, $7; to south-shore hotels, $19; and to the West End, $26. A surcharge of 25¢ is added for each piece of luggage stored in the trunk or on the roof. Between 10 PM and 6 AM, and on Sundays and public holidays, fares are 25% higher. Depending on traffic, the driving time to Hamilton is about 20 minutes, and about 45 minutes to the West End.

By Bus

Bermuda Aviation Services Ltd. (tel. 809/293–2500; fax 809/293–0513) operates an eight-passenger Volkswagen minibus to the smaller hotels and a 26-passenger bus to the large resorts. You must make reservations two weeks prior to your arrival. At the airport, look for the BAS sign after you leave customs. Fares and driving times are as follows: Zone 1—a 15-minute trip to the Grotto Bay Beach Hotel—costs $5; Zone 2—a 20-minute trip stopping at St. George's and Flatts Village—is $7; Zone 3—a 35-minute ride to hotels in Smith's, Devonshire, Pembroke, Hamilton, and Paget parishes—costs $13; Zone 4—a 45-minute journey to Warwick and half of Southampton Parish—is $16; and Zone 5—a 90-minute trip to hotels in the other half of Southampton and in Sandys Parish—costs $21.

From the U.K. by Plane

The options for flying to Bermuda from Great Britain are limited. Only **British Airways** (tel. 071/897–4000) flies direct, with six flights a week from Gatwick. Flying time is approximately seven hours. No charter flights are available, but travel packages offer reduced fares on the British Airways flights. Peak-season round-trip economy fares range from £589 to £914; in first class, tickets are as much as £2,464. Flying to New York, and then taking a connecting flight to Bermuda, takes longer and costs as much—even with the cheapest fares—as the scheduled British Airways flight direct to Bermuda.

From the U.S. by Cruise Ship

Bermuda has long been a favorite destination of cruise lines, and (except for a few cruises that continue down to the Caribbean) it is usually a ship's only port of call. Most ships make seven-day loops from New York, with four days spent at sea and three days in port; other cruises leave from Baltimore, Philadelphia, Boston, and Charleston. The cruise season in Bermuda runs from March to October. (For more information on cruises to Bermuda, *see* Chapter 3, Cruising in Bermuda.) Concerned about overcrowding, the Bermudian government recently limited the number of regularly scheduled visits by cruise ships to four per week, none on weekends. The restrictions will probably make it more difficult to find cabins on cruises to Bermuda, and prices are likely to rise. At the same time, however, passengers will be able to enjoy the island without being jostled by other tourists, and many of the island's attractions are relatively empty during the week.

Ships tie up at one of three harbors on Bermuda: Hamilton, St. George's, or the West End. The traditional port is Hamilton, the capital and the most commercial area on the island. If you want to shop until you drop, choose a cruise that anchors here. Passengers whose ship ties up at St. George's walk off the vessel into Bermuda's equivalent of Colonial Williamsburg. Located at the east end of the island, St. George's is a charming town of 17th-century buildings, narrow lanes, and small boutiques. West End is the farthest cruise port from Bermuda's main attractions. A new tourist complex is under construction in the West End, however, including a shopping mall, museums, and crafts stores. (For more information about Bermuda's ports and attractions, *see* Chapter 4, Exploring Bermuda.)

Shore Excursions   Shore excursions are usually group tours arranged for passengers by their cruise ship. Almost all ships sell these tours, which tend to follow well-established formulas. Information about the shore excursions offered by a ship is sent to passengers before the cruise. Depending upon availability, shore excursions can be booked from the time you first reserve your cruise until right before the excursion begins. Listed below are the shore excursions offered by cruise lines in Bermuda, although not all excursions are offered by all cruise lines. (For more information about the attractions listed below, *see* Chapter 4, Exploring Bermuda.) Times quoted are approximate, and passengers should check with their travel agent or cruise director for tour prices.

Boats and Beaches   **Bermuda Glass-Bottom Boat Cruise:** A tame but pleasant cruise through the harbor and over reefs that includes feeding the fish from the boat. *2 hrs.*

Coral Reef and Calypso Cruise: Rum swizzles and island music set the tone for a cruise aboard a glass-bottom party boat. *2½ hrs.*

Reef Roamer Island Party: A beach party that includes snorkeling, dancing, and rum swizzles. *3½ hrs.*

Sailing Cruise: A relaxing, romantic, and quiet sailing trip, with a short stop to allow guests to swim. *3 hrs.*

Snorkeling Tour: Equipment, lessons, and underwater guided tour are included. Underwater cameras are available for an extra charge. *3¾ hrs.*

South Shore Beaches: This is a sightseeing tour along scenic South Road, with an hour for swimming at Horseshoe Bay Beach. Wet bathing suits are not allowed on the bus, but changing facilities are available. *4 hrs.*

Cultural and Scenic   **West End Highlight Tour:** Visit the Island Pottery, Art Centre, Crafts Market, Maritime Museum, Heydon Trust Chapel, and Gibb's Hill Lighthouse during a drive through Sandys Parish. This tour is recommended for passengers whose ships dock in Hamilton or St. George's and who are unlikely to travel to the West End on their own. *4 hrs.*

St. George's Highlight Tour: A quick overview of the area around St. George's includes Fort St. Catherine, Fort William, Gates Fort, the Unfinished Church, Somers Garden, Tobacco Bay, and the government housing complex. The guide is informative and will point out the popular shopping areas. *2 hrs.*

Bermuda's Attractions Tour: Visit Leamington or Crystal caves and the Aquarium, Museum and Zoo. The tour ends at the Bermuda Perfumery, where the essence of flowers is made into perfume. *4 hrs.*

Entertainment   **Coca-Cola Steel Band at the New Clayhouse Inn:** An evening of island music played on homemade instruments, limbo, and fire dancing. Two free drinks are included.

Hamilton Princess "Big, Bad and Beautiful" Revue: A salute to famous female performers such as Ella Fitzgerald and Anita Baker. Two free drinks are included. *4 hrs.*

Staying in Bermuda

Important Addresses and Numbers

Tourist Information   **Visitors Service Bureaus,** which provide tourist information and assist with reservations and ticketing, can be found at the following locations:

Hamilton. *Ferry Terminal Bldg., Front St., tel. 809/295–1480. Open weekdays 9–4:45.*

Civil Air Terminal-Airport. *Tel. 809/293–0030. Open daily 9–5.*

Visitors Information Centres, which offer tourist information but no other services, are at the following locations:

St. George's. *King's Sq., next to Town Hall, tel. 809/297–1642. Open Mon.–Wed., Fri, and Sat. 10–3; closed Thurs. and Sun.*

Somerset. *Nr. St. James's Church, tel. 809/234–1388. Open April–November, weekdays 10–4.*

Consulates   Neither the Canadian nor the British government has a consulate in Bermuda.

American Consulate General. *Crown Hill, 16 Middle Rd., Devonshire, tel. 809/295–1342. Open weekdays 9–noon and 1:30–4.*

Emergencies   Dial 911 for the **police, fire brigade,** or an **ambulance. Air/Sea Rescue** (tel. 809/297–1010).

Hospitals   The **King Edward VII Memorial Hospital** (7 Point Finger Rd., outside Hamilton near the Botanical Gardens, tel. 809/236–2345) is a fully equipped medical facility with a 24-hour emergency room.

Doctors and Dentists   Contact the hospital or the **Government Health Clinic** (67 Victoria St., Hamilton, tel. 809/236–0224) for referrals to a doctor or dentist.

Late-Night Pharmacies   **Hamilton Pharmacy.** *Church and Parliament Sts., Hamilton, tel. 809/295–7004. Open weekdays and Sat. 8AM–9PM.*
Phoenix Store. *Marriott's Castle Harbour Resort, tel. 809/293–8119. Open weekdays and Sat. 9AM–10PM.*
Collector's Hill Apothecary. *Collector's Hill, Smith's, tel. 809/236–8664. Open weekdays and Sat. 8–8, Sun. 7:30–9 PM.*

Travel Agencies   The American Express agent is **L. P. Gutteridge Ltd.** (L. P. Gutteridge Bldg., Bermudiana Rd., Hamilton, tel. 809/295–4545). Thomas Cook is represented by **Butterfield Travel Ltd.** (75 Front St., Hamilton, tel. 809/292–1510).

Telephones

Local Calls Pay phones, identical to those found in the United States, can be found on the streets of Hamilton, St. George's, and Somerset, as well as at ferry landings and some bus stops. Deposit 20¢ (U.S. or Bermudian) in the meter as soon as your party answers. Most hotels charge 20¢–75¢ for local calls.

International Calls Direct dialing is possible from anywhere on the island. Most hotels impose a surcharge for long-distance calls, even those made collect. Many of the small guest houses and apartments have no central switchboard; if you have a phone in your room, it's a private line from which you can make only collect or credit-card calls (and local calls, of course). Some of the small hotels have a telephone room or kiosk where you can make long-distance calls. Specially marked **AT&T USA Direct** phones can be found at the airport, the cruise-ship dock in Hamilton, and at King's Square and Ordnance Island in St. George's. International calls can also be made from the **main post office** (Church and Parliament Sts., Hamilton, tel. 809/295–5151) and from the **Cable & Wireless Office** (20 Church St., opposite City Hall, Hamilton, tel. 809/297–7000), which makes its overseas telephone, telex, cable, and fax facilities available to the public weekdays and Saturdays from 9 to 5.

To call the United States, Canada, Hawaii, and most Caribbean countries, dial 1 (or 0 if you need an operator's assistance), plus the area code and the number. For all other countries, dial 011 (or 01 for an operator), the country code, the area code, and the number. Using an operator for an overseas call is more expensive than dialing direct. For calls to the United States, rates are highest between 10 AM and 7 PM, and discounted between 7 PM and 11 PM; the lowest rates are from 11 PM to 7 AM. (No rate reductions are given for calls to Alaska and Hawaii.) Calls to Canada are cheapest from 9 PM to 7 AM, and to the United Kingdom from 6 PM to 7 AM.

Operators and Information To find a local number or to request information, dial 902. For information about international calls, dial 01.

Mail

Postal Rates Airmail letters and postcards to the United States and Canada require 55¢ postage per half ounce, and 70¢ per half ounce to the United Kingdom.

Receiving Mail If you have no address in Bermuda, you can have mail sent care of General Delivery (General Post Office, Hamilton HM GD, Bermuda).

Tipping

A service charge of 10% (or an equivalent per diem amount), which covers everything from baggage handling to maid service, is added to your hotel bill. Most restaurants, too, tack on a 15% service charge; otherwise a 15% tip is customary (more for exceptional service). Porters at the airport expect about a dollar, while taxi drivers usually receive 15% of the fare.

Opening and Closing Times

Banks   All branches of the **Bank of Bermuda** are open Monday–Thursday 9:30–3, and Friday 9:30–4:30. The exception is the airport branch, which is open Monday–Friday 11–4. All other banks on the island operate from Monday to Thursday 9:30–3, and Friday 9:30–3 and 4:30–5:30. All branches of the Bank of Bermuda have automatic teller machines, where travelers can obtain Visa cash advances up to $500 (in Bermudian currency) at any time of day.

Museums   Hours vary greatly, but generally museums are open weekdays and Saturday from 9 or 9:30 until 4:30 or 5; some museums close on Wednesday or Saturday. Check with the Visitors Information Centre or with the museum itself for exact hours.

Stores   Most stores are open weekdays and Saturday from around 9 until 5 or 5:30. Some Hamilton stores keep evening and Sunday hours when cruise ships are in port.

Convention and Business Services

Its proximity to U.S. East Coast cities and its diverse range of attractions—from sea and sun to shopping, sightseeing, tennis, and golf—have made Bermuda a popular center for conventions and conferences. In fact, meetings and incentives account for 33% of the island's tourism. Many hotels and resorts offer comprehensive meeting facilities and help expedite customs procedures for business and convention materials. The **Bermuda Chamber of Commerce** (tel. 809/295–4201; fax 809/292–5779) will help group organizers plan a variety of activities for group participants and/or spouses, including lectures, shopping tours, fashion shows, and sightseeing excursions. In 1988, Bermuda and the United States signed a tax treaty, giving business meetings in Bermuda the same tax privileges as those held in the United States. For more information about convention facilities and services in Bermuda, obtain a copy of *Bermuda: A Meeting and Incentive Travel Planner's Guide*, available free from the Bermuda Department of Tourism. Listed below are some of the business services available on the island.

Dry Cleaners   Full-service hotels and cottage colonies have laundry and drycleaning services, but guest houses and housekeeping apartments do not. **Hamilton Valcleners Ltd.** (Bermudiana Rd., Hamilton, tel. 809/292–3063) and **Paget Dry Cleaners Ltd.** (Lovers La., Paget, tel. 809/236–5142) both provide free pick-up and delivery, and express service on request.

Flowers and Gift Baskets   Concierges in the major hotels can arrange delivery of flowers and gift baskets. **The Flower Shop** (14 Reid St., Hamilton, tel. 809/295–2903) is an FTD florist. Fruit baskets, gift baskets, and flowers are also available at **House of Flowers** (Washington Mall, Hamilton, tel. 809/292–4750). **Designer Flowers** (Windsor Pl., Queen St., Hamilton, tel. 809/295–4380 and Market Place Plaza, Heron Bay, tel. 809/238–1490) creates special floral designs for any occasion.

Formal Wear   Formal wear by After Six, for both men and women, can be rented at **Karl's/Guys 'n Dolls** (Church St., Hamilton, tel. 809/292–5948).

Group Tours   Comprehensive group tours of the island are available through **L. P. Gutteridge Ltd.** (tel. 809/295–4545), **Butterfield Travel** (tel. 809/292–1510), **Penboss Associates** (tel. 809/295–3927), and **Meyer's Holiday Tours** (tel. 809/295–4176).

The **Bermuda National Trust** (tel. 809/236–6483) offers a variety of events for groups, including private house and garden tours, a champagne reception at the Verdmont house, walking tours, and slide shows and lectures.

Group Transportation From March to November, **Bermuda Aviation Services** (tel. 809/293–2500) provides group transport from the airport in eight-passenger minibuses and 26-passenger motorcoaches. From December through February, only taxis are available on the island. Taxi companies offering group service include **Bermuda Taxi Operators Company Ltd.** (tel. 809/292–4175), **Trott Travel Ltd.** (tel. 809/295–0041), and **B.I.U. Taxi Co-op Transportation** (tel. 809/292–4476).

Messenger Services Radio-dispatched messengers of **International Bonded Couriers** (Mechanics Bldg., Hamilton, tel. 809/295–2467) offer guaranteed pick-up and delivery of packages island-wide within 90 minutes. Two-day international deliveries are available through **Federal Express** (Par-la-Ville Rd., Hamilton, tel. 809/295–3854) and **DHL Worldwide Express** (Express Centre, 22 Washington Mall, tel. 809/295–3300).

Photocopying **The Copy Shop** (The Walkway, Reid St., Hamilton, tel. 809/292–5355) makes photocopies. The store is open weekdays 8:30–5, and Saturday 8:30–1.

Secretarial Services **Business Services of Bermuda** (tel. 809/295–5175) provides secretarial services, as well as photocopying and translation services.

Cranleigh Limited (tel. 809/292–3458) specializes in secretarial, translation, and messenger/telephone-answering services.

ExecuTemps (tel. 809/295–8608, fax 809/292–7783) offers secretarial services, meeting transcripts, conference-recording equipment, and word-processing and color photocopying services.

Video and Film Services **Electronic Services** (tel. 809/295–3885) has audiovisual equipment and operators for hire. **Panatel VDS Ltd.** (tel. 809/292–1600) is a full-service film and video production house.

Getting Around Bermuda

Despite its small size (20 square miles), Bermuda does pose some transport problems. Most important, rental cars are not allowed, so visitors must travel by bus, taxi, ferry, moped, bike, or on foot. Furthermore, narrow, winding roads—more than 1,200 miles of them—and a 20-mph speed limit (15 mph in town) that is strictly enforced make moving around the island a time-consuming process. Traveling the length of this long, skinny island takes particularly long: The trip from St. George's to Hamilton takes an hour by bus, and the onward journey to the West End takes another hour, although a new express bus service from Hamilton to the West End takes only 30 minutes. Hiring a taxi can cut down the amount of time you spend on the road, but the cost may discourage you. Fortunately, Hamilton, St. George's, and Somerset are all manageable on foot. Anyone who plans to do a lot of traveling around the island should pick up a copy of the *Bermuda Islands Guide,* an atlas of every road, alley, lane, and landmark on the island. Available

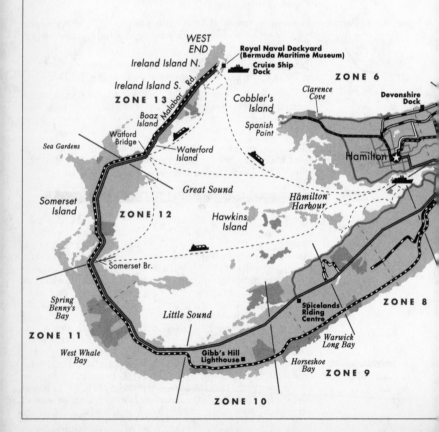

ATLANTIC OCEAN

WEST
END
Ireland Island N.

Royal Naval Dockyard
(Bermuda Maritime Museum)
Cruise Ship
Dock

ZONE 6

Clarence
Cove

Devonshire
Dock

Ireland Island S.
ZONE 13

Cobbler's
Island

Malabar Rd.

Boaz
Island

Spanish
Point

Watford
Bridge

Waterford
Island

Sea Gardens

Hamilton

Great Sound

Somerset
Island

ZONE 12

Hawkins
Island

Hamilton
Harbour

Somerset Br.

Spring
Benny's
Bay

ZONE 11

West Whale
Bay

Little Sound

Gibb's Hill
Lighthouse

Spicelands
Riding
Centre

ZONE 8

Warwick
Long Bay

Horseshoe
Bay

ZONE 9

ZONE 10

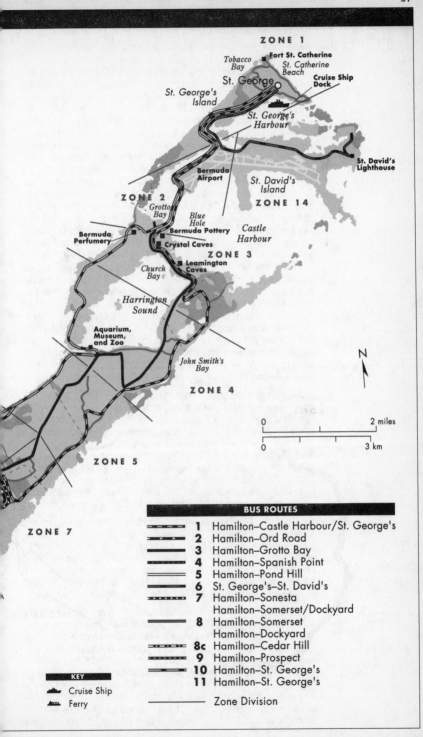

ZONE 1

Tobacco Bay Fort St. Catherine
St. Catherine Beach
St. George Cruise Ship Dock
St. George's Island
St. George's Harbour
St. David's Lighthouse
Bermuda Airport
ZONE 2
St. David's Island
Grotto Bay ZONE 14
Blue Hole
Bermuda Perfumery Bermuda Pottery *Castle Harbour*
Crystal Caves
ZONE 3
Leamington Caves
Church Bay
Harrington Sound
Aquarium, Museum, and Zoo
John Smith's Bay
ZONE 4
N
0 ——— 2 miles
0 ——— 3 km
ZONE 5
ZONE 7

	BUS ROUTES
1	Hamilton–Castle Harbour/St. George's
2	Hamilton–Ord Road
3	Hamilton–Grotto Bay
4	Hamilton–Spanish Point
5	Hamilton–Pond Hill
6	St. George's–St. David's
7	Hamilton–Sonesta
	Hamilton–Somerset/Dockyard
8	Hamilton–Somerset
	Hamilton–Dockyard
8c	Hamilton–Cedar Hill
9	Hamilton–Prospect
10	Hamilton–St. George's
11	Hamilton–St. George's

KEY
Cruise Ship
Ferry
——— Zone Division

at the Bermuda Book Store (Queen and Front Sts., Hamilton, tel. 809/295–3698), it is well worth the $4.95 price tag.

By Bus Bermuda's modern pink-and-blue buses tour the island from east to west, grinding up hills and squeezing through alleys. Hamilton buses arrive and depart from the **Central Bus Terminal** (Washington and Church Sts., Hamilton, tel. 809/292–3854), a small kiosk that is open daily 7:30–5. Finding a bus stop outside Hamilton can be difficult. Some are easily identifiable stone shelters, but others are marked only by striped poles by the road. These poles can be short or tall, green and white, or black and white, but the net effect is confusing. Remember to wait on the proper side of the road—driving in Bermuda is on the left. Exact change is necessary when boarding a bus and, to make matters worse, the fare depends on your destination. Bermuda is divided into 14 bus zones, each about 2 miles in length. Within the first three zones, adults pay $1.50 (coins, tickets, or tokens only; no dollar bills). For greater distances, the fare is $3. Children 3–12 pay 65¢ for all zones. If you plan to do much bus travel, it makes sense to buy a booklet of 15 14-zone tickets for $16 (or 15 three-zone tickets for $9). Ticket booklets and packets of discounted tokens are available at the Hamilton bus terminal and at post offices. Three- and seven-day passes ($15 and $25, respectively) are available at the bus terminal and the visitor's center in Hamilton. Buses run about every 15 minutes, except on Sunday when they usually come every hour. Bus schedules, which also contain ferry timetables, are available at the bus terminal in Hamilton and at many of the hotels. Bermudian bus drivers are sometimes rude, but they do answer questions about fares and destinations; upon request, they will also tell you when you've reached your stop.

In addition to the public buses to and from Hamilton, private minibuses serve the eastern and western ends of the island. In the West End, **Sandys Taxi Service** (tel. 809/234–2344) operates a minibus service hourly between Somerset Bridge and Dockyard. The fare depends upon the destination, although you won't have to pay more than $3 (half price for senior citizens). Minibuses, which you can flag down on the road or summon by phone, drop passengers wherever they want to go. The service operates from 7:20 AM until 7 PM between December and March, and from 7:20 AM until 10:20 PM between May and mid-October.

St. George's Transportation (tel. 8909/297–8199) has a similar minibus service around St. Geroge's and St. David's in the east. The minimum fare is $1.35 for adults, 85¢ for senior citizens, and 75¢ for children. Buses are available in King's Square in St. George's's, or they can be flagged down from the roadside. The service operates between 7 AM and 11 PM from March to November, and betwenn 7 AM and 10 PM from December to February.

By Ferry Quick and enjoyable, ferries sail every day from the **Ferry Terminal** (tel. 809/295–4506) in Hamilton, with routes to Paget, Warwick, and across the Great Sound to Somerset in the West End. On weekdays, most ferries run until 11 PM, although the last ferry from Hamilton to Somerset leaves at 6 PM; on Sunday, ferry service is limited and ends around 7 PM. A one-way fare to Paget or Warwick is $1.50, $3 to Somerset; children 3–13 pay 50¢. The turnstiles leading to the ferries accept only tokens, which are available at the terminal. Bicycles can be brought aboard free, but passengers must pay $2 extra to take a motor scooter to Somerset; motorized cycles are not allowed on the smaller Paget and Warwick ferries. The ferry operators, among the friendliest and most helpful people on the island, will answer questions about routes and schedules, and they'll even help get your bike aboard. Schedules, posted at each landing, are available at the Ferry Terminal, Central Bus Terminal, and most hotels.

By Taxi Taxis are metered and offer the fastest and easiest way around the island—and also the costliest. Taxis charge $4 for the first mile, and $1.40 for each subsequent mile. A half-hour trip costs about $20, including tip. Between 10 PM and 6 AM, or on Sunday and public holidays, a 25% surcharge is added to the fare. There is a 25¢ charge for each piece of luggage stored in the trunk or on the roof. For radio-dispatched taxis, contact **Radio Cabs Bermuda** (tel. 809/295–4141) and **Bermuda Taxi Operators** (tel. 809/292–5600).

By Moped Mopeds, or motor-assisted vehicles as Bermudians call them, offer visitors the most flexibility for moving about the island. Riding a moped, however, is not without hazards—especially for first-time riders. The roads are narrow, winding, and full of blind curves, and accidents occur frequently. The best way to avoid a mishap is to obey the 20-mph speed limit and to remember to stay on the left-hand side of the road, especially at traffic circles (or roundabouts as they're known in Bermuda). In addition, avoid riding in the rain and at night. The law requires all riders to wear a crash helmet with the chin strap fastened. Single- or double-seat mopeds and scooters can be rented from cycle liveries by the hour, the day, or the week. The cycle liveries will show first-time riders how to operate the mopeds. Rates vary from livery to livery, but single-seat mopeds cost about $21 per day, or $74 per week (plus a mandatory $12 repair waiver). The fee includes helmet, lock, key, third-party insurance, breakdown service, pick-up and delivery, and a tank of gas. A $20–$50 deposit is required for the lock, key, and helmet, and you must be at least 16 to rent. Recommended liveries are **Oleander Cycles** (Valley Rd., Paget, tel. 809/236–5235, and Gorham Rd., Hamilton, tel. 809/295–0919); **Eve's Cycle Livery** (Middle Rd., Paget, tel. 809/236–6247); **Devil's Hole Cycles** (Harrington Sound Rd., Smith's, tel. 809/293–1280); and **St. George's Cycles** (Water St., St. George's, tel. 809/297–1463). Major hotels have their own cycle liveries, and all hotels and guest houses will make rental arrangements. Gas stations are open weekdays and Saturday from 7 AM to 7 PM; you will be lucky to find one open on Sunday.

By Bicycle Push bikes, as Bermudians call bicycles, are a pleasant way to travel around the island, provided you don't mind the hilly terrain (*see* Chapter 6, Sports and Fitness). Bikes can be rented at **Eve's Cycle Livery** (Middle Rd., Paget, tel. 809/236–6247), **St. George's Cycles** (Water St., St. George's, tel. 809/297–1463), and **Georgiana Cycles** (Cambridge Rd., Somerset, tel. 809/234–2404). Rentals cost $10–$15 for the first day and $5 for each subsequent day.

By Limousine A limousine isn't the cheapest way to tour the island, but it is the most luxurious. If you reserve 24 hours in advance, **London Taxi Limousine Service** (tel. 809/292–3691) will provide a London-type cab, replete with liveried chauffeur, to drive you around for $70 per hour; corporate rates are available.

Guided Tours

Orientation Tours **Butterfield Travel Ltd.** (tel. 809/292–1510), the local Gray Line representative, runs custom-designed tours for groups and individual tours for cruise passengers seeking an alternative to prearranged shore excursions. Among the tours are a glass-bottom boat trip ($25 per person), a three-hour taxi tour around Harrington Sound ($30), and a five-hour island cruise with stops at Dockyard and St. George's ($50).

L. P. Gutteridge Ltd. (tel. 809/295–4545), the American Express representative on the island, specializes in group tours, but individual packages can also be arranged.

Taxi Tours A blue flag on the hood of a cab indicates that the driver is a qualified tour guide. These cabs can be difficult to find, but most of their drivers are friendly, entertaining, and well informed about the island and its history. Ask your hotel to arrange a tour with a knowledgeable driver. Tours are a minimum of three hours long. The legal rate is $20 per hour for one to four passengers, and $30 per hour for five or six passengers. A 25% surcharge is added between 10 PM and 6 AM, and on Sunday and public holidays.

Bus and **Penboss Associates Ltd.** (tel. 809/295–3927) conducts narrated
Minibus Tours motorcoach tours of both St. George's and Hamilton. The five-hour St. George's tour ($30), which circles Harrington Sound, includes admission to the Aquarium, Museum and Zoo, and Leamington Caves. The three-hour tour of Hamilton ($22) covers Verdmont, the Botanical Gardens, and sights in the capital city.

St. George's Transportation (tel. 809/297–8199) runs minibus tours of St. George's and St. David's, leaving from King's Square in St. George's. A one-hour tour costs $12 per person, and the two-hour tour is $17.50.

Carriage Tours There are only a few horse-drawn carriages on the island, but they are still a romantic way to see the sights. The raconteurs at the reins dispense a wealth of local lore and information—or misinformation. Regardless of the veracity of their tales, you'll enjoy the telling. Carriages can be hired on Front Street in Hamilton; for tours of the West End and Dockyard, contact **Bermuda Carriages** (tel. 809/238–2640). Rates for a one-horse carriage are $15 for a half hour, and $10 for each additional half hour. For a two-horse carriage, the fee is $20 for the first half hour, and $15 for each half hour thereafter.

Special-Interest For six weeks each spring, several Bermudian homes and gar-
Tours dens are open for public tours, offering visitors a delightful
Open Houses and glimpse of how the locals live. Most of the homes date from the
Garden Tours 17th century, and all have lovely lawns and gardens. Arranged by the **Garden Club of Bermuda** (tel. 809/295–1301), tours visit three different houses each Wednesday between 2 and 5. A $8 admission fee helps sponsor the club's conservation projects and horticultural scholarships.

Free guided tours of the **Botanical Gardens** leave at 10:30 AM from the parking lot just inside the Berry Hill Road entrance. These 90-minute tours are conducted year-round on Tuesday and Wednesday (Tuesday and Friday between November 15 and March 31).

Boat Trips   A host of boats offers sightseeing, snorkeling, and swimming excursions. Major attractions include the Sea Gardens, with their splendid underwater scenes, and the coral-wrapped wreck of HMS *Vixen*, both of which lie off the West End. Many of the boats operate only during high season, so call in advance for schedules.

The *Looking Glass* (tel. 809/236–8000), an 85-passenger glass-bottom boat owned by Beau Evans, heads out to the Sea Gardens twice daily from Hamilton on a two-hour cruise known as the "Reef and Wreck Adventure." En route, Evans offers an entertaining commentary on the islands of Hamilton Harbour and the Great Sound. Tours depart from Front Street and cost $25 for adults and $12.50 for children under 12; senior citizens receive a 20% discount. A four-hour dinner cruise ($55 adults, $27.50 for children, 20% discount for senior citizens) includes complimentary cocktails on board the *Looking Glass* and a four-course meal—accompanied by a calypso guitarist—at the Somerset Village Inn. The "Cruise of Lights" ($30 adults, $15 children, 20% discount for seniors) is a late-night outing with views of reefs, sea creatures, and constellations.

Bermuda Island Cruises (tel. 809/292–8652) operates the 120-passenger *Reef Explorer*, which leaves Hamilton on Monday, Wednesday, and Saturday night for a "Pirate Party Cruise" ($60 adults, $30 children under 12). The boat travels along the reefs, stopping at Hawkins Island for dinner, dancing, and a show featuring limbo dancers and calypso music. Two-hour glass-bottom-boat tours of the Sea Gardens ($25 adults, $12.50 children) leave twice daily from the Ferry Terminal in Hamilton. The "Starlight Reef & Wreck Cruise" ($25) leaves Hamilton Monday, Wednesday, Thursday, and Saturday at 10 PM and returns at midnight. And departing Monday and Wednesday–Saturday at 10:30 AM, a six-hour cruise stops at Dockyard and St. George's ($50 adults, $25 children), with a rum swizzle party on the return leg. From Albuoy's Point in Hamilton, a five-hour Somerset cruise ($40 adults, $20 children) features shopping in Somerset Village and a rum-swizzle party on the return trip. A six-hour tour to St. George's ($50 adults, $25 children), including sightseeing, shopping, and rum swizzles, also operates from Albuoy's Point, Tuesday–Sunday.

Submarine *Enterprise* (tel. 809/234–3547) takes passengers on sightseeing submarine dives offshore of the west end. The 44-passenger air-conditioned submarine has large viewing ports that overlook spectacular views; however, this trip is definitely not for the claustrophobic. Dives take in the wreck of the *Lartington*, which sank in 1878 and is now home to schools of tropical fish. The *Enterprise* itself does not put in to Dockyard, and the two-hour excursion ($70 adults, $35 children under 12) includes travel time from Dockyard to the submarine and back. Weather conditions must be ideal, and you must call ahead to find out if the submarine will be operating. Dive updates are available from the Visitor Service Broadcasting Radio, 1160 AM.

Whistler Charters (tel. 809/234–7038) offers sailing parties and charters aboard the *Whistler of Paget*, a 10-passenger, 38-foot sloop. Half-day sailing parties and two-hour sunset sails cost $30 per person; private charters are $325 for a full day and $180 for a half day. Snorkeling gear is provided.

Williams Marine Ltd. (tel. 809/238–0774) operates half-day tours ($30) and sunset sails ($20) on the *Alibi*, a 40-foot ketch that can carry 15 passengers, and the *Sundancer*, a 50-foot ketch that carries 24. Rum swizzles, soda, and beer are complimentary.

Salt Kettle Boat Rentals Ltd. (tel. 809/236–4863) offers sailing parties aboard the 55-foot sloop *Brightstar* for $30 per person.

Butterfield Travel Ltd. and **L. P. Gutteridge Ltd.** (*see* Orientation Tours, above) also arrange boat trips.

Walking Tours   The Bermuda Department of Tourism publishes brochures for self-guided tours of Hamilton, St. George's, the West End, and the Railway Trail. Available free at all Visitors Information Centres and at hotels and guest houses, these brochures contain detailed directions for walkers and cyclists, historical notes, and anecdotes.

From November 15 to March 31, the **Bermuda National Trust** (tel. 809/236–6483) conducts one-hour walking tours of Hamilton, St. George's, and Somerset. The tours of Hamilton and St. George's take in the large number of 17th- and 18th-century buildings in the two towns, while the tour in Somerset focuses more on the island's flora. Hamilton tours begin from the Visitors Information Centre in the Ferry Terminal on Front Street every Monday at 10 AM; tours of St. George's are conducted Wednesday and Saturday, starting at 10:30 AM in King's Square; the Somerset walk departs from the Country Squire Restaurant (Mangrove Bay, Somerset, tel. 809/234–0105) on Thursday at 10 AM.

Other free guided walks during the low season include a 2-mile walk through woodlands and scenic areas, leaving from the Clock Tower Building at Dockyard at 11:30 AM; and a tour around Dockyard, departing from the Craft Market on Sunday at 2 PM.

2 Portraits of Bermuda

Bermuda at a Glance: A Chronology

1503 Juan de Bermudez discovers the islands while searching for the New World. The islands are eventually named after him.

1603 Diego Ramirez, a Spanish captain, spends several weeks on Bermuda making ship repairs.

1609 An English fleet of nine ships, under the command of Admiral Sir George Somers, sets sail for Jamestown, Virginia, with supplies for the starving colony. Struck by a hurricane, the fleet is scattered, and the admiral's ship, the *Sea Venture*, runs aground on the reefs of Bermuda. The colonization of Bermuda begins.

1610 After building two ships, *Deliverance* and *Patience*, from the island's cedar trees, the survivors depart for Jamestown, leaving behind a small party of men. Admiral Sir George Somers returns to Bermuda a few weeks later but dies soon afterward. He requests that his heart be buried on the island.

1612 Asserting ownership of the islands, the Virginia Company sends 60 settlers to Bermuda under the command of Richard Moore, the colony's first governor. The Virginia Company sells its rights to the islands to the newly formed Bermuda Company for £2,000.

1616 The islands are surveyed and divided into shares (25 acres) and tribes (50 shares per tribe). The tribes, or parishes, are named after investors in the Bermuda Company. The first slaves are brought to Bermuda to dive for pearls.

1620 The Bermuda Parliament meets for the first time, in St. Peter's Church in St. George's, making it the third oldest parliament in the world after Iceland and Great Britain.

1684 The Crown takes over control of the colony from the Bermuda Company. Sir Robert Robinson is appointed the Crown's first Governor.

1775 The American Continental Congress announces a trade embargo against all colonies remaining loyal to the Crown. Dependent on America for food, Bermuda negotiates to give the rebellious colonies salt if they will lift the embargo. The colonies refuse, but state that they will end sanctions in exchange for gunpowder. Without the knowledge of Governor George Bruere, a group of Bermudians breaks into the magazine at St. George's and steals the island's supply of gunpowder. The gunpowder is delivered to the Americans, who lift the embargo.

1780 The "Great Hurricane" hits Bermuda, driving ships ashore and leveling houses and trees.

1784 Bermuda's first newspaper, *The Bermuda Gazette & Weekly Advertiser*, is started by Joseph Stockdale in St. George's.

1804 Irish poet Thomas Moore arrives in Bermuda for a four-month stint as registrar of the admiralty court. His affair with the married Hester Tucker was the inspiration for his steamy love poems to her (the "Nea" in his odes), which have attained legendary status in Bermuda.

1810 The Royal Navy begins work on Dockyard, a new naval base on Ireland Island.

1812 In response to American raids on York (now Toronto) during the War of 1812, the British fleet attacks Washington, DC, from its base in Bermuda.

1815 Hamilton becomes the new capital of Bermuda, superseding St. George's.

1834 Slavery is abolished.

1846 The first lighthouse in the colony, the 133-foot Gibb's Hill Lighthouse, is built at the western end of the island in an effort to reduce the number of shipwrecks in the area.

1861 Bermuda enters a period of enormous prosperity with the outbreak of the American Civil War. Sympathetic to the South, Bermudians take up the lucrative and dangerous task of running the Union blockade of southern ports. Sailing in small, fast ships, Bermudians ferry munitions and supplies to the Confederates and return with bales of cotton bound for London.

1883 Princess Louise, daughter of Queen Victoria, visits Bermuda. In honor of her visit, the new Pembroke Hotel changes its name to The Princess.

1901 Afrikaner prisoners from the Boer War are incarcerated in Bermuda. By the end of the war, approximately 4,000 prisoners are housed on the islands.

1915 A 120-man contingent of the Bermuda Volunteer Rifle Corps (B.V.R.C.) departs for service in France during World War I. In action at the battles of the Somme, Arras, and the Third Battle of Ypres, the unit loses more than 30% of its men. In 1916, the Bermuda Militia Artillery also heads for France.

1931 Constructed at a cost of £1 million, the Bermuda Railway opens years behind schedule. Maintenance problems during World War II cripple train service, and the whole system is sold to British Guiana in 1948.

1937 Imperial Airways begins the first scheduled air service to Bermuda from Port Washington in the United States.

1940 During World War II, mail bound for Europe from the Americas is off-loaded in Bermuda and taken to the basement of The Princess hotel, where it is opened by British civil servants trying to locate German spies. Several spies in the United States are unmasked. As part of the Lend-Lease Act between Prime Minister Churchill and President Roosevelt, the United States is awarded a 99-year lease for a military base on St. David's Island. Construction of the base begins in 1941.

1944 Women landowners are given the vote.

1946 For the first time, automobiles are permitted by law on Bermuda.

1951 The Royal Navy withdraws from Dockyard and closes the base.

1953 Winston Churchill, Dwight D. Eisenhower, and Prime Minister Joseph Laniel of France meet on Bermuda for the "Big Three Conference."

1959 NASA opens a space tracking station on Coopers Island, which is part of the American base.

1971 Edward Richards becomes Bermuda's first black government leader (a title later changed to premier).

1973 Governor Sir Richard Sharples and his aide, Captain Hugh Sayers, are shot dead. In 1976, Erskine "Buck" Burrows is convicted of the murder, as well as several other murders and armed robberies. He is hanged in 1977.

1979 Gina Swainson, Miss Bermuda, wins the Miss World Contest. An official half holiday is announced and Gina Swainson postage stamps are released in 1980.

1987 Hurricane Emily hits Bermuda, injuring more than 70 people and causing millions of dollars in damage.

1990 President Bush and Prime Minister Thatcher meet on Bermuda.

Bermuda's Hidden Landscapes

by William G. Scheller

William G. Scheller is a contributing editor to National Geographic Traveler; his articles have also appeared in the Washington Post Magazine, Islands, and numerous other periodicals.

At the pub on the square in St. George's, Bermuda, there is a sign on the second-floor veranda that everyone ignores. "Do not feed the birds," it says, but the clientele keeps handing out crumbs to the sparrows that dart through the open railings.

I sat on that veranda on a sultry October afternoon, finishing a pint of Watney's and looking out over King's Square. I had just enjoyed my first cup of Bermuda fish chowder, which the Pub, like most local restaurants, lets you fine-tune with cruets of dark rum and a fiery concoction called sherry peppers.

At the next table an English toddler was singing a song about a little duck. The 18th-century square below was quiet, partly because it had just rained and partly because at the moment there was no cruise ship anchored at St. George's. I crumbled a few morsels from the bun of my fish sandwich, tossed them to the sparrows, and made up my mind on another Watney's. After all, I wasn't playing golf that afternoon.

Not playing golf? The Bermuda Islands, conventional wisdom has it, are a place where you live on the links. But I was after a different place—a traveler's Bermuda, if I could find it.

On an archipelago roughly 22 miles long and seldom more than a mile wide, traveling can be a difficult order—unless you severely limit your pace. Fortunately, automobiles are out of the question. Visitors can't rent them (even residents weren't allowed to own cars until 1946), and the only option for exploring Bermuda on four wheels is to engage a taxi driven by an accredited guide. But why risk seeing the whole place in a day? If you move at a speed faster than a walk, you miss details like the sign I saw on a small, shuttered yellow building: "Dot & Andy's Restaurant. Operated by Barbara and Donna."

Until recently, walking in Bermuda has meant edging gingerly along the nearly nonexistent shoulders of narrow lanes, ready to press yourself into the hibiscus hedges when a car comes by. A few years ago, though, some enterprising Bermudians got the idea of turning the right-of-way of the abandoned Bermuda Railway into an island-length hiking trail. (The entire railway, down to the spikes, was sold to British Guiana, now Guyana, in 1948).

My first choice, as a rail enthusiast, would have been to have the narrow-gauge locomotive and cars still rattling along the tracks. But being able to walk the route, or part of it, is clearly the next best thing. My problem was that I chose a section that skirted a residential district along Bailey's Bay, near the northeastern end of the main island. Here the old roadbed was frequently severed by sharp inlets of the sea, and the trestles that had once bridged them had long since gone to South America. I'd walk a hundred yards or so and have to go back to the road, often finding no signs to tell me when I could pick up the trail again. (Farther west on the islands, the old route is less frequently broken.) On one side was the ocean, on the other a series of relentlessly suburban backyards—there are no raffish little shacks here, like the ones you find on other islands. Finally, after I had inadvertently wandered into my fourth backyard, it began to rain. It was the kind of rain that makes you so wet in the first couple of minutes that there's no sense in hurrying out of it. I walked to a bus shelter, and admitted defeat…and some success, having got into a situation in which I could hardly be mistaken for a tourist, even in Bermuda.

It was in the bus shelter that I met a young American, who was waiting out the storm with his two toddlers. He was a civilian worker at the U.S. naval air station, a submarine-watching facility now largely dedicated to operating the islands' commercial airport. His most telling comment had to do with his younger child, who had been born in Hamilton: "She's a real Bermuda Onion."

He knew, of course, that genuine Bermudian citizenship requires at least one native parent, or jumping through more bureaucratic hoops than most people would care to deal with, but the fact that he liked thinking of his little girl as a Bermudian meant that he wasn't just serving a remunerative sentence in a faraway place. To a wet traveler like me, the message was that there was a community here, and foreigners could become part of it.

The rain that ended my railway trail walk was part of the tail end of Hurricane Nana, which had threatened to strike the island in full force before being pushed off track by a continental cold front. "We don't have hurricanes in Bermuda," a hotel bartender had told me with a wink, obviously remembering 1987's Emily, with her 116-mph winds, 50 injuries, and $35 million damage.

"No," I replied. "I live in Vermont, and we don't have snow."

Nana was a hurricane that missed, although she faded and veered away with great theatrical effect. By nine that evening the rain returned, sheeting sideways against the windows of the hotel restaurant while tall palms thrashed in wild abandon. From the hotel bar the storm was a terrific backdrop—the room was all *Key Largo* atmosphere heightened by the adrenal tingle that comes with a sudden pres-

sure drop. It didn't last long. Within an hour, all that remained of Nana in Bermuda was a random gusting among
the palm tops, and it was fine outside for a walk down to the
bay.

The next day I reverted to the vehicle of choice for covering
ground in Bermuda. Motorized or "auxiliary" cycles, and
the more modern motor scooters—none for rent with en-
gines larger than 50cc, but powerful enough for islands with
a 21-mph speed limit—have become a virtual postcard cli-
ché in Bermuda, and to strap on your de rigueur white helmet is to feel as if you've somehow become part of the
landscape.

A lot of visitors are afraid the scooters can too easily help
them accomplish just that, but the bikes aren't all that dangerous, once you learn the controls and remember to stay
on the left, British style. There is, however, a common
motorbike injury the locals call "road rash," a nasty abra-
sion of whatever appendage happens to meet with the road,
or with one of Bermuda's limestone walls, during a badly
executed turn.

What I most wanted the bike for was exploring
the Bermuda hinterlands. I had already visited
St. George's, the islands' oldest settlement and
former capital, with its narrow meandering streets, lovely
State House (built in 1620), and cedar-beamed, 18th-centu-
ry church of St. Peter. I had been particularly intrigued
with a local attraction called the Confederate Museum,
headquarters of blockade-running operations during the
U.S. Civil War. (What really caught my interest there was
the attitude of the black docent, "proud," as she put it, of a
building that housed the branch office of a desperate effort
to keep her ancestors in chains. In Bermudian race relations, bygones are bygones to a remarkable degree.)

Towns are best explored on foot, even though it did get to be
great fun to breeze into the capital for dinner after dark and
have maître d's take my helmet. The bike, though, would let
me discover the countryside, with its quiet lanes and
tended meadows and fragments of old estates. One of those
estates—Verdmont, in Smith's Parish, now a Bermuda National Trust property—lay at the end of a delightfully convoluted route I had devised, one that was designed to take
me buzzing along as many back roads as possible.

It was on St. Mark's Road, rounding Collector's Hill while I
was more or less on the way to Verdmont, that the essence
of this miniature landscape suddenly came clear: I was looking, I realized, at a near-perfect combination of Martha's
Vineyard and the Cotswolds. On the Vineyard account was
the gently rolling countryside with the sea not far away, as
on a New England seacoast farm; the Cotswolds element
was provided by a little jewel of a limestone Gothic church,
by narrow byways with names like Pigeon Berry Lane, and

by the faultless juxtaposition of every stand of trees, half-acre of greensward, and carefully clipped hedgerow.

As it turned out, I wasn't the first to get this feeling about the place: I saw later that two of the local streets were named Nantucket Lane (close enough) and Cotswold Lane. And why not? The Cotswold Hills, Bermuda, and the Massachusetts islands are all essentially English places, the latter two offering their settlers an Englishness of landscape even before any art was applied to it. And that art, in all three locales, was the particular English genius for conjuring tremendous diversity within the most compact of areas. Consummately ordered yet always romantically picturesque, the English landscape aesthetic depends on constant variety and small surprises, and never upon great vistas.

The result is a sense of much in little, of no space wasted; the effect in Bermuda is to shrink the visitor into the islands' scale, rather than to leave him feeling like a scooter-mounted giant in a hibiscus garden.

There was another aspect of Bermuda to consider, one that counters the islands' persona as a serene, ocean-borne fragment of English countryside. This is its past history as fortress Bermuda, a 21-square-mile dreadnought permanently anchored in the Atlantic. Fort St. Catherine, at the colony's extreme northeastern tip, is now decommissioned and restored to reveal its vast warren of tunnels, built to feed shells to guns commanding the northern and eastern approaches to the islands. St. David's Island, too, has its battery, a rusting line of World War II-era shore artillery where feral housecats pad about the empty magazines.

From the 17th to the 20th century, dozens of promontories and harbor entrances throughout Bermuda bristled with guns, reflecting Britain's confrontations with forces that ranged from imperial Spain to the newly independent United States to the U-boats of the Third Reich. And no single installation loomed so mightily as the Royal Navy Dockyard, at the barb of Bermuda's fishhook-shaped western end.

From 1810 to 1950 the dockyard was the "Gibraltar of the West," providing a heavily fortified anchorage for British warships and a citadel of massive limestone support structures. Approaching by ferry from Hamilton, I immediately was struck by the orderliness and permanence of it all, by the twin towers of the main building with clock faces showing the time and the hour of the next high tide, and by the ubiquitous initials V.R.—"Victoria Regina," shorthand for one of history's most remarkable imperial achievements. The dockyard looks as if it were built to last a thousand years, and it may, though now it houses a cluster of museums, craft galleries, restaurants, and boutiques. Like the rest of Bermuda's defenses, the dockyard was never tested by a serious attack; its bristles were too formidable a challenge.

Time and again in Bermuda, one encounters the opposing tidal pull of British and American influences. This, after all, is a place where they still refer to the panorama of harbor islands as seen from the top of Gibb's Hill as the "Queen's View," because Elizabeth II admired it in 1953. But this British colony also conducts its financial affairs in dollars, not sterling, and nearly 90 percent of its visitors are American.

There is a continuing Bermudian tradition that many residents link with the long British military presence, and that is a certain formality of dress. I was reminded of it one day in downtown Hamilton, when I saw a white-haired gentleman wearing a blue blazer, a white shirt, and a rep silk tie, along with pink Bermuda shorts, white knee socks, and pink tassels on his garters. The shorts themselves are a throwback to the military, and got their start as a local trademark when Bermuda tailors began refining officers' baggy khaki shorts for civilian wear. They are now ubiquitous as Bermudian business attire, but the most striking thing about them is not the fact that they expose gentlemen's knees but that they are integrated into a very correct, very formal men's civilian uniform. I never once saw a businessman's collar and tie loosened on a hot day in Bermuda—a sure sign that the stiff upper lip can outlast even the presence of the Royal Navy.

I thought about where I might find the quintessence of Bermudian formality and local tradition, and concluded that the place to look was probably afternoon tea at the venerable Hamilton Princess hotel. I was staying elsewhere, and thought it might be appropriate to call the Princess first to see if outsiders were welcome. "Are you serving tea at four?" I asked the English-accented woman who answered the telephone.

"Yes."

"Is it all right to come if you're not registered at the hotel?"

"Are you registered at the hotel?"

"No. That's why I'm asking."

"I'll switch you to dining services."

"Hello?" (Another Englishwoman's voice.)

"Hello, I'm wondering if I can come to tea if I'm not registered at the hotel."

"What is your name, sir?" I gave her the name and spelling. At this point, I was tempted to add "Viscount."

"I don't have you listed as a guest."

"I know that. I'm calling to ask if it's all right to come to tea if I'm not a guest."

"No, sir."

Now we were deep in Monty Python territory, and I had the John Cleese part. Clearly, there was nothing to do but get dressed, scoot into Hamilton, and crash tea at the Princess. But when I sauntered into the hotel with my best ersatz viscount air, all I found was a small antechamber to an empty function room where a dozen people in tennis clothes stood around a samovar and a tray of marble pound cake slices. I poured a cup, drank it, and was gone in five minutes. Crashing tea at the Princess had been about as difficult, and as exciting, as crashing lunch at my late grandfather's diner in New Jersey.

Hamilton is a tidy, cheerful little city, but as the days drew down I returned more and more to the countryside, particularly to the back roads where small farms survive. Bermuda was once a midocean market garden, in the days before the United States restricted imports, and property values skyrocketed beyond the reach of farmers; now, an occasional neat patch of red earth still produces root crops, broccoli, cabbage, and squash. I even saw a truck loaded with onions go by—a reminder of a Bermuda before golf.

America's Rebel Colonies and Bermuda: Getting a Bang for Their Buckwheat

by William Zuill

A native Bermudian and a member of the Bermuda House of Assembly, William Zuill is the author of several historical works about the island. This excerpt about the role of Bermuda in the American War of Independence is taken from his book, Bermuda Journey. *William Zuill died in July 1989.*

When the War of American Independence began, Bermudians at first felt little personal concern. There was some sympathy for the colonists; quarrels between arbitrary executive power and people, which in America had now led to real trouble, had also been part of Bermuda's history, and besides this there were ties of blood and friendship to make for a common understanding. But for all that, Bermudians, while expressing discreet sympathy, were chiefly concerned for their ships and carrying trade, and realizing their helpless position, they believed their wisest course lay in continued loyalty to the Crown. The wisdom of this policy was suddenly brought into question when the Continental Congress placed an embargo on all trade with Britain and the loyal colonies, for as nearly all essential food supplies came from the Continent, the island faced starvation unless the decree was relaxed. Thus there was a swift realization that Bermuda's fate was deeply involved in the war.

The drama now began to unfold and soon developed into a struggle between the governor, George Bruere, and the dominant Bermuda clique led by the Tuckers of the West End. Bruere's chief characteristic was unswerving, unquestioning loyalty, and the fact that two of his sons were fighting with the royalist forces in America—one of them was killed at Bunker Hill—made the ambiguous behavior of Bermudians intolerable to him, both as a father and as an Englishman.

Of the Tuckers, the most prominent member of the family at this time was Colonel Henry, of the Grove, Southampton. His eldest son, Henry, colonial treasure and councillor, had married the governor's daughter, Frances Bruere, and lived at St. George's. There were also two sons in America, Thomas Tudor, a doctor settled in Charleston, and St. George, the youngest, a lawyer in Virginia. The two boys in America, caught up in the events around them and far removed from the delicacies of the Bermuda situation, openly took the side of the colonists.

Up to the time of the outbreak of the war there had been warm friendship between the Tuckers and the Brueres, a relationship made closer by the marriage of Henry Tucker to Frances Bruere. But when it became known in Bermuda that the Tuckers abroad were backing the Americans, Bruere publicly denounced them as rebels and broke off relations with every member of the family except his son-in-law. But Colonel Henry was more concerned with the situation in Bermuda than he was with the rights and wrongs of the conflict itself, and he believed that unless someone acted, the island was facing serious disaster. So, privately, through his sons in America, he began to sound out some of the delegates to the Continental Congress as to whether the embargo would be relaxed in exchange for salt. This move, never in any way official, had the backing of a powerful group, and before long it was decided to send the colonel with two or three others to Philadelphia to see what could be arranged. Meanwhile another but less powerful faction took form and likewise held meetings, the object of which was to oppose in every way these overtures to rebels.

Colonel Henry and his colleagues reached Philadelphia in July 1775 and on the 11th delivered their appeal to Congress. Though larded with unctuous flattery, the address met a stony reception, but a hint was thrown out that although salt was not wanted, any vessel bringing arms or powder would find herself free from the embargo. The fact that there was a useful store of powder at St. George's was by now common knowledge in America, for the Tucker boys had told their friends about it and the information had reached General Washington. Thus, before long, the question of seizing this powder for the Americans was in the forefront of the discussions.

Colonel Henry was in a tight corner. Never for an instant feeling that his own loyalty was in question, he had believed himself fully justified in coming to Philadelphia to offer salt in exchange for food. But these new suggestions which were now being put to him went far beyond anything he had contemplated, and he was dismayed at the ugly situation that confronted him. It is evident that the forces at work were too strong for him. The desperate situation in Bermuda, verging on starvation, could only be relieved by supplies from America, and an adamant Congress held the whip hand. In the end, after some agonizing heart-searching, he gave in and agreed with Benjamin Franklin to trade the powder at St. George's for an exemption of Bermuda ships from the embargo.

Colonel Henry returned home at once, arriving on July 25. His son St. George, coming from Virginia, arrived about the same time, while two other ships from America, sent especially to fetch the powder, were already on their way.

On August 14, 1775, there was secret but feverish activity among the conspirators as whaleboats from various parts of the island assembled at Somerset. As soon as it was dark, the party, under the command, it is believed, of son-in-law Henry and a Captain Morgan, set off for St. George's. St. George, lately from Virginia and sure to be suspect, spent the night at St. George's, possibly at the home of his brother Henry, and at midnight was seen ostentatiously walking up and down the Parade with Chief Justice Burch, thus establishing a watertight alibi. Meanwhile the landing party, leaving the boats at Tobacco Bay on the north side of St. George's, reached the unguarded magazine. The door was quickly forced, and before long, kegs of powder were rolling over the grass of the Governor's Park toward the bay, where they were speedily stowed in the boats. The work went on steadily until the first streaks of dawn drove the party from the scene. By that time 100 barrels of powder were on the way to guns that would discharge the powder against the king's men.

When Bruere heard the news he was frantic. A vessel which he rightly believed had the stolen powder on board was still in sight from Retreat Hill, and he determined to give chase. Rushing into town, the distraught man issued a hysterical proclamation:

POWDER STEAL

Advt

Save your Country from Ruin, which
may hereafter happen. The Powder
stole out of the Magazine late last
night cannot be carried far as the
wind is so light.

A GREAT REWARD

will be given to any person that can
make a proper discovery before the
Magistrates.

News of the outrage and copies of the proclamation were hurried through the colony as fast as rider could travel. The legislature was summoned to meet the following day. Many members of the Assembly doubtless knew a good deal, but officially all was dark and the legislature did its duty by voting a reward and sending a wordy message expressing its abhorrence of the crime.

But no practical help was forthcoming, and after several days of helpless frustration Bruere determined to send a vessel to Boston to inform Admiral Howe what had happened. At first no vessels were to be had anywhere in the island; then, when one was found, the owner was threatened with sabotage, so he withdrew his offer. Another vessel was found, but there was no crew, and for three whole weeks, in an island teeming with mariners, no one could be found to go to sea. At last, on September 3, the governor's ship put to sea, but not without a final incident, for she was boarded offshore by a group of men who searched the captain and crew for letters. These had been prudently hidden away in the ballast with the governor's slave, who remained undiscovered. The captain hotly denied having any confidential papers, so the disappointed boarders beat him up and then left.

In due course the ship reached Boston, and Admiral Howe at once sent the *Scorpion* to Bermuda to help Bruere keep order. Thereafter for several years His Majesty's ships kept a watchful eye on the activities of Bermudians, and in 1778 these were replaced by a garrison. It has always seemed extraordinary that no rumor of this bargain with the Americans reached the ears of Bruere before the actual robbery took place. It is even more amazing that within a stone's throw of Government House such a desperate undertaking could have continued steadily throughout the night without discovery.

The loss of the powder coincided with the disappearance of a French officer, a prisoner on parole. At the time it was thought that he had been in league with the Americans and had made his escape with them. But 100 years later when the foundation for the Unfinished Church was being excavated, the skeleton of a man dressed in French uniform was disclosed. It is now believed that he must have come on the scene while the robbery was in progress and, in the dark, been mistaken for a British officer. Before he could utter a sound he must have been killed outright by these desperate men and quickly buried on the governor's doorstep.

Following in the Tracks of the Bermuda Railway

by Ben Davidson

A former travel editor for Sunset Travel *magazine, Ben Davidson specializes in travel writing and photography.*

Bermuda is lovely, but a walk along its narrow roads can involve close encounters with countless madcap moped drivers and a stream of cars. A more serene way to sample Bermuda's lush terrain, stunning seascapes, and colorful colonies of island homes is to follow the route of the railroad that once crossed this isolated archipelago. The Bermuda Railway Trail goes along the old train right-of-way for 18 miles, winding through three of the several interconnected islands that make up Bermuda.

Opened in 1931, the railway provided smooth-running transportation between the quiet village of Somerset at the west end and the former colonial capital of St. George's to the east. But by 1948 it had fallen a victim to excessive military use during World War II, soaring maintenance costs, and the automobile. The railroad was closed down, and all its rolling stock was sold to Guyana (then called British Guiana). In 1984, Bermuda's 375th anniversary, the government dedicated the lands of the old railway for public use and began to clear, pave, and add signs to sections of its route.

The trail's most enchanting aspect is that it reveals a parade of island views hidden from the public for nearly 30 years, scenes similar to what the first colonists must have found here in the early 1600s. In a few places the trail joins the main roads, but mostly it follows a tranquil, car-free route from parish to parish, past quiet bays, limestone cliffs, small farms, and groves of cedar, allspice, mangrove, and fiddlewood trees. Short jaunts on side trails and intersecting tribe roads (paths that were built in the early 1600s as boundaries between the parishes, or "tribes") bring you to historic forts and a lofty lighthouse, coral-tinted beaches, parks, and preserves.

I explored the Railway Trail on foot, moped, and horseback, using an 18-page guide available free at the Visitors Service Bureau in Hamilton. (You can also find the guide at some of the big hotels.) The booklet contains historical photos, a brief history of the railroad, maps, and descriptions of seven sections of trail, which range from 1¾ to 3¾ miles.

Sporting a pair of proper Bermuda shorts, I revved up my rented moped and headed out to the Somerset Bus Terminal, one of eight former railroad stations and the westernmost end of the trail. From there I followed the paved path to Springfield—an 18th-century plantation house used by the Springfield Library. A leisurely stroll in the adjoining five-acre Springfield & Gilbert Nature Reserve took me through thick forests of fiddlewood. I also saw stands of Bermuda cedars that once blanketed the island but were nearly wiped out by blight in the 1940s.

Back on the trail I spotted oleander, hibiscus, bougainvillea, and poinsettia bursting through the greenery at every turn. In backyards I could see bananas, grapefruit, oranges, lemons, and limes growing in profusion, thanks to Bermuda's consistent year-round subtropical climate.

I parked the moped at the trailhead to Fort Scaur—a 19th-century fortress built by the Duke of Wellington, conqueror of Napoleon at Waterloo—and strolled up to its mighty walls and deep moat. Through a dark passage I reached the grassy grounds with their massive gun mounts and bunkers. A telescope atop the fort's walls provided close-up views of the Great Sound and Ely's Harbor, once a smuggler's haven. A caretaker showed me around the fort, one of the three largest in Bermuda.

On my moped again, I motored past Skroggins Bay to the Lantana Colony Club, a group of beachside cottages. I stopped to sip a Dark and Stormy—a classic Bermudian rum drink—and to enjoy the view of the sail-filled Great Sound. My post-swizzle destination: Somerset Bridge. Only 32 inches wide, this tiny bridge was built in 1620 and looks more like a plank in the road than the world's smallest drawbridge—its opening is just wide enough for a sailboat's mast to pass through.

I ended my first Railway Trail ride at the ferry terminal near the bridge, where I boarded the next ferry back to Hamilton. Had I continued, the trail would have taken me through what was once the agricultural heartland of Bermuda. The colony's 20 square miles of gently rolling landscape, graced by rich volcanic soil and a mild climate, once yielded crops of sweet, succulent Bermuda onions, potatoes, and other produce. But tourism has become bigger business here, and today only some 500 acres are devoted to vegetable crops.

Just west of Sandys Parish the trail runs for some 3¾ miles through Warwick Parish. The path, now dirt, overlooks Little Sound and Southampton, where fishing boats are moored. Here the Railway Trail begins to intersect many of Bermuda's tribe roads, which make interesting diversions. Tribe Road No. 2 brings you to the Gibb's Hill Lighthouse, built around 1846. This 133-foot structure is one of the few lighthouses in the world made of cast iron. You pay $2 for the dubious privilege of climbing 185 steps to the lens house, where you're rewarded with far-reaching views of the island and Great Sound. The 1,500-watt electric lamp can be seen as far away as 40 miles.

Spicelands, a riding center in Warwick, schedules early-morning rides along sections of the Railway Trail and South Shore beaches. I joined a ride to follow part of the trail where it cuts deep into the rolling limestone terrain—so deep that at one point we passed through the 450-foot Paget Tunnel, whose walls are lined with roots of rubber trees.

We rode through woodlands and fields, past stands of Surinam cherry trees and houses equipped with domed water tanks and stepped, pyramid-shaped roofs designed to catch rainwater. As we trotted through the cool darkness beneath a dense canopy of trees it was hard to imagine a time when noisy rolling stock rattled along the same route, carrying some of the 14 million passengers who rode the railway while it was in operation. Finally, a tribe road led us through tropical vegetation to the clean, coral-pink beaches of Bermuda's beautiful South Shore.

East of Hamilton, the Railway Trail follows the North Shore, beginning in Palmetto Park in the lush, hilly parish of Devonshire. It hugs the coastline past Palmetto House (a cross-shaped, 18th-century mansion belonging to the Bermuda National Trust) and thick stands of Bermuda cedar to Penhurst Park, where there are walking trails, agricultural plots, and good swimming beaches.

Farther east the trail hits a wilder stretch of coast. The Shelley Bay Park and Nature Reserve along here has native mangroves and one of the few beaches on the North Shore. After a short walk on North Shore Road, the trail picks up again at Bailey's Bay and follows the coast to Coney Island. The park here has an old lime kiln and a former horse-ferry landing.

The remaining sections of the trail are in St. George's. Start at the old Terminal Building (now called Tiger Bay Gardens) and stroll through this historic town. The trail passes by Mullet Bay and Rocky Hill Parks, then heads to Lover's Lake Nature Reserve, where nesting longtails can be seen amid the mangroves. The end of the trail is at Ferry Point Park, directly across from Coney Island. In the park there's a historic fort and a cemetery.

Evenings are perhaps the most enchanting time to walk along the Railway Trail. As the light grows dim, the moist air fills with songs from tiny tree frogs hidden in hedges of oleander and hibiscus. The sound sets a tranquil, tropical mood that, for nearly a half century, has been undisturbed by the piercing whistle and clickety-clack of Bermuda's bygone railroad.

3 Cruising in Bermuda

Choosing Your Cruise

Cruise Information

Cruise Travel Magazine, (Box 3767, Escondido, CA 92025) which is published every two months, is a glossy magazine with feature articles about ships and ports of call. Subscriptions are $9.97 for six issues.

Ocean & Cruise News (World Ocean & Cruise Liner Society, Box 92, Stamford, CT 06901) is a newsletter that features profiles of a ship of the month.

The **Center for Environmental Health and Injury Control** performs regular sanitation inspections on all cruise ships sailing in American waters. Ships are given a rating between 1 and 100, and scores under 85 fall in the Not Satisfactory category. The latest sanitation summary is available free from the Department of Health and Human Services (Public Health Service, Centers for Disease Control, Atlanta, GA 30333).

Types of Ships

The bigger the ship, the more it can offer: more on-board activities, larger cabins, a greater number of public rooms, a wider variety of dining options, and a broader range of shore excursions. Large ships invariably hold more people, which may be a plus for sociable individuals. Also, passage on these ships may be slightly cheaper, because larger, newer ships are significantly less expensive per passenger to operate. Some ships, though, are too big to dock in port, and passengers may have to wait in line to take one of the tenders that commute between ship and shore. Smaller cruise ships offer a level of intimacy virtually impossible on larger vessels; the crew may be more informal, and the level of activity is usually less intense. Small ships can often slip into tiny, shallow harbors and dock right at quayside. A small ship, however, may not have a swimming pool, a movie theater, a casino, or a library, and the cabins are almost always smaller.

When considering a ship's size, don't forget other variables, such as the passenger/crew ratio (or service ratio), which indicates how many passengers each crew member must serve. If a ship's service ratio is 2:1, there is one crew member for every two passengers on a ship. A low service ratio means you will receive more personal service.

Another factor to consider is on-board facilities. Most ships have certain standard facilities: swimming pools, entertainment lounges, movie theaters, and exercise rooms. Ships with more lounges usually have more entertainment.

Mainstream Ships A **mainstream cruise ship** carries between 400 and 2,000 passengers and is similar to a self-contained, all-inclusive resort. Vast quantities of food are served, and guests can enjoy swimming pools, spas and saunas, movie theaters, exercise rooms, Las Vegas–style entertainment, a casino, shore excursions, and plenty of planned group activities.

Mainstream ships charge from $150 to $600 per diem, although **economy ships**—generally older and smaller mainstream ships—offer lower per-diem prices, ranging from under $100 for the smallest inside cabins to about $350 for top-of-the-line suites.

Upscale ships justify higher prices—from $150 to $620—by offering a level of service, accommodations, and cuisine that's a cut above the average. Passengers on upscale ships tend to be older and more sedate.

Luxury ships have more spacious staterooms, most of which are outside cabins, complemented by white-glove service, formal or semiformal dining with three- and four-star cuisine, and a low service ratio. Per diem prices range from $200 to $750 and up.

The **megaship** is a vessel that is 60,000 tons or larger and carries 1,500 or more passengers. There will be an increasing number of these big ships on the water because the economics of cruising make them more profitable, whether they offer standard, upscale, or luxury cruises. The only difference between these and other mainstream ships is that megaships have more of everything: more cabins, more entertainment areas, more restaurants, more shops, and more lounges and bars.

Cost

The entire cost of your trip (aside from tips, shopping, bar bills, and other incidentals), is covered in one all-inclusive price. The axiom "the more you pay, the more you get" doesn't always hold true with cruises, and most mainstream ships are generally one-class vessels on which the passenger in the cheapest inside cabin eats the same food, sees the same shows, and shares the same amenities as the passenger in the top suite. (An exception worth noting is the *Queen Elizabeth 2*, which has four different restaurants and makes dining-room assignments depending upon the per diem paid for a cabin or stateroom: the higher the cabin category, the more elegant the dining room.)

A larger cabin (and a higher price) may not be all that important because the average cruise passenger uses his or her cabin only for sleeping, showering, and changing clothes. Where price does make a difference is in the choice of ship.

A handy way to compare costs of different cruises, ships, or cabins is to look at the per diem cost—the price of a cruise on a daily basis for each passenger, when two people occupy one cabin. In other words, if a seven-day cruise costs $700 per person, then the per diem for each person is $100. To select a cruise you can afford, consider the following elements.

Pre- and post-cruise arrangements: If you plan to arrive at the port of embarkation a day or two early, or linger a few days for sightseeing after the cruise is over, estimate the cost of your hotel, meals, car rental, sightseeing, and other expenditures. Cruise lines sell packages for pre- and post-cruise stays that can include hotel accommodations, transportation, tours, and other extras, such as car rentals, access to golf courses, and some meals. These packages usually cost significantly less than similar stays that you would arrange on your own.

Airfare: Airfare and transfers are often included in the basic price of a cruise. There is usually a reduction of $50–$200 for passengers not using the whole transportation package.

Pretrip incidentals: Trip insurance, flight insurance, the cost of boarding your pets, airport or port parking, departure tax, visas, long distance calls home, cruise clothing, film, and other miscellaneous expenses.

Shore excursions: Estimate an average of $70–$100 per passenger on a seven-day cruise.

Gambling allowance: Losses in the casino, on bingo, or for other forms of gambling average about $400 per family. (Children are not permitted to gamble on cruise ships, but you should include in your budget how much the kids are likely to spend in the video arcade.)

Shopping: Include what you expect to spend both for inexpensive souvenirs and large duty-free purchases.

On-board incidentals: According to the Cruise Lines International Association (CLIA), the typical tip total works out to $7–$11 per person per day. Daily on-board expenditures, including bar tabs, wine with meals, laundry, beauty parlor services, and gift shop purchases, average about $22.50 per person.

Accommodations

Where you sleep matters only if you enjoy extra creature comforts and are willing to pay for them; on most of today's one-class cruise ships no particular status or stigma is attached to your choice of cabin. Having said that, there's certainly an advantage in selecting the best cabin within your budget, rather than allowing your travel agent or cruise line representative to book you into the next available accommodation. The earlier you book, the better the selection will be: The best cabins are often reserved a year or more in advance.

Cabin Size A few ships use the term "stateroom" to indicate a high-price cabin, but on most ships the terms "cabin" and "stateroom" are nearly interchangeable. The price of a cabin is directly proportional to how large it is, and the overwhelming majority of ship cabins are *tiny*—certainly far smaller than the average American bedroom.

Suites are the roomiest and best-equipped accommodations, although there may be a considerable difference in size, facilities, and prices among each ship's various suites. Most suites have a sitting room or an area with a sofa and chairs, and they may receive more attentive steward service (top suites on some ships are even assigned private butlers). Some have two bathrooms, possibly with a Jacuzzi bathtub. The most expensive suites may be priced as complete packages, regardless of the number of passengers occupying them.

Furnishings Almost all modern cabins are equipped with private bathrooms—usually closet-size, with a toilet, tiny shower, and washbasin. More expensive cabins, especially on newer ships, may have bathtubs and double sinks. Most cabins also have miniscule closets, a small desk or dresser, a reading light, and, on many ships, a telephone and television.

Depending upon the ship and category, a cabin may have beds or berths. The beds may be twins, either side-by-side or at right angles to each other. Less expensive cabins and cabins on smaller or older ships may have upper and lower bunks, or berths, especially when three or four people share the same accommodation. To provide more living space in the daytime, the room stewards fold the berths into the wall and frequently convert single beds into couches. More and more ships are reconfiguring their cabins to offer double beds; if that is what you want, get an assurance in writing that you have been assigned a cabin with a double bed.

Sharing The great majority of cabins are designed for two people. Smaller, one-person cabins usually carry a premium price. If more than two people share a cabin, there can often be a substantial saving for the third or fourth person. Children sharing a cabin with their parents often get an extra discount. When no single cabins are available, passengers traveling on their own must pay a single supplement, which is usually 125%–200% of the double-occupancy rate. If requested, however, many cruise lines will match up two strangers of the same sex in a cabin at the double-occupancy rate.

Location On all ships, regardless of size or design, the bow (front) and stern (back) bounce up and down on the waves far more than amidships (middle). Similarly, the closer your deck is to the true center of the ship—about halfway between the bottom of the hull and the highest deck—the less you will feel the ship's movement. Some cruise lines charge more for cabins amidships; most charge more for the higher decks.

Outside cabins have portholes or windows (which, often as not, cannot be opened); on the upper decks, the view from outside cabins may be partially obstructed by lifeboats or look out onto a public deck. Because outside cabins are more desirable, many newer upscale and luxury ships are configured with outside cabins only. On a few cruise ships more expensive outside cabins may feature a private veranda that overlooks the sea.

Inside cabins, which are less expensive than outside ones, are frequently smaller and sometimes oddly shaped to fit around the ship's particular configuration. Because they are situated closer to the working innards of the ship, they might be noisy, subject to vibration, or near busy steward workstations. Also, some passengers may feel claustrophobic sleeping in windowless inside cabins.

Cruise brochures show the ship's layout, deck by deck, and the approximate location and shape of every cabin and suite. Study the map to make sure the cabin you pick is not near the noise of public rooms or the ship's engine and that it is near stairs or an elevator. If detailed layouts of typical cabins are printed, you can determine what kind of beds the cabin has, if it has a window or a porthole, and what furnishings are provided. Be aware that configurations within each category can differ.

Booking Your Cruise

Most cruise ships sail at or near capacity, especially during the high season, so consider making reservations as much as a year or even two years in advance. On the other hand, you may be able to save hundreds of dollars by booking close to the sailing date, especially if you go through a cruise broker or a discount agent.

Travel Agents

A travel agent can help you in selecting a cruise and will deal directly on your behalf with all airlines, cruise companies, car-rental agencies, hotels, and resorts. Travel agents do not charge you for booking cruises—they make their money on commissions (usually 10%) from the cruise lines. A good travel agent should save you money by eliminating such expenses as long-distance telephone calls, postage, and express mail, not to mention throwing in extras such as flight bags and bon voyage champagne.

Not all travel agents or agencies are equal, of course. Some specialize in cruises, which means that the agent with whom you deal has actually sailed on the specific ship you wish to take, has visited the ports you plan to see, and has personally checked all the logistics beforehand. Less experienced agents get most of their cruise information from the same brochures and booklets available to you. It's a good idea to deal either with a large travel agency in which at least one agent is thoroughly familiar with the cruise industry or to select a smaller firm that specializes in cruise holidays. A growing number of travel agencies now handle cruises only and are usually more experienced than regular agencies in finding bargains and available cabins. Check your yellow pages for these specialized agencies. Ask friends, family, and colleagues—especially those who have been on cruises before—which agent they use, and if their last experience was a positive one. Otherwise, interview various agents to locate one who seems genuinely interested in finding the right cruise for you. To make sure your visits to your agent are productive, make an appointment for each. Don't just walk in off the street.

All travel agents should charge you identical prices for identical services; differences in price, if any, usually come in tacked-on extras, such as limousine service to and from the local airport, pre- or post-cruise stays, or stopovers at the port city. If prices quoted by two agents are significantly different, then one may be more knowledgeable and thus better able to take advantage of the cruise lines' fare structures and various hotel and airfare discounts.

In order to get your business, however, some travel agents may discount tickets to you, despite the fact that it's against regulations. Beware of such practices: The sort of agency that engages in shady dealings may end up suddenly closing its doors before your cruise—leaving you with a ruined vacation, or even with a loss of your money. Reputable agencies make sure your vacation is secured.

Because travel agents make their money from commissions, they have a vested interest in selling you a more expensive cruise. And because some cruise lines offer sales incentives or higher commission rates, an agent might have an ulterior motive for directing you to one ship over another. But if you use a professional, respectable firm, especially one that prides itself on its expertise in designing cruise holidays, such unethical practices should not be a problem.

Cruise Brokers

When cabins are unsold or empty because of cancellations, cruise companies recoup lost revenue by unloading these berths onto cruise brokers who buy the space wholesale and try to resell it to the public at modest markups. The nearer it is to the sailing date, the bigger the saving usually is. There are scores of large cruise-broker agencies throughout the country, and you work with them just as you would with a travel agent. Some deal only with specific cruise lines or book only on certain ships. Although the broker will quote a rate, the price is rarely fixed and you may be able to negotiate.

What are the risks of dealing with a cruise broker? Financially, there are few risks. Brokers work for reputable companies and handle money with the same responsibility as travel agents, although they rarely provide the comprehensive service that a good travel agency does. You may never see your broker face to face, since many work over the telephone. The chief caveat in dealing with a broker is that you can't book very far in advance—usually less than a month and in most instances just a couple of weeks. By waiting, you might luck into the travel bargain of a lifetime, or you might end up spending your vacation at home.

Know how much your cruise would cost at normal rates so you can judge how good the bargain is. Be flexible about your travel dates and accommodations, and consider whatever cruises are available. To save the most money, be prepared to take off on short notice—sometimes as little as 24 hours' warning—when (and if) something comes the broker's way.

You can find names and numbers of travel brokers in most newspaper travel sections. Major cruise publications, such as *Cruise Travel Magazine*, also carry listings for travel brokers. Here are a few that specialize in cruises:

CruiseMasters (3415 Sepulveda Blvd., Suite 645, Los Angeles, CA 90034, tel. 800/242–9444, or 800/242–9000 in CA).
Cruise Pro (2900 Townsgate Rd., Suite 103, Westlake Village, CA 91361, tel. 800/222–7447 or 800/258–7447 in CA).
Cruise Quarters of America (4840 Irvine Blvd., Irvine, CA 92720, tel. 800/648–2444 or 714/730–8934 in CA).
The Travel Company (333 W. El Camino Real, Suite 250, Dept. CM, Sunnyvale, CA 94087, tel. 800/367–6090, 800/858–5888 in CA, 800/336–8320 in Canada).

Videotapes

Over the past several years, cruise companies have discovered that fast-paced promotional videotapes showing off their ships can be an effective marketing tool. Most travel agencies have a library of travel tapes, including some on specific cruise ships; usually you can also borrow, rent, or buy tapes directly from the cruise line. As you view the tape, keep in mind that the cruise company made this tape to show its ship to the best advantage. Still, you will get a visual idea of the size and shape of the cabins, dining room, swimming pool, and public rooms; and the kinds of attractions, amenities, and entertainment on board.

Cruise Brochures

Like a videotape, a brochure is obviously promotional in nature, but it can provide invaluable information about a ship and what it has to offer. Make sure the brochures you select are the most recently published versions: Schedules, itineraries, and prices change constantly. Study the maps of the decks and cabin layouts, and be sure to read the fine print to find out just what you'll be getting for your money. Check out the details on fly/cruise programs; optional pre- and post-cruise packages; the ship's credit card and check-cashing policy; embarkation and debarkation procedures; and legal matters of payment, cancellation, insurance, and liability.

Payment

Deposit Most cruises must be reserved with a refundable deposit of $200–$500 per person, depending on the price of the cruise; the balance is to be paid one to two months before you sail. Don't let a travel agent pressure you into paying a larger deposit or paying the balance earlier. However, if the cruise is less than a month away, you may have to pay the entire amount immediately.

If possible, pay your deposit and balance with a credit card. This gives you some recourse if you need to cancel, and you can ask the credit card company to intercede on your behalf in case of problems. Don't forget to get a receipt.

Handing money over to your travel agent constitutes a contract, so before you pay your deposit, study the cruise brochure to find out the provisions of the cruise contract. What is the cancellation policy? Will there be any additional charges before you can board your ship, such as transfers, port fees, local taxes, or baggage charges? If your air connection requires you to spend an evening in a hotel near the port before or after the cruise, is there an extra cost?

Cancellation If you cancel your reservation 45–60 days prior to your scheduled cruise (the grace period varies from line to line), you may receive your entire deposit or payment back. You will forfeit some or even all of your deposit if you cancel any closer to cruise time. In rare cases, however, if your reason for canceling is unavoidable, the cruise line may decide, at its discretion, to waive some or all of the forfeiture. An average cancellation charge would be $100 one month before sailing, $100 plus 50% of the ticket price 15–30 days before sailing, and $100 plus 75% of the ticket price between 14 days and 24 hours before sailing. If you simply fail to show up when the ship sails, you will lose the entire amount you've paid.

Insurance Cruise lines sell cancellation insurance for about $50 per ticket (the amount varies according to the line, the number of days in the cruise, and the price you paid for the ticket). Such insurance protects you against cancellation fees; it may also reimburse you, with a deductible, if your luggage is lost or damaged. There are usually some restrictions. For instance, the trip cancellation policy may insure that you receive a full refund only if you cancel and notify the cruise line no less than 72 hours in advance.

Before You Go

Tickets, Vouchers, and Other Travel Documents

Some cruise companies will give you your cruise ticket and transfer vouchers (which will get you from the airport to the ship and vice versa) at the time you make the final payment to your travel agent. Depending upon the airline, and whether or not you have purchased a fly/cruise package, you may receive your plane tickets or charter flight vouchers at the same time; you may also receive vouchers for any shore excursions, although most cruise lines prefer to hand those over when you board your ship. There are some cruise companies that mail tickets, either to you or your travel agent, only after they have received payment in full. Should your travel documents not arrive when promised, contact your travel agent or call the cruise line directly on its toll-free line. Occasionally tickets are delivered directly to the ship for those who book late.

Once you board your ship you may be asked to turn over your passport for group immigration clearance or to turn over your return plane ticket so the ship's staff may reconfirm your flight home. Otherwise, be sure to keep all travel documents in a safe place, such as a shipboard safe-deposit box.

Cruise Ships

Chandris Cruise Lines, Celebrity Cruises

SS Horizon
Specifications

Type of ship: Upscale mainstream
Type of cruise: Traditional
Size: Large (46,811 tons)
Number of cabins: 677
Outside cabins: 84%

Passengers: 1,354
Passenger/crew ratio: 2.1 to 1
Crew: 642 (international)
Officers: Greek
Year built: 1990

Itinerary Between April and November the *Horizon* offers seven-night cruises from New York to Hamilton (two nights) and St. George's, Bermuda (two nights). Two days are spent at sea. The cruise line warns that poor weather may force them to avoid the narrow entry into St. George's. But, so far, all *Horizon* cruises to Bermuda have included the St. George's stop.

Overview Like most huge modern cruise ships, the *Horizon*'s exterior looks ungainly, primarily because of the long rows of large windows and portholes along the side, squared-off stern, and boxy smokestack (which, like all Chandris and Celebrity ships, is marked with a large, distinctive X). However, the interior is surprisingly gracious, airy, and comfortable. Because there is no central architectural focus (such as an atrium), the *Horizon* seems more intimate than other ships that carry 1,600 passengers. The ship's design makes the most of natural light through 7 strategically placed oversize windows, especially in the Star-

Chart Symbols. The following symbols are used in the charts in this chapter. D: Double bed; K: King-size bed; Q: Queen-size bed; T: Twin bed; U/L: Upper and lower berths; ●: All cabins have this facility; ○: No cabins have this facility; ◐: Some cabins have this facility

light Restaurant and America's Cup Club. The nine passenger decks sport a generous number of bars, entertainment lounges, and ample deck space. Wide corridors, broad staircases, seven elevators, and well-placed signs make it a relatively easy ship on which to get around. The furnishings are contemporary and attractive, the art work pleasant rather than memorable. The *Horizon* does an excellent job with children and teens, who are thoroughly entertained— so much so that parents often don't see them except at dinner.

Cabins and Rates	Beds	Phone	TV	Sitting Area	Fridge	Tub	Per Diem
Starlight Suites	D or T	●	●	●	○	●	$302–$314
Deluxe Suites	D	●	●	●	○	●	$266–$278
Deluxe Cabins	D or T	●	●	●	○	○	$231–$242
Outside	D or T	●	●	○	○	○	$188–$221
Inside	T, D or	●	●	○	○	○	$138–$194

The cabins are modern rather than traditional and are roomier than those on the average cruise ship. In the upper priced cabins, many bathtubs are fitted with whirlpool jets. The view from many of the outside cabins on Bermuda Deck is partially obstructed by lifeboats. Voltage is 110 AC. The single supplement is 150% of the double-occupancy rate. The rate for a third or fourth passenger in the cabin is $64 each per day. The rate for children under 12 traveling with two full-paying adults is $42 per day, and under 6 years, free. Repositioning cruises are more expensive.

Sports and Fitness **Health club:** The upper deck's spa is bright and sunny and has sauna, massage, weight machines, stationary bicycles, rowing machine, treadmill, separate mirrored aerobics area, fitness programs, and classes.
Walking/jogging: Five laps around Marina Deck equals a mile.
Other sports: Exercise classes, putting green and driving range, shuffleboard, snorkeling, trapshooting, ping pong, three adjacent whirlpools, two adjacent swimming pools.

Facilities **Public rooms:** Eight bars, three showrooms, disco, teen room/juice bar, casino, restaurant, library/reading room, card room, video arcade.
Shops: Mini-shopping mall with gift shop, specialty boutique, perfume shop, cigarette/liquor store, and photo shop.
Health care: On-board hospital staffed by doctor and nurse. Limited dispensary for prescriptions. Refrigerated insulin storage provided.
Child care: Children's playroom, separate teen room on the sun deck, preteen and teen youth programs supervised by counselors. Baby-sitting can be arranged privately with a crew member.

Cruise Facilities

Ship	Cruise Line	Principle Cruising Regions	Size (in tons)	Type of Ship	Type of Cruise	Per Diem Rates	Length of Cruise	Number of Passengers	Passenger/Crew Ratio	Sanitation Rating*	Disabled Access	Special Dietary Options	Gymnasium	Jogging Track	Swimming Pool	Whirlpool	Sauna/Massage	Deck Sports	Casino	Disco	Cinema/Theater	Library	Boutiques/Gift Shops	Video Arcade	Child Care
Horizon	Celebrity Cruises	Caribbean & Bermuda	45,000	Upscale mainstream	Traditional	$134–$324	8-day	1354		98	●	●	●	●	2	3	●	●	●	●	○	●	●	●	●
Meridian	Celebrity Cruises	Caribbean & Bermuda	30,000	Upscale mainstream	Traditional	$112–$324	8-day	1008		92	◑	●	●	◑	2	3	●	●	●	●	●	●	●	●	●
Nordic Prince	Royal Caribbean Cruise Line	Caribbean & Bermuda	23,000	Mainstream	Traditional/Party	$160–$373	8-day	1014		93	◑	●	●	●	1		●	●	●	●	○	○	●	○	◑
Queen Elizabeth 2	Cunard Line	Worldwide	67,139	Luxury/Up. mainstream	Traditional	$185–$767	4.5-day	1864		92	◑	●	●	●	4	4	●	●	●	●	●	●	●	◑	●

*Sanitation ratings are provided by the Vessel Sanitation Program, Center for Environmental Health and Injury Control. Ships are rated on water, food preparation and holding, potential contamination of food, and general cleanliness, storage, and repair. A score of 86 or higher indicates an acceptable level of sanitation. According to the center, "a low score does not necessarily imply an imminent outbreak of gastrointestinal disease." Chart ratings come from the center's March 15, 1991 report. Not all ships are covered.

Services: 24-hour room service from a limited menu, photographer, valet laundry, barber/beauty shop.
Other: Safety-deposit boxes.

Access for the Disabled Four cabins with 39½-inch doorways can accommodate wheelchair-bound passengers. Public elevators are 35½ inches wide. Certain areas may not be wide enough for wheelchairs. The captain cannot guarantee that wheelchair-bound passengers will be accommodated at every port. Disabled passengers are asked to provide their own small collapsible wheelchairs and to travel with a fellow passenger.

SS Meridian *Specifications*

Type of ship: Upscale mainstream	*Passengers:* 1,008
Type of cruise: Traditional	*Crew:* 580 (international)
Size: Large (30,440 tons)	*Officers:* Greek
Number of cabins: 544	*Passenger/crew ratio:* 1.7 to 1
Outside cabins: 54%	*Year built:* 1967

Itinerary In summer the *Meridian* sails on seven-night loops out of New York (or, occasionally, Baltimore, Boston, Charleston, Philadelphia, Wilmington, or Fort Lauderdale) to Bermuda, where she ties up for three days at King's Wharf in Somerset. Three days at sea are included in the cruise. Port tax is $82 per person.

Overview Originally the *Galileo*, this former transatlantic liner was stretched and totally refurbished before reemerging as the *Meridian*. Whatever grace and charm the old liner once possessed has unfortunately been lost. The interior looks like the maritime equivalent of a Howard Johnson's—garish oranges and pinks abound, and many of the public rooms are uniform and characterless. Unlike on many ships, however, the public rooms are spacious. The same cannot be said for the tanning decks, which are cluttered and unattractive.

Cabins and Rates

	Beds	Phone	TV	Sitting Area	Fridge	Tub	Per Diem
Presidential Suite	T	●	○	●	○	●	$342–$371
Starlight Suite	T	●	○	●	○	●	$285–$321
Deluxe Suite	D	●	○	●	○	○	$249–$292
Deluxe Cabin	T or D	●	○	●	○	○	$196–$242
Outside	T or D	●	○	○	○	○	$156–$221
Inside	T, D, or U/L	●	○	○	○	○	$99–$182

The bathtubs in the Presidential, Starlight, and Deluxe Suites all have whirlpool jets. The outside cabins on Captain's and Horizon Decks have picture windows. Many outside cabins on the Atlantic deck have an obstructed or partially obstructed view. The single supplement is 150% of double-occupancy rate. Adding a third or fourth passenger in a cabin costs about $60 per diem for each additional person. Children under 12 years of age, sharing a cabin with two full-paying adults, pay about $50 per diem. Children under 2 years travel free.

Sports and Fitness **Health club:** Stationary bicycles, weight machines, treadmill, and rowing machines, plus sauna and massage.
Walking/jogging: A jogging track is on Captain Deck; 8 laps make a mile.
Other sports: Exercise classes, putting green and driving range, shuffleboard, snorkeling, trapshooting, ping pong. One swimming pool, plus a children's pool. Three adjacent outdoor whirlpools.

Facilities **Public rooms:** Seven bars, four entertainment lounges (including the main showroom), card room/library, casino, chapel/synagogue, cinema, dining room, disco, Lido, video arcade.
Shops: Boutique, perfumerie, drug store, photo shop, beauty salon/barber shop.
Health care: A doctor is on call.
Child care: Children's playroom. Youth programs with counselors are offered whenever there are enough children on board to warrant it. Baby-sitting can be arranged privately with a crew member.
Services: 24-hour room service from a limited menu, photographer, valet laundry, barber/beauty shop.
Other: Safe-deposit boxes, Friends of Bill W.

Access for the Disabled Two cabins are designed for wheelchair access. Celebrity suggests that passengers confined to wheelchairs travel with another adult who will take full responsibility for them in case of emergency.

For More Information Brochures and sailing schedules are available from travel agents or Chandris Cruise Lines (900 Third Ave., New York, NY 10017, tel. 800/621–3446).

Cunard Line Limited

RMS Queen Elizabeth 2 Specifications

Type of ship: Luxury/ upscale mainstream
Type of cruise: Traditional
Size: Megaship/liner (67,396 tons)
Number of cabins: 957
Outside cabins: 70%

Passengers: 1,864
Crew: 1,025 (international)
Officers: British
Passenger/crew ratio: 1.8 to 1 (varies according to cabin price)
Year built: 1969

Itinerary In summer the *QE2* has two sailings from New York to Bermuda. The first is a five-night cruise with one night in Hamilton (Bermuda); the second cruise is four nights with a stop for the day in Hamilton. Port tax is $103 per person.

Overview Built in 1969 as the last of the true ocean liners, the *QE2* is designed as both a two-class crossing ship and a one-class cruise ship. Even on cruises, however, passengers are assigned to one of the four restaurants aboard (each offering a different level of quality and service) according to the type of cabin they have taken. Outside the cabin or restaurants, however, all passengers enjoy the same level of facilities and amenities, whether they are in the cheapest inside cabin or in the Penthouse Suite.

The ship has undergone numerous refits over the years, including one that transformed it into a troop carrier for the Falklands War. Taking the *QE2*'s unique historical and social position to heart, Cunard continues to invest its flagship with the best, the most, and the largest of whatever can fit into this floating city. Big as it is—13 stories high, three football fields long—the *QE2* possesses a grace that the new megaships don't. With its high ceilings, wood paneling, and expensive furnishings, the interior of the *QE2* looks less like a ship than it does a grand hotel. The ship features a magnificent shopping arcade with stores like Harrods and Elizabeth Arden. In addition, you'll find the famous Golden Door Spa at Sea, an American Express bank, a flower shop, a nursery run by professional nannies, and a large, well-equipped computer learning center. Passengers on the transatlantic run have use of a 30-car garage and even a dog kennel. If you look closely, you will see signs of its age. Still, everything that a passenger could want is on board somewhere. Some passengers may find the ship too large, others too proud, but amid the wealth of space, service, and options, the *QE2* remains a beautiful ship, filled with pizzazz and excitement, that still reserves a few private corners to remind you of its essentially British dignity.

Activities. Without diverging from the traditional cruise formula of bingo, get-togethers, games, "horse racing," and similar events, the *QE2* offers more activities than any ship afloat, partly because of its size and partly because Cunard's pride in its flagship wouldn't accept less. These amenities include numerous lectures and seminars, classical-music concerts, four outdoor swimming pools, fashion shows, computer courses, and an extensive exercise and fitness program under the auspices of the Golden Door Spa.

Dining. The quality of the restaurant to which you are assigned depends on the price of your cabin. The gourmet Queen's Grill and Princess Grill are elegant, single-seating restaurants that are reserved for occupants of the suites and the luxury and ultra-deluxe cabins. In these two restaurants passengers can order anything they want. They are consistently awarded four stars by international food critics—and with good reason, since they serve the finest food afloat. The larger, single-seating Columbia Restaurant is for the occupants of the deluxe and higher-priced outside cabins, and while the cuisine is beautifully prepared and served, it isn't quite up to the standards of the Queen's Grill or Princess Grill. All others are served in two seatings in the Mauritania Restaurant. Were it on any other ship, the Mauritania Restaurant would be rated very highly, but it suffers by comparison with the *QE2*'s other restaurants. Each of the restaurants offers two dinner seatings. In addition, on transatlantic crossings there is a special early dinner for children so that parents may dine on their own. Spa meals are available, but other dietary requests should be made at least three weeks before sailing. Two formal evenings are held each week, though dinners in the Queen's Room and the Princess Grill are never casual. Unsupervised kosher meals are available only in the Columbia Restaurant. The ship's wine cellar stocks more than 20,000 bottles of wine.

The Lido serves early morning coffee and pastries, a buffet breakfast and lunch, plus hamburgers and hot dogs. Health-conscious passengers can take their breakfast, and sometimes their lunch, from a spa buffet. An International Food Bazaar is dished up occasionally in the Mauritania Restaurant. Other food service includes midmorning bouillon, a traditional British high tea, and a midnight buffet.

Entertainment. The nightlife is diverse, including variety shows in the Grand Lounge, cabaret, classical-music concerts, disco parties, and a piano bar. Celebrity talks feature such big names as Jeremy Irons, Meryl Streep, Jason Robards, Art Buchwald, and Barbara Walters. Dance contests, passenger talent contests, and a costume party are also held on each voyage. The liner has its own 20-station TV network with color sets in every cabin. A daily newspaper is published on board.

Service and Tipping. Service in the first-class staterooms and restaurants is impeccable because that's where the most—and the best—staff members work. The service at all levels of the ship, however, is higher than on most ships. Unfortunately, Cunard suffers from occasional labor problems, and there have been a few incidents of work slowdowns or stoppages. Also some passengers find the very British attitude of the staff a bit stuffy and unspontaneous. If you are in the Mauritania Restaurant, your cabin steward and waiter will each expect $3 per passenger per day. In the Columbia Restaurant it's $4 each per passenger per day. Those who dine in the Queen's and Princess grills are expected to tip the cabin steward and the waiter each $5 per passenger per day. A 10% service charge is automatically added to bar bills.

Cabins and Rates

	Beds	Phone	TV	Sitting Area	Fridge	Tub	Per Diem*
Suite *Queen's Grill*	Q or T/D	●	●	●	●	●	$2,305–$4,706 (*per suite*)
Luxury *Queen's Grill*	Q or T	●	●	●	●	●	$526–$1,344
Ultra Deluxe *Queen's/Princess*	T	●	●	●	●	●	$361–$795
Deluxe *Columbia Restaurant*	T	●	●	○	○	●	$291–$527
Outside *Columbia/Mauritania*	T	●	●	○	○	◑	$230–$505
Inside *Mauritania Restaurant*	T or U/L	●	●	○	○	○	$190–$370

The wide range of daily rates reflects differences between cabins in the lower-priced categories as well as differences between itineraries. More exotic cruises tend to be more expensive. Prices are for Western Hemisphere cruises only.

The prices for suites cover the accommodation of as many as four passengers. They are, therefore, actually more economical than paying for two luxury cabins for a family of four. The *QE2*'s Penthouse Suites, complete with verandas and Jacuzzis, are the largest, most luxurious accommodations afloat; the first-class cabins can compare with the rooms of any luxury-hotel chain. All Luxury cabins, except No. 8184, have private verandas. All first-class cabins have VCRs. Lifeboats partially obstruct the view from some of the cabins on the Sports Deck, and the cabins on the Boat Deck look out onto a public promenade rather than the open sea. Outlet voltage is 110 AC. The single supplement is 175%–200% of the double-occupancy rate, although several single cabins are available at $179–$726 a day. A third or fourth passenger in a cabin pays half the minimum fare in that restaurant grade.

Sports and Fitness   **Health club:** The Golden Door Spa maintains two fitness centers that include health and beauty programs for men and women, numerous exercise classes, weight machines, bicycles, treadmills, sauna, whirlpools, one indoor swimming pool that is equipped for hydrocalisthenics, massage.
Walking/jogging: Jogging track; 3.5 laps equals 1 mile.
Other sports: Aerobics and exercise classes, putting green and electronic golf driving course, paddle tennis, table tennis, shuffleboard, tetherball, trapshooting, volleyball, two outdoor and two indoor swimming pools, child's wading pool, four whirlpools, private Jacuzzis in suites. The sports area also has separate clubhouses for adults and teens.

Facilities   **Public rooms:** Six bars, five entertainment lounges, card room, casino, chapel/synagogue, cinema, computer learning center (IBM), disco, executive boardroom, library/reading room, Lido, piano bar, video-game room.
Shops: Extensive arcade that includes men's formal rental shop, a branch of Harrods, designer boutiques (Gucci, Christian Dior, Louis Vuitton), florist, QE2 logo shop, beauty center, barber shop.
Health care: The ship hospital is the most extensive on any cruise ship and is fully staffed by doctors and nurses.
Child care: Children's playroom, teen center, baby-sitting. Youth programs run by counselors are offered all year.
Services: 24-hour room service, full-service laundry, dry-cleaning, valet service, self-serve laundromat, ironing room, photographer, film-developing service.
Other: American Express foreign exchange and cash center, garage, kennel, safe-deposit boxes, Friends of Bill W (occasionally).

Access for the Disabled   A few cabins have been equipped with wide doors, low threshold ledges, and special bathrooms. However, wheelchairs may not be carried aboard tenders in those numerous ports where the *QE2* must anchor offshore, so wheelchair-bound passengers may not be able to see all the ports on the itinerary.

For More Information   Brochures and sailing schedules are available from travel agents or from Cunard Line Limited (555 Fifth Ave., New York, NY 10017, tel. 800/221–4770).

Royal Caribbean Cruise Line

MS Nordic Prince
Specifications

Type of ship: Mainstream
Type of cruise: Traditional/
Party
Size: Medium (23,000 tons)
Number of cabins: 531
Outside cabins: 66.2%

Passengers: 1,014
Crew: 400 (international)
Officers: Norwegian
Passenger/crew ratio: 2.5 to 1
Year built: 1971

Itinerary In summer the *Nordic Prince* sails every Sunday from New York to spend three days in Hamilton (Bermuda), two days in St. George's, and two days at sea. Port tax is $88 per person.

Overview Built in 1971, the *Nordic Prince* was split and stretched in 1981 to accommodate more passengers and to increase the size and number of public rooms. The stretching also created a superb sun deck, with a larger pool that allows passengers to swim laps.

Like every RCCL ship, the *Nordic Prince* features the Viking Crown Lounge, a dramatic bar wrapped around the very top of the funnel, for the best view on the ship. Considering RCCL's emphasis on glitzy entertainment, the interior is surprisingly conservative, relying on muted pastels, wood panels, and many mirrors and chandeliers.

Cabins and Rates

	Beds	Phone	TV	Sitting Area	Fridge	Tub	Per Diem
Owner's Suite	D or T	●	○	●	●	●	$281–$390
Deluxe Outside	T	●	○	○	●	●	$237–$269
Larger Outside	D or T/D	●	○	○	●	○	$186–$241
Outside	D/U or T	●	○	○	○	○	$143–$233
Larger Inside	D/L or T	●	○	○	○	○	$164–$223
Inside	D, D/U, or T	●	○	○	○	○	$106–$210

Cabins 604 and 704 are larger outside staterooms with one double bed plus upper and lower berths. The suites and outside cabins on the Promenade Deck look out onto a public area rather than the open sea. All cabins are above the waterline. Outlet voltage is 110 AC. The single supplement is 150% of the double-occupancy rate; however, less expensive singles plans are available if you are willing to wait for your cabin assignment until embarkation time. The addition of a third or fourth passenger in a cabin (including children) costs $49–$64 each per day.

Sports and Fitness **Health club:** Stationary bikes, rowing machines, treadmills, separate men's and women's saunas and massage rooms.
Walking/jogging: The Compass Deck (above the Sun Deck) has an unobstructed circuit for fitness walks.
Other sports: Aerobics, basketball, dancercise, golf driving and putting, table tennis, shuffleboard, skeet shooting, yoga, swimming pool.

Facilities **Public rooms:** Five bars, three entertainment lounges, casino, disco, Lido Deck.
Shops: Gift shop, drugstore, beauty salon/barber.
Child care: Youth programs with counselors are offered only during holidays or in summer. Baby-sitting can be arranged privately with a crew member.
Health care: A doctor is on call.
Services: 24-hour room service from a limited menu, full-service laundry, dry-cleaning, photographer, film-developing service.
Other: Safe-deposit boxes.

Access for the Disabled Wheelchair access is limited. The Viking Crown Lounge is inaccessible via wheelchair. Doorways throughout the ship have lips, and public bathrooms have no facilities for the handicapped. Disabled passengers must bring their own traveling wheelchair, and they must be escorted by a companion.

For More Information Brochures and sailing schedules are available from travel agents or from Royal Caribbean Cruise Line (903 South America Way, Miami, FL 33132, tel. 800/327–2055).

4 Exploring Bermuda

Orientation

by Honey Naylor

The major contributor to Fodor's New Orleans *and* Caribbean, *Honey Naylor has worked on various other Fodor's guides. Her featured articles have appeared in* Travel & Leisure, USA Today, New Orleans Magazine, Travel-Holiday, *and other national publications.*

Bermuda is nothing if not colorful. The streets are lined with hedges of hibiscus and oleander, and rolling green hills are shaded by tall palms and casuarina trees. The limestone buildings are painted in pretty pastels (pink and white seem to be most popular), and their gleaming white roofs are steeply pitched to channel the rain upon which Bermudians depend—the island has no freshwater lakes or streams. In addition, many houses have quaint butteries, miniature cottages that were once used as ice houses. House numbers are a relatively new phenomenon on the island, although most houses have names, such as Tranquillity, Struggle, and Last Penny. Another architectural feature indigenous to Bermuda is moon gates. These free-standing stone arches can be found in gardens all over the island, and Bermudians favor them as backdrops for wedding pictures.

For exploring purposes, we've divided Bermuda into four separate tours. The first tour is of Hamilton, the island's capital. Hamilton is of primary interest for its harbor, its shops—housed in small pastel-colored buildings—and the government buildings, where visitors can watch sessions of Parliament. In addition, the town is the major departure point for sightseeing boats, ferries, and the pink-and-blue buses that ramble all over the island. Don't confuse Hamilton town with the parish of the same name—Hamilton town is in Pembroke Parish. The second tour is of St. George's town on the eastern end of the island, near the site of Bermuda's first settlement. History mavens will find much of interest in St. George's, which boasts several noteworthy 17th-century buildings. The third tour explores the West End, the site of the sleepy hamlet of Somerset and the Royal Naval Dockyard, a former British naval shipyard that is home to the Maritime Museum and a developing tourist center. The West End is in Sandys Parish, which can be pronounced either "Sandies" or "Sands."

The fourth tour is a rambling journey through the island's other parishes that is best done by moped, bicycle, or taxi. The parishes date back to 1616, when Bermuda was first surveyed and the island was divided into eight tribes or parishes, each named for an investor in the Bermuda Company, an offshoot of the Virginia Company, which controlled the island until 1684. The parishes are Sandys, Southampton, Warwick, Paget, Smith's, Hamilton, Pembroke, and Devonshire. St. George's, which was considered public land in the early days, is the ninth parish and includes the town of St. George's. Bermudians customarily identify sites on the island by the parish in which they are located: "It's in Pembroke," a resident will say, or "It's in Warwick." The main roads connecting the parishes are self-explanatory: North Shore Road, Middle Road, South Road, and Harbour Road. Almost all traffic traversing the island's 20-mile length uses these roads, although some 1,200 smaller roads crisscross the island. Visitors will see several "tribe roads" that date back to the initial survey of the island; many of these are now no more than country lanes, and some are dead ends. As you travel around the island you'll see small brown-and-white signs pointing to the Railway Trail. Built along the route of Bermuda's old railway line, the trail is now a peaceful route reserved for pedestrians and cyclists (*see* Off the Beaten Track, below).

Tour 1: Hamilton

Numbers in the margin correspond to points of interest on the Hamilton map.

Historically, Bermudians were seafarers, and the government relied for revenues on the duties paid on ships' cargoes. Ships were required by law to anchor in the harbor at St. George's to declare their goods, but most captains preferred to anchor closer to their homes, and the law was largely ignored. To combat the loss of revenues, legislation was passed in 1790 to establish a second port and customs house at Crow Lane Harbour (now Hamilton Harbour). Largely because of Hamilton's excellent harbor and central location, the seat of government was moved from St. George's to Hamilton on January 1, 1815. Today, the capital is home to about a quarter of the island's 54,000 residents.

❶ Your first stop should be the **Visitors Service Bureau** in the Ferry Terminal Building, where the friendly staff can provide you with maps and brochures. Step out of the bureau onto the capital's main avenue, **Front Street.** Running alongside the harbor, Front Street bustles with small cars, mopeds, bicycles, buses, pedestrians, and the occasional horse-drawn carriage. It's fun to imagine what the street must have looked like prior to the arrival of automobiles in 1946. From 1931 to 1946, railroad tracks ran along Front Street, carrying "Old Rattle and Shake," as the Bermuda Railway was called. Today, Front Street is lined with colorful little buildings, many with balconies and arcades that house shops and boutiques selling everything from imported woolens to perfumes and cosmetics. This is the main shopping area on the island, and shoppers will probably want to spend plenty of time—and money—here (*see* Chapter 5, Shopping).

The docks behind the Ferry Terminal are the departure points for ferries making the short trip to Paget and Warwick parishes, or the longer trip across the Great Sound to the West End. Next to the terminal are the slips for glass-bottom boats and other sightseeing vessels that take passengers on excursions to the Sea Gardens, St. George's, and Dockyard. Beyond these is **No. 1 Shed,** the pink passenger-ship terminal (two other terminals are situated farther east on Front Street). During high season, a cruise ship is usually moored in the harbor—all but the largest ships, such as the *QE2*, can sail right into Hamilton Harbour. During the low season (mid-November–March 31), No. 1 Shed is the site of regularly scheduled afternoon teas, fashion shows, and performances by the Gombey Dancers (*see* Chapter 10, The Arts and Nightlife).

The oddly shaped traffic box at Heyl's Corner, at the intersection of Front and Queen streets, is known as the **"Birdcage,"** from which the police (locally known as "bobbies" as in Great Britain) sometimes direct traffic. Named for its designer, Michael "Dickey" Bird, the traffic box has been a Hamilton landmark for more than 20 years. The corner itself is named for J. B. Heyl, a Southerner who came to Bermuda in the 19th century and opened an apothecary shop on Queen Street.

Visitors interested in coins should cross Point Pleasant Road
❷ and go up to the mezzanine of the **Bank of Bermuda**. British and Spanish coins, many of them ancient, are displayed in glass

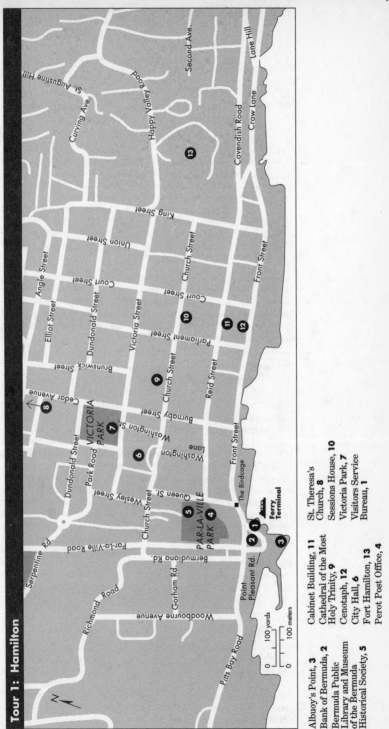

Tour 1: Hamilton

Albuoy's Point, **3**
Bank of Bermuda, **2**
Bermuda Public
Library and Museum
of the Bermuda
Historical Society, **5**

Cabinet Building, **11**
Cathedral of the Most
Holy Trinity, **9**
Cenotaph, **12**
City Hall, **6**
Fort Hamilton, **13**
Perot Post Office, **4**

St. Theresa's
Church, **8**
Sessions House, **10**
Victoria Park, **7**
Visitors Service
Bureau, **1**

cases. The collection includes some pieces of "hog money," Bermuda's first currency, which was issued by the Bermuda Company in 1615. Hog money, the oldest of all British colonial coins, is stamped on one side with a replica of the *Sea Venture* and on the other with an unattractive wild hog ringed with the words "Somer Ilands." Pigs, which had survived a shipwreck or been released by Spanish sailors, were the only inhabitants encountered by Sir George Somers and his crew when they foundered on Bermuda's shores in 1609. *Admission free. Open weekdays. 9:30–3.*

Following Point Pleasant Road toward the water, you'll come to **③ Albuoy's Point,** a pleasant waterfront park with benches, trees, and a splendid view of the activity in the harbor. Nearby is the **Royal Bermuda Yacht Club,** which was built in the 1930s. The idea for the yacht club was conceived in 1844 beneath the Calabash Tree at Walsingham (*see* Tour 4: The Parishes, below), and Prince Albert gave permission for the club to use the word "Royal" in 1845. Today, royalty, international yachting celebrities, and the local elite hobnob at the posh club, which sponsors the Newport–Bermuda Yacht Race.

If you plan to do a lot of exploring, visit the **Bermuda Book Store,** on Front and Queen streets, to buy a copy of the *Bermuda Islands Guide* ($4.95). The paperback atlas contains every lane, tribe road, alley, and landmark on the island. The bookstore, a marvelous Dickensian place with creaky wood floors, is filled with books about the island.

④ From the bookstore, continue along Queen Street to the **Perot Post Office,** a white two-story edifice that dates back to around 1842. Still a post office, this shuttered building is where Bermuda's first postage stamps originated. The island's first postmaster was William Bennet Perot. Appointed in 1821, Perot used to meet arriving steamers to collect the mail, stash it in his beaver hat, and then stroll around Hamilton to deliver it. Customers wishing to post a letter paid Perot, who hand-stamped each letter. Obviously, the postmaster had to be at his station to do this, which annoyed Perot, who preferred pottering around in the garden. Local historians credit Perot's friend, the pharmacist J. B. Heyl, for the idea for Bermuda's first book of stamps. Heyl suggested that Perot make a whole sheet of postmarks, write "Wm B. Perot" on each postmark, and sell the sheet for a shilling. People could then tear off a postmark, paste it on a letter, and post it—without having to extricate Mr. Perot from the garden shrubbery. The extremely rare Perot stamps, some of which are in the Queen's Royal Stamp Collection, are now coveted by collectors. In 1986, one of them sold at auction in Chicago for $135,000. *Queen St., tel. 809/295–5151. Admission free. Open weekdays 9–5.*

Time Out The garden where Perot liked to pass his time is now **Par-la-Ville Park,** a pleasant spot that occupies almost an entire block. The Queen Street entrance (there's another on Par-la-Ville Road) is next to the post office. Paths wind through the luxuriant gardens, and the park benches are ideal for picnicking or a short rest. At noon you may have trouble finding a place to sit, because this is a favorite lunch spot of Hamilton office workers. One block along Queen Street is a Kentucky Fried Chicken franchise (open daily 11–10).

Next to the post office is a giant rubber tree from British Guiana (now Guyana) that was planted by Perot. On a visit to Bermuda, Mark Twain lamented that the rubber tree didn't bear fruit in the form of hot-water bottles and rubber overshoes. The tree is in the front yard of the Georgian house where Mr.

❺ Perot and his family lived. Now the **Bermuda Public Library** and **Museum of the Bermuda Historical Society**, the house is a wonderful find for history buffs. The library, which was founded in 1839, moved to its present quarters in the 1940s. One early librarian was an eccentric gentleman with the Pickwickian name of Florentius Frith, who rode in from the country on horseback and struck terror into the heart of anyone who interrupted his chess games to check out a book. The reference section of the library has virtually every book ever written about Bermuda, as well as a collection on microfilm of Bermudian newspapers dating back to 1787. The collection of rare books contains a 1624 edition of John Smith's *Generall Histoire of Virginia, New England and the Somers Isles*. In the museum's entrance hall are portraits of Sir George Somers and his wife, painted about 1605; portraits of Postmaster Perot and his wife can be seen in the back room. Notice Admiral Sir George Somers's lodestone (circa 1600), used for magnetizing compass needles, and a Bermuda map from 1622 that shows the division of the island into 25-acre shares by the original Bermuda Company. The museum also contains an eclectic collection of old English coins and Confederate money; Bermuda silver; Oriental porcelains; portraits of the major investors in the Bermuda Company; and pictures of horse-and-buggy Bermuda juxtaposed with modern-day scenes. There are several cedar pieces, including two Queen Anne chairs from about 1740; a handsome grandfather clock; a Waterford chandelier; handmade palmetto hats; and a sedan chair from around 1770 that is beginning to show its age. Ask to see the letter from George Washington, written "to the inhabitants of Bermuda" in 1775, asking for gunpowder. *13 Queen St. Library: tel. 809/295–2905. Admission free. Open weekdays 9:30–6, Sat. 9:30–5. Museum: tel. 809/295–2487. Donation: $2. Open Mon., Tues., and Thurs.–Sat. 9:30–4:30; closed Wed. and Sun.*

Time Out Decorated with lace curtains and white iron furniture, **Fourways Pastry Shop** (Reid St., at the entrance to Washington Mall) serves irresistible, diet-destroying pastries. The **Fourways Grill** (Windsor Pl., across Queen St. from the library) serves light lunches as well as desserts.

Continue up Queen Street, or cut through Washington Mall, to Church Street. Set back from the street behind a lawn, fountains, and a lily pond is **City Hall**. Built in 1960, the large white

❻ structure is topped by a weather vane shaped like the *Sea Venture*. Massive cedar doors open into a large lobby that boasts huge chandeliers, high ceilings, and a portrait gallery. The regal portrait of Queen Elizabeth II was painted by Curtis Hooper and unveiled on April 29, 1987, by the Duke of Gloucester. Oil paintings of all Bermuda's mayors hang here as well. Behind tall cedar doors on the right is the Benbow Collection of stamps. A handsome cedar staircase leads to an exhibition gallery where the Bermuda Society of Arts holds frequent shows. The City Hall Theatre is often the venue for musical, dance, and theatrical performances. *Church St., tel. 809/292–1234. Admission free. Open weekdays 9:30–5.*

➐ Behind City Hall on Victoria Street, **Victoria Park** has a sunken garden, trees, and a Victorian bandstand, where concerts are sometimes held in the summer. The 4-acre park, built in 1887 in honor of Queen Victoria's Golden Jubilee, opened with great fanfare in 1890. The park is perfectly safe when filled with people, but it isn't a good place to wander alone—some fairly seedy-looking characters hang out here.

Cedar Avenue forms the eastern border of Victoria Park. Follow it north for two blocks to **St. Theresa's Church**, a Roman Catholic church built in 1927 in Spanish Mission style. St. Theresa's serves as head of the island's six Roman Catholic churches. During a visit in 1968, Pope Paul VI presented Bermuda's Roman Catholic diocese with a gold and silver chalice that is housed in this church. *Cedar Ave. and Elliot St., tel. 809/292–0607. Open daily 8–7.*

Return to Victoria Street and walk down Washington Street, a one-block boulevard that is the site of the **Central Bus Terminal**. Pink-and-blue buses depart from here to all points on the island. Stop at the kiosk on the median to pick up bus and ferry schedules, and to buy discounted bus tokens for future use.

Time Out Executives, secretaries, shoppers, and store owners flock to **The Spot** for breakfast, plate lunches, burgers, sandwiches, and coffee. In business for more than 40 years, this simple little restaurant serves full meals for about $8 and sandwiches for about $3. *6 Burnaby St., tel. 809/292–6293. Open Mon., Tues., Thurs.–Sat. 6:30–8. Closed Wed. and Sun.*

➒ One of the island's most impressive structures is the **Cathedral of the Most Holy Trinity**, the seat of the Anglican Church of Bermuda. The cathedral is the second church to have been built on this site: Twelve years after its completion in 1872, Trinity Church was burned to the ground by an arsonist who torched several houses of worship on the island. Work began on the present church the following year, and it was consecrated in 1911. Designed in Early English style with Gothic flourishes, the church is constructed of Bermuda limestone and materials imported from Scotland, Nova Scotia, France, Ireland, and Indiana. The tower rises to a height of 143 feet, and the clerestory in the nave is supported by piers of polished Scottish granite. The four smaller columns in each aisle were added after a hurricane shook the cathedral—and its architect—during construction. The altar in the Lady Chapel is of Italian marble, and above it is a copy of Andrea del Sarto's *Madonna and Child*. In the south transept, the Warrior Chapel was dedicated in 1977 to honor those who serve in the armed forces of the Crown, and to commemorate those who died in service to their country. The Great Warrior Window is a memorial to 85 Bermudian men who died in World War I; the flags represent military units of Bermuda and England. The choir stalls and bishop's throne are of carved English oak, and the pulpit is a replica of the one in St. Giles Cathedral, Edinburgh. On a wall near the lectern, the Canterbury Cross, set in stone taken from the walls of Canterbury Cathedral, is a copy of one made in Kent in the 8th century. The stained-glass windows are lovely; note especially the Angel Window on the east wall of the north transept, which was made by local artist Vivienne Gilmore Gardner. *Church St., tel. 809/292–4033. Open daily 8–7.*

➓ The eye-catching Italianate edifice on the next block is **Sessions House**, home of the House of Assembly (the lower house of Parliament) and the Supreme Court. The original two-story structure was built in 1817; the Florentine towers and colonnade, decorated with red terra-cotta, were added in 1887 to commemorate Queen Victoria's Golden Jubilee. The Victoria Jubilee Clock Tower made its striking debut at midnight, December 31, 1893. Bermuda's Parliament, which is the world's third oldest after Iceland's and England's, met for the first time in 1620 in St. Peter's Church in St. George's. It later moved to the State House, where deliberations were held for almost 200 years until the capital was moved to Hamilton. In its present location, the House of Assembly meets on the second floor, where business is conducted in a style befitting such a venerable body. The Sergeant-at-Arms precedes the Speaker into the chamber, bearing a silver-gilt mace. Introduced in 1921, the mace is fashioned after a James I mace in the Tower of London. The Speaker, in wig and flowing black robe, solemnly calls the meeting to order with a cedar gavel made from an old belfry tree that has been growing in St. Peter's churchyard since 1620. The proceedings are no less ceremonious and colorful in the Supreme Court on the lower floor, where judges in red robes and full wigs hear the arguments of barristers in black robes and wigs. Visitors are welcome to watch the proceedings in the Assembly and the Supreme Court, but you must call to find out when sessions are scheduled. *Parliament St., between Reid and Church Sts., tel. 809/292-7408. Admission free. Open weekdays 9–5. Closed holidays.*

The next street over from Reid Street is Court Street. Although Court Street is safe during daylight hours, it is not advisable to wander around here at night. Bermuda doesn't have much of a drug problem, but what traffic there is centers on Court and Victoria streets after dark.

⓫ The Senate, which is the upper house of Parliament, sits in the **Cabinet Building**, a dignified two-story structure surrounded by trees and gardens. Amid great ceremony, the official opening of Parliament takes place in the Senate Chamber in late October or early November. His Excellency the Governor, dressed in a plumed hat and full regalia, arrives on the grounds in a landau drawn by magnificent black horses and accompanied by a military escort. A senior police officer, carrying the Black Rod made by the Crown jewelers, summons the elected representatives to convene. The governor makes his Throne Speech from in front of a tiny cedar throne crudely carved with the words "Cap Josias Forstore Govornour of the Sumer Islands Anodo 1642" (Josias Foster was governor in 1642). The portraits above the dais are of King George III and Queen Charlotte. The chamber is open to visitors, but come on a Wednesday if you want to watch the Senate in action; call first to find out about scheduling. *Front St., tel. 809/292-5501. Admission free. Open weekdays 9–5. Closed holidays.*

⓬ In front of the Cabinet Building, the **Cenotaph** is a memorial to the war dead; on Remembrance Day (November 11), the governor and other dignitaries lay wreaths at the base of the monument. The Cenotaph is a smaller version of the famous one in Whitehall, London. The cornerstone was laid in 1920 by the Prince of Wales, who as King Edward VIII abdicated to wed Mrs. Simpson.

⓭ On the eastern outskirts of Hamilton is **Fort Hamilton,** an imposing old fortress, complete with a moat, 18-ton guns, and underground passageways that were cut through solid rock by Royal Engineers in the 1870s. If you've done enough walking, consider taking a taxi or moped there, because it's quite far. Head east on East Reid Street, turn left on King Street, and then right onto Happy Valley Road. The restored fort is one of several built by order of the Duke of Wellington. Outdated even before its completion, the fort never fired a shot in anger. Today, it affords splendid views of the capital and the harbor. Accompanied by drummers and dancers, the kilted Bermuda Isles Pipe Band performs a stirring skirling ceremony on the green every Monday at noon during the low season. Afterward the fort's "Tea Shoppe" is open for light refreshments. *Happy Valley Rd., Pembroke, no phone. Admission free. Open weekdays 9:30–5.*

Tour 2: The Town of St. George's

Numbers in the margin correspond to points of interest on the Town of St. George's map.

The settlement of Bermuda began on the eastern end of the island in 1609, when the *Sea Venture* was wrecked off the coast. Despite its small size, St. George's encompasses much of historical interest, and visitors should plan to spend a full day poking around in the houses and museums. Much of the fun of St. George's is exploring the little alleys and walled lanes that wind through the town. The tour of the town is easily managed on foot.

⓮ **King's Square** is the hub of St. George's, although it is comparatively new. For 200 years after St. George's was settled, the square was a marshy part of the harbor—the area was filled in
⓯ only in the last century. Stop at the **Visitors Information Centre** for maps, brochures, and advice. A combination ticket for $6 buys admission to Tucker House and the Confederate Museum (and to Verdmont in Smith's Parish), which are all operated by the Bermuda National Trust.

Prominently displayed in King's Square is a cedar replica of the stocks and pillory originally used to punish criminals. Today, they serve as props for tourist photos and for the street theater staged here on Wednesdays during the low season. If you decide to take the walking tour (*see* Guided Tours in Chapter 1, Essential Information), you will be greeted in the square by the mayor of St. George's. The town crier, who has a voice to wake the dead (his voice is in the *Guinness Book of World Records)*, is on hand in full colonial costume. After the official welcome, the crier bellows a few pronouncements and places any perceived malefactors in the stocks.

⓰ Stroll across the bridge to **Ordnance Island** and the splendid Desmond Fountain statue of Sir George Somers, titled *Land Ho!* The **ducking stool** on the island is a replica of the one used to dunk gossips, nagging wives, and suspected witches in the water. Demonstrations are sometimes given, although volunteers say that getting dunked is no fun, even in fun.

Also on the island is the *Deliverance II,* a replica of the *Deliverance* built by the survivors of the wreck. After their shipwreck in 1609, Somers and his crew built two ships, the *Deliverance*

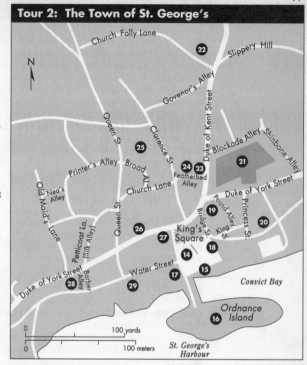

Tour 2: The Town of St. George's

and the *Patience*, to carry them to Jamestown, Virginia. Below deck, life-size mannequins in period costume are used to depict the realities of ocean travel in the 17th century—it's not the *QE2*. *Ordnance Island, no phone. Admission: $2 adults, 50¢ children under 12. Open daily 10–4. Closed Good Friday, Easter, and Christmas.*

17 The waterside **White Horse Tavern** is a popular restaurant today, but it was the Davenport home for much of the 19th century. After his arrival in St. George's in about 1815, John Davenport opened a small dry-goods store on the square. He was able to wangle a profitable contract to supply beef to the garrison, and gold and silver began to pour in. There were no banks on Bermuda, but Davenport wasn't the trusting sort anyway. He stashed the money in a keg that he kept beneath his bed. When the keg was full, he took it down to the cellar and put another one under his bed. By the time he was an old man, Davenport would spend hours each day gloating over the kegs that now filled his cellar. After his death, it was discovered that the old miser had amassed a fortune in gold and silver worth £75,000.

18 Across the square is **Town Hall**, a two-story building that houses administrative offices. Constructed in 1808 and subsequently restored, the hall is paneled and furnished with cedar, and there's a delightful collection of photographs of former mayors. Many years ago Town Hall was the scene of a memorable con. A gentleman calling himself Professor Trott appeared in town and announced a spectacular production of *Ali Baba and the Forty Thieves*. A great crowd collected at Town

Hall for the play, and thievery was duly performed: Having lured the residents away from their homes, the wily "professor" made off with an iron safe. *The Bermuda Journey*, a worthwhile audiovisual presentation, is shown in the second-floor theater. *King's Sq. Admission to Town Hall free. Open Mon.–Sat. 9–4. Closed holidays. Bermuda Journey, tel. 809/ 297–0526. Admission: $3.50 adults, $2 senior citizens and children under 12. Open Mon.–Sat. 10:30–4:30, Sun. and public holidays noon–4:30 (shows every 45 min).*

Time Out **Pub on the Square** (King's Sq., tel. 809/297–1522) is exactly what its name implies. The balcony overlooking the square is a great place to knock back a beer, have a burger, and watch the action below.

⑲ On your left as you walk up King Street is **Bridge House,** so named for a bridge that once crossed a small creek here. Built around 1700, the house is a fine example of Bermudian architecture, has two verandas, and was the home of several governors. Now an art gallery and souvenir shop, the house is furnished with 18th- and 19th-century pieces. *King St., tel. 809/297–8211. Admission free. Open Mon., Thurs., Fri., Sat. 10–5, Tues.–Wed. 10–9, Sun. 11–3. Closed Christmas and Dec. 26. From mid-Jan. to mid-Feb. open Wed. and Sat. 10–5 only.*

⑳ At the top of King Street, the **Old State House** is the oldest stone house in Bermuda. Constructed in 1620 in what Governor Nathaniel Butler believed was the Italian style, the limestone building used a mixture of turtle oil and lime as mortar and set the style for future Bermudian buildings. Upon completion, it became home to the Parliament, which had been meeting in St. Peter's Church; dances and social gatherings were also held there. After the capital was moved to Hamilton, the old State House was rented to Lodge St. George's No. 200 of the Grand Lodge of Scotland. The annual rent charged by the city was one peppercorn, the payment of which is still made upon a velvet pillow amid much pomp and circumstance. The Peppercorn Ceremony takes place each April. *Princess St., no phone. Admission free. Open Wed. 10–4.*

Proceeding down Princess Street, you'll pass the place where a hotheaded tailor named Joseph Gwynn gunned down one Henry Folger in 1826. Enraged after his son had been sentenced to jail, Gwynn went out one night looking for the magistrate who had punished his son. Apparently blind with rage, he mistook Folger for the magistrate and shot him dead. A few months later, Gwynn was hanged near the very spot where the murder took place.

㉑ Nearby is **Somers Garden,** a pleasant tree-shrouded park where the heart of Sir George Somers is said to be buried. After sailing to Jamestown and back in 1610, Somers fell ill and died. According to local lore, Somers told his nephew Matthew Somers that he wanted his heart buried in Bermuda, where it belonged. Matthew, who never seemed to pay much attention to his uncle's wishes, sailed for England soon afterward, sneaking Somers's body aboard in a cedar chest to avoid alarming the superstitious seamen. (Somers's body is buried near his birthplace in Dorset.) When the tomb where Somers's heart was supposedly interred was opened many years later, only a few bones, a pebble, and some bottle fragments were found—no one knows if Matthew Somers ever carried out his uncle's wishes. Nevertheless, ceremonies were held at the empty grave upon the 1920 visit of the Prince of Wales, during which the prince christened the park Somers Garden. *Bordered by Shinbone Alley, Blockade Alley, Duke of Kent and Duke of York Sts., no phone. Admission free. Open daily 7:30–4:30.*

Time Out   Off the tourist beat, **Clyde's Cafe** (Duke of York St. at Somers Garden, tel. 809/297–0158) is popular with locals as a lunch spot. Nothing fancy is served here—just plate lunches, sandwiches, and burgers—but the prices aren't fancy, either.

Walk through Somers Garden and up the steps to Blockade Alley. On the hill ahead is the **Unfinished Church**. Considering how much attention and affection are lavished on St. Peter's these days, it's hard to believe that residents in the 19th century wanted to replace the old church with a new one. Work began on this church in 1874, but construction was halted when a schism developed in the church. Money for construction was later diverted to rebuild Trinity Church in Hamilton when it burned down; work on the new church in St. George's was abandoned by the turn of the century.

At the corner of Featherbed Alley and Duke of Kent Street is **St. George's Historical Society Museum.** A typical Bermudian structure from the early 1700s, the house is furnished much the same as when it was a private home. One of Bermuda's oldest pieces is a table believed to have been used as the High Court bench in the State House. The house is also filled with documents (including a doctor's bill from 1790), old letters, and displays of pewter, china, and rare books; there's even a whaleblubber cutter. A torpedo raft is one of the relics from the American Civil War. Constructed of heavy timber with projecting arms to hold torpedoes, the raft was part of a Union plan to blow up the submarine barricade in Charleston harbor. After breaking loose from its towing ship during a gale, the raft drifted for six years before washing ashore in Dolly's Bay on St. David's Island. When the captain of the towing ship later visited Bermuda, he recognized the raft and explained its purpose to the puzzled Bermudians. On the south wall of the house is an iron grate that is said to have come from the cell where Bermuda's first Methodist missionary, the Reverend John Stephenson, was confined for preaching to slaves. The persistent missionary continued to preach from his cell to a crowd that collected outside. Local artist Carole Holding has her studio and craft's shop in the former slave quarters of the house. *Featherbed Alley, tel. 809/297–0423. Admission: $2 adults, $1 children 6–16, children under 6 free. Open weekdays 10–4. Closed holidays.*

Around the corner, the **Featherbed Alley Printery** is as quaint as its name. Inside the cottage is a working printing press of the kind invented by Johann Gutenberg in the 1450s. *Featherbed Alley, tel. 809/297–0009. Admission free. Open Mon.–Sat. 10–4. Closed holidays.*

Cross Clarence Street to Church Lane, and then turn right on Broad Alley to reach the **Old Rectory,** now a private residence but owned by the Bermuda National Trust. Built around 1705 by a reformed pirate, it's a charming little house with Dutch doors, shutters, chimneys, and a welcoming-arms staircase.

For many years it was the home of Alexander Richardson, the "Little Bishop," who was rector of St. Peter's from 1755 to 1805, except for a five-year stint on St. Eustatius. Richardson's diary is filled with anecdotes about 18th-century St. George's. *Broad Alley, tel. 809/297–0879. Admission free (donations appreciated). Open Wed. and Fri. 10–5. Closed holidays.*

Straight ahead (if "straight" is applicable among these twisted alleys) is **Printer's Alley**, where Bermuda's first newspaper was published. On January 17, 1784, less than a year after his arrival on the island, Joseph Stockdale printed the first copy of the *Bermuda Gazette*. The paper was published weekly for 20 years until Stockdale's death in 1805. The house where Stockdale worked is now a private home.

Nea's Alley is a short street connecting Printer's Alley with Old Maid's Lane. The 19th-century Irish poet Tom Moore lived on this street, then known as Cumberland Lane, during his four-month tenure as registrar of the admiralty court. Moore, who was endowed with considerable charm, had an impact on the island that endures to this day. He was invited to stay in the home of Admiral Mitchell, the neighbor of Mr. William Tucker and his wife, Hester—the "Nea" to whom Moore pours out his heart in several poems. Moore is thought to have first seen her in Cumberland Lane, which he describes in one of his odes as "the lime-covered alley that leads to thy home." However discreet Nea and Moore may have been about their affair, his odes to her were on the steamy side—much to the dismay of her husband. Although it was rather like locking the barn door after the horse has bolted, William Tucker refused to allow his former friend into his house again. Some Bermudians speculate that Nea was very much in love with Tom, but that he considered her merely a pleasant divertissement. He returned to Ireland after his assignment, and Nea died in 1817 at the age of 31. Bermudians are much enamored of the short-lived romance between Hester and Moore, and visitors are likely to hear a good deal about it.

❷❻ Return to Church Lane and enter the churchyard of **St. Peter's Church.** The tombstones in Bermuda's oldest churchyard tell some interesting tales, indeed—this is the resting place of governors, doctors, simple folk, and pirates. East of the church is the grave of Hester, or "Nea," marked "Mr. William Tucker's Family Vault." One of the best-known monuments stands over the grave of Richard Sutherland Dale, who died in 1815 at age 20. An American navy midshipman, Dale was mortally wounded during a sea battle with the British in the War of 1812. The monument was erected by his parents as a tribute to the St. Georgians whose "tender sympathy prompted the kindest attentions to their son while living and honoured him when dead." In an enclosure to the west of the church is the slaves' graveyard. The ancient cedar tree, which dates back to 1620, is the old belfry tree. St. Peter's is the oldest Anglican church in the Western Hemisphere, constructed in 1620. It was not the first church to stand on this site, however; it replaced a 1612 structure of posts and palmetto leaves that was destroyed in a storm. The present church was extended in 1713, and the galleries on either side were added in 1833. The oldest part of the church is the area around the 17th-century triple-tier pulpit. The dark-red cedar altar is the oldest piece of woodwork in the colony, carved under the supervision of Richard Moore, a ship-

wright and the first governor. The font, brought to the island
by the early settlers, is about 500 years old, and the late-18th-
century bishop's throne is believed to have been salvaged from
a wreck. Among the treasures displayed in the vestry are a
1697 William of Orange communion set and a Charles I chalice,
sent from England by the Bermuda Company in 1625. Commemorative plaques hang on the walls, and some of the names
are wonderfully Pickwickian: One large memorial is to Governor Allured Popple. If you enter through the back door, be sure
to look at the front of the church when you leave. *Duke of York
St., tel. 809/297–8359. Donations appreciated. Open daily.*

㉗ Across the street, the **Confederate Museum** has a colorful history. Built in 1700 by Governor Samuel Day, the building served
for 150 years as the Globe Hotel. During the American Civil
War, the house was occupied by Major Norman Walker, who
came to Bermuda as a Confederate agent. St. George's—which
had suffered a depression after the capital moved to Hamilton
in 1815—sided with the South for economic reasons, and the
town became a hotbed of blockade-running activity. The first
woman to run the blockade was Major Walker's pregnant wife,
who risked capture by the North to join him in Bermuda. She
was determined to have their baby born on Confederate soil,
however, beneath the Stars and Bars. In the room where she
gave birth, therefore, the four-poster bed was draped with the
Confederate flag, and it's said that Confederate soil was spread
beneath the bed. A wall map, designed by Desmond Fountain,
shows the blockade-running routes from Bermuda to Southern
ports. Also on display are a model of a blockade-runner, a replica of the Great Seal of the Confederacy, and an antique Victorian Seal Press, which makes reproductions of the Great Seal as
souvenirs for visitors. *Duke of York St., tel. 809/297–1423. Donation: $3. Open Mon.–Sat. 10–5. Closed holidays.*

Continuing down Duke of York Street, you come to **Barber Alley**, named for Joseph Hayne Rainey, a former slave from South
Carolina. Rainey's father had bought him his freedom, so when
the Civil War broke out, Rainey and his French wife fled to Bermuda. Living in the kitchen of the Tucker House, Rainey became a barber and his wife made fashionable clothes. After the
Civil War, they returned to South Carolina, where he went into
politics. Elected to the House of Representatives in 1870, Rainey was the first black to serve in Congress.

Petticoat Lane, which is also called Silk Alley, received its name
in 1834 after the emancipation of Bermudian slaves. Legend
has it that two freed slaves, who had always wanted petticoats
like those worn by their mistresses, strolled down the lane on
Emancipation Sunday amid much rustling of petticoat skirts.

㉘ Antiques aficionados will find much of interest in the **Tucker
House,** one of the showplaces of the Bermuda National Trust.
Built of native limestone in 1711, the house sat above green hills
that sloped down to the waterside (the area is now all built up).
Henry Tucker, president of the Governor's Council, lived in the
house with his family from 1775 to 1800. His grandson donated
most of the furnishings, which date from the mid-18th and early 19th centuries. Much of it is cedar, but there are some handsome mahogany pieces as well: The mahogany dining table was
crafted from a tree grown in Cuba, and an English mahogany
breakfront holds a collection of Tucker-family silver engraved
with their coat of arms. Notice the tiny wig rooms off the dining

room, where ladies and gentlemen went to fix their wigs after dinner. A short flight of stairs leads down to the kitchen, where Joseph Rainey lived and ran his barber shop. There is a small bookstore in the cellar. The Tucker name has been important in Bermuda since the island's beginnings (Henry Tucker's son St. George built the Tucker House in Williamsburg, Virginia), and a number of interesting family portraits hang in the house. Henry Tucker's father and brother were both involved in the famed "Gunpowder Plot" of 1775. The Continental Congress had imposed a ban on exports to all British colonies not taking part in the revolt against England. Bermuda depended upon the American colonies for grain, so a delegation of Bermudians traveled to Philadelphia offering salt in exchange for the resumption of grain shipments. Congress rejected the salt but agreed to lift the ban if Bermuda sent gunpowder instead. A group of Bermudians, including the two Tuckers, then sneaked into the island's arsenal, stole the gunpowder, and shipped it to Boston. The ban was soon lifted. *Water St., tel. 809/297–0545. Donation: $3. Open Mon.–Sat. 10–5. Closed holidays.*

With the arrival of cars on Bermuda in 1946, horse-drawn carriages were put out to pasture, so to speak. Across the street ㉙ from the Tucker House, the **Carriage Museum** offers a fascinating look at some of the island's old carriages. Yes, there's a surrey with a fringe on top as well as isinglass curtains that roll down. Among the other displays are a dignified Brougham; a six-passenger enclosed Opera Bus; and a small two-wheeler for children, called the Little Red Dog Cart. The carriages are labeled, but it's fun to hear the curator, Mr. Frith, describe them. *Water St., tel. 809/297–1367. Admission free (donations appreciated). Open Mon.–Sat. 10–4. Closed holidays.*

Somers Wharf, where the Carriage Museum is located, is part of a multimillion-dollar waterfront restoration that includes several shops and the pleasant Carriage House Restaurant. St. George's new passenger-ship terminal, scheduled for completion in June 1991, is in this area.

Tour 3: The West End

Numbers in the margin correspond to points of interest on the West End map.

In contrast to Hamilton and St. George's, the West End is a rather bucolic part of Bermuda. With the notable exception of Dockyard, many of the attractions here are natural rather than manmade: nature reserves, wooded areas, and beautiful harbors and bays. In the waters off Daniel's Head, the Sea Gardens are regularly visited by glass-bottom boats from Hamilton: With its bow jutting out of the water, the coral-wrapped wreck of HMS *Vixen* is a major attraction. The ship was deliberately sunk by the British to block the channel and protect Dockyard from attack. The West End is part of Sandys Parish, named after Sir Edwin Sandys, an investor in the Bermuda Company. Local lore contends that Sir George Somers took a keen interest in this region, and in the early days it was known as "Somers's seate"—hence the name of Somerset Village. Today, Somerset is a sleepy little hamlet with a few shops and not much else. The West End's big attraction is Dockyard, a bastion of the British Royal Navy for 150 years. You should plan to spend at least a day exploring this area.

If you take the ferry to Somerset, look closely at the ferry schedule: The trip can take anywhere from a half hour to more than an hour, depending on which ferry you take. However, there are worse ways to while away an hour than churning across Bermuda's Great Sound. Take your bicycle or moped aboard the ferry, too, because you will need wheels in the West End. Bus service is available for those without their own transport.

The Somerset ferry stops at Somerset Bridge, Cavello Bay, Watford Bridge, and Dockyard. This tour begins at **Dockyard** on Ireland Island, a sprawling complex housing several notable attractions. After the American Revolution, Britain found itself with neither an anchorage nor a major ship-repair yard in the western Atlantic. When Napoleon started to make threatening noises in Europe and British ships became increasingly vulnerable to pirate attack, Britain began construction of a major stronghold in Bermuda in 1809. The work was done by slaves and English convicts toiling under appalling conditions—thousands of workers died before the project was completed. The Royal Navy maintained a presence here for nearly 150 years, finally leaving in 1951. With the opening of the Maritime Museum (*see* below) in 1975, the decision was made to transform the entire naval port into a tourist attraction. Dockyard is currently under development as a minivillage. Bermudians are enormously proud of the Dockyard project, but the area lacks the warmth and charm of, for example, Nelson's Dockyard in Antigua; instead it has the barren feel of a shopping mall. Dockyard is still being developed, however, and it may blossom over time. New additions include a shopping arcade and visitor center in the century-old Clock Tower (which *is* a handsome edifice); a cruise-ship terminal; a marina and deepwater berth. Also planned are scuba-diving facilities and a snorkel park; horse-drawn carriage tours; and the tourist submarine *Enterprise*. A new half-hour express bus service leaves Hamilton for Dockyard every 15 minutes. Hold on to your hair when you're strolling around Dockyard—it's very windy, particularly along the water.

Opened by Queen Elizabeth II in 1975, the sprawling 6-acre **Maritime Museum** is housed in the huge fortress built to defend Dockyard. Entry to the museum is over a moat. The exhibition rooms are in old magazines and munitions warehouses arranged around the parade grounds. Several exhibits pertain to the *Sea Venture* and the early history of the island. Treasures and relics from some of the approximately 300 ships wrecked on the island's reefs are exhibited, as are maps, diving gear, ship models, uniforms, and costumes. Sailors will particularly enjoy the Bermuda dinghies (14-foot sailboats which can carry as much as 1,000 feet of canvas) on display in the Boat Loft. Visitors can also explore the ramparts, although this walk is only for dedicated (and hardy) fortress buffs. Currently undergoing renovation, the 19th-century Commissioner's House is an elaborate cast-iron affair set high on a bluff. The house is slated for completion by 1992, in time for the 500th anniversary of Christopher Columbus's voyage to the New World. *Dockyard, tel. 809/234–1418. Admission: $5 adults, $2 senior citizens and children under 12. Open daily 10–5. Closed Christmas.*

Across the street from the Maritime Museum is the Old Cooperage, or barrel-maker's shop. Dating back to 1831, the recon-

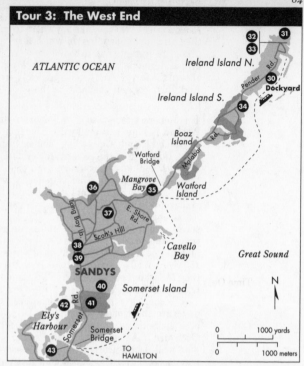

Tour 3: The West End

❸❷ structed building houses the **Neptune Cinema** and **Craft Market.**

The Neptune Cinema features *The Attack on Washington*, a spirited multimedia show detailing the role Bermuda and Dockyard played in the War of 1812. Angered by American raids on York (now Toronto), the British laid plans to retaliate. Bermuda was the departure point for a mighty fleet and some 35,000 troops that sailed over to sack and burn the U.S. capital in 1814. Shows are run continuously every half hour. *Neptune Cinema, the Cooperage, tel. 809/234–2923. Admission: $2.50 adults, $1.50 senior citizens and children under 12. Shows daily 10–4. Closed Easter and Christmas Day.*

Adjacent to the theater, the Craft Market displays the works of local artists. Jaded tourists, for whom "craft" usually means tacky souvenirs, are in for a pleasant surprise. Despite a poor presentation and layout, some delightful items are on sale here, including stained glass and miniature cedar furniture (*see* Chapter 5, Shopping). *Dockyard, tel. 809/234–3208. Admission free. Open daily 11–4. Closed Christmas, Boxing Day, New Year's Day, Good Friday.*

❸❸ Since its opening by Princess Margaret in 1984, the **Bermuda Arts Centre** has been a showcase for local artists and artisans, and an excellent place to see Bermudian work (*see* Chapter 5, Shopping). Exhibits, which cover such subjects as underwater photography, change monthly. *Dockyard, tel. 809/234–2809. Admission: $1 adults, 50¢ senior citizens, students, and children under 12. Open Tues.–Fri. 10–4:30; weekends 10–5.*

Closed Christmas, Boxing Day, New Year's Day, and Good Friday.

㉞ Take the main road out of Dockyard along Ireland Island South. Turn left on Craddock Road and cycle down to **Lagoon Park.** Hidden in the mangroves are a lovely lagoon, footpaths, wild birds, and places to picnic. Next to the park, **The Crawl** is a picturesque inlet with fishing boats bobbing in the water and lobster pots on the dock. The park is always open, and there's no admission charge.

Cross over Boaz and Watford islands to Somerset Island. The largest of all these islets, Somerset Island is fringed on both sides with beautiful secluded coves, inlets, and bays. Beside **㉟** pretty Mangrove Bay, **Somerset Village** is a quiet retreat, quite different from St. George's, Hamilton, and Dockyard. Only one road runs through the village, and the few shops are mostly branches of Hamilton stores. During the low season walks, tour guides concentrate on the area's natural beauty and the unusual and medicinal plants on the island. Somerset Island itself is heavily populated, laced with roads and pathways through quiet residential areas.

Time Out Overlooking Mangrove Bay, the **Somerset Country Squire Restaurant** (Mangrove Bay Rd., tel. 809/234–0105) is an English-style pub with a great atmosphere. Diners can rely on good sandwiches and burgers, as well as such traditional British dishes as steak and kidney pie and bangers (sausages) and mash. Desserts are sensational.

Cambridge Beaches, Bermuda's original cottage colony, sits on its own 25-acre peninsula northwest of Somerset Village. Nestled among the trees near the entrance is a branch of the **Irish Linen Shop** (Cambridge Rd., tel. 809/234–0127). The little cottage was one of the original units of Cambridge Beaches.

㊱ A short distance farther along Cambridge Road is **Long Bay Park and Nature Reserve,** which has a great beach, shallow water, and picnic areas. The Bermuda Audubon Society owns the adjacent nature reserve and its pond, which attracts migrating birds in the spring and fall. Peaceful as this area is now, it was the scene of one of Bermuda's most sensational murders. Skeeters' Corner, at the end of Daniel's Head Road, was the site of a cottage once owned by a couple of the same name. One night in 1878, Edward Skeeters strangled his wife and dumped her in the water. His long, rambling confession revealed that he was irked because she talked too much!

Continue along Cambridge Road (which becomes Somerset Road), until you see the arched gateway leading to the **㊲** **Springfield Library and Gilbert Nature Reserve.** Set in 5 heavily wooded acres, Springfield is an old plantation home that dates back to around 1700. The restored house and outbuildings— the kitchen, slave quarters, and buttery—are built around an open courtyard. The most interesting rooms are in the main house, which also contains the Somerset branch of the public library. Named after the family that owned the property from 1700 to 1973, the nature reserve was acquired by the Bermuda National Trust in conjunction with the Bermuda Audubon Society. *Main Rd., Somerset, tel. 809/234–1980. Admission free. Nature reserve always open. Library open Mon. and Wed. 9–5, Sat. 10–5. Closed 1–2 PM, and holidays.*

38 Somerset Road winds around to the **Somerset Visitors Information Centre** (Somerset Rd., tel. 809/234–1388), where you can get information about this area from May through November.

39 High atop a promontory against a backdrop of the sea, **St. James Church** is one of the loveliest churches on the island. The entrance on the main road is marked by handsome iron gates that were forged by a Royal Engineer in 1872; the long driveway curls past glistening white tombs in the churchyard. The first church on this site was a wood structure destroyed by a hurricane in 1780. The present church was consecrated in 1789, and its tall, slender spire was added in 1880. *Main Rd., Somerset, no phone. Open daily 8–7.*

40 Shortly after the church, you'll see the entrance to the **Heydon Trust property,** opposite Willowbank guest house. Among its 43 acres are citrus orchards, banana groves, flower and vegetable gardens, and bird sanctuaries. The quiet, peaceful property has been maintained as undeveloped "open space"—a reminder of what the island was like in its early days. Pathways dotted with park benches wend through the preserve, affording some wonderful views of the Great Sound. If you persevere along the main path, you'll reach the tiny, rustic **Heydon Chapel,** which dates from before 1620. An old rugged cross is planted in the hillside, and a welcome mat lies at the door. Inside are a few wooden pews, cedar beams, and an ancient oven and hearth in a small room behind the altar. Services are still held in the chapel. *Somerset Rd., tel. 809/234–1831. Admission free. Open during daylight hours.*

41 Just around the bend on your left is **Scaur Hill Fort.** Perched on the highest hill in Somerset, the fort was built in the 1870s to protect the Royal Naval Dockyard. Little remains to be seen here, although the 22 acres of gardens are quite pretty, and the view of the Great Sound is fantastic. Almost worth the long climb is the Early Bermuda Weather Stone, the "perfect weather indicator." The plaque reads: "A wet stone means . . . it is raining; a shadow under the stone . . . means the sun is shining; if the stone is swinging, it means there is a strong wind blowing; if the stone jumps up and down it means there is an earthquake; if ever it is white on top . . . believe it or not . . . it is snowing." *Somerset Rd., Ely's Harbour, tel. 809/234–0908. Admission free. Open daily 10–4:30. Closed Christmas and Boxing Day.*

42 At the bottom of the hilly, twisting road lies spectacular **Ely's Harbour,** with pleasure boats dotting its brilliant turquoise waters. Pronounced "Ee-lees," the small sheltered harbor was once a hangout for smugglers. From the main road you can take a right turn on rugged Scaur Hill Drive to visit the aptly named **Cathedral Rocks,** which overlook the harbor. This is one of the prettiest scenes in Bermuda.

43 Linking Somerset Island with the rest of Bermuda is **Somerset Bridge,** reputed to have the smallest draw in the world. It opens a mere 18 inches, just wide enough to accommodate a sailboat mast. Near the bridge is the Somerset ferry landing, where you can catch a ferry back to Hamilton. Across the bridge, Somerset Road becomes Middle Road, which leads into Southampton Parish (*see* Tour 4: The Parishes, below).

Time Out At the Somerset Bridge Hotel, the **Blue Foam** (162 Somerset Rd, tel. 809/234–2892) is a pleasant lunch spot in a greenhouse setting. In high season, an expensive alternative is the sumptuous lunch at the **Lantana Colony Club** (Somerset Rd., tel. 809/234–0141). Reservations are necessary at Lantana.

Tour 4: The Parishes

Numbers in the margin correspond to points of interest on The Parishes map.

Bermuda's other points of interest—and there are many—are scattered across the island's parishes. This final tour takes you across the length and breadth of the colony, commenting only on the major sights. Half the fun of exploring Bermuda, though, is wandering down forgotten lanes or discovering some little-known beach or cove. A moped or bicycle is ideal for this kind of travel, although most of the island is covered by bus and ferry service. It would be foolish to try to see all the sights here in just one day. The tour, which leaves from Hamilton, can easily be broken into two halves: The first half explores those parishes in the eastern part of the island; the second travels through the western parishes. Even so, vacationers may find it more rewarding to do the tour piecemeal—a couple of sites here, a church there, and a day at the beach in between.

44 Follow Cedar Avenue north out of Hamilton to **St. John's Church,** consecrated in 1826 as the parish church of Pembroke. Another church, which dated to 1625, stood on this site before. During a funeral in 1875, the churchyard was the scene of a verbal duel between the Anglican rector and a Wesleyan minister. The Anglican church insisted that all burial services in parish churchyards be conducted by the rector, but the Wesleyans challenged the church in the case of a deceased woman named Esther Levy. Claiming he'd been asked by her friends to perform the funeral service, a Wesleyan minister appeared in the churchyard despite the efforts of the Anglican rector to stop him. Simultaneous services were held over poor Mrs. Levy's body, with the minister and the adamant Anglican trying to out-shout each other. The rector subsequently filed charges of trespassing against the Wesleyan, and the celebrated case went before the Supreme Court. The jury found for the rector, and fined the minister one shilling. *St. John's Rd., Pembroke. Open daily 8–7.*

45
46 By following Marsh Folly Road, which runs between the church and Bernard Park, you'll come to **Black Watch Pass.** The Public Works Department excavated about 2.5 million cubic feet of solid limestone during construction of the pass. The tunnel received its name from **Black Watch Well,** at the intersection of Black Watch Pass and North Shore Road. During a severe drought in 1849, the governor ordered a well dug on government ground to alleviate the suffering of the poor in the area. Excavated by a detachment of the famed Black Watch regiment, the well is marked by a commemorative plaque and shaded by a tiered concrete slab. The site is not particularly inspiring, however, and only the most dedicated well-wishers will want to make the pilgrimage to see it.

47 From its position on Langton Hill, imposing **Government House** overlooks North Shore Road, Black Watch Well, and the sea.

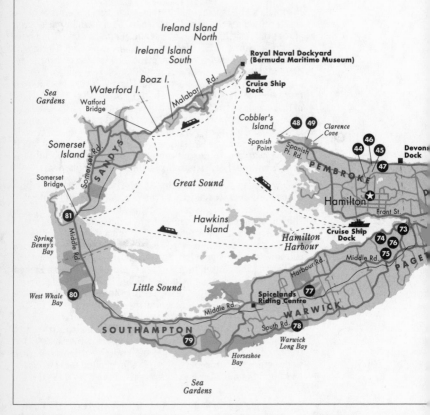

ATLANTIC OCEAN

Ireland Island
North

Ireland Island
South

Boaz I.

Waterford I.

Malabar Rd.

Royal Naval Dockyard
(Bermuda Maritime Museum)

Cruise Ship
Dock

Sea
Gardens

Watford
Bridge

Somerset
Island

Somerset
Rd.

SANDYS

Cobbler's
Island

Spanish
Point

Spanish
Pt. Rd.

Clarence
Cove

48 **49**

44 **46**
45
47

PEMBROKE

Devons
Dock

Somerset
Bridge

81

Middle Rd.

Great Sound

Hamilton

Front St.

Spring
Benny's
Bay

Hawkins
Island

Hamilton
Harbour

Cruise Ship
Dock

73
74
76
75

West Whale
Bay

80

Little Sound

Harbour Rd.

Middle Rd.

PAGET

Spicelands
Riding Centre

77

Middle Rd.

WARWICK

South Rd. **78**

Warwick
Long Bay

SOUTHAMPTON

79

Horseshoe
Bay

Sea
Gardens

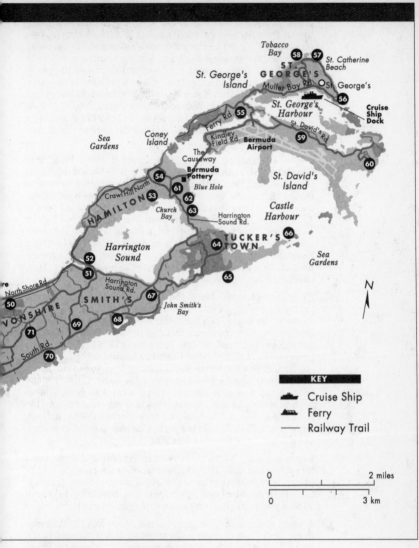

The house is the residence of the governor and is not open to the public. The land was purchased when the capital was transferred from St. George's to Hamilton in 1815. A simple, two-story house served as the governor's home until the present, rather austere mansion was built. Various royals and other distinguished visitors planted the trees and shrubs on the pretty landscaped lawns. Among the guests who have been entertained in Government House are Queen Elizabeth II and Prince Philip, Prince Charles, Winston Churchill, and President Kennedy. The mansion was also the scene of the 1973 assassination of Governor Richard Sharples and his aide, Captain Hugh Sayers.

48 North Shore Road merges with Spanish Point Road near **Spanish Point,** at the tip of the peninsula. The survivors of the wrecked *Sea Venture* thought they found evidence here of an earlier visit by the Spanish. Apparently they were right: Historians now believe that Captain Diego Ramirez landed here in 1503. There is a small park for picnicking, a sheltered bay for swimming, public facilities, and a lovely view of Somerset across the sound. Cobbler's Island, across Cobbler's Cut from Spanish Point, has a grisly history—executed slaves were exhibited there as a warning to others of the consequences of disobedience.

49 En route to Spanish Point you pass **Admiralty House Park,** a pretty spot with several caves and sheltered coves. Little remains of the house, originally the 19th-century estate of John Dunscombe. Dunscombe, who later became lieutenant governor of Newfoundland, sold the property in 1816 to the Bermuda government, which decided to build a house for the commanding British admiral of the naval base at Dockyard. The house was reconstructed several times over the years, notably in the 1850s by an eccentric admiral with a weakness for subterranean tunnels—he had several caves and galleries cut into the cliffs above the sea. The house was closed when the Royal Navy withdrew in 1951. Within the park, Clarence Cove offers a sheltered beach and pleasant swimming.

Head back along North Shore Road to Devonshire Parish. Ideal for cycling and quiet picnics, Devonshire is a serene part of the island, with much to offer in the way of natural beauty. Locals come to **Devonshire Dock** to buy fresh fish (something to bear in mind if you're staying in a housekeeping apartment).

50 A short distance farther along North Shore Road is **Palmetto House,** an 18th-century cruciform house. It was believed that a house built in the shape of a cross warded off evil spirits. Three rooms, furnished with fine pieces of Bermudian furniture, are on view. *North Shore Rd., tel. 809/295–9941. Admission free. Open Thurs. 10–5.*

51 If you continue along North Shore Road, you will reach **Flatts Village,** one of the earliest settlements on the island. The House of Assembly sometimes met in Flatts, although much of the village's activities involved flaunting the law rather than making it. Hoping to avoid customs officers, Bermudians returning from the West Indies would sometimes sail into the village in the dead of night to unload their cargoes.

52 The **Aquarium, Museum and Zoo** at Flatts Village is one of the island's most popular attractions. Pick up an audio "wand" at the aquarium entrance for a self-guided tour of the tanks and exhibits. Sea creatures native to Bermudian waters are on display, including sharks, barracuda, and grumpy-looking giant grouper. Just outside the aquarium, you'll see three harbor seals (Charlotte, Archie, and their pup) splashing in a small pond. The natural-history museum features a geology display that explains Bermuda's volcanic origins, and a deep-sea exhibit that documents the half-mile dive of marine biologist Dr. William Beebe in the early 1930s. The odd-looking contraption outside the museum is the bathosphere in which Dr. Beebe made his dive. In the zoo, a reptile walkway gives visitors a close look at alligators, Galapagos tortoises, and lizards. Other attractions include an aviary, a monkey house, and a number of Caribbean flamingos and strutting peacocks. A petting zoo is open only in the summer. *Flatts, tel. 809/293–2727. Admission: $4 adults, $1 senior citizens and children 5–12. Open daily 9–5 (last admission at 4:30). Closed Christmas.*

Continuing east, North Shore Road climbs **Crawl Hill**, a high point offering spectacular views over the island and sea. "Crawl" derives from the Afrikaans word "kraal," meaning animal enclosure; on Bermuda, the word was applied to several ponds containing turtles and fish. This part of Hamilton Parish was also a site for shipbuilding during the early days of the colony.

53 Turn right on Trinity Church Road to see **Holy Trinity Church.** Built in 1623 as one long room with a thatched roof, it is said to be the oldest Anglican church on Bermuda. The church has been much embellished over the past 368 years, but the original building remains at its core. The small graveyard is encircled by palms, royal poinciana, and cherry trees. *Church Bay, Harrington Sound, no phone. Not open to the public.*

Just off Trinity Church Road is **Mount Wyndham**, the peak from which Admiral Sir Alexander Cochrane surveyed the British fleet prior to its attack on Washington, DC, in 1814.

54 Follow North Shore Road as it dips south to the **Bermuda Perfumery and Gardens.** On a guided tour, visitors learn how the Lili Perfume Factory, which began extracting natural fragrances from the island's flowers in 1929, blossomed into the present perfumery/tourist attraction. The factory is in a 200-year-old cottage with cedar beams, but the biggest draw is the aromatic nature trail that you can walk on your own. A complimentary map helps you sniff your way around the oleanders, frangipani, jasmine, orchids, and passionflower that are the raw material for the factory. *212 North Shore Rd., tel. 809/293–0627. Admission free. Open Apr.–Oct., Mon.–Sat. 9–5, Sun. 10–4; Nov.–Mar., Mon.–Sat. 9–4:30, closed Sun. and holidays.*

Time Out Just up the road, **Bailey's Ice Cream Parlour & Food D'Lites** (Blue Hole Hill, tel. 809/293–9333) offers 40 varieties of freshly made natural ice cream, as well as shakes, sodas, yogurts, and sorbets. For something a bit stronger, cross the road for a rum swizzle and a "swizzleburger" at the **Swizzle Inn** (Blue Hole Hill, tel. 809/293–9300).

Blue Hole Hill leads to the causeway over Castle Harbour. Once on the other side you are in St. George's Parish. Take Kindley Field Road around the airport, turn left onto Mullet Bay Road, and cross Swing Bridge over Ferry Reach. The

⑤⑤ Bermuda Biological Station for Research will be of interest to anyone who cares about the environment. Scientists here have conducted research on marine life since 1932, and the center has been given a five-year, $2 million grant from the U.S. National Science Foundation to study the greenhouse effect. Extensive research has been conducted here on acid rain. Guided tours of the grounds and laboratory are conducted every Wednesday at 10 AM, beginning in the main building. Coffee and snacks are served. *17 Biological La., Ferry Reach, St. George's, tel. 809/297–1880.*

The scenery is magnificent along the stretch of road that runs between Mullet Bay and the sea. A little farther east, Mullet Bay Road becomes Wellington Road, and finally Duke of York Street when you reach St. George's (*see* Tour 2: The Town of St. George's, above). East of town, Duke of York Street becomes Barrack Hill Road. From the road, the views of the town, St. David's Island, and Castle Harbour are splendid. Barrack Hill **⑤⑥** Road turns into Cut Road, which leads all the way to **Gates Fort.** St. George's has always had the greatest concentration of fortifications on the island. Gates Fort is a reconstruction of a small militia fort dating from the 1620s. Don't expect turrets, towers, and tunnels, however; there is little to see here apart from the sea. The fort and Gates Bay, which it overlooks, were named for Sir Thomas Gates, the first of the survivors of the *Sea Venture* to reach dry land. Upon doing so, he is reputed to have shouted, "This is Gates, his bay!" Public speaking was obviously not his forte, although Gates was by profession a politician—he later became governor of Virginia. *Cut Rd., no phone. Admission free. Open daily 10–4.*

The main camp of the *Sea Venture* survivors is believed to have been in this general area. Leaving Gates Fort via Barry Road, you'll pass **Buildings Bay**. One of the two ships that carried Sir George Somers and his crew to Virginia was built here in 1610, hence the bay's name.

⑤⑦ Continue up Barry Road to **Fort St. Catherine.** Apart from Dockyard, this restored fortress is the most impressive on the island: It has enough cannons, tunnels, and ramparts to satisfy the most avid military historian. One of a host of fortifications constructed in St. George's, the fort was begun around 1614 and work continued on it throughout the 19th century. As you travel through the tunnels, you'll come across some startlingly lifelike figures tucked into niches. Several dioramas depict the island's development, and an audiovisual presentation describes the building and significance of the fort. There is also a small but elaborate display of replicas of the crown jewels of England. *Barry Rd., tel. 809/297–1920. Admission: $2.50 adults, children under 12 free, but must be accompanied by an adult. Open daily 10–4:30. Closed Christmas.*

St. Catherine's Beach, where the survivors from the *Sea Venture* scrambled ashore, is a pleasant place for a swim and quiet contemplation of the events of July 28, 1609. Another fine beach, with changing facilities and a refreshment stand, is **⑤⑧** at nearby **Tobacco Bay,** where the Tuckers secretly loaded the gunpowder bound for Boston in 1775 (*see* Tour 2: The Town of St. George's, above). Retrace your route through St. George's to Swing Bridge that connects St. George's with St. David's Island. In addition to Bermuda's airport, about 2 square miles of St. David's is occupied by a U.S. Naval Air Station. In 1940, during World War II, Churchill agreed to give the United States a 99-year lease to operate a base on Bermuda in exchange for destroyers. The entire area taken up by the air station is now called St. David's, but construction of the base actually required linking three separate islands—St. David's, Longbird, and Cooper's—with landfills.

Christopher Carter, one of three men left behind when the *Deliverance* and the *Patience* sailed for Jamestown in 1610, was offered St. David's Island in 1612 as a reward for revealing the "Ambergris Plot." Before the ships returned to Bermuda, it seems, one of the three men, Edward Chard, found 80 pounds of ambergris (a precious sperm-whale product used for perfumes) washed up on the beach. In collusion with Carter and the third man, Chard planned to smuggle the ambergris off the island (when a ship arrived) and sell it in London at enormous profit. At the last minute, however, Carter squealed on his co-conspirators to Governor Moore, who had arrived in 1612 with new settlers. Instead of St. David's Island, Carter opted for Cooper's Island, which is also now part of the naval base. Built

59 by Carter's descendants in 1640, **Carter House** is one of the oldest houses in Bermuda and should not be missed. The stone-and-cedar house has been refurbished with new floors and period furnishings, including a 17th-century bedding chest, a mortar and pestle, and an 18th-century tavern table, and is maintained by the naval base as a museum. You can reach Carter House through the main gate of the air station; you'll need a photo identification and proof of vehicle insurance to get in. *Kindley Field Rd., tel. 809/297–1150 (ask for Ms. Lyndell O'Dey). Admission free. Open Wed. 11–4.*

Apart from the naval base, St. David's is a rustic spot where the inhabitants have always led an isolated life—some are said to have never visited St. George's, let alone the other end of the island. A number of residents had to be relocated when the base was built, but they refused to leave St. David's. Therefore, a section of St. David's called "Texas" was purchased by the government, which built cottages there for the displaced islanders. The area is just off the naval base; you can see Texas Road at the tip of the island near the lighthouse.

60 **St. David's Lighthouse** occupies the highest point on the island's eastern end. Built in 1879 of Bermuda stone, the lighthouse rises 280 feet above the sea. Although only about half the height of Gibb's Hill Lighthouse in Southampton Parish, it nevertheless affords spectacular views: From the balcony you can see St. David's and St. George's, Castle Harbour, and the reef-fringed south shore. The lighthouse is not always open; check with the Visitors Service Bureau in the Visitors Information Centre in Hamilton or St. George's.

Time Out Right on the water near the lighthouse, the **Black Horse Tavern** (Clarkes Hill, tel. 809/293–9742) is a spot that's popular with the locals. Seafood is the specialty, and shark hash and curried conch stew are featured items. The fish sandwiches are delicious. There are outdoor picnic tables as well as indoor dining.

Head back across the causeway and turn left on Wilkinson Avenue. A network of caves, caverns, and subterranean lakes runs beneath the hills in this part of the island. Two of them are on the property of the nearby Grotto Bay Beach Hotel (*see* Chap-

⑥ ter 8, Lodging). Just south of the hotel are the **Crystal Caves,** discovered in 1907 by two boys playing ball. When the ball disappeared down a hole, the boys burrowed after it and found themselves in a vast cavern 120 feet underground, surrounded by fantastic stalagmite and stalactite formations. Today, the approach is along a wet, sloping walkway and a wood pontoon bridge across the underground lake. After explaining the formation of stalactites and stalagmites, a tour guide uses a lighting system to make silhouettes. People who suffer from claustrophobia will probably want to give the caves a miss, because space can be quite tight. *8 Crystal Caves Rd., off Wilkinson Ave., tel. 809/293–0640. Admission: $3 adults, $1.50 senior citizens and children 5–11. Open daily 9:30–4:30. Closed Dec. 24–26 and Jan. From mid-Nov. to mid-March, hours may vary.*

Harrington Sound Road runs along the strip of land between the Sound and Castle Harbour. At Walsingham Lane, you'll see
⑥ a white sign for **Tom Moore's Tavern,** a popular restaurant. The restaurant was originally the home of Samuel Trott, who constructed it in the 17th century and named it Walsingham. (The harbor nearby was named for Robert Walsingham, a sailor on the *Sea Venture* who apparently became enamored of the bay.) The house is surrounded by woods that are much the same as they were three centuries ago. When Tom Moore, the Irish poet, arrived in Bermuda in 1804, the house was occupied by a descendant of the original owner (also named Samuel Trott) and his family. The Trotts befriended the poet, who became a frequent visitor to the house. In Epistle V, Moore immortalized the Calabash Tree on the Trott estate under which he liked to write his verses. In 1844, the idea for the Royal Bermuda Yacht Club was conceived under the very same tree.

⑥ Harrington Sound Road leads southward to the **Amber Caves of Leamington,** smaller and less impressive than Crystal Caves. However, they do have their share of stalagmites and stalactites in fanciful formations, one of them an amber-tinted Statue of Liberty. Above ground, the Plantation Restaurant serves some of the island's best food—worth a trip whether you visit the caves or not. *Harrington Sound Rd., tel. 809/293–1188. Admission: $3 adults, $1.50 senior citizens and children 4–12. Open Mon.–Sat. 9:30–4:30, Sun. noon–3. Closed late Nov.–late Feb., holidays.*

⑥ Farther south on Harrington Sound Road is **Tucker's Town,** named for Governor Daniel Tucker, who wanted to abandon St. George's in 1616 in favor of a new settlement on the shores of Castle Harbour. A few streets were laid out and some cottages were built, but the plan was eventually shelved. For 300 years Tucker's Town remained a small fishing and farming community: Cotton was grown for a while, and a few whaling boats operated from here. Dramatic change overtook the community soon after World War I, however. Seeking to raise the island's appeal in order to attract passengers on its luxury liners to Bermuda, a steamship company called Furness, Withy & Co. purchased a large area of Tucker's Town for a new country club. The result was the exclusive Mid Ocean Club, with its fine golf course. Members of the club started building residences nearby, and the Tucker's Town boom began. Today, only members of the club can buy a house in the area, and private residences have been known to sell for more than $2 million.

65 Below the clubhouse on the south shore are the **Natural Arches,** one of the island's oldest and most photographed attractions. Carved over the centuries by the wind and ocean, the two limestone arches rise 35 feet above the beach. Look for the signs near the end of South Shore Road pointing to Castle Harbour Beach and the Natural Arches.

A chain of islands dots the entrance channel to the harbor between St. David's and Tucker's Town Bay. In the colony's early days, these islands were fortified to protect Castle Harbour from possible enemy attack. Soon after his arrival in 1612, Gov-

66 ernor Moore built his first and best fort on **Castle Island.** According to an oft-told tale, two Spanish ships appeared outside the channel in 1614 and attempted to attack the colony. Two shots were fired from the fort: One fell into the water, and the other hit one of the ship's hulls. The Spaniards fled, unaware that the fortress had expended two-thirds of its stock of ammunition—the colonists had one cannonball left.

67 Touted as Bermuda's first tourist attraction, **Devil's Hole Aquarium** was started by a Mr. Trott in 1830. After building a wall around his fish pond—manifestly to prevent people from fishing in it—Mr. Trott was besieged with questions about what he was hiding. In 1843, yielding to the curiosity of the Bermudians, Mr. Trott permitted people to view his fish pond—at a fee. These days, the deep pool contains about 400 sea creatures, including giant grouper, sharks, and huge turtles. Visitors can play at fishing, using baited—but hookless— lines. *Harrington Sound Rd., tel. 809/293-2072. Admission: $5 adults, $3 children 6-12. Open Apr.-Oct., Sun.-Fri. 9-5; Nov.-Mar., Sun.-Fri. 10-4. Closed Good Friday and Christmas Day.*

68 Take steep Knapton Hill Road, which leads westward to South Shore Road and **Spittal Pond.** A showcase of the Bermuda National Trust, this nature park has 60 acres in which visitors can roam, although visitors are requested to keep to the walkways. More than 25 species of waterfowl winter here between November and May. On a high bluff, overlooking the ocean, is an oddity known as Spanish Marks. Early settlers found a rock crudely carved with the date 1543 and other markings that were unclear. It is now believed that a Portuguese ship was wrecked on the island in 1543, and that her sailors built a new ship on which they departed. The carvings are thought to be the initials *RP* (for Rex Portugaline), and the cross to be a badge of the Portuguese Order of Christ. The rock was removed to prevent further damage by erosion, and a plaque now marks the spot. A plaster-of-paris cast of the Spanish Marks is on display at the Museum of Bermuda Historical Society in Hamilton (*see* Tour 1: Hamilton, above). *South Shore Rd., no phone. Admission free. Open daily sunrise-sunset.*

West of Spittal Pond on South Shore Road is the turnoff to **Collector's Hill**, which is a very steep climb indeed. The hill is named for Gilbert Salton, a 19th-century customs collector who lived in a house near the top; the house has long since disappeared.

69 At the very top of Collector's Hill is **Verdmont,** Bermuda's finest house museum. It was built around 1710, possibly by a prominent shipowner named John Dickinson. At the end of the War of Independence, Verdmont was the home of John Green, an American Loyalist who fled to Bermuda from Philadelphia. Green married one of Dickinson's granddaughters and was appointed judge of the Court of Vice Admiralty. Green was also a portrait painter, and the only furnishings in the house from the 18th century are family portraits by him. The house, which resembles a small English manor house, has an unusual double roof and four large chimneys—all eight rooms have their own fireplace. Elegant cornice moldings and paneled shutters grace the two large reception rooms downstairs, originally the drawing room and formal dining room. The sash windows reflect a style that was fashionable in English manor houses. Although it contains none of the original furnishings, Verdmont is a treasure house of Bermudiana. Some of the furniture is mahogany imported from England—there are two exquisite early 19th-century pianos—but most of it is fine 18th-century cedar, crafted by Bermuda cabinetmakers. In particular, notice the desk in the drawing room, the lid and sides of which are made of single planks. Also displayed in the house is a china coffee service, said to have been a gift from Napoleon to President Madison. The president never received it: The ship bearing it across the Atlantic was seized by a Bermudian privateer and brought to Bermuda. Look carefully, too, at the handmade cedar staircase, with its handsomely turned newels and posts. The newel posts on each landing have removable caps to accommodate candles in the evening. Upstairs is a nursery: It's easy to imagine a child at play with the antique toys, riding the hand-propelled tricycle (circa 1840), or napping in the cedar cradle. The last occupant of Verdmont was an eccentric old woman, who lived here for 75 years without electricity or any other modern trappings. After her death, her family sold the house to the Bermuda Historic Monuments Trust—the forerunner of the Bermuda National Trust—which opened it as a museum in 1956. *Collector's Hill, tel. 809/236-7369. Admission: $3. Open Mon.-Sat. 9-5. Closed holidays.*

Time Out Popular with the locals, **Speciality Inn** (South Shore Rd., foot of Collector's Hill, tel. 809/236-3133) is a simple spot that serves pasta, pizza, sandwiches, soups, shakes, ice cream, and good breakfasts.

A singular delight of Devonshire Parish are the gardens at ⑦⓪ **Palm Grove,** a private estate. There is a splendid pond, within which is a relief map of the island—each parish is divided by carefully manicured grass sections. Desmond Fountain statues stand around the edge, peering into the pond's depths. *South Shore Rd., across from Brighton Hill, no phone. Admission free. Open weekdays 9-5.*

Brighton Hill Road, just west of Palm Grove, runs north to ⑦① Middle Road and the **Old Devonshire Church,** the parish's biggest attraction. A church has stood on this site since 1612, although the original was replaced in 1716. That replacement church was almost completely destroyed in an explosion on Easter Sunday in 1970, and the present church is a faithful reconstruction. A small, simple building of limestone and cedar, it looks much like an early Bermuda cottage. The three-tier pulpit, the pews, and the communion table are believed to be from the original church. Some pieces of church silver date back to 1590 and are said to be the oldest on the island. A cedar chest, believed to have once held the church records, dates from the early 17th century. Other pieces that have survived include an old cedar armchair, a candelabra, a cross, and a cedar screen. *Middle Rd., Devonshire, tel. 809/236–3671. Admission free. Open daily, 9–5:30.*

Turn left off Middle Road onto Tee Street, and then right onto Berry Hill Road. One mile farther on the left is the turnoff to **72** Point Finger Road and the **Botanical Gardens,** a landscaped park laced with roads and paths. The gardens are a fragrant showcase for the island's exotic subtropical plants, flowers, and trees. Within the 36 acres are a miniature forest, an aviary, a hibiscus garden (with more than 150 species of the flower), and a special Garden for the Blind, which is filled with the scent of lemon, lavender, and spices. Ninety-minute walking tours of the gardens leave the parking lot at 10:30 AM on Tuesday, Wednesday, and Friday (Tuesday and Friday only from November 15 to March). *Point Finger Rd., tel. 809/236–4201. Admission free. Open daily sunrise–sunset.*

The pretty white home on the grounds of the Botanical Gardens is **Camden,** the official residence of Bermuda's premier. A large two-story house, Camden is more typical of West Indian estate architecture than traditional Bermudian building. The house is open for tours, except when official functions are scheduled. *Botanical Gardens, tel. 809/236–5732. Admission free. Open Tues. and Fri. noon–2 PM.*

73 A few minutes away by moped are the offices of the **Bermuda National Trust,** a nonprofit organization that oversees the restoration and preservation of many of the island's gardens and historic homes. The trust is also a wonderful source of information about the island. The offices and "Trustworthy" gift shop are in a rambling 18th-century house built by the Trimingham family. Island crafts, novelties, and Trust logo items are sold in the shop; all proceeds go to the Trust. *"Waterville," 5 The Lane, Paget, tel. 809/236–6483. Open weekdays 9–4:30. Gift shop open Tues.–Sat. 10–4.*

The first half of the tour ends here: Hamilton is just a few hundred yards up the road. The second part of the tour heads west through the parishes of Paget, Warwick, and Southampton.

74 On Harbour Road near the Lower Ferry Landing, **Clermont** is an imposing house noted for its fine woodwork. Once the residence of Sir Brownlow Gray, Chief Justice of Bermuda, the house is also famous for having Bermuda's first tennis courts. During a visit from New York in 1874, Miss Mary Outerbridge learned to play here. Upon her return to the United States, she asked the Staten Island Cricket Club to build a court; armed with her racquet and a book of rules, she introduced tennis to America. This house is not open to the public, although it is sometimes included in the spring House and Gardens Tour (*see* Guided Tours in Chapter 1, Essential Information).

75 Turn left on Valley Road to reach **St. Paul's,** built in 1796 to replace an earlier church on the site. Around the turn of the century, the "Paget Ghost" began to be heard in and around St. Paul's. Nothing could be seen, but the mysterious sound of tinkling bells was plainly audible, coming from several directions. The ghost became quite famous, and a veritable posse—armed with firearms and clubs— gathered to find it; vendors even set up refreshment stands. Finally, a visiting American scientist proclaimed that the tinkling sound came from a rare bird, the

fililo. According to the scientist, the fililo was a natural ventril-
oquist, which explained why the sound jumped around. No one
ever saw the fililo, however, and no one saw the ghost either—
it disappeared as mysteriously as it had appeared.

76 St. Paul's sits on the edge of **Paget Marsh,** 18 acres of unspoiled
woodland that look much as they did when the first settlers arrived. Protected by the Bermuda National Trust, the marsh
contains cedars and palmettos, endangered plants, and a mangrove swamp. *Middle Rd., tel. 809/236–6483. Admission by arrangement with the Bermuda National Trust.*

From St. Paul's, head west into Warwick Parish along Middle
Road. Just after the intersection with Ord Road (opposite the
Belmont Hotel, Golf & Country Club), look to your left to see
77 **Christ Church.** Built in 1719, it is reputedly the oldest Presby-
terian church in any British colony or dominion.

Turn left off Middle Road onto Camp Hill Road, which winds
down to the south shore beaches. Along the way is **Warwick
Camp,** built in the 1870s to guard against any enemy landing on
the beaches. The camp was used as a training ground and rifle
range during World War I. In 1920, Pearl White of *The Perils of
Pauline* fame came to Bermuda to shoot a movie, bringing
along an entourage that included lions, monkeys, and a host of
other exotic fauna. Scenes for the film were shot on Warwick
Bay, below the rifle range. Most Bermudians had never seen
either a lion or a movie star, and huge crowds collected to watch
the filming.

Time Out An inexpensive roadside restaurant, **Tio Pepe's** (South Shore
Rd., near the entrance to Horseshoe Bay, tel. 809/238–1897)
serves Spanish and Italian foods and pizza to go. It's closed on
Tuesday.

Bermuda's beaches tend to elicit the most effusive travel-writ-
ing clichés—simply because they are so good. A 3-mile chain of
sandy beaches, coves, and inlets begins at Warwick Long Bay
and extends to Horseshoe Bay in the east (*see* Chapter 6,
78 Beaches and Water Sports). Just east of Warwick Bay, **Astwood
Park** is a lovely public park with picnic tables and two beaches,
one of them ideal for snorkeling.

Two miles west along South Shore Road is the turnoff for Light-
79 house Road. High atop Gibb's Hill, **Gibb's Hill Lighthouse** is the
second cast-iron lighthouse ever built. Designed in London and
opened in 1846, the tower stands 133 feet high and 360 feet
above the sea. The original light mechanism had to be wound
every three hours, a process that took three minutes. Today,
the beam from the 1,500-watt bulb can be seen by ships 40 miles
out to sea, and by planes 120 miles away at 10,000 feet. You can
climb to the top of the lighthouse, although this is not a trip for
anyone who suffers from vertigo. It's a long haul up the 185 spiral stairs—you have to climb another 30 steps just to reach the
entrance—but you can stop to catch your breath at platforms
along the way, where photographs and drawings of the lighthouse are displayed. At the top you can stroll on the balcony for
a spectacular view of Bermuda. The wind may snatch you bald-
headed—the tower is known to sway in high winds—and you
may find it hard to concentrate on the view knowing that a tiny
guard rail is the only thing between you and a swan dive. (An
alternative is to inch around with your back pressed against the

tower, clinging to it for dear life). *Lighthouse Rd., Southampton, tel. 809/238–0524. Admission: $2 adults, children under 6 free. Open daily 9–4:30. Closed Christmas.*

If you're still feeling adventurous, turn left off Middle Road onto Whale Bay Road (just before the Port Royal Golf & Country Club), and go down the hill to **Whale Bay Fort.** Overgrown with grass, flowers, and subtropical plants, this small 19th-century battery offers little in the way of a history lesson, but it does overlook a secluded pink-sand beach, gin-clear water, and craggy cliffs. The beach is accessible only on foot, but it's a splendid place for a swim. Bear in mind that you have to climb back up the hill to your moped or bike.

Just before Somerset Bridge is a little street with the odd name of **Overplus,** which harks back to the 17th century. When Richard Norwood surveyed the island in 1616, he divided the island into shares and tribes. He allotted 25 acres to each share, and 50 shares to each tribe. When the survey was completed, 200 acres (too small to form a tribe) remained unalloted and were listed as "overplus." Governor Tucker apparently directed the surveyor to keep an eye peeled for an attractive chunk of territory that could be designated as the surplus land. Norwood recommended a piece of real estate in the western part of the island, whereupon the governor claimed it and built a fine house on it. Upon hearing of the governor's action, the Bermuda Company lodged a complaint, forcing Tucker to return to London to sort everything out. The surplus land was eventually divided into seven parts, with Tucker retaining the section on which his house sat; the remainder was given to the church.

Across Somerset Bridge is the West End (*see* Tour 3: The West End, above). If you are traveling by bike or by moped, you can catch a ferry from Somerset Bridge back to Hamilton. Otherwise, take your choice of Middle, Harbour, or South Shore roads, to find your way back to the capital.

Bermuda for Free

Bermuda is an expensive vacation destination. The cost of lodging and food aside, however, many of the island attractions are free. Certainly, Bermuda's greatest attractions—the sea and its beaches—don't cost a penny, but there is also a host of historical sites and museums that don't charge admission fees. Large portions of the exploring tours in this guide can be enjoyed for a few dollars at most. During the low and shoulder seasons (October–April), the government and the Department of Tourism sponsor a whole range of free or inexpensive activities, from walking tours and house tours to fashion shows. Listed below are attractions described in the exploring tours and elsewhere that can be enjoyed for free.

Astwood Park (*see* Tour 4: The Parishes)
Beaches (*see* Chapter 5, Beaches and Water Sports)
Bermuda Public Library (*see* Tour 1: Hamilton)
Black Watch Well (*see* Tour 4: The Parishes)
Botanical Gardens (*see* Tour 4: The Parishes)
Cabinet Building and Sessions House (*see* Tour 1: Hamilton)
Camden (*see* Tour 4: The Parishes)
Carter House (*see* Tour 4: The Parishes)
City Hall (*see* Tour 1: Hamilton)

Featherbed Alley Printery (*see* Tour 2: The Town of St. George's)

Fort Hamilton (*see* Tour 1: Hamilton)

Gates Fort (*see* Tour 4: The Parishes)

Heydon Chapel (*see* Tour 3: The West End)

Old Rectory (*see* Tour 2: The Town of St. George's)

Par-la-Ville Park (*see* Tour 1: Hamilton)

St. Peter's Church (*see* Tour 2: The Town of St. George's)

Scaur Hill Fort (*see* Tour 3: The West End)

What to See and Do with Children

Bermuda is not an ideal vacation spot for children. Aside from the obvious attractions of surf and sand, Bermuda does not offer much in the way of fairs, amusement parks, or other diversions. Two books are available, however, that can make exploring the island with children much easier. The first, *The Bermuda Coloring Book*, by Diana Watlington Ruetenik, is an educational book with historical sites for small children to color. The second, *A Child's History of Bermuda*, by E. M. Rice, puts the island's history into words that are easy to understand. Both books are available at A. S. Cooper & Son (59 Front St., Hamilton, 809/295–3961). Listed below are some of the attractions in the exploring tours and elsewhere that will appeal to children.

Aquarium, Museum and Zoo (*see* Tour 4: The Parishes)

Beaches (*see* Chapter 5, Beaches and Water Sports)

Botanical Gardens (*see* Tour 4: The Parishes)

Ferries (*see* Getting Around Bermuda in Chapter 1, Essential Information)

Glass-bottom boat ride (*see* Guided Tours in Chapter 1, Essential Information)

Off the Beaten Track

The **Railway Trail** is a secluded 18-mile track that runs the length of the island along the route of the old Bermuda Railway. Restricted to pedestrians, horseback riders, and cyclists, the trail is a delightful way to see the island, away from the traffic and noise of the main roads. The Bermuda Department of Tourism has published *The Bermuda Railway Trail Guide*, which is available at all Visitors Service Bureaus and Information Centres. The pamphlet includes seven separate walking tours, ranging from about two to four hours, and an outline of what you can expect to see along the way. (For more information about sights along the way, refer to the appropriate section of the exploring tours, above. See also "Following in the Tracks of the Bermuda Railway," in Chapter 2, Portraits of Bermuda.) It should be noted that many of the trails are quite isolated, and none is heavily trafficked. Although Bermuda has no major crime problem, unpleasant incidents do sometimes occur; women travelers especially should avoid striking out on remote trails alone. Apart from reasons of safety, the Railway Trail is much more enjoyable shared with a companion.

The history of the railway that ran along this trail is fascinating. Aside from horse-drawn carriages, boats, and bikes, the Bermuda Railway—"Old Rattle and Shake" as it was called—was the primary means of transportation on the island from 1931 to 1948. As early as 1899, however, the Bermuda Public

Works Department bandied about proposals for a railroad. In 1922, over the objections of livery stable owners, the Bermuda Parliament finally granted permission for a narrow-gauge railroad to run from Somerset to St. George's.

The laying of the tracks was a formidable undertaking, requiring the construction of long tunnels and swing bridges. By the time it was finished in 1931, the railway had cost the investors $1 million. Mile for mile it was the most expensive railroad ever built, and the construction, which proceeded at a somnolent 2½ miles per year, was the slowest ever recorded. Nevertheless, on October 31, 1931, the little train got off to a roaring start with festive opening ceremonies at Somerset Bridge.

Passengers in the first-class carriages sat in wicker chairs, and the second-class cars were outfitted with benches. An American visitor reported in glowing terms of her first train ride in Bermuda, waxing lyrical about rolling cedar-covered hills, green velvet lawns, and banks of pink oleanders. Certainly, it was a vast improvement over the 19th-century horse buses that lumbered from Somerset to St. George's, carrying freight as well as passengers. Not everyone was happy, however. One writer groused that the train was "an iron serpent in the Garden of Eden." "Old Rattle and Shake" began going downhill during World War II. While the train was put to hard use by all the military personnel on the island, it proved impossible to obtain the necessary maintenance equipment. At the end of the war, the government acquired the distressed railway for £115,000. After the arrival of the automobile on Bermuda in 1946, the government sold the railway in its entirety to British Guiana (now Guyana).

Sightseeing Checklists

Historical Buildings and Sights

"Birdcage" (*see* Tour 1: Hamilton)
Black Watch Well (*see* Tour 4: The Parishes)
Bridge House (*see* Tour 2: The Town of St. George's)
Cabinet Building (*see* Tour 1: Hamilton)
Camden (*see* Tour 4: The Parishes)
Cenotaph (*see* Tour 1: Hamilton)
City Hall (*see* Tour 1: Hamilton)
Clermont (*see* Tour 4: The Parishes)
Deliverance II (*see* Tour 2: The Town of St. George's)
Featherbed Alley Printery (*see* Tour 2: The Town of St. George's)
Gibb's Hill Lighthouse (*see* Tour 4: The Parishes)
Government House (*see* Tour 4: The Parishes)
Old Rectory (*see* Tour 2: The Town of St. George's)
Old State House (*see* Tour 2: The Town of St. George's)
Palmetto House (*see* Tour 4: The Parishes)
Perot Post Office (*see* Tour 1: Hamilton)
Printer's Alley (*see* Tour 2: The Town of St. George's)
Royal Bermuda Yacht Club (*see* Tour 1: Hamilton)
Sessions House (*see* Tour 1: Hamilton)
St. David's Lighthouse (*see* Tour 4: The Parishes)
Tom Moore's Tavern (*see* Tour 4: The Parishes)
Town Hall (*see* Tour 2: The Town of St. George's)
White Horse Tavern (*see* Tour 2: The Town of St. George's)

Churches

Cathedral of the Most Holy Trinity (*see* Tour 1: Hamilton)
Christ Church (*see* Tour 4: The Parishes)
Heydon Chapel on the grounds of the Heydon Trust property (*see* Tour 3: The West End)
Holy Trinity Church (*see* Tour 4: The Parishes)
Old Devonshire Church (*see* Tour 4: The Parishes)
St. James Church (*see* Tour 3: The West End)
St. John's Church (*see* Tour 4: The Parishes)
St. Paul's (*see* Tour 4: The Parishes)
St. Peter's Church (*see* Tour 2: The Town of St. George's)
St. Theresa's Church (*see* Tour 1: Hamilton)
Unfinished Church (*see* Tour 2: The Town of St. George's)

Forts

Castle Island (*see* Tour 4: The Parishes)
Fort Hamilton (*see* Tour 1: Hamilton)
Fort St. Catherine (*see* Tour 4: The Parishes)
Gates Fort (*see* Tour 4: The Parishes)
Maritime Museum (*see* Tour 3: The West End)
Scaur Hill Fort (*see* Tour 3: The West End)
Warwick Camp (*see* Tour 4: The Parishes)
Whale Bay Fort (*see* Tour 4: The Parishes)

Museums and Galleries

Aquarium, Museum and Zoo (*see* Tour 4: The Parishes)
Bank of Bermuda (*see* Tour 1: Hamilton)
Bermuda Public Library and Museum of the Bermuda Historical Society (*see* Tour 1: Hamilton)
Carriage Museum (*see* Tour 2: The Town of St. George's)
Carter House (*see* Tour 4: The Parishes)
Confederate Museum (*see* Tour 2: The Town of St. George's)
Maritime Museum (*see* Tour 3: The West End)
St. George's Historical Society Museum (*see* Tour 2: The Town of St. George's)
Tucker House (*see* Tour 2: The Town of St. George's)
Verdmont (*see* Tour 4: The Parishes)

Parks and Gardens

Admiralty House Park (*see* Tour 4: The Parishes)
Astwood Park (*see* Tour 4: The Parishes)
Botanical Gardens (*see* Tour 4: The Parishes)
Gilbert Nature Reserve (*see* Tour 3: The West End)
Heydon Trust property (*see* Tour 3: The West End)
Lagoon Park (*see* Tour 3: The West End)
Long Bay Park and Nature Reserve (*see* Tour 3: The West End)
Paget Marsh (*see* Tour 4: The Parishes)
Palm Grove (*see* Tour 4: The Parishes)
Par-la-Ville Park (*see* Tour 1: Hamilton)
Somers Garden (*see* Tour 2: The Town of St. George's)
Spittal Pond (*see* Tour 4: The Parishes)
Victoria Park (*see* Tour 1: Hamilton)

5 Shopping

by Honey Naylor

If you're looking for colorful street markets where you can haggle over the price of low-cost goods and souvenirs, find another island. Shopping in Bermuda is characterized by sophisticated department stores and boutiques that stock top-quality—and expensive—merchandise. Cheap bargains are a rarity, and only products actually made in Bermuda (and antiques more than 100 years old) can be sold duty-free. If you're accustomed to shopping in Saks Fifth Avenue, Neiman-Marcus, and Bergdorf-Goodman, the prices in Bermuda's elegant shops won't come as a surprise. Actually, the prices on many items in Bermuda's stores are discounted, but a $600 dress discounted by 20% is still $480. But if you are looking for high-end merchandise, Bermuda does offer substantial savings on many items, particularly British-made clothing. Woolens and cashmere are good buys, especially in February when there is a host of sales during which many stores offer two-for-one sweater deals. Bermuda shorts are hot items, obviously, as are kilts.

European-made crystal and china—Wedgwood, Royal Crown Derby, Villeroy & Boch, Waterford, and Orrefors, to name a few—are available at prices at least 25% lower than those in the United States. Figurines from Lladro, Royal Doulton, and Hummel are also sold at significantly discounted prices. European fragrances and cosmetics are priced about 20%–25% less than in the United States, as are Rolex, Tissot, Patek Philippe, and other watches.

Bermuda has a thriving population of artists and artisans, whose work ranges from sculpture and paintings to miniature furniture, hand-blown glass, and dolls (*see* Arts and Crafts, below). Bermuda also has a number of noteworthy products to offer. Outerbridge's Sherry Peppers condiments add zip to soups, stews, drinks, and chowders. The original line has been expanded to include Bloody Mary mix, pepper jellies, and barbecue sauce; gift packs are available all over the island.

Bermuda rum is another popular item, and a variety of rum-based liqueurs is available, including Bermuda Banana, Banana Coconut Rum, and Bermuda Gold. Gosling's Black Seal Rum is excellent mixed with ginger beer to make a Dark 'n' Stormy, a famous Bermuda drink that should be treated with respect and caution. Rum is also found in quantity in Horton's Rum Cakes, which are made from a secret recipe and sold island-wide. U.S. citizens aged 21 or older, who have been out of the country for 48 hours, are allowed to bring home one liter of duty-free liquor each (*see* Customs and Duties in Chapter 1, Essential Information). In a bizarre catch-22, however, Bermuda requires a minimum purchase of two liters. Some liquor stores tell tourists that they must buy a minimum of four or five bottles to qualify for in-bond (duty-free) prices, but it isn't true. Although liquor prices are identical island-wide, some stores allow customers to create their own mixed packs of various liquors at in-bond prices, while others offer a selection of prepackaged sets (the five-pack is most common). Duty-free liquor must be purchased at least 24 hours before your departure, and it can be picked up only in the airport departure lounge or on board your cruise ship. The airport has no duty-free shop of its own. Below are some sample prices at press time for one liter of liquor: Tia Maria, $13.55; Grand Marnier, $20.40; Chivas Regal, $20.85; J&B Rare, $14.25; Johnnie Walker Black, $21.20;

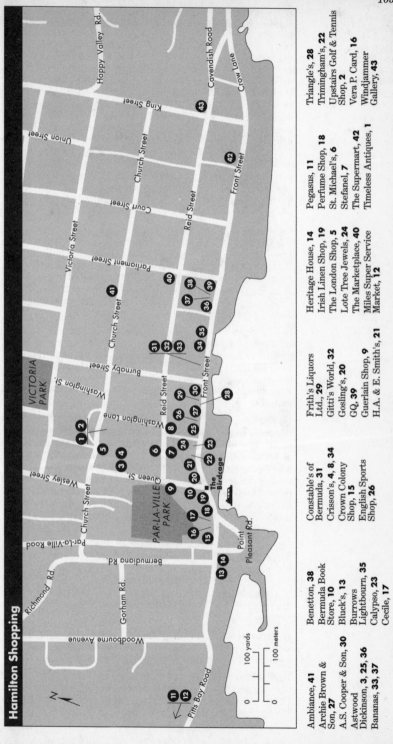

Hamilton Shopping

Ambiance, **41**
Archie Brown &
Son, **27**
A.S. Cooper & Son, **30**
Astwood
Dickinson, **3, 25, 36**
Bananas, **33, 37**

Benetton, **38**
Bermuda Book
Store, **10**
Bluck's, **13**
Burrows
Lightbourn, **35**
Calypso, **23**
Cecile, **17**

Constable's of
Bermuda, **31**
Crisson's, **4, 8, 34**
Crown Colony
Shop, **15**
English Sports
Shop, **26**

Frith's Liquors
Ltd, **29**
Gitti's World, **32**
Gosling's, **20**
GQ, **39**
Guerlain Shop, **9**
H.A. & E. Smith's, **21**

Heritage House, **14**
Irish Linen Shop, **19**
The London Shop, **5**
Lote Tree Jewels, **24**
The Marketplace, **40**
Miles Super Service
Market, **12**

Pegasus, **11**
Perfume Shop, **18**
St. Michael's, **6**
Stefanel, **7**
The Supermart, **42**
Timeless Antiques, **1**

Triangle's, **28**
Trimingham's, **22**
Upstairs Golf & Tennis
Shop, **2**
Vera P. Card, **16**
Windjammer
Gallery, **43**

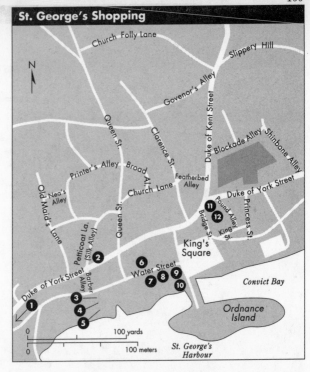

Stolichnaya vodka, $8.80; Beefeater gin, $12.15; and Bermuda rum, $7.

Comparison shopping is probably a waste of time in Bermuda because the merchants' association keeps prices almost identical island-wide. However, it's worth checking the price of items at home—especially crystal and china—before you embark on a shopping spree in Bermuda. Ask your local department store if any sales are scheduled and check the prices of designer and name-brand products at local factory outlets. Remember that Bermuda, unlike most U.S. states, has no sales tax, which means that the price on the tag is the price you pay.

Buildings and houses in Bermuda are numbered rather whimsically. If you check the phone directory for a store address, you may find a listing on Front Street or Water Street, for example, but no street number. To complicate matters further, some Front Street buildings have two numbers, one of them an old historic address that has nothing to do with the building's present location. Fortunately, almost all Bermudians can give you precise directions.

In general, shops are open Monday–Saturday 9–5 or 9–5:30. Some of the Front Street shops in Hamilton stay open until about 10:30 AM, and open on Sunday when cruise ships call.

In most cases in this chapter, if a store has several branches or outlets, only the main branch phone number has been listed. Unless otherwise noted the shops listed below accept American Express, MasterCard, and Visa.

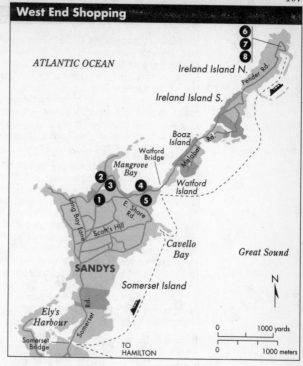

Shopping Districts

Hamilton boasts the greatest concentration of shops in Bermuda, and **Front Street** is its pièce de résistance. Lined with small, pastel-colored buildings, this most fashionable of Bermuda's streets houses sedate department stores and snazzy boutiques, with several small arcades and shopping alleys leading off it. **The Emporium** on Front Street, a renovated old building arranged around an open atrium, is home to an eclectic collection of dress and jewelry stores. The statue on top of the atrium fountain is of Bermudian Gina Swaison, who ruled as Miss World in 1979–80. **Windsor Place** is a new mall on Queen Street where customers can shop while taped classical music plays in the background.

In St. George's, **Water Street and Somers Wharf** are the site of numerous renovated buildings that now house boutiques and branches of Front Street stores. **King's Square** is also dotted with shops selling everything from dresses to sweaters and ties. In the West End, **Somerset Village** has a few shops, but they hardly merit a special shopping trip. Restoration continues on the 19th-century **Dockyard** area, however, where additions include a large split-level luxury mall. Dockyard is also home to the Craft Market, the Bermuda Arts Centre, and Island Pottery, where local artisans display their wares and visitors can sometimes watch them at work. Several other small plazas are sprinkled over the island, featuring a few shops, and often a grocery store and post office.

Department Stores

Bermuda's three leading department stores are A. S. Cooper &
Son, Trimingham's, and H. A. & E. Smith's, the main branches
of which are on Front Street in Hamilton. These elegant, venerable institutions are operated by the third or fourth generation of the families that founded them, and customers stand a
good chance of being waited on by a Cooper, a Trimingham, or a
Smith. In addition, many of the salespeople have worked at the
stores for two or three decades; they tend to be unobtrusive,
but polite and helpful when you need them.

A. S. Cooper & Son (59 Front St., Hamilton, tel. 809/295–3961)
is best known for Wedgwood bone china, which is sold exclusively on the island by this store. A five-piece place setting of
the Wedgwood strawberry-and-vine pattern costs $51.20, or
$64 (including duty, freight, and insurance) if you want it
shipped to the United States. Prices on other well-known
brands of china, as well as crystal, are similarly attractive. The
store's own private-label collection of clothing can be found in
the well-stocked men's and women's departments. Hungry
shoppers can head for The Balcony, a tiny pink-and-white restaurant just off the second floor that has a magnificent view of
the harbor. Open Monday–Friday from noon to 2, The Balcony
serves quiches, salads, and sandwiches. Other branches of the
department store can be found in all major hotels and in St.
George's at 22 Water Street.

H. A. & E. Smith's (35 Front St., Hamilton, tel. 809/295–2288),
founded in 1889 by Henry Archibald and Edith Smith, is
arguably the best men's store in Bermuda—and exclusive
agents for Burberry and Alan Paine. Burberry raincoats are
priced from $295 to $495, and Alan Paine cable-knit sweaters
sell for about $375; a Chester Barrie cashmere jacket costs
around $650. You can buy Harris Tweed jackets for $175 and
Italian silk ties for $12. There is a large selection of Shetland
sweaters, which go for about $30 each. Smith's is also a good
place to buy kilts. Ladies can find Christian Dior handbags for
about $300, but the store also stocks Bermuda bags—the kinds
with the detachable cedar handle and interchangeable cloth
satchel—for about $30. Ladies' cashmere-lined leather gloves
cost $65 (unlined $45). Unfortunately, the store's confusing
layout makes it easy to get lost. The staff here is especially gen-
teel, however, and they will help orient you. Branches can be
found in the Belmont and Southampton Princess hotels and at
18 York Street in St. George's.

St. Michael's (7 Reid St., Hamilton, tel. 809/295–0031), an offshoot of Britain's Marks & Spencer, is called Marks and Sparks
by everyone in Bermuda. This large store is usually filled with
thrift-minded Britons attracted by its moderate prices for
men's, women's, and children's clothing. Summer wear, including swimsuits, cotton jerseys, and polo shirts, is a good buy.
High-quality men's and women's cashmere and woolen sweaters are also sold at substantial discounts.

Trimingham's (37 Front St., Hamilton, tel. 809/295–1183) has
been a Hamilton fixture since 1842. The first store in the world
to tailor madras for Western clothing, this is the place to look
for men's colorful madras blazers and trousers. The store also
has its own line of sportswear, and Bermuda shorts are good
buys. In womenswear, savings can be found on Shetland and

lamb's wool sweaters, but prices for Dean's of Scotland woolens
are about the same, or even a bit less, in the United States. Liberty of London and Hermès scarves are definitely worth a look.
The store has an impressive display of perfumes and cosmetics,
and it is the exclusive Bermuda distributor for Tiffany and
Boucheron fragrances. La Prairie, the beauty treatment from
Montreux, is discounted by about 20%. Head for the excellent
gift boutique to buy Outerbridge's Sherry Pepper Sauce or a
box of Trimingham's hand-baked assorted cookies. Trimingham branches have sprouted up all over the island, including at
Somers Wharf in St. George's and in Somerset Village.

Grocery Stores

Most of the accommodation on Bermuda, from cottage colonies
to guest houses and housekeeping apartments, offers guests
the opportunity to do their own cooking. Self-catering vacations are cheaper than those where you pay full board or dine
out at every meal; considering how expensive Bermuda is, this
option has widespread appeal for both families and budget
travelers. Don't expect the same prices as at home, however—
foodstuffs in Bermuda are also quite expensive. For example, a
dozen large eggs costs $2.30, a six-pack of Coke is $4.10, a
pound of Maxwell House coffee $4.50, and a quart of Tropicana
orange juice $3.10 (a local brand is slightly cheaper). Listed be-
low are some of the major supermarkets in Bermuda.

A-1 Fine Food Market (South Shore Rd., Paget, tel. 809/236–
0351) features a take-out counter that serves inexpensive
($6–$9) chicken dinners, French fries, burgers, hot dogs, and
sandwiches. The store is near Barnsdale Guest Apartments
and the Sky Top Cottages, but you will need a vehicle to carry
heavy groceries up the hill.

The Friendly Store (Middle Rd., Warwick, tel. 809/236–1344) is
a medium-size convenience store within walking distance of the
Pretty Penny guest house.

Harrington Hundreds Grocery & Liquor Store (South Rd.,
Smith's, tel. 809/293–1635) is near Spittal Pond, not far from
Angel's Grotto apartments; it may be too far to walk, however.

The Marketplace (Reid St., near Parliament St., Hamilton, tel.
809/292–3163) is part of a moderately priced chain with stores
around the island. Customers can get hot soups to go.

Miles Market (Pitts Bay Rd., near The Princess, Hamilton, tel.
809/295–1234) has expensive steaks and Häagen-Dazs ice
cream. The market makes deliveries anywhere on the island.

The Supermart (Front St., near King St., Hamilton, tel.
809/292–2064) has a well-stocked salad bar, prepackaged sandwiches, and hot coffee. This store and Miles Market are a five-
minute ferry ride across the harbor from the Greenbank Cottages and Salt Kettle House.

Specialty Stores

Antiques **Heritage House** (2 W. Front St., Hamilton, tel. 809/295–2615).
Browsers will find it difficult to tear themselves away from this
small shop, which features an array of both antique and modern
pieces. Among the antiques recently featured were a 17th-cen-
tury chest for $9,000, an 18th-century harp for $2,250, a 19th-

century sewing machine for $277, and a six-piece Royal Worcester demitasse set priced at $575. Staffordshire silver is usually available, too; a Spode plate goes for about $75. The shop is also home to the Litchfield Collection, a fascinating array of tall ships in glass bottles, including a beautiful model of HMS *Victory* (Admiral Nelson's ship) for $325. The original works of several local artists are also on display. Shoppers who don't want to make a major purchase can search through bins of prints. The shop has its own framing department.

Pegasus (63 Pitts Bay Rd., Hamilton, tel. 809/295–2900). A Dickensian place with creaky wood floors, this store has racks and racks of antique prints and maps. In particular, look for the "Spy" *Vanity Fair* caricatures from the late 19th and early 20th centuries ($10–$100) and the Dickens characters by 19th-century artist Frederick Barnard ($50–$100). Among the antique maps are some 18th-century representations of the United States priced at $300, and others showing the castles of Ireland, Scotland, and England. There are several racks of children's books (about $4) by British authors, as well as a good selection of postcards. Shoppers can browse here to their hearts' content. Diners Club cards are accepted here in addition to those credit cards mentioned above.

Timeless Antiques (26 Church St., Hamilton, tel. 809/295–5008). Across the street and down the steps from City Hall, you'll find this small, Old World shop, where the walls are lined with 200- to 300-year-old grandfather (or long-case) clocks. Among the store's collection of antiques are carved Early English oak tables, chests, chairs, candelabra, and exquisite reproductions of medieval tapestries. Time is of the essence here, however, and clock aficionados will want to spend hours talking with proprietor Peter Durhager. If $8,000 for a long-case clock is a little too rich for your blood, take a look at the collection of antique pocket watches.

Arts and Crafts
Artists

Buying artwork by someone you know is always more satisfying than buying it blind, and some of Bermuda's resident artists encourage visits to their studios. Call ahead first, however, to find out if it's convenient to stop by, and be sure to check which credit cards each artist accepts. Remember that there are no duties levied on Bermudian arts and crafts.

Celia and Jack Arnell (tel. 809/236–4646). The miniature cedar furniture crafted by this husband-and-wife team is displayed in a dollhouse at the Craft Market (*see* below). The fine details on the breakfronts and chests of drawers include tiny metal drawer knobs, and the wonderful four-poster bed comes complete with a canopy. A breakfront sells for $140; the four-poster bed for $100; and chairs for $27.

Kathleen Kemsley Bell (tel. 809/236–3366). A director of the Bermuda Arts Centre, Ms. Bell creates exquisite dolls of a particular person or period in Bermuda's history. Each doll is researched for historical accuracy and is unique. The bodies are sculpted of papier-mâché and hand-painted. The faces of the dolls are marvelously expressive, and the costumes are all hand-stitched. The base of each doll is signed and carries a description of the historical period on which the doll's fashions are based. Ms. Bell works on commission and will visit your hotel with samples of her work. Prices start at $185.

Alfred Birdsey Studio ("Stowe Hill," Paget, tel. 809/236–6658). An island institution, Mr. Birdsey is a recipient of the Queen's Certificate of Honour and Medal in recognition of "valuable services given to Her Majesty for more than 40 years as an artist of Bermuda." His watercolors of Bermuda hang in the Bank of Bermuda and Cambridge Beaches cottage colony, as well as in the building at 2 Wall Street in New York. His studio is open weekdays 9–5.

Liz Campbell (tel. 809/236–8539). Lovely stained-glass butterflies, mirrors, panels, and boxes created by Ms. Campbell are displayed at the Dockyard Craft Market (*see* below). Prices range from $30 to about $200 for larger, more elaborate pieces.

Ronnie Chameau (tel. 809/292–1387). Ms. Chameau creates Christmas angels and dolls from dried palm, banana, and grapefruit leaves gathered from her yard. The 9-inch dolls ($35), with palmetto leaf baskets and hats, Spanish moss hair, and pecan heads with painted faces, are intended as table ornaments, while the dainty little 4-inch angels ($5–$20) are designed to hang on the Christmas tree. The angels and dolls are available year-round at Trimingham's (*see* above) and at Carole Holding's studio in St. George's (*see* below).

Joan Forbes (Art House, South Shore Rd., Paget, tel. 809/236–6746). Watercolors and lithographs are the specialty of Ms. Forbes, whose work focuses on Bermudian architecture, horticulture, and seascapes. Her lithographs sell for $10–$45. She also produces cards, notepaper, and envelopes.

Desmond Fountain (tel. 809/292–3955). This award-winning sculptor's works are on display all over the island, whether it's a life-size bronze statue perched beside a lagoon or a lolling figure seated in a garden chair. Fountain created the *Land Ho!* statue of Sir George Somers on Ordnance Island in St. George's, and other of his works can be seen in the Sculpture Gallery on the mezzanine of the Southampton Princess. Prices start at about $5,000 for a small bronze and soar to dizzying heights.

Carole Holding Studio (3 Featherbed Alley, St. George's, tel. 809/297–1833, after hours 809/236–6002). Ms. Holding uses pastel watercolors to paint the flowers and homes of Bermuda. In addition to her own watercolors, signed prints, and limited editions, her studio displays works, including cedar crafts, by local artists. Housed in the slave quarters of an 18th-century home that now serves as the St. George's Historical Society, Holding's studio is open to the public Monday–Saturday 10–4.

Graeme Outerbridge (tel. 809/238–2411). A photographer who contributed to the acclaimed *Day in the Life* book series, Mr. Outerbridge captures Bermuda in original photographic prints, silk screens, and posters.

Mary Zuill (10 Southlyn La., Paget, tel. 809/236–2439). In a tiny studio attached to her house, Ms. Zuill paints delightful watercolors of Bermuda's flowers, alleyways, and cottages. She accepts commissions and will either design a painting or work from a photograph you've taken in Bermuda. Original watercolors cost from $60 to $600. She welcomes visitors Tuesday–Friday from April to November only.

Galleries and Crafts Shops **Bermuda Arts Centre** (Dockyard, Ireland Island, tel. 809/234–2809). Sleek and modern, with well-designed displays of local art, this gallery is housed in one of the stone buildings of the former naval yard. The walls are adorned with pictures and photographs, and glass display cases contain costume dolls, jewelry, and other crafts. Visitors are provided with a printed list with descriptions and prices of the various works. Changing exhibits are frequently held.

Bermuda Glass-Blowing Studio & Show Room (Blue Hole Hill, Hamilton Parish, tel. 809/293–2234). A Bermuda cottage in the Bailey's Bay area houses this glassblower's studio. Glass plates, bowls, cups, and ornaments are created here in vibrant, swirling colors. Prices range from $15 to more than $200. Shoppers can watch glassblowers at work daily.

Bridge House Gallery (1 Bridge St., St. George's, tel. 809/297–8211). Housed in a Bermuda mansion that dates to 1700, this gallery is of historical and architectural interest in its own right. In the 18th century, the two-story white building was the home of Bermuda's governors; today it is maintained by the Bermuda National Trust. Displayed amid 18th- and 19th-century furnishings are works of Bermudian artists: original paintings, hand-blown glass, Bermuda costume dolls, antique bottles and maps, jewelry, and books.

Craft Market (Dockyard, Ireland Island, tel. 809/234–3208). Occupying part of what was once the cooperage, this large stone building dates to 1831. Although some lovely work is to be found here—miniature cedar furniture, stained glass, and costume dolls, in particular—the displays are poorly arranged on simple wooden tables and in drab booths. As a result, even high-quality work seems unimpressive.

Island Pottery (Dockyard, Ireland Island, tel. 809/234–3361). This workshop establishment takes up a single room in a large stone building. A counter separates the workshop from the gift shop in the front of the room, where crude tables and shelves are piled with ashtrays, bowls, and vases. Behind the counter, artisans in aprons and work clothes toil over potter's wheels.

Windjammer Gallery (King and Reid Sts., Hamilton, tel. 809/292–7861). A cluttered, three-room shop on the ground floor of a small cottage, this is the place to go to find out about upcoming art shows. The staff can help you choose from the huge range of prints, lithographs, oils, watercolors, and photographs that fill the walls and bins. Jewelry and sculpture—most notably by Desmond Fountain—are also on display.

Bookstores   **Bermuda Book Store** (Queen and Front Sts., Hamilton, tel. 809/295–3698). Book lovers, beware! Once you set foot inside this musty old place, you'll have a hard time tearing yourself away. Stacked on a long table are a host of books about Bermuda. Proprietor Jim Zuill, whose father wrote the acclaimed *Bermuda Journey*, can probably answer any questions you have about the island.

Boutiques   **Ambiance** (Armoury Bldg., Reid St., Hamilton, tel. 809/292–4132). Ladies who like hats should head for this tiny shop. Prices average around $75.

Archie Brown & Son (49 Front St., Hamilton, tel. 809/295–2928). Top-quality woolens, Pringle of Scotland cashmeres, Shetland and lamb's wool sweaters, and 100% wool tartan kilts are among the specialties at this store.

Bananas (93 W. Front St., 7 E. Front St., Hamilton, and 3 King's Sq., St. George's, tel. 809/295–1106 or 809/292–7268). Sportswear and T-shirts make this place a teenager's dream. Brightly colored Bermuda umbrellas cost about $25.

Benetton (95 Front St., Hamilton, tel. 809/292–5878). In this link in the ever-lengthening Italian chain are colorful Benetton fashions at prices considerably lower than in the United States.

Calypso (45 Front St., Hamilton, tel. 809/295–2112). Available only in Bermuda, owner Polly Hornburg's ladies' fashions are created from splashy fabrics imported from Europe, India, and Africa. Her casually elegant dresses sell for $145 and more. The store has an exclusive arrangement to sell Louis Vuitton merchandise in Bermuda. Expect to shell out $180 for a small wallet; $1,145 for an attaché case.

Cecile (15 Front St., Hamilton, tel. 809/295–1311). Specializing in upscale off-the-rack ladies' fashions, this shop carries designer labels such as Ciao and Ciaosports, Nina Ricci, Geiger of Austria, and Louis Feraud of Paris. There's a good selection of swimwear, too, including swimsuits by Gottex.

Constable's of Bermuda (Emporium, Front St., Hamilton, tel. 809/295–8060). Icelandic woolen clothing is the specialty of this store, and prices are generally 30%–50% lower than those in the United States. This is *the* place to come for heavy woolen coats, ski sweaters, ponchos, jackets, and skirts in smoky colors. Travel blankets are also a hot item.

Cow Polly (Somers Wharf, St. George's, tel. 809/297–1514). Phoebe and Sam Wharton's store is an upscale novelty shop that carries only imported items. You won't find their unusual pottery, jewelry, or men's ties sold anywhere else on the island.

English Sports Shop (95 Front St., Hamilton, tel. 809/295–2672). Bermuda has several branches of this store, which specializes in British woolens: Harris Tweed jackets for men cost $175, while Shetland woolen sweaters are priced at $45; more expensive cashmere sweaters go for $99. The Crown Colony Shop (1 Front St., Hamilton, tel. 809/295–3935), a branch of the store that focuses on women's clothing, sells Lady Clansmen Scottish Shetland sweaters for $45 and silk dresses made in Hong Kong for about $300.

Frangipani (Water St., St. George's, tel. 809/297–1357). Exotic men's and women's clothing from Greece and Indonesia give this little shop a distinctly non-Bermudian feel. Colorful cotton sweaters from Greece come in more than 100 designs. The shop also has a collection of unusual jewelry.

Gitti's World (Emporium, Front St., Hamilton, tel. 809/295–8056). This tiny, rather inconspicuous boutique is a real find. It's overflowing with modestly priced hand-embroidered blouses, beaded sweaters, sequined evening bags, and tie-dyed dresses. Casual cottons cost $30; cocktail dresses are about $60. The shop also has a collection of chunky costume jewelry and children's dresses and sleepwear for about $15.

GQ (99 Front St., Hamilton, tel. 809/292–7703). Rap and rock music attract a trendy young crowd to this small boutique, which stocks the latest fashions from Smak and Williwear, Italian shoes, knit suits, high-quality leather jackets (around $275), and jazzy cocktail dresses.

The London Shop (22 Church St., Hamilton, tel. 809/295–1279). This small, cluttered shop has shelves piled high with Pierre Cardin dress shirts for about $35 and sweaters for $45. Countess Mara short-sleeve sport shirts are priced at $19, and herringbone caps cost $35.

Stefanel (12 Reid St., Hamilton, tel. 809/295–5698). This very smart, very expensive boutique stocks the snazzy cotton knits of Italian trendsetter Carlo Stefanel. Imported from Italy, the clothing includes men's cotton and linen suits and cotton dress shirts; women's patterned wool skirts with handknit, contrasting jackets; and children's sweaters and sweats.

Triangle's (55 Front St., Hamilton, tel. 809/292–1990). The star attractions of this boutique are Diane Freis's original, colorful, and crushable mosaic dresses, priced between $220 and $260—almost half what they cost in the United States.

Upstairs Golf & Tennis Shop (26 Church St., Hamilton, tel. 809/295–5161). As befits Bermuda's role as a golfing paradise, this store stocks clubs and accessories from some of the best brands available including Hogan, Ping, MacGregor, and Spalding. Tennis players can choose a racquet by Head, Wilson, Square Two, or Nike. Men's and women's sportswear is also available.

Crystal, China, and Porcelain **Bluck's** (4 W. Front St., Hamilton, tel. 809/295–5367). A dignified establishment that has been in business for more than 140 years, this is the only store on the island devoted exclusively to the sale of crystal and china. Royal Doulton, Royal Copenhagen, Villeroy & Boch, Herend, Lalique, Minton, Waterford, Baccarat, and others are displayed on two floors. The courteous staff will provide you with price lists upon request. As an example, a five-piece place setting of Limoges Roulette costs $119.75, while eight place settings of Hermès Peonies are priced at $1,587.

Vera P. Card (11 Front St., Hamilton, and 9 Water St., St. George's, tel. 809/295–1729). Lladro and Royal Doulton's "Reflections" figurines are widely available all over the island at almost identical prices, but this store has the most extensive selection. The shop's collection of Hummel figurines is, without a doubt, the best on the island.

Jewelry **Astwood Dickinson** (83–85 Front St., Windsor Pl. on Queen St., and Walker Arcade, Hamilton, tel. 809/292–5805). In addition to 18-karat gold Omega watches that sell for $7,125, this store carries less expensive items such as Le Clip Swiss quartz watches ($35) and alarm Le Clips ($60). Most interesting of all, however, is the store's Bermuda Collection of 18-karat gold mementos that sell for $50–$600. The collection includes the Bermuda dinghy pendant for $300 (earrings are $230); a tall ship pin or pendant for $600; a Bermuda Island pendant for $50; and a Gibb's Hill Lighthouse tie-pin for $150.

Crisson's (71 Front St., 20 Reid St., Hamilton, and five other locations, tel. 809/295–2351). The exclusive Bermuda agent for Rolex, Cartier, and Raymond Weil, this upscale establishment offers discounts of 20%–25% on expensive merchandise, but don't expect to find cheap Timex or Swatch watches. The gift department carries English flatware, Saint Louis crystal, and imported baubles, bangles, and beads.

Lote Tree Jewels (Walker Arcade, Hamilton, tel. 809/292–8525). Opened by owner Mary Walker in 1980 to showcase her own Marybeads—14-karat gold beads intertwined with semi-precious gems or freshwater pearls—the shop now emphasizes ethnic jewelry from around the world: African trade beads combined with tooled silver beads from Afghanistan, Bali, and India; and handmade, hand-painted Peruvian clay beads strung with hand-carved stone beads from Ecuador. There are baskets of bangles from Burkina Faso, Mali, and Kenya; a "jungle collection" that includes tortoise twin combs and hair bows; and tribal jewelry from Afghanistan that features lapis lazuli and silver chokers, earrings, rings, and brooches. Marybeads are still available—a 14-karat necklace sells for $495.

Linens **Irish Linen Shop** (31 Front St., Hamilton, tel. 809/295–4089; Cambridge Rd., Somerset, tel. 809/234–0127). In a cottage that looks as though it belongs in Dublin, the Hamilton branch is *the* place for Irish linen double damask tablecloths. Prices range from $38 to $410 (not including napkins), although antique tablecloths can cost as much as $1,600. From Madeira come exquisite hand-embroidered handkerchiefs ($17); cotton and organdy pillowcases; and a cotton organdy christening robe with slip and bonnet, hand embroidered with garlands and tiers of Valenciennes lace ($210). Pure linen hand-rolled handkerchiefs from Belgium with Belgian lace are priced under $20, while Le Jacquard Français cotton kitchen towels cost less than $10. The shop's Bermuda Cottage Collection includes quilted place mats, tea cozies, and pot holders—most for less than $12. The store has an exclusive arrangement with Souleiado, maker of the vivid prints from Provence that are available in skirts, dresses, place mats, bags, as well as by the yard.

Liquors and Liqueurs The following liquor stores sell at identical prices, and each will allow you to put together your own package of Bermuda liquors at in-bond (duty-free) prices: **Burrows Lightbourn** (Front St., Hamilton, tel. 809/295–0176), **Frith's Liquors Ltd.** (57 Front St., Hamilton, tel. 809/295–3544), **Gosling's** (33 Front St., Hamilton, tel. 809/295–1123).

Perfumes **Bermuda Perfumery** (212 North Shore Rd., Bailey's Bay, tel. 809/293–0627 or 800/527–8213). This highly promoted perfumery is on all the taxi-tour itineraries. Guided tours of the facilities are given continuously, during which you can see how the fragrances of flowers are distilled into perfume and take a walk through the ornamental gardens. At the Cobweb gift shop you can purchase the factory's Lili line of fragrances.

The **Perfume Shop** (23 W. Front St., Hamilton, tel. 809/295–0570) and the **Guerlain Shop** (19 Queen St., Hamilton, tel. 809/295–5535 and 6 Water St., St. George's, tel. 809/297–1525), which is the exclusive agent for Guerlain products, stock more than 127 lines of French and Italian fragrances, as well as soaps, bath salts, and bubble bath.

6 Beaches and Water Sports

Introduction

by Peter Oliver

*Peter Oliver is a
New York–based
freelance writer,
specializing in
sports and the
outdoors. His
articles have
appeared in*
Backpacker, The
New York Times,
Skiing, *and*
Travel-Holiday.

Bermuda boasts that it has "water scientifically proven to be
the clearest in the western Atlantic." Whether this is true or
not, the water is certainly clear enough to make Bermuda one
of the world's great centers for snorkeling and scuba diving.
Clear water also gives fishermen a distinct advantage—a fish
has almost nowhere to hide in the island's shallow, translucent
water. For whatever reasons, however, the water around Bermuda was apparently *not* clear enough to allow many ship
captains to see the barrier reefs encircling the island.
Consequently, the reefs today are a veritable smorgasbord of
marine wreckage, guaranteed to whet the appetite of any diving enthusiast. Some wrecks are in less than 30 feet of water
and are accessible even to snorkelers. The reefs also help keep
the water close to shore relatively calm, acting as a fortress
wall against the pounding swells of the Atlantic and reducing
beach erosion. And Bermuda's beaches are definitely worth
saving—fine-grain sand tinted pink with crushed coral. But
Bermuda's reefs remain as dangerous as ever. Boat rentals are
available at several island locations, but only the most experienced yachtsmen should venture beyond the safe waters of
Great Sound, Harrington Sound, and Castle Harbour. To go
anywhere else without a full knowledge of Bermuda's considerable offshore hazards is pure folly.

Thanks to Bermuda's position close to the Gulf Stream, the water stays warm year-round, although Bermudians consider
anything under 75°F frigid. In summer, the ocean is usually
above 80°F, and even warmer in the shallows between the reefs
and shore. In winter, the water temperature only occasionally
drops below 70°F, but it seems cooler because the air temperature is usually in the mid-60s—a wet suit is recommended for
anyone who plans to spend an extended period of time in the
water. Lack of business, more than a drop in water temperature, is responsible for the comparative dearth of water-sports
activity during the winter months. The winter does tend to be
windier, however, which means water conditions can be less
than ideal. Rough water creates problems anchoring or stabi-
lizing fishing and diving boats, and visibility underwater is often clouded by sand and debris. High season runs from April
through October, during which time fishing, diving, and yacht
charters fill up quickly. Most boats carry fewer than 20 passengers, so it's advisable to sign up early. March–April and
October–November are shoulder seasons, and December–
February is the off-season, when many operators close to make
repairs and perform routine maintenance. During these
months, a few operators stay open on a limited basis, scheduling charters only when there are enough people to fill a boat; if
too few people sign up, the charter is canceled. For this reason,
water-sports enthusiasts have to be flexible during the winter
months.

Take advantage of the activities director at your hotel or your
ship's cruise director—he or she can make arrangements for
you long before you arrive. The **"Sportsman's Guide,"** a 24-page
booklet available free from the Bermuda Department of Tourism (*see* Chapter 1, Essential Information), has extensive listings and information on all water sports in Bermuda; it's worth
obtaining a copy before you make any plans.

Water Sports

Boating and Sailing

Visitors to Bermuda can either rent their own boat or charter a boat with a skipper. Rental boats, which are 17 feet at most, range from sailboats (typically tiny Sunfish) to motorboats (typically 13-foot Boston Whalers), glass-bottom boats, kayaks, and pedal boats. Such vessels are ideal for exploring the coves and harbors of the sounds or, in the case of motorboats, waterskiing. In **Great Sound,** several small islands, such as Hawkins Island and Long Island, have tiny secluded beaches that are usually empty during the week. If the wind is fresh, the islands are about a half hour's sail from **Hamilton Harbour** or **Salt Kettle.** These beaches are wonderful places to have a picnic, although many are privately owned and visitors are not always welcome. Check with the boat-rental operator before planning an island outing.

The trade winds pass well to the south of Bermuda, so the island does not have predictable air currents. Channeled by islands and headlands, the winds around Hamilton Harbour and the Great Sound can be particularly unpredictable; **Mangrove Bay** has far more reliable breezes. The variability of the winds has no doubt aided the education of Bermuda's racing skippers, who are traditionally among the world's best. To the casual sailor, however, wind changes can be troublesome, although you can be fairly confident you won't be becalmed: The average summer breeze is 10–15 knots, usually out of the south or southwest. Encircled by land, **Harrington Sound** has the calmest water, ideal for novice sailors, pedal boaters, and waterskiers. Anyone wanting a small taste of open water should head for **Pompano Marina** (Pompano Beach Club, Southampton, tel. 809/234–0222) on the western ocean shore.

Boat Rentals Rates for small powerboats range between $25 and $35 an hour, or about $110 for a full day; sailboat rentals cost $12–$20 an hour, or $50–$80 for a full day. A refundable deposit of about $50 is usually required. Several of the larger hotels, such as **Marriott's Castle Harbour Resort** (Paynters Rd., Hamilton Parish, tel. 809/293–2040), the **Sonesta Beach Hotel & Spa** (Sinky Bay Rd., Southampton, tel. 809/238–8122), and the **Southampton Princess** (off South Rd., Southampton, tel. 809/238–8000) have their own fleets of rental boats. Otherwise, the best places for renting sailboats or powerboats are **Grotto Bay Water Sports** (Grotto Bay Hotel, 11 Blue Hole Hill, Hamilton Parish, tel. 809/293–8333, ext. 37), **Mangrove Marina** (Cambridge Rd., Sandys, tel. 809/234–0914), **Robinson's Marina** (Somerset Bridge, Sandys, tel. 809/234–0709), and **Salt Kettle Boat Rentals** (off Harbour Rd., Salt Kettle Rd., Paget, tel. 809/236–4863).

Charter Boats More than 20 large power cruisers and sailing vessels, piloted by local skippers, are available for charter. Typically between 35 and 50 feet long, charter sailboats can carry up to 18 passengers, with overnight accommodations available in some cases. Meals and drinks can be included on request, and a few skippers offer dinner cruises for the romantically inclined. Rates generally range between $225 and $300 for a half-day cruise, or $350–$600 for a full-day cruise, with additional per-person charges for large groups. Where you go and what you do—exploring, swimming, snorkeling, cruising—is up to you and your skipper. In most cases, cruises travel to and around the islands of Great Sound. Several charter skippers advertise year-round operations, but the off-season (December–February) schedule can be haphazard. Skippers devote periods of the off-season to maintenance and repairs or close altogether if bookings lag. Be sure to book well in advance. A full listing of charter-boat operators is included in the "Sportsman's Guide," available from the Bermuda Department of Tourism (*see* Chapter 1, Essential Information).

Diving

Bermuda has all the ingredients necessary for classic scuba diving—reefs, wreckage, underwater caves, a variety of coral and marine life, and clear, warm water. Although diving is possible year-round, the best months are May–October, when the water is calmest and warmest. No prior certification is necessary; novices can learn the basics and be diving in water up to 25 feet deep on the same day. The easiest day trips, offered by **South Side Scuba** (Sonesta Beach Hotel, Sinky Bay Rd., Southampton, tel. 809/238–1833) and **Nautilus Diving Ltd.** (Southampton Princess Hotel, off South Rd., Southampton, tel. 809/238–2332), involve exploring the south-shore reefs that lie close inshore. These reefs may be the most dramatic in Bermuda: In places, the oceanside drop-off exceeds 60 feet, and the coral is so honeycombed with caves, ledges, and holes that exploratory possibilities are infinite. Also infinite are the chances of becoming lost in this coral labyrinth, so it is important to stick with your guide. Despite concerns in recent years about dying coral and fish depletion, most of Bermuda's reefs are still in good health—anyone eager to swim with multicolored schools of fish or the occasional barracuda will not be disappointed. In the interest of preservation, however, the removal of coral or coral objects is illegal.

Prominently displayed in any dive shop in Bermuda is a map of nautical carnage, showing the outlying reef system and wreck sites. The map shows 38 wrecks spanning three centuries, but these are only the larger wrecks that are still in good condition. There are reportedly more than 300 wreck sites in all, many of them well preserved. As a general rule, the more recent the wreck or the more deeply submerged it is, the better its condition. Most of the well-preserved wrecks are to the north and east, and dive depths range between 25 and 80 feet. Several wrecks off the western end of the island are in relatively shallow water—30 feet or less—making them accessible to novice divers and even snorkelers. The major dive operator for wrecks on the western side of the island is **Blue Water Divers Ltd.** (Robinson's Marina, Somerset Bridge, Sandys, tel. 809/234–1034); for wrecks off the east coast, contact **Grotto Bay Diving** (Grotto Bay Beach Hotel, 11 Blue Hole Hill, Hamilton Parish, tel. 809/293–2915). Costs range from $45 for a one-tank dive to $70 for introductory dives for novices or two-tank dives for experienced divers. With two tanks, divers can explore two or more wrecks during the same four-hour outing. Rates usually include all equipment—mask, fins, snorkel, scuba apparatus, and wet suit (if necessary). Some operators also offer night dives.

Beaches and Water Sports

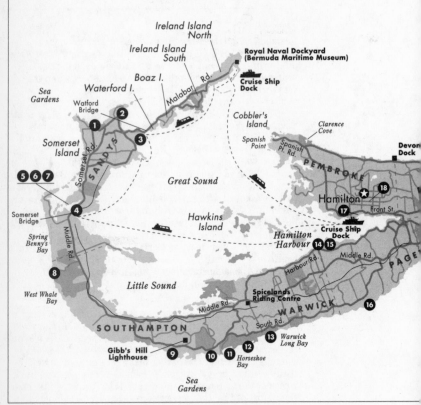

ATLANTIC OCEAN

Ireland Island North

Ireland Island South

Boaz I.

Waterford I.

Royal Naval Dockyard
(Bermuda Maritime Museum)

Cruise Ship Dock

Sea Gardens

Watford Bridge

Cobbler's Island

Clarence Cove

Spanish Point

Devonshire Dock

Somerset Island

Great Sound

Hamilton

PEMBROKE

Front St.

Somerset Bridge

Hawkins Island

Hamilton Harbour

Cruise Ship Dock

Middle Rd.

Spring Benny's Bay

Harbour Rd.

PAGET

West Whale Bay

Little Sound

Spicelands Riding Centre

WARWICK

Middle Rd.

South Rd.

Warwick Long Bay

SOUTHAMPTON

Gibb's Hill Lighthouse

Horseshoe Bay

Sea Gardens

Beaches
Chaplin Bay, **12**
Elbow Beach Hotel, **16**
Horseshoe Bay Beach, **11**
John Smith's Bay, **21**
St. Catherine Beach, **27**
Shelley Bay Beach, **19**
Somerset Long Bay, **1**
Tobacco Bay Beach, **26**
Warwick Long Bay, **13**

Water Sports
A & J Watersports, **20**
Bermuda Waterski Centre, **5**
Bermuda Water Skiing, **22**
Bermuda Water Tours Ltd., **17**
Blue Hole Water Sports, **24**
Blue Water Divers Ltd., **7**

Fly Bridge Tackle, **18**
Greg Hartley's Under Sea Adventure, **3**
Mangrove Marina, **2**
Grotto Bay Diving, **23**
Nautilus Diving Ltd., **10**
Pitman's Snorkelling, **4**
Pompano Marina, **8**
Robinson's Marina, **6**

Salt Kettle Boat Rentals, **15**
South Side Scuba, **9**
Tobacco Bay Beach House, **25**
Watlington's Windsurfing Bermuda, **14**

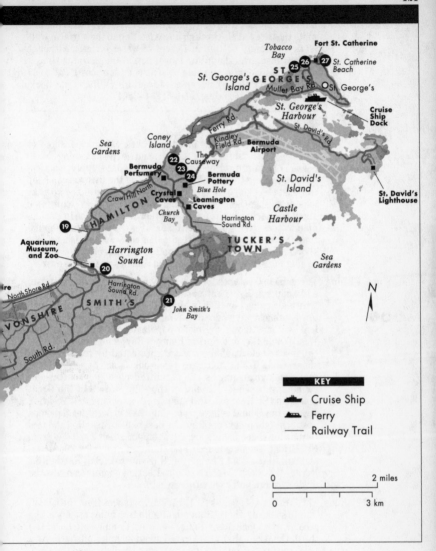

Tobacco Bay
Fort St. Catherine
25 26 27 *St. Catherine Beach*
St. George's Island
ST. GEORGE'S ISLAND
Mullet Bay Rd. St. George's
St. George's Harbour
Cruise Ship Dock
Sea Gardens
Coney Island
Ferry Rd.
Kindley Field Rd.
St. David's Rd.
22
The Causeway
23
Bermuda Perfumery 24 **Bermuda Pottery**
Blue Hole
Bermuda Airport
St. David's Island
Crawl Hill North
HAMILTON
Crystal Caves
Church Bay
■ **Leamington Caves**
Harrington Sound Rd.
Castle Harbour
19
Aquarium, Museum, and Zoo
Harrington Sound
TUCKER'S TOWN
Sea Gardens
North Shore Rd.
20
Harrington Sound Rd.
SMITH'S
21 *John Smith's Bay*
DEVONSHIRE
South Rd.

N

KEY
⛴ Cruise Ship
⛴ Ferry
— Railway Trail

0   2 miles
0   3 km

Helmet Diving A different, less technical type of diving that is popular in Bermuda is "helmet diving." Underwater explorers, wearing helmets that are fed air through hoses leading to the surface, walk along the sandy bottom in 15 feet of water or less. Although cruises last three hours or more, actual underwater time is about a half hour. A morning or afternoon tour costs $32. Contact **Greg Hartley's Under Sea Adventure** (Village Inn dock, Bridgeview La., Sandys, tel. 809/234–2861).

Fishing

Fishing in Bermuda falls into three basic categories: shore or shallow-water fishing, reef fishing, and deep-sea fishing. No license is required, although some restrictions apply, particularly regarding the use of spear guns and the fish you can keep (for instance, only commercial fishers are permitted to take lobsters). In recent years, some concern has been expressed about the decline in the number of reef and shore fish in Bermudian waters. New government measures to restore fish populations have adversely impacted some commercial fishers, but sportfishing has been largely unaffected. Indeed, the deep-sea fishing for which Bermuda is famed remains as good as ever.

Shore Fishing The principal catches for shore fishers are pompano, bonefish, and snapper. Excellent sport for saltwater fly-fishing is the wily and strong bonefish, which is found in coves, harbors, and bays—almost anywhere it can find food and shelter from turbulent water. Among the more popular spots for bonefish are **West Whale Bay** and **Spring Benny's Bay,** which feature large expanses of clear, shallow water, protected by reefs close inshore. Good fishing holes are numerous along the south shore, too, although fishing is not permitted on major south-shore swimming beaches. Fishing in the calm waters of the **Great Sound** and **St. George's Harbour** can be rewarding, but enclosed **Harrington Sound** is less promising. Ask at local tackle shops about the latest hot spots and the best baits to use. Rod and reel rentals for shore fishing are available for about $10 a day from **Fly Bridge Tackle** (Church St., Hamilton, tel. 809/ 295–1845) and **Salt Kettle Boat Rentals** (off Harbour Rd., Salt Kettle Rd., Paget, tel. 809/236–4863). Rental arrangements can also be made through hotel activities directors.

Reef Fishing Three major reef bands lie at various distances from the island: The first is anywhere from a half mile to 5 miles offshore; the second, the Challenger Bank, is about 15 miles offshore; the third, the Argus Bank, is located about 30 miles offshore. As a rule, the farther out you go, the larger the fish—and the more expensive the charter. Most charter fishers work the reefs and deep water to the north and northwest of the island, because most of Bermuda's harbors face in those directions. Catches over the reefs include snapper, amberjack, grouper, and barracuda. Of the most sought-after deep-water fish—marlin, tuna, wahoo, and dolphin—wahoos are the most common and blue marlin the least. Trolling is the usual method of deep-water fishing, and charter-boat operators offer various tackle setups, with test-line weights ranging from 20 to 130 pounds. The boats, which range between 35 and 55 feet long, are fitted with a wide array of gear and electronics to track fish, including depth sounders, lorans, video fish finders, radar, and computer scanners. Half-day or full-day charters are offered by most operators, but full-day trips offer the best chance for a big catch, because the boat can reach waters that are less frequently fished. Rates vary widely, as do policies about keeping the catch. The Bermuda Game Fishing Association runs a year-long **Game Fishing Tournament,** open free to all fishers. Catches of any of 26 game varieties can be registered with the Bermuda Department of Tourism, and prizes are awarded at the end of the year. Charter bookings can be arranged through three organizations: the **Bermuda Charter Fishing Boat Association** (Box SB 145, Sandys SB BX, tel. 809/292–6246); the **Bermuda Sport Fishing Association** ("Creek View House," 8 Tulo La., Pembroke HM 02, tel. 809/295–2370); and the **St. George's Game Fishing & Cruising Association** (Box GE 107, St. George's GE BX, tel. 809/297–1622). In addition, several independent charter boats operate out of Hamilton Harbour and harbors in Sandys at the western end of the island. For more information about chartering a fishing boat in Bermuda, obtain a copy of the "Sportsman's Guide" from the Bermuda Department of Tourism (*see* Chapter 1, Essential Information).

Snorkeling

The clarity of the water, the stunning array of coral reefs, and the shallow resting places of several wrecks make snorkeling in the waters around Bermuda—both close inshore and offshore—particularly rewarding. Snorkeling is possible year-round, although a wet suit is advisable for anyone planning to spend a long time in the water in winter, when the water temperature can dip into the 60s. During the winter, too, the water tends to be rougher, often restricting snorkeling to the protected areas of Harrington Sound and Castle Harbour. Underwater caves, grottoes, coral formations, and schools of small fish are the highlights of these areas. When Bermudians are asked to name a favorite snorkeling spot, however, **Church Bay** is invariably ranked at or near the top of the list. A small cove cut out of the coral cliffs, this protected bay is full of nooks and crannies in the coral, and the reefs are relatively close to shore. Snorkelers should exercise caution here, as they should everywhere along the south shore, because the water can be rough. Other popular snorkeling areas close inshore are the beaches of **John Smith's Bay** at the eastern end of the south shore, and **Tobacco Bay** at the eastern end of the north shore. Despite its small size, **West Whale Bay** is also worth a visit.

Having a boat at your disposal can improve your snorkeling experience immeasurably. Otherwise, long swims are necessary to reach some of the best snorkeling sites from shore, while other sites are inaccessible from anything but a boat. Small boats, some with glass bottoms, can be rented by the hour, half day, or day (*see* Boat Rentals, above). As the number of wrecks attests, navigating around Bermuda's reef-strewn waters is no simple task, especially for inexperienced boaters. If you rent a boat yourself, stick to the protected waters of the sounds, harbors, and bays. For trips to the reefs, let someone else do the navigating—a charter-boat skipper (*see* Charter Boats, above) or one of the snorkeling-cruise operators (*see* Snorkeling Cruises, below). Some of the best reefs for snorkeling, complete with shallow-water wrecks, are to the west. Where the tour guide or skipper goes, however, often depends on the tide, weather, and water conditions. For snorkelers who demand freedom of movement and privacy, a boat charter (complete

with captain) is the only answer, but the cost is considerable—
$450 a day or more. Divided among eight or more passengers,
however, the expense may be worthwhile. By comparison, half-
day snorkeling cruises (*see* Snorkeling Cruises, below) generally cost $35 or less, including equipment and instruction.

Snorkeling equipment is available for rental at most major hotels; the **Grotto Bay Hotel, Palmetto Hotel, Sonesta Beach Hotel,** and **Southampton Princess** have dive operators on site.
Rates for mask, flippers, and snorkel are usually $6 per hour, or
$18 per day from the dive operators; however, snorkels and
masks can be rented for $2 an hour at the concession stand at
Horseshoe Bay Beach. Equipment, including small boats and
underwater cameras, can also be rented at several dive shops or
marinas. The two best places for equipment rentals on the
western end of the island are **Blue Water Divers Ltd.** (Robinson's Marina, Somerset Bridge, Sandys, tel. 809/234–1034) and
Mangrove Marina (Cambridge Rd., Sandys, tel. 809/234–
0914), both of which also rent small boats. In the central part of
the island, boats and gear can be rented at **Salt Kettle Boat Rentals** (off Harbour Rd., Salt Kettle Rd., Paget, tel. 809/236–
4863). At the eastern end of the island, contact **Tobacco Bay
Beach House** (Tobacco Bay, Naval Tanks Hill, St. George's, tel.
809/293–9711).

Snorkeling Cruises   Snorkeling cruises, which are offered from May to November,
may be too touristy for many visitors. Some boats carry 20 passengers or more, and feature music and bars (complimentary
beverages are usually served on the return trip from the reefs).
Smaller boats limit capacity to 10 passengers, but they offer
few amenities and their travel range is shorter. To make sure
you choose a boat that's right for you, ask for all the details before booking. Half-day snorkeling tours cost approximately
$35. **Bermuda Water Tours Ltd.** (Albuoy's Point, Hamilton, tel.
809/295–3727) operates two boats out of Hamilton, and
Pitman's Snorkelling (Somerset Bridge Hotel, Main Rd.,
Sandys, tel. 809/234–0700) offers half-day and shorter evening
cruises, departing from the Somerset Bridge Hotel dock next
to Robinson's Marina. Half-day cruises are also available from
Salt Kettle Boat Rentals Ltd. (off Harbour Rd., Salt Kettle
Rd., Paget, tel. 809/236–4863).

Waterskiing

Winds on the island vary considerably, making it difficult to
predict when the water will be calmest, although evening
breezes are usually the lightest. Head for the **Great Sound**
when the winds are coming from the south or southwest, the
prevailing winds on Bermuda. In the event of northerly winds,
however, **Castle Harbour** and **Harrington Sound** are protected
bodies of water. If possible, make friends with a Bermudian
with a boat—many visitors are invited boating by Bermudians
they have only recently met. Otherwise, contact **Bermuda Water Skiing** (Grotto Bay Hotel, 11 Blue Hole Hill, Hamilton Parish, tel. 809/293–8333, ext. 37) or **Bermuda Waterski Centre**
(Robinson's Marina, Somerset Bridge, Sandys, tel. 809/234–
3354). Rates fluctuate with fuel costs, but average $75–$80 an
hour, with lessons extra.

Windsurfing

Great Sound, Somerset Long Bay, Mangrove Bay, and **Harrington Sound** are the favorite haunts of board sailors in Bermuda. For novices, the calm, enclosed waters of Harrington Sound are probably the best choice. The Great Sound, with its many islands, coves, and harbors, is good for board sailors of all abilities, although the quirky winds that sometimes bedevil yachts in the sound obviously affect sailboards as well. When the northerly storm winds blow, the open bays on the north shore are popular among wave-riding enthusiasts. Only experts should consider windsurfing on the south shore. Wind, waves, and reefs make the south shore so dangerous that rental companies are prohibited from renting boards there. Experienced board sailors might want to try their luck in the open races at **Salt Kettle** from April through mid-October every Thursday at 6 PM.

Even the most avid board sailors should rent sailboards rather than attempt to bring their own. Transporting a board around the island is a logistical nightmare: There are no rental cars on Bermuda, and few taxi drivers are willing to see their car roofs scoured with scratches in the interest of sport. Rental rates range between $15 and $20 an hour, or about $80 a day. Contact **Blue Hole Water Sports** (Grotto Bay Hotel, 11 Blue Hole Hill, Hamilton Parish, tel. 809/293–3328), **Mangrove Marina** (Cambridge Rd., Sandys, tel. 809/234–0914), **Pompano Marina** (Pompano Beach Club, Southampton, tel. 809/234–0222), or **A & J Watersports** (Palmetto Hotel & Cottages, Flatts Village, Smith's, tel. 809/293–2323). **Watlington's Windsurfing Bermuda** (Glencoe Harbour Club, Salt Kettle La., Paget, tel. 809/236–5274 or 809/295–0808) rents high-performance boards at a premium. A & J Watersports and Watlington's also offer instruction: A two- or three-lesson program costs about $105, including on-land simulation and instruction on water.

Beaches

The beaches of Bermuda fall into two categories: those on the south shore and those on the north shore. The water on the southshore beaches tends to be a little rougher, because the prevailing winds come from the south and southwest. However, most people would agree that the typical south-shore beach is also more scenic—fine pinkish sand, coral bluffs topped with summer flowers, and gentle, pale-blue surf. Most Bermudian beaches are relatively small compared with ocean beaches in the United States. Although sizes vary considerably, an average Bermudian beach might be 300 yards long and 30 yards wide. In winter, when the weather is more severe, beaches may erode—even disappear—only to be replenished as the climate eases into spring.

Bermudian beaches offer little shade, either in the way of palm trees or thatched shelters, so bring hats, umbrellas, and plenty of sunscreen. Below are reviews of the major beaches on the island that are open to the public. (For information about the many private beaches owned by hotels on the south shore, *see* Chapter 8, Lodging.)

South-Shore Beaches

Chaplin Bay. In a secluded bay east of Horseshoe Bay (*see* below), this tiny beach disappears almost entirely at high tide or after a storm. Its most distinguishing feature is a high coral wall that reaches across the beach to the water, perforated by a 10-foot high, arrowhead-shaped hole. Like Horseshoe Bay, the beach fronts South Shore Park. *Off South Rd., Southampton. Bus no. 2 or 7 from Hamilton.*

Elbow Beach Hotel. The $3 fee for nonguests ensures that this beach remains relatively quiet, even on weekends. (Nonguests must call first.) Shielded from big ocean swells by reefs, the beach has almost no surf, except in heavy winds. The Elbow Beach Surf Club sells refreshments, and has umbrellas and beach chairs to rent; toilet facilities are available. A free public beach lies adjacent. *Off South Rd., Paget, tel. 809/236–3535. Bus no. 2 or 7 from Hamilton.*

Horseshoe Bay Beach. Horseshoe Bay has everything you would expect of a Bermudian beach: A ¼-mile crescent of pink sand, clear water, a vibrant social scene, and an uncluttered backdrop provided by South Shore Park. This is the most popular beach with visitors and locals alike, a place where adults arrive with coolers and teenagers come to check out the action. The presence of lifeguards—the only other beach with lifeguards is John Smith's Bay (*see* below)—and a variety of rentals, a snack bar, and toilet facilities add to the beach's appeal; in fact, it can become uncomfortably crowded here on summer weekends. Parents should keep a close eye on their children in the water: The undertow can be strong, especially when the wind is blowing. *Off South Rd., Southampton, tel. 809/238–2651. Bus no. 2 or 7 from Hamilton.*

John Smith's Bay. Backed by houses and South Road, this beach consists of a pretty strand of long, flat, open sand. The presence of a lifeguard in summer makes this an ideal place to bring children. As the only public beach in Smith's Parish, John Smith's Bay is also popular among locals. *South Rd., Smith's. Bus no. 1 from Hamilton.*

Warwick Long Bay. Very different from covelike Chaplin and Horseshoe bays, this beach features the longest stretch of sand—about ½ mile—of any beach on the island. And instead of a steep backdrop, low grass- and brush-covered hills slope away from the beach, exposing the beach to the wind. Despite the wind, the waves are rarely big here because the inner reef is close inshore. An interesting feature of the bay is a 20-foot coral outcrop, less than 200 feet offshore, that looks like a sculpted boulder balancing on the surface of the water. The emptiness of South Shore Park, which surrounds the bay, heightens the beach's sense of isolation and serenity. *Off South Rd., Southampton. Bus no. 2 or 7 from Hamilton.*

North-Shore Beaches

St. Catherine Beach. Nestled beneath Fort St. Catherine and St. George's Golf Club, this is the prettiest beach near St. George's. This eastern-facing beach was the property of a nearby hotel, most recently managed by Club Med. At press time, however, the hotel was not in operation and swimmers could use the beach at their discretion. Whether the beach will be open to the public in future years remains unclear. *Off Barry Rd., St. George's. Bus no. 10 or 11 from Hamilton.*

Shelley Bay Beach. As at Somerset Long Bay (*see* below), the water at this beach near Flatts is well protected from prevailing southerly winds. In addition, a sandy bottom and shallow water make this a good place to take small children. Shelley Bay also boasts shade trees—something of a rarity at Bermudian beaches. A beach house has rest rooms, showers, and changing areas. One drawback is the traffic noise from busy North Shore Road, which runs nearby. *North Shore Rd., Hamilton Parish, tel. 809/293–1327. Bus no. 10 or 11 from Hamilton.*

Somerset Long Bay. Popular with Somerset locals, this beach sits on the quiet northwestern end of the island—far from the airport, the bustle of Hamilton, and major tourism hubs. In keeping with the area's rural atmosphere, the beach is low-key and unprepossessing. Undeveloped parkland shields the beach from light traffic on Cambridge Road. The main beach is crescent-shaped and long by Bermudian standards—nearly ¼ mile from end to end. Instead of the great coral outcroppings common on the south shore, grass and brush make up the main backdrop here. Although exposed to northerly storm winds, the bay water is normally calm and shallow—ideal for children. However, the bottom is not sandy everywhere nor is it even. *Cambridge Rd., Sandys. Bus no. 7 or 8 from Hamilton.*

Tobacco Bay Beach. The most popular beach near St. George's, this small north-shore beach is huddled in a coral cove similar to those found along the south shore. Like Shelley Bay (*see* above), Tobacco Bay has a beach house with a snack bar, equipment rentals, toilets, showers, and changing rooms. *Naval Tanks Hill, St. George's, tel. 809/293–9711 (public phone). Bus no. 10 or 11 from Hamilton.*

7 Sports and Fitness

by Peter Oliver

When high jumper Nicky Barnes won a gold medal in the 1990 Commonwealth Games, Bermuda welcomed him home with a degree of adoration normally reserved for martyrs and deities. Bermudians champion their sports heroes, but—more significantly—they champion sports, both as participants and spectators. Every taxi driver seems to be a single-handicap golfer; tennis courts outnumber banks by more than three to one; and runners, cyclists, and horseback riders fill the roads and countryside in the mornings, especially on weekends. Bermuda might not have the world's fittest population but, at sunrise on Saturday, it certainly seems that way.

Washed by the Atlantic, Bermuda is probably best known as a beach destination, offering a host of water sports and activities (*see* Chapter 5, Beaches and Water Sports). However, the island is also a golfing center—eight courses are jammed onto this tiny island—and the popularity of tennis, squash, and riding are a further testament to Bermudians' love affair with land-based sports. Britain's oldest colony tends to favor pursuits with a British flavor. In addition to several golf tournaments, cricket, soccer, rugby, field hockey, equestrian events, and even badminton, are popular spectator sports in season. Visitors can enter some of these events, primarily races and golf and tennis tournaments, although it is usually necessary to qualify.

Perhaps more than any other single factor, climate is what makes Bermuda such a sporting hive. In winter (December–February), temperatures hover between 50°F and 70°F, often climbing higher. While this might prove too chilly for many water sports, the cool air is ideal for activities on land. And although it is not immune to the occasional hurricane or storm, Bermuda does not have an extended storm season. Island residents like to boast, with some justification, that if you enjoy sport, you can enjoy it here 365 days of the year.

Most visitors can arrange sporting activities (tee times, for example) through their hotel's or ship's activities director, although arrangements can be made independently as well. For this purpose, the Bermuda Department of Tourism issues two excellent publications, the *Sportsman's Guide* and *Golfer's Guide*. Available through the Department of Tourism (*see* Government Tourist Offices in Chapter 1, Essential Information), the guides offer descriptions of sports facilities and golf courses on the island, addresses, phone numbers, and prices.

Participant Sports

Bicycling

In Bermuda, bicycles are called pedal or push bikes, to distinguish them from the more common motorized two-wheelers. Many of the cycle liveries around the island (*see* Chapter 1, Essential Information) also rent three-speed and 10-speed pedal bikes, but they can be difficult to find—it makes sense to reserve a bike a few days in advance. Rental rates start at $10–$15 for the first day, and $5 per day thereafter.

Bermuda is not the easiest place in the world to bicycle. Riders should be prepared for some tough climbs—the roads running

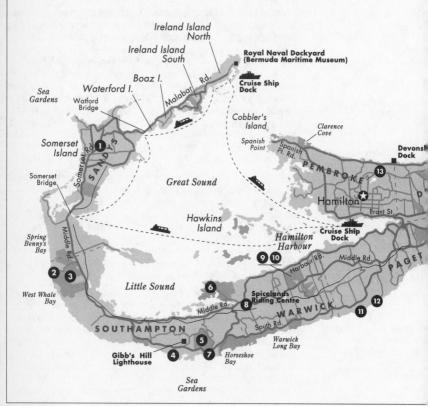

ATLANTIC OCEAN

Ireland Island
North

Ireland Island
South

Royal Naval Dockyard
(Bermuda Maritime Museum)

Cruise Ship
Dock

Boaz I.

Sea
Gardens

Waterford I.

Watford
Bridge

Cobbler's
Island

Clarence
Cove

Devons
Dock

Somerset
Island

Spanish
Point

Spanish
Pt. Rd.

PEMBROKE

Great Sound

Somerset
Bridge

Hamilton

Front St.

Spring
Benny's
Bay

Hawkins
Island

Hamilton
Harbour

Cruise Ship
Dock

West Whale
Bay

Little Sound

Middle Rd.

Harbour Rd.

PAGET

Spicelands
Riding Centre

WARWICK

SOUTHAMPTON

Middle Rd.

South Rd.

Warwick
Long Bay

Gibb's Hill
Lighthouse

Horseshoe
Bay

Sea
Gardens

Golf Courses

Belmont Golf &
Country Club, **9**

Castle Harbour Golf
Club, **18**

Mid Ocean Club, **19**

Ocean View Golf &
Country Club, **14**

Port Royal Golf &
Country Club, **3**

Princess Golf Club, **5**

Riddell's Bay Golf &
Country Club, **6**

St. George's Golf
Club, **21**

**Tennis and Squash
Courts**

Belmont Hotel, Golf &
Country Club, **10**

Bermuda Squash
Club, **16**

Coral Beach & Tennis
Club, **11**

Elbow Beach Hotel, **12**

Government Tennis
Stadium, **13**

Marriott's Castle
Harbour Resort, **17**

Pompano Beach
Club, **2**

Sonesta Beach Hotel
& Spa, **4**

Southampton
Princess Hotel, **7**

Horseback Riding

Spicelands Riding
Centre, **8**

Spectator Sports

National Sports
Club, **15**

St. George's Cricket
Club, **20**

Somerset Cricket
Club, **1**

Tobacco Bay

Fort St. Catherine
St. Catherine Beach

ST **㉑** **GEORGE'S**

St. George's Island

Mullet Bay Rd. ⚓ ○ St. George's

㉒

St. George's Harbour

Cruise Ship Dock

St. David's Rd.

Ferry Rd.

Sea Gardens

Coney Island

Kindley Field Rd.

Bermuda Airport

Bermuda Perfumery

The Causeway

Bermuda Pottery

St. David's Island

Crawl Hill North

Crystal Caves

Blue Hole

Leamington Caves

㉗

Harrington Sound Rd.

Church Bay

St. David's Lighthouse

Castle Harbour

HAMILTON

㉘

TUCKER'S TOWN

Aquarium, Museum, and Zoo

Harrington Sound

㉙

Sea Gardens

North Shore Rd.

㉖

Harrington Sound Rd.

SMITH'S

㉕

4

VONSHIRE

John Smith's Bay

South Rd.

N

KEY	
🚢	Cruise Ship
⛴	Ferry
—	Railway Trail

0 ——————————— 2 miles

0 ——————————— 3 km

north–south across the island are particularly steep and winding—and the wind can sap even the strongest rider's strength, especially along South Road in Warwick and Southampton parishes. Bermudian roads are narrow, with heavy traffic (especially near Hamilton during rush hours) and no shoulder. Most motorists are courteous to cyclists—arbitrary horn-honking is against the law—and stay within 10 mph of the 20-mph speed limit. Despite the traffic, bicycle racing is a popular sport in Bermuda, and club groups can regularly be seen whirring around the island on evening and weekend training rides. Bermudian roads are no place for novice riders, however, and parents should think twice before allowing preteen children to hop on a bike.

Bermuda's premier cycling route, the Railway Trail (*see* Chapter 3, Exploring Bermuda), requires almost no road riding. Restricted to pedestrian and bicycle traffic, the paved trail runs intermittently for almost the length of the island along the route of the old Bermuda Railway. The Bermuda Department of Tourism publishes *The Bermuda Railway Trail Guide*, a free pamphlet that features a series of short exploring tours along the trail. The pamphlet is available at all Visitors Service Bureaus and Information Centres.

Tribe roads—small side roads that are often unpaved—are also good for exploring, although don't be surprised if many of these roads, which date back to the earliest settlement of Bermuda, are dead ends. Well-paved South Road has relatively few climbs and some excellent ocean views, although it is one of Bermuda's most heavily traveled thoroughfares. The "Bermuda Handy Reference Map," also available at Visitors Service Bureaus and Information Centres, is as essential to cyclists as two inflated tires and an oiled chain.

Golf

Bermuda is justifiably renowned for its golf courses. The scenery is spectacular, and the courses are challenging. However, visitors should not expect the manicured, soft fairways and greens typical of U.S. courses. Just as courses in Scotland have their own identity, the same is true of courses on this Atlantic isle. Bermudian golf courses are distinguished by plenty of sand, firm fairways and greens, relatively short par fours, and wind—*especially* wind. Elsewhere, golf courses are usually designed with the wind in mind—long downwind holes and short upwind holes. Not so on Bermuda's eight courses, where the wind is anything but consistent or predictable. Quirky air currents make a Bermudian course play differently every day. On some days, a 350-yard par four may be driveable; on other days, a solidly hit drive may fall short on a 160-yard par three. Regardless, the wind puts a premium on being able to hit the ball straight; any slice or hook becomes disastrously exaggerated in the wind.

The island's water supply is limited, so irrigation is done sparingly and the ground around the green tends to be quite hard. For success in the short game, therefore, players need to run the ball to the hole, rather than relying on high, arcing chips, which require plenty of club face under the ball. Typically, Bermudian greens are elevated and protected by sand traps rather than thick grass. Most traps are filled with the pulverized coral that has made the island's beaches so famous. Such fine sand may be unfamiliar to visiting golfers, but it tends to be consistent from trap to trap and from course to course.

Greens are usually seeded with Bermuda grass and then overseeded with rye. Golfers putt on Bermuda grass during the warmer months (March–November) and on rye when the weather cools and the Bermuda grass dies out. Greens are reseeded anytime from late September to early November, according to the weather. (Castle Harbour Golf Club's greens are reseeded in early January.) Some courses use temporary greens for two to four weeks; others keep the greens in play while reseeding and resurfacing. Greens in Bermuda tend to be much slower than the bent-grass greens prevalent in the United States, and putts tend to break less.

Another characteristic of Bermudian courses is the preponderance of rolling, hummocky fairways, making a flat lie the exception rather than the rule. Little effort has been made to flatten the fairways, because much of the ground beneath the island's surface is honeycombed with caves; bulldozer and backhoe operators are understandably uneasy about doing extensive landscaping.

How should golfers prepare for a Bermuda trip? In anticipation of the wind, practice hitting lower shots—punching the ball or playing it farther back in the stance may be helpful. Working on chip-and-run shots (a seven iron is ideal for this), especially from close-cropped lies, should also help. You can save yourself some strokes, too, by practicing iron shots from awkward, hillside lies. On the greens, a long, firm putting stroke may save you from the bugaboo that haunts many first-time visitors: gently stroked putts dying short of the hole or drifting off-line with the grain of the Bermuda grass. As Allan Wilkinson, the professional at the Princess Golf Club, says: "In Bermuda, ya gotta slam 'em into the back of the cup."

Tournaments for pros, seniors, juniors, women, and mixed groups fill Bermuda's golfing schedule from February through December. Some competitions, such as the Bermuda Open in early October, are high-level competitions with prize money for professional participants. Handicap limits are usually imposed for the more serious tournaments, and entry fees range between $90 and $120 (not all events are open to non-Bermudian players). A schedule, with entry forms, is available from the **Bermuda Golf Association** (Box HM 433, Hamilton HM BX, tel. 809/238–1367). A low-key event for golfers of all abilities is the **Bermuda Golf Festival**, a two-week affair in late February that gives players a chance to compete on several of the island's courses. Greens fees are reduced for festival participants, and several hotels offer reduced package rates. For more information, contact the Bermuda Golf Festival (GD/T Sports Marketing, 5520 Park Ave., Box 395, Trumbull, CT 06611, tel. 203/373–7154 or 800/282–7656). Another easygoing tournament in mid-February is the **Valentine's Mixed Foursomes**, for which tournament/hotel packages are also available. For information or entry forms, contact the tournament chairman, Kim Swan (St. George's Golf Club, 1 Park Rd., St. George's GE 03, tel. 809/297–8067).

Be sure to pack proper golf attire—long pants (no jeans) or Bermuda shorts (no cutoffs) are required for men. Lessons, available at all courses, usually cost $25 for a half hour, and club rentals range between $10 and $22. Caddies are a thing of the past, except at the Mid Ocean Club. Below are reviews and ratings of all eight of Bermuda's golf courses. The ratings, devised and administered by the United States Golf Association (USGA), "represent the expected score of an expert amateur golfer based upon yardage and other obstacles." For example, a par-72 course with a rating of 68 means that a scratch golfer would hit a four-under-par round—and ordinary hackers would probably score a little better, too. Ratings below are given for the blue tees (championship), white tees (men's), and red tees (women's).

Belmont Golf & Country Club

Length: 5,777 yards from the blue tees
Par: 70
Rating: blue tees, 68.9; white tees, 67.9; red tees, 69.1

Of Bermuda's eight courses, the layout of the public Belmont Golf & Country Club is perhaps the most maddening. The first two holes, straight par fours, are a false preview of what lies ahead—a series of doglegs and blind tee shots. Playing with an experienced Belmont player, who knows where to hit drives on such blind holes as the sixth, 11th, and 16th, and how best to play a dogleg hole such as the eighth, can help a newcomer trim six or more shots from a round. Despite the layout, Belmont remains one of Bermuda's easier courses, and it is ideal for inexperienced players. Belmont is an inland course and has few ocean panoramas. Instead, most holes overlook pastel houses with white roofs, a few of which have taken a beating from errant golf balls. A new irrigation system has improved the course dramatically in recent years. Fairway grass tends to be denser—and the clay soil moister—than the grass on the close-cropped, sandy fairways typical of other Bermudian courses. The rough, too, is generally deeper, snaring any wild tee shots. For this reason, and because Belmont is a short course (only one par four in more than 400 yards), it makes sense to use a three or five wood, or even a low iron, from the tee. Belmont's chief drawback, especially on the weekend, is slow play—weekend rounds of five hours or more are common.

Highlight hole: The par-five 11th features a severe dogleg left, with a blind tee shot—Belmont in a nutshell. A short but straight drive is the key; trying and failing to cut the corner can be disastrous. The approach to the green is straight, although a row of wispy trees on the left awaits hooked or pulled shots. *Belmont Rd., Warwick, tel. 809/236–1301. Greens fees: $45 for the public; $30 for hotel guests. Cart rentals, $32; hand carts, $7.*

Castle Harbour Golf Club

Length: 6,440 yards from the blue tees
Par: 71
Rating: blue tees, 71.3; white tees, 69.2; red tees, 69.2

The only course on Bermuda that requires players to use golf carts is the Castle Harbour Golf Club—with good reason. The only flat areas on the course, it seems, are the tees. The first tee, a crow's-nest perch by the clubhouse, offers an indication of things to come: Looking out over the fairway, with the harbor beyond, is like peering onto a golf course from a 20th-story window. Wind can make this course play especially long. Although most par fours feature good landing areas despite all the hills, holes such as the second, 16th, and 17th require players to drive over fairway rises. A wind-shortened drive can mean a long, blind shot to the green. Carrying the rise, on the other hand, can mean a relatively easy short shot, especially on the second and 17th holes. Elevated greens are a common feature of Castle Harbour. The most extreme example is the 190-yard, par-three 13th, with the green perched atop a steep, 100-foot embankment. Balls short of the green inevitably roll back down into a grassy basin between the tee and the green. On the other hand, sand traps at Castle Harbour are mercifully few and far between by Bermudian standards; 10 holes feature two or fewer bunkers around the green.

With a $70 greens fee, plus $32 for the required cart, Castle Harbour is Bermuda's most expensive course. However, the money is clearly reinvested in the course. Greens are well maintained—firm, consistently cropped, and generally faster than most Bermudian greens. The course also rewards golfers with several spectacular views, such as the hilltop panorama from the 14th tee, where blue water stretches into the distance on three sides.

Highlight hole: The 235-yard, par-three 18th is the most difficult finishing hole on Bermuda, especially when the wind is blowing from the northwest. On the right are jagged coral cliffs rising from the harbor; on the left are a pair of traps. When the course was revamped a few years ago, a small, flower-lined pond was added on the front right of the green, making this hard hole even harder. *Marriott's Castle Harbour Hotel, Paynters Rd., Hamilton Parish, tel. 809/293–8161 or 809/293–0795. Greens fees: $70 ($40 after 4:30 PM), plus mandatory $32 cart rental. Shoe rentals.*

Mid Ocean Club **Length:** 6,547 yards from the blue tees
Par: 71
Rating: blue tees, 72; white tees, 70; red tees, 72

It isn't Bermuda's oldest course—that honor belongs to Riddell's Bay—and other Bermudian courses are equally difficult, but the elite Mid Ocean Club is generally regarded as one of the top 50 courses in the world. Quite simply, this course has charisma, embodying everything that is golf in Bermuda—tees on coral cliffs above the ocean, rolling fairways lined with palms and spice trees, doglegs around water, and windswept views. It is rich in history, too. At the dogleg fifth hole, for example, Babe Ruth is said to have splashed a dozen balls in Mangrove Lake in a futile effort to drive the green. The course rewards long, straight tee shots and deft play around the green, while penalizing—often cruelly—anything less. The fifth and ninth holes, for example, require that tee shots (from the blue tees) carry 180 yards or more over water. And while length is not a factor on two fairly short par fives, the 465-yard second and the 487-yard 11th, accuracy is: Tight doglegs ensure that any wayward tee shot ends up in trees, shrubbery, or rough. The course may have mellowed with age, however. The course lost hundreds of trees to a tornado in 1986 and was battered again by Hurricane Emily in 1987. The tight, tree-lined fairways have become more open as a result, and the rough less threatening.

Highlight hole: The 433-yard fifth is a par-four dogleg around Mangrove Lake. The elevated tee overlooks a hillside of flowering shrubbery and the lake, making the fairway seem impossibly far away. Big hitters can take a short cut over the lake (although the green is unreachable, despite the Babe's heroic efforts), but anyone who hits the fairway has scored a major victory. To the left of the green, a steep embankment leads into a bunker that is among the hardest in Bermuda from which to recover. *Mid Ocean Dr., off South Rd., Tucker's Town, tel. 809/ 293–0330. Greens fees: $70 ($35 when accompanied by a member). Nonmembers must be introduced by a hotel activities director or a club member; nonmember starting times available only on Mon., Wed., and Fri. Cart rental, $30; caddies, $20 per bag (tip not included).*

Ocean View Golf &   **Length:** 3,000 yards (nine holes) from the blue tees
Country Club   **Par:** 35; ladies, 37
  Rating: none

Work on the Ocean View Golf & Country Club is still in progress. Founded nearly 40 years ago as a club for blacks, the nine-hole course fell into neglect as other courses in Bermuda began admitting black players. In 1988, the Bermudian government took over management of Ocean View and committed roughly $3 million to its refurbishment. In addition to restoring the course to good playing condition and altering a few holes, the government's plans include a new clubhouse, possibly to be finished by the end of 1991. Also under consideration is the addition of a second nine holes. Although the old clubhouse is indeed a dank place, the course is better—and in far better shape—than its reputation would suggest. Several holes challenge and intrigue: The second is a tough par four that runs up and along the side of a hill; the sixth is a wind-buffeted par five, with a 40-foot coral wall on one side, and a slope leading down to the Great Sound on the other. Some holes have as many as six tees, offering players the opportunity for considerable variation. Locals crowd the course on weekends, although Ocean View is relatively empty on weekdays. That could change, however, if the course continues to improve as expected.

Highlight hole: The green on the 177-yard, par-three fifth hole has been cut out of a coral hillside draped with flowering vines, giving players the sensation of hitting into a grotto. Club selection can be tricky—winds off the Great Sound might seem insubstantial on the tee, but they can be much stronger over the coral wall near the green. *Off North Shore Rd., Devonshire, tel. 809/236–6758. Greens fees: $22 for 9 or 18 holes. Cart rental, $11 per 9 holes, $22 per 18 holes; hand carts, $5.*

Port Royal Golf &   **Length:** 6,425 yards from the blue tees
Country Club   **Par:** 71; ladies, 72
  Rating: blue tees, 72; white tees, 69.7; red tees, 72.5

Such golfing luminaries as Jack Nicklaus rank the Port Royal Golf & Country Club among the world's best public courses. A favorite among Bermudians as well, the course is well laid out, and the greens fees are modest. By Bermudian standards, Port Royal is also relatively flat. Although there are some hills, on the back nine in particular, the course has few of the blind shots and hillside lies that are prevalent elsewhere. Those holes that do have gradients tend to run either directly uphill or downhill. In other respects, however, Port Royal is classically Bermudian, with close-cropped fairways, numerous elevated tees and greens, and holes raked by the wind, especially the eighth and the 16th. The 16th hole, one of Bermuda's most famous, is frequently pictured in magazines. The green sits on a treeless promontory overlooking the blue waters and pink-white sands of Whale Bay, a popular boating and fishing area. When the wind is blowing hard onshore, as it frequently does, a driver may be necessary to reach the green, which is 163 yards away. One complaint often raised about Port Royal is the condition of the course, which can become chewed up by heavy usage—more than 55,000 rounds a year.

Highlight hole: Like the much-photographed 16th hole, the 371-yard, par-four 15th skirts the cliffs along Whale Bay. In addition to the ocean view, the remains of Whale Bay Battery, a 19th-century fortification, lie between the fairway and the bay. Only golf balls hooked wildly from the tee have any chance of a direct hit on the fort. The wind can be brutal on this hole. *Off Middle Rd., Southampton, tel. 809/234–0974. Greens fees: $32; discount rates after 4 PM. Except for groups, tee times can be arranged no more than 2 days in advance. Cart rental, $22; hand cart, $6. Shoe rentals.*

Princess Golf Club **Length:** 2,684 yards from the blue tees
Par: 54
Rating: none

The Princess Golf Club unfolds on the hillside beneath the Southampton Princess. The hotel has managed to sculpt a neat little par-three course from the steep terrain, and players who opt to walk around will find their mountaineering skills and stamina severely tested. The vertical drop on the first two holes alone is at least 200 feet, and the rise on the fourth hole makes 178 yards play like 220. Kept in excellent shape by an extensive irrigation system, the course is a good warm-up for Bermuda's full-length courses, offering a legitimate test of wind and bunker play with a minimum of obstructions and hazards. Ocean views are a constant feature of the front nine, although the looming presence of the hotel does detract from the scenery.

Highlight hole: The green of the 174-yard 16th hole sits in a cup ringed by pink-blooming oleander bushes. Less than a mile away, the Gibb's Hill Lighthouse dominates the backdrop. *Southampton Princess, South Rd., tel. 809/238–0446. Greens fees: $24 ($20 for hotel guests). Cart rental: $20 ($18 for hotel guests). Shoe rentals.*

Riddell's Bay Golf **Length:** 5,588 yards from the blue tees
& Country Club **Par:** 69; ladies, 71
Rating: blue tees, 67.7; white tees, 66.4; red tees, 70.6

Built in 1922, the Riddell's Bay Golf & Country Club is Bermuda's oldest course. In design, however, it more nearly approximates a Florida course—relatively flat, with wide, palm-lined fairways. You don't need to be a power hitter to score well here, although the first four holes, including a 427-yard uphill par four and a 244-yard par three, might suggest otherwise. The par fours are mostly in the 360-yard range, and the fairways are generously flat and open. Despite the course's position on a narrow peninsula between Riddell's Bay and the Great Sound, water only comes into play on holes eight through 11. With the twin threats of wind and water, these are the most typically Bermudian holes on the course, and accuracy off the tee is important. This is especially true of the par-four eighth, a 360-yard right dogleg around the water. With a tail wind, big hitters might try for the green, but playing around the dogleg on this relatively short hole is the more prudent choice. As at the Belmont course, a few tees are fronted with stone walls—an old-fashioned touch that harks back to the old courses of Great Britain. Like Mid Ocean, Riddell's is a private club that is open to the public only at certain times, but the clubbish atmosphere is much less pronounced here.

Highlight hole: The tees on the 340-yard, par-four 10th are set on a grass-topped quay on the harbor's edge. The fairway narrows severely after about 200 yards, and a drive hit down the right-hand side leaves a player no chance to reach the green in two. Two ponds guard the left side of a sloped and elevated green. The hole is rated only the sixth most difficult on the course, but the need for pinpoint accuracy probably makes it the hardest to par. *Riddell's Bay Rd., Warwick, tel. 809/238-1060. Greens fees: $20 ($15 when accompanied by a member). Cart rental, $25; hand carts, $4.*

St. George's Golf Club

Length: 4,502 yards from the blue tees
Par: 63 (formerly 64)
Rating (based on par 64): blue tees, 62.8; white tees, 61.4; red tees, 62.8

Built in 1985, St. George's Golf Club dominates a secluded headland at the northeastern end of the island. The 4,502-yard course is short, but it makes up for its lack of length with sharp teeth. No course in Bermuda is more exposed to wind, and no course has smaller greens—some are no more than 25 feet across. To make matters trickier, the greens are hard and slick from the wind and salty air. Many of the holes have commanding views of the ocean, particularly the eighth, ninth, 14th, and 15th, which run along the water's edge. Wind—especially from the north—can turn these short holes into club-selection nightmares. Don't let high scores here ruin your enjoyment of some of the finest views on the island. The scenery, the course's shortness, and the fact that it gets little play midweek, make St. George's Golf Club a good choice for couples or groups of varying ability.

Highlight hole: Pause to admire the view from the par-four 14th hole before you tee off. From the elevated tee area, the 326-yard hole curls around Coot Pond, an ocean-fed cove, to the green on a small, treeless peninsula. Beyond the neighboring 15th hole is old Fort St. Catherine's, and beyond that lies the sea. With a tail wind, it's tempting to hit for the green from the tee, but Coot Pond leaves no room for error. *1 Park Rd., St. George's, tel. 809/297-8067 or 809/297-8148. Greens fees: $25; $13 after 4 PM. Cart rental, $22; hand carts, $5.*

Horseback Riding

Because most of the land on Bermuda is residential, opportunities for riding through the countryside are few. The chief exception is **South Shore Park,** between South Road and the Warwick beaches. Sandy trails, most of which are open only to riders or people on foot, wind through stands of dune grass and oleander, along beaches and over coral bluffs. Nearby is the **Spicelands Riding Centre** (Middle Rd., Warwick, tel. 809/238-8212 or 809/238-8246), the main riding facility on the island. The center's most popular trail ride is the two-hour south-shore breakfast ride, departing at 7 AM; breakfast is included in the

$37.50 fee. Evening rides are also offered, although it's wise to confirm all rides from October through April, when low demand can force the cancellation of certain trail rides. Spicelands also offers instruction in its riding ring.

Jogging and Running

Many of the difficulties that cyclists face—hills, traffic, and wind—also confront runners in Bermuda. The presence of pedestrian sidewalks and footpaths along roadsides, however, does make the going somewhat easier. Runners who like firm pavement will be happiest on the Railway Trail (*see* Bicycling, above) or on South Road, a popular route. For those who like running on sand, the trails through **South Shore Park** are relatively firm, while the island's beaches obviously present a much softer surface. **Horseshoe Beach** is frequented by a large number of runners, although their interest in the beach may be more social than physical, because Horseshoe Beach is where the action is. A better beach for running is ½-mile **Warwick Long Bay,** the longest uninterrupted stretch of sand on the island. By using South Shore Park trails to skirt coral bluffs, runners can create a route that connects several beaches, although trails in some places can be winding and uneven.

The big race on the island is the **Bermuda International Marathon & 10K Race,** held in mid-January. The race attracts world-class distance runners from several countries, but it is open to everyone. For information, contact the Bermuda Track & Field Association (Box DV 397, Devonshire DV BX). The association can also provide information on other races held throughout the year. Another event for fitness fanatics is the **Bermuda Triathlon** in late September. Held in Southampton, the event combines a 1-mile swim, a 15-mile cycling leg, and a 6-mile run. For information, contact the Bermuda Triathlon Association (Box HM 1002, Hamilton HM DX). Less competitive—and certainly less strenuous—are the 2-mile **"fun runs,"** held every Tuesday evening from April through October. Runs begin at 6 PM in front of Camden House on Berry Hill Road, Botanical Gardens. No entry fee is charged.

Squash

The **Bermuda Squash Club** (Middle Rd., Devonshire, tel. 809/292–6881) makes its four courts available to nonmembers between 9 AM and 11 PM by reservation. A $5 fee per person includes racquet, ball, and towel. Soft-ball players will enjoy the two English courts (larger than U.S. courts) at the **Coral Beach & Tennis Club** (South Rd., Paget, tel. 809/236–2233). In mid-November, the Bermuda Squash Racquets Association (tel. 809/292–6881) sponsors the **Bermuda Open Squash Tournament**, in which top international players compete.

Tennis

Bermuda has a tennis court for every 600 residents, a ratio that even the most tennis-crazed countries would find difficult to match. Many of the tennis courts are private, but the public has access to more than 80 courts in 20 locations island-wide. Courts are inexpensive and seldom full. Hourly rates for nonguests are about $10–$15. Bring along a few fresh cans of balls, because balls in Bermuda cost $6–$7 per can—about three times the rate in the United States. Among the surfaces used in Bermuda are Har-Tru, clay, cork, and hard composites, of which the relatively slow plexipave composite is the most prevalent. Considering Bermuda's British roots, it's surprising that there are no grass courts on the island.

Wind, heat (in summer), and humidity are the most distinguishing characteristics of Bermudian tennis. From October through March, when daytime temperatures rarely exceed 80°F, play is comfortable throughout the day. In summertime, however, the heat radiating from the court (especially hard-surface ones) can make play uncomfortable between 11 AM and 3 PM. At such times, the breezes normally considered a curse in tennis can become a cooling blessing. Early morning or evening tennis presents players with an entirely different problem, when tennis balls grow heavy with moisture from Bermuda's humid sea air, always at its wettest early and late in the day. On clay courts, the moist balls become matted with clay, making them even heavier. In strong winds, inland courts, such as the clay and all-weather courts at the **Government Tennis Stadium** (Cedar Ave. and St. John's Rd., Pembroke, tel. 809/292–0105) or the clay courts at the **Coral Beach & Tennis Club** (off South Rd., Paget, tel. 809/236–2233 or 809/236–6495) are preferable. Despite their position at the water's edge, the plexipave courts of the **Southampton Princess Hotel** (South Rd., Southampton, tel. 809/238–1005) are reasonably well shielded from the wind (especially from the north), although the breeze can be swirling and difficult. High on a bluff above the ocean, the courts at the **Sonesta Beach Hotel & Spa** (off South Rd., tel. 809/238–8122) offer players one of the more spectacular settings on the island, but the courts are exposed to summer winds from the south and southwest. Other hotels with good tennis facilities open to the public are the **Elbow Beach Hotel** (South Shore, Paget, tel. 809/236–3535), with five courts, and **Marriott's Castle Harbour Resort** (Paynters Rd., Hamilton Parish, tel. 809/293–2040), with six cork courts. All of the above facilities have some floodlit courts for night play, as do the **Pompano Beach Club** (off Middle Rd., Southampton, tel. 809/234–0222) and the **Belmont Hotel, Golf & Country Club** (Belmont Rd., Warwick, tel. 809/236–1301). An additional fee of $2–$5 is usually charged to play under lights. Most tennis facilities offer lessons, ranging from $15 to $25 for 30 minutes of instruction, and racquet rentals for $3–$5 per day (a few hotels lend racquets to hotel guests for free.)

Spectator Sports

Bermuda is a great place for sports enthusiasts seeking relief from an overdose of baseball, football, and basketball—sports that mean little to Bermudians. In addition to golf and tennis, the big spectator sports here are cricket, rugby, soccer, field hockey, and yacht racing. The Bermuda Department of Tourism (*see* Government Tourist Offices in Chapter 1, Essential Information) can provide exact dates and information about all major sporting events.

Cricket   Cricket is the big team sport in summer, and the **Cup Match Cricket Festival** is *the* event on Bermuda's summer sports calendar. Held in late July or early August at the Somerset Cricket

Club (Broome St., off Somerset Rd., 809/234–0327) or the St. George's Cricket Club (Wellington Slip Rd., tel. 809/297–0374), the competition features teams from around the island. Although cricket is taken very seriously, the event itself is a real festival, attended by thousands of colorful picnickers and party goers. Admission is free. The regular cricket season runs from April through September.

Field Hockey   Hockey games between local teams can be seen at the National Sports Club (Middle Rd., Devonshire, tel. 809/236–6994) on Sunday from October through April. In early September, the National Sports Club is the site of the **Hockey Festival**, a tournament with teams from Bermuda, the United States, Great Britain, Holland, and Germany. Admission is free.

Golf   Golf tournaments are held throughout the year at various courses on the island. The highlight of the golf year is the **Bermuda Open** in early October, which attracts a host of professionals and amateurs. A schedule of events is available from the Bermuda Golf Association (*see* Golf in Participant Sports, above).

Rugby   The **Easter Rugby Classic** is the final event in Bermuda's rugby season, which runs from September to April. Held at the National Sports Club (Middle Rd., Devonshire, tel. 809/236–6994), the competition attracts teams from Great Britain, France, New Zealand, and Australia, as well as Bermuda. Admission is $5. During the rest of the season, matches between local teams can be seen on weekends at the National Sports Club.

Soccer   In early April, teams from countries around the Atlantic, including the United States, Canada, Great Britain, and several Caribbean nations, compete for the **Diadora Youth Soccer Cup**. Teams play in three age divisions, and games are held on fields around the island.

Yachting   Bermuda has a worldwide reputation as a yacht-racing center. Spectators, particularly those on land, may find it difficult to follow the intricacies of a race or regatta, but the sight of the racing fleet, with brightly colored spinnakers flying, is always striking. The racing season runs from March to November. Most races are held on weekends in the Great Sound, and several classes of boats usually compete. Good vantage points for viewing races are around Spanish Point, Hamilton Harbour, and the islands northeast of Somerset. Anyone wanting to get a real sense of the action, however, should be aboard a boat near the race course.

In late June, Bermuda acts as the finish for ocean-going yachts in two major races beginning in the United States—the **Newport–Bermuda Race** and the **Annapolis–Bermuda Race**. Of the two, the Newport–Bermuda Race is considered the more prestigious, but both provide the spectacular sight of the island's harbors filled with yachts, which range in length from 30 to 100 feet. For those more interested in racing than expensive yachts, the **King Edward VII Gold Cup International Match Racing Tournament** is the event to see. Held in late October or early November in the Great Sound, the tournament features many of the world's best skippers in one-on-one races, similar to the competition style used in the America's Cup.

8 Dining

Introduction

by John DeMers

The former food editor for United Press International, John DeMers is the author of three cookbooks, the most recent of which is Caribbean Cooking.

With 150 restaurants from which to choose, visitors to this tiny island will have little difficulty satisfying their cravings for everything from traditional English fare to French, Italian, Greek, Indian, and Chinese. A quest for Bermudian food, however, is likely to be as extended and elusive as the search for the Holy Grail. And if you persist, you'll discover the single greatest truth about Bermudian cuisine: There's no such thing, but everybody on the island loves it. Waiters, in particular, prove inspirational. While heaping your plate, they will wax lyrical about their mother's turtle stew, their late uncle's fish chowder, or their great aunt's codfish and potatoes. And no islander seems to remember ever tasting anything better than a mysterious concoction called hash shark or—more intelligibly— shark hash.

In moments of candor, islanders will confide that Bermudian cuisine is really a collection of dishes showing English, American, and West Indian influences. But whatever the origins of the recipes, the island's cuisine begins and ends with Bermudian ingredients—and therein lies the island's claim to a culinary identity. Seafood is extraordinary here, especially the local lobster that is best eaten during the winter. This is the spiny lobster familiar in the Caribbean, usually prepared with a minimum of seasoned stuffing, broiled, and served drizzled with butter. Menus also feature Bermuda rockfish, the flesh of which is firm and white; red snapper, often served with onions and potatoes; shark; and mussels steamed in white wine or made into a pie or fritters. Another local variety of seafood is the guinea chick. Although it sounds more like poultry, the guinea chick is a Bermudian cross, in taste and texture, between a crayfish and a prawn. This delicate shellfish is worth ordering whenever you find it; unfortunately, you won't find it often. (At press time, a ban has been placed on the harvesting of both lobsters and guinea chicks because of overfishing. It is unknown when these shellfish will be available again.) You should also try the fish chowder, laced at the table with local black rum and sherry peppers (sherry in which hot peppers have been marinated). The result is unforgettable. Conch fritters, too, are a good bet when you can find them. Unless you venture to St. David's Island on the island's East End, you may never get to taste shark hash. The best approach is to hang around the Black Horse Tavern or Dennis's Hideaway until somebody announces that the hash is ready. The passion that East Enders hold for this dish means the pot won't be full for long.

Without doubt, the most famous vegetable is the Bermuda onion, hailed by onion lovers as a more heavenly version of the sweet Vidalia onion from Georgia. It is most commonly found in onion pie and cheese and onion sandwiches, and glazed in sugar and rum. Bermuda's soil works miracles with most common vegetables. Don't be put off if your meal is accompanied by potatoes, broccoli, or even carrots. Rarely will these vegetables taste better or fresher in their natural flavors.

In addition to onion pie and mussel pie, cassava pie is a tradition dating back three centuries. Made from dough flavored with ground cassava root, this meat pie is a Christmas standard, nearly always paired with a traditional English plum

144

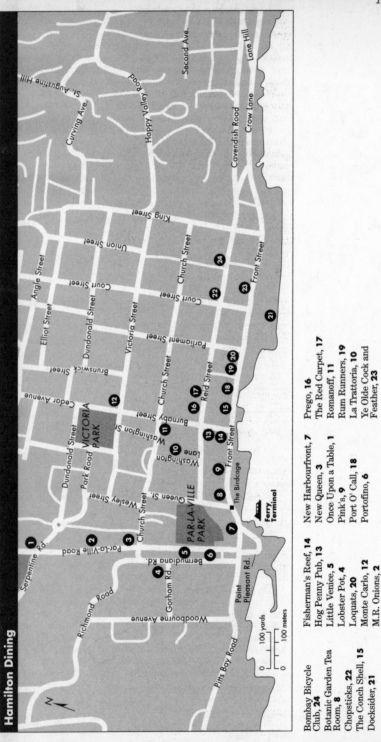

Hamilton Dining

Bombay Bicycle
Club, **24**
Botanic Garden Tea
Room, **8**
Chopsticks, **22**
The Conch Shell, **15**
Docksider, **21**

Fisherman's Reef, **14**
Hog Penny Pub, **13**
Little Venice, **5**
Lobster Pot, **4**
Loquats, **20**
Monte Carlo, **12**
M.R. Onions, **2**

New Harbourfront, **7**
New Queen, **3**
Once Upon a Table, **1**
Pink's, **9**
Port O' Call, **18**
Portofino, **6**

Prego, **16**
The Red Carpet, **17**
Romanoff, **11**
Rum Runners, **19**
La Trattoria, **10**
Ye Olde Cock and
Feather, **23**

pudding. Other island dishes turn up just when you despair of ever finding any. At breakfast, ask for codfish and bananas, made with the salt cod commonly known as Portuguese bacalao. Revived by soaking in water, the cod is cooked with a savory tomato sauce and usually served with boiled potatoes and sautéed bananas. Hoppin' John, a Bermudian dish that's also popular in the Carolinas, is rice cooked with chicken, beans or peas, bacon, onion, and thyme. Another traditional favorite is syllabub, a sweet treat of guava, wine, and cream served either as a liquid or a jelly.

For the most part, however, dining on the island is fairly non-Bermudian, and it's expensive: Dinner at the island's best restaurants can cost as much as $100 per person, excluding a 15% service charge. During the summer season, reservations are essential at these restaurants. Of course, if you are staying in one of the major resorts, you can usually choose from several restaurants without ever leaving the property, and most hotels and cottage colonies offer a variety of meal plans ranging from full board to Continental breakfasts (*see* Chapter 9, Lodging).

Dining in Bermuda tends to be rather formal. In the more upscale restaurants, men should wear jackets and ties, and women should be comparably attired. Credit cards are widely accepted in the major hotels and restaurants, while the small taverns and lunch spots only take cash.

Highly recommended restaurants are indicated by a star ★.

Category	Cost*
Very Expensive	over $50
Expensive	$36–$50
Moderate	$20–$35
Inexpensive	under $20

per person, excluding drinks and service (a 15% service charge is sometimes added)

The following credit card abbreviations are used: AE, American Express; D, Discover; DC, Diners Club; MC, MasterCard; V, Visa.

Asian

Expensive **Mikado.** This fun restaurant in Marriott's Castle Harbour Hotel brings Japanese cooking to very English Bermuda. The decor is stark, using simple lines and colors to great effect. As at many Japanese-style steak houses, the enjoyment lies less in the food than in the dazzling flash of twirling knives, slapping mallets, and airborne salt and pepper shakers—it's like judo you can eat. Although à la carte dining is available, you're better off with one of the complete dinners: a shrimp or scallop appetizer with ginger sauce, miso or *tori* soup, a seafood or beef entrée selection, salad, steamed rice, *teppan-yaki* vegetables, and Japanese tea. *Castle Harbour Hotel, Tucker's Town, tel. 809/293–2040. Reservations required. Dress: neat but casual. AE, DC, MC, V.*

Moderate **Bombay Bicycle Club.** The culinary scene of any British colony would be woefully incomplete without a curry house. Named after a private gentleman's club in the waning days of the Raj, this burgundy-hued restaurant captures the flavor of the sub-continent without becoming a caricature. All the traditional Indian favorites are offered here and prepared remarkably well. Order the *peeaz pakora* (onion fritters) and mulligatawny soup as starters, then opt for the *jhinga vindaloo* (shrimp in hot curry), *mutton saagwala* (braised lamb in creamy spinach), or anything from the clay tandoor oven. *Nan*, *paratha*, and *papadums* are terrific breads and snacks to accompany the meal. *Reid St., Hamilton, tel. 809/292–0048. Reservations suggested. Dress: neat but casual. AE, DC, MC, V.*

Chopsticks. An alternative to New Queen (*see* below) at the east end of Hamilton, this Chinese restaurant features an intelligent mix of Szechuan, Hunan, and Cantonese favorites. The decor is utilitarian—red-upholstered chairs and tables—and mercifully devoid of calendars of Hong Kong's skyline. Top selections include the mandarin butterfly steak, lemon chicken Macau, and ribs in a mandarin orange sauce. For dessert, order nothing but the freshly baked pastries described as "Betty's pies." *Reid St. E, Hamilton, tel. 809/292–0791. Reservations suggested. Dress: neat but casual. AE, DC, MC, V.*

New Queen. This Chinese restaurant is the current favorite of Bermudians, who flock here for the hot and spicy fare. The emphasis is on the food rather than the decor, but the interior is attractive, clean, and subdued. Try the Szechuan duck, steamed until tender, then pressed with black mushrooms and potato flour, deep-fried, and served with a peppery mushroom sauce. Another great choice is *wor suit* chicken—boneless chicken pressed with minced meat, lightly battered and fried, and served on a bed of vegetables. *Par-la-Ville Rd., Hamilton, tel. 809/295–4004 or 809/292–3282. Reservations suggested. Dress: neat but casual. AE, DC, MC, V.*

Bermudian

Expensive **Glencoe.** The Salt Kettle ferry from Hamilton drops you off just two minutes' walk from this popular restaurant overlooking the harbor in Paget. Part of a cottage colony owned by Reggie and Margot Cooper, the restaurant offers truly stylish dining: Lunch is almost always served on the patio, and dinner is in an impressive manor house that dates back to the 1700s. The lunch menu is in English, and the dinner menu in French—a sure sign that the dining becomes fussier after sunset. Start with the *gaspacho Andaluz* (chilled vegetable soup) in summer or the fish chowder in any season. The vichyssoise is excellent at dinner, too, as are the local fish in a sauce of tomatoes, capers, and white wine, and the crispy roast duckling in a dark cherry sauce. Another dish worth considering is the chicken breast wrapped around a lobster tail, served in a red-wine sauce. *Salt Kettle, Paget, tel. 809/236–5274. Reservations required. Dress: casual at lunch, jacket and tie required at dinner. AE, DC, MC, V.*

★ **Plantation.** Chris and Carol West call their trendy, clublike establishment a "truly Bermudian restaurant"; if that means the emphasis is on fresh seafood, they are absolutely right. Island wicker, flickering candles, and a glass-enclosed atrium filled with plants give the restaurant a cool, exotic look that works well with the ambitious, tropical menu. Some of the dishes can

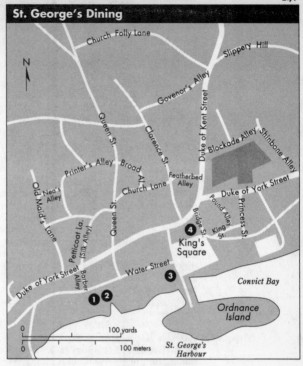

St. George's Dining

be overly exotic, however—monkfish poached with pineapple, raisins, and a host of other curry condiments, for example—but the chef's art is in the right place. Panfried fish with prawns and coconuts offers a delightful tropical taste, as does the creative lamb loquat. *Bailey's Bay, Hamilton Parish, tel. 809/293–1188. Reservations suggested. Jacket and tie required. AE, DC, MC, V.*

Moderate **Black Horse Tavern.** Long a secret among Bermudians who
★ flock here for the good, plentiful food, this place was finally discovered by Americans from the next-door Naval Air Station. Nothing has changed much as a result. A menacing shark, with jaws agape, still hangs on the white-plaster wall, along with an assortment of other mounted island fish. And islanders still fill the casual dining room and the six outside picnic tables to savor the culinary magic of chef Bernel Pitcher. Curried conch stew with rice is a favorite, as are Pitcher's straightforward renderings of amberjack, rockfish, shark, tuna, wahoo, and—in season—Bermuda lobster. For lunch, the fish sandwich is a taste sensation. If you want to try a Bermuda original, ask for shark hash, the chef's most popular specialty—the kitchen can never keep it in stock. *St. David's Island, tel. 809/293–9742. Reservations unnecessary. Dress: casual. No credit cards.*

Loquats. A popular lunch spot for businesspeople, this chic restaurant becomes far more romantic at night, serving well-prepared meals to the accompaniment of a pianist. Bright colors and eye-catching graphics will appeal to the MTV generation. The extensive menu is thoroughly international, but the best dishes have a Bermudian touch. In other words, choose the conch fritters over the Norway prawn cocktail, the fish chowder over the cucumber and watercress, and the broiled Bermuda rockfish over the so-called scampi tempura. *Front St., Hamilton, tel. 809/292–4507. Reservations suggested. Dress: neat but casual. AE, DC, MC, V.*

Inexpensive ★ **Dennis's Hideaway.** Of all the eccentric characters who call St. David's home, Dennis Lamb may be the most eccentric. Piratical in appearance, he hunches over his pots grousing about everything from the plumbing and the government to the fate of man. The place consists of little more than a ramshackle pink building, a scattering of homemade picnic tables, and a few yapping dogs, but it serves probably Bermuda's best food. Don't come here if you're a stickler for cleanliness, however—the place is decidedly grubby. Dennis's son does most of the cooking these days, but Dennis still potters around the kitchen. If you want to make Dennis's day, order his "fish dinner with the works"—$28.50 for a feast of shark hash on toast, conch fritters, mussel stew, conch stew, fish chowder, fried fish, conch steak, shark steak, shrimp, scallops, and perhaps a bit of mussel pie. He may even include some bread-and-butter pudding for good measure. *Cashew City Rd., St. David's, tel. 809/297–0044. Reservations unnecessary. Dress: casual. No credit cards.*

British

Expensive **Carriage House.** Hearty English food is the daily bread of this attractive slice of the Somers Wharf restoration. With its exposed brick walls, the interior looks rather like the exterior; try to secure a table by a window so you can watch the action on the docks. The price of dinner can add up quickly, especially if you choose something like the Bermuda Triangle—shrimp, filet mignon, and chicken breast, each prepared with its own sauce. Don't overlook the fresh Bermuda rockfish. On Sunday, a much less expensive brunch features a generous buffet of eggs, pancakes, meat and seafood entrées, pastas, salads, and desserts. There's even unlimited wine. *Somers Wharf, St. George's, tel. 809/297–1270. Reservations suggested. Jacket required at dinner. AE, DC, MC, V.*

Henry VIII. As popular with locals as it is with tourists from the nearby Southampton resorts, this lively restaurant affects an Old England look that stops just short of "wench" waitresses and contrived Tudor styling. The food is terrific, an eclectic mix of English and Bermudian favorites. Order the mussel pie if it's offered, or opt for the lighter steamed mussels in wine. The fish chowder is wonderful, as are the very British lamb, beef, and steak and kidney pies. Save room for the dessert of bananas flamed in dark rum. *South Shore Rd., Southampton, tel. 809/238–1977. Reservations suggested. Jacket and tie required. AE, DC, MC, V.*

Moderate **Botanic Garden Tea Room.** One of Bermuda's most pleasant traditions is afternoon tea at Trimingham's department store in Hamilton. Like many tearooms, it has seen better days, but its faded elegance is now part of its appeal. Managed by the Fourways Inn, the tearoom also serves light lunches. A wide variety of teas, coffee, and soft drinks is available. *Front St., Hamilton, tel. 809/295–1183. Reservations unnecessary. Dress: casual. No credit cards.*

★ **Colony Pub.** A favorite meeting place for Hamilton's business and government communities, this cozy nook is an excellent place for visitors to gain an understanding of how Bermuda works. Tourists are readily accepted by the lunching locals, although more as honored spectators than participants. Part of the Princess Hotel, the pub is redolent of Britain and the history of this tiny island. Rich shades of brown and green, and plenty of polished brass, give the restaurant an appealing clublike atmosphere. Food at the luncheon buffet is unpretentious but good, and the prices are very reasonable. *Princess Hotel, Hamilton, tel. 809/295–3000. Reservations unnecessary. Dress: casual. AE, DC, MC, V.*

Hog Penny Pub. Veterans of a London pub crawl might wonder about some of the dishes offered at this atmospheric watering hole off Front Street in Hamilton—"escargots pub-style" is, after all, something of an oxymoron. Nevertheless, die-hard aficionados of British cooking (if such animals actually exist) will also be rewarded with shepherd's pie, steak and kidney pie, and bangers (sausages) and mash; there's even a small but passable sampling of curries. But look for good fun more than good food: Sunburned strangers mingle freely in this dark and smoky den, and entertainment is offered nightly. *Burnaby Hill, Hamilton, tel. 809/292–2534. Reservations suggested. Dress: casual. AE, DC, MC, V.*

Port Royal Golf Club. This white dining room, on the 19th hole of the Port Royal Golf Club, overlooks the golf course through large plate-glass windows. Ask for a steak sandwich and English beer, although don't hesitate to order something more sophisticated from the main menu—the food is quite good. *Port Royal, Southampton, tel. 809/234–0236. Reservations suggested. Dress: casual. AE, DC, MC, V. Open until dusk.*

Pub on the Square. After a morning wandering around St. George's, this pub on King's Square is perfect for a slaking pint of English beer. The draft beer is better than anything that comes from the kitchen, although hamburgers and fish-and-chips are reasonably prepared. Warehouse brick and plenty of dark wood give the pub a warm atmosphere. *King's Sq., St. George's, tel. 809/297–1522. Reservations unnecessary. Dress: casual. No credit cards.*

Somerset Country Squire. Overlooking Mangrove Bay in the West End, this typically English tavern is all dark wood and good cheer, with a great deal of malt and hops in between. The food isn't good enough to warrant a special trip across the island, but you won't be disappointed if you do stop by. Steak and kidney pie is fine, but the curried mussel pie is much better. Desserts are excellent: The hot apple pie with whipped cream approaches mythical status. *Mangrove Bay, Somerset, tel. 809/234–0105. Reservations unnecessary. Dress: casual. No credit cards.*

Wharf Tavern. Like most dockside restorations in Bermuda, this English-style watering hole is nondescript, with a stale atmosphere; it should be much better than it is. The mainstays are a selection of so-called Black Beard's pizzas (of which the privateer would surely disapprove) and an equally varied selection of burgers. The quality and service are typical of a pub, but the menu and prices are what you would expect in a proper restaurant. *Somers Wharf, St. George's, tel. 809/297–1515. Reservations unnecessary. Dress: casual. AE, DC, MC, V (with a $25 minimum).*

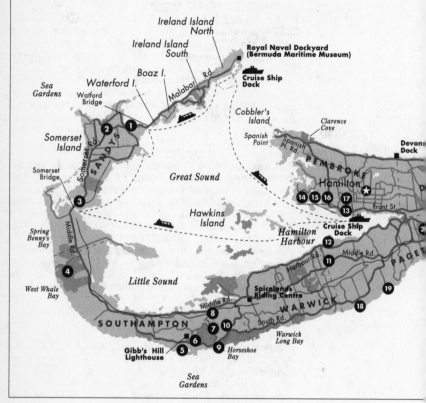

ATLANTIC OCEAN

Ireland Island North

Ireland Island South

Boaz I.

Waterford I.

Sea Gardens

Watford Bridge

Royal Naval Dockyard (Bermuda Maritime Museum)

Cruise Ship Dock

Malabar Rd.

Cobbler's Island

Clarence Cove

Somerset Island

SANDY'S

Somerset Rd.

Spanish Point

Spanish Pt. Rd.

Devons Dock

PEMBROKE

Somerset Bridge

Great Sound

Hamilton

Front St.

Spring Benny's Bay

Middle Rd.

Hawkins Island

Little Sound

West Whale Bay

Hamilton Harbour

Cruise Ship Dock

Harbour Rd.

Middle Rd.

PAGE

Spicelands Riding Centre

WARWICK

Middle Rd.

SOUTHAMPTON

South Rd.

Warwick Long Bay

Gibb's Hill Lighthouse

Horseshoe Bay

Sea Gardens

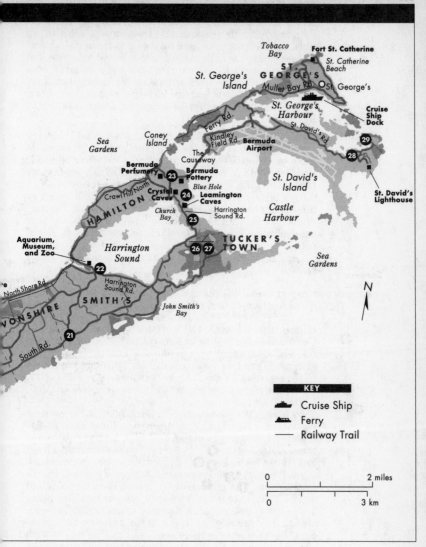

Tobacco Bay

Fort St. Catherine

St. Catherine Beach

St. George's Island

ST. GEORGE'S

Mullet Bay Rd. St. George's

St. George's Harbour

Cruise Ship Dock

Ferry Rd.

St. David's Rd.

Sea Gardens

Coney Island

Kindley Field Rd.

Bermuda Airport

The Causeway

Bermuda Perfumery

Bermuda Pottery

23

Crystal Caves

Blue Hole

24

Leamington Caves

St. David's Island

Castle Harbour

29

28

St. David's Lighthouse

Crawl Hill North

Harrington Sound Rd.

Church Bay

25

HAMILTON

Aquarium, Museum, and Zoo

Harrington Sound

22

26 27

TUCKER'S TOWN

Sea Gardens

N

North Shore Rd.

Harrington Sound Rd.

SMITH'S

John Smith's Bay

DEVONSHIRE

21

South Rd.

KEY

Cruise Ship

Ferry

Railway Trail

0   2 miles

0   3 km

Ye Olde Cock and Feather. One of the busiest spots along Front Street in Hamilton, this is a favorite meeting place for locals. Patrons sit either in a room that is a cross between a British pub and a Key West–style tropical outpost or on the upstairs balcony overlooking the harbor. Food here is served pub-style, but the eclectic menu spans several cuisines and continents, from gazpacho Andaluz to steak and kidney pie and chicken Kiev. Live entertainment is featured nightly. *Front St., Hamilton, tel. 809/295–2263. Reservations suggested. Dress: casual. AE, DC, MC, V.*

Inexpensive **Docksider.** This Front Street hangout boasts that it has the widest selection of draft beers on the island, which says a lot about its priorities and the priorities of its young clientele. However, that's no reason to steer clear of the fish-and-chips or the hamburgers. The club sandwiches are a good bet, too, although taste just won't matter once you've drunk your way through the bar's large selection of European brews. The interior is crowded with hundreds of beer bottles, labels, and beer paraphernalia. *Front St., Hamilton, tel. 809/292–4088. Reservations unnecessary. Dress: casual. No credit cards.*

French

Very Expensive **Newport Room.** With its nautical theme, this lovely restaurant in the Southampton Princess has occupied a special place in the hearts of the island's elite for several years. French cuisine is the specialty. Glistening teak and models of previous America's Cup winners set the tone for some culinary winners, especially the grilled snapper with ratatouille and garlic quenelles (dumplings), and the venison medallions with orange sauce and fresh pasta. *South Shore Rd., Southampton, tel. 809/238–8167. Reservations suggested. Jacket and tie required. AE, DC, MC, V. Dinner only.*

Tiara Room. After something of an identity crisis, the gourmet restaurant in Bermuda's historic Princess Hotel has rediscovered those elements of dining that make for fine cuisine and theater. Renovations in 1990 have given the restaurant a fresh look, utilizing clean lines and bright colors (particularly mauve), but the highlight remains the stunning view of Hamilton Harbour. The emphasis is on classic French cuisine and service that can be overwhelming. Whenever possible, dishes are finished tableside, often flambéed dramatically. These tableside theatrics may not be chic in Paris or New York nowadays, but they work in these surroundings. The rack of lamb carved tableside is always an excellent choice, as are the cherries Jubilee and the crepes suzette. *Princess Hotel, Hamilton, tel. 809/295–3000. Reservations suggested. Jacket and tie required. AE, DC, MC, V.*

★ **Waterlot Inn.** Housed in a graceful, single-story manor house that dates back to 1670, this restaurant is a Bermudian treasure. Like most Bermudian restaurants, it has good days and bad, but it works hard to live up to its reputation and age. Chef Regis Neaud watches over the kitchen, while the dining room staff has just enough island exuberance to take the edge off their European-style training. The menu's French selections are far superior to most of the cuisine that passes for French on the island, although the chef seldom misses an opportunity to prepare dishes indigenous to Bermuda. Waterlot serves one of the best fish chowders on the island, while the Bermuda rockfish, wrapped in spinach leaves and baked in puff pastry, is spectacular. For dessert, try the chocolate domino—white chocolate mousse in a domino of dark chocolate. *Middle Rd., Southampton, tel. 809/238-0510. Reservations suggested. Jacket and tie required. AE, DC, MC, V.*

Expensive   **Monte Carlo.** Southern French cooking is the trademark of this bright new restaurant just behind City Hall in Hamilton. Beams of old Bermuda cedar add a touch of local color, as does the unusual original artwork on the walls. There is a good selection of pizzas, but the main emphasis is on a sprightly collection of hot and cold appetizers. The carpaccio (thinly sliced raw beef served with lemon) and the stuffed mussels are superb. Favorite entrées include roast duck in mango sauce, and veal breaded with Parmesan and served with two sauces. *Victoria St., Hamilton, tel. 809/295-5453. Reservations suggested. Dress: neat but casual. AE, MC, V.*

Waterloo House. A private home a century ago, this restaurant/guest house on Hamilton Harbour serves Bermudian and Continental cuisine. Guests can eat either on the waterside patio adjoining the flower-shaded buildings, or in the uncluttered English dining room, where a fire is kept burning during the winter. Chef Bruno Heeb usually offers a special or two, but don't overlook such appetizers as St. Jacques ravioli and sautéed periwinkles in a pink champagne sauce. For an entrée, consider one of the stranger dishes on the island: Bermuda rockfish stuffed with oysters and wrapped in fresh salmon, with caviar sauce and an avocado rice timbale. *Pitt's Bay Rd., Pembroke, Hamilton, tel. 809/295-4480. Reservations suggested. Jacket and tie required at dinner. No credit cards.*

International

Very Expensive   **Fourways Inn.** This restaurant has risen to preeminence on the island in recent years, as much for its lovely 18th-century surroundings as anything coming out of the kitchen. The decor is evocative of a wealthy plantation home, with plenty of expensive china, crystal, and silver. Order the local mussels simmered in white wine and cream, and any of the sautéed veal dishes. The Caesar salad is a good choice, too, but leave enough room for strawberry soufflé, if it's available. For a slightly different cocktail, try a Fourways Special, made with the juice from the Bermuda loquat and other fruits, and a dash of bitters. *1 Middle Rd., Paget, tel. 809/236-6517. Reservations suggested. Jacket and tie required. AE, DC, MC, V.*

Romanoff. Elegant European meals served in a theatrical Russian setting are the specialty of this restaurant run by Anton Duzavic. A deep rich red is the restaurant's predominant color, providing a dramatic backdrop for the vodka and black caviar that Duzavic himself presents to each diner. Stick to the well-known dishes or select a seafood special from the cart that is wheeled around the tables. *Church St., Hamilton, tel. 809/295-0333. Reservations suggested. Jacket and tie required. AE, DC, MC, V.*

Expensive   **Norwood Room.** Don't be put off that this restaurant in the Stonington Beach Hotel is run by students of the Bermuda Department of Hotel Technology. Under the supervision of their mentors, the students offer a dining experience notable for the high quality of the food and superb service. The kitchen uses local ingredients and European culinary techniques to create a whole range of bright, fresh tastes. Seafood is the best bet here, well prepared and served with excellent sauces. Enjoy a preprandial cocktail at the sunken bar overlooking the swimming pool. *South Shore Rd., tel. 809/236-5416. Reservations suggested. Jacket and tie required. AE, DC, MC, V.*

Tavern on the Green. No connection to the famous restaurant in New York's Central Park, this stylish tavern is hidden away in Bermuda's Botanical Gardens. Tables overlook the gardens, a waterfall, and a statue of Caesar. Additional seating for 100 was recently added, and there's a small dance floor and a honeymoon retreat. The eight-page menu focuses on dishes with a Mediterranean flair, including such specialties as duck breast sautéed in a fruit sauce and garnished with kiwi, and beef sirloin served with a sauce of green peppercorns and Bermuda's own sherry peppers. *Botanical Gardens, Paget, tel. 809/236-7731. Reservations suggested. Dress: neat but casual. AE, DC, MC, V.*

Tom Moore's Tavern. Set in an old home that dates to 1652, this restaurant overlooking Bailey's Bay clearly enjoys its colorful past. Irish poet Tom Moore visited friends here frequently during his stay on the island in 1804 and wrote several of his odes under the nearby Calabash Tree. Today, fireplaces, casement windows, and copper appointments capture a sense of the building's history. The cuisine, however, labors under none of history's baggage—it is fresh, light, and innovative. Seafood lovers should try the Treasures of St. David's Island, a marriage of local fish, flame fish, and lobster tail. *Bailey's Bay, Hamilton Parish, tel. 809/293-8020. Reservations suggested. Jacket required. AE, DC, MC, V.*

Windsor. Overlooking Castle Harbour Resort, this elegant dining room in Marriott's Castle Harbour Hotel features an international blend of cuisines with a strong European underpinning. Try the salmon, fettuccine Alfredo, escargot Café de Paris, or prime rib with Yorkshire pudding. Don't expect too much innovation, however; as a hotel dining room, the restaurant must hedge its culinary bets. Nevertheless, with its unhurried atmosphere, live piano music, and view of Castle Harbour, the Windsor makes for a fine night out. *Castle Harbour Resort, Tucker's Town, tel. 809/293-2040. Reservations required. Jacket and tie required. AE, DC, MC, V. No lunch.*

Moderate **The Conch Shell.** This attractive, modern restaurant is the setting for an unusual mix of cuisines and ingredients, from seafood and steaks to Asian specialties—the latter are done so well that the restaurant could easily be classified as Chinese. Egg rolls, ginger beef, and lamb curry are served alongside fried seafood platters and conch fritters. *Emporium Bldg., Front St., Hamilton, tel. 809/295-6969. Reservations recommended. Dress: casual. AE, DC, MC, V.*

The Inlet. With beautiful views over Harrington Sound, this restaurant in the Palmetto Hotel is filled with sunlight and fresh air. None of the dishes is likely to find its way into a gourmet magazine, but the quality is reasonable and guests have a wide selection from which to choose. In winter, there are good steaks and rack of lamb. *Palmetto Hotel, Flatts Village, tel. 809/293-2323. Reservations suggested. Jacket and tie required. AE, DC, MC, V.*

M. R. Onions. The Bermudian equivalent of TGIFriday, this fun restaurant got its name from the phrase "Him are Onions," meaning "he's one of us" (Bermudians are referred to as Onions, after the sweet onion that grows on the island). Friendly service and good spirits (both from the heart and the bar) make for an enjoyable evening here. Finger foods, such as potato skins, zucchini sticks, and breaded mushrooms, are especially good, although don't hesitate to order anything from fish chowder to charbroiled fish, steaks, and barbecued ribs. A special children's menu is available until 8 PM, but children are discouraged any later than that. *Par-la-Ville Rd. N, Hamilton, tel. 809/292–5012. Reservations suggested. Dress: casual. AE, DC, MC, V.*

Harbourfront. Few of the restaurants along Front Street have the courage to be so inventively Continental or ambitious as this thoroughly modern restaurant, where unusual architectural elements clash with a tropical decor. The menu has recently traded its Mediterranean flavors for more basic European fare; the veal chops are exceptional, as is the roast duck in a sauce of seasonal fruit. *Front St., Hamilton, tel. 809/295–4207. Reservations recommended. Dress: casual. AE, DC, MC, V.*

★ **Once Upon a Table.** Hailed by many Bermudians as the finest restaurant on Bermuda, this delightful restaurant offers elegant service in an 18th-century island home, complete with elegant china and crystal. Dinner here is theatrical—the restaurant is not unlike a theme park in its use of costumes and setting to create a sense of a bygone era. From the menu, consider rack of lamb, roast duckling, or pork, although you can also order a dinner of Bermudian specialties with 48-hours' notice. *Serpentine Rd., Hamilton, tel. 809/295–8585. Reservations recommended. Jacket and tie required. Dinner only. AE, DC, MC, V.*

Rum Runners. This popular Front Street restaurant assumes different personalities throughout the day. It is at its most formal at dinner, when it becomes a full-service restaurant with terrific seafood and well-coached waiters. The best bets are the seafood brochette and the fish pot, both combination plates of immense proportions. Meat patrons will be amply satisfied by the mixed English grill. Lunch is far more casual, with traditional pub fare as well as sandwiches, salads, and the unavoidable array of burgers. *Front St., Hamilton, tel. 809/292–4737. Reservations suggested for dinner. Dress: casual. AE, DC, MC, V.*

Seahorse Grill. With rustic decor reminiscent of old Bermuda, this casual restaurant at the Elbow Beach Hotel in Paget is a winner. In addition to overwhelmingly large burgers and pizzas, the Seahorse's diverse menu includes breast of chicken in fruit-tinged curry sauce, lamb chops in Provencale herbs, and beef fillet in green peppercorn sauce. Don't overlook the dessert trolley. *Elbow Beach Hotel, Paget, tel. 809/236–3535. Reservations recommended. Dress: casual. AE, DC, MC, V.*

Swizzle Inn. People come to this outwardly nondescript place as much to drink as to eat. Just west of the airport near the Bermuda Perfume Factory, the inn created one of Bermuda's most hallowed drinks—the rum swizzle. Sit in the shadowy bar—plastered with business cards from all over the world—sipping one of these delightful concoctions, and watch the mopeds whiz by. If you get hungry, try a "swizzleburger." *Blue Hole Hill, Bailey's Bay, tel. 809/293–9300. Reservations unnecessary. Dress: casual. MC, V.*

White Horse Tavern. Set on the water's edge overlooking the harbor in St. George's, this restaurant has such a great location and atmosphere that a little more local color in the menu would work wonders. As it is, however, you can only get high-quality burgers, steaks, and a small selection of fish—nothing that sets the place apart. Still, the memorable chocolate cake makes the tavern worth a visit. *King's Sq., St. George's, tel. 809/297–1838. Reservations unnecessary. Dress: casual. AE, DC, MC, V.*

Inexpensive **Pink's.** This deli in the heart of Hamilton is certain to make your day—or at least your lunch. Salads are wide-ranging, from tabouleh to tarragon chicken and pasta; creative sandwich combinations are available. Try the country pate. *55 Front St., Hamilton, tel. 809/295–3524. Reservations unnecessary. Dress: casual. No credit cards. Breakfast and lunch Mon.–Sat.*

Italian

Expensive **Little Venice.** The name of this restaurant may refer to the lovely city of canals, but the atmosphere is strictly Roman—stylish, self-confident, and urbane. Bermudians head for this trattoria when they want more from Italian cooking than pizza. Little Venice can be expensive, but the food is decent enough to command higher prices and the service is expert. In particular, try the eggplant with grilled cheese and herbs as an appetizer, or perhaps the crepes filled with ricotta and spinach. Marinated in fresh mint and simmered with scallions, wine, and fresh tomatoes, the swordfish makes an excellent main course. A special early evening dinner deal, featuring appetizer, main course, dessert, and coffee, is available for $16.75—less than most of the à la carte entrées. *Bermudiana Rd., Hamilton, tel. 809/295–3503 or 809/295–8279. Reservations suggested. Dress: neat but casual. AE, DC, MC, V.*

Moderate **Il Palio.** A ship's spiral staircase leads upstairs from the bar to the dining room at this West End restaurant. Some of the best pizzas on the island are served here, with all the usual trimmings. Among the other offerings are a wide range of good antipasti and pasta dishes, including cannelloni and pasta primavera. The selections of veal, chicken, and beef are straightforward. *Main Rd., Somerset, tel. 809/234–1049 or 809/234–2323. Reservations suggested. Dress: casual. AE, DC, MC, V.*

Primavera. White and burgundy dominate this pleasing Mediterranean dining room in the west end of Hamilton. Ultimately, however, it's the food that makes a visit here worthwhile. A spectacular starter is baked mushrooms in garlic butter with paprika and cream, followed by one of the house specialties: breast of duck with black peppercorns, brandy, and cream. Guests can also choose from a wide variety of consistently good pastas. *Pitt's Bay Rd., Hamilton, tel. 809/295–2167. Reservations suggested. Dress: neat but casual. AE, DC, MC, V. No lunch weekends.*

The Red Carpet. Very popular at lunch, this tiny restaurant sports a few New York touches, such as a ravioli dish named for Frank Sinatra, but otherwise the flavor is Old World Italian. The clever use of mirrors dispels a sense of claustrophobia, while plentiful brass gives the place a stylish look. Among the culinary highlights are the veal, the Bermuda fish dishes, an incongruous beef Stroganoff, and chicken Normand (prepared with Calvados apple brandy). *Armoury Bldg., Reid St., Ham-*

ilton, tel. 809/292–6195. Reservations suggested. Dress: neat but casual. AE, DC, MC, V.

Inexpensive **Portofino.** Busy for both lunch and dinner, this popular Italian restaurant, with its traditional red-check tablecloths, is really a fancy pizza parlor. A wide selection of pizza toppings is available, and customers are asked to phone 15 minutes ahead if they want their pie to go. If you're not in the mood for pizza, however, try the excellent sirloin steak with olives, capers, and tomato sauce, or the fried calamari in a delicate batter. More adventurous diners will enjoy the octopus, cooked in red sauce with olives and capers and served on a bed of rice. *Bermudiana Rd., Hamilton, tel. 809/292–2375 or 809/295–6090. Reservations suggested. Dress: casual. AE, DC, MC, V. Closed for lunch weekends.*

Prego. Accented with brass and burgundy, this cozy restaurant on Hamilton's east side is usually very busy. There's nothing on the menu that you couldn't find at most Italian restaurants, but the prices are quite reasonable. Pizzas are a specialty, as is the excellent rendition of *penne puttanesca*, pasta with tomatoes, anchovies, capers, olives, and hot peppers. *Reid St. E, Hamilton, tel. 809/292–1279. Reservations suggested. Dress: casual. AE, DC, MC, V.*

Specialty Inn. A favorite with locals, this south-shore restaurant is cheerful, clean, and cheap. The low prices are reflected in the fact that the restaurant is almost totally lacking in decoration. Try the fish chowder or the red-bean soup. Otherwise, all the dishes are just what you would expect of a family-style Italian restaurant, plus milk shakes and ice cream. *Collectors Hill, Smith's, tel. 809/236–3133. Reservations suggested. Dress: casual. No credit cards.*

Tio Pepe. You don't need to spend a lot of money for a satisfying meal at this Italian restaurant with a Mexican name. Photocopied menus and flourishes of red and green (also rather Mexican) create an easygoing atmosphere ideal for bathers returning from a day at Horseshoe Bay Beach. Try an appetizer such as spicy eggplant baked in tomato sauce and cheese, followed by a small pizza or pasta dish. *South Shore Rd., Southampton, tel. 809/239–1897 or 809/238–0572. Reservations suggested. Dress: casual. AE, DC, MC, V.*

La Trattoria. Tucked in a Hamilton alley, this comfortable trattoria is typical of every no-nonsense Italian restaurant with red-check tablecloths: Veal parmigiana is the staple, and tortellini is a typical starter. However, this restaurant also serves an interesting "diet" pizza, made with whole-wheat flour and topped with zucchini and tomatoes, and an antidiet Italian buffet every Thursday night from 5 PM to 10 PM; eat as much as you want for $15.75. *Washington La., Hamilton, tel. 809/292–7059 or 809/295–1877. Reservations suggested. Dress: casual. AE, DC, MC, V.*

Seafood

Expensive **Lillian's.** Part of the Sonesta Beach Hotel, this elegant art nouveau restaurant gains much of its character from testimonials and mementos in honor of Aunt Lillian, whose counsel appears on the menus advising diners to "be wonderful or be horrible, but for heaven's sake, don't be mediocre." Lillian's is neither mediocre nor horrible, and it is well worth a visit. Seafood is the specialty, starting with the so-called Bermuda Fish Market—two fresh fish cooked as you wish and topped with the sauce of your choice. The grilled swordfish, with its herb and spice marinade, is also excellent. *Sonesta Beach Hotel, Southampton, tel. 809/238–8122. Reservations suggested. Jacket required. AE, DC, MC, V. Closed Mon.*

Whaler Inn. Perched above the rocks and surf at the Southampton Princess, this seafood house has one of the most dramatic settings on the island. The table d'hôte menu ($32 per person, plus a 15% gratuity) entitles you to an appetizer, a salad, a main course, dessert, and a beverage. Start with the crisp, lightly battered Bermuda rockfish and the fish chowder. Cooked the way you want, any of the selections of fresh wahoo, yellowfin tuna, barracuda, shark, or dolphinfish makes an excellent main course. *Southampton Princess Hotel, South Shore Rd., Southampton, tel. 809/238–0076. Reservations suggested. Dress: neat but casual. AE, DC, MC, V.*

Moderate **Blue Foam.** Don't let its location at the motel-like Somerset Bridge Hotel put you off this restaurant. Grilled, baked, sautéed, or fried, the local fish served here needs nothing more than a drizzle of lemon and butter. In summer, do your best to secure one of the tables on the terrace overlooking Ely's Harbour and the world's smallest drawbridge, or settle for the cozy, greenhouse atmosphere of the dining room. For something other than grilled food, try the seafood brochette—fish, shrimp, and scallops fried Asian-style in a light batter and served with sweet-and-sour sauce. *Somerset Bridge, Sandys, tel. 809/234–1042. Reservations required. Dress: neat but casual. AE, DC, MC, V.*

Fisherman's Reef. Located above the Hog Penny Pub, this restaurant has a predictable nautical motif. The Reef draws a crowd of locals, who are attracted by the restaurant's high-quality seafood and steaks, for lunch and dinner. The fish chowder is excellent, as is the St. David's conch chowder. Of the wide selection of seafood entrées, the best are the Bermuda lobster, the wahoo Mangrove Bay (seasoned and broiled with slices of Bermuda onions and banana), and the dolphinfish Cardinal (panfried and coated with a rosy pink lobster sauce). *Burnaby Hill, just off Front St., Hamilton, tel. 809/292–1609. Reservations recommended. Dress: casual for lunch, neat but casual for dinner. AE, DC, MC, V.*

Harley's. Mildly nautical in theme, this pleasant restaurant in the Princess emphasizes fresh fish and simple presentation. Best bets are the grilled grouper, snapper, and dolphinfish, or the scallops en brochette. The restaurant stopped short of placing the grill in the open as entertainment, but the muted sea and sand tones bespeak a consultant's touch. *Princess Hotel, Hamilton, tel. 809/295–3000. Reservations recommended. Dress: casual. AE, DC, MC, V.*

Lobster Pot. Locals swear by this place, which serves local lobster in winter, excellent Maine lobster, and a host of other local shellfish and fish. In keeping with its specialty, the restaurant sports a nautical decor, including shining brass instruments and sun-bleached rope. The menu is a little too cute for its own good ("Frankie's Fish and Fun" belongs in a fast-food restaurant), but it features some of the best versions of the local standards. *Bermudiana Rd., Hamilton, tel. 809/292–6898. Reservations suggested. Dress: casual. AE, DC, MC, V. Closed Sun.*

Port O' Call. For lunch or dinner, this restaurant is one of

Hamilton's elegant new favorites. While there are some spectacular lighter dishes for the midday meal, dinner is the time for abandonment. The roast veal shank with red cabbage is unforgettable, as is the pan fried or broiled black grouper. *87 Front St., Hamilton, tel. 809/295-5373. Reservations recommended. Jacket required at dinner. AE, DC, MC, V. Closed Sun.*

9 Lodging

by Honey Naylor   If all the accommodations available on Bermuda were reviewed here, this book would barely qualify as carry-on luggage. Visitors to this tiny island can choose from a huge array of full-service resort hotels, cottage colonies, small inns, guest houses, and housekeeping apartments. It is the beachfront cottage colonies for which Bermuda is probably most famous, however—free-standing cottages clustered around a main building housing a restaurant, a lounge, and an activities desk. Many properties, especially these cottage colonies, are sprawling affairs set in extensive grounds and connected by walkways and steps; at some of the smaller guest houses and housekeeping apartments visitors must carry their own luggage on the long walk to their rooms. Disabled visitors or anyone unwilling to climb hills may be happier at a conventional hotel with elevators and corridors.

Like everything else in Bermuda, lodging is expensive. The rates at Bermuda's luxury resorts are comparable to those at posh hotels in New York, London, and Paris. The high prices would be easier to swallow if you received first-class service in return. However, such features as 24-hour room service and same-day laundry service are rare; in most instances, you pay extra for room service when it is available. You can shave about 40% off your hotel bill by visiting Bermuda during the low or shoulder seasons, which run from October to April. Temperatures rarely dip below 60°F during this period, and the weather is ideal for tennis, golf, and shopping, although the water is a bit chilly for swimming. Low-season packages are attractively priced, and during this time a host of government-sponsored special events (many of which are free) are staged for tourists.

The greatest concentration of accommodations is along the south shore, in Paget, Warwick, and Southampton parishes, where the best beaches are located. If shopping is your bag, however, there are several hotels just a stone's throw from the main shopping area in Front Street in Hamilton, as well as a host of properties clustered around Hamilton Harbour, a five-to 10-minute ferry ride from the capital. The West End is a bit remote, but it is ideal for boaters, fishermen, and those who want to get away from it all. The East End has its share of nautical pursuits, too, but its major attraction is the charming, historic village of St. George's. In truth, the island is so small that it's possible to see and do everything you want, regardless of where you unpack your bag.

Whether or not they are officially classified as cottage colonies, a large number of guest accommodations are in cottages—usually pink with white trim and gleaming white, tiered roofs. There are some sprawling resorts, but no high rises and no neon signs. An enormous property like the Southampton Princess is hard to miss, but many hotels and guest houses are identified only by small, inconspicuous signs or plaques. The island is noted for its lovely gardens and manicured lawns, and the grounds of almost every hotel and cottage are filled with subtropical trees, flowers, and shrubs.

A 6% tax is tacked onto all hotel bills, and a service charge is levied in lieu of tipping: Some hotels calculate the service charge as 10% of the bill, others charge a per diem dollar amount. Some of the smaller guest houses and housekeeping units have also instituted a 5% "energy surcharge." All guests

Lodging

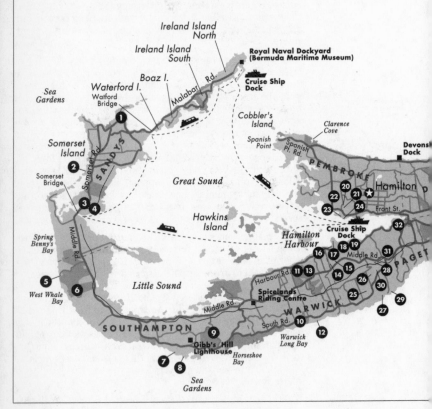

ATLANTIC OCEAN

Ireland Island North

Ireland Island South

Boaz I.

Waterford I.

Watford Bridge

Sea Gardens

Royal Naval Dockyard (Bermuda Maritime Museum)

Cruise Ship Dock

Cobbler's Island

Clarence Cove

Spanish Point

Spanish Pt. Rd.

Devonsh Dock

PEMBROKE

Somerset Island

SANDYS

Somerset Rd.

Somerset Bridge

Great Sound

Hawkins Island

Hamilton Harbour

Hamilton

Front St.

Cruise Ship Dock

PAGET

Spring Benny's Bay

Middle Rd.

Little Sound

West Whale Bay

Harbour Rd.

Middle Rd.

WARWICK

Spicelands Riding Centre

South Rd.

Warwick Long Bay

SOUTHAMPTON

Gibb's Hill Lighthouse

Horseshoe Bay

Sea Gardens

Middle Rd.

KEY

🚢 Cruise Ship

⛴ Ferry

— Railway Trail

0		2 miles
0		3 km

Marriott's Castle Harbour Resort, **37**

Newstead, **19**

Oxford House, **20**

Palmetto Hotel & Cottages, **34**

Pink Beach Club & Cottages, **36**

Pompano Beach Club, **5**

Pretty Penny, **15**

The Princess, **23**

The Reefs, **7**

Rosedon, **21**

The St. George's Club, **40**

Salt Kettle House, **18**

Sky Top Cottages, **26**

Somerset Bridge Hotel, **3**

Sonesta Beach Hotel & Spa, **8**

Southampton Princess, **9**

Stonington Beach Hotel, **29**

Waterloo House, **24**

Whale Bay Inn, **6**

Willowbank, **2**

are required to make a two-night deposit two to three weeks before their arrival; those accommodations that don't take credit cards for payment—and many do not—may accept them for the deposit. Virtually every hotel on the island offers at least one vacation package—frequently some kind of honeymoon special—and many of these are extraordinarily good deals. It's worth learning about the various policies and programs at the properties that interest you before booking.

Bermuda is not noted as a great family destination, and some hotels discourage parents from bringing small children. In 1990, however, three properties inaugurated family packages during high season: The Grotto Bay Beach Hotel & Tennis Club, the Sonesta Beach Hotel & Spa, and the Southampton Princess offer free room and board for children up to age 16 staying in the same room as their parents on the Modified American Plan (MAP). All packages include free, supervised day camps for children. The Elbow Beach Hotel also offers a MAP package that includes daily supervised children's activities. Many of the hotels on the island can arrange for baby-sitters, but only these four hotels offer special programs for children.

Most lodgings offer their guests a choice of meal plans, and the hotel rate varies according to the meal plan you choose. Under the American Plan (AP), breakfast, lunch, and dinner are included in the hotel rate; the Modified American Plan (MAP) offers breakfast and dinner; the Bermuda Plan (BP) includes a full breakfast but no dinner, while the Continental Plan (CP) features a breakfast of pastries, juice, and coffee. The rates quoted below are based on the European Plan (EP), which includes no meals at all. Many hotels also have a variety of "dine-around" plans that allow guests to eat at other restaurants on the island as part of their meal plan. During the low season, there is an island-wide dine-around program, in which 25 participating restaurants—including Italian, Japanese, English, and Continental establishments—offer three-course, prix fixe meals for $18.50, $23.50, and $29 per person. The Princess and the Southampton Princess offer a Royal Dine-Around program year-round, which allows guests to eat at any of the several Princess restaurants. The eight properties in the Bermuda Collection (Cambridge Beaches, Lantana, the Reefs, Horizons, Newstead, Glencoe Harbour Club, Stonington Beach, and the Pompano) have a similar arrangement, known as the Carousel Dine-Around program, as do Horizons, Newstead, and Waterloo House. Dinner is usually formal in restaurants at hotels and cottage colonies, and men are asked to wear jackets and ties; neat but casual dress is suggested for women. Many hotels will pack a picnic lunch for those guests who want to get out and about.

Cottage colonies and hotels offer entertainment at least one night a week during high season, staging everything from calypso to classical music; barbecues and dinner dances are also popular. Afternoon tea is served daily in keeping with British tradition, and a rum-swizzle party is usually held on Monday night. Featuring the Bermudian beverage of choice, these parties present a pleasant opportunity to welcome new arrivals, get acquainted—and, of course, knock back some rum. Guest houses and housekeeping apartments do not have regularly scheduled entertainment, although informal gatherings are not uncommon.

Most of the large hotels have their own water-sports facilities where guests can rent Windsurfers, Sunfish, paddle boats, and other equipment. Even the smallest property, however, can arrange sailing, snorkeling, scuba, and deep-sea fishing excursions, as well as sightseeing and harbor tours. The Coral Beach & Tennis Club and the Mid Ocean Club are posh private clubs, where an introduction by a member is necessary to gain access to their excellent beach, tennis, and golf facilities. However, many hotels have arrangements with one or the other to allow guests certain club privileges.

Highly recommended lodgings are indicated by a star ★.

Category	Cost*
Very Expensive	over $200
Expensive	$125–$200
Moderate	$90–$125
Inexpensive	under $90

All prices are for a standard double room for two (EP) during high season, excluding 6% tax and 10% service charge (or equivalent).

The following credit card abbreviations are used: AE, American Express; DC, Diners Club; MC, MasterCard; V, Visa.

Resort Hotels

Very Expensive **Elbow Beach Hotel.** Set amid 34 acres of botanical gardens overlooking the superb south-shore beach for which it is named, this large sports-oriented resort is popular with tour groups and is a major venue for College Weeks events. Guests are given a map to help them sort out the myriad paths and roads that wind down the hillside to the beach, past cottages, lanais, bars, and the pool. The main building, a five-story white stone edifice perched on top of the hill, houses a dining room, a nightclub, a shopping mall, library, health club, and a game room. Two hundred guest rooms and suites are also contained in this building, and the majority of these rooms have balconies or patios with ocean views. However, 71 are tiny "landside" rooms that have no balconies and overlook rooftops. Those guests who seek peace and quiet should avoid the ground-floor rooms off the main hallway—the area sees plenty of activity and can be noisy. The remainder of the rooms and suites are in duplex cottages and multi-unit lanais set amid the gardens or by the beach. Three types of suites are available: junior suites, with one bedroom, a small sitting room, and a patio; royal suites, with one or two bedrooms, a Jacuzzi, a lounge, and a large private patio; and family suites, with two bedrooms, a lounge, and private patio. The decor throughout is contemporary, with thick carpeting, sofas and chairs upholstered in flame-stitch fabrics, and attractive framed prints. Each room has a minibar. There are cabanas and showers on the beach, and weekly scuba lessons are offered at the Sea Horse Club. A playground is provided for children, and the swimming pool has a shallow area; during July and August special children's programs are held. Use of the health club, with its exercise machines and whirlpool, is free, but there's a $5-per-hour fee for the tennis courts ($8 for night play) and racquet rentals cost $3. A shuttle bus is available for those guests who don't want to tackle the surrounding hills on foot, and there are taxi stands at the hotel entrance and by the beach. *Box HM 455, Hamilton HM BX, tel. 809/236–3535; in U.S. and Canada, 800/223–7434. 223 rooms, 75 suites, all with bath. Meal plans: BP, MAP. Facilities: 3 restaurants, 3 bars, nightclub, private beach, beauty salon, moped rental, heated freshwater pool, shopping mall, game room, playground, 5 tennis courts (3 lighted), water sports, health club with exercise room and whirlpool. AE, DC, MC, V.*

Marriott's Castle Harbour Resort. Bordered by Harrington Sound on one side and the Castle Harbour golf course on the other, this whitewashed hilltop resort is an impressive sight from the air. If "castle" conjures up images of King Ludwig, though, forget it. This is a big, busy, modern hotel geared to groups and conventions. The original Castle, which opened in 1931, was built by the Furness Withy Steamship Line as a hotel for steamship passengers traveling between U.S. and British ports. Since 1984 Marriott has spent $60 million in renovation and expansion, and four new wings are now connected to the original building by glass-enclosed skywalks: the two-story Golf Club wing, the Bay View wing, and the two nine-story Harbour View wings, which descend in terraces to the water. Rooms throughout the hotel are identical, featuring upholstered wing-back chairs, windows dressed in ruffled valances, and heavy drapes with matching quilted bedspreads. All rooms have minifridges, and many have balconies. Most suites boast wet bars, refrigerators, and huge balconies. The resort's two beaches are miniscule, but guests have access to a private beach on the south shore and to three pools, including an Olympic-size lap pool and a cascading pool. Tennis courts are $8 an hour (plus $4 for racquet rental), but the well-equipped health club is free to guests. The big draw is the 18-hole Castle Harbour golf course; designed by Robert Trent Jones, it is one of the best courses on the island. *Box HM 841, Hamilton HM CX, tel. 809/293–2040; in U.S., 800/228–9290. 375 rooms, 27 suites, all with bath. Meal plan: EP. Facilities: 4 restaurants; 3 bars; 2 beaches; beauty/barber shop; concierge; moped rental; 3 heated freshwater pools; 6 all-weather tennis courts; 18-hole golf course; shops; same-day laundry/dry cleaning; marina and water sports; health club with exercise room, sauna, and whirlpool. AE, DC, MC, V.*

Sonesta Beach Hotel & Spa. A sloping, serpentine drive leads through landscaped lawns to this hotel, the only property on the island where you can step directly from your room onto a sandy south-shore beach. Set on a low promontory fringed by coral reefs, the six-story modern building has a stunning ocean view and direct access to three superb beaches. Totally refurbished in 1989, the Sonesta caters to guests who want an action-packed vacation: A social director coordinates bingo games, theme parties, movies, water sports, and other diversions. Vacationers seeking a quiet beachfront retreat will probably be happier elsewhere—perhaps at The Reefs (*see* below), adjacent to the Sonesta. A glass-enclosed entranceway leads to the enormous, low-ceiling lobby, where large groups are, it seems, always checking in or out. Guest rooms and suites are decorated in creams, island prints, and light woods. The two natural beaches on the 25-acre property are at Cross Bay and Sinky Bay, but beach lovers should insist on a Bay Wing minisuite that opens onto a private, man-made sandy beach. The split-level minisuites feature lacquered art deco and art nouveau furnishings, hair dryers, and VCRs. Sports facilities include an indoor pool under a huge glass dome, a well-equipped health spa (extra charge), and six tennis courts ($8 an hour; $5 for racquet rental). A shuttle bus transports guests between the hotel and South Road, at the top of the hill. *Box HM 1070, Hamilton HM EX, tel. 809/238–8122; in U.S., 800/ 343–7170. 365 rooms, 37 suites, all with bath. Meal plan: MAP. Facilities: 3 restaurants; 3 bars; nightclub; 2 beaches; beauty salon; concierge service; moped rental; heated indoor and outdoor freshwater pools; 6 tennis courts (2 lighted); shuttle bus; health spa with steam room, saunas, whirlpool, exercise and massage rooms; shopping arcade; game rooms; children's playground; water sports. AE, DC, MC, V.*

Expensive– Very Expensive **Southampton Princess.** This hotel is much larger and livelier than its older sister, The Princess (*see* below) in Hamilton. This is not the place for those seeking a quiet retreat, but it's an excellent choice for anyone who enjoys planned activities, such as theme parties, bingo, aerobics, cooking demonstrations, and tennis matches. For families, it offers the island's best children's program, including parties and baby-sitting services. The six-story, ultramodern main building, which contains all rooms and suites, dominates a hilltop near Gibb's Hill Lighthouse; the 300-year-old Waterlot Inn restaurant (*see* Chapter 7, Dining) occupies a dockside spot on the north side, and the beach club is perched above the surf at South Shore Beach. A jitney churns over hill and dale to connect them all, and a regiment of staffers is on hand to assist you if you get lost. Rooms vary in size, but they're all decorated in soft corals and light woods, and all have plenty of marble in their spacious bathrooms. Obviously, oceanfront deluxe rooms are preferable; if possible, avoid rooms on the first three floors of the west and north wings, which overlook rooftops. Some of the elegant suites feature kitchens, dishwashers, and four-poster beds. Perks in the 55-room Newport Club include private check-in/ out, complimentary Continental breakfast, hair dryers, bathrobes, and a business center. Guests pay a one-time $10 fee to use the health club; the greens fee is $16, and tennis costs $10 an hour ($6 an hour for racquet rental). *Box HM 1379, Hamilton HM FX, tel. 809/238–8000; in U.S., 800/223–1818. 598 rooms, 36 suites, all with bath. Meal plan: MAP. Facilities: 6 restaurants, 4 bars, nightclub, disco, 2 beaches, beauty salon, concierge, moped rental, heated indoor and outdoor freshwater pools, dive shop, 18-hole par-54 golf course, 11 tennis courts (3 lighted), health club, croquet, boccie court, shopping arcade, water sports. AE, DC, MC, V.*

Belmont Hotel, Golf & Country Club. Occupying 110 acres between Harbour and Middle roads, this large, gray hotel was built at the turn of the century and has a distinctly British personality. As its name suggests, it's also a sports-minded resort: Golf and tennis pros are on hand to give lessons and organize golf scrambles and tennis round-robins (hotel guests pay a $10 greens fee and $5 an hour for lighted tennis courts). A social director coordinates a range of other activities. The enormous lobby, decorated with chandeliers and fresh flowers, bustles with the golf groups that frequent the hotel. Refurbished in 1990, the rooms are average in size (bathrooms are quite small), but their large windows admit plenty of light and create a sense of spaciousness. Mahogany Queen Anne furniture is mixed with wicker, and the bedspreads and drapes sport bold floral patterns on dark backgrounds. With views over the harbor and the resort's gardens and pool—one of the largest on the island—the rooms on the fourth floor are probably the best. The Hamilton ferry stops at the Belmont Wharf; it's a long haul up the hill from the wharf to the hotel, but a shuttle bus makes the trip regularly. *Box WK 251, Warwick WK BX, tel. 809/236–1301; in U.S., 800/225–5843. 149 rooms, 1 suite, all with bath. Meal plans: BP, MAP. Facilities: 2 restaurants, bar, beauty salon, heated saltwater pool, 18-hole golf course, 3 lighted tennis courts, shops, ferry dock, water sports. AE, DC, MC, V.*

Grotto Bay Beach Hotel & Tennis Club. Only a mile from the airport, this is the smallest and least luxurious of the hotels in this price category. Set in 20 acres of gardens, it appeals to a young crowd that likes the hotel's informal atmosphere and the romantic coves and natural caves in the nearby enclosed bay. Also in the bay are a fish-feeding aquarium and two illuminated underground attractions: the Cathedral Cave for swimming, and Prospero's Cave disco for dancing beneath the stalactites. The hotel itself consists of a main building and 11 three-story pink lodges dotting a hill that slopes to the waters of Ferry Reach. The lobby is subdued, with tile floors, wicker furniture, and low ceilings; adjacent are the large dining room and lounge, where floor shows and dancing are held nightly in season. You can avoid a long hike across the hotel grounds by requesting a room in a lodge near the main building. Each lodge contains 15–30 sunny rooms featuring light woods and fabrics, private balconies, and views of the water. Most rooms have a TV, coffee maker, and hair dryer. The four suites have two bedrooms, three bathrooms, a living room, and a balcony. Regardless of the location of your room, you will be forced to do a fair amount of walking at this sprawling resort; and the lodges don't have elevators. The hotel has its own sightseeing excursion boat and offers scuba diving and snorkeling from a private deep-water dock. The beach—not the island's best by any means—is a small strip of sand just below the pool. Guests can play on the resort's four tennis courts for $5 an hour, and racquets can be rented for $5 an hour. There is a children's playground, and children's activities are held in season. *11 Blue Hole Hill, Hamilton Parish CR 04, tel. 809/293–8333; in U.S. and Canada. 197 rooms, 4 suites, all with bath. Meal plans: BP, EP, MAP. Facilities: restaurant, 3 bars, nightclub, disco, beach, 2 coves, 4 cork tennis courts (2 lighted), freshwater pool, gift shop, children's playground, excursion boat, water sports. AE, MC, V.*

★ **The Princess.** Named in honor of Princess Louise, Queen Victoria's daughter who visited the island in 1883, this large pink landmark opened in 1884 and is credited with starting Bermuda's tourist industry. Refurbished in 1989, this traditional grand hotel retains a slightly formal atmosphere, and its staff provides swift, courteous service. The walls at the entrance to the Tiara Room restaurant are covered with pictures of the politicians and royals who have visited the hotel. Ideally located on Hamilton Harbour, the hotel now caters to business and professional people, convention groups, and other visitors who want to be near downtown Hamilton. Mahogany dominates the original six-story main building, and the two three-story wings are filled with light woods and art deco touches. Plush cream-colored upholstery, bedspreads, and drapes are used throughout the hotel, and most of the rooms and suites have balconies. There are several categories of suites, and all are large and sumptuous—the penthouse suite has a Jacuzzi. The Princess Club's amenities include Continental breakfast, and showers and changing facilities for travelers with late flights who want to swim after morning check-out. In high season a ferry makes regular runs across the harbor to the Southampton Princess (*see* above), which has excellent sports facilities (none of which is free to guests). The Hamilton Princess has no beach, but there are stretches of lawn with deck chairs for relaxing and sunning. In season, glittery Vegas-style shows are presented in the Gazebo Lounge. Details of the Royal Dine-Around plan are somewhat Byzantine, but essentially there are nine Princess restaurants from which guests can choose. *Box HM 837, Hamilton HM CX, tel. 809/295–3000; in U.S., 800/223–1818; in Canada, 800/268–7176. 422 rooms, 28 suites, all with bath. Meal plans: BP, EP, MAP. Facilities: 3 restaurants; 2 bars; nightclub; beauty salon; concierge; moped rental; heated freshwater pool; saltwater pool; putting green; private dock and ferry; shopping arcade; water sports; access to Southampton Princess for golf, tennis, health and beach clubs. AE, DC, MC, V.*

Small Hotels

Very Expensive **Harmony Club.** Nestled in lovely gardens, this two-story pink-and-white hotel was built in the 1930s as a private home and extensively renovated in 1990. The hotel has a couples-only policy, but a couple can be two aunts, two friends, or any other combination—only children are not welcome. The base rate covers everything, including meals, alcohol, and even two-seater scooters. Although such a package is ideal for people who don't like to stray too far from their accommodations, food lovers might prefer to experiment with the interesting cuisine offered elsewhere on the island. The spacious reception area has warm wood paneling; and the club lounge has a big-screen TV and an assortment of games, including cards, darts, and backgammon. Upon arrival, guests find complimentary champagne in their rooms, which are luxuriously decorated with Queen Anne furnishings and feature hair dryers, bathrobes, and coffee makers. All but 12 of the rooms have a patio or balcony. The hotel is not on the water, but it's only about a five-minute scooter ride to the south-shore beaches. Guests can partake of a host of activities during high season, from informal barbecues to twice-weekly tennis clinics to formal dances. *Box PG 299, Paget PG BX, tel. 809/236–3500; in U.S., 800/225–5843. 72 rooms with bath. Meal plan: AP. Facilities: restaurant, bar, freshwater pool, whirlpool, sauna, moped rental, putting green, 2 tennis courts. AE, DC, MC, V.*

Pompano Beach Club. Expect a friendly, personal welcome when you arrive at this informal seaside hotel, owned and operated by the American-born Lamb family. Located on the western end of the island, adjacent to the Port Royal Golf & Country Club, the hotel was a fishing club until 1950. Today, it still appeals primarily to fishermen, water-sports enthusiasts, and anyone in search of a quiet, remote getaway. The main building is a crescent-shape, split-level structure of pink and white stone, containing the main dining room, a British-style pub, and a cozy lounge with a large stone fireplace. Spread across the luxuriant hillside are cabanas, one-bedroom suites, and deluxe rooms, all with balconies and ocean views. Living rooms in the suites have Queen Anne furnishings and velvet chairs, but elsewhere the decor is tropical, featuring rattan, light woods, and glass-top tables. All guest rooms have minifridges, irons, and ironing boards; some have kitchenettes. The cabanas are the best choice, not only because the rooms are larger than in the suites, but also because guests wake in the morning to a splendid ocean view through the bedroom window (suites have an ocean view through the living room window). Perched on a hill adjacent to the main building is an attractive pool and a small conference center. There's only a small patch of beach for sunbathing, and it's not easily accessible; serious beach goers are advised to head elsewhere. The hotel's new water-sports facility offers Sunfish, Windsurfers, paddle boats, and small glass-bottom boats for rent; at low tide guests can stroll 250 yards into the ocean, in waist-deep water. Sunsets viewed from this hotel are spectacular events. *32 Pompano Beach Rd., Southampton SB 03, tel. 809/234–0222; in U.S., 800/343–4155. 33 rooms, 21 suites, all with bath. Meal plans: BP, MAP. Facilities: restaurant, bar, heated freshwater pool, Jacuzzi, water sports, conference center. No credit cards.*

★ **The Reefs.** The pink lanais of this small, casually elegant resort are set in cliffs above the beach at Christian Bay, adjacent to the Sonesta Beach Hotel & Spa (*see* above). The pace here is sedate, offering guests a restful stay in a spectacular beachfront setting. Vacationers looking for action are better off at such sports-oriented resorts as the Sonesta, Elbow Beach, or the Southampton Princess (*see* above). In the pink Bermuda cottage that serves as the clubhouse, a small registration area opens onto a spacious, comfortable lounge, where a pianist or guitarist entertains nightly. Beyond the lounge lies the main dining room, with additional seating in a tropical glass-ceiling conservatory and on a large terrace. Dinner dances are held frequently during the high season. Another restaurant is the waterside Coconuts, which is popular for casual lunches and candlelight dinners under the stars. Two guest rooms are located in the clubhouse, but the best rooms are in the lanais around the pool and on the hillside above the sandy beach. Lanais near the beach are the most expensive. Earth tones and rattan predominate in the guest rooms; bathrooms are small, with beige-marble vanities and an adjoining dressing area. All rooms have balconies and a stunning ocean view. In addition to the lanais, there are seven secluded cottages, one a three-bedroom, two-bathroom unit. Changing rooms near the beach are available for travelers with late flights who want to swim after morning check-out. The tennis courts are free to guests. *56 South Rd., Southampton, SN 02, tel. 809/238–0222; in U.S., 800/223–1363; in Canada, 800/268–0424. 49 rooms, 7 cottage suites, all with bath. Meal plans: BP, MAP. Facilities: 2 restaurants, 2 bars, beach, moped rental, heated freshwater pool, 2 tennis courts, water sports. No credit cards.*

Stonington Beach Hotel. A training ground for students of the Bermuda Department of Hotel Technology, this south-shore hotel has one of the friendliest, hardest-working staffs on the island. Like students everywhere, they make mistakes, but if you have a little patience and a sense of humor your stay here should be most enjoyable. The place has a warm, gracious atmosphere; the formal restaurant is excellent; and the beach at the bottom of the hill rivals any on the island. However, the hotel is terribly overpriced—it's one of the most expensive properties on the south shore—and simply does not offer the kind of amenities guests expect for the money. In size and style guest rooms can be compared with those in an upscale Holiday Inn. Set in two-story terraced lodges leading to the beach, each room features a balcony with an ocean view. The furnishings are modern, and the decor includes heavy drapes and quilted bedspreads in matching fabrics; a minibar is tucked into the small dressing area adjacent to the bathroom. The small hotel lobby gains much of its character from its beamed ceiling and large windows with graceful fanlights. The adjoining library features Regency furnishings, bookshelves, a fireplace, and TV. Weekly champagne receptions are held during the high season, and classical music is played in the attractive Norwood Dining Room. Use of the tennis courts is free. *Box HM 523, Hamilton HM CX, tel. 809/236–5416; in U.S., 800/223–1588; in Canada, 800/268–0424. 64 rooms with bath. Meal plans: BP, MAP. Facilities: restaurant, bar, beach, moped rental, heated freshwater pool, 2 tennis courts, library, game room, gift shop, water sports. AE, DC, MC, V.*

Expensive– Very Expensive

Glencoe Harbour Club. Located in a manor house dating to the 1700s, this quiet, secluded inn on Salt Kettle Bay is a favorite of boaters. It is not a beachfront hotel, however: A tiny man-made beach offers deep-water swimming, sailing, and windsurfing, but for other beach activities guests must head to the Coral Beach & Tennis Club, where they are welcome. The lobby is small and unprepossessing, but a few steps away is a cozy wood-paneled lounge with a fireplace and nautical decor. Dining (and dancing in season) is in a chic room with velvet chairs, candlelight, and crisp napery. The waterside terrace is open for meals and frequent barbecues during high season. Rooms are in the main house (Number 10 has its original fireplace and Old World charm) or across the road in two-story pink-stone buildings with rambling decks. The individually decorated rooms have cathedral ceilings and elegant wicker furniture with bold plaid or flame-stitch fabrics. All rooms have balconies or patios, but the best rooms are those with a view of the harbor; the least expensive rooms overlook the garden. TVs can be rented. *Box PG 297, Paget PG BX, tel. 809/236–5274; in U.S., 800/468–1500; in Canada, 416/622–8813; in U.K., 071/730–7144. 33 rooms, 7 suites, all with bath. Meal plans: BP, MAP. Facilities: 2 restaurants, 2 bars, 2 heated freshwater pools, man-made beach. AE, MC, V.*

Newstead. This renovated manor house could accommodate only 12 people when it opened as a guest house in 1923. Since then the elegant harborside hotel has expanded considerably, with brick steps and walkways now leading to several poolside units and cottages. Set amid tall trees and a profusion of flowering shrubs and plants, the main house and cottages are typically Bermudian—in fact, some of the cottages were originally private residences. The spacious drawing room boasts handsome wing chairs, traditional furnishings, fresh flowers, and a fireplace, and the less-formal lounge has large windows overlooking the harbor. A harpist entertains during dinner. The large guest rooms feature polished mahogany campaign chests with brass drawer-pulls, framed prints, and fresh flowers; sliding glass doors open onto a balcony. The units are oddly designed—the front door opens into the large dressing area adjoining the bathroom—but there is ample vanity space, as well as a coffee maker, trouser press, hair dryer, and heated towel rack. Radios and TVs can be rented. The hotel has no beach, but a private dock is available for deep-water swimming in the harbor, and guests have use of the facilities at the Coral Beach & Tennis Club, on the south shore, about 10 minutes away by cab. Men's and women's changing rooms by the pool allow guests to go straight from swimming to the Hamilton ferry at Hodsdon's Landing. Tennis costs $3.50 an hour, and tennis whites are mandatory. *Box PG 196, Paget PG BX, tel. 809/236-6060; in U.S., 800/468-4111. 47 rooms, 3 suites, all with bath. Meal plans: BP, MAP. Facilities: restaurant, bar, freshwater pool, private dock for deep-water swimming, men's and women's saunas, putting green, 2 tennis courts. No credit cards.*

★ **Waterloo House.** About a three-minute walk from the Hamilton ferry and the Front Street shops, this quiet retreat is so secluded you can easily pass by without noticing it. A pink archway and steps leading to the flower-filled patio from Pitts Bay Road were later additions to a house that predates 1815, when it was renamed in honor of the defeat of Napoleon. The white-column house faces the harbor, and a spacious harborside terrace filled with umbrellas and tables is used for outdoor dining and entertainment. The stately lounge is furnished traditionally, with oil paintings, wing chairs, and a large fireplace. The majority of the rooms are in the main house; others are in pink two-story stone buildings beside the pool and patio. The quietest rooms are on the second floor of the main house. Matching fabrics are used in the rooms' quilted bedspreads, dust ruffles, draperies, and valances. Bathrooms are large, and most have double vanities. TVs can be rented. Guests on MAP have dine-around privileges at Horizons & Cottages (*see* below) and Newstead (*see* above); the short golf course at Horizons is also open to guests. *Box HM 333, Hamilton HM BX, tel. 809/295-4480; in U.S., 800/468-4100. 28 rooms, 6 suites, all with bath. Meal plans: BP, MAP. Facilities: restaurant, bar, heated freshwater pool. No credit cards.*

Expensive **Palmetto Hotel & Cottages.** Set amid tall shade trees on the banks of Harrington Sound, this casually elegant property was once a private home. The main building is a sprawling two-story pink-and-white structure typical of Bermuda. Adjoining the small reception area is the Ha'Penny, a very British pub, where tea is served in the afternoon. Twenty-four rooms are located in the main building, but the 16 rooms in cottages on the banks of the sound are the most luxurious. Most rooms have balconies with a good view of the water. The hotel's beach is small, but a complimentary shuttle ferries guests to a south-shore beach. In addition, guests can swim or snorkel off the hotel's private dock; windsurfing lessons are available. *Box FL 54, Flatts FL BX, tel. 809/293-2323; in U.S., 800/982-0026. 42 rooms with bath. Meal plans: BP, EP, MAP. Facilities: restaurant, bar, beach, private dock, saltwater pool. No credit cards.*

★ **Rosedon.** Notable for its spacious veranda and white iron furniture, this stately Bermuda manor attracts an older crowd—mostly of women—that appreciates the hotel's ambience, service, and proximity to Front Street shops. Some of the four rooms in the main house have leaded-glass doors and other Old World touches; all other rooms are in two-story buildings arranged around a large pool in the back garden. Rooms are rather dark, despite their white wicker furniture and bright prints and wallpaper. Each has a minifridge, a coffee maker, and a small dining table. There is no restaurant, but breakfast, sandwiches, and light meals are served either in your room or under umbrellas by the pool. Afternoon tea is served in the large lounges in the main house, where a TV and an honor bar are also located. The hotel has no beach of its own, but use of the beach and tennis courts at the Elbow Beach Hotel (*see* above) is free; transportation is provided for the 15–20 minute drive. *Box HM 290, Hamilton HM AX, tel. 809/295–1640; in U.S., 800/225–5567. 43 rooms with bath. Meal plans: BP, EP. Facilities: 2 lounges, heated freshwater pool, complimentary shuttle to beach, same-day laundry service. No credit cards.*

Somerset Bridge Hotel. About a three-minute walk from the Somerset Bridge ferry landing and within walking distance of Scaur Hill Fort, this three-story building resembles the kind of motels found on U.S. turnpikes. Its position on pretty Ely's Harbour makes it ideal for water-sports enthusiasts and those who want to explore the West End. The hotel has no charm, however, except for its idyllic setting in Ely Harbour, and no appeal whatsoever for anyone primarily interested in Hamilton's shops or the south-shore beaches. It's also overpriced. All of the apartments have kitchenettes and utensils, and most have Murphy beds, which leave little room for moving about when they're pulled down. This is the home of the Blue Foam (*see* Chapter 7, Dining), a good place to eat when you're ambling around this part of the island. *Box SB 149, Sandys SB BX, tel. 809/234–1042; in U.S., 800/468–5501. 24 apartments with bath. Meal plans: CP, EP, MAP. Facilities: restaurant, bar, small beach, freshwater pool, Jacuzzi. AE, DC, MC, V.*

Moderate– Expensive

Willowbank. On a high promontory overlooking Ely's Harbour, this former home is essentially a Christian religious retreat. Morning devotionals are held in a lounge, for those who wish to attend, and grace is said before meals, which are announced by an ancient ship's bell and are served family-style. There is no proselytizing, however, and no pressure to participate in religious activities. The hotel is simply a serene alternative to the glitzy resorts; anyone who likes plenty of action will not be happy here. With their cedar paneling and fireplaces, the two large lounges in the main building are the focal point for quiet conversations, TV viewing, and afternoon tea; there are also a restaurant and library. Guests may have liquor in their rooms, but there is no bar. Located in one-story white cottages, the guest rooms are large and simply furnished—they have neither phones nor TVs. Rooms with an ocean or harbor view are the most desirable and expensive. No service charge is added to the bill and tipping is not expected, but the staff is friendly and helpful nonetheless. *Box MA 296, Sandys MA BX, tel. 809/ 234–1616 or 800/752–8493. 58 rooms with bath; 2 double rooms share bath. Meal plan: MAP. Facilities: restaurant, 2 lounges, 2 small beaches, 2 tennis courts, heated freshwater pool. No credit cards.*

Cottage Colonies

Very Expensive
★

Cambridge Beaches. Within walking distance of Somerset Village in the West End (*see* Chapter 4, Exploring Bermuda), this outstanding resort occupies a beautifully landscaped peninsula edged with private coves and six pink-sand beaches. The original cottage colony (it opened in 1958), it remains a favorite among British and Saudi royalty, as well as a host of commoners. Many guests return year after year, attracted by the elegant style, superior water-sports facilities, and those unsurpassed pink-sand beaches. Registration is in a Bermuda-style clubhouse with large, elegantly furnished lounges. Candlelight dining and dancing take place in the lower-level restaurant and on the terrace, which has a splendid view of Mangrove Bay. A wide range of accommodations is offered—the entire peninsula is dotted with cottages—and prices vary considerably. Pegem is a 300-year-old, two-bedroom Bermuda cottage with a cedar-beam ceiling, English antiques, a den, and a sunporch. On the other end of the spectrum is Windswept, a two-unit cottage near the pool, that features one of the smallest, least expensive units in the colony. The decor differs from cottage to cottage, but antiques and fireplaces are common throughout; 30 cottages have Jacuzzis. Don't fret about being far from Front Street: A shopping launch makes twice-weekly trips from the resort's private dock. Ferry tokens are complimentary, as are the use of tennis courts, racquets, and balls. *Somerset MA 02, tel. 809/234–0331; in U.S., 800/468–7300. 61 rooms, 17 suites, all with bath. Meal plan: MAP. Facilities: restaurant, 2 bars, 6 beaches, heated saltwater pool, private marina, ferry, 3 tennis courts, putting green, water sports. No credit cards.*

Fourways Inn. About a five-minute ride from the ferry landing and the south-shore beaches, this luxury hotel has a sedate, formal ambience. Look elsewhere if you want exciting nightlife or if you plan to bring the kids—children under 16 are discouraged at the inn, and nothing here would interest them anyway. The architecture is typically Bermudian: The main building is a one-time family home that dates from 1727; the five cottages, set in a profusion of greenery and flowers, each contain a poolside suite and a deluxe upper-floor room. Marble floors and marble bathrooms are common throughout, and plenty of flowers give the rooms a bright freshness. In addition, each room has a balcony or terrace, a stocked minibar, a bar/kitchenette, and large closets paneled with full-length mirrors. Amenities in the suites include hair dryers, bath phones, bathrobes, and slippers. Guests receive a complimentary bottle of champagne on arrival, and homemade pastries and the morning paper are delivered daily to the door. The hotel serves a sumptuous Sunday brunch. *Box PG 294, Paget, PG BX, tel. 809/236–6517; in U.S., 800/962–7654. 5 rooms, 5 suites, all with bath. Meal plan: CP. Facilities: restaurant, bar, freshwater pool. AE, DC, MC, V.*

★ **Horizons & Cottages.** Oriental rugs, polished wood floors, cathedral ceilings, and knee-high open fireplaces are elegant reminders of the 18th century, when the main house in this resort was a private home. Today, the cottage colony maintains a formal atmosphere that appeals to an older crowd. Horizons Restaurant is a chic place for intimate candlelight dining; in pleasant weather, tables are set on the terrace. Monday-night rum swizzling is done downstairs in a wood-panel pub, where Austrian-born manager Wilhelm Sack makes every effort to see that guests (many of whom are European) are introduced. Guest cottages dot the terraced lawns, and each cottage has a distinct personality and decor: Most have two or three rooms and a large common room with a fireplace, library, and shelves of board games. Some of the spacious guest rooms feature white wicker furnishings, and others have an Old European flavor. Most cottages also have a kitchen, where a maid prepares breakfast before bringing it to your room. The hotel has no beach of its own, but guests may use the facilities of the Coral Beach & Tennis Club, within walking distance along South Road. Tennis courts cost $3.50 per hour and the greens fee for the short nine-hole golf course is also $3.50. *Box PG 198, Paget, PG BX, tel. 809/236–0048; in U.S., 800/468–0022. 45 rooms, 5 suites, all with bath. Meal plans: BP, MAP (combination also available). Facilities: restaurant, bar, heated freshwater pool, 3 tennis courts, 9-hole golf course, 18-hole putting green. No credit cards.*

Lantana Colony Club. A short walk from the Somerset Bridge ferry landing in the West End, this cottage colony is known for its lavish gardens and impressive (if sometimes bizarre) objets d'art. Several life-size sculptures by Desmond Fountain are dotted through the grounds, including a delightful rendering of a woman seated on a bench reading a newspaper. The solarium dining area in the main house is dazzling, with hanging plants and wall brackets of frosted Bohemian glass grapes. Rooms and suites come in a variety of sizes and configurations: lanais, split-levels, garden cottages, and "family houses" with two bedrooms, two bathrooms, and a living/dining room. Many guest rooms have parquet or tile floors and beamed ceilings and all have private balconies or patios. Lunch is a featured attraction here, something to bear in mind when you're tooling around the West End. *Box SB 90, Somerset Bridge SB BX, tel. 809/234–0141; in U.S., 800/468–3733. 56 suites, 6 cottages, all with bath. Meal plans: BP, MAP. Facilities: 2 restaurants, 2 bars, beach, freshwater pool, private dock, 2 tennis courts, putting green, croquet lawn, shuffleboard, water sports. No credit cards.*

Pink Beach Club & Cottages. With its two pretty pink beaches, this secluded, relaxing colony is a favorite of international celebrities. The location is a bit remote, however, and might not appeal to those who want to be near the shops of Front Street or the swinging resorts. Built as a private home in 1947, the main house has a clubby ambience derived from its dark-wood paneling, large fireplace, and beamed ceilings. Paved paths lace the attractively landscaped grounds and lead to 23 pink cottages and to the beaches. Each cottage contains four units, ranging from single rooms to two-bedroom suites with two bathrooms and twin terraces. Each spacious unit has wall-to-wall carpeting, wood paneling, and sliding glass doors that open onto a balcony or terrace. Extensive use is made of marble, complemented by white rattan furniture and light woods in some rooms, and by dark woods and velvet upholstery in others. The best accommodations are, of course, those near the beach. Breakfast is prepared by a maid and served in your room. Use of the tennis courts is free. *Box HM 1017, Hamilton HM DX, tel. 809/293–1666; in U.S., 800/422–1323; in Canada, 800/268–0424. 14 rooms, 67 suites, all with bath. Meal plan: MAP. Facilities: restaurant, bar, 2 beaches, saltwater pool, 2 tennis courts, water sports. MC, V.*

The St. George's Club. Within walking distance of King's Square in St. George's, this ultramodern time-share property adjoins an 18-hole golf course designed by Robert Trent Jones. The sleek, three-story main building contains the office, activities desk, a game room, a restaurant, a pub, and the Club Shop, where you can buy everything from champagne to suntan lotion. In two-story white cottages sprinkled over 18 acres, the individually decorated apartments are huge and filled with sunlight. In some, stark white walls are offset by bright accent pieces and fabrics in muted colors. In others, sweeping bold designs draw upon the entire spectrum of colors. Each apartment has a full kitchen with dishwasher, fine china, and crystal. Bathrooms are large and lined with marble; some feature double Jacuzzis in dramatic settings. In 1991, eight new units and another restaurant were added. *Box GE 92, St. George's GE BX, tel. 809/297–1200. 69 suites with bath. Meal plan: EP. Facilities: 2 restaurants, bar, 3 freshwater pools (1 heated), 18-hole golf course, putting green, tennis court, convenience store. AE, DC, MC, V.*

Expensive– Very Expensive **Ariel Sands Beach Club.** This most informal of the cottage colonies surrounds Cox's Bay in Devonshire Parish, not far from the Edmund Gibbons Nature Reserve. The beach here is large and sandy, and a graceful statue of Ariel perches on a rock in the sea. The one-story white-limestone clubhouse, designed in Bermudian cottage style, contains the dining room and a lounge. A grand piano, a fireplace, and Oriental rugs give the resort an air of distinction. The large patio is ideal for outdoor dining, dancing, and barbecues in season. Two- to six-unit white cottages are set in the sloping, tree-shaded grounds. Guest rooms are small and furnished with white or natural rattan and island prints. Shakespeare's Dream has two bedrooms, one of which has a single bed. Rooms in the lowest price bracket have no ocean view. Tennis is free to guests. *Box HM 334, Hamilton HM BX, tel. 809/236–1010; in U.S., 800/468–6610. 48 rooms with bath. Meal plans: BP, MAP. Facilities: restaurant, bar, beach, freshwater pool, saltwater lagoon, 3 tennis courts (2 lighted), putting green, water sports. AE, MC, V.*

Housekeeping Cottages and Apartments

Expensive– Very Expensive **Marley Beach Cottages.** Scenes from the films *Chapter Two* and *The Deep* were filmed here, and it's easy to see why—the setting is breathtaking. Near Astwood Park on the south shore, the resort sits high on a cliff overlooking a lovely beach and dramatic reefs; a long path leads down to the sand and the sea. If you plan to stay here, pack light—there are a lot of steep steps, and you may have to carry your own luggage. The price is also steep, considering that you have to prepare your own meals. Each cottage contains a suite and a studio apartment, which can be rented separately or together, by families or friends. This is not a good place for children, and there's little to occupy them except the pool and the beach. The rooms are individually decorated, but all have large rooms, superb ocean views, private porches or patios, and fully equipped kitchens. Heaven's Above, the deluxe suite, is a spacious affair with two wood-burning fireplaces, tile floors, upholstered rattan furniture, and ample kitchen facilities. TVs can be rented, and groceries delivered. *Box PG 278, Paget PG BX, tel. 809/236–1143 (ext. 42); 809/236–8910; in U.S., 800/541–7426. 7 suites, 6 studios, all with bath. Meal plan: EP. Facilities: private beach, heated freshwater pool, whirlpool. No credit cards.*

Expensive ★ **Longtail Cliffs.** Don't be put off by the small office and the concrete parking lot that serves as the front yard of this motel-like establishment. Although it may not have the personality or splendid beach views of Marley Beach Cottages (*see* above), its relatively flat setting makes it much more suitable for elderly people or anyone who doesn't want to do a lot of climbing. Housed in a modern, two-story building, guest apartments are large, light, and airy, with balconies and ocean views. Each has two bedrooms and two spacious bathrooms decorated with brightly colored tiles. A small but well-equipped kitchen features a microwave oven, an iron, and an ironing board. Italian-tile floors grace the living areas and are accented by scatter rugs and high-quality white wicker furniture. Many units have beamed ceilings and some have fireplaces. There's a coin-operated laundry and a gas barbecue grill for cookouts. Despite its location on the south shore, the complex does not have a beach, although Horseshoe Bay is not far away. *Box HM 836, Hamilton HM CX, tel. 809/236–2864; 809/236–2822; in U.S., 800/541–7426. 14 apartments with bath. Meal plan: EP. Facilities: freshwater pool. AE, MC, V.*

Moderate–Expensive   **Angel's Grotto.** Some 30 years ago this was a swinging nightclub and one of the hottest spots on the island. Now, it's a quiet residential apartment house close to Devil's Hole Aquarium on the south shore of Harrington Sound. Don't come here if you want to spend a lot of time in Hamilton or on the beach—it's a long way from the best south-shore beaches. None of the one- or two-bedroom efficiencies (each with full kitchen facilities) is glamorous, but all are well-maintained by owner Daisy Hart and her efficient staff. Most of the guests are couples; the secluded Honeymoon Cottage is particularly appealing to those who want privacy. A large patio is ideal for cocktails in the evening, and there is also a barbecue. Deep-water swimming is possible in Harrington Sound. *Box HS 62, Smith's HS BX, tel. daytime, 809/295–6437; evening, 809/293–1986; in U.S., 800/541–7426. 7 apartments with bath. Meal plan: EP. Facilities: swimming in Harrington Sound. AE, MC, V.*

Moderate   **Pretty Penny.** A three-minute walk from the ferry dock at
★   Darrell's Wharf and 10 minutes by scooter from the south-shore beaches, this upscale lodging has one of the friendliest, most helpful staffs on the island. A two-story cottage next to a small shaded pool serves as the office. The grounds are small and offer no good views, but guest cottages are surrounded by trees and shrubs. Each room is brightened by a colorful tile floor and has a dining area and private patio. A small kitchen area features a microwave oven, refrigerator, and cupboards well-stocked with china, cooking utensils, and cutlery. TVs can be rented. The property was completely refurbished in 1991; the Shilling, a room in a cottage across from the main building, is a charmer. If you want absolute privacy ask for the Play Penny, which is tucked away by itself. Across the street from the main house are a couple of quaint cottages that were being renovated at press time. Owner Steve Martin throws frequent cocktail parties so guests can get acquainted. *Box PG 137, Paget PG BX, tel. 809/236–1194; in U.S., 800/541–7426. 6 apartments with shower bath. Meal plan: EP. Facilities: freshwater pool. AE, MC, V.*

Inexpensive–Moderate   **Barnsdale Guest Apartments.** Budget travelers who want to be near the south-shore beaches would do well to consider the small apartments in this two-story white cottage. The setting may not be spectacular, and the amenities are less than luxurious, but the units are clean and neat, and each has a private entrance. All were redecorated in 1990. Apartments with sofa beds can sleep four, but the four people must be able to get along well—the quarters are close. Kitchenettes have sufficient utensils to prepare light meals, and each has an iron and ironing board. Apartment Number 5 is a charmer—a somewhat larger, light, airy room decorated with colorful prints—but it's next to the pool area, which can become noisy. Long-distance calls can be made from a phone kiosk at the side of the house. *Box DV 628, Devonshire DV BX, tel. 809/236-0164; in U.S., 800/514-7426. 5 apartments with bath. Meal plan: EP. Facilities: freshwater pool. AE, MC, V.*

★ **Sky Top Cottages.** This establishment is aptly named—guests will be happy to have a scooter or taxi to climb the high hill on which the cottages sit. The ascent is worthwhile, though, because the views of the ocean from here are spectacular. Neat sloping lawns, paved walks bordered by geraniums, and a nearby citrus grove provide a pleasant setting for studio and one-bedroom apartments that are only five minutes by scooter from Elbow Beach. Although the furnishings are basic, the individually decorated units do have character. The friendly owners, Marion Stubbs and Susan Harvey, have decorated the rooms with attractive prints and carefully coordinated colors, and the property is well-maintained. Studio apartments have full kitchens and shower baths; one-bedroom apartments have limited kitchen facilities and full baths. Frangipani is furnished in white wicker and rattan and has an eat-in kitchen, a king-size bed, and a sofa bed. Honeysuckle is a three-level apartment with a sitting room, kitchen, dining room, and a bedroom and bathroom upstairs; each room is small but decorated in bright colors. A barbecue grill is available for guests' use. *Box PG 227, Paget PG BX, tel. 809/236-7984; in U.K., 071/242-9964. 11 apartments with bath. Meal plan: EP. No facilities. MC, V.*

Inexpensive **Greenbank Cottages.** Located on a quiet dead end two minutes' walk from the Salt Kettle ferry landing, these one-story green cottages nestle among tall trees beside Hamilton Harbour. This is not a grand hotel—it's small and family-owned—but guests can count on plenty of personal attention from the Ashton family. In the 200-year-old main house, the guests' lounge has Oriental rugs, hardwood floors, a TV, and a grand piano; a billiards room is across the hall. There are two guest rooms in the main house; all other units are self-contained, with private entrances and shaded verandas. Most units have fully equipped kitchenettes for preparing light meals. The waterside cottages are the best choice, especially The Pink One—the view of the harbor from the dining table in the kitchen is lovely. Some simply furnished rooms are not air-conditioned, and none has a phone. There is no beach, but there is a private dock suitable for deep-water swimming, and Salt Kettle Boat Rentals is located on the property. *Box PG 201, Paget PG BX, tel. 809/236-3615; in U.S., 800/541-7426. 2 rooms and 7 apartments, all with bath. Meal plans: CP, EP. Facilities: private dock for deep-water swimming, billiards room. AE, MC, V.*

Whale Bay Inn. Golfers approaching the 14th hole of the Port Royal course are sometimes baffled to find golf balls other than their own dotting the green. Little do they know that it's a mere chip shot from the front lawn of this new inn, and some guests can't resist the challenge to play through. Vacationers who want to be near good beaches or Hamilton's shops are better served elsewhere, however. The friendly Metschnabel family owns, operates, and lives on the premises of this small, attractive property in the remote West End. The ocean is visible beyond beds of flowers and the rolling lawn that surrounds the Bermuda-style pink building. At the bottom of the hill, a tiny patch of pink beach is tucked under the rugged cliff; it's pretty and private, but you'll have to do a fair amount of climbing to reach it. The decor of the guest rooms is contemporary, relying on rattan and muted prints. All five ground-floor units have a bedroom, a separate sitting room, and a private entrance. The two end units have larger bathrooms and are better-suited to families. Small, modern kitchens are equipped with microwave ovens, two-burner stoves, small refrigerators, cutlery, dinnerware, and cooking utensils. Groceries can be delivered from nearby markets. *Box SN 544, Southampton SN BX, tel. 809/238-0469; in U.S., 800/541-7426. 5 apartments with bath. Meal plan: EP. No facilities. No credit cards.*

Guest Houses

Moderate **Edgehill Manor.** Atop a high hill surrounded by gardens and shrubs, this large colonial house is within easy walking distance of downtown Hamilton. Anyone wanting to spend a lot of time on the beach should stay elsewhere, however—the best south-shore beaches are 15–20 minutes away by scooter. The staff is friendly and helpful, and guests are guaranteed plenty of personal attention. In the morning, feast on home-baked muffins and scones in the cheery breakfast room, which is decorated with white iron chairs, glass-top tables, and vivid wallpaper. The individually decorated guest rooms feature French provincial furniture, colorful quilted bedspreads, large windows, and terraces. If you want air-conditioning be sure to request it—the four upstairs rooms have ceiling fans only. A large poolside room has a kitchen and is suitable for families. Anyone traveling alone on a tight budget should ask for the small ground-level room that offers a kitchen and private terrace. *Box HM 1048, Hamilton HM EX, tel. 809/295-7124. 9 rooms with bath. Meal plan: CP. Facilities: freshwater pool. No credit cards.*

Granaway Guest House & Cottage. In the 18th and 19th centuries, this 1734 manor house on Hamilton Harbour was used as a storehouse for pirate's booty. Surrounded by mounds of shrubbery, the house is a bit hard to find even today. A pay phone, a coffee maker, and disposable cups (guests can help themselves to coffee), set the tone for the poky entrance hall. The Continental breakfast, served in the garden with antique silver and Herend china, is far more pleasant. The large Pink Room, in the main house, has a king-size bed, white wicker furniture, and soft prints. The Strawberry Room was once the kitchen of the main house. The old hearth remains, and the room is now decorated with a patchwork quilt and scarred cedar beams; the walls and rafters are adorned with ceramic strawberries and other gifts from repeat guests. The Cottage, formerly the slave quarters, has a fully equipped modern kitchen, a phone, hand-painted tile floors, and its own entrance and lawn. The other guest rooms are nondescript. There is no beach—south-shore beaches are 10–15 minutes away by scooter—but the waterside patio can be used for deep-water swimming and snorkeling. In the evening, guests gather on the patio for cocktails. *Box WK 533, Warwick WK BX, tel. 809/236-1805; in U.S., 800/541-7426. 4 rooms, 1 cottage, all with bath. Meal plans: CP,*

EP. Facilities: waterside patio, TVs provided on request. MC, V.

★ **Oxford House.** This is the closest you can get to downtown Hamilton without pitching a tent. The two-story establishment is popular with older people and is an excellent choice for shoppers. It is family-owned and operated, and guests receive friendly, personal attention. Just off the small entrance hall a fireplace and colorful floral tablecloths lend warmth to the breakfast room, where guests sample scones, English muffins, fresh fruit, and cereal in the morning; tea is served here in the afternoon. The rooms (doubles, triples, and quads) are bright and airy and are decorated with white rattan and bold fabrics. Two of the rooms have shower baths only. A small bookcase in the upstairs hall is crammed with paperbacks and serves as a library for guests. *Box HM 374, Hamilton HM BX, tel. 809/295–0503; in U.S., 800/548–7758. 12 rooms with bath. Meal plan: CP. No facilities. No credit cards.*

Inexpensive– Moderate **Loughlands Guest House & Cottage.** Built in 1920, this stately white mansion sits on a green hill above South Road, a mere 5-minute ride by scooter from the best beaches. The house contains an eclectic collection of fine antiques and flea-market bric-a-brac. China figurines grace the mantelpiece in the formal parlor; grandfather clocks stand in corners; and handsome breakfronts display Wedgwood and cut glass. There are an Empire chaise longue, an elegant pink-satin prie-dieu, and a refrigerator for guests' use in the upstairs hallway. A Continental breakfast of cereals, fresh fruit, croissants, and coffee is served in the enormous, well-appointed dining room. The guest rooms are not nearly as interesting as the public rooms, however. No two are alike—there are singles, doubles, triples, and quads—but the furnishings are functional at best. Some rooms are unattractively adorned with large overstuffed chairs and chenille spreads. There are additional rooms in a large cottage near the main house. *79 South Rd., Paget PG 03, tel. 809/236–1253. 19 rooms with bath, 6 with shared bath. Meal plans: CP, EP. Facilities: freshwater pool, tennis court. No credit cards.*

Inexpensive **Hillcrest Guest House.** Set back from Nea's Alley in St. George's, behind a gate and gardens, this green double-gallery house dates to the 18th century. It's been a guest house since 1961, but owner Mrs. Trew Robinson says her father took in shipwrecked sailors in 1914, when this was a private home. Today, Mrs. Robinson offers personal attention and helpful advice to budget travelers. The upstairs and downstairs lounges are spacious and homey, decorated with Oriental rugs, treasured family pictures, and heirlooms. Although they are spotlessly clean, guest rooms lack the charm of the public rooms— they are Spartan, and merely functional. No meals are served, but guests can keep refreshments in the refrigerator. The house is far from Hamilton and the best beaches. *Box GE 96, St. George's GE BX, tel. 809/297–1630. 10 rooms with bath. No facilities. No credit cards.*

★ **Little Pomander Guest House.** A little jewel in a quiet residential area near Hamilton Harbour, this is a find for budget travelers seeking accommodations near Hamilton. The house was professionally decorated with a keen eye for detail—nothing here is out of place. Soft colors, fresh flowers, and tastefully arranged sofas and chairs make the living room spacious and airy. Guest rooms are decorated in French provincial style: Plump pastel-colored comforters cover the beds; the shams, dust ruffles, drapes, headboards, and shower curtains are made of matching fabrics. Continental breakfast is served family-style in a sunny room where tables are set with china in a blue-and-white floral design. Guests may use the microwave oven and refrigerator, as well as a barbecue grill in the backyard. There's also a soda machine. *Box HM 384, Hamilton HM BX, tel. 809/ 236–7635; in U.S., 800/541–7426. 5 rooms with bath. Meal plan: CP. No facilities. No credit cards.*

★ **Salt Kettle House.** Set behind a screen of palm trees on Hamilton Harbour, this small secluded guest house attracts plenty of repeat visitors and is popular with boating enthusiasts. Just to the left of the entrance is a cozy lounge with a fireplace where guests gather for cocktails (BYOB) and conversation. A hearty English breakfast is served family-style in the adjacent dining room. Two guest rooms are located in the main house, and an adjoining apartment features a double bedroom, bathroom, living room, and kitchen. The best accommodations are in the waterside cottages, which have shaded patios and lounge chairs. Two of the cottages have a bed/sitting room and a kitchen. The Starboard, which accommodates four people, is a two-bedroom, two-bathroom unit with a living room, fireplace, and kitchen. Guest rooms overall are small, however, and are arranged haphazardly. The tiny kitchens have adequate utensils for preparing light meals. Only a few of the units are air-conditioned—some have heaters only. *10 Salt Kettle Rd., Paget PG 01, tel. 809/236–0407. 6 rooms with bath. Meal plan: BP. Facilities: deep-water swimming, lounge. No credit cards.*

10   The Arts and Nightlife

The Arts

by Honey Naylor

Available in all hotels and tourist information centers, *This Week in Bermuda*, *Preview Bermuda*, and *Bermuda Weekly*, are free publications that list what's happening around the island. *The Bermudian* ($4) is a glossy monthly magazine that also carries a calendar of events. The Bermuda Channel (Channel 4), a local television station, broadcasts a wealth of information about sightseeing, restaurants, cultural events, and nightlife on the island. Tourist-related information can also be heard on an AM radio station, VSB-1160, between 7 AM and 12:30 PM. The island is so small, however, that virtually everyone knows what's going on—taxi drivers, in particular, have a good idea of what's hot and what's not. In truth, the arts scene in Bermuda is not extensive, and many of the events and performing groups listed below operate on a casual or part-time basis. **City Hall Theatre** (City Hall, Church St., Hamilton) is the major venue for a number of top-quality cultural events each year, although performances and productions are sometimes staged elsewhere on the island. Contact the **Box Office** (Visitors Service Bureau, tel. 809/295–1727) for reservations and information about all cultural events on the island. American Express, MasterCard, and Visa are accepted.

In January and February the **Bermuda Festival** brings internationally renowned artists to the island for a series of performances. The two-month program includes classical and jazz concerts and theatrical performances. Recent festivals have included appearances by classical and jazz trumpeter Wynton Marsalis, the Dance Theatre of Harlem, the Royal Shakespeare Company, and the Flying Karamazov Brothers. Most of the performances take place in City Hall, although some are held in major hotels. Ticket prices range from $17 to $25 ($12 for students). For information and reservations, contact Bermuda Festivals, Ltd. (Box HM 297, Hamilton HM AX, tel. 809/295–1291) or the Bermuda Department of Tourism (*see* Government Tourist Offices in Chapter 1, Essential Information).

Concerts

The Bermuda Philharmonic Society presents several programs throughout the year, including classical music concerts by the full Philharmonic and by soloists. Students of the Menuhin Foundation, established in Bermuda by virtuoso violinist Yehudi Menuhin, sometimes perform with the orchestra. Concerts take place either in City Hall Theatre (*see* above) or the Cathedral of the Most Holy Trinity in Hamilton (*see* Chapter 4, Exploring Bermuda).

The Gilbert & Sullivan Society of Bermuda mounts a musical production each year, usually in October. In addition to Gilbert and Sullivan operettas, the group occasionally does Broadway shows.

Dance

The **Gombey Dancers,** a Bermudian dance group, perform each week as part of the off-season (mid-November–March 31) festivities. Gombey (pronounced "gum-bay") dancing is a blend of African, West Indian, and American Indian influences. The

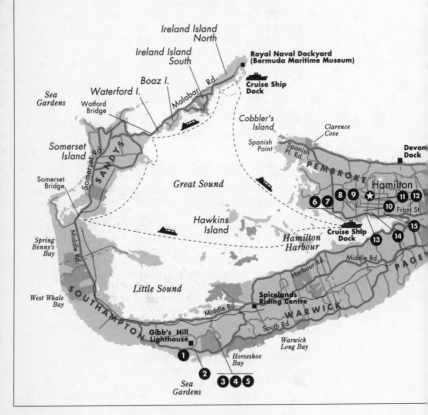

ATLANTIC OCEAN

Ireland Island North

Ireland Island South

Royal Naval Dockyard (Bermuda Maritime Museum)

Boaz I.

Cruise Ship Dock

Waterford I.

Sea Gardens

Watford Bridge

Malabar Rd.

Cobbler's Island

Spanish Point

Clarence Cove

Spanish Pt. Rd.

PEMBROKE

Devon Dock

Somerset Island

Somerset Rd.

SANDYS

Great Sound

Hamilton

Somerset Bridge

Spring Benny's Bay

Middle Rd.

Hawkins Island

Front St.

Cruise Ship Dock

Hamilton Harbour

Middle Rd.

PAGET

West Whale Bay

SOUTHAMPTON

Little Sound

Harbour Rd.

Spicelands Riding Centre

WARWICK

Gibb's Hill Lighthouse

Middle Rd.

South Rd.

Warwick Long Bay

Horseshoe Bay

Sea Gardens

Blossoms Bar, **19**	Gazebo Lounge, **6**
Casey's, **9**	Henry VIII, **2**
City Hall Theatre, **11**	Hog Penny Pub, **13**
The Clayhouse Inn, **16**	Lillian's, **1**
The Club, **8**	Load of Mischief Pub, **10**
Colony Pub, **15**	Neptune Lounge, **3**
Empire Room, **5**	The Oasis, **14**

Prospero's Cave, **18**
Ram's Head Inn, **7**
Scandal, **12**
Swizzle Inn, **17**
Touch Club, **4**
Wharf Tavern, **20**

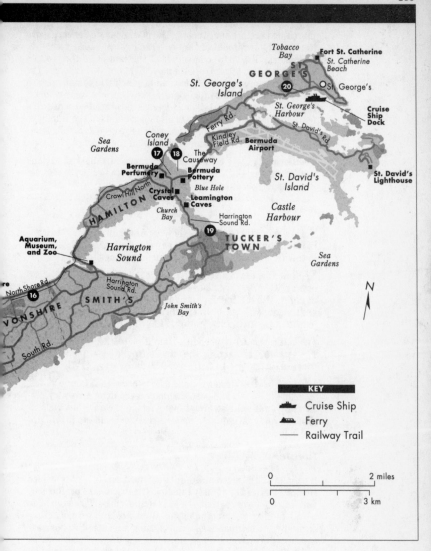

Tobacco Bay

Fort St. Catherine

St. Catherine Beach

ST. GEORGE'S

St. George's Island

20

St. George's

St. George's Harbour

Cruise Ship Dock

St. David's Rd.

Sea Gardens

Coney Island

17   18

The Causeway

Ferry Rd.

Kindley Field Rd.

Bermuda Airport

Bermuda Perfumery

Bermuda Pottery

Blue Hole

St. David's Island

St. David's Lighthouse

Crawl Hill/North

Crystal Caves

Leamington Caves

Church Bay

Harrington Sound Rd.

Castle Harbour

HAMILTON

19

TUCKER'S TOWN

Aquarium, Museum, and Zoo

Harrington Sound

Sea Gardens

North Shore Rd.

16

Harrington Sound Rd.

SMITH'S

VONSHIRE

John Smith's Bay

South Rd.

N

KEY

Cruise Ship

Ferry

Railway Trail

0   2 miles

0   3 km

Gombey tradition in Bermuda dates to the mid-18th century, when costumed slaves celebrated Christmas by singing and marching through the streets. The masked male dancers move to the accompaniment of skin-covered drums, called gombeys, and the shrill whistle commands of the captain of the troupe. The ritualistic, often frenetic movements of the dancers, the staccato drum accompaniment, and the whistle commands are passed from generation to generation. Dancers wear colorful costumes that include tall headdresses decorated with peacock feathers and tiny mirrors. On all major holidays the Gombeys dance through the streets, attracting large crowds of followers. It's traditional to toss coins at the feet of the dancers.

The Bermuda Civic Ballet performs classical ballets at various venues during the year. Internationally known artists sometimes appear as guests.

Movies

Bermuda has three cinemas showing first-run movies—two are in Hamilton and the third is in the West End. Check the listings in the *Royal Gazette* for movies and show times.

Neptune Cinema (The Cooperage, Dockyard, tel. 809/234–2923 or 809/234–1709) is a 250-seat cinema that shows feature films at night. During the day, it runs *The Attack on Washington*, a multimedia account of Bermuda's role in the sacking of Washington, DC, during the War of 1812.

The Little Theatre (Queen St., Hamilton, tel. 809/292–2135) is a 173-seat theater across the street from Casey's Bar. Show times are usually 2:15, 7:15, and 9:30 daily.

Liberty Theatre (corner Union and Victoria Sts., Hamilton, tel. 809/292–7296) is a 270-seat cinema located in an unsavory section of Hamilton. The area is safe during the day, but visitors should avoid it after dark. Show times are usually at 2:15, 7:15, and 9:30.

Theater

Bermuda is the only place outside the United States where **Harvard University's Hasty Pudding Theatricals** are performed. For almost 30 years, the satirical troupe has performed on the island during Bermuda College Weeks (March–April). Produced by the estimable Elsbeth Gibson, an American-born actress/producer who lives in Bermuda, each show incorporates political and social themes and issues of the past year. The Hasty Pudding Theatricals are staged in the City Hall Theatre (*see* above); ticket prices are about $17.

Nightlife

During high season all hotels and cottage colonies feature entertainment—barbecues, steel bands, dinner dancing, and other diversions. Otherwise, the island's nightlife is fairly subdued; there are no casinos and only a few nightclubs and discos. Much of the action occurs in the pubs and lounges, which range from hotel bars to local hangouts. Some places close during the off-season, so check *This Week in Bermuda* and *Preview of Bermuda* (*see* above) for the latest information about what's happening each night. As a general rule, men should wear a jacket and tie to clubs; for ladies the dress code is smart but casual. Pubs and discos begin to fill up around 9:30 or 10.

The music scene is dominated by local acts and bands playing the island's hotel and pub circuits. Occasionally, outside performers are billed, particularly during the Bermuda Festival (*see* above). The island superstar is **Gene Steede,** a guitarist, singer, and comedian who has been described as Tony Bennett, Harry Belafonte, and Johnny Carson rolled into one. Steede and his trio often headline the local shows at the two Princess hotels (*see* Cabaret, below). Among the other popular entertainers to watch for are the **Talbot Brothers,** calypso singers and instrumentalists, the **Bermuda All-Star Steel Band,** the **Coca-Cola Steel Band,** and the **Bermuda Strollers.** You can catch **Mike Meredith,** a popular folk singer/political satirist, at the Hog Penny, Henry VIII (*see* below), and other pubs on the entertainment circuit. **Electronic Symphony** is a glitzy show band that performs an eclectic selection of pop, country, gospel, rock, and island music. **Jimmy O'Connor** heads a band that plays Kenny Rogers and Neil Diamond tunes, as well as island music and '50s hits. The **Shinbone Alley Cats** play Dixieland jazz, and the flamboyant trio of **Tino and Friends** plays a mix of classics and standards. **Sharx** is a rock band; the **Travellers** straddle country and rock music.

Around 3 AM, when the bars and discos close, head for the **Ice Queen** (Middle Rd., Paget, tel. 809/236–3136). This place is like a drive-in movie without the movie—the parking lot is jammed with cars and mopeds. The main attraction is the $2.50 burgers, which are probably the best on the island. You don't sit down here—there's just a take-out window where you line up to place your order—but it's *the* place to be after hours.

Bars and Lounges

Almost anyone will tell you that **Casey's** (Queen St., across from the Little Theatre, Hamilton, tel. 809/293–9549) is the best bar on the island. It's not fancy, nor is it touristy by any means. It's just a bar—a narrow room with a juke box and a few tables—but the place packs them in, especially on Friday night. It's open 10–10 every day except Sunday. **Blossoms Bar** (Marriott's Castle Harbour Resort, Paynters Rd., Hamilton Parish, tel. 809/293–2040) is a popular meeting place for young professionals, as is the **Colony Pub** (The Princess, Pitts Bay Rd., Hamilton, tel. 809/295–3000), where the lights are low and the piano music is soft and soothing. **Henry VIII** (South Shore Rd., Southampton, tel. 809/238–1977) is a wild and popular place with a devoted following of locals of all ages, who like its piano player, its sing-alongs, and its British ambience. The **Hog Penny Pub** (Burnaby St., between Front and Reid Sts., Hamilton, tel. 809/292–2534) has a nightly lineup of local talent, and the **Load of Mischief Pub** at Rum Runners (93 Front St., Hamilton, tel. 809/292–4737) hosts local bands nightly, attracting a crowd of young locals and tourists. In the Bailey's Bay area, the **Swizzle Inn** (Middle Rd., Hamilton Parish, tel. 809/293–9300) is strictly for the young, with a dart board, a juke box that plays soft and hard rock, and business cards from all over the world tacked on the walls, ceilings, and doors. The yachting crowd gathers at the **Wharf Tavern** (Somers Wharf, St. George's, tel. 809/297–1515) for rum swizzling and nautical talk. **Lillian's**

(Sonesta Beach Hotel & Spa, off South Rd., Southampton, tel. 809/238–8122) is a chic, art nouveau restaurant where a sedate crowd dances to the music of a trio.

The Club Scene

Cabaret There are Las Vegas–style tourist shows at the Hamilton Princess and Southampton Princess hotels during high season. The **Gazebo Lounge** (The Princess, Pitts Bay Rd., Hamilton, tel. 809/295–3000), a 280-seat nightclub, and the 750-seat **Empire Room** (Southampton Princess, South Rd., Southampton, tel. 809/238–8000) feature two shows nightly from mid-April to mid-November. Local entertainers perform at the 9:30 show, and the glitz-and-glitter international show takes the stage at 10:45. At both places, a $29 cover charge includes two drinks and the two shows.

Calypso The **Clayhouse Inn** (North Shore Rd., Devonshire, tel. 809/292–3193) is a dark dive that packs in locals and tourists for a rowdy show involving limbo dancers, calypso singers, fire eaters, steel bands, and an occasional top-name entertainer. The pace picks up around 9:30. A $12.50 cover charge includes one drink. The ambience is considerably more sophisticated at the **Neptune Lounge** (Southampton Princess, South Rd., Southampton, tel. 809/238–8000), a posh establishment with a small dance floor, large-screen TV, and live calypso music nightly until 1 AM during high season.

Discos

A snappy canopy covers the entrance to **Scandal** (119 Front St., Hamilton, tel. 809/292–4040), Bermuda's newest and hottest night spot. The decor is shocking pink and black, and a sophisticated crowd gathers to sip wine and champagne and dance nightly till the wee small hours. **The Club** (Bermudiana Rd., Hamilton, tel. 809/295–6693) is a ritzy room with red velvet, brass, and mirrors, that attracts an older professional crowd. Open for dancing every night from 10 PM to 3 AM , the disco also hosts Club Hour, on Friday from 5 PM to 7 PM. The $8 admission fee is waived if you have dinner at The Harbourfront, La Trattoria, Tavern on the Green, or Little Venice beneath the disco (*see* Chapter 8, Dining). **The Oasis** (Emporium Bldg., Front St., Hamilton, tel. 809/292–4978 or 809/292–3379) is a hot spot for a slightly younger crowd that gladly pays the $8 cover charge. Another trendy place where the young come to show off the latest fashions is the **Touch Club** (Southampton Princess, South Rd., Southampton, tel. 809/238–8000), a club-by disco decorated with glass bricks and leather. The $10, two-drink-minimum charge is waived during the off-season; dancing is from 9 PM to 1 AM. At **Prospero's Cave** (Grotto Bay Beach Hotel & Tennis Club, 11 Blue Hole Hill, Hamilton Parish, tel. 809/293–8333), you can dance from 9 PM to 1 AM beneath the stalactites in a huge underground cave. A DJ spins the disks for a young crowd.

Index

Personal Itinerary

Departure *Date*

Time

Transportation

Arrival *Date*   *Time*

Departure *Date*   *Time*

Transportation

Accommodations

Arrival *Date*   *Time*

Departure *Date*   *Time*

Transportation

Accommodations

Arrival *Date*   *Time*

Departure *Date*   *Time*

Transportation

Accommodations

Personal Itinerary

Arrival *Date*   *Time*

Departure *Date*   *Time*

Transportation

Accommodations

Arrival *Date*   *Time*

Departure *Date*   *Time*

Transportation

Accommodations

Arrival *Date*   *Time*

Departure *Date*   *Time*

Transportation

Accommodations

Arrival *Date*   *Time*

Departure *Date*   *Time*

Transportation

Accommodations

Personal Itinerary

Arrival *Date*   *Time*

Departure *Date*   *Time*

Transportation

Accommodations

Arrival *Date*   *Time*

Departure *Date*   *Time*

Transportation

Accommodations

Arrival *Date*   *Time*

Departure *Date*   *Time*

Transportation

Accommodations

Arrival *Date*   *Time*

Departure *Date*   *Time*

Transportation

Accommodations

Personal Itinerary

Arrival *Date*   *Time*

Departure *Date*   *Time*

Transportation

Accommodations

Arrival *Date*   *Time*

Departure *Date*   *Time*

Transportation

Accommodations

Arrival *Date*   *Time*

Departure *Date*   *Time*

Transportation

Accommodations

Arrival *Date*   *Time*

Departure *Date*   *Time*

Transportation

Accommodations

Personal Itinerary

Arrival	*Date*	*Time*
Departure	*Date*	*Time*
Transportation		
Accommodations		

Arrival	*Date*	*Time*
Departure	*Date*	*Time*
Transportation		
Accommodations		

Arrival	*Date*	*Time*
Departure	*Date*	*Time*
Transportation		
Accommodations		

Arrival	*Date*	*Time*
Departure	*Date*	*Time*
Transportation		
Accommodations		

Name	Name
Address	Address
Telephone	Telephone
Name	Name
Address	Address
Telephone	Telephone
Name	Name
Address	Address
Telephone	Telephone
Name	Name
Address	Address
Telephone	Telephone
Name	Name
Address	Address
Telephone	Telephone
Name	Name
Address	Address
Telephone	Telephone
Name	Name
Address	Address
Telephone	Telephone
Name	Name
Address	Address
Telephone	Telephone

Addresses

Name	Name
Address	Address
Telephone	Telephone
Name	Name
Address	Address
Telephone	Telephone
Name	Name
Address	Address
Telephone	Telephone
Name	Name
Address	Address
Telephone	Telephone
Name	Name
Address	Address
Telephone	Telephone
Name	Name
Address	Address
Telephone	Telephone
Name	Name
Address	Address
Telephone	Telephone
Name	Name
Address	Address
Telephone	Telephone

Addresses

Name	Name
Address	Address
Telephone	Telephone
Name	Name
Address	Address
Telephone	Telephone
Name	Name
Address	Address
Telephone	Telephone
Name	Name
Address	Address
Telephone	Telephone
Name	Name
Address	Address
Telephone	Telephone
Name	Name
Address	Address
Telephone	Telephone
Name	Name
Address	Address
Telephone	Telephone
Name	Name
Address	Address
Telephone	Telephone

Notes

Fodor's Travel Guides

U.S. Guides

Alaska
Arizona
Boston
California
Cape Cod, Martha's
  Vineyard, Nantucket
The Carolinas & the
  Georgia Coast
The Chesapeake
  Region
Chicago
Colorado
Disney World & the
  Orlando Area
Florida
Hawaii

Las Vegas, Reno,
  Tahoe
Los Angeles
Maine, Vermont,
  New Hampshire
Maui
Miami & the
  Keys
National Parks
  of the West
New England
New Mexico
New Orleans
New York City
New York City
  (Pocket Guide)

Pacific North Coast
Philadelphia & the
  Pennsylvania
  Dutch Country
Puerto Rico
  (Pocket Guide)
The Rockies
San Diego
San Francisco
San Francisco
  (Pocket Guide)
The South
Santa Fe, Taos,
  Albuquerque
Seattle &
  Vancouver

Texas
USA
The U. S. & British
  Virgin Islands
The Upper Great
  Lakes Region
Vacations in
  New York State
Vacations on the
  Jersey Shore
Virginia & Maryland
Waikiki
Washington, D.C.
Washington, D.C.
  (Pocket Guide)

Foreign Guides

Acapulco
Amsterdam
Australia
Austria
The Bahamas
The Bahamas
  (Pocket Guide)
Baja & Mexico's Pacific
  Coast Resorts
Barbados
Barcelona, Madrid,
  Seville
Belgium &
  Luxembourg
Berlin
Bermuda
Brazil
Budapest
Budget Europe
Canada
Canada's Atlantic
  Provinces

Cancun, Cozumel,
  Yucatan Peninsula
Caribbean
Central America
China
Czechoslovakia
Eastern Europe
Egypt
Europe
Europe's Great Cities
France
Germany
Great Britain
Greece
The Himalayan
  Countries
Holland
Hong Kong
India
Ireland
Israel
Italy

Italy 's Great Cities
Jamaica
Japan
Kenya, Tanzania,
  Seychelles
Korea
London
London
  (Pocket Guide)
London Companion
Mexico
Mexico City
Montreal &
  Quebec City
Morocco
New Zealand
Norway
Nova Scotia,
  New Brunswick,
  Prince Edward
  Island
Paris

Paris (Pocket Guide)
Portugal
Rome
Scandinavia
Scandinavian Cities
Scotland
Singapore
South America
South Pacific
Southeast Asia
Soviet Union
Spain
Sweden
Switzerland
Sydney
Thailand
Tokyo
Toronto
Turkey
Vienna & the Danube
  Valley
Yugoslavia

Wall Street Journal Guides to Business Travel

Europe
International Cities
Pacific Rim
USA & Canada

Special-Interest Guides

Bed & Breakfast and
  Country Inn Guides:
Mid-Atlantic Region
New England
The South
The West

Cruises and Ports
  of Call
Healthy Escapes
Fodor's Flashmaps
  New York

Fodor's Flashmaps
  Washington, D.C.
Shopping in Europe
Skiing in the USA &
  Canada

Smart Shopper's
  Guide to London
Sunday in New York
Touring Europe
Touring USA